ZURICH INTERNATIONAL CHESS TOURNAMENT, 1953

by
DAVID BRONSTEIN

Translated from the
Second Russian Edition by
JIM MARFIA

Dover Publications, Inc.
New York

Zurich International Chess Tournament, 1953 is a new English translation by Jim Marfia of the second, corrected Russian edition as published by Gosudarstvennoe Izdatel'stvo "Fizkul'tura i Sport" [State Publishing House "Physical Culture and Sports"], Moscow, in 1960 under the title *Meždunarodnyǐ turnir grossmeǐsterov; kommentarii k partiyam turnira pretendentov na matč s čempionom mira.*

International Standard Book Number: 0-486-23800-8
Library of Congress Catalog Card Number: 78-74881

International Standard Book Number

ISBN-13: 978-0-486-23800-5
ISBN-10: 0-486-23800-8

Library of Congress Catalog Card Number: 78-74881

Manufactured in the United States by LSC Communications
23800820   2017
www.doverpublications.com

A WORD FROM THE TRANSLATOR

Surely, this is no ordinary chess book that you hold, dear Reader. Myself, I have read chess books that were entertaining, and those that were instructive; some that were historic, and a few that were downright bad. But never have I encountered a book written with such powerful style and such obvious passion for the game.

The passion is infectious. The translation you hold is the final product of ten years' work and four revisions — and still, I feel that it wanted more effort...so you can see the fascination Bronstein's book had for its translator! If my translation can infect you, the Reader, with half of that fascination, then it will be a job well done.

I must thank Jack O'Keefe for his meticulous proofreading and priceless editorial work.

Jim Marfia

INSTEAD OF A PREFACE

As I began work on my first chess book, I put myself mentally in the reader's place, recalling the excitement with which I used to open each new chess book, hoping to find vital thinking there, clear words, and a wondrous tale of the art of chess. I absorbed a great deal from books, and to this day I cherish the memory of the best of them.

Books about chess tournaments belong to a special class of literature, which would seem at first blush to be rather restrictive of the author's creative possibilities, since he must write, not on themes of his own choosing, but about chess material already created. But this is not quite true. The author is free to treat the games any way he wishes, to make generalizations, and to uncover the ideas and plans actually executed, as well as those that could have occurred in the actual or some other game.

The book of a strong tournament is more than just a games collection. When its participants are the world's strongest players, then the games are mutually interdependent, and brimming with ideas, which crystallize and develop as the event progresses. Thus, the tournament as a whole represents a step forward in the development of chess creativity. We may take as examples of such tournaments the events at Hastings 1895, St Petersburg 1914, New York 1924, Moscow 1935, and Groningen 1946. Beyond doubt, Zurich-Neuhausen 1953 deserves a place among them.

In working on this book, I started from the premise that every full-bodied game of chess is an artistic endeavor, arising out of a struggle between two masters of equal rank. The kernel of a game of chess is the creative clash of plans, the battle of chess ideas, which takes on its highest form in the middlegame.

This book examines a number of standard positions which occur as a result of the collision of plans; also examined are such strategic concepts as darksquare weaknesses, the advantage of the two bishops, play and counterplay on opposite wings, the relative strengths of the pieces, overprotection, and so forth. Such elements of the struggle as intuition, resourcefulness, and determination are discussed too.

The games of a tournament of grandmasters bring the reader into the creative circle of the contemporary leaders of chess, showing him the rise and fall of battle as well as the manner in which a game of chess is created. It is the author's intention to discourse upon the least explored and most interesting stage of the game: the middlegame, and the way it is handled by today's grandmasters. That is the basic aim of this book.

The author has tried to avoid weighing down his book with variations. Variations can be interesting, if they show the beauty of chess; they become useless when they exceed the limits of what a man can calculate; and they are a real evil when they are substituted for the study and clarification of positions in which the outcome is decided by intuition, fantasy and talent.

Along with this, it was my hope that the player who read this book would raise himself thereby to a rather higher level of playing strength.

The reader will see errors, too, in the games of this tournament; but he will not be too severe in his judgment of the masters if he pictures to himself the peculiar nature of the chess struggle. At the board there sits a living person, with all his everyday thoughts and worries, sometimes far removed from chess. While selecting his plan, or even his next move, he cannot help thinking about his standing in the tournament, remembering yesterday's result, looking at other games. A game is not an analysis: everything must be worked out in one's head, without moving the pieces, without consulting a book or asking advice from anyone...

The grandmaster thinks and thinks — one last look at the clock — "Time to decide; I'll risk it!" — and the knight goes to e5. Of course it's easy, a whole year later, after studying all of the analyses and spending days on the position, to tell the reader, with absolute certainty: "A mistake; the careful Ne1 was to be preferred..."

It may be that mistakes will turn up in my analyses and evaluations as well, although I have tried to keep them to a minimum. It is my hope that the reader will be indulgent, and help me to correct them.

It is with trepidation, then, that I submit my work to the judgment of the readers. I will consider my ends achieved if the contents of this book expand the reader's chess horizon, increase his mastery of the game, give him some idea of the state of the art, and help him more fully to value — and still more to love — the depths of chess.

PREFACE TO THE SECOND EDITION

Now that my book is ready for its second edition, I would like to explain today what I had to pass over in the preface to the first edition four years ago. The work I submitted to the readers' judgment at that time was a work which had little in common with the commentaries usually seen in the chess press. "Rotework" is a thing abhorrent to art and literature alike; thus, it should be still less acceptable in chess, which actually falls somewhere in an intermediate zone between art and literature. I do not wish to say anything against the numerous tournament and reference books that are being published, but for some years now a considerable decline has been noticed in the appetite of chessplayers for this type of literature, and yesterday's insatiable demand has slackened. Under these circumstances, how would the public accept a large and unfortunately rather expensive tournament book, such as this one?

I had no wish to become a variations-monger; nor did I want the role of annotator-cum-guide. I felt that the author's ideas and conclusions should form the basis of this book, with the moves played in each game serving to annotate them, as it were. I tried to let the book's contents display the richness and limitless expanse of chess ideas, and to let the format resemble that of a literary work.

To judge from all the accepted indicators, the author appears to have accomplished his purpose, at least in part: the book sold out very quickly, and the reviews were favorable. Most valuable to me, however, were the many letters and opinions I received from readers (and I regret not having answered nearly enough of them). There I found, along with justified criticism of my book's shortcomings, approval of the basic principles by which it was written. Those letters have been the finest possible reward for my labors, and I should like to take this opportunity to offer my heartfelt thanks to all who wrote me. I should like especially to thank Peter Romanovsky for his detailed review (helpful to readers and the author alike) which appeared in "Shakhmaty v SSSR".

I was happy to agree to the publishers' suggestion of a second edition; I intended to excise all obsolete and unimportant materials, to develop other material a bit more fully, and to expand the preface to reflect the most recent developments in the world of chess.

Thus, this second edition devotes a great deal less space to text, in games which did not serve my purpose of uncovering and describing the ideas of the art of chess. This applies especially to games from the later rounds, when the final standings of the tournament had already been largely determined, and the tension had slackened somewhat. Additionally, two or three errors in analysis, discovered by the readers and the author, have been corrected; the proofreading has been upgraded, and some diagrams revised.

I would like to close this segment with the hope that in the future my chessplaying audience will continue to aid the author in his work with their alert criticism, as well as their words of praise.

*****

Since this is a book devoted mainly to the middle phase of the game of chess, it might be appropriate to begin with a few words about the evolution of opening ideas and the modern openings repertoire.

In former times — shall we say, the latter half of the preceding century — a game generally opened with the king's pawn, to which Black would, in the majority of cases, reply 1..e7-e5. Such defenses as the Sicilian and the French were also employed, of course, but less frequently. With some exceptions, over half of the games played in any tournament would be open games, and sometimes a much greater percentage than that. At the close of the last century and the beginning of the present one, the closed games for White and the semi-open games for Black became very popular. Thus, in the Cambridge Springs tournament of 1904, the Queen's Gambit was the most common opening, with the Ruy Lopez second and the Sicilian third. The Indian defenses also began to appear in the tournaments of the 1890's and 1900's: these were the harbingers of new ideas.

The 1920's witnessed the almost total disappearance of the open games, with the exception of the Ruy Lopez, from important tournaments, and the rise of the Queen's Gambit and other Queen's Pawn games. White's success with the Queen's Gambit and the Ruy led gradually to the popularization of the asymmetrical defensive systems: the Indian against 1 d2-d4, and the Sicilian against 1 e2-e4. This was a very fruitful period for the development of opening ideas. The victories of the young grandmasters were closely bound up with their discovery of new openings: the Nimzo-Indian, Reti's Opening, Grunfeld's Defense, Alekhine's Defense.

At the strong double-round tournament at Bled 1931, which included Alekhine, Bogolyubov, Nimzovich, Vidmar, Flohr, Tartakover, Spielmann and Maroczy, among others, 77 Queen's Gambits and other Queen's Pawn games were played; of these, White won 29, and Black only 13. In the same event, 21 games used Indian Defenses, of which White could win only 2, while losing 14. Is in any wonder that, in the era that followed, encompassing the 1930's and 1940's, fewer and fewer Queen's Gambits would be seen? The careers of many Soviet and non-Soviet players owed a great deal to the creation and development of new systems in the King's Indian and Sicilian, as well as in the Nimzo-Indian and Grunfeld Defenses. Today, one may separate all openings, Black and White, into three major groupings.

In the first grouping, both sides follow classical principles, developing pieces, occupying space, creating a pawn center, avoiding weaknesses, etc. This is the shape of the struggle in the great majority of variations of the Queen's Gambit, Ruy Lopez, French, and some systems of the Sicilian and Nimzo-Indian Defenses. Black knows that in these variations, especially in symmetrical positions, the advantage of the first move counts heavily, and he faces a long and patient struggle for equality. He has few winning chances, but if he works hard and plays cautiously, he may get a draw. The results of the World Championship match between Capablanca and Alekhine may be taken as typical for such openings. Of the thirty-four games of that match, thirty-three opened with the queen's pawn; twenty-five games were drawn, White won six, and Black two. Masters nowadays tend to avoid such openings, shunning symmetrical setups in favor of defenses which offer counterchances.

Thus we come to the second group of openings, in which one side follows classical principles, while the other side consciously flouts a few, in order to obtain active play for his pieces, or an attack on the enemy pawn center, or sometimes simply for the sake of complicating. Such are the main lines of the King's Indian, Sicilian, Grunfeld and Nimzo-Indian, and some forcing lines of the Queen's Gambit.

To the third group we may assign those openings in which White uses the opening phase not to occupy, but to control, the center squares, avoiding early definition of the pawn structure, and retaining maximum flexibility, while preparing for a war of maneuver. While this is going on, White is ready to stir up complications at an appropriate moment, or — should he secure some positional plus — to boil the game down to a technical stage. This group comprises the Closed Variation of the Sicilian, a number of lines in the Reti, the English, the King's Indian Reversed, and a few others.

It should be noted here that giving an opening a name does not automatically set the course of the opening struggle. For example: in the Queen's Gambit, one may play the Orthodox Defense, which is a typical form of the struggle on a classical footing. But one may also play Botvinnik's line, or the risky "Peruvian" variation, with forcing play and counterchances for Black. The Queen's Indian is not one of the symmetrical openings, but it does not give Black any real counterchances at all. And the Nimzo-Indian, one of the most outstanding and hardiest of defenses the "Hypermodern" school of the 1920's ever produced, allows a flexible transition either to positional schemes or to sharp variations.

*****

These changes in our conception of the opening closely paralleled the development of chess ideas in general. The Queen's Gambit's greatest popularity coincided with the period when chess was completely dominated by the principles of the positional school. With all the good these principles have done, their one major shortcoming must be pointed out: the evaluation of positions by externals alone. In the eyes of Tarrasch's disciples — and he was the propagandist of Steinitz' ideas — such factors as a backward pawn, or a powerful pawn center, or an advantage in development, were decisive, both in the evaluation of one's own position and in setting up a plan of action. "If one piece stands poorly, the whole game stands poorly," said Tarrasch. The principles of the positional school, expressed in simple instructional form by Tarrasch, became inviolable axioms of chess to many of his contemporaries. And thus arose the misconception, which persists to this day, of the so-called "consistent" game, in which one player carries out, from beginning to end, his logical plan, almost as if he were demonstrating a theorem of geometry.

In the annotations to such an "ideal" game, one player always appears as the keeper of principle, the other as its transgressor. The "good" player then accumulates positional advantages and places them in a vault, much as if he were saving to buy a motorcycle. Having accumulated the proper amount, he then launches a combinative attack, winding it up with an instructive mate, or with a still more instructive win of the exchange. And just what, you may ask, was his opponent doing all this time? Why, gazing phlegmatically at his backward pawns and poorly-placed pieces, shrugging his shoulders, and then finally: "Black resigns."

I doubt if it needs to be demonstrated that such games never occur between two grandmasters of equal ability, and that the annotators — a role generally assumed by the winner — turned what they wished to be into what actually happened.

The views of the positional school held sway in chess for a long time, but their weak side came to light in the 1920's. As the Queen's Gambit began to fade from the openings lists, so the names of Nimzovich, Reti, Tartakover and other masters began to appear more and more frequently at the top of tournament crosstables, while these players came out strongly against one-sided understanding and exaggeration of the role of positional principles.

Around 1935, the young masters of our country made their international debut, with Botvinnik at their head; later, they were to advance to the forefront of the world's players. Their continuing successes gave some observers the impression of a Soviet school of chess, some sort of aggregate of identical chess ideas and views. I don't find this to be entirely true. As a matter of fact, the Soviet family of chess masters includes players of the most diverse styles. For example, Spassky and Petrosian, to judge from their styles of play and differing conceptions of the game, are as unlike one another as were Spielmann and Schlechter; and Tal as is far removed from Botvinnik as Lasker was from Capablanca.

Now, what sort of ideas characterize the 1950's? What contribution did this tournament in Switzerland make to the development of these ideas? And what is to be the direction of further progress in chess?

First, let us note the great erudition of chessplayers who have absorbed the experience of previous generations, allowing them now to fight with still more courage, forethought, fantasy and risk — all based on sober assessment of the pros and cons of the intended operation.

Our understanding of positional play has matured immeasurably. Where Tarrasch taught us to avoid weaknesses in our own position while striving to create them in our opponent's position, to accumulate small advantages, to occupy open lines, and never to begin an attack without sufficient grounds, today things are sometimes done altogether differently. We might give ourselves weak spots and weak pawns, in order to distract our opponent; give up open lines, in order to save the rooks for other, more promising plans; or mount an attacking demonstration, in order to hide our real intentions.

The number of standard defensible positions, which every chessplayer knows he can fall back on in case of need, has also grown by leaps and bounds. We now find that many positions which were formerly considered lost can be defended successfully, even actively; but this requires, firstly: a tense game of calculation, and secondly: the ability to perceive the proper moment to abandon the weakness to its fate and carry the fight to a new sector. Only now has it become clear that this was precisely Emanuel Lasker's standard approach to the game, and that one of his major advantages over his rivals lay in the fact that none of them understood it.

On the other hand, this approach was hardly Lasker's only distinguishing characteristic. He was the game's great psychologist, who knew better than anyone how to make the pendulum of battle swing left, then right, never overstepping the bounds of safety himself, while imperceptibly goading his opponent over the edge. He would deliberately play second-rate moves, practically inviting his orthodox opponent to punish him. Nowadays, even this style has been analyzed and superseded. Today's players are ready at times to give their opponents what would appear to be a positional advantage from the very first moves.

Clear examples of this are the positions that arise in the King's Indian after ..e5:d4, as well as the group of positions after 1 d4 Nf6 2 c4 c5 3 d5 e6 4 Nc3 ed 5 cd. The Boleslavsky Variation of the Sicilian, with its gaping hole at d5 and the hopelessly backward pawn on d6, might seem unbelievably daring, but nonetheless it withstands every assault. In this book, we will find a number of such examples.

The reader will also find here descriptions of the technical ways and means employed by the contemporary master in the middlegame. The concept of technique is much broader now than it was a few decades ago, and what was once a rare occurrence, a lucky find, is now the tool of the masses.

Without technique, one cannot attain mastery of any form; it is no less impossible in chess.

However, the importance of technique in chess should not be exaggerated, either. The end phase of the game, frequently described as "a matter of technique", is certainly not always that clear and simple. Thirty years ago, Capablanca was considered the greatest technical player in the world; today it is Smyslov. After analysis of the so-called technical games of Capablanca and Smyslov, I concluded that they are based on the combinative element and on far-seeing and accurate analysis, and that as a consequence their technique is of an unusually high order. The same could be said, to a greater or lesser degree, of the endgames played by many grandmasters. I will mention only two here from this tournament: Euwe's against Stahlberg, and Gligoric's against Euwe.

Another characteristic quality of the contemporary creative output, which the reader will note more than once in the games of this tournament, is a readiness to react instantly to any change in the opponent's plans, and to make radical alterations in one's own plan, if given sufficient justification.

One of the most prominent — and promising — tendencies which came forward in the course of this tournament was a penchant for wide-open piece play almost from the first moves. Apparently Morphy's style retains an irresistible fascination for chessplayers in every age, and a return to this style, refined perhaps to a higher level, is the dream of all players, grandmasters included. To me, it appears that we are closer to this ideal now than we have been at any time in the past century.

This new tendency, whose representatives have blazed a trail through the USSR Championships, the 1955 and 1958 Interzonal tournaments, and the 1959 Candidates' tournament, is characterized by an effort to take the game out of its logical channels at any cost, redirecting it into the combinative — or, more accurately, the calculative. The material side of the question — a pawn more or an exchange less — has no special significance. There is absolutely no need to demonstrate the combination's correctness in every variation. More likely the reverse may be true: in the majority of cases, it turns out that the defending side could have held out by finding a series of saving moves. But here the New Wave grandmaster trusts in himself and in his phenomenal ability to calculate a vast number of long and complicated variations.

Sometimes this can give the game a very strange turn indeed. As one positional master said, "I fought him (a master of the calculative style) for thirty-two moves, and never guessed his reply, except once, when he had to take my queen."

The foremost advocates of this dynamic style today are undoubtedly Mikhail Tal and Boris Spassky. Of course, complicating and turning the game into a war of calculation are not the only weapons in the arsenal of these unusually talented and well-rounded players. They are past masters of the techniques of positional play, conduct brilliant endgames, know the openings well, and surpass other masters precisely in their skill at giving the game a dynamic twist, making it the sort of game which is absolutely impossible to evaluate by landmarks; willy-nilly, one must then play "move by move", or perhaps even "variation by variation".

The time came for one of them to try his mettle, and the viability of his personal style, in single combat against the most powerful player of the past two decades: Mikhail Moiseevich Botvinnik. The results of that encounter and of the tournaments that led to it show, first of all, that in Mikhail Nekhemevich Tal we have the representative of a definite new direction; and second, that the existence of this direction does not by any stretch of the imagination signify an end to the kind of chess struggle that is based not only on the computation of variations, but on logic and principle as well.

The author of this book, in the course of his twenty-year life in chess, has played quite a few sharp, tense games, where he had to balance for a while on a sword edge; but I would certainly be the last to conclude that chess consists solely of calculating variations. And I would hope that, rather than see the further course of chess history bear out such a conclusion, the new style of play will instead become but one of many elements in the arsenal of creative techniques that are comprised in the art of chess.

*****

CONTENTS

[xv]

ROUND ONE

1. Szabo—Geller
(Catalan Opening)

I have long suspected, whenever the books I have read began
discussing darksquare weaknesses
or an attack on the dark squares,
that the subject under discussion
was not only beyond my understanding, but beyond the author's as
well. "Certainly,", I would say
to myself, "it must be true that
the enemy dark squares will be
weak if his pawns stand on light
squares and he loses his darksquare bishop. But if he then
removes all of his pieces from
the dark squares, what will be
left for me to attack?"

Such was my line of reasoning,
until the day I realized that a
weakness of the dark squares is
also a weakness of the pieces and
pawns on the light squares. Lightsquare weaknesses are also possible, resulting in a weakening of
the enemy pieces and pawns on the
dark squares — as occurred, for
example, in the Geller - Najdorf
game in Round 13. The point of an
attack on the dark squares is
that, by placing my pawns and
pieces on the dark, I attack my
opponent's pieces and pawns on
the light.

The Szabo - Geller game provides a clear example of the method of exploiting a darksquare
weakness; and the combination
which was possible after Black's
24th fairly begs to be included
in a textbook, taking place as
it does entirely on light squares.

1.	c2-c4	Ng8-f6
2.	g2-g3	e7-e6
3.	Bf1-g2	d7-d5
4.	d2-d4	d5:c4
5.	Qd1-a4+	Nb8-d7
6.	Ng1-f3	a7-a6
7.	Qa4:c4	b7-b5
8.	Qc4-c6	...

Having hatched a plan to weak-
en the enemy dark squares, Szabo
undertakes a delicate maneuver
aimed at bringing about the exchange of the darksquare bishops,
which will further strengthen
his grip on the dark squares.

8.	...	Ra8-b8
9.	Bc1-f4	Nf6-d5

10.	Bf4-g5	Bf8-e7
11.	Bg5:e7	Qd8:e7
12.	0-0	Bc8-b7
13.	Qc6-c2	c7-c5
14.	d4:c5	Nd7:c5
15.	Rf1-c1	Rb8-c8
16.	Nb1-c3	Nd5-f6

A small but serious inaccuracy:
Black removes this piece from the
main theater of operations. Additionally, the combination 17 N:b5
ab 18 b4 now becomes possible, due
to the insufficiently protected
rook at c8. Szabo, however, continues with his plan, fixing the
pawns at a6 and b5 on their light
squares. 16.. Nb6 would have been
much better for Black: increasing
his control of c4 would have made
it more difficult for White to
decide on b2-b4.

17.	b2-b4	Nc5-a4
18.	Qc2-b3	Na4:c3
19.	Rc1:c3	Rc8:c3
20.	Qb3:c3	0-0
21.	Ra1-c1	Rf8-d8

Geller cannot take the c-file
away from his opponent, for if
21.. Rc8, White would simply take
the rook: 22 Q:c8+ B:c8 23 R:c8+
Ne8 24 Ne5!, and there is no
stopping 25 Bc6.

22.	a2-a3	Nf6-d5

Seeing that White's positional squeeze could become very dangerous, should he succeed in occupying the seventh rank or in
establishing his knight on c5,
Geller decides to complicate (his
move also stops both threats).

23.	Qc3-d4	f7-f6
24.	Nf3-e1	e6-e5
25.	Qd4-c5	...

A consistent, though rather un-inspired, continuation. 25 Qa7! would certainly have been much prettier, retaining his hold on the dark squares while attacking the enemy pieces and pawns on the light squares. Black would be un-able to smoke the queen out, since 25..Ra8 would obviously fail ag-ainst 26 B:d5+; while after 25..Kf8 26 Nd3 Ra8 27 Qc5, the ex-change of queens would bring the white knight to c5. And finally, 25..Rd7 brings on an elegant lit-tle combination: 26 Q:b7! If Black takes the queen, then 27 B:d5+, followed by 28 Rc8+ leads to the complete extermination of Black's pieces — curiously enough, all of them perish on light squares.

Black may have intended to ans-wer 25 Qa7 with 25..e4, and if 26 B:e4, not 26..Nf4? (which would be nicely refuted by 27 Bf3), but simply 26..Q:e4 27 Q:b7 Q:e2, with an unclear game. On 25..e4, how-ever, White's bishop would leave the blocked diagonal for an equ-ally successful career on its neighbor (with 26 Bh3).

25.	...	Qe7:c5
26.	b4:c5	

White would have maintained a clear advantage with 26 R:c5, but Szabo probably thought that his pin on the knight, combined with his threat to advance the c-pawn would assure him victory. However, Black finds the defensive maneu-ver ..Rd8-d7-e7.

26.	...	Bb7-c6
27.	Rc1-d1	Rd8-d7
28.	Bg2-h3	Rd7-e7
29.	Ne1-c2	a6-a5
30.	Bh3-g2	Re7-d7
31.	Bg2-h3	Rd7-e7
32.	Kg1-f1	...

Szabo declines the repetition, although he no longer has the bet-ter position. This is a psycho-logical error common to chess-players of all ranks from begin-ner to grandmaster: to lose one's objectivity is almost invariably to lose the game as well.

32.	...	Kg8-f7
33.	Kf1-e1	

This was White's last chance to force the draw with Bh3-g2-h3.

33.	...	Re7-c7
34.	Rd1-d3	Bc6-b7

And now White will lose his c-pawn.

35.	Nc2-e3	Rc7:c5
36.	Ne3-f5	Bb7-c6
37.	Nf5-d6+	Kf7-f8
38.	Bh3-g2	g7-g6
39.	Ke1-d2	Kf8-e7
40.	Nd6-e4	Rc5-c4
41.	f2-f3	f6-f5
42.	Ne4-f2	Rc4-a4
43.	Nf2-d1	e5-e4
44.	f3:e4	f5:e4
45.	Rd3-b3	Ra4-d4+
46.	Kd2-c1	b5-b4

Black's plan is simple: to cre-ate a passed pawn and queen it. White can offer no real resistance to this.

47.	Nd1-e3	Nd5-c3
48.	a3:b4	Nc3-e2+
49.	Kc1-b1	Bc6-a4
50.	Rb3-b2	Ne2-c3+
51.	Kb1-c1	a5:b4
52.	Rb2-d2	Rd4:d2
53.	Kc1:d2	Ke7-d6
54.	Ne3-g4	Kd6-c5
55.	h2-h4	Kc5-d4
56.	h4-h5	g6:h5
57.	Ng4-e3	Nc3-b1+

| 58. | Kd2-e2 | Ba4-b5+ |
| 59. | Ke2-f2 | b4-b3 |

WHITE RESIGNED

******

2. Najdorf—Reshevsky
(Nimzoindian Defense)

1.	d2-d4	Ng8-f6
2.	c2-c4	e7-e6
3.	Nb1-c3	Bf8-b4
4.	e2-e3	...

Aron Nimzovich, who invented this defense, could hardly have thought that thirty years later the masters of chess still would not have solved the basic problem: whether putting the question to Black's bishop with an immediate 4 a3 is good or bad. Naturally, if we knew it to be good, that would render all other tries pointless, to say the least.

4.	...	c7-c5
5.	Bf1-d3	0-0
6.	Ng1-f3	d7-d5

Nimzovich never used to advance his c-pawn to c5 without need; he hoped that, after he gave White doubled pawns by means of the exchange at c3, sooner or later he could induce White to play d4-d5, after which he could establish his knight at c5. A lot of water has gone under the bridge since, and the modern master puts no great stock in that far-off prospect of capitalizing on the doubled c-pawns. Instead, the immediate counterattack on the center with every means available has become one of the standard ideas for Black in the Nimzo-Indian.

7.	0-0	Nb8-c6
8.	a2-a3	Bb4:c3
9.	b2:c3	d5:c4
10.	Bd3:c4	Qd8-c7

Today, this position has been studied as thoroughly as were the Muzio and Evans Gambits a century ago. What are the basic features of this position, and how does the evaluation of those features give rise to the further plans for both sides?

The placement of White's pieces radiates a great deal of potential energy, which ought to be converted into kinetic — White must set his center pawns in motion, activating both his rooks and his deeply-buried darksquare bishop. The most logical plan would seem to be the advance of the e-pawn, first to e4, and then to e5, to drive Black's knight from f6 and lay the groundwork for a kingside attack.

Black in turn must either prevent the e-pawn's advance or counterattack the white pawn center, which will lose some of its solidity the moment the pawn advances from e3 to e4.

In this game, Reshevsky combines both of Black's ideas to achieve a favorable disposition of his forces, while Najdorf does not put nearly enough vigor into the execution of his plan.

| 11. | a3-a4 | ... |

Of all the possible continuations that have been used here, this one may well be the least logical: it resolves only one minor problem, the development of the queen's bishop — and to a poor square, at that. The pawn at c5 will find defenders easily enough, and the bishop will find itself out of the action. That outflung pawn at a4 will not be a jewel in White's position either.

11.	...	b7-b6
12.	Bc1-a3	Bc8-b7
13.	Bc4-e2	Rf8-d8
14.	Qd1-c2	Nc6-a5
15.	d4:c5	b6:c5
16.	c3-c4	Bb7-e4
17.	Qc2-c3	Ra8-b8

(See diagram next page)

Another weak point in White's position: Black now controls b3. White cannot play 18 Rb1, and 18 Nd2 is not attractive either.

| 18. | Rf1-d1 | Rd8:d1+ |

(Position after 17..Rab8)

| 19. | Ra1:d1 | Be4-c6! |

Initiating a straightforward siege of the a-pawn.

| 20. | Qc3-c2 | h7-h6 |
| 21. | h2-h3 | Na5-b3 |

Black hasn't the time to bring the knight to b6: if 21..Nd7, then 22 Bb2 Nb6 23 Qc3, forking g7 and a5.

| 22. | Ba3-b2 | Nf6-d7 |
| 23. | Qc2-c3 | f7-f6 |

Strategically, Black already has a won game: the a-pawn is falling, while White has yet to find useful employment for his bishops. In this difficult situation, Najdorf employs the resiliency of his position to work up one last tactical try.

| 24. | Nf3-h2 | ... |

As time-pressure approaches, the less strategy and the more tactics.

| 24. | ... | Nd7-b6 |

How to meet the threat of 25..N:a4 is a question White was never called upon to answer, because Reshevsky, having four minutes left to make his last 16 moves, offered a draw. Evidently he was unable to calculate fully the consequences of White's combination 25 Ng4 N:a4 26 N:f6+ gf 27·Q:f6.

Right after the game, and later in his published commentaries as well, Najdorf showed that he had a guaranteed draw: for example, 27.. N:b2 28 Bg4, and there is no escaping the perpetual after 29 B:e6+ and 30 Bf5+, etc. One pretty variation is 28..Qg7 29 B:e6+ Kh7 30 Bf5+ Kh8 31 Rd8+ R:d8 32 Q:d8+ Qg8 33 Qf6+.

If Black had not taken the pawn at move 25, playing 25..e5 instead, then 26 Qc2 and 27 Qg6 also leads inevitably to a perpetual check.

White would have had a harder time if, instead of 24..Nb6, Black had simply played 24..B:a4, leaving the knight to defend the king side. Now 25 Ng4 would not have nearly the same effect, in view of 25.. e5 26 Qc2 Nf8. Another possibility after 24..Nb6 25 Ng4 would be 25..Nd4; for example: 26 ed N:a4, etc. The aim of 25..Nd4 is to close off the c3-f6 diagonal, thereby cancelling out White's N:f6+ gf; Q:f6. Since such variations are impossible to calculate accurately in time-pressure, Reshevsky preferred the

DRAW

******

3. Petrosian—Keres
(English Opening)

1.	c2-c4	c7-c5
2.	Ng1-f3	Ng8-f6
3.	d2-d4	c5:d4
4.	Nf3:d4	e7-e6
5.	g2-g3	d7-d5
6.	Bf1-g2	e6-e5

In contrast to his opponent's somewhat slothful play, Keres is handling the opening energetically: taking advantage of a tactical nuance (7 Nf3 d4 8 N:e5 Qa5+), he obtains a brace of powerful center pawns, just waiting for the chance to push onward.

```
 7.  Nd4-c2      d5-d4
 8.  0-0         Nb8-c6
 9.  Nb1-d2      Bc8-g4
10.  Nd2-f3      a7-a5
```

It was time to start thinking about castling and developing the rooks to support the further advance of the pawns. One attractive line, involving long castling — 10..B:f3 11 B:f3 e4 12 Bg2 h6 13 b3 Qd7 14 Bb2 0-0-0 — fails to come off, because on the 11th move White recaptures, not with the bishop, but with the pawn, which he then advances to f4, breaking up the enemy center pawns. After the text move, Black no longer has to worry about an eventual b2-b4.

```
11.  Bc1-g5      Bf8-c5
```

Black sets up the threat of 12..e4, but grants White the opportunity to stop this pawn cold. After 11..Be7!, White would not have had this blockading opportunity. In order to meet the threatened advance of the e-pawn, White would have been practically forced to make the exchange on f6.

```
12.  e2-e4       h7-h6
13.  Bg5:f6      Qd8:f6
14.  Nc2-e1      Qf6-e6
```

The most important point in this position is unquestionably d4: it marks the intersection of the lines of force from the black bishop to the white king and from the black rook to the white queen; also, if the black knight could get to d4, it would take away four squares from the white queen and strengthen the pin on the knight at f3. White's next — and quite obvious — move will reduce the value of this communications nexus to a minimum, if not to zero. The blockaded d-pawn will frustrate both the bishop on c5 and the rook on a8 with its aspirations to d8. The nexus could have been cleared for the price of a pawn: 14..d3

would have given Black a very promising game.

```
15.  Ne1-d3      Bc5-e7
16.  h2-h3       Bg4:f3
```

Black could not capture the h-pawn, since 17 B:h3 Q:h3 18 Nd:e5 N:e5 19 N:e5 would have deprived him of either the castling privilege or his d-pawn; and retreating to h5 would have permitted 17 N:d4!

```
17.  Qd1:f3      Qe6:c4
18.  Rf1-c1      Qc4-e6
```

```
19.  Qf3-f5      ...
```

A pretty final stroke, based on combinative motifs, to the defensive system White has devised. If Black exchanges queens and continues with ..f7-f6, he will lose: 19..Q:f5 20 ef f6 21 R:c6! bc 22 B:c6+ Kf7 23 Bd5+!, followed by the capture of the rook at a8. If, after exchanging queens, Black defends the e-pawn with his bishop instead, then White has a positional advantage. And if 19..Qd6, then 20 f4 g6 21 fe, or 20 Rc5 are strong.

19..Bd6 20. Q:e6+ fe 21. a3 Kd7 22. Bf1 a4 23. Ne1 Ra5 24. Rc2 Rc8 25. Rac1 Na7 26. R:c8 N:c8 27. Bc4 Be7

The position is now a clear draw: White's knight returns to d3 presently, leaving Black no place to penetrate. Keres plays it out to the 41st move and adjourns, hoping to find some hidden resource at his leisure.

28. Nd3 Nd6 29. f3 N:c4 30. R:c4
Bd6 31. Kf2 Ra6 32. Ke2 g5
33. Kd1 Ra8 34. Ke2 h5 35. Rc1
Rh8 36. Rh1 h4 37. g4 b5 38. Rc1
Rb8 39. Kd1 Rb6 40. Rc2 Rb8
41. Rc1 Rc8

The game was agreed a

DRAW

without further play.

******

4. Averbakh—Smyslov
(Ruy Lopez)

1.	e2-e4	e7-e5
2.	Ng1-f3	Nb8-c6
3.	Bf1-b5	a7-a6
4.	Bb5-a4	Ng8-f6
5.	0-0	Bf8-e7
6.	Rf1-e1	b7-b5
7.	Ba4-b3	d7-d6
8.	c2-c3	0-0
9.	h2-h3	Nc6-a5
10.	Bb3-c2	c7-c5
11.	d2-d4	Qd8-c7

Chigorin's System in the Ruy
Lopez is a frequent guest in international competition, but it
appeared in Zurich only six
times. White marshals his forces
for a kingside attack which generally doesn't have much bite to
it, since today's grandmasters
have learned quite well how to
set up a defensible position.
Not surprisingly, therefore, most
of the games played with this
variation have lately been winding up drawn.

12.	Nb1-d2	Bc8-d7
13.	Nd2-f1	Rf8-e8
14.	Nf1-e3	Be7-f8
15.	Bc1-d2	g7-g6
16.	Ra1-c1	...

I find it hard to tie White's
last two moves in with his strategic plan: the bishop on d2 and
the rook on c1 are not one whit
better placed than they were at
their original positions. After
this loss of two tempi, White's
diversion on the kingside can
have no serious future. Averbakh
decides to generate piece play
on this wing without taking on
additional responsibilities with
the advance of the g-pawn.

16.	...	Na5-c6
17.	d4:c5	d6:c5
18.	Nf3-h2	Ra8-d8

19.	Qd1-f3	Bf8-g7
20.	Re1-d1	Bd7-e6
21.	Bc2-b1	Qc7-e7

This being the first round,
both players wage rather blood-
less battle: neither has yet
pushed a man past the boundary
of his own territory. Both sides
are concealing, as much as possible, the area in which they intend to take action.

22.	Nh2-g4	Nf6:g4

23.	Ne3:g4	...

In the event of 23 hg, Black
had prepared the reply 23.. Qh4.

23.	...	Nc6-a5
24.	b2-b3	Na5-c6
25.	Bd2-e3	Rd8:d1+
26.	Qf3:d1	Re8-d8
27.	Qd1-f3	Rd8-d7
28.	Rc1-d1	b5-b4

As a result of White's slow
play, Black has obtained a slight
advantage. Now he wishes to secure d4 for his knight, but he
might well have considered a plan
involving ..c5-c4, which could be
prepared here with 28..a5.

29.	Rd1:d7	...

(See diagram, top of next page)

29.	...	Be6:d7
30.	Ng4-h6+	...

Smyslov wasn't worried about
the check at h6, intending simply to move his king to f8; but

at the last moment he noticed the textbook stroke 31 B:c5!, and the queen is lost. Now he must give up his darksquare bishop instead, which might have proved decisive under other circumstances.

30.	...	Bg7:h6
31.	Be3:h6	b4:c3
32.	Qf3:c3	Nc6-d4

DRAW

Black's centralized knight fully compensates for White's powerful bishop at h6.

******

5. Talmanov—Bronstein
(Benoni Defense)

It's a difficult thing to maintain objectivity when commenting on one's own games. Variations running in the commentator's favor are always interesting, so details flow quick and plentiful from the pen; variations which favor one's opponent, however, are often unclear as can be. For one's own mistakes, one seeks (and generally finds) justification; while the opponent's errors seem so natural as to need no explanation whatever. So even before beginning to comment on my game from Round One, I feel compelled to note that Black did not have a decisive advantage until very late in the game, almost the very end. Psychologically, White's loss can be traced to the fact that he missed the turning point of the game, at which it was necessary for him to begin giving serious thought to the problem of how to get a draw. As regards the purely chessic reasons for his loss, these I shall try to illuminate in my notes.

1.	d2-d4	Ng8-f6
2.	c2-c4	c7-c5
3.	d4-d5	g7-g6
4.	Nb1-c3	d7-d6
5.	e2-e4	b7-b5

What does Black achieve by sacrificing a pawn? First, he undermines the spearhead of the white pawn chain, the pawn on d5; in addition, after the unavoidable ..a7-a6 and b5:a6, he obtains the good diagonal a6-f1 for his bishop, which would have far fewer prospects along the c8-h3 diagonal. The two open files Black obtains on the queenside, allowing him active play against White's a- and b-pawns, also speak in favor of the sacrifice. Nor ought we to forget Black's bishop at g7: since Black intends to leave his e-pawn at e7 in this system, the bishop's sphere of activity is automatically increased. And finally, there is the interesting strategic idea (encountered also in other variations of the King's Indian) of developing the queen's rook without moving it from its original square.

Of course, the sacrifice has its deficiencies as well, chief among these being the pawn deficit. Should White gradually succeed in overcoming all his difficulties, and reach an endgame, he will have excellent winning chances. It is for this last reason that this variation was not seen in any more games from this tournament. I used it here, partly because I did not want to begin this tournament with the sort of protracted defense Black is usually forced to put up with in one of the "normal" lines.

6.	c4:b5	Bf8-g7
7.	Ng1-f3	0-0
8.	Bf1-e2	a7-a6

Up to this point, Black might still have hoped to regain his pawn, but now it becomes a real sacrifice.

5.	c4:d5	d7-d6
6.	Ng1-f3	g7-g6
7.	g2-g3	Bf8-g7
8.	Bf1-g2	0-0
9.	0-0	a7-a6

The system Black has selected is not without its drawbacks, positionally speaking, but he does possess several trumps: the open e-file, good diagonals for both his bishops, and three pawns against two on the queenside. For his part, White can usually establish a knight at c4, putting the squeeze on the d-pawn, the keystone of Black's entire fortress. In this game, Euwe decides he would rather play on the queenside, creating weaknesses there for occupation by his pieces. Later, the game gets interesting, thanks to bold play — bold to the point of sacrifices — by both sides.

10.	a2-a4	Nb8-d7
11.	Nf3-d2	...

A typical maneuver in this position: White brings the knight to c4, and then plays a4-a5 to neutralize Black's queenside majority by blockade; should Black then play ..b7-b5, White's knight gains access to a5 and c6.

11.	...	Rf8-e8
12.	a4-a5	b7-b5
13.	a5:b6	Nd7:b6
14.	Nd2-b3	Qd8-c7
15.	Nb3-a5	Bc8-d7
16.	h2-h3	Bd7-b5
17.	Bc1-e3	Nf6-d7

Black activates his pieces, intending to bring the knight on d7 via e5 to c4, or else to play ..c5-c4 followed by ..Nd7-c5.

18.	Qd1-b3	...

Halting Black's plan. White is not worried about the loss of the e-pawn, since he would obtain an attack on the dark squares as compensation: for instance, 18..B:c3 19 Q:c3 B:e2 20 Rfe1 Bb5 21 Bh6 f6 22 Re6; or 22 b3 first, with the threat of 23 Re6.

18.	...	Nd7-f6

Black had a strong move at his disposal, namely 18..Rab8, underscoring the white queen's insecure position: for example, 19 N:b5 ab 20 Nc6 Rb7, and White cannot play 21 Q:b5 in view of 21..N:d5. After 18..Rab8, the threat of 19..c4 would carry more weight also.

The plan Black actually selects is not as good: he intends to sacrifice an exchange, hoping to obtain complications.

19.	Rf1-c1	Bb5-d7
20.	Qb3-d1	...

White prepares the decisive break b2-b4, which Black prevents by giving up his rook for the bishop.

20.	...	Re8:e3
21.	f2:e3	Bg7-h6
22.	Qd1-d3	Ra8-e8
23.	Kg1-h2	Re8:e3
24.	Qd3:a6	...

24. ..Re5 25. Rf1 Bc8 26. Qb5 Bd7
27. Nc6 Kg7

The d-pawn could not have been captured, here or on the previous move: if 27..Nb:d5, White takes twice and checks with the knight at e7.

28. Ra6 Nc8 29. Qb8 Q:b8 30. N:b8
Bf5 31. Rc6 Re8 32. e4 Bd7 33. e5
R:e5 34. N:d7 N:d7 35. R:c8 Re3
36. Rc6 Ne5 37. R:d6 Rd3 38. Rd1
Re3 39. Rc6

BLACK RESIGNED

******

7. Stahlberg—Boleslavsky
(King's Indian)

1.	d2-d4	Ng8-f6
2.	c2-c4	g7-g6
3.	g2-g3	Bf8-g7
4.	Bf1-g2	0-0
5.	Nb1-c3	d7-d6
6.	Ng1-f3	Nb8-d7
7.	0-0	e7-e5
8.	e2-e4	Rf8-e8
9.	h2-h3	e5:d4
10.	Nf3:d4	Nd7-c5
11.	Rf1-e1	a7-a5
12.	Qd1-c2	...

Fifteen years ago, the King's Indian Defense was played in Soviet tournaments only by those wishing to avoid the passive, thoroughly analyzed variations of the Queen's Gambit Declined; outside our borders, it was hardly played at all. As recently as the 1948 World's Championship, the King's Indian figured in only two games out of fifty. Here

in Zurich, one out of three games opened with 1 d2-d4 turned into a King's Indian, and foreign players used it just as often as ours did.

The diagrammed position is a familiar one to theory; the text move is one of the latest discoveries. Wishing to develop his bishop to e3, White also overprotects his e-pawn!

The knight at d4 is temporarily undefended, of course, and Black could win a center pawn by 12 ..Nf:e4 13 N:e4 B:d4; but then it would be White's turn to move, and he would seize the key square f6 with 14 Bg5 Qd7 15 Nf6+ B:f6 16 B:f6, removing Black's "Indian" bishop, without which all Indian configurations become pointless. The extra pawn would be no consolation: occasional attempts to prove otherwise have nearly all wound up disastrously for Black, so no one snaps at the e-pawn anymore.

12.	...	a5-a4
13.	Bc1-e3	c7-c6
14.	Ra1-d1	Nf6-d7

Characteristically, the King's Indian Defense features a tense battle waged on all fronts simultaneously. The system used here secures White considerable territory, not only in the center, but on the kingside as well.

I do not wish to leave the reader the false impression that White's further task, which is to transform his sizable spatial plus into a material advantage, will be an easy one. The secret of the King's Indian's hardihood is that, while conceding space, Black builds a few small but weighty details into his configuration. Foremost among these are his long-range bishops at g7 and c8, his firmly entrenched knight at c5 and the rook at e8, which maintain constant watch on the e-pawn. Nor ought we to forget his pawns. The "weak" pawn on d6 is just waiting for the chance to push to d5, so White must continually keep an eye on that. The pawn at a4 also has an important role: the threat to advance it to a3 can upset his opponent's plans for that sector at any time, so White must take extra precautions regarding the defense of c3 and c4. If 12 Qc2 was White's latest theoretical discovery, then the same might justifiably be said of Black's 14..Nfd7. 14..Qa5 was the old move, but after 15 Bf4, either the bishop at g7 or the rook at e8 had to move to an inferior position, whereas now the pawn can be covered with 15..Ne5.

15.	f2-f4	Qd8-a5
16.	Be3-f2	Nd7-b6
17.	Bg2-f1	Bc8-d7
18.	a2-a3	...

Stahlberg decides to rid his position once and for all of the threat of a black pawn advance to a3. This move deprives the square b3 of pawn protection, but it also strengthens the position of the pawn at b2 and generally of the whole constellation a3-b2-c3.

The next stage of the game — roughly to move 30 — consists of skillful maneuvers from both sides, inducing weaknesses, White's preparation for e4-e5 and Black's for ..d7-d5 or ..f7-f5, and mutual prevention of these breaks.

18.	...	Ra8-d8
19.	Kg1-h2	Bd7-c8
20.	Nc3-a2	Nb6-d7
21.	Bf1-g2	Nd7-f6
22.	Na2-c3	Rd8-d7
23.	Nd4-f3	Rd7-e7

The next two moves are somewhat unusual, both for White and for Black: Black concentrates maximum firepower against the pawn at e4, an assault which White tries to divert by threatening to take on d6. It is entirely characteristic that, in order to carry out this idea, White can find no better retreat square for his centralized knight at d4, the pride of his position, than back to its original square g1, since all other retreat squares would interfere, in one way or another, with the coordination between his pieces.

This seems an appropriate time to impart to the reader the secret of the d6-pawn in the King's Indian Defense. This pawn, although backward on an open file, proves nevertheless a tough little nut to crack, because it is so hard to reach. It might seem that nothing could be simpler than dropping the knight back from d4, but the problem is that White needs his knight precisely on d4, where it observes the squares b5, c6, e6 and f5, and neutralizes the power of the bishop at g7. Only after White has taken precautions against all of Black's possible attacks (..a4-a3, ..Bc8-e6, ..f7-f5) can his knight allow itself to leave the center; but meanwhile Black has time to regroup.

So the weakness of the d6-pawn turns out to be largely fictive. Modern methods of opening play allow for many such fictive weak pawns, but it was precisely this "permanent" weakness at d6 which so long condemned the King's Indian to the list of dubious openings.

24.	Nf3-g1	...

The knight will return, five moves later, to help the pawn on e4 cross the Rubicon. The pawn could have been pushed at once, but that would have given up control of the f5 square; Black's bishop could go there, and after 24 e5 Bf5, White would have had to sacrifice his queen by taking the knight at f6 with his pawn — but that would win for White. The simple 24..de, on the other hand, would give Black excellent play.

White could have taken the a-pawn here, but at too great a price: White needs his darksquare bishop as much as Black does.

Boleslavsky's 24th move is an invitation to White's rook to capture that long-disputed point at last; after 25..Nb6, however, Black's knight enters c4. Stahlberg's decision is most probably the correct one: before proceeding with the siege of the d-pawn, he exchanges off the "Indian" bishops.

24.	...	Nf6-d7
25.	Bf2-d4	Nd7-b6
26.	Bd4:g7	Kg8:g7
27.	Rd1:d6	Nb6:c4
28.	Rd6-d1	Bc8-e6

The position appears basically unchanged, but an important event

has taken place: the disappearance of the darksquare bishops,
and of the pawns at c4 and d6.
With the bishops' disappearance,
both sides must now make some ad-
justments in their basic strategies. Black, for example, must
give top priority to securing
his position on the long diagonal, and against the incursion
of a white pawn to f6 and queen
to h6. Considering the seriousness of this threat, Boleslavsky's
last move was a very good one:
the bishop is ready for action
on the a2-g8 diagonal, and the
f-pawn, by going to f6, covers
the king against any attacks
from the main road; the bishop
replaces the pawn at f7. White,
for his part, must punch a hole
in this new defensive line at any
cost, or else the initiative will
pass to his opponent, and all the
weaknesses in White's position,
which were of only passing interest so long as he was on the
offensive (b3, the lack of pawn
control of d3, c3 and f3, and
the passive bishop at g2), might
become the basis for combinations.

29.	Qc2-f2	f7-f6
30.	Ng1-f3	Be6-f7
31.	e4-e5	...

Stahlberg is a consummate tactician, and a master of the kingside attack, and this sacrifice
is in his style. White cannot be
left master of e5, so the pawn
must be taken; but this opens the
f-file, and Black's king comes

under fire.

31.	...	f6:e5
32.	Nf3:e5	Nc4:e5
33.	Re1:e5	Re7:e5
34.	f4:e5	Re8:e5

| 35. | Rd1-f1 | Re5-f5 |

In the heat of battle, Boleslavsky disregards his fierce
time-pressure and declines the
draw he could probably have secured by means of the accurate
retreat 35..Qc7, defending against both threats, 36 Q:f7 and
36 Qf6+. Black's dream of capitalizing on his extra pawn is
impractical, considering his exposed king. Even if Black should
successfully run the gauntlet,
warding off all assaults, White
could still, in all probability,
find a perpetual check.

| 36. | Qf2-d4+ | ... |

White's task is now partially
complete: the queen has attained
the long diagonal.

36.	...	Kg7-g8
37.	Rf1:f5	g6:f5
38.	Qd4-e5	...

Judging from his next two
moves, it seems quite likely that
Black simply overlooked this modest little move, which shakes his
position to its foundations.

| 38. | ... | Qa5-b6! |

The pin on the knight must be
liquidated at once. The threat

was not so much 39 Q:f5 as 39 g4, and if 39.. fg 40 Ne4. With this timely retreat of his queen to b6, Black avoids the worst. Attempting to save his f-pawn by 38.. Bg6 might have had tragic consequences, since besides 39 g4, White could also have exploited the new pin motif to drive the black king into a mating net almost by force: 39 Bf1 Qb6 40 Bc4+ Kf8 41 Qf6+ Ke8 42 Nd5 — such variations are certainly not for time-pressure. Now White restores the material balance, and Black's king is in as much danger as before.

39.	Qe5:f5	Bf7-g6
40.	Qf5-e5	Nc5-d3

Black uses his last move before the time control to remind White that there are targets in his own camp too. Black's queen is ready to take the b-pawn, or, circumstances permitting, to enter at f2 with the threat of ..Ne1.

41.	Qe5-e6+	...

41.	...	Kg8-g7?

This was the move Black wrote on his scoresheet, then sealed in the envelope which was handed to the chief arbiter of the tournament. Stahlberg, of course, without any knowledge of that sealed move, had to analyze both of Black's possible replies, 41.. Kg7 and .. Bf7.

42.	Qe6-e7+	...

When he adjourned, Boleslavsky considered the possibility 42 Nd5,
but felt that after 42.. Q:b2 White would have, at most, a perpetual check. This powerful move, however, changes matters completely. Black cannot retreat to g8, since 43 Nd5 would follow; so the bishop has to interpose, but then the knight can enter d6 via e4. So 41.. Bf7 was a better move than 41.. Kg7: White could give perpetual check or win the a-pawn with 42 Qg4+, but this would be fully compensated by the black queen's entry into f2. The most likely outcome would then be a draw. Well, the game was a draw here, too, but only after some interesting new adventures.

42.	...	Bg6-f7
43.	Nc3-e4	Qb6:b2
44.	Ne4-d6	Qb2-f2
45.	Nd6-e8+	...

Certainly the obvious, "what-else" moves are not always best.

45.	...	Kg7-g8
46.	Ne8-f6+	Kg8-g7
47.	Nf6-h5+	Kg7-g6
48.	g3-g4	Nd3-c5

DRAW

— on Stahlberg's offer. The attempt to end the game with a queen-sacrifice mating combination: 49 h4 h6? 50 Q:c5!! Q:c5 51 Be4+, is refuted by 49..Ne6.

48 h4 would not have won either: Black replies 48.. h6, and after 49 Qe4+ K:h5 50 Kh3, with the apparently unstoppable threat of mate by 51 g4, Black liquidates the threat with the surprising counterstroke 50.. Nf4+.

However, 45 h4, instead of 45 Ne8+, would have led to victory.

******
******

ROUND TWO

8. Kotov—Stahlberg
(Queen's Gambit)

1.	d2-d4	Ng8-f6
2.	c2-c4	e7-e6
3.	Ng1-f3	d7-d5
4.	Nb1-c3	Bf8-e7
5.	c4:d5	e6:d5

White usually enters the Exchange Variation of the Orthodox Queen's Gambit with the intention of playing a minority attack, in which he stations his rooks on the b- and c-files, and then advances his b-pawn and trades it off on c6 to create a backward black pawn. A number of master games have demonstrated that this is too direct a plan to pose any great danger to Black, who may, in his turn, expand upon his control of the e-file to carry an active piece game to the kingside, establishing approximate equality.

For this game, Kotov is not after a draw: he has other reasons altogether for trading off the center pawns. In the tradition of the old masters, he intends castling long, followed by a kingside pawn storm — an idea he conceals quite well for the next 5-7 moves.

6.	Bc1-f4	c7-c6
7.	Qd1-c2	g7-g6
8.	e2-e3	Bc8-f5
9.	Bf1-d3	Bf5:d3
10.	Qc2:d3	Nb8-d7
11.	h2-h3	Nd7-f8

Black's last five moves are all part of one plan. Stahlberg is perhaps the only grandmaster of our day who retains the Orthodox Defense as part of his repertoire, and he plays it like a virtuoso. This system, with 7.. g6 and the knight transfer to e6 prior to castling, is his invention. Neither Kotov, in the present game, nor the author, in the tournament's second half, nor even the World Champion, Botvinnik himself, in the Budapest tournament of 1952, could find any weak spot in the Swedish grandmaster's favorite defense.

12.	g2-g4	...

Kotov has kept his battle plans encoded long enough: now at last his true intentions are revealed.

12.	...	Nf8-e6
13.	Bf4-g3	...

This move is more than a little inconsequent. It would be good, if White were carrying out the queenside minority attack; but here, after the pawn has been pushed to g4, the more provocative 13 Be5 is better.

13.	...	Qd8-a5
14.	Nf3-d2	0-0

Fearlessly castling into it.

15.	0-0-0	...

White answers in kind. The battle is joined...

15.	...	Be7-b4
16.	Kc1-b1	Bb4:c3
17.	Qd3:c3	Qa5:c3
18.	b2:c3	...

... and ends straightway. As a result of this exchange, a pawn has moved from b2 to c3. Both sides prefer the new situation, each for his own reasons: White, because he has a new open file, and the pawn is closer to the center; and Black, because he need no longer fear the pawn storm, and he now controls the key square e4.

18.	...	Nf6-e4
19.	Nd2:e4	d5:e4
20.	Kb1-c2	Ra8-d8
21.	a2-a4	...

The game has gone into an ending which favors White a bit,

and requires accurate play from Black. White would have done better to play 21 Rb1, answering 21..Rd7 with 22 Rb2; then, after the f-file opened, he could obtain counterpressure on the b-pawn, saving his a2-a4 until after Black's ..b7-b6.

21.	...	f7-f5
22.	g4:f5	Rf8:f5
23.	c3-c4	Rd8-d7
24.	Kc2-c3	Ne6-g7
25.	Rd1-d2	Kg8-f7
26.	Bg3-b8	b7-b6
27.	Rd2-a2	Rf5-a5

White's inappropriately active play has resulted in a slight deterioration of his position.

28.	Bb8-e5	Ng7-f5
29.	Rh1-g1	h7-h5
30.	Be5-f4	...

30 Bg3 was correct: the exchange of minor pieces (.. N:g3) holds no terrors for White. Now, however, the knight gets to f3 via h4, and the white bishop's situation becomes precarious (even the longest of diagonals can sometimes grow too short).

30.	...	Nf5-h4
31.	Rg1-g5	Ra5:g5
32.	Bf4:g5	Nh4-f3
33.	h3-h4	...

If 33 Bf4 g5, followed by ..Ng1.

33.	...	Nf3:g5
34.	h4:g5	Kf7-e6
35.	a4-a5	h5-h4
36.	Ra2-a1	...

White's game is lost: he has nothing to match Black's passed pawn. However, he would have some practical chances of a draw in the following variation: 36 ab ab 37 Ra1 h3 38 Rh1 Rh7 39 Rh2; pawns are equal for the moment, and White's rook is unapproachable; to play for the win, therefore, Black's king must go for the g-pawn, which time White could use to attack the b- and c-pawns: 39.. Kf5 40 Kb4 K:g5 41 c5, and if 41.. bc+, White gets his draw; but on 41.. b5, he is one tempo short: 42 d5 cd 43 K:b5 Kh4 44 c6 — with the white king on b6, this would be a draw. But he should still have tried it, especially since the whole variation occurs just before the time control.

36.	...	b6:a5
37.	Kc3-d2	h4-h3
38.	Kd2-e2	h3-h2
39.	f2-f3	Rd7-h7
40.	Ra1-h1	e4:f3+
41.	Ke2:f3	a5-a4

WHITE RESIGNED

******

9. Geller—Euwe
(Nimzoindian Defense)

One of the tournament's best games, and the recipient of a brilliancy prize. White initiated a powerful attack on the king by sacrificing his c4-pawn. This attack gave Geller every hope of success, provided Black held to the traditional sort of queen-side counterattack. Euwe, however, carried out two remarkable ideas: 1) utilizing his queen-side lines of communication for an attack on the king's wing, and 2) decoying the enemy's forces deep into his own rear area, with the aim of cutting them off from the defense of their king.

It's a most diverting spectacle to watch White's pieces in their frontal assault on the king, burrowing further and further, while Black is transferring his forces by roundabout routes.

1.	d2-d4	Ng8-f6
2.	c2-c4	e7-e6
3.	Nb1-c3	Bf8-b4
4.	e2-e3	c7-c5
5.	a2-a3	Bb4:c3+
6.	b2-c3	b7-b6
7.	Bf1-d3	Bc8-b7

8.   f2-f3   ...

A small but significant opening
subtlety: Black substituted .. b6
and .. Bb7 for the more usual
.. Nc6 and .. 0-0; and White, who
failed to notice in time to react
correctly with 7 Ne2, must now
spend an extra tempo preparing
e3-e4. Such details should never
be underestimated, but neither
should they be overvalued. Occasionally it is said that White's
advantage consists of his right
to the first move: should he lose
a tempo, then, the advantage must
necessarily pass to Black. Practically speaking, however, the advantage of playing White boils
down to greater freedom in selecting a plan to suit one's tastes;
once the game has settled into
its ordained track, the loss of
a single tempo is not always so
serious.

8.	...	Nb8-c6
9.	Ng1-e2	0-0
10.	0-0	Nc6-a5
11.	e3-e4	Nf6-e8

Black retreats his knight to
forestall the pin with 12 Bg5, and
to be able to answer f3-f4 with
.. f7-f5, blockading the king's
wing. White therefore secures f5
before advancing his f-pawn. It
would be senseless to defend the
pawn at c4 now: that pawn was
doomed by White's fifth move.

12.	Ne2-g3	c5:d4
13.	c3:d4	Ra8-c8
14.	f3-f4	Na5:c4
15.	f4-f5	f7-f6
16.	Rf1-f4	...

White's attack has become rather threatening. Black's previous move was necessary to forestall White's intention to push
his pawn to f6, and then, after
16.. N:f6, to pin the knight after all, piling up on the king
with the combined firepower of
queen, rooks and three minor
pieces. Even now, White needs
only two moves to transfer his
rook and queen to the h-file, and
then it might appear that nothing
could save the black king.

Euwe, however, is not easily
flustered. Remember that in his
lifetime he played more than
seventy games with Alekhine, the
most feared attacking player of

our time.

16.   ...   b6-b5!

The beginning of a remarkable
plan. Clearly, any defensive maneuvers on the kingside are fore-
doomed, since they involve pieces
with an inconsequential radius of
activity (.. Rf7, .. Qe7, etc.).
But Black does have another defensive resource, and that is
counterattack! The bishop at b7,
the rook at c8, and the knight at
c4 are all well-based; all that
remains is to bring up the queen.
The basis for this counterattack
is Black's preponderance on the
central squares. With 16..b5,
Black reinforces the knight on c4
and opens a path for the queen
to b6. Still, one cannot help
feeling that his operations are
too little and too late ...

17. Rf4-h4   Qd8-b6

Pinning White's queen to the
defense of the d-pawn, Black
prevents the intended 18 Qh5.
After 17 Qh5 Qb6 18 Ne2 Ne5, we
get the echo-variation, with the
white rook unable to get to h4.

18.	e4-e5	Nc4:e5
19.	f5:e6	Ne5:d3
20.	Qd1:d3	Qb6:e6

All of White's moves required
detailed and precise analysis.
Here, for example, the natural
20 ed would fail to 20.. Qc6.

21. Qd3:h7+   ...

Thus, White has broken through after all, at an insignificant cost. Once again, Black's position appears critical.

| 21. | ... | Kg8-f7 |
| 22. | Bc1-h6 | Rf8-h8 |

If Black's 16th move was the beginning of his strategic plan of counterattack, then this rook sacrifice is its fundamental tactical stroke, with the aim of drawing the white queen still further afield and decoying it away from the c2 square, meanwhile attacking the king.

| 23. | Qh7:h8 | Rc8-c2 |

Threatening mate in a few moves: 24.. R:g2+, 25.. Qc4+, etc. Detailed analysis, requiring more than just one week's time, showed that White could have saved himself from mate by finding a few "only" and very difficult moves. First, he has to play 24 d5; if then 24.. Qb6+ 25 Kh1 Qf2 26 Rg1 B:d5, White saves himself with 27 Re4!; and on the immediate 24.. B:d5, not 25 Rd4 — only 25 Rd1! works: after 25.. R:g2+ 26 Kf1 gh, neither 27 R:h6 nor 27 R:d5 once again, the only move is 27 Q:h6. Black would still have bishop and two pawns for his rook then, which would leave him good winning chances, considering the open position of White's king. It goes without saying that Geller had no practical chance to find all of these moves over the board.

The analysts also showed that the ..Rf8-h8 idea was actually a little premature, and that .. Rc4 first was better. However, those who love chess will find it difficult to agree with this. Moves like 22.. Rh8 are not forgotten.

24.	Ra1-c1	Rc2:g2+
25.	Kg1-f1	Qe6-b3
26.	Kf1-e1	Qb3-f3

WHITE RESIGNED

******

10. Smyslov—Szabo
(Reti Opening)

1. c4 Nf6 2. g3 c6 3. Nf3 d5
4. b3 g6 5. Bb2 Bg7 6. Bg2 Qb6
7. Qc1 0-0 8. 0-0 Nbd7 9. cd cd
10. Bd4 Qd6 11. Qa3 Ne4 12. B:g7
K:g7 13. Q:d6 N:d6

With the queens and darksquare bishops gone, White is banking on the open c-file and chiefly on the advantage of his "good" bishop over Black's, which will be hemmed in by its own pawns.

14. Rc1 e6 15. Nc3 b6 16. d4 Ba6
17. Ne5 N:e5 18. de Nb5 19. N:b5 B:b5 20. Rc2 Rfc8 21. Rac1 R:c2
22. R:c2 Ba6 23. f4 Rc8 24. R:c8 B:c8 25. Kf2 Ba6 26. Ke3 h6
27. Bf3 f5

White's plan is too tame, and insufficient for winning purposes. Black needs only to keep his bishop on the a6-f1 diagonal and his king at e7: most importantly, he must not advance any of his pawns. His last two moves only help his opponent to create a passed pawn.

28. ef+ K:f6 29. Kd4 g5 30. fg+ hg 31. e4 de 32. K:e4 Bb5 33. h4 gh 34. gh a5 35. Kd4 a4 36. b4 a3

Allowing Black's pawn to get to a3 cost White his winning chances: he had to push his own pawn to a3 on move 35.

37. Be4 Be8 38. Bb1 Bf7 39. Kc3 e5 40. b5 Bd5 41. Kb4 e4 42. K:a3 e3 43. Bd3 Bf3 44. Kb4 e2
45. B:e2 B:e2 46. a4

DRAW

******

11. Keres—Averbakh
(Nimzoindian Defense)

1. d4 Nf6 2. c4 e6 3. Nc3 Bb4
4. e3 0-0 5. Bd3 d5 6. Nf3 c5
7. 0-0 Nc6 8. a3 B:c3 9. bc b6
10. Ne5 Bb7 11. f4 Na5 12. cd
Q:d5 13. Qe2 cd 14. ed Nb3
15. Rb1 N:c1 16. Rb:c1 Rac8
17. Qb2 Qd6 18. f5 ef 19. B:f5
Rc7 20. c4 Rd8 21. Rf4 g5

A surprising and correct decision. Black leaves his knight on
f6 without pawn protection and
exposes his king to win a pawn.
Averbakh's calculations have convinced him that the pawn cannot
be recovered, and Black's weaknesses will not be much of a
problem to him with the queens
off. White also has weak pawns
of his own on the queenside.

22. Rf2 Q:d4 23. Q:d4 R:d4
24. Rcf1 Rd6 25. h4 gh 26. Rf4
Rc5 27. Ng4 N:g4 28. R:g4+ Kf8
29. B:h7 Ba6 30. Rff4 Rh6 31. Bd3
h3 32. gh R:h3 33. Rd4 Bc8
34. Rd8+ Ke7 35. Rgd4 Be6 36. Kg2
Rg5+ 37. Kf2 Ra5 38. Rb8 R:a3
39. Be2 Rh2+ 40. Ke1 Ra1+ 41. Rd1
R:e2+

WHITE RESIGNED

******

12. Reshevsky—Petrosian
(Nimzoindian Defense)

1.	d2-d4	Ng8-f6
2.	c2-c4	e7-e6
3.	Nb1-c3	Bf8-b4
4.	e2-e3	0-0
5.	Bf1-d3	d7-d5
6.	Ng1-f3	c7-c5
7.	0-0	Nb8-c6
8.	a2-a3	Bb4:c3
9.	b2:c3	b7-b6

The text is thought to give
Black a cramped game, but if a
player likes precisely that sort
of "cramped game", then he will
get better results with it than
with a "freer" game. Generally
speaking, such evaluations, even
though they may sway the opinions
of the theoreticians, have far
less of an influence on practical
tournament games than is commonly
supposed.

10.	c4:d5	e6:d5
11.	Bc1-b2	...

Trying to improve one's position, and finding the correct

idea to accomplish that end, is
one of the bases of chess strategy in every phase of the game.
The proper move order also plays
an important part, but this falls
under the heading of tactical im-
plementation, which of course is
a major determinant of the eventual success of the strategic
plan.

Here, White's basic idea is
obvious: he needs a good development for both his bishops. He
can accomplish this in two ways:
either by playing a4 followed by
Ba3, or by taking dc bc, and then
playing c4. Apparently against
all logic, however, White places
his bishop on a diagonal which is
occupied by pawns, seemingly inviting Black to play ..c4 himself, and shut the bishop in for
good.

Why? As it turns out, 11 a4
would have been met by 11.. cd
12 cd Bg4, or 12 ed Ne4, attacking the c-pawn; and 11 dc bc
12 c4 would allow the reply
12.. Rb8, preventing 13 Bb2.

Having played 11 Bb2, however,
White can go ahead with his c3-c4,
either at once or after the preliminary 12 dc bc; so Black's reply is not merely useful, but almost obligatory. The next phase
of the struggle is defined by the
new pawn structure: already it
has much less to do with the
tastes and preferences of the
two players than it has to do
with their choice of opening.
White will set his f- and e-
pawns in motion, creating a
passed d-pawn and combining the
advance of these central pawns
with an attack on the f-file.
Black, with three pawns to two
on his right wing, cannot do too
much with them for the moment,
since he must first battle the
white bishop pair and central
preponderance.

11.	...	c5-c4
12.	Bd3-c2	Bc8-g4
13.	Qd1-e1	Nf6-e4

Black could have altered the
course of the struggle here by
taking the knight: 13.. B:f3
14. gf Nh5; but he refrained
from doing so. The standard explanation — White would be left
with the two bishops, a strong

pawn center, and the open g-
file — could hardly have de-
terred him, since one bishop
would be blocked by its own
pawns, and the pawn center is
not dangerous for the moment.
If 15 e4, for example, then
15.. Nf4 16 Kh1 Qh4 17 Bc1 Nd3
18 B:d3 cd 19 Qe3 de 20 fe Rfe8
21 f3 f5 22 e5 Rad8, and the
pawn at d3 is taboo.

However, after 13..B:f3 14 gf
Nh5 White could systematically
strengthen his position with
f4, f3, Qf2, Rae1, Bc1, Kh1 and
e4, in that or in some other order, depending on how Black replies (Rg1 might also prove necessary, etc.). A direct attack
on the king would be Black's
only possible counter, and it
would have had very small chances
of success, considering his restricted maneuvering space: the
pawn barriers hamper the mobility
of his knights.

Petrosian continues following
his own line, figuring that as
long as he has made no unsound
moves, nor upset the positional
balance, he will not risk finding
himself in a losing position.

14.	Nf3-d2	Ne4:d2
15.	Qe1:d2	Bg4-h5
16.	f2-f3	Bh5-g6
17.	e3-e4	Qd8-d7
18.	Ra1-e1	d5:e4
19.	f3:e4	Rf8-e8

On 20 a4 there could follow
20.. Ne5! 21 Ba3 Nd3 22 B:d3 cd
23 Q:d3 Q:a4.

| 20. | Qd2-f4 | b6-b5 |

Black prevents the maneuver
21 a4 and 22 Ba3, and reminds his
opponent that he has a queenside
pawn majority.

| 21. | Bc2-d1 | ... |

We have grown accustomed to
seeing this bishop on d3 or c2 —
or b1, at least — participating
in a kingside attack. Reshevsky
undertakes a roundabout maneuver
which further strengthens White's
position and prepares the advance
of his pawns, hitherto impossible.

21.	...	Re8-e7
22.	Bd1-g4	Qd7-e8
23.	e4-e5	a7-a5

| 24. | Re1-e3 | Ra8-d8 |
| 25. | Rf1-e1 | Re7-e6 |

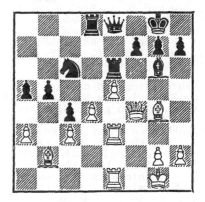

Reshevsky's clever play combined with Petrosian's iron logic make this game one of the
tournament's jewels. Black must
stop White's pawns, so Petrosian
gives up the exchange at a spot
of his own choosing, freeing e7
for the transfer of his knight to
d5. Of course, Black gets good
compensation for the exchange:
his knight is much stronger on
d5, as is his bishop, which no
longer has an opponent. Note
that here, or even on the previous move, White might have
launched a direct attack with
h4 followed by h5 and Rg3, with
good winning chances; but he expects to win a different way.

| 26. | a3-a4 | ... |

Provoking 26.. b4, when there
would follow 27 d5 R:d5 28 B:e6
fe 29 Q:c4 (28 Q:c4 Rd:e5 would
have been weaker), but Petrosian
perseveres with his plan.

26.	...	Nc6-e7
27.	Bg4:e6	f7:e6
28.	Qf4-f1	...

Keeping an eye on the pawn at
c4, and preparing to return the
exchange — for a pawn. On 28 Qf2
Nd5 29 Rf3 b4 is unpleasant.

| 28. | ... | Ne7-d5 |
| 29. | Re3-f3 | Bg6-d3 |

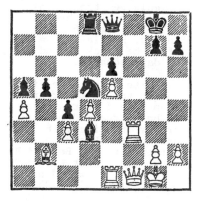

| 30. | Rf3:d3 | c4:d3 |
| 31. | Qf1:d3 | b5-b4 |

Black, naturally, had no choice, since taking the a-pawn would have been senseless. But now it is White who must solve a difficult psychological problem: should he exchange on b4, which practically guarantees the draw, or advance the pawn, driving out the knight and obtaining winning chances, as well as losing ones?

With no time left in which to calculate variations, it is understandable that Reshevsky chose the simpler continuation. After 32 c4 Nb6 33 Rc1 N:a4 34 Ba1 Qc6 or 33 d5 ed 34 c5 N:a4 35 Bd4 Rc8 36 Qf3 Qe6, White's pawns would have been blockaded, and Black's would become extremely dangerous.

| 32. | c3:b4 | a5:b4 |

32.. N:b4 33 Qb3 Nd5 was also possible, or 33 Qb5 Q:b5 34 ab Nd3 35 Re2 Rb8 36 Rd2 R:b5 37 R:d3 R:b2 38 d5, with a draw.

33.	a4-a5	Rd8-a8
34.	Re1-a1	Qe8-c6
35.	Bb2-c1	...

Tempting Black to go into the unclear line 35.. R:a5? 36 R:a5 Q:c1+ 37 Qf1 Qe3+ 38 Kh1 h6 39 Ra8+ Kh7 40 Qb1+ g6 41 Ra7+ Kh8 42 h3 — but Black has no need to speculate, since he does not stand worse.

| 35. | ... | Qc6-c7 |
| 36. | a5-a6 | Qc7-b6 |

37.	Bc1-d2	b4-b3
38.	Qd3-c4	h7-h6
39.	h2-h3	b3-b2
40.	Ra1-b1	Kg8-h8

| 41. | Bd2-e1 | ... |

Black has a small advantage, but not enough to convert. After analysis at home, both players agreed to the

DRAW

******

13. Bronstein—Najdorf
(King's Indian)

1.	d2-d4	Ng8-f6
2.	c2-c4	g7-g6
3.	Nb1-c3	Bf8-g7
4.	e2-e4	d7-d6
5.	Bc1-g5	c7-c5
6.	d4-d5	Nb8-a6

A lot has already happened in the first six moves. Taking advantage of the white queen's bishop's development to g5, instead of the usual e3, where it participates in the struggle for d4, Black quickly counterattacked the white center with 5.. c5. Since 6 d5 kept Black's knight from developing to c6, Najdorf now intends to bring it to c7, so he can prepare ..b7-b5 with ..a7-a6. This costs a lot of time, however, and the result obtained is disproportionately small, compared with the amount of effort expended. The knight occupies a passive position on c7, where it remains unemployed for some time. In the end, it nearly costs Black the game.

7.	Bf1-d3	Na6-c7
8.	Ng1-e2	a7-a6
9.	a2-a4	Ra8-b8
10.	0-0	0-0
11.	Qd1-c2	Bc8-d7
12.	h2-h3	b7-b5

13. f2-f4   ...

The positions of Black's pieces give the e- and f-pawns an insensate urge to advance. White is acquiring more and more territory; the pawn now at b5 is hardly compensation for Black's cramped position: for instance, compare the rooks at f8 and f1.

13.	...	Nf6-e8
14.	a4:b5	a6:b5
15.	Ra1-a7	b5:c4
16.	Bd3:c4	Rb8-a8

17 Rfa1 could not be allowed; but now White trades off Black's only active piece.

| 17. | Ra7:a8 | Nc7:a8 |
| 18. | Qc2-b3 | f7-f6 |

Since the queen cannot remain tied forever to the pawn at e7, Black decides upon a weighty step: shutting in his own bishop.

19.	Bg5-h4	Qd8-b6
20.	Qb3-a3	Ne8-c7
21.	b2-b3	Nc7-b5
22.	Nc3:b5	Bd7:b5
23.	f4-f5	...

Small advantages, patiently accumulated, have grown into a sizable stack; now with this move, White begins his search for the decisive strengthening of his position. The threat is 24 Nf4 g5 25 Ne6 gh 26 N:f8; additionally, his last move helped fix the black e- and f-pawns on dark squares.

Still, White might have given some thought to the transfer of his bishop to a different diagonal. It has already done its work here by inducing ..f6, and might have caused Black considerable grief after 23 Be1. 23 Ra1 was also possible, but although an immediate 23..f5 would not work in view of 24 e5 de 25 d6+ Kh8 26 de etc., White would always have had to consider an eventual ..f5 anyway.

23.	...	Bg7-h6
24.	f5:g6	h7:g6
25.	e4-e5	Bb5:c4
26.	b3:c4	d6:e5
27.	Qa3-d3	...

Why did White sacrifice that pawn? Can't Black begin a counterattack now? Not yet; and, meanwhile, White needs only two or three moves — Nc3 and Rb1, for example — to take over all the key points on the queenside, and then to pick up the c5- or the e7-pawn. The knight's poor placement at a8 helps White greatly in the execution of this plan.

| 27. | ... | Kg8-h7 |
| 28. | Ne2-c3 | Qb6-b3 |

White's last two moves weren't bad, but they could have been a little better: for instance, 27 Bf2 Rc8 28 Qd3 Kg7 29 h4. Now Najdorf finds a way to introduce tactical complications, and, more importantly, to exchange queens, which eases his defense.

29.	Rf1-b1	e5-e4
30.	Rb1:b3	e4:d3
31.	Rb3-b7	Kh7-g8
32.	Kg1-f2	...

Of course White does not take the pawn, which would allow the knight out of its distant corner at last.

32.	...	Bh6-f4
33.	Kf2-f3	Rf8-b8
34.	Rb7:b8+	...

Practically all of White's advantage disappears after the exchange of rooks. Better was 34 R:e7 Rb3 35 B:f6 or 34..Bd6 35 Re6 Be5 36 B:f6 B:c3 37 B:c3 Rb3 38 Ba5!

White overestimated the strength of the pawn at d3 in rejecting this continuation, although his pawn on d5 would have been much more dangerous.

The best line of all would have been 33 Bg3, instead of 33 Kf3, offering to exchange bishops. However, White had overlooked Black's reply, 33..Rb8.

34.	...	Bf4:b8
35.	Nc3-a4	Bb8-d6
36.	Bh4-f2	Kg8-f7
37.	Kf3-e3	Na8-c7
38.	Ke3:d3	Nc7-a6
39.	Kd3-e4	f6-f5+
40.	Ke4-f3	e7-e6
41.	Na4-b6	...

DRAW

******

14. Gligoric—Taimanov
(Nimzoindian Defense)

1.	d2-d4	Ng8-f6
2.	c2-c4	e7-e6
3.	Nb1-c3	Bf8-b4
4.	Ng1-f3	...

In the overwhelming majority of this tournament's Nimzo-Indians, White continued with 4 e3: such is the pull of fashion — which, as I suspected, was to persist long after this tournament. Gli-

goric's choice, 4 Nf3, is also quite playable. Although Black managed to equalize swiftly and even to seize the initiative in this game, Gligoric himself was to blame for that.

4.	...	b7-b6
5.	Bc1-g5	h7-h6
6.	Bg5-h4	g7-g5
7.	Bh4-g3	Nf6-e4
8.	Qd1-c2	Bc8-b7
9.	e2-e3	d7-d6

Hasn't Taimanov blundered a piece — 10 Qa4+ Nc6 11 d5? No, since the white knight is insufficiently defended — 11..N:c3.

| 10. | Bf1-d3 | Bb4:c3+ |
| 11. | b2:c3 | f7-f5 |

| 12. | 0-0 | ... |

Gligoric is not afraid of the further advance of Black's pawns, correctly judging that this will only weaken Black's position. So he invites 12..h5, and where is the player who could resist such temptation? Taimanov saw just in time, however, that after 12..h5? 13 h4!, it is not Black who has the attack, at any rate. So he increases the pressure on e4 by means of the quiet maneuver Nb8-d7-f6, which results in a slight advantage for Black.

However, White might have cast doubt on Black's whole system of development if he had played something more concrete than his clever castling idea: that being 12 d5, cutting communications be-

tween the bishop at b7 and the
knight at e4. After 12.. ed,
White would play 13 Nd4 (which
would also meet most of Black's
other replies), with a very powerful attack: he threatens, among other things, simply 14 f3.

Though I know I'm anticipating,
I still can't resist mentioning
that less than two years after
this game, in the 22nd USSR Championship, Taimanov reached precisely this position against Keres, for which the Estonian had
prepared (as he himself tells us)
the improvement 12 d5! Keres'
idea and the author's thus coincided — and immediately diverged:
White answered 12..ed, not with
13 Nd4, but with 13 cd B:d5, and
only then 14 Nd4 Nd7 15 f3 N:g3
16 hg Qf6 17 B:f5 0-0 18 Qa4,
with an excellent position: Black
had to lay down his arms in 29
moves.

12.	...	Nb8-d7
13.	Nf3-d2	Nd7-f6
14.	Nd2:e4	Bb7:e4
15.	Bd3:e4	Nf6:e4
16.	f2-f3	Ne4:g3
17.	h2:g3	Qd8-d7
18.	a2-a4	...

Taimanov has kept his pawn oc-
tave whole, while White's is
slightly marred in two places —
which more or less defines the
extent of Black's positional advantage. All the minor pieces
having been traded off in the
preceding phase of the game, now
the pawns' turn comes: twelve of

them will disappear in the next
twelve moves! This statistic is
also a reflection of the essential point of White's strategy:
to denude the black king and
also to give Black some queenside pawn weaknesses with the
break c4-c5.

18.	...	a7-a5
19.	c4-c5	b6:c5
20.	d4:c5	0-0
21.	Rf1-d1	Qd7-c6
22.	c5:d6	c7:d6
23.	g3-g4	Ra8-c8
24.	g4:f5	Rf8:f5

The pawn skirmishes have gone
in White's favor: Black now has
a weakness at d6, and his king
is starting to feel the draft.

| 25. | e3-e4 | Rf5-f7 |

White had planned the further
advance of his e-pawn, opening
the diagonal for the queen to
invade at g6. At the moment, this
would not work, since on 26 e5
Black gives check and takes off
the e-pawn with his queen. More
pawn exchanges follow shortly,
and the game begins to look like
a draw.

26.	Rd1-d3	g5-g4
27.	f3:g4	Qc6:e4
28.	Qc2-d2	Qe4:g4
29.	Ra1-e1	Rf7-g7

Black throws all of his pieces over to the g-file, but to
no avail.

30.	Rd3:d6	Rc8:c3
31.	Rd6:e6	Rc3-g3
32.	Re1-e2	Rg3:g2+

DRAW,

since after 33 R:g2 Q:e6
34 R:g7+ K:g7 35 Q:a5, both
generals will be left practically without soldiery.

******
******

ROUND THREE

15. Najdorf—Gligoric
(Grunfeld Defense)

1.	d2-d4	Ng8-f6
2.	c2-c4	g7-g6
3.	g2-g3	c7-c6
4.	Nb1-c3	d7-d5
5.	c4:d5	c6:d5

The choice of opening indicates mutual lack of aggressive intent. The nearly symmetrical deployments and the immobile pawn center largely presage the outcome of this game.

6.	Ng1-h3	Bf8-g7
7.	Nh3-f4	0-0
8.	Bf1-g2	e7-e6
9.	0-0	Nb8-c6
10.	e2-e3	b7-b6
11.	b2-b3	Bc8-a6
12.	Rf1-e1	Ra8-c8
13.	Bc1-b2	Rf8-e8
14.	Ra1-c1	Ba6-b7

Here or a move earlier, White might have tried to stir up at least the semblance of a fight by playing g3-g4, with h2-h4 to follow. The risk would have been small; but on the other hand, it is not likely he could have broken into Black's position either. So both captains decide to steer with the wind into quiet harbor.

15.	Nf4-d3	Bb7-a6
16.	Bb2-a3	Bg7-f8
17.	Ba3:f8	Re8:f8
18.	Nd3-f4	Nc6-e7
19.	h2-h4	h7-h5
20.	Qd1-d2	Qd8-d6

DRAW

******

16. Petrosian—Bronstein
(Catalan Opening)

1.	d2-d4	Ng8-f6
2.	c2-c4	e7-e6
3.	g2-g3	d7-d5
4.	Bf1-g2	d5:c4
5.	Ng1-f3	...

The Catalan only appears to be a harmless opening: in reality, it conceals a number of subtleties, which is why it is so often played by such as Keres, Smyslov and Petrosian. White's move, 5 Nf3, is one such nuance. Usually, check is given here, and the pawn recaptured, but this allows Black to develop his bishop

via d7 to c6. Now, however, White has the choice, depending upon circumstances, of recovering his pawn by Nf3-e5:c4 or Nb1-d2:c4, or going back to Qd1-a4:c4.

If Black plays it like a Queen's Gambit, and tries to "equalize" by means of the standard maneuver ..c7-c5, the fianchettoed bishop unleashes tremendous power: for example, 5..c5 6 0-0 Nc6 7 Qa4 Bd7 8 dc Na5 9 Qc2 B:c5 10 Ne5 Rc8 11 Nc3 b5 12 Bg5, and White has an outstanding game.

5.	...	Bf8-b4+

A new line. Black wants to draw the bishop out to d2 to prevent the knight from using that square. On 6 Nbd2 White was afraid of 6..c3 7 bc B:c3, when Black retains his pawn; but it would be interesting to see what would happen after 8 Ba3 B:a1 9 Q:a1.

6.	Bc1-d2	Bb4-e7
7.	Qd1-c2	...

By not giving check, White avoids 7..Bd7 and 8..Bc6. Now if 7..Bd7 he intends 8 Ne5, removing Black's lightsquare bishop and thereby strengthening his own.

7.	...	Bc8-d7

Anyway! On 8 Ne5, Black replies 8..Nc6, allowing his pawns to be shattered: after 9 N:c6 B:c6 10 B:c6+ bc 11 Q:c4, however, Black has 11..Qd5, forcing the trade of queens, which levels the game completely. If 9 Q:c4 in this line, 9..N:e5 10 de Nd5 11 B:d5 ed 12 Q:d5 Qc8 13 0-0 Bc6, with a fine attack for the sacrificed pawn.

8.	0-0	Bd7-c6
9.	Qc2:c4	Bc6-d5
10.	Qc4-c2	Nb8-c6
11.	Bd2-c3	Bd5-e4
12.	Qc2-d1	0-0
13.	Nb1-d2	Be4-g6
14.	Nd2-c4	Bg6-e4
15.	Nc4-d2	Be4-g6
16.	Nd2-c4	Bg6-e4
17.	Nc4-d2	

The transition phase from opening to middlegame has arrived. White does not wish to continue the fight with an enemy piece on e4, nor does Black care to allow White's knight to get to e5. Unable to reach an agreement as to the placing of these two pieces, both sides repeat moves...

DRAW

******

17. Averbakh—Reshevsky
(Nimzoindian Defense)

1.	d2-d4	Ng8-f6
2.	c2-c4	e7-e6
3.	Nb1-c3	Bf8-b4
4.	e2-e3	c7-c5
5.	Bf1-d3	0-0
6.	Ng1-f3	d7-d5
7.	0-0	Nb8-c6
8.	a2-a3	Bb4:c3
9.	b2:c3	d5:c4
10.	Bd3:c4	Qd8-c7

After obtaining a good position with Black in the first round against Najdorf, Reshevsky repeats the opening exactly against Averbakh. Here Najdorf played 11 a4; Averbakh plays the more logical 11 Re1, which prepares 12 e4. The first skirmish flares, concluding some ten moves later with White on top. Along the way, however, he will have to occupy e4 with a piece, in order to prevent Black's pawn from doing so.

11.	Rf1-e1	Rf8-d8
12.	Qd1-c2	e6-e5
13.	Nf3-g5	...

13.	...	Rd8-f8
14.	d4-d5	...

Black counterattacked White's pawn center, playing 11..Rd8 to prevent White's d4-d5, but his plan failed: the rook had to go back in order to defend the f-pawn, and White advanced his d-pawn. The position also admits of a different, and sharper, handling: 14 Bd3 would maintain the tension at c5 and e5, force a weakening of Black's king's wing, and prepare an attack with his pieces: for example, 14..h6 15 Ne4 N:e4 16 B:e4 cd 17 cd ed 18 Bb2.

14.	...	Nc6-a5
15.	Bc4-a2	h7-h6
16.	Ng5-e4	Nf6:e4
17.	Qc2:e4	Bc8-d7

White threatens to play f2-f4, when taking the pawn would be inadvisable for Black, since it would open up the game in White's favor. Defending the pawn with ..f7-f6 would also be poor in view of Bb1, when the white queen will invade at h7. So Black begins the construction of a defensive perimeter based on his pawn at e5. 17..Bd7 is necessary to meet the threat of 18 f4, for now Black could reply 18..ef 19 ef? Rae8; the move is also useful for control of the diagonal a4-e8.

18.	c3-c4	b7-b6
19.	Qe4-d3	Ra8-e8
20.	e3-e4	Qc7-d6

An audit of the last ten moves would show a strong positive balance for White, with good showings in all his ventures: he has gotten in 20 e4, and closed the center, so that now he is ready to storm the king's position; and in the event of an endgame, he is ready with his protected passed pawn at d5. On the negative side, of course, there is that bishop at a2, but that can always be redeployed via b1 to d3. How is Black to meet the impending attack on his king? He must ready himself to weather the storm by placing his pawns on dark squares, his rooks on the e-file, and his knight at d6, where it blockades the pawn and covers the light squares.

21.	Qd3-g3	Re8-e7
22.	Bc1-d2	Na5-b7

23.	f2-f4	Rf8-e8
24.	Bd2-c3	f7-f6

Black shores e5 up with might and main, pressing simultaneously on e4 in the hope of inducing f4-f5.

25. f4-f5 ...

Correctly evaluating the position, Averbakh does not capture on e5, even though he would hold a clear advantage after 25 fe fe 26 Rf1, followed by the doubling of the rooks on the f-file, since one of the black rooks would have to remain tied to the defense of the e-pawn. The reason he didn't take the pawn is that Black would have answered 25 fe with 25..R:e5, and the black knight which would soon enter d6 would be not a bit weaker than a white rook. Now, with Black's bishop immured, White can bring up his rooks and push his g- and h-pawns.

25.	...	Re8-b8
26.	Bc3-d2	...

Before beginning his attack, White would like to ascertain which direction Black's king will move in order to meet the threatened 27 B:h6.

26. ... Kg8-h8

Now everything is in readiness for White to begin his pawn storm (with h2-h4 and g2-g4) immediately. Of course he must watch out for his opponent's play, but still Black would have had a very difficult time of it. White's next move, however, slows the pace of the attack, allowing Reshevsky to slip in a little reminder of his own counterchances (his extra pawn on the queenside, the possible attack on the pawn at c4, and the weakness at b3).

27.	Ba2-b1	Nb7-a5
28.	Qg3-d3	Bd7-a4
29.	Bb1-c2	Ba4:c2
30.	Qd3:c2	Na5-b7
31.	a3-a4	Qd6-d8
32.	Ra1-a3	Nb7-d6
33.	Ra3-h3	Nd6-f7

DRAW

White's attack would now involve some risk, while Black need only prepare the advance ..b6-b5 to assure himself good counterplay on the opposite wing.

******

18. Szabo—Keres
(Queen's Gambit)

1.	d2-d4	d7-d5
2.	Ng1-f3	Ng8-f6
3.	c2-c4	d5:c4
4.	Nb1-c3	a7-a6
5.	Qd1-a4+	...

Practically speaking, the shortest game of the tournament: even though it did continue until the 41st move, after this check Szabo might as well have resigned, since in effect he is now giving Keres odds of pawn and move (odds once given by masters to first-category players in the handicap tourneys of Chigorin's day). One wonders how, after prolonged consideration, Szabo could blunder a pawn as early as move five. Keres was more than a little amazed himself: he spent fifteen minutes considering his reply.

5.	...	b7-b5
6.	Qa4-c2	...

The whole problem is that White has not yet played e2-e3. With the bishop's diagonal open, ..b7-b5 would require extensive analysis, since White could then simply take the pawn with his knight and meet ..Bd7 with B:c4. But now his choice is either to remain a pawn down, or to give up a piece: 6 N:b5 Bd7 7 N:c7+ Q:c7 8 Qc2, hoping to pick up the c-pawn as well eventually. Even in that highly problematical event, however, he would still have only two pawns for his piece.

6.	...	Nb8-c6
7.	e2-e4	e7-e6
8.	Bc1-g5	...

A pawn down, Szabo panics: why not 8 Be3, when his two center pawns, e4 and d4, promise White plenty of opportunities to complicate? Szabo's 8 Bg5 gives up a second pawn, in hopes that if it is taken he will gain several tempi to complete his development. However, Keres easily repels the attack, remaining two pawns up.

8.	...	Nc6:d4
9.	Nf3:d4	Qd8:d4
10.	Ra1-d1	Qd4-c5
11.	Bg5-e3	Qc5-c6
12.	Bf1-e2	Bc8-b7
13.	Be2-f3	e6-e5
14.	0-0	Bf8-c5
15.	Nc3-d5	Bc5:e3
16.	Nd5:e3	0-0
17.	g2-g4	Rf8-e8
18.	Ne3-f5	Nf6-d7
19.	b2-b3	Nd7-b6
20.	Qc2-c1	c4:b3
21.	a2:b3	Qc6:c1
22.	Rd1:c1	Ra8-c8
23.	Rf1-d1	g7-g6
24.	Nf5-h6+	Kg8-g7
25.	g4-g5	c7-c5
26.	Bf3-g4	Rc8-c7
27.	Rd1-d6	Nb6-c8

White's threats do require a bit of alertness from Keres.

28.	Rd6-f6	Bb7:e4
29.	Rc1-d1	c5-c4
30.	b3:c4	b5:c4
31.	f2-f3	Be4-d3
32.	Rf6:a6	Nc8-e7
33.	Ra6-d6	Ne7-g8
34.	Rd1-c1	Rc7-b7
35.	Bg4-d7	Re8-d8
36.	Nh6:g8	Kg7:g8
37.	Bd7-c6	Rd8-d6
38.	Bc6:b7	Rd6-b6
39.	Bb7-d5	Kg8-f8
40.	Rc1-a1	c4-c3
41.	Ra1-a8+	Kf8-e7

WHITE RESIGNED

******

19. Euwe—Smyslov
(Grunfeld Defense)

| 1. | d2-d4 | Ng8-f6 |
| 2. | c2-c4 | g7-g6 |

3.	g2-g3	Bf8-g7
4.	Bf1-g2	d7-d5
5.	c4:d5	Nf6:d5
6.	e2-e4	Nd5-b6
7.	Ng1-e2	c7-c5

Smyslov makes frequent use of this line of the Grunfeld, where Black attacks the center pawns with ..c5 and ..e6, trades off on d5 and blockades the pawn by planting his knight at d6. Isolated and blockaded though it may be, the white d-pawn remains very strong nevertheless. Black must always be prepared for its advance, especially considering how difficult it will be for him to actually get either one of his knights from b6 or b8 to d6. The outcome of this game will depend on whether White finds an appropriate moment to advance the pawn to d6 and secure it there. If he can, then he will have the advantage; if not, Black will obtain good counterchances.

In my personal opinion, the system looks good for White. It is possible that Smyslov now shares this opinion, since, despite the successful outcome of this game, he did not employ the system again, either at Zurich or at any other tournament thereafter.

8.	d4-d5	e7-e6
9.	0-0	0-0
10.	a2-a4	...

Smyslov is dealing with a great expert on the Grunfeld. At the Amsterdam 1950 tournament, Euwe played a similar game against Pilnik, continuing here with 10 Nbc3. In the tournament book Euwe noted that the move was not good, and recommended the continuation 10 a4! Na6 11 Na3 ed 12 ed Nb4 13 Nc3! Smyslov goes into the line nonetheless, which gives this game added interest.

Curiously enough, in Game 129 (Round 19) against Keres, Euwe played 10 Nec3, and in his notes calls this move stronger than 10 a4.

Both moves seem adequate to me.

10.	...	Nb8-a6
11.	Nb1-a3	e6:d5
12.	e4:d5	Bc8-f5
13.	Ne2-c3	...

13 a5 would have been a trifle more accurate, but Euwe was expecting the knight to go to d7 on its own, with: 13 Nc3 Nb4 14 Be3 Nd7 15 Qd2.

| 13. | ... | Na6-b4 |
| 14. | Bc1-e3 | Ra8-c8 |

Smyslov plays an active defense: now he threatens to occupy d3 with a piece, severing the enemy communications between flanks. Advancing his pawn to d6, with the exchange sacrifice that follows, appears to be the logical end of White's entire setup, but it would have had more effect after 15 a5.

| 15. | d5-d6 | Bf5-d3 |
| 16. | Bg2:b7 | ... |

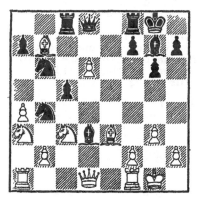

The strategic idea is correct, but its tactical formulation is wrong. Now 16 a5 was necessary in order to meet 16.. B:f1 17 K:f1 Nd7 18 B:b7 Rb8 with 19 a6. After the text, an interesting battle of the pieces ensues, where calculation reigns supreme, and where Black's chances are objectively no worse.

| 16. | ... | Rc8-b8 |
| 17. | Bb7-g2 | Bd3:f1 |

A brave choice. Many would have preferred 17.. Q:d6, which equalizes, and is in any event easier to calculate.

18.	Kg1:f1	Nb6-d7
19.	Na3-c4	Nd7-e5
20.	Nc4:e5	Bg7:e5

| 21. | Be3:c5 | Qd8-a5 |

Two pawns, one of them passed and on the sixth rank, are sufficient compensation for the exchange; the maneuver Smyslov begins with this move, however, underscores the weakness of the pawn at d6. 22 Nb5 is now impossible, in view of 22.. R:b5, so the bishop has to retreat.

| 22. | Bc5-e3 | Rf8-d8 |
| 23. | Nc3-e4 | Be5:d6 |

The scales tip first one way, then the other: just when Black has obtained the upper hand, Euwe begins a complex combination with a pretty zwischenzug, 26 Nd7.

| 24. | Ne4-f6+ | Kg8-h8 |

As will later become clear, 24.. Kg7 was better: it is important in one variation that the king defend the pawn on f7.

| 25. | Be3-d4 | Bd6-e5 |

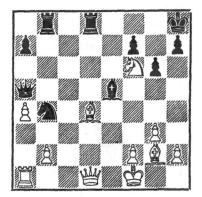

The picture looks hopeless for White, but his next move is quite pretty.

| 26. | Nf6-d7 | ... |

The idea is to decoy the rook onto an unprotected square. Now if 26.. R:d7 27 B:e5+ Q:e5 28 Q:d7 Q:b2 29 Re1, and two of Black's pawns are *en prise*; also poor is 26.. B:d4 27 Q:d4+ Kg8 28 Nf6+ Kh8 29 Nd5+ Kg8 30 Ne7+ Kf8 31 Qh8+ K:e7 32 Re1+.

[29]

| 26. | ... | f7-f6 |

After 26.. Qa6+ 27 Kg1 B:d4
28 Q:d4+ f6 or 28.. Kg8, White
obtains the better endgame with
29 N:b8 R:d4 30 N:a6.

| 27. | Bd4:e5 | f6:e5 |
| 28. | Qd1-d2 | ... |

Smyslov's determination to play
for complications has borne fruit:
Euwe fails to find the better
move 28 Qd6, whose main continuation runs: 28.. Rb6 29 Qe7 Nc6
30 Qf6+ Kg8 31 Rd1, which threatens the killing 32 Bd5+. Black
would be forced to trade queens
and try to save himself in a difficult pawn-down endgame: 28.. Qa6+
29 Q:a6 N:a6 30 N:b8 R:b8 31 Re1.

| 28. | ... | Rb8-c8 |

With the queen on d6, White
could have continued 29 Qf6+ and
30 Bh3 here (forcing 30..Qa6+),
traded queens, recovered the exchange, and come out a pawn up.

| 29. | Kf1-g1 | Qa5-c5 |

A brilliant resource which
White overlooked. Black's queen
reenters the fray elegantly and
decisively, threatening to win
the pinned knight.

| 30. | Bg2-h3 | Qc5-e7 |

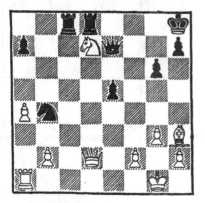

| 31. | Qd2-e2 | ... |

Euwe thinks 31 Rd1 would have
been better, but I do not see
any great difference: 31.. Rc7

32 Qe1 Nc6 33 b4 Q:b4 34 N:e5
Q:e1+ 35 R:e1 N:e5 36 R:e5 Rd2,
and Black must win.

31.	...	Rd8-d7
32.	Bh3:d7	Qe7:d7
33.	Qe2:e5+	Kh8-g8

Now Black is a piece up, and
the win is, as they say, a matter of technique. In the present
instance, however, the technique
will be anything but simple; for
the piece White has, besides two
pawns, some other chances as
well: his king is better sheltered, and Black's knight has
no support points in the center.

In general, Black's plan will
be to avoid exchanging queenside
pawns, to find shelter for his
king, to bring his knight to the
kingside, and finally, to attack
the white pawns at f2 and b2 (or
b3) with overwhelming force.

The fulfilment of this plan
requires exceptional restraint,
deep calculation, and rapid assessment of the positions that
occur along the way.

34.	Qe5-e4	a7-a5
35.	h2-h4	Qd7-d5
36.	Qe4-g4	Rc8-f8
37.	Ra1-d1	Qd5-f3
38.	Qg4-c4+	Qf3-f7
39.	Qc4-c5	Qf7-f5
40.	Qc4-c4+	Qf5-f7
41.	Qc4-c5	Qf7-f5
42.	Qc4-c4+	Kg8-g7

These last moves were played
in grievous time-pressure, and
Black has thus far achieved nothing beyond pinning the white
queen to the protection of the
f2 square. Now he must secure c6
for the transfer of his knight.

43.	Qc4-d4+	Qf5-f6
44.	Qd4-c5	Rf8-f7
45.	Rd1-d2	Qf6-e7

The threat of 46.. Qe1+ gains
Black a tempo to regroup.

46.	Qc5-c3+	Rf7-f6
47.	Rd2-d4	Nb4-c6
48.	Rd4-d5	...

White could have gotten a third
pawn for the piece by 48 Rf4 Qe5
49 R:f6 Q:c3 50 R:g6+ K:g6 51 bc,
but he would have had a lost ending all the same. Euwe gives the

line 51.. Ne5 52 Kf1 Kf5 53 Ke2 Ke4 54 h5 h6, and White's pawns die.

48.	...	Qe7-e6
49.	Rd5-c5	h7-h5
50.	b2-b3	Kg7-f7
51.	Rc5-b5	Qe6-d7
52.	Kg1-g2	Qd7-e7
53.	Qc3-c4+	Kf7-g7
54.	Qc4-d3	Kg7-h6
55.	Rb5-d5	Rf6-f7
56.	Rd5-d6	Nc6-e5

Gradually, the knight works its way to g4.

| 57. | Qd3-e3+ | Kh6-h7 |
| 58. | Rd6-b6 | ... |

58 Rd5 would not have helped either, in view of 58.. Rf5 59 R:a5 Qb7+ 60 f3 Nc4. The text leads to an immediate loss.

| 58. | ... | Qe7-c7 |

After 58.. Ng4 59 Q:e7 R:e7 60 b4, White might have had a slim chance; but now 59.. Ng4 is threatened, and if 59 f3, then 59.. Qc2+ decides.

WHITE RESIGNED

Smyslov showed a high level of mastery and an incredible will to win in every phase of this tense game.

******

20. Stahlberg—Geller
(King's Indian)

1.	d2-d4	Ng8-f6
2.	Ng1-f3	g7-g6
3.	g2-g3	Bf8-g7
4.	Bf1-g2	0-0
5.	0-0	d7-d6
6.	Nb1-d2	...

An unusual and somewhat passive system Stahlberg employs occasionally against the King's Indian. The e-pawn is kept at home, and the c-pawn advanced but one square; the d-pawn is traded off, as White refrains absolutely from either creating a pawn center or participating in the fight for the central squares. Not infrequently this results in a great deal of maneuvering, followed by exchanges, and a draw; but for this game, Geller will have none of it. Instead, he wages a very active campaign for more terri-

tory, first on the kingside, and then over the entire board.

6.	...	Nb8-c6
7.	c2-c3	e7-e5
8.	d4:e5	d6:e5
9.	Nd2-b3	Qd8-e7
10.	Bc1-e3	Rf8-d8
11.	Qd1-c1	...

The first result of his passive strategy is that White cannot move his queen to c2 in view of 11.. Bf5.

11.	...	e5-e4
12.	Nf3-d4	Nc6-e5
13.	Be3-g5	Ne5-c4
14.	Nd4-c2	c7-c6

Stahlberg's maneuverings are not dictated by any strategic plan, but rather by practical guidelines he has derived from his enormous tournament experience and chess-sense: advance no pawns, create no glaring weaknesses, show not the slightest aggressive intent; but meanwhile, do not avoid exchanges, and be ready to set a tactical snare at any moment. So now, despite a whole series of planless (but also harmless) moves, White's position is not yet bad, on the whole. Geller shows great resourcefulness and determination in breaking down Stahlberg's skilled — and not entirely toothless — defense.

| 15. | Nc2-e3 | Nc4-d6 |
| 16. | Rf1-d1 | h7-h6 |

Now, while the knight temporarily blocks the diagonal, Black breaks the pin, puts his king on h7, and then plays .. f5.

17.	Bg5-f4	Nf6-e8
18.	Ne3-f1	Kg8-h7
19.	Qc1-c2	f7-f5
20.	Bf4-e3	Bc8-e6
21.	Be3-d4	Ne8-f6

Black's advantage has crystallized somewhat: White's pieces are corralled, his light square bishop is locked out of play, and the powerful chain of Black's kingside pawns is always ready to be set in motion. All of this put together, however, is not yet enough to win with. Black undertakes a queenside pawn advance as well, in order to restrict still further his opponent's pieces;

then he trades off all White's active pieces, leaving him only the bishop on g2 and the knight on f1. Stahlberg maintains his composure, and holds to his passive course, believing himself to be running no danger of losing yet.

| 22. | Bd4-c5 | b7-b6 |
| 23. | Bc5:d6 | Rd8:d6 |

For trading's sake, Stahlberg does not grudge even the dark-square bishop, so important for White against the King's Indian. This might eventually have cost White the game.

24.	Rd1:d6	Qe7:d6
25.	Ra1-d1	Qd6-c7
26.	Nf1-e3	c6-c5
27.	Nb3-d2	Ra8-d8
28.	Nd2-f1	Rd8:d1
29.	Ne3:d1	Qc7-f7
30.	Nd1-e3	...

A transparent trap: if the bishop takes the pawn, White cuts off its retreat by 31 c4.

30.	...	b6-b5
31.	a2-a3	a7-a5
32.	Nf1-d2	Nf6-d5

Since Geller plans to close up the game, he ought not to exchange his last knight; on the other hand, having traded it off now, he ought not to close up the game.

| 33. | Ne3:d5 | Be6:d5 |
| 34. | e2-e3 | ... |

Stahlberg breaks his rule of no

pawn advances, and wrongly so: nothing required that he weaken his d3 square and give the black queen an inroad. A better plan would have been 34 Nf1, 35 Ne3 and 36 Qd2.

34.	...	c5-c4
35.	Bg2-f1	a5-a4
36.	Bf1-g2	Qf7-d7
37.	g3-g4	...

To give the knight a way out, via f1, to g3 — and, as we shall see, White will soon get the opportunity to avail himself of it.

37.	...	Bd5-e6
38.	g4:f5	g6:f5
39.	Nd2-f1	...

Wearying of his dull drawing play, Stahlberg wishes to hurry matters by transferring the knight via g3 and e2 to d4. At this moment, a crevice appears in his defensive wall; 39 Bf1 was the proper move to keep the queen out of d3.

| 39. | ... | Qd7-d3 |
| 40. | Qc2-c1 | h6-h5 |

Geller's last move before the time control destroys the fruits of all his labors, throwing away a well-earned win. He could have exploited the power of his two bishops with 40.. b4, putting White in a hopeless predicament: 41 ab a3 42 ba B:c3, and Black's pawn will cost White a piece; or 41 cb c3, and Black gets to the a-pawn.

| 41. | Nf1-g3 | h5-h4 |

[32]

Now the break would come too late, since f1 has been cleared for White's bishop: he could answer 41.. b4 with 42 Bf1, driving away the queen.

A move earlier wins; a move later draws — that's what the time element means in chess.

42.	Ng3-h5	Be6-f7
43.	Nh5:g7	Kh7:g7
44.	Bg2-f1	Qd3-d8
45.	Bf1-e2	Qd8-g5+
46.	Kg1-f1	h4-h3
47.	Qc1-d1	...

After adjournment and analysis, White bravely sacrifices a pawn, knowing full well that he still gets a perpetual check.

47.	...	Qg5-g2+
48.	Kf1-e1	Qg2:h2
49.	Qd1-d4+	Kg7-h7
50.	Be2-f1	Qh2-g1
51.	Qd4-d7	Kh7-g8
52.	Qd7-d8+	Kg8-g7
53.	Qd8-d4+	Kg7-g6
54.	Qd4-d6+	...

DRAW

******

21. Boleslavsky—Kotov
(Queen's Gambit)

1.	d2-d4	d7-d5
2.	c2-c4	d5:c4
3.	Ng1-f3	Ng8-f6
4.	e2-e3	e7-e6
5.	Bf1:c4	c7-c5
6.	0-0	a7-a6
7.	Qd1-e2	c5:d4

7.. b5 is usually played here, but Kotov holds back with this, intending to play it only after White's Nc3; if then a2-a4, Black can reply .. b5-b4 with tempo.

Black's central exchange aims at securing an unhampered development for his pieces, followed by the establishment of a piece on d5. This relieves White of his main headache in the Queen's Gambit Accepted, namely: the development of his queen's bishop; it also opens up the e-file.

Boleslavsky amasses a great pile of pieces in the center, and then sets off some interesting complications, with the d-pawn acting as a fuse.

8.	e3:d4	Bf8-e7
9.	Nb1-c3	b7-b5
10.	Bc4-b3	Bc8-b7
11.	Bc1-g5	0-0
12.	Rf1-e1	...

A typical move in this opening: White attacks not only the pawn at e6 but also the bishop behind it at e7. For example, if 12.. Nbd7 13 Rad1 Nb6, White can already play 14 B:e6 fe 15 Q:e6+ Rf7 16 Ne5.

Kotov therefore tries to liquidate the threat of B:e6 as quickly as possible by exchanging or else driving the bishop away from b3.

12.	...	Nb8-c6
13.	Ra1-d1	Nc6-a5

All the commentators agreed this move was a mistake, since it allowed White to carry out the pretty breakthrough that follows, with its lively play leading to a win for White, some thirty moves hence. Stahlberg, and Euwe as well in his earlier commentaries, suggest that 13.. Nb4 was the required response here. However, Rauzer showed in some rather old analysis that the continuation 13.. Nb4 14 d5 Nb:d5 15 N:d5 B:d5 16 B:d5 N:d5 17 B:e7 Q:e7 18 R:d5 favors White. Najdorf therefore recommended 13..Nd5 14 N:d5 B:g5 15 Nc3 Nb4, a view later adopted by Euwe also.

We should like to go a little more deeply into the concept of "mistake", as it is applied to chess. To begin with, the mistakenness of 13.. Na5 was only demonstrated as a result of White's clever and by no means obvious continuation. His advantage finally boiled down to his possession of a strong bishop against Black's knight in an endgame: certainly not all that simple, nor all that much!

Secondly, it's not clear how the battle might have gone after 13.. Nd5, since White had the secret weapon 14 N:d5 B:g5 15 Nb6. If Black plays 15.. Rb8, instead of taking the knight, he loses the exchange after 16 N:g5 and 17 Nd7; and on 15.. Ra7 16 d5 is very strong. If he takes the knight on b6, however, Black will be in a real predicament after 16 N:g5: 16.. h6 loses to the sacrifice at f7 followed by 18 Q:e6, and there seems to be no clear defense to the thematic push d4-d5, since 16.. N:d4 fails against 17 Qd3 Nf5 18 N:e6 fe 19 B:e6+ Kh8 20 B:f5, or 18..Qc6 19 Nf4, etc.

Had the game in fact taken such a course, then 13.. Nd5 would have been labeled the mistake, and 13.. Na5 recommended instead, since it does not appear to be too dangerous.

Black's difficulties appear to have another cause entirely. Compared with Black's pieces, White's have made three extra moves! — both rooks to central files, and the bishop to an attacking diagonal. If there is logic in chess, then those three powerful developing moves must tell somehow. It is a grandmaster's task to demonstrate White's advantage, and in this case the proof was of the complicated combinative sort.

Such melding of logic and combinative powers is the hallmark of Boleslavsky.

14. d4-d5   Na5:b3

It is easy to see that taking the d-pawn with bishop, knight or pawn would cost a piece.

15. d5:e6   ...

15.   ...   Qd8-b6

If the bishop takes the knight at f3, there follows 16 ef+ Kh8 17 R:d8 B:e2 18 R:a8 R:a8 19 R:e2 and Black has two pieces en prise; when one falls, White will be two pawns ahead. If that's not enough for White, he can also play 16 Q:f3 Nd4 17 Qe3.

16. a2:b3   f7:e6
17. Nf3-d4   ...

White does not need the pawn so much as the square e6.

17.   ...   Be7-d6
18. Qe2:e6+   Kg8-h8
19. Nd4-f3   Ra8-d8
20. Bg5-f4   ...

Credit is due White also for selecting precisely this out of all the possible continuations here. The phrase which comes to mind is: "Black's two bishops and good development in an open position fully compensate his pawn minus." But now, it turns out, the two bishops will disappear, and the bad knight remain, compensating nothing — but all this had to be foreseen!

20.   ...   Bb7:f3

20.. Rfe8 21 R:d6 R:e6 22 R:b6 R:b6 23 Bc7 was bad too.

21. Rd1:d6   Rd8:d6

22.	Qe6:d6	Qb6:d6
23.	Bf4:d6	Rf8-e8
24.	Re1:e8+	Nf6:e8
25.	Bd6-e5	...

Now Boleslavsky must demonstrate his endgame skill. White begins with a typical technique in such bishop/knight endings: placing his bishop three squares distant from the enemy knight on an opposite-colored square, thereby totally depriving the knight of moves.

Getting out via f6 would be absolutely hopeless, since the knight/bishop ending with an extra pawn is a dead win for White.

Boleslavsky continues by fixing the a- and b-pawns on light squares and bringing up his king; then, after a few more preparatory moves, he can pick off the a-pawn with his knight.

25..Bc6 26. b4 h5 27. f3 Kh7
28.Ne2 g5 29. Kf2 h4 30. g3 hg+
31. hg Kg6 32. g4 Bb7 33. Ke3
Bc6 34. Nc3 Bb7 35. Ne4 Bd5
36. Nc5 Kf7 37. N:a6 Ke6 38.Bc3
Ba8 39. Nc5+ Kf7 40. Ne4 Kg6
41. Be5 Bd5 42. Nd2 Kf7

BLACK RESIGNED

White would continue: 43 Kd4
Ke6 44 Ne4.

******

******

ROUND FOUR

22. Geller—Boleslavsky
(Queen's Indian Defense)

1.	d2-d4	e7-e6
2.	Ng1-f3	Ng8-f6
3.	c2-c4	b7-b6
4.	Nb1-c3	Bc8-b7
5.	Bc1-g5	h7-h6
6.	Bg5:f6	Qd8:f6
7.	e2-e4	...

Other things being equal, it's always advantageous to occupy the center with pawns. Unwilling to lose time retreating the bishop, Geller decides to see whether the two bishops really do counterbalance a strong pawn center.

7.	...	Bf8-b4
8.	Bf1-d3	c7-c5

Black opens the center, to give his bishops more room.

9.	0-0	c5:d4
10.	Nc3-b5	Qf6-d8

The best defense to the threat of 11 Nc7+.

11.	Nc5:d4	0-0
12.	Qd1-e2	Nb8-c6
13.	Ra1-d1	Nc6:d4
14.	Nf3:d4	...

In many variations of the Nimzo-Indian, an exchange on c3 leaves White with the two bishops. In this case, it is Black who has the two bishops, but White has the better position. He has a lead in development, with prospects of capitalizing on it, since Black has a backward pawn at d7 and the weak square d6. Geller occupies d6 with his knight, and then uses his rook to fix the weak pawn at d7. Boleslavsky's counterplay is based on his strong bishop, which will sweep a long diagonal after White's coming e4-e5, and on the possibility of opening the g-file for his major pieces.

14.	...	Bb4-c5
15.	Bd3-c2	Ra8-c8
16.	e4-e5	Qd8-g5
17.	f2-f4	...

White throws himself into his assault on the d-pawn, thinking that the fianchettoed queen's bishop will be no danger to him, but that bishop will avenge the insult later. 17 Be4, liquidating the long-diagonal threats once and for all, would have been a good idea.

17.	...	Qg5-e7

Now if 18 Be4 Ba6 19 b3 d5 20 ed Q:d6, and Black rids himself, not only of his weak pawn, but of White's knight as well.

18.	Kg1-h1	f7-f5
19.	Nd4-b5	a7-a6
20.	Nb5-d6	Bc5:d6
21.	Rd1:d6	Rc8-c6
22.	Rf1-d1	...

Geller's decision to trade rooks here is contrary to logic. White is pressing on the d-pawn, and for this two rooks are clearly better than one. After the rook's retreat, followed by 23 Rfd1, one of Black's pieces would be forced into a passive position: either .. Rc7, .. Bc8, or .. Rd8.

22.	...	Rc6:d6
23.	Rd1:d6	Bb7-c6
24.	b2-b4	...

This queenside diversion (b2-b4, followed by a2-a4 and b4-b5) would have been a good idea under more peaceful circumstances —with the queens gone, for example. This was a good time to think of defense with 24 Qe3 or 24 Kg1; but Geller, more from inertia than for any other reason, continues to press, hoping to force a win from a position not yet ripe for it. Now Bole-

[36]

slavsky lays his trumps on the
table.

24.   ...   Qe7-h4

First comes this attack on the
pawn at f4, exploiting the
back-rank mate threat: if 25 b5,
for example, then Black takes
twice.

25.   Rd6-d4   g7-g5

Another pair of trumps: the g-
file is opened, and Black also
demonstrates that the rook at d4
is no defender of the pawn at f4.

26.   Kh1-g1   ...

The sudden turn of events has
affected Geller's nerve and self-
possession. There was no need to
give the pawn away: 26 Qe3 was
still playable. Even though White
has to submit to a powerful attack — 26 Qe3 gf 27 R:f4 Qg5
28 Qf2 Kh8 — Black has no forced
win yet.

26.   ...   g5:f4
27.   Qe2-f2   Qh4-e7
28.   a2-a3   Qe7-g7

A pretty maneuver.

29.   Rd4:f4   Qg7:e5
30.   Rf4-d4   Rf8-f7
31.   Bc2-d3   ...

With queens exchanged, the endgame would also be hopeless for
White. Both sides were now in
time-pressure, but Boleslavsky
plays very exactly.

31.   ...   f5-f4

The pawns start to roll: this
is the beginning of the end.

32.   Bd3-f1   Qe5-f6
33.   Rd4-d2   b6-b5
34.   c4-c5   Qf6-a1

Pushing the e-pawn to e3 would
have decided at once. In time-
pressure, Black wants to trade
queens first.

35.   Qf2-h4   Qa1-f6
36.   Qh4:f6   Rf7:f6
37.   Kg1-f2   e6-e5
38.   g2-g3   f4:g3+

In his time-pressure, Geller
probably failed to notice that

his bishop on f1 was hanging.

39.   Kf2-e1   Rf6-f3
40.   h2:g3   Rf3:g3
41.   Rd2-d6   Kg8-g7
42.   Bf1-d3   e5-e4
43.   Bd3-e2   Rg3:a3
44.   Be2-g4   Ra3-d3

WHITE RESIGNED

******

23. Smyslov—Stahlberg
(French Defense)

1.	e2-e4	e7-e6
2.	d2-d4	d7-d5
3.	Nb1-c3	Ng8-f6
4.	Bc1-g5	d5:e4
5.	Nc3:e4	Bf8-e7
6.	Bg5:f6	Be7:f6
7.	Ng1-f3	Nb8-d7
8.	Bf1-c4	0-0
9.	Qd1-e2	Nd7-b6
10.	Bc4-b3	Bc8-d7
11.	0-0	...

For this game, the chessboard
becomes a battleground of principle between Smyslov and Stahlberg, who are repeating their
game from the Budapest 1950 tournament. There, Stahlberg continued with 11.. Ba4, only to discover, after 12 N:f6+, that he
could not recapture with his
queen because of 13 B:a4 and
14 Qc4, winning a pawn. So here,
he delays the exchange of lightsquare bishops for two moves, but
without achieving any substantial
improvement.

White has a palpable advantage
in space and complete freedom of
maneuver, while Black's bishop
remains under attack by White's
knight and requires the queen's
protection; the black knight's
movements are quite restricted
too. Under these circumstances,
the slightest misstep could be
fatal for Black.

11.	...	Qd8-e7
12.	Rf1-e1	Ra8-d8
13.	Ra1-d1	Bd7-a4
14.	Bb3:a4	Nb6:a4
15.	Qe2-b5	Na4-b6
16.	c2-c4	c7-c6
17.	Qb5-b3	Qe7-c7

White threatened 18 N:f6+,
forcing the pawn recapture,
since on 18.. Q:f6 19 c5 would
win the b-pawn. 17.. Qc7 does
not meet this threat, however.

[37]

But it is hard to criticize Stahlberg for not playing the more accurate 17.. Rd7, since in this case also White would have many ways to strengthen his position, such as 18 a4, or 18 Nc5 and 19 Nd3, to say nothing of the simple 18 N:f6+, followed by Ne5 and Rel-e3-h3 for an attack.

18.	Ne4:f6+	g7:f6
19.	Qb3-e3	Kg8-g7

Smyslov's logical play has been making Black's defense more and more difficult. He cannot take the c-pawn, of course, because of 20 Qh6, which leaves him no time to defend the f6-pawn: for example, 19.. N:c4 20 Qh6 Qe7 21 Nh4, threatening 22 Nf5 and 22 Rd3. Nor does 19.. Kh8 save him, in view of 20 Qh6 Nd7 21 d5, and the exchange of pawns brings White's rook to d5 and thence to h5; or 20.. Qe7 21 Nh4. After the text, White must bring his knight to g4 in order to continue his attack — but how?

20. Nf3-e5   ...

A beautiful move, captivating in its simplicity: since the only route to g4 lies through e5, the knight runs full tilt onto the bayonets — what could be simpler! The point is, of course, that taking the knight would open the door for White's queen and rook to set up a mating attack: 20.. fe 21 Qg5+, followed by 22 Qf6+ and 23 Re3.

(In this line we find a pretty forcing maneuver to keep the king in the corner which you may find useful: 21 Qg5+ Kh8 22 Qf6+ Kg8 23 Re3 Rfe8 24 Qh6 — a quiet move — 24.. Kh8 25 Rg3, threatening Qg7 mate, and on 25.. Rg8, obviously, there follows 26 Qf6+.)

20.	...	Qc7-e7
21.	Ne5-g4	Rf8-g8
22.	Ng4-h6	...

A small concluding combination: the rook cannot escape, due to the threat of 23 Nf5+. In addition to the text, whereby White wins the exchange, and thus renders the remainder of the game a matter of technique, there was also 22 Qh6+, a reasonable move which maintains the attack.

22.	...	Qe7-c7
23.	Nh6:g8	Rd8:g8
24.	b2-b3	Kg7-h8
25.	Qe3-h6	Rg8-g6
26.	Qh6-h4	Nb6-d7
27.	Rel-e3	Qc7-a5
28.	Re3-h3	Nd7-f8
29.	Rh3-g3	Qa5:a2
30.	Rg3:g6	Nf8:g6
31.	Qh4:f6+	Kh8-g8
32.	Qf6-f3	Qa2-c2
33.	Qf3-d3	

BLACK RESIGNED

******

24. Keres—Euwe
(Nimzoindian Defense)

1.	d2-d4	Ng8-f6
2.	c2-c4	e7-e6
3.	Nb1-c3	Bf8-b4
4.	e2-e3	c7-c5
5.	Bf1-d3	0-0
6.	Ng1-f3	d7-d5
7.	0-0	Nb8-d7

A little reshaping of a fashionable variation: instead of c6, the knight is brought to d7. For this game, Euwe makes his appearance as Theoretician: he wishes to demonstrate that by keeping both his bishops and forcing the trade of pieces, Black has an easy draw.

8.	a2-a3	d5:c4
9.	Bd3:c4	...

If White takes the bishop, there is a good in-between move: 9.. c5:d4, when two of White's

pieces are en prise. After 10 B:c4
dc, neither 11 Qb3 nor the immediate 11 bc gives White any noticeable advantage.

9.	...	c5:d4
10.	e3:d4	Bb4-e7
11.	Bc4-a2	Nd7-b6
12.	Nf3-e5	Nb6-d5
13.	Qd1-f3	Nd5:c3
14.	b2:c3	Nf6-d7
15.	Ne5-g4	Nd7-f6
16.	Ng4:f6+	Be7:f6
17.	Bc1-f4	Bf6-g5

An amusing situation! Black
methodically trades off every
piece White brings out — first
the two knights, and now comes
the bishops' turn. White cannot
avoid the exchange; he can only
choose the square on which it
will occur.

| 18. | Bf4-g3 | Bg5-h4 |
| 19. | Bg3-e5 | Bh4-f6 |

Persistent as a mosquito.

20.	Rf1-e1	Bf6:e5
21.	Re1:e5	Qd8-f6
22.	Qf3-e4	...

Trading queens is not a good
idea here: the a- and c-pawns
would be a lot of trouble to
White in a rook ending.

| 22. | ... | Ra8-b8 |

White has some advantage in
development, but no place to focus his energies, since Black
has no weaknesses anywhere; and
there are so few pieces left...
Meanwhile, Black intends to bring
his bishop out to a good position
on c6 via d7, or by ..b7-b6 and
.. Bc8-b7.

| 23. | d4-d5 | ... |

With many pieces on the board,
this push always promises action;
here, it seems more like a fleeting glimpse of what might have
been.

23.	...	e6:d5
24.	Ba2:d5	Bc8-d7
25.	Ra1-e1	Bd7-c6

26.	c3-c4	g7-g6
27.	g2-g3	Rb8-e8
28.	Kg1-g2	Re8:e5
29.	Qe4:e5	Qf6:e5
30.	Re1:e5	Bc6:d5
31.	c4:d5	Rf8-d8
32.	Re5-e7	Rd8:d5
33.	Re7:b7	Rd5-a5
34.	Rb7-b3	...

DRAW

This drawn position represents
a victory for Euwe the Theoretician — but we won't call it the
last word...

******

25. Reshevsky—Szabo
(Grunfeld Defense)

1.	d2-d4	Ng8-f6
2.	c2-c4	g7-g6
3.	Nb1-c3	d7-d5
4.	Bc1-f4	Bf8-g7
5.	e2-e3	0-0

Offering a pawn (6 cd N:d5
7 N:d5 Q:d5 8 B:c7) for the
quick development of his queenside; but Reshevsky prefers a
quieter continuation.

6.	Qd1-b3	c7-c5
7.	c4:d5	c5:d4
8.	e3:d4	e7-e6

Having begun the game in gambit style, Szabo sees no point in
half-measures, and sacrifices a
second pawn. This gambit is an
idea of Trifunovic's, and is
based on the fact that White has
not one kingside piece developed
yet. Black seeks to destroy the

enemy pawn center and create
threats against the king. In
the present instance, however,
the price paid for all this —
two pawns — is too high.

9.	d5:e6	Nb8-c6
10.	e6:f7+	Kg8-h8
11.	Ng1-f3	Nc6:d4
12.	Nf3:d4	Qd8:d4
13.	Bf4-e3	Qd4-e5

You will find this diagram in
the book "Grunfelda Odbrana" by
Trifunovic, Gruber and Bozic
(Section One, System Two, Variant
18, Continuation A), with a note
stating that Black, for his two
sacrificed pawns, has two threats:
.. Ng4 and .. Be6. Clearly, both
sides are playing a prepared line;
now we shall see how Reshevsky
uses one bishop to meet both
threats.

14.	Bf1-e2	Bc8-e6
15.	Be2-c4	Be6-d7

Szabo's first independent move
of this game, and it loses immediately. Trading bishops in order
to develop the rook to c8 with
tempo would have been more in
the spirit of this variation. If
17 Qb3 Ng4 18 Nd1 Rc7, and Black
recovers one of his pawns; and
if 17 Qd4 Qh5, when Black's threat
of .. Ng4 prevents White from castling and allows the recovery
of one of Black's pawns.

White would probably have played
17 Qf4, but then 17.. Qe6 was possible, with reasonable counterplay.

16.	h2-h3	b7-b5
17.	Bc4-e2	Bd7-e6
18.	Qb3:b5	Nf6-d5
19.	Nc3:d5	a7-a6
20.	Qb5-c5	Ra8-c8
21.	Qc5-a3	Be6:d5
22.	0-0	Rf8:f7

Black hurriedly removes the
more dangerous pawn: if 22..Q:b2
White trades queens and plays
24 Rad1, and then 24.. B:a2 allows an elegant mate: 25 Rd2 Rb8
26 R:b2 R:b2 27 Bd4. Black would
be forced to take the f-pawn off
on move 24, when White would remain a healthy pawn up.

23.	Rf1-d1	Bd5-b7
24.	Be2:a6	...

A small combination: if 24..Ra8
25 Qb3, forking f7 and b7.

24.	...	Qe5-e4
25.	Ba6:b7	Rf7:b7
26.	Ra1-c1	Rc8-e8
27.	Rd1-d2	Bg7-e5
28.	Rc1-d1	Kh8-g8
29.	b2-b3	Be5-c7
30.	Qa3-a6	Rb7-b4
31.	Qa6-d3	Qe4-e5
32.	Qd3-d5+	

BLACK RESIGNED

******

26. Bronstein—Averbakh
(Nimzoindian Defense)

1. d4 Nf6 2. c4 e6 3. Nc3 Bb4
4. e3 0-0 5. Nf3 b6 6. Be2 Bb7
7. 0-0 d5 8. cd ed 9. Bd2 Bd6
10. Rc1 a6 11. Ne5 c5 12. Ng4 Nbd7
13. N:f6+ N:f6 14. dc bc

White's passive play, his premature exchange on d5, and the
unfortunately posted queen's bishop, render any effective play
against Black's hanging pawns impracticable.

15. Bf3 Re8 16. Na4 Rc8 17. Qb3
Ba8 18. Rfd1 Ne4 19. Be1 Rb8
20. Qd3 Qh4 21. g3 N:g3

Rather than wait until his opponent collects himself sufficiently to be able to organize an
attack on the c- and d-pawns,
Black simplifies the position by
a series of exchanges.

22. hg Q:a4 23. Bc3 Be5 24. B:e5
R:e5 25. R:c5 Q:a2 26. b4 Ree8

*****

27. Gligoric—Petrosian
(Benoni Defense)

1.	d2-d4	Ng8-f6
2.	c2-c4	c7-c5
3.	d4-d5	e7-e6
4.	Nb1-c3	e6:d5
5.	c4:d5	d7-d6
6.	Ng1-f3	g7-g6
7.	Nf3-d2	...

White violates one of the classic principles of the opening by thus moving the same piece twice; as a matter of fact, he is preparing to move the knight yet a third time, in order to bring it to c4. Is this the end of the principle, then? Of course not! Black, you see, has already violated classical principles twice himself, by exchanging a center pawn for a wing pawn and by giving himself a backward pawn at d6; with his last move, furthermore, he has saddled himself with weaknesses on the dark squares as well. If one side were to play concretely, however, while the other side contented himself with following the rules, the winner would not be difficult to predict..

(Let's take an extreme case: 1 f2-f3? e7-e6 2 g2-g4? What should Black do? Moving the queen so early in the game is not generally recommended, but in this instance, taking White's errors into consideration, 2.. Qd8-h4 does not look bad.)

The knight maneuver from f3 via d2 to c4 in this position was played by Nimzovich in a famous game against Marshall from the New York 1927 tournament; since then, it has become popular. Its point is to generate enough pressure on the d-pawn and the square b6 to prevent Black from carrying out his only possible active plan here: .. a7-a6, .. b7-b5, etc., which, with the knight on c4, can be met with a2-a4-a5. Additionally, from d2 the knight can support the advance e2-e4: combined with f2-f4 and e4-e5, this is White's main strategic idea in this position.

7.	...	Nb8-d7

In order to answer 8 Nc4 with 8.. Nb6.

8.	g2-g3	Bf8-g7
9.	Bf1-g2	0-0
10.	0-0	Qd8-e7
11.	Nd2-c4	Nd7-e5
12.	Nc4:e5	Qe7:e5
13.	a2-a4	a7-a6
14.	a4-a5	...

White has the better position. Black has no immediate prospects of exploiting his "extra" queenside pawn, since the pawn at a5 restrains two of Black's pawns. Meanwhile, White can begin the pawn roller with e4, f4 and e5 at the first available opportunity, clearing the way for the d-pawn. Gligoric, however, prefers piece maneuvers to all-out pawn assaults, so the e-pawn never even gets as far as the fourth rank.

14.	...	Rf8-e8
15.	Bc1-f4	Qe5-e7
16.	Qd1-b3	...

It's hard to win games without moving any pawns at all. One good line here would appear to be 16 Na4 Nd7 17 Rb1, followed by b2-b4, opening up the b-file with the intention of turning the d-pawn's flank. Or he might try to induce Black's pawn to advance to c4 and then try to win it.

16.	...	Nf6-d7
17.	Rf1-e1	Nd7-e5
18.	Nc3-a4	Bc8-d7
19.	Na4-b6	Ra8-b8
20.	Bf4-d2	Bd7-b5
21.	Bd2-c3	...

White still has the advantage. He intends to smoke the knight out of e5 and weaken Black's king position by the exchange of bishops, and then play e2-e4-e5. Sensing real danger, Petrosian tries some tactics; his next two moves, ..c5-c4 and ..f7-f5, complicate his position, but do not improve it.

21.	...	c5-c4
22.	Qb3-c2	f7-f5
23.	h2-h3	Qe7-c7
24.	f2-f4	Ne5-d7
25.	Nb6:d7	Bb5:d7
26.	Bc3:g7	Kg8:g7
27.	Qc2-c3+	Kg7-g8
28.	Kg1-h2	Qc7-c5
29.	e2-e3	b7-b5
30.	a5:b6	Rb8:b6
31.	Ra1-a5	Qc5-b4
32.	Re1-e2	Qb4:c3

The weakness of Black's a- and c-pawns, along with the concrete threat of 33 Q:b4 and R:a6, forces him to exchange queens and take on a somewhat inferior endgame, but one in which he does have a passed pawn. The next part of the game takes place in a time-scramble, where both sides play inaccurately.

| 33. | b2:c3 | Kg8-f8 |
| 34. | Kh2-g1 | ... |

This move allows Black time to regroup, freeing his rook from defending the a-pawn.

34.	...	Rb6-b1+
35.	Kg1-f2	Bd7-b5
36.	g3-g4	Rb1-c1

The pawn would have been better attacked from the side with 36.. Rb3 37 Rc2. Then Black could have continued the plan begun by 33.. Kf8 — to bring his king to the queenside and try to put some life into his passed pawn.

| 37. | Ra5-a3 | Kf8-f7 |

Here too, 37.. Rb1, intending .. Rb3, was better: Black would not have had to display so much ingenuity to get a draw.

38.	Bg2-f3	Re8-e7
39.	h3-h4	Rc1-d1
40.	g4-g5	Rd1-d3

The rook stands poorly here. Black will now have to find just the right move to draw.

| 41. | h4-h5 | ... |

Here the game was adjourned. After home analysis, both players concluded that the draw was within Black's capabilities, so Gligoric only asked to see what move Black had sealed. Petrosian, of course, was not about to allow a pawn on h6.

| 41. | ... | g6:h5 |

DRAW

******

28. Taimanov—Najdorf
(King's Indian)

Let the reader be forewarned: this was one of the tourney's most interesting games, and the recipient of a brilliancy prize. Both of its phases — opening and middlegame — were conducted by Najdorf with such a high degree of erudition and mastery that the need of a third phase never arose.

1.	d2-d4	Ng8-f6
2.	c2-c4	g7-g6
3.	Nb1-c3	Bf8-g7
4.	e2-e4	d7-d6
5.	Ng1-f3	0-0
6.	Bf1-e2	e7-e5
7.	0-0	Nb8-c6
8.	d4-d5	...

Not too long before this tournament, Taimanov employed this opening variation — 7.. Nc6 8 d5 — twice in the 20th USSR Championship. In both cases, he

scored with one and the same
plan: a pawn break on the c-
file, followed by an outflanking
and turning maneuver around the
entire grouping of Black's pieces on the d- through g-files,
leaving only the darksquare bishop to guard his king. These
games made the rounds of the
chess press, and the general
consensus was that they had been
lost in the opening.

However, a few players still
ventured this "refuted" variation of the King's Indian; at
the Mar del Plata tournament of
1953, for example, Najdorf fell
victim to fashion: playing White,
in this variation, he lost to
Gligoric and only drew with difficulty against Trifunovic. At
the start of the tournament in
Zurich, however, these games were
not known to Taimanov.

Thus, both sides played the
opening with great expectations:
Najdorf, having absorbed the Yugoslav analyses, which ran at
least to move 21, and Taimanov,
still flushed with his previous
successes.

8.	...	Nc6-e7
9.	Nf3-e1	Nf6-d7
10.	Bc1-e3	f7-f5
11.	f2-f3	f5-f4
12.	Be3-f2	...

Taimanov's kingside defensive
array appears most imposing: the
pawns on light squares form a kind
of toothed fortress wall, with the
darksquare bishop covering the
gaps between the teeth. But if
the position be examined without
prejudgment, then it would be
naive to speak of any sort of advantage to White. Could Black
hope to obtain more from the opening than the development of all
his pieces, the advance .. f7-f5-
f4, occupation of the dark squares,
and substantial attacking prospects on the kingside? Naturally,
in view of the extreme sharpness
of the position, Black must play
exactly, combining his attack with
defense of the queen's wing, especially d6 and c7 — and seize every tactical chance.

12.	...	g6-g5
13.	Ne1-d3	Nd7-f6
14.	c4-c5	Ne7-g6
15.	Ra1-c1	Rf8-f7

16.   Rc1-c2   Bg7-f8

This was the system employed
by Gligoric and Trifunovic at
Mar del Plata. Now the d-pawn is
defended, the rook can go to the
g-file, and Black's knights hov-
er over the king's wing. Taimanov, however, trusts the invulner-
ability of his position, and continues with his cavalier assault
on the queenside.

17.	c5:d6	c7:d6
18.	Qd1-d2	g5-g4
19.	Rf1-c1	g4-g3!

A pawn sacrifice with an enormous future.

20.	h2:g3	f4:g3
21.	Bf2:g3	Nf6-h5
22.	Bg3-h2	Bf8-e7
23.	Nc3-b1	Bc8-d7
24.	Qd2-e1	Be7-g5
25.	Nb1-d2	Bg5-e3+
26.	Kg1-h1	Qd8-g5

Black's pieces march onto the
battlefield like soldiers in column, one after the other. Here
Taimanov ought to have rid himself of the bishop at e3, even
at the cost of the exchange, by
playing 27 Nc4.

27.	Be2-f1	Ra8-f8
28.	Rc1-d1	b7-b5
29.	a2-a4	a7-a6
30.	a4:b5	a6:b5
31.	Rc2-c7	Rf7-g7
32.	Nd2-b3	Ng6-h4
33.	Rc7-c2	Bd7-h3

What a picture! The queen's

34.	Qe1-e2	Nh4:g2
35.	Bf1:g2	Bh3:g2+
36.	Qe2:g2	Qg5-h4

White cannot save his queen, since if it retreats Black has a knight check at g3.

37.	Qg2:g7+	Kg8:g7
38.	Rc2-g2+	Kg7-h8
39.	Nd3-e1	Nh5-f4
40.	Rg2-g3	Be3-f2
41.	Rg3-g4	Qh4-h3
42.	Nb3-d2	h7-h5

Here the game was adjourned; after sealing

43. Rg4-g5

WHITE RESIGNED

wing is by now completely deserted, while seven pieces assail the white king; now the square g2 is attacked four times, and there is obviously nothing left to defend it with: on 34 gh there follows mate in three moves, and 34..R:f3 is threatened too.

without further play. After 43..Rg8 44 R:g8+ K:g8 he has no defense against mate.

*****

*****

ROUND FIVE

29. Petrosian—Taimanov
(Queen's Indian Defense)

1.	d2-d4	Ng8-f6
2.	c2-c4	e7-e6
3.	Ng1-f3	b7-b6
4.	Nb1-c3	Bc8-b7
5.	e2-e3	d7-d5
6.	c4:d5	e6:d5
7.	Bf1-b5+	...

White must develop the bishop anyway; so, making hay out of the fact that it would not be in Black's best interest to interpose a piece, he induces 7.. c6, shutting in Black's bishop without loss of tempo. Black therefore ought not to have been in so much of a hurry to push his d-pawn; 5.. Be7 instead was better.

7.	...	c7-c6
8.	Bb5-d3	Bf8-e7
9.	0-0	0-0
10.	b2-b3	Nb8-d7
11.	Bc1-b2	Be7-d6

Not very logical. White quite evidently intends to bring his knight to f5, when the bishop will be forced to retreat: better to have prepared a place for it on f8 while also playing the useful move 11.. Re8.

12.	Nf3-h4	Rf8-e8
13.	Nh4-f5	Bd6-f8
14.	Ra1-c1	Nf6-e4

Positional evaluation alone is not sufficient grounds for such a decision: deep and accurate calculation is necessary too. Feeling that his position is gradually worsening, and knowing Petrosian's power in just such positions, Taimanov changes key, and invites his opponent to trip the light combinative. Psychologically correct, this decision is also very much in accord with Taimanov's style.

15.	Bd3:e4	d5:e4

(See diagram next column)

16.	Qd1-g4	...

The inviting 16 d5 cd 17 N:d5 would lead nowhere after the exchange of bishop for knight: 17.. B:d5 18 Q:d5 Nc5. However. 17 Nb5 was well worth a try:

(Position after 15.. d5:e4)

the threats are 18 Nc7 and 18 Nd6, and if 17.. Rc8 18 Qg4. On the other hand, Black loses after 16 d5 cd 17 N:d5 Nc5 18 Nh6+ gh 19 Nf6+, etc. Curiously, the pawn at c6, blocking the bishop's diagonal as a result of Black's barely noticeable opening inaccuracy, provides the basis for this combination, as well as for the one which actually occurs in the game.

16.	...	g7-g6

The threat was Nh6+, N:f7+, and N:d3.

17.	Nc3:e4	...

White indicates his readiness to sacrifice a piece: Black could play 17.. h5, when White's queen would have to leave either the g-file, unpinning the pawn and thereby losing the knight at f5, or the fourth rank, losing the knight at e4. Taimanov, however, feels that the risk is too great, and so he contents himself with the trade of rook and two pawns for both the knights. Material equality is maintained, and the struggle flares anew.

17.	...	Re8:e4
18.	Qg4:e4	g6:f5
19.	Qe4:f5	Bf8-g7
20.	e3-e4	...

Intending to transfer the rook by way of c3 to attack the kingside.

20.	...	Ne7-f8
21.	e4-e5	...

Petrosian wants to throw his e- and f-pawns into the attack too, but this requires one more move than the laws of chess will allow him. As Najdorf suggests, what was required was 21 Rc3 c5 22 Rg3 cd 23 Rd1 Ne6 24 Qg4, or 21.. Q:d4 22 Ba1 Bc8 23 Qf3, with a powerful attack.

The text blocks White's bishop, while giving Black a long diagonal for the operation of the harmonious duet of Bb7 and Qd5.

21.	...	Qd8-d5
22.	f2-f4	c6-c5

Forcing White back on the defensive. Black already has the advantage.

23.	Qf5-h3	c5:d4
24.	Rc1-d1	Qd5-e4
25.	Rd1-e1	Qe4-d5
26.	Re1-d1	Ra8-c8
27.	Rd1:d4	Qd5-a5
28.	Rd4-c4	...

White must accede to this exchange of rooks, with the consequent weakening of both his queenside pawns, in view of the terrible threat of 28.. Rc2.

28.	...	Rc8:c4
29.	b3:c4	Qa5-c5+
30.	Rf1-f2	Qc5:c4
31.	Qh3-b3	Qc4-e4
32.	Qb3-c2	Nf8-e6
33.	f4-f5	...

The ending would be in Black's favor, but the queens should still have been exchanged, as this at least would have freed White of the direct threats on his king, which are growing more and more dangerous.

33.	...	Ne6-c5
34.	Qc2-d2	Qe4-b1+
35.	Rf2-f1	Qb1-d3
36.	Qd2-e1	Qd3-d5
37.	Qe1-g3	Nc5-e4
38.	Qg3-h4	Ne4-c3
39.	Qh4-g4	h7-h5

Leaving, as usual, only one bodyguard for his king, Taimanov has established all of his other pieces in their best positions.

White's queen must simultaneously defend both g2 and e2. Black's last move deflects it from one of these two squares, and Black carries out his deciding combination.

40.	Qg4-h3	Nc3-e2+
41.	Kg1-f2	...

On 41 Kh1 there would come 41.. Nf4 42 Qf3 N:g2. But now, Black has 41.. Qd2, so

WHITE RESIGNED

******

30. Averbakh—Gligoric
(King's Indian)

1.	c2-c4	Ng8-f6
2.	Nb1-c3	g7-g6
3.	g2-g3	Bf8-g7
4.	Bf1-g2	0-0
5.	d2-d4	d7-d6
6.	Ng1-f3	Nb8-d7
7.	0-0	e7-e5
8.	e2-e4	e5:d4
9.	Nf3:d4	...

A position which occurs so often these days that it might be worthwhile to say a few words about it here: not about systems, or variations to boggle the memory, but about the ideas which will direct the play on both sides for many moves to come.

By this exchange in the center, Black has opened his bishop's diagonal to attack the d4 square; shortly, he will also attack the pawn at e4 with rook and knight. The knight's position on c5 will be secured with .. a5, and this pawn may also be pushed further: to a4, and even to a3.

For the moment, White attacks nothing, but he does dispose of a strong center and freedom to maneuver. Look at the board: White's pieces and pawns occupy four ranks, and Black's, three, with a "no-man's-land" between. These geometrical features largely reflect the character of the opening, as the opposing forces have not yet come into contact. White's further plans are simple: to develop the bishop and the queen, to connect his rooks, prepare an attack on the weak pawn at d6 with which Black must eventually saddle himself in this deployment, and keep an eye on the defense of the e-pawn. The differing ways to defend this pawn lead to different systems of play. Qc2 would be a handy move, but this would leave the knight on d4 en prise for a moment, which Black might be able to exploit; if Be3 is played first, then Black has .. Ng4. It is this sort of tempo-play, with its many combinative possibilities (due to the fact that all of the pieces and nearly all of the pawns are still on the board), that makes the King's Indian Defense such a delight to its adherents.

9.   ...   Nd7-c5
10.   f2-f3   ...

Before leaving for this tournament, every one of its participants prepared a few new systems, especially in the popular openings such as the King's Indian, the Sicilian and the Nimzo-Indian. One of the best of these must be the system Averbakh introduced in the present game: f3, and Rf2-d2. White prepares an attack on the d-pawn, but practice has shown that it makes little sense to take it with the queen, since on d6 the queen itself becomes vulnerable to attack, and must quickly retreat. The enemy camp must therefore be invaded with a weaker piece first. The move 10 f3 also secures the pawn at e4, while the fianchettoed bishop's diagonal is only closed temporarily.

10.   ...   a7-a5
11.   Bc1-e3   a5-a4
12.   Rf1-f2   c7-c6

13.   Nd4-c2   Qd8-e7
14.   Rf2-d2   ...

White's position is solid as a rock. Now Black can only defend the d-pawn by tactical means, since 14.. Rd8 obviously loses to 15 B:c5. Gligoric proves equal to the challenge: his is not a mechanical but a creative mastery of every nuance of the King's Indian. It's hard to believe that ten moves hence Black still will not have had to give up his d-pawn!

14.   ...   Nf6-d7
15.   Ra1-c1   ...

The pawn capture here would run into 15.. a3, and if 16 N:a3 B:c3, winning a piece. White neutralizes this threat, and what else does Black have now?

15.   ...   Bg7-e5

This looks senseless: surely the bishop cannot stay here very long — but stay here it does.

16.   Be3-f2   ...

If 16 f4 B:c3 17 bc N:e4 18 B:e4 Q:e4 19 R:d6, Black's kingside may be weakened, but White's is no better off, and pawns are still even.

16.   ...   Rf8-e8
17.   Nc2-e3   ...

In order to drive out the bishop with 18 Ng4.

17.   ...   Nd7-f8

18.	Nc3-e2	Qe7-c7
19.	Rc1-b1	a4-a3
20.	b2-b3	...

If 20 b4 Na4.

20.	...	h7-h5
21.	Qd1-c2	Bc8-e6
22.	Ne2-c3	Nf8-h7

The position certainly is ripe for decisive action, but it might have been worth the trouble to make one more preparatory move: 23 Rbd1.

23.	b3-b4	Nc5-a6
24.	f3-f4	Be5-g7
25.	f4-f5	...

The sort of move that is either very good or very bad. Its drawbacks are so obvious that the advance of this pawn to f5 is only playable when a forcing line has been calculated, resulting in a clear advantage. In the present instance, Averbakh probably assessed the position after Black's 33rd move incorrectly.

25.	...	Be6-d7
26.	Qc2-b3	...

The tempo of the attack slackers somewhat here. A better idea might have been 26 fg fg 27 e5 R:e5 28 Q:g6, getting close to the black king and paralyzing Black by threats like 29 R:d6, 29 Nf5, 29 Ne4, etc.

26.	...	Nh6-f6
27.	f5:g6	...

But now this exchange is a mistake. It was not yet too late to play 27 Rad1, continuing, in the event of 27.. Bf8, with 28 c5.

27.	...	f7:g6
28.	c4-c5+	Bd7-e6
29.	c5:d6	Be6:b3
30.	d6:c7	Bb3-f7

A number of weaknesses have cropped up in White's position.

31.	b4-b5	Na6:c7
32.	b5:c6	b7:c6
33.	Rb1-b7	Ra8-c8

Averbakh may have thought a rook on the seventh would give him the better of it, but the pawn at a3 is now so dangerous that this position should probably be considered as favoring Black.

34.	Rd2-c2	...

The threat was 34.. Ng4.

34.	...	Nc7-a6
35.	Bg2-f1	Na6-c5
36.	Rb7:f7	...

Averbakh's resourcefulness does not abandon him, even in the most difficult situations. In time pressure, he sets a trap, but Gligoric finds the proper rebuttal.

36.	...	Kg8:f7
37.	Bf1-c4+	Kf7-f8
38.	Ne3-f5	....

Hoping for 38.. gf 39 B:c5+.

38.	...	Nc5:e4
39.	Nf5:g7	Kf8:g7
40.	Nc3:e4	Re8:e4
41.	Bc4-a6	Rc8-d8
42.	h2-h3	Re4-b4
43.	Rc2:c6	Nf6-e4
44.	Rc6-c7+	Kg7-h8
45.	Bf2-e3	Rb4-b2

WHITE RESIGNED

******

31. Szabo—Bronstein
(Old Indian Defense)

1.	d2-d4	Ng8-f6
2.	c2-c4	d7-d6
3.	Ng1-f3	Nb8-d7
4.	g2-g3	e7-e5
5.	Bf1-g2	c7-c6

White's seemingly irreproachable development turns out to have a hole in it after all: he has failed to take control of e4, and Black exploits this immediately by preparing ..e5-e4 and .. d6-d5. Szabo prefers to exchange pawns at e5, but this gives Black an easy game, and he begins at once to lay plans to assume the initiative.

6.	d4:e5	d6:e5
7.	0-0	Bf8-c5
8.	Nb1-c3	0-0
9.	Qd1-c2	Qd8-e7
10.	Nf3-h4	Rf8-e8
11.	Nc3-a4	...

One of those dynamic positions characteristic of contemporary chess, in which one may evaluate the possibilities for both sides, but find it difficult to determine which side has the advantage. Usually, both sides feel they stand better; occasionally, both sides think that they stand worse. In the present instance, the pivotal factor is the pawn at e5. With the support of rook and queen, it may easily advance to e3. To counteract this, White tries to disorganize the enemy ranks by carrying out flanking raids with his cavalry. Black decides not to waste time retreating the bishop, since the exchange on c5 would develop his knight to a good position and uncover his queen's bishop as well. Black's move also cuts off the retreat at f3 from the white king's knight. All of these advantages are more than enough compensation for the "sacrifice" of his Indian bishop.

11.	...	e5-e4
12.	Nh4-f5	Qe7-e5
13.	Bg2-h3	...

With the unsubtle threat of 14 Bf4; but now Black succeeds in spiriting his bishop away, not only giving his queen the square a5, but also underscoring the misplaced state of the knight at a4. After 13 N:c5 N:c5 14 Ne3 the game would have been roughly even, while now Black has the initiative firmly in hand. Unwilling to settle for a titmouse, Szabo goes after an entire crane— and sure enough, soon one flies down for him.

13.	...	Bc5-f8
14.	Bc1-d2	Qe5-c7
15.	Bh3-g2	...

Forced: after Black carries out his threat to move his queen's knight, an unpleasant pin would arise along the diagonal h3-c8.

15.	...	g7-g6
16.	Nf5-e3	Qc7-e5
17.	f2-f4	Qe5-h5

Another strong line was 17.. ef 18 ef Qd4.

| 18. | h2-h3 | ... |

In view of Black's positional threat of .. Nf8 and .. Bh3, etc., White is practically forced to sacrifice his e-pawn.

| 18. | ... | Qh5:e2 |

With this, Black's queen sets out on a long and hazardous journey. Five queen moves for a single pawn: even the arithmetical balance is clearly unfavorable to Black. Still, what can White accomplish with those five moves?

19.	Ra1-d1	Qe2-d3
20.	Qc2-c1	Qd3-d6
21.	g3-g4	Qd6-c7

So, White has made just one useful move: 19 Rd1; and as for those kingside pawn moves, those might better be called double-edged than favorable to White.

To which we might add that Black could have made still better use of his pieces, with 19.. Nc5 20 Nc3, and now 20.. Qd3. In that event Black's knight would stand actively on c5, the queen's bishop would have been uncovered, and White's bishop would have been temporarily deprived of the c3 square.

What conclusion may we draw from all of this? That when one is well developed, one can afford to spend a few moves to capture an important enemy pawn; but bear in mind that one must also evaluate the position correctly, and calculate accurately...

| 22. | Bd2-c3 | ... |

| 22. | ... | Bf8-g7 |

Black breaks both of the rules

laid down in the previous note, in his distracted determination to exploit the position of the white knight on a4. The obvious 22.. b5 would have forced White to trade off his best piece, the bishop on c3. But 23 B:f6 N:f6 24 cb Qa5 didn't seem clear enough to me, so I decided to make some sort of waiting move. Now Black also threatens .. b5, but —

23.   g4-g5   .b7-b5

Alas! Black must give up the knight, in order to avoid getting mated: 23.. Nh5 24 B:g7 N:g7 25 Ng4, followed by 26 Qc3, and White is master of the diagonal a1-h8. Knowing Szabo's skill with a direct attack, I had no illusions as to the outcome, were I to enter that line. Now Black fights on with the energy of despair.

24.   g5:f6   Bg7-f8
    The bishop returns,
    Shorn of honor,
    For his steed has fallen
    By the road...

25.   c4:b5   c6:b5
26.   Ne3-d5   Qc7-c6
27.   f4-f5   ...

The idea behind this pawn move appears in the variation 27.. ba 28 fg hg 29 Ne7+ B:e7 30 fe R:e7 31 Qh6 Ne5 32 Rd8+ Re8 33 B:e5! That also explains Black's reply: by connecting his rooks, he protects the eighth rank.

27.   ...   Bc8-b7
28.   f5:g6   h7:g6
29.   Nd5-e7+   Bf8:e7
30.   f6:e7   b5-b4

In order to distract that awful bishop from the long diagonal, if only for a moment.

31.   Bc3:b4   ...

31 Qf4 wasn't bad, either.

31.   ...   Qc6:a4
32.   Bb4-c3   ...

Szabo is dead set on a checkmate. Also quite sufficient to win was 32 Ba3, holding on to the e-pawn.

32.   ...   Re8:e7

33.   Qc1-h6   ...

A bit of tactics: White draws the knight to e5 in order to set up the following fork. Strangely enough, however, this move gives Black defensive chances, since the diagonal a1-h8 is briefly closed. 33 Qg5 Rae8 34 R:d7 and 35 Qf6 was stronger.

33.   ...   Nd7-e5
34.   Qh6-g5   Qa4-e8

Black is now so terrorized by the bishop on c3 that all he can think about any more is how soon he can play .. Ra8-c8:c3. I played 34.. Qe8 without thinking, but here was the place to try 34.. Rae8, answering Euwe's recommendation of 35 Rd8 simply by 35.. Re6, continuing to balance somehow on cliff's edge.

35.   Rf1-f4   Ra8-c8
36.   Rf4-h4   ...

(See diagram, top of next page)

36.   ...   Rc8:c3

For the first time since move 23, I breathed a sigh of relief — only to notice 37 Qf6!, and mate next move...

37.   Qg5-h6   f7-f6
38.   b2:c3   Re7-g7

Up to this point, Black was battling the bishop on c3; now he continues the fight with its ghost. 38.. Kf7 was correct, although White would still have

(Position after 36 Rh4)

retained sufficient advantage to win.

39.	Rd1-d8	Qe8:d8
40.	Qh6-h8+	Kg8-f7
41.	Qh8:d8	g6-g5
42.	Rh4-h6	

After checking the scoresheet to make sure that no one had forfeited,

BLACK RESIGNED

******

32. Euwe—Reshevsky
(Nimzoindian Defense)

1.	d2-d4	Ng8-f6
2.	c2-c4	e7-e6
3.	Nb1-c3	Bf8-b4
4.	e2-e3	c7-c5
5.	Bf1-d3	0-0
6.	a2-a3	Bb4:c3+
7.	b2:c3	b7-b6

Perhaps an appropriate continuation with a different move-order — for instance. that which occurred in Game 9, Geller-Euwe, where Bd3 had not yet been played and Black had not yet castled. There, White had to expend a move on f2-f3, whereas here he could play 8 e4, easily carrying out an advance that would ordinarily have cost him a good deal of trouble. It is amazing that Reshevsky, who is such an expert on the Black side of the Samisch line, should have allowed such a possibility, and also that Euwe should not have exploited it. After 8 e4, 9 Bg5

is threatened, and if Black's knight retreats to e8, then 9 Qh5! begins White's attack before castling.

The reader will find just such a development of events in Game 77, when Reshevsky ventured a repeat of this variation against Keres.

8.	Ng1-e2	Bc8-b7
9.	0-0	d7-d6
10.	Qd1-c2	d6-d5

One might assume Reshevsky had forgotten that pawns may also move two squares! However, the gradual advance of this pawn has its logic too. With White playing slowly (10 Ng3! was best), Reshevsky amends his error on move 7, stopping White's e3-e4 for some time to come. After 10 Ng3, 10.. d5 could have been met by 11 cd ed 12 Nf5, so the correct reply would have been 10.. Nc6. But now, Black answers the exchange of central pawns by a clever maneuver which is only possible with the queen at c2.

| 11. | c4:d5 | Qd8:d5 |

Black threatens mate at g2, no more and no less. The natural 12 f3 allows 12.. c4; that leaves White only 12 Nf4, when the knight will not be very well placed. Thus, the mate threat wasn't so naive after all: it led to a substantive change in the position which was definitely not in White's favor.

[51]

| 12. | Ne2-f4 | Qd5-c6 |
| 13. | c3-c4 | c5:d4 |

13.. g5 would be bad, of course: after 14 d5 Black's position crumbles.

14.	e3:d4	Nb8-d7
15.	Bc1-b2	Rf8-e8
16.	Rf1-e1	Ra8-c8
17.	Ra1-c1	Nd7-f8
18.	Bd3-f1	...

The changing of the guard.

| 18. | ... | Nf8-g6 |
| 19. | Nf4:g6 | ... |

The only possible explanation for this exchange must be that Euwe wanted to try to mate Black on the opened h-file. 19 Nd3 would have been much better, maintaining the option of driving out Black's queen with either Ne5 or Nb4, thus freeing the bishop at f1 for work along its proper diagonal: b1-h7.

19.	...	h7:g6
20.	Re1-e3	Re8-d8
21.	Qc2-e2	Qc6-d6
22.	Re3-h3	...

It seems our guess was correct.

22.	...	Qd6-f4
23.	Rc1-d1	Bb7-a6
24.	Rh3-f3	Qf4-e4
25.	Rf3-e3	Qe4-g4
26.	f2-f3	...

Reshevsky's skillful queen maneuvers have induced first one weakening, then another. White does not want to trade queens, fearing to go into an endgame with his hanging pawns.

26.	...	Qg4-f4
27.	g2-g3	Qf4-h6
28.	Re3-c3	Qh6-g5
29.	Qe2-f2	Rd8-d7
30.	Rd1-c1	...

White absolutely must bring his bishop out via c1 to f4, and then to e5. Now was the time: 30 Bc1 Qa5 31 Qb2 Rdd8 32 Bf4, and 32.. Nd5 doesn't work, while 32.. Rc7 is now rendered impossible.

30.	...	Rd7-c7
31.	Rc1-c2	Qg5-a5
32.	Bb2-c1	...

But this is very much the wrong time: 32 Rc1 was the proper continuation of his defense, although White's game is, by and large, already ruined. Black would have brought up his knight via e8 to d6, continuing the assault on White's hanging pawns.

| 32. | ... | Nf6-d5 |

No doubt Euwe overlooked this decisive stroke.

33.	c4:d5	Rc7:c3
34.	Rc2:c3	Qa5:c3
35.	Bc1-b2	Qc3-b3
36.	Bf1:a6	Rc8-c2
37.	d5-d6	Rc2:f2
38.	d6-d7	Qb3-d5
39.	Kg1:f2	...

WHITE RESIGNED

******

33. Stahlberg—Keres
(Queen's Gambit)

The reader has certainly noticed by this time, and will probably continue to note, that we avoid detailed examination of opening variations. When two armies march to the battlefield, there are so many roads they can take that one could never describe all of them.

In the present game, however, we shall make an exception, since Keres employs a defense that is not found in the opening books.

| 1. | d2-d4 | Ng8-f6 |

2.	c2-c4	e7-e6
3.	Ng1-f3	d7-d5
4.	Nb1-c3	c7-c5
5.	c4:d5	c5:d4

Theory examines only 5.. N:d5, and considers that White gets a small advantage with the continuation 6 e3 Nc6 7 Bc4. Keres' move has never been seen in major tournaments, and must have been something Keres whipped up himself, especially for this tournament. Is it any good? Apparently, no worse than anything else; at any rate, Keres used it three times, and the 2½ points it brought him speak for themselves.

| 6. | Qd1:d4 | ... |

White has gained the time to develop his queen, but Black wins it back shortly with 8.. Nc6. There would have been no point in sacrificing a piece for three pawns by 6 de dc 7 ef+ Ke7 8 Q:d8+ K:d8 9 bc, since the pawn on f7 will fall sooner or later.

| 6. | ... | e6:d5 |
| 7. | Bc1-g5 | ... |

In later games (Nos. 155 and 210), Najdorf and Geller played 7 e4 against Keres, but they came prepared. In his first encounter with an unfamiliar variation, Stahlberg could not risk a sharp continuation.

7.	...	Bf8-e7
8.	e2-e3	Nb8-c6
9.	Qd4-d2	0-0
10.	Bf1-e2	Bc8-e6
11.	0-0	Nf6-e4

This freeing possibility is an important link in this system, and doubtless Keres had foreseen it. If now 12 B:e7 Q:e7 13 N:d5?, then 13.. Qd7, winning a piece.

| 12. | Nc3:e4 | d5:e4 |
| 13. | Bg5:e7 | ... |

Danger still stalks White: 13 Q:d8 B:d8, and once again, White comes out a piece down.

| 13. | ... | Qd8:e7 |
| 14. | Nf3-d4 | Rf8-d8 |

A final snare: if 15 N:c6, then 15.. R:d2 16 N:e7+ Kf8, and Black recovers his piece with

the superior position.

| 15. | Rf1-d1 | Nc6:d4 |
| 16. | e3:d4 | Rd8-d6 |

Keres' new system has successfully withstood its baptism of fire. The game's further course revolves around the pawn at d4. It is isolated, but also passed; Black would like to capture it, but he must blockade it first.

17.	Qd2-e3	Be6-d5
18.	Ra1-c1	Ra8-d8
19.	Be2-c4	h7-h6
20.	h2-h3	a7-a6
21.	Bc4:d5	Rd6:d5
22.	Rc1-c4	f7-f5
23.	f2-f3	...

Stahlberg wants to give his opponent a weak pawn too.

23.	...	b7-b5
24.	Rc4-c6	Qe7-d7
25.	Rc6:a6	e4:f3
26.	Qe3:f3	Rd5:d4
27.	Rd1-f1	Rd4-d2
28.	Ra6-a8	Rd8:a8
29.	Qf3:a8+	Kg8-h7
30.	Qa8-f3	g7-g6

Black has a small but clear positional advantage, which may be explained, but is hard to put into any sort of concrete form. The black king is better sheltered from possible checks, with the pawn at f5 rendering special service in this regard by protecting against diagonal checks. (A similar disadvantage nearly cost Keres his Round 29 game against Taimanov.) In the present case, however, the white pieces are solidly placed, and the last move, 30.. g6, which laid bare the seventh rank, certainly did not increase Black's winning chances.

| 31. | Rf1-e1 | Rd2:b2 |
| 32. | Qf3-a3 | ... |

Now White has some threats of his own.

32.	...	Qd7-d4+
33.	Kg1-h1	h6-h5
34.	Qa3-e7+	...

White could easily have played 34 Qf8, too: Black would then have had nothing but to play 34.. Re2, when 35 R:e2 Qd1+ 36 Kh2 Q:e2 37 Qf7+ Kh6 38 h4 probably leads to a draw.

| 34. | ... | Kh7-h6 |
| 35. | Qe7-f8+ | ... |

Here and two moves later White misses a simple draw: 35 h4, with the threat 36 Qg5+ and 37 Qe7+.

35.	...	Kh6-g5
36.	Qf8-e7+	Kg5-h6
37.	Qe7-f8+	Qd4-g7
38.	Qf8-c5	...

With queens off, the rook ending would be a loss for White.

38.	...	Qg7-f6
39.	a2-a3	Rb2-b3
40.	Re1-d1	f5-f4
41.	Rd1-f1	f4-f3
42.	Rf1:f3	Rb3:f3
43.	g2:f3	Qf6:f3+
44.	Kh1-h2	...

It is possible to draw queen endings with very accurate play. Keres intends to set up a position in which White will not be able to avoid the exchange of queens. For this purpose, the king must be brought to the queen's wing. The winning method is interesting, and a useful bit of knowledge to have, but its execution in this game was abetted by an inaccuracy from White.

44... h4 45. Qe5 Qf2+ 46. Kh1 Qf5 47. Qh8+ Kg5 48. Qd8+ Kf4 49. Qd2+ Kf3 50. Qd1+ Ke3 51. Qe1+ Kd3 52. Qb1+ Ke2 53. Qb2+ Ke3 54. Qc1+ Ke4 55.Qb1+ Kf3 56. Qd1+ Kf4 57. Qd2+

An error that helps Black set up the winning position. 57 Qc1+ was correct, so as to meet 57.. Ke5 with 58 Qc5+, keeping the king out of the queenside.

57... Ke5 58. Qc3+ Kd5 59. Qb3+ Kc6 60.Qc3+ Kb7 61. Qg7+ Ka6 62. Qc3 Qf1+ 63. Kh2 Qf2+ 64.Kh1 Kb6 65. Qc8 Qe1+ 66. Kg2 Qe4+ 67. Kg1 Qd4+

WHITE RESIGNED

— since Black now has every point on the c-file from c7 to c4 to support an exchange of queens. After 68 Kg2 Qd5+ 69 Kh2 Qd6+ forces the trade.

*****

34. Boleslavsky—Smyslov
(Queen's Gambit)

1. d4 d5 2. c4 c6 3. Nf3 Nf6 4. Nc3 dc 5. a4 Bf5 6. e3 e6 7. B:c4 Bb4

A defensive system prepared by Smyslov for the Zurich event. Although he used it four times, drawing all four games in short order, I still consider this a difficult variation for Black. Smyslov had to display a great deal of resourcefulness in order to equalize, and his opponents did not always exploit their opportunities to the fullest. After this tournament, neither Smyslov nor the other masters made much further use of this defense, so it has disappeared from practice.

8. 0-0 Nbd7 9. Qe2 0-0 10. e4 Bg6 11. e5 Nd5 12. N:d5 cd 13. Bd3

a6 14. B:g6 fg 15. Be3 Qe7
16. Rfc1 Rfc8 17. Bd2 h6

DRAW

******

35. Kotov—Geller
(Sicilian Defense)

1. e4 c5 2. Nf3 Nc6 3. d4 cd
4. N:d4 Nf6 5. Nc3 d6 6. Bg5 e6
7. Qd2 Be7 8. 0-0-0 0-0 9. f4 e5

A theoretical novelty, introduced in this game, which received further development in
the USSR Championships, and was

finally found not quite satisfactory for Black. In this game,
Kotov avoids risk by quick simplification.

10. N:c6 bc 11. fe de 12. Q:d8
R:d8 13. R:d8+ B:d8 14. Bc4 Be7
15. h3 Bd7 16. Rd1 Be8 17. a3 Kf8
18. Be3 Nh5 19. Ne2 Nf6 20. Nc3
Nh5 21. Ne2 Nf6 22. Nc3

DRAW

******

·

36. Smyslov—Kotov
(Sicilian Defense)

1.	e2-e4	c7-c5
2.	Ng1-f3	d7-d6
3.	d2-d4	c5:d4
4.	Nf3:d4	Ng8-f6
5.	Nb1-c3	a7-a6
6.	Bf1-e2	e7-e5

The outcome of a game between Smyslov and Kotov may be hard to predict, but there can never be any doubt about what the opening will be: Smyslov feels honor-bound to play 1 e4, and Kotov invariably replies 1.. c5.

This time, Kotov alters the tradition a bit: instead of his usual Scheveningen, in which ..e5 is played only at the last minute, with White's threats already hanging overhead, he tips his hat to fashion and plays .. e5 on move six. One idea behind this rather eccentric move is that here 7 Nf5 is unfavorable, due to the reply 7.. B:f5 and 8.. d5.

7.	Nd4-b3	Bf8-e7
8.	Bc1-e3	Nb8-d7
9.	0-0	0-0
10.	f2-f3	Qd8-c7
11.	Qd1-e1	...

Smyslov's omission of a2-a4 on this or the preceding move allows Black too much leeway. Had Black played 10.. b5, White still might have replied 11 a4 b4 12 Nd5 N:d5 and retaken with the queen; but now .. b5 is wholly unobjectionable. All that White has gotten out of the opening is safe and solid control of e4. That's something — we shall have numerous occasions to remember it during the course of the game — but still one might have hoped for more.

11.	...	b7-b5
12.	a2-a3	Nd7-b6
13.	Qe1-f2	Ra8-b8
14.	Ra1-b1	...

14.. Nc4 and 14.. Na4 were both threatened. That White should be forced to make such a move as 14 Rab1 indicates that there is something disharmonious in his position.

14.	...	Bc8-e6

15.	Kg1-h1	Nb6-c4

This has its logic, but 15..d5 looks far more attractive, demonstrating as it does that the pawn on d6 wasn't really weak at all. It gives Black more than just the moral victory of proving that he could bring more force to bear on d5 than White: it would have given Black a free game for his pieces as well (15.. d5 16 ed Nb:d5 17 N:d5 N:d5 18 Bc5 Nf4).

16.	Be2:c4	b5:c4
17.	Nb3-c1	Rb8-b7

Smyslov comes up with an excellent antidote to this straightforward plan of doubling rooks and winning the b-pawn; here too, 17.. d5 was good with the same ideas as noted before.

18.	Nc1-a2	d6-d5

At the most inappropriate moment. 18.. a5 was now necessary; only after 19 a4 Qb8 20 Nb5 would 20.. d5 be possible.

19.	e4:d5	Be6:d5
20.	Na2-b4	Be7:b4
21.	a3:b4	...

21.	...	Qc7-c6
22.	Be3-g5	...

Exploiting the fact that the bishop is tied up temporarily, White begins a kingside attack. 22..R:b4 23 B:f6 gf 24 Qd2 Be6 25 Ne4 is bad for Black, so the rook beats a disappointed retreat from b7.

22.	...	Rb7-d7
23.	Rf1-e1	Rf8-e8
24.	Rb1-d1	...

Smyslov plays simply and directly; gradually, his pieces assume better and better positions. Now 25 B:f6 is a threat.

24.	...	Nf6-h5
25.	Qf2-h4	g7-g6
26.	Nc3:d5	Rd7:d5
27.	Rd1:d5	Qc6:d5
28.	Qh4-e4	...

Now that White has induced .. g6, one might expect him to attack this weakening; but instead, judging correctly that Black's castled position would prove very difficult to penetrate, Smyslov suggests a transition into an endgame that is slightly better for him, based on his control of the square e4.

| 28. | ... | Qd5:e4 |

Kotov agrees, mistakenly, to the trade of queens: the weak pawns at a6 and c4 leave him little chance to save the endgame. With queens still on, Black might eventually get a chance to play .. f5 and .. e4.

29.	Re1:e4	f7-f6
30.	Bg5-e3	Re8-c8
31.	g2-g4	Nh5-g7
32.	g4-g5	...

32 Bc5 would not have won a pawn in view of 32.. a5 33 R:c4 ab, and the pawn cannot be taken, either by rook or bishop; if then 34 b3 Ne6 35 B:b4 R:c4 36 bc Nd4, and this endgame is most probably a draw.

However, White has found a way to exploit the weakness at e5.

32.	...	Kg8-f7
33.	g5:f6	Kf7:f6
34.	Be3-d2	Ng7-f5
35.	Bd2-c3	Nf5-d4
36.	f3-f4	...

Nothing would come of 36 B:d4 ed 37 R:d4 c3 38 b3 Re8: the rook invades the second rank and wins the c-pawn, which draws. Now Kotov wins the c-pawn at once, but his knight gets driven to a1, and Black's position becomes critical.

| 36. | ... | Nd4:c2 |

| 37. | Re4-e2 | Nc2-a1 |

| 38. | Re2:e5 | ... |

Smyslov's fine play has brought the game to this winning position, but now time-pressure puts him on the wrong path. 38 fe+ Ke6 39 Rf2 would have led to swift victory for White — or perhaps 38 Kg2 first, and only then 39 fe+, would have been yet more thematic. Smyslov's plan appears powerful, but leaves Black a hidden drawing resource.

38.	...	Kf6-f7
39.	Re5-a5	Na1-c2
40.	Ra5:a6	Rc8-b8
41.	Ra6-c6	Nc2-b4
42.	Rc6-c7+	...

An essential check: if 42 R:c4 is played at once, then 42..Nd5 43 Be5 Rb3, and Black's king goes to f5 via e6. Now, after 42..Ke6 43 R:c4, 43.. Nd5 is no longer possible, because of 44 Re4+, when 44.. Kf5 loses the knight, and 44.. Kd6 allows 45 Be5+. Even after this check, however, the draw is still there, with

42.	...	Kf7-e6
43.	Rc7:c4	Nb4-d3
44.	b2-b4	Rb8-f8

DRAW

******

37. Keres—Boleslavsky
(Old Indian Defense)

1.	d2-d4	Ng8-f6
2.	c2-c4	d7-d6

3.   Nb1-c3   e7-e5

A radical means of avoiding
both the Samisch and the Four
Pawns' Attack. Whatever White
plays, the pure Samisch setup is
now unattainable: for example,
after 4 d5, Black is by no means
obliged to fianchetto his bishop,
but may play instead 4.. Bf5,
and if 5 f3 e4.

If 4 e4, Black gains a tempo
for development with 4.. ed 5 Q:d4
Nc6, after which he may play either 6.. Be7 or 6.. g6. And on
4 de de 5 Q:d8+ K:d8, Black's
king forfeits castling, but will
find shelter at c7.

However, White still has ways of
exploiting Black's early e-pawn
push, and the one Keres has in
mind is 5 Bg5, a rarely-played
line which is nevertheless one of
White's most solid positional
ideas.

4.   Ng1-f3   Nb8-d7
5.   Bc1-g5   ...

If Black's 2.. d6 and 3.. e5
prevented the strongest of the
anti-King's Indian attacks, then
White, in turn, prevents Black
from obtaining the modern form of
the King's Indian (with a fianchettoed king's bishop), since
5.. g6 6 de de 7 N:e5 costs a
pawn. Black, of course, could
play 5.. Be7, but that sort of
development for this bishop grates
on a King's Indian player. In
that case, White would have a simple program: 6 e3, 7 Be2 and 8 0-0
with no fear of .. e5-e4, since
his queen's bishop is already
outside his pawn chain.

Boleslavsky, who has worked
steadily and with immense success at improving the King's Indian for Black, feels himself mor-
ally obligated to correct extant
opinions; for this game, he has
prepared a dizzying new line involving the sacrifice of his
queen's rook.

5.   ...   h7-h6
6.   Bg5-h4   g7-g5
7.   d4:e5   ...

If the bishop retreats again,
the e-pawn rushes to the third
rank, with the well-known idea
of retarding White's kingside

development: 7 Bg3 e4 8 Nd2 e3;
but now we enter Boleslavsky's
main line.

7.   ...   g5:h4
8.   e5:f6   Qd8:f6
9.   Nc3-d5   Qf6:b2

Some pieces in the King's Indian appear on a "special price"
list: the darksquare bishops are
at the top of that list. This
means that Black has achieved
something, in removing White's
bishop while retaining his own,
even at the cost of shattering
his own pawns. With his last move,
Black initiates his previously
prepared sharp attacking line,
sacrificing a rook for the attack.

The attack will be based on the
fact that the centralized knight
is out of play at a8; the whole
question is whether Black can
work up decisive threats in the
short time it will take White to
develop his bishop and get his
knight back to the center.

Boleslavsky had mainly considered the following line, in which
his darksquare bishop plays the
lead: 10 N:c7+ Kd8 11 N:a8 d5!
12 Rc1 Bb4+ 13 Nd2 Nc5 14 Rc2 Qe5
15 e3 Bf5. Najdorf's recommendation, returning the queen to d8,
is not appealing. His variation:
9.. Qd8 10 Qd4 Ne5 11 N:e5 Bg7
12 N:f7 K:f7 13 Qf4+ Kg8 14 0-0-0
c6 15 Nc3 Qa5, only appears playable; in actuality, Black's one
threat, 16.. B:c3, is no threat
at all, and White can cheerfully
take on d6 with his queen, one

possible continuation being:
16 Q:d6 B:c3 17 bc Q:c3+ 18 Kb1
Bf5+ 19 e4 B:e4+ 20 Bd3.

| 10. | Ra1-b1 | ... |

The simple move which Boleslavsky overlooked in his preparatory
analysis. After 10 N:c7+ Kd8, the
move 11 Rb1 would be no problem
for Black, since he would have the
check on c3; here, however, with
the knight on d5, the check is
impossible, and Black's whole attack is refuted.

10.	...	Qb2:a2
11.	Nd5:c7+	Ke8-d8
12.	Nc7:a8	Nd7-c5

Blushing furiously at his mistake, Boleslavsky commits another.
True, 12.. d5 would have been useless now without the check on b4,
but 12.. Bg7 would still have kept
up some semblance of an attack:
for example, 13 Rc1 Qa3 14 Qd2 Nc5.
If Black can pick up the knight on
a8, he will have a pawn for the
exchange. Now, however, Keres can
force the exchange of queens with
a series of precise moves, and all
danger is liquidated.

13.	Rb1-a1	Qa2-b2
14.	Qd1-d4	Qb2:d4
15.	Nf3:d4	Bf8-g7
16.	e2-e3	Rh8-e8
17.	Bf1-e2	Bg7:d4
18.	e3:d4	Nc5-b3
19.	Ra1:a7	Nb3:d4
20.	Ra7-a2	h4-h3
21.	Rh1-g1	Re8-g8
22.	g2-g4	

BLACK RESIGNED

******

38. Reshevsky—Stahlberg
(Queen's Gambit)

1.	d2-d4	d7-d5
2.	c2-c4	e7-e6
3.	Nb1-c3	c7-c5
4.	c4:d5	e6:d5
5.	Ng1-f3	Nb8-c6
6.	g2-g3	c5-c4

The Swedish Variation, a great
favorite of Stahlberg and Stoltz.
Black's further plans are to dim-
inish the pressure on the d5-pawn
with .. Bb4, and to strengthen its
defense with .. Ne7, avoiding the
pin with Bg5 that would be possible after .. Nf6. However, 6..c4
gives the d4-pawn great addition-

al strength: after e2-e4, it will
become passed, and tie down some
black pieces. The black pawn at
c4 cannot be considered its equal
by any stretch of the imagination,
since it is not passed, and is
hardly likely ever to attain that
status.

7.	Bf1-g2	Bf8-b4
8.	0-0	Ng8-e7
9.	e2-e4	d5:e4
10.	Nc3:e4	0-0
11.	Qd1-c2	...

A Reshevsky novelty: 11 a3 Ba5
12 Qa4 was usual here, but then
comes 12.. Bg4, indirectly attacking, and then capturing, the
d-pawn in return for his c-pawn.
The point of 11 Qc2 is not the
sacrifice of a pawn, of course:
that's so obviously bad for Black
as to render it a mere footnote
(11..N:d4 12 N:d4 Q:d4 13 Rd1 Qe5
14 Bf4, and White recovers the
pawn with a colossal lead in development); the idea is that White
can use his attack on the c-pawn
to gain a tempo to bring his rook
to d1. With the support of the
rook, that pawn gets very lively
indeed, and runs quickly down to
the seventh rank, setting up dangerous tactical possibilities.

| 11. | ... | Qd8-d5 |
| 12. | Bc1-e3 | ... |

Giving his opponent the opportunity to play his bishop to f5,
when there would follow 13 Nh4
N:d4 14 B:d4 Q:d4 15 N:f5 N:f5
16 Rfd1 Qe5 17 Rd5 Q:d5 18 Nf6+;
or 16.. Qb6 17 a3 Ba5 18 Q:c4,

and the white pieces would be much more harmoniously placed than the black : 19 b4 is a threat, to which capturing on b2 is no adequate defense, in view of 20 Qd5, forking bishop and knight.

12.	...	Ne7-g6
13.	Nf3-h4	Qd5-b5
14.	Nh4:g6	h7:g6
15.	a2-a3	Bb4-e7
16.	d4-d5	Nc6-a5
17.	d5-d6	...

Playing forcefully and concretely, Reshevsky allows his opponent not a single free breath; Black is continually forced to ward off direct threats. The game is vintage Reshevsky, and without doubt one of the tourney's best.

17.	...	Be7-d8
18.	Ne4-c3	Qb5-a6
19.	Ra1-d1	Bc8-g4
20.	Rd1-d4	Bg4-f5
21.	Qc2-a4	Ra8-b8

With the obvious intention of getting a little air by means of 22.. b5, but White does not allow this either.

22.	Rd4-d5	Bf5-e6
23.	Rd5-e5!	b7-b6

The pawn at d6 is loose, and the rook may be attacked four different ways — every one of which would lose material for Black. Stahlberg contents himself with the modest 23.. b6, defending the knight and allowing the queen to get back to c8.

I would not have been able to resist 24 R:e6, with Black's queen and knight so far away from their king, his pawns weak, and the pair of white bishops sweeping the board. Variations would have to be calculated too, naturally, but I don't believe they'd look too bad. I would recommend that the reader examine 25 Nb5, as well as 25 Qc2 and 25 Bh3, for himself.

24. d6-d7 ...

Reshevsky's actual move is also strong, and partly the product of time-pressure. Having no time left for calculations, Reshevsky preferred to convert the game into a technical exercise, in which there could be no doubt as to his advantage.

24... b5 25. R:b5 R:b5 26.Q:b5 Q:b5 27. N:b5 a6 28. Nc3 B:d7 29. Rd1 Bc8

White's pieces are beautifully developed, while Black's pawns are weak, and must fall before the marauding bishops and rook.

30. Ne4 Be7 31. Bc5 B:c5 32.N:c5 Bf5

An admission of helplessness, or simple oversight? Most likely, the latter.

33. N:a6 Re8 34. Bf3 Nb3 35.Kg2 Bc2 36. Rd7 Bf5 37. Rd1 Bc2 38. Rd7 Bf5 39. Rd6 Be6 40. Nc7 Re7 41. N:e6

BLACK RESIGNED

******

39. Bronstein—Euwe
(Nimzoindian Defense)

Generally, it makes sense to sacrifice a pawn, sometimes even a piece, in order to keep the enemy king in the center and assail it with rooks and queen. However, two general classes of such attacks must be distinguished: in the first category, the king is kept to the eighth rank, hemmed in by its own pawns and pieces; while in the second category, the king is driven out to the sixth rank — sometimes even to the fifth — and attempts to find shelter on one wing or the other.

The present game is an example of the latter type. The defender's chief resource is a cool head, and my opponent made full use of his here. At one point, I had to break off my calculations in order to ask myself: Just who is attacking whom here?

During the game, and afterwards as well, I was unable to shake the feeling that somewhere I had had a win. Perhaps some concrete variation did flicker momentarily through my mind, but it tarried not... In any event, neither I, nor the commentators (Euwe, Najdorf and Stahlberg) have been able to find an improvement for White, which would mean that my promising piece sacrifice was not enough for a win. Perhaps the win may yet be found in analysis; but even if I did not get the point, I did get a lively and interesting game.

1.	d2-d4	Ng8-f6
2.	c2-c4	e7-e6
3.	Nb1-c3	Bf8-b4
4.	e2-e3	c7-c5
5.	Bf1-d3	d7-d5
6.	Ng1-f3	0-0
7.	0-0	Nb8-c6
8.	a2-a3	Bb4:c3
9.	b2:c3	d5:c4
10.	Bd3:c4	Qd8-c7

All of these opening moves were played almost automatically by both sides. Now White begins preparations for e3-e4.

| 11. | Bc4-d3 | e6-e5 |
| 12. | Qd1-c2 | Rf8-e8 |

This, to me, seems stronger than 12.. Qe7, as Euwe played in Game 176 against Averbakh, and later in the 11th Olympiad against Botvinnik. Comparing the two continuations: 12.. Qe7 13 de N:e5 14 N:e5 Q:e5, and 12.. Re8 13 de N:e5 14 N:e5 Q:e5 — Black has an extra tempo in the latter line. Of course, Black temporarily prevents 13 e4 with his 12..Qe7, but is that move really so dangerous?

| 13. | e3-e4 | e5:d4 |

Euwe could have forced the trade of queens here, with considerably simpler play after 13.. c4 14 B:c4 ed 15 cd Na5 16 Bd3 Q:c2 17 B:c2 N:e4; but

instead, he accepts the challenge to play a more complex game, full of interesting combinations.

| 14. | c3:d4 | Bc8-g4 |

14.. cd would have been met by 15 e5. Euwe wants White to try 15 e5 B:f3 16 ef N:d4 17 B:h7+ Kh8 18 fg+ K:g7 19 Bb2 Rad8, considering his position capable of withstanding the attack. After the game, the complications were found to favor White, but I was drawn to another, more intriguing possibility.

15.	Qc2:c5	Nf6:e4
16.	Bd3:e4	Re8:e4
17.	Nf3-g5	...

Beginning an attack on the king (of course not 17 d5? B:f3 18 gf Rh4 19 f4 Qd7). Black could capture the d-pawn here, but he refrained, fearing 17..R:d4 18 Bb2 Rd7 19 Qc2 g6 20 Ne4. I was a little uncertain about 17.. R:d4 18 Bb2 Qf4, but this exchange sacrifice didn't look convincing enough to my opponent.

17.	...	Re4-e7
18.	Qc5-c2	g7-g6
19.	Ng5-e4	Bg4-f5

Both sides have played into this line, which involves the sacrifice of a piece. Black weakened the long diagonal by playing 18.. g6 instead of the more natural 18.. f5, because he wanted the f5 square kept free for his bishop; and White is giving up the piece in order to get the black king out to f6 and e6, and then assail him with all his pieces. The battle waxes uncommonly fierce.

| 20. | Ne4-f6+ | Kg8-g7 |
| 21. | Qc2-d2 | ... |

At this moment, I was quite pleased with my position. Indeed, after

| 21. | ... | Kg7:f6 |

Black's king can never get back to g7, but must remain in the center, assailed by both rooks, queen, bishop and perhaps even by pawns. However, my opponent's face showed no sign of despair either — an object lesson for the young player who finds himself in difficulties (especially when facing a mating attack), and chokes up at once, thereby rendering his defensive task still more difficult.

22. d4-d5 ...

Here I examined 22 Bb2 and 22Qh6 too. The text is stronger: it retains both those threats while creating a third: 23 d6.

22. ... Ra8-d8

A remarkable move: Black brings up the last of his defensive reserves, and obviates all three of White's threats at a stroke. 23 Qh6 would now be met by the calm 23.. R:d5, and on 23 Bb2+, Black plans to return the piece. Even here, I was quite optimistic still, feeling that with material equality restored White's attack would be all the stronger.

23. Bc1-b2+ Nc6-e5
24. f2-f4 ...

24 Rad1 was worth a look, but I could not see anything forcing and decided not to take any unnecessary risk.

24. ... Qc7-c5+
25. Kg1-h1 ...

Since the d-pawn is doomed anyhow, there's no sense in putting the bishop en prise as well: after 25 Bd4, Euwe would have continued 25.. R:d5 26 B:c5 R:d2 27 B:e7+ K:e7 28 fe Be4, which draws; or

26 fe+ Ke6 27 B:c5 R:d2 28 B:e7 K:e7, and Black can still draw, even though he is the exchange down.

25. ... Rd8:d5
26. f4:e5+ Kf6-e6

Having recovered his piece, White now attacks the exposed king; however, he encounters strategical difficulties in developing his attack. The king is surrounded by its own pieces, which display a sharp tendency to counterattack at the first available opportunity. The king also has many more open squares about him than would be the case if White were attacking the castled position. And finally, with White's king tucked away at h1, his own first rank has become weak.

Nonetheless, White still has one strong trump: the opposite-colored bishops, which normally ensure an advantage to the attacking side. It may have been this chance that White failed fully to exploit.

27. Qd2-g5 Ke6-d7

Black would find himself ensnared after 27.. Qc2 28 Rac1, since he is not really threatening the bishop: 28.. Q:b2? 29Qf6+ and 30 e6+.

28. Ra1-c1 ...

28 a4, to exploit his strategic advantage (the darksquare bishop) would have been stronger, and possibly decisive: his opponent would have had to oppose his rook. After 28 a4, Black would be practically forced to give up the exchange; he would get a second pawn for it, but then the attack of the queen and two rooks would have become fierce indeed: for example, 28 a4 Re6 29 Ba3 Qc4 30 Bd6 Re:d6 31 ed R:d6 32 Rad1; or 28.. Re:e5 29 B:e5 R:e5 30 Rac1.

28. ... Qc5-b6
29. Bb2-c3 Re7-e8
30. Bc3-b4 Re8:e5

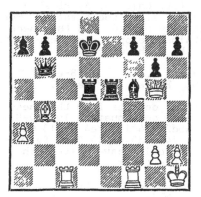

To compare this with the 28 a4 line: White has brought his bishop to the strong diagonal here too, but he has given up the e-pawn for nothing. Now he could try 31 R:f5 gf 32 Qg8, but after 32.. Qc6!, this leads to a perpetual.

31. Qg5-h4   a7-a5

At this point I began to suspect that Black had started to play for the win. Having determined that 32 Q:h7 ab 33 Q:f7+ was simply bad for me, I decided on one last attacking try: to bring the bishop via e1 to g3, creating a threat to c7.

32. Bb4-e1   h7-h5
33. Be1-f2   Qb6-a6
34. Bf2-g3   Re5-e4

One last detail, to complete the picture : neither side had more than two minutes left until flag-fall. 35 Qg5 Ke6 looked worse than unclear, so I decided to stop tempting fate.

35. Rf1:f5   ...

All of the commentators gave this move an exclamation mark, since it was by now White's only means of forcing a draw. Nevertheless, I feel bound to admit to the reader that I sacrificed more from inspiration than from calculation. 35.. gf 36 Rc7+ Ke8 37 Rc8+ appeared to me to be very dangerous for Black, for instance: 37.. Kd7 38 Qd8+ Ke6 39 Qe8+ Kf6

40 Qh8+ Ke6 41 Re8+ Kd7 42 Rd8+ Kc6 43 Qh6+ Re6 44 Qc1+ Rc5 45 Rc8+ Kd7 46 R:c5. Later it was shown that not all of Black's moves in this line were forced, and that with exact play he could draw.

Had Euwe taken the rook, there would have been no practical reason why he should lose, since this variation would lie, for the most part, beyond the time control; however, he chose the more natural continuation.

35.   ...   Re4:h4

For a moment, I forgot that Black's queen had moved to a6, attacking the square f1, and very nearly went in for 36 R:d5+ Ke6 37 Re5+?? Kf6 38 Rf1+. Do not imagine, dear reader, that the grandmasters are spotless creatures; they too, get into time-trouble; sometimes they fail to calculate a variation completely; and occasionally, they even blunder...

36. Rf5:d5+   Kd7-e6

37. Rc1-d1   Qa6-c4
38. Rd5-d6+   Ke6-e7
39. Rd6-d7+   Ke7-f6

39.. Kf8 looked too risky: 40 Rd8+ Kg7 41 Be5+ f6 42 R8d7+ Kh6 43 B:f6, threatening 44 Bg7+; but 43.. Rf4 would stop everything.

40. Bg3:h4+   Qc4:h4
41. Rd1-f1+   ...

The game was adjourned here, and Black sealed

41.   ...   Kf6-g5

but there was no further play, since after 42 Rd5+ and 43 R:a5 the

DRAW

is obvious.

******

40. Gligoric—Szabo
(Ruy Lopez)

The prime consideration in one's choice of an opening plan should be the harmonious development of the pieces, but sometimes we forget about the development of the queen. Since the queen is, after all, the most important and the most valuable of the pieces, the success of the whole piece configuration may depend on how well the queen plays its part.

In some openings, the move .. c5 is important not only as a means of attacking the enemy pawn center, but also in order to give the queen an exit to c7, b6 or a5. This applies especially to systems in which the bishop is developed to e7, thus blocking the queen's other diagonal: for example, the Orthodox Queen's Gambit, the Chigorin Ruy Lopez, or the Classical Variation of the French Defense.

In the game Gligoric - Szabo, the development of Black's queen became the central theme of the opening and middlegame struggle: White maintained a clear advantage as long as the queen was relegated to the eighth rank, and found his game sliding downhill as soon as the queen obtained some <u>lebensraum</u>.

1.	e2-e4	e7-e5
2.	Ng1-f3	Nb8-c6
3.	Bf1-b5	a7-a6
4.	Bb5-a4	Ng8-f6
5.	0-0	Nf6:e4
6.	d2-d4	b7-b5
7.	Ba4-b3	d7-d5
8.	d4:e5	Bc8-e6
9.	c2-c3	...

Here the Open Defense to the Ruy branches off into two main

lines: 9.. Be7 and 9.. Bc5. To me, the latter seems more natural (cf. Game 70, Averbakh - Szabo), since the bishop is more actively posted, and the queen retains the option of developing on the d8-h4 diagonal.

9.	...	Bf8-e7
10.	Bc1-e3	Ne4-c5

Szabo departs from the theoretical continuation 10.. 0-0 11 Nbd2 Bg4 12 N:e4 de 13 Qd5 Q:d5 14 B:d5 ef 15 B:c6 fg 16 Rfe1, which would leave White with much the freer game.

11.	Bb3-c2	Be6-g4
12.	Nb1-d2	Nc5-e6

Black cannot take the pawn because of the continuation 13 B:c5 B:c5 14 Qe1, winning a piece (13.. N:f3+ 14 gf Bh3 15 Re1 is no improvement). So he retreats the knight first. Now the e-pawn is really threatened; but Gligoric proceeds to refute Black's entire opening configuration by means of a pretty and original queen maneuver, unpinning his knight and preventing Black from castling.

13.   Qd1-b1   ...

13.	...	Bg4-h5
14.	a2-a4	b5-b4

Thus, Black has developed all of his minor pieces well, holds the advanced e-pawn under observation, and could now play 14.. Bg6 and castle without giv-

[64]

ing himself any pawn weaknesses.
But there is one significant
piece weakness in his position,
and that is the queen, which is
not developed, and has no good
prospect of ever doing so —
something which White could have
attempted to exploit with 15 c4.
Whether Black takes or pushes
his pawn, 16 Be4 would be White's
reply; and on 15.. Bg6, White
would have traded bishops and proceeded with 17 Rd1. Black would
then have faced some difficult
problems, but 16 Be4 would not
have settled the outcome of the
game: 15.. d4 16 Be4 Qd7 would
pose the dilemma for White of
whether to sell his fine game
for a mere pawn. After 17 B:c6
Q:c6 18 N:d4 N:d4 19 B:d4 Bg6,
I rather prefer Black.

The positional text move does
not cost White his advantage, but
it does slow the game somewhat.

15.	a4-a5	Bh5-g6
16.	Nd2-b3	b4:c3
17.	b2:c3	Qd8-b8

Szabo has spotted the basic
shortcoming of his position,
and decides to postpone castling
until his queen has found a way
to the battlefield (the threat
was 18 Rd1 and 19 c4).

18.	Qb1-a2	0-0
19.	Bc2:g6	h7:g6
20.	Ra1-b1	Qb8-b5

A chessmaster's skill lies not
so much in perceiving the correct
plan as in carrying it out with
exact and sometimes "only" moves.
In the present case, we have
White proceeding with his strategically correct play against
the undeveloped queen, but selecting a technically inexact se-
quence: 20 Rfb1 was stronger. In
that event, the a-pawn would have
been defended, and the reply
20.. Qb5, obviously, rendered impossible; while Vukovic's recommendation of 20.. Qd8 would be
pointless, since the queen would
be as it was before, with no
field of activity; one possible
line might be 21 Rd1, and if
21.. Qd7, then 22 Nc5 N:c5
23 R:d5, etc., or 21.. Rb8 22 Nbd4
Ne:d4 23 N:d4 N:e5 24 Bf4, or
21.. Na7 22 c4.

| 21. | Qa2-c2 | ... |

Gligoric's desire to win this
game exclusively by positional
means, without recourse to any
of the combinative possibilities, leads eventually to his
downfall. 21 Nbd4 might fail to
21.. Q:a5, but 21 Nfd4 was good:
after 21.. Ne:d4 22 N:d4 Q:a5,
White sacrifices his queen —
23 N:c6 Q:a2 24 N:e7+ Kh7 25 Rb4
g5 26 B:g5 g6 27 Rh4+ Kg7 28 Bf6
mate! — a finale that could be
labeled the consistent conclusion to his plan. Of course,
21 Nfd4 would be better met by
21.. Nc:d4 22 cd Qd7 23 Rfc1,
with a minimal edge.

21.	...	Qb5-c4
22.	Nf3-d2	Qc4-g4
23.	f2-f4	Qg4-f5
24.	Qc2:f5	g6:f5

Black's queen needed a long
trek (Qd8-b8-b5-c4-g4-f5) to
achieve the opportunity to exchange itself for White's queen;
only then were the two queens
of equal value. After the trade,
Black has the better of it, since
the a-pawn is weak, and the pawns
at e5 and f4 hem in White's bishop. Summarizing the course of
the struggle through the opening
and middlegame, we could say that
White's powerful and consistent
play netted him an advantage,
which he might have exploited
with 20 Rfb1; on the 21st move,
White might have maintained approximate equality, or if Black
were careless, a pretty combination could have been played. Having let slip all these opportunities, White must now endure a
difficult endgame.

25.	Nd2-f3	Rf8-b8
26.	Nf3-d4	Nc6:d4
27.	Nb3:d4	Ne6:d4
28.	c3:d4	...

Taking with the pawn hems in
the bishop still more severely,
but 28 B:d4 would result in a
lost position after 28.. Rb5
29 R:b5 ab 30 Ra1 Ra6 31 Kf1 Kf8.

28.	...	Be7-b4
29.	Rb1-a1	Rb8-b5
30.	Ra1-a4	Ra8-b8
31.	Rf1-a1	...

After 31 Rc1, Black simply
takes the pawn, and the pseudo-
sacrifice of the exchange to recover it falls short: 31..R:a5

32 R:b4 R:b4 33 Bd2 Rab5 34 B:b4
R:b4 35 R:c7 R:d4, and Black now
has two passed pawns.

31.	...	Bb4-c3
32.	Ra1-c1	Rb5-b1
33.	Rc1:b1	Rb8:b1+
34.	Kg1-f2	Rb1-a1

34.. Rb5 would leave White the
reply 35 Ra3 Bb4 36 Ra4, forcing
the bishop to take the a-pawn;
then, in order to untangle his
pieces, Black would have to bring
his king up from g8 all the way
to b7 or b6.

35.	Ra4:a1	Bc3:a1
36.	Kf2-e2	Ba1-c3
37.	Ke2-d3	Bc3-a5
38.	h2-h3	...

Despite his pawn minus, Gligoric had a beautiful positional
draw here with 38 Bd2, and if
38.. Bb6 39 Bb4, when it would
be very difficult for Black to
bring his king to the center,
39.. f6 being met by 40 e6. In
the pawn endgame after 38.. B:d2
39 K:d2, the draw is clearer yet:
for example, 39.. Kf8 40 Kc3 Ke7
41 Kb4 Kd7 42 Kc5. White would
not have had this chance, if
Black had played 34.. Rb5 instead
of 34.. Ra1 — yet another example demonstrating how one must
always note and exploit the tiniest details in an endgame, and
how useful it can be to know
problem ideas.

| 38. | ... | Ba5-e1 |

Now the exchange of bishops
does not come off, since Black
can answer 39 Bd2 with 39.. Bg3,
gaining the tempo he needs to
play 40.. Kf8.

39.	g2-g4	g7-g6
40.	Kd3-c2	Kg8-f8
41.	Kc2-d1	Be1-g3

WHITE RESIGNED

******

41. Taimanov—Averbakh
(Nimzoindian Defense)

One of the tournament's most
interesting games, characterized
by White's persistent efforts to
clear a path, by combinative
means, for his fianchettoed
queen's bishop to reach the weakened kingside dark squares. Pre-

sentday defensive technique being what it is, however, the ex-
ploitation of a single weakness
is not enough to win. White
therefore had to accumulate other
small advantages as well; at the
decisive moment, all were necessary for the conclusive combination. The game acquires special
interest, due to Averbakh's exceptionally staunch and resourceful defense: at one point, it
looked as though he had weathered every threat, but just then
White found the means of reviving
his attack. The finish was quite
pretty.

1.	d2-d4	Ng8-f6
2.	c2-c4	e7-e6
3.	Nb1-c3	Bf8-b4
4.	e2-e3	0-0
5.	Bf1-d3	d7-d5
6.	Ng1-f3	b7-b6
7.	0-0	Bc8-b7
8.	a2-a3	...

When Taimanov played this same
line with Black against Szabo in
the following round, White continued 8 Qe2, and Black was unable to save his king's bishop
from exchange, whereas here he
could have played it back to d6.
Averbakh, being unwilling to
lose the time, gives up the bishop for the knight, to open his
fianchettoed bishop's diagonal
by trading pawns on c4; only
thereafter does he counterattack
White's center with his pawn on
c5 and strategically placed
pieces.

This plan is harmless enough
to leave White's hands free for
operations on both flanks.

8.	...	Bb4:c3
9.	b2:c3	d5:c4
10.	Bd3:c4	c7-c5
11.	Bc4-d3	Nb8-d7
12.	Rf1-e1	...

White quietly prepares e3-e4,
for which Black has no better
remedy than mechanical prevention. If he places his bishop on
e4, then White can play 13 Bf1
(which would have been impossible after 12 Qe2), and the coming Nf3-d2 will make it impossible for Black's bishop to keep
White's pawn on e3 for long.

| 12. | ... | Nf6-e4 |
| 13. | Bc1-b2 | Ra8-c8 |

14.   c3-c4   Nd7-f6

.. Rc7, .. Qa8, .. Rfc8, and
.. Nf8 would have made a more
rational defensive setup. A
knight on f8 is one of the most
economical ways of defending h7,
and sometimes g7. The knight is
much less well placed on f6 for
defensive purposes, since it can
be more easily attacked and driv-
en away. The Qa8/Bb7 battery
would not only control the a8-
e4 diagonal, but might also
threaten the pawn on g2 in certain lines. By removing his
knight from d7, Black also gives
e5 over too soon. Averbakh later
concludes that the knight has to
return.

15.   Nf3-e5   Rc8-c7
16.   a3-a4   ...

Before continuing with his
kingside operations, White creates favorable queenside pawn
tension; by opening the a-file,
he also greatly increases the
scope of his rooks.

16.   ...   Ne4-d6
17.   a4-a5   Nf6-d7
18.   a5:b6   a7:b6
19.   Qd1-h5   ...

Black has a number of defenses
to this direct threat of mate. The
problem is not so much the threat
per se as the nature of the positional advantage White will derive from Black's various replies.
19.. Be4 suggests itself, but then
there comes 20 Red1, and the line-
up of queen on d8, knights on d7

and d6, and rook on d1 would be
none too comfortable for Black.
If 19.. h6, then 20 Ng4, with
the powerful threat 21 N:h6+,
either immediately or after a
preparatory d4-d5; and 19.. f5
would deprive Black of the possibility of defending his king
position at some future time by
means of .. f7-f6. Averbakh did
not want to bring the knight back
to f6, because after 20 Qh3 he
would still have to consider such
threats as 21 Ng4 and 21 d5; on
f6 the knight is exposed, and
may easily be driven away from
the defense of h7, as we have
seen. The continuation Averbakh
selects obviously weakens the
dark squares, but he had a concrete variation in mind which
brings a white pawn to e5, and
thereby denies White's bishop
access to the squares f6, g7 and
h6. Indeed, after

19.   ...   g7-g6
20.   Qh5-h6   Nd7:e5
21.   d4:e5   Nd6-e4

any retreat of the white king's
bishop allows 22.. Qd2, and in
this position, with its immobil-
ized pawn chain, White's bishops
would pose no problem. But Taimanov's brilliant

22.   Bd3:e4   ...

ushers in a new and truly grand-
masterly phase of the struggle,
wherein both sides will have ample opportunity to display fantasy, calculation and technique.

22.   ...   Bb7:e4
23.   Re1-d1   Rc7-d7

Thinking that the d-file
threats had been met and that
White would no longer be able
to reach Black's king after the
exchange of rooks, Averbakh offered a draw. No doubt White's
self-evident reply must have escaped him completely.

24.   Rd1-d6   ...

White has taken over the d-
file! If Black now exchanges
rooks and stops the mate by
25.. f6, then the other rook
enters Black's position via the
a-file White was farsighted enough to have opened back on the
18th move.

```
24.    ...         Be4-b7
25.    Ra1-d1      ...
```

There are players who think
"such moves cannot be bad"; curiously, however, this move is
a clear loss of tempo. After
25.. R:d6, White recaptures with
the pawn, not the rook, and for
that he does not need a rook on
d1. In order to keep up the pace
of his attack, Taimanov should
have substituted either 25 e4
or 25 h4.

```
25.    ...         Rd7:d6
```

Passive defense would allow
White to strengthen his position
decisively. One way would be to
play e3-e4 and then transfer the
rook via d3 to h3; another might
be to bring the bishop via c1 and
g5 to f6. In either event, f2-f4-
f5, intending further exposure of
Black's king, would be a useful
plan.

```
26.    e5:d6       f7-f6
```

Now the a1-h8 diagonal is
blocked, and Black needs only
one move, 27.. Qd7, to parry his
opponent's main threats.

```
27.    d6-d7       ...
```

A powerful move! The pawn advances to certain death, but it
will destroy the coordination of
the black pieces. While Black occupies himself in dealing with
the pawn, White's pieces will
take up still more active positions.

Let's make it White's move
here. Do you see a pretty queen
sacrifice? — 28 Q:f8+ K:f8
29 B:f6. To meet this threat,
Black could move his rook to f7,
attacking the pawn as well, but
then we get the echo-variation
28 Qh3 f5 29 Qh6 R:d7 30 Qg7+
(the queen sacrifices itself on
a different dark square)30..R:g7
31 R:d8+. Black's move draws the
sting from the threatened 28 Q:f8+,
since he can now meet 28.. K:f8
29 B:f6 with 29.. Q:d7.

```
27.    ...         Bb7-c6
```

I believe there was a more
radical solution to the problem
of defending the entire diagonal
in 27.. e5, which would also flow
quite logically from Black's last
few moves. For example:

I. 28 h4 Rf7 29 h5 R:d7 30 R:d7
Q:d7 31 hg hg 32 Q:g6+ Qg7

II. 28 f4 Rf7 29 fe R:d7 30 Rf1
Rd1

III. 28 Qh3 Qe7, and White seems
to have no means of preventing
the maneuver .. Rd8, ..Bc6 and
.. R:d7.

27.. Bc6 solves part of the
problem by getting rid of the
pawn on d7, but that's not enough for this complex position.
Now Taimanov injects new life into his attack: throwing his pawns
into the fray, he finally succeeds in breaking through to the
black king.

```
28.    h2-h4       Bc6:d7
29.    h4-h5       ...
```

By now, the atmosphere has become so thick that the combinations have begun to flicker here
and there, like heat-lightning.
If the pawn advances now (29.. g5),
the pawn that stood on d7 makes
possible the sacrifice 30 B:f6.
If the queen takes, White obtains
a winning rook endgame with the
positional capital accumulated in
the very beginning of the game;
and if the rook takes, then
31 Q:g5+ Kf7 32 h6 e5 (32.. Qe7
33 R:d7) 33 Rd6.

```
29.    ...         g6:h5
30.    e3-e4       ...
```

Opens the high road, d1-d3-g3,

for his rook. In reply, Black opens the road to g4 for his bishop, so as to stop the rook here, at least, but it won't be here...

| 30. | ... | e6-e5 |
| 31. | f2-f4 | ... |

King's Gambit, Taimanov's Interpretation: a complete success.

| 31. | ... | e5:f4 |

On 31.. Qe7 32 fe fe 33 Rd5 decides, as Black can no longer defend the e-pawn; but now the a1-h8 diagonal is open again, and even though the pawn still stands at f6, Black can no longer evade catastrophe.

32.	Rd1-d6	Qd8-e8
33.	Bb2:f6	Rf8-f7
34.	Rd6-d5	

BLACK RESIGNED

******

42. Najdorf—Petrosian
(King's Indian)

1.	d2-d4	Ng8-f6
2.	c2-c4	d7-d6
3.	Ng1-f3	g7-g6
4.	g2-g3	Bf8-g7
5.	Bf1-g2	0-0
6.	0-0	Nb8-c6

An idea peculiar to the King's Indian: Black immediately joins battle for d4, inviting White to push his pawn to d5 with gain of time. What does this lead to, however? One fianchettoed bishop begins irritating White's most sensitive spots, while its opposite number gets walled in behind its own pawn. There would be some point to 7 d5 if the knight had to return to b8 or at least to go to e5, when White could exchange knights and then set up a majority attack with his queenside pawns. But the knight goes to a5 instead, from which it can never be driven: for instance, 7 d5 Na5 8 Qa4 c5!, with an excellent game.

| 7. | Nb1-c3 | Bc8-g4 |

Continuing the fight for d4, Black next trades off the knight which controls that square.

| 8. | h2-h3 | Bg4:f3 |
| 9. | Bg2:f3 | Nf6-d7 |

Repeating his invitation to advance the pawn to d5. 10 e3 is met by 10.. e5, and if 11 d5 then, not 11.. Na5, but 11.. Ne7, with .. f7-f5 to follow. And if White continues to fight for d4 with 10 e3 e5 11 Ne2, then 11.. ed 12 ed Qf6.

| 10. | Bf3-g2 | ... |

Najdorf wearies of this obstinacy; so, with a negligent wave at the d4-pawn, he retreats his bishop, so that now, after e2-e3 etc., Black's queen will no longer come out to f6 with an attack on the bishop at f3. If White was in some way forced to exchange his d-pawn for Black's b-pawn, then Black has gained a signal strategical success in the opening, for the two pawns are worlds apart in value.

10.	...	Nc6:d4
11.	Bg2:b7	Ra8-b8
12.	Bb7-g2	c7-c5

A serious positional error; just how serious it is will be made clear to the reader by the explanation which follows.

Black controls an open queenside file, and can easily force White to play b2-b3. After that, his plan will be to advance his a-pawn to attack the pawn at b3. This plan can only succeed if Black can support his pawn to a4, but with what? He no longer has his lightsquare bishop, and his last move deprived his knight of its proper square. It will also

become clear quite soon that his knight cannot be maintained on d4 for long, and the light squares on the queenside are under the control of White's fianchettoed bishop — thus, Black's knights have no good squares. As a matter of fact, Black's knights end up in pitiable positions.

Thus, Black has no plan with a future to it. He can make moves — some of them, no doubt, will be fairly good; he still need not lose the game, but he has already lost the guiding thread, so his position is consequently inferior. We recommend that the reader study this game in conjunction with the Najdorf — Geller game from Round 28. There Black played 12.. Rb4!, and followed this up with .. Ne5, inducing both f2-f4 and b2-b3; then he re-positioned his knight on c5, and, despite Najdorf's resourceful counterplay on the queenside, carried out the required attack on the pawn at b3.

13.	e2-e3	Nd4-e6
14.	Qd1-c2	a7-a5
15.	Bc1-d2	Nd7-e5
16.	b2-b3	Qd8-d7
17.	Kg1-h2	Ne5-c6
18.	Ra1-d1	Ne6-d8
19.	Bd2-e1	Kg8-h8

Black has done all one could ask: he has induced 16 b3 and advanced his pawn to a5 — what he can do further, however, is a mystery. Nor can one find any

advice to offer him, other than to avoid weaknesses and not to leave pieces en prise (which was the principle behind such moves as 18.. Nd8 and 19.. Kh8). Meanwhile, White is all set for many moves' worth of straightforward, logical strengthening of his position: for example, Na4, Bc3 and the exchange of bishops, followed by f2-f4, Bf3, Kg2, h3-h4-h5, Rh1, etc. This is only a sketch, of course; in actual play, Black would not likely stand still, but there can be no denying that all the chances in this fight would be with White, the more so in that any attempt to bring the pawn at e7 into the fight would result in an irreparable weakening of the pawn at d6.

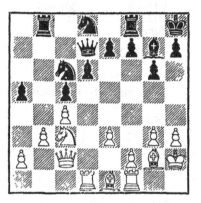

20.	Nc3-a4	Qd7-c8
21.	Be1-c3	Bg7:c3
22.	Na4:c3	Qc8-f5

Petrosian undoubtedly saw that he would lose a pawn after the exchange of queens, but he hoped to start using his tactical chances to go rook-hunting.

23.	Qc2:f5	g6:f5
24.	Rd1-d5	Nd8-e6
25.	Rd5:f5	Nc6-b4
26.	Rf5-h5	Ne6-g7
27.	Rh5-h4	Ng7-f5
28.	Rh4-f4	e7-e6
29.	Rf1-d1	Rb8-b6
30.	Nc3-a4	Rb6-b8
31.	Bg2-e4	Nf5-g7
32.	Rd1:d6	Nb4:a2
33.	Na4:c5	

BLACK RESIGNED

☆☆☆☆☆☆
☆☆☆☆☆☆

ROUND SEVEN

43. Averbakh—Najdorf
(King's Indian)

1.	d2-d4	Ng8-f6
2.	c2-c4	g7-g6
3.	g2-g3	Bf8-g7
4.	Bf1-g2	0-0
5.	Nb1-c3	d7-d6
6.	Ng1-f3	c7-c5
7.	d4-d5	Nb8-a6

A setup quite similar to that of Bronstein - Najdorf, from Round Two, the only difference being that here the white king's bishop is on g2, not d3. This circumstance promises Black better chances from his idea of .. Nb8-a6-c7 followed by .. a7-a6 and .. b7-b5, since the white bishop is less effective here, and White has spent an extra tempo on 3 g3.

8.	0-0	Na6-c7
9.	e2-e4	a7-a6
10.	a2-a4	Ra8-b8
11.	Rf1-e1	b7-b5

The opening battle grows very tense: if White takes twice on b5, his center will end up very sad-looking indeed: 12 ab ab 13 cb N:b5 14 N:b5 R:b5. Following classical principles, Averbakh answers this wing attack with a counterblow in the center, even at the cost of material.

12.	a4:b5	a6:b5
13.	e4-e5	Nf6-g4
14.	e5:d6	e7:d6
15.	Bc1-g5	Ng4-f6
16.	Nc3-e4	b5:c4
17.	Nf3-d2	...

Bravery, verging on bravado: Black cannot take on b2 or on d5, in view of the terrific threat of 18 N:c4, when the pawn at d6 must fall as well. Najdorf must hold on to c4 at all costs, while simultaneously keeping track of how many pieces are attacking and defending his pinned knight on f6.

17.	...	Rb8-b4
18.	Ra1-c1	...

18 Qf3 leads to nothing: after the surprising 18.. Nc:d5, it is Black who wins.

DRAW

It's hard to predict who might have won, had the game continued, but certainly a draw would have been the least likely outcome.

Najdorf offered the draw because he considered his position insecure, and Averbakh may have agreed because he could not see precisely how he was going to recover his pawn. The players should have exchanged places — more than likely, they would have continued the game then. Najdorf gave the following variations to justify the draw: 18.. Ba6 19 Bf1 h6 20 N:f6+ B:f6, followed by either 21 B:h6 Re8 22 R:e8+ Q:e8 23 N:c4 B:c4 24 B:c4 B:b2 25 Rc2, or the better line 21 B:f6 Q:f6 22 Ne4 Qd8 23 Qd2 Kh7 24 Qf4 Ne8 25 Rc2, with even chances.

It seems to me that 18 Rc1 was the mistake: the rook stood well on the a-file too. A good move with the same idea of attacking the c-pawn would have been 18 Bf1, especially since the bishop does not defend the d-pawn anyway. In this line, almost every white piece would stand well, and the threat of 19 Qf3 would be strengthened. A rough idea of the seriousness of the pin on Black's king's knight may be gathered from the following variation: 18 Bf1 Ba6 19 R:a6 N:a6 20 Qf3, and there is no further defense available for f6 (the proper move would be 18 .. Bf5, and not 18.. Ba6).

*****

44. Szabo—Taimanov
(Nimzoindian Defense)

1. d4 Nf6 2. c4 e6 3. Nc3 Bb4
4. e3 0-0 5. Bd3 d5 6. Nf3 b6
7. 0-0 Bb7 8. Qe2 Nbd7 9. a3
B:c3 10. bc c5 11. Bb2 dc
12. B:c4 Qc7 13. Bd3 Be4 14. B:e4
N:e4 15. Qd3 Qb7 16. c4 Rac8

Here or on the next move,
White could — indeed, by the
logic of things he must — start
his central pawns moving: for example, with 17 d5 ed 18 cd Ndf6
19 B:f6 N:f6 20 e4. His next two
moves do little to improve his
position: the rooks would have
been better posted a little to
the right.

17. Rac1 h6 18. Rfd1 cd 19. ed
Rfd8 20. Qb3 Nd6 21. Qb4 Nb8
22. d5 ed 23. cd R:c1 24. B:c1
Na6

The pawns have advanced, under
less favorable conditions than
before, but still White stands
rather well: he has a passed pawn
and some attacking chances.

25. Qh4 Re8 26. Bf4

26 Bb2 was better.

26. ... Qd7 27. B:d6 Q:d6
28. Qa4 Nc7

DRAW

*****

45. Euwe—Gligoric
(King's Indian)

1.	d2-d4	Ng8-f6
2.	c2-c4	g7-g6
3.	g2-g3	Bf8-g7
4.	Bf1-g2	0-0
5.	Nb1-c3	d7-d6
6.	Ng1-f3	Nb8-d7
7.	0-0	e7-e5
8.	e2-e4	e5:d4
9.	Nf3:d4	Nd7-c5
10.	h2-h3	Rf8-e8
11.	Rf1-e1	a7-a5
12.	Qd1-c2	a5-a4
13.	Bc1-e3	c7-c6
14.	Ra1-d1	Nf6-d7

One of the ritual lines of the
King's Indian. Deviate one step
from the "correct" move order,
and the theoreticians will instantly brand the offending game
with that most dread taboo: either "±" or "∓".

15. g3-g4?! ...

But what's this? The High Priest
of Theoreticians himself, making
the sort of move to baffle his
opponent, and the reader too —
and to what end? Firstly, to hinder the usual .. f7-f5; secondly,
to swing the knight over to g3,
and only then to play f2-f4, since
this advance would be premature
here (it was Tarrasch's opinion
that f2-f4 is nearly always premature); and thirdly, to push the
pawn up to g5, if circumstances
warrant.

These are the surface points
of 15 g4, but we may also guess
at something bolder: to station
the knight on g3 and the bishop
on e2, and at the right moment
go over to the assault with h3-
h4-h5... It's amazing that a move
with so many good ideas behind it
could be bad, but there is so
much piece tension in the center
that such a wing attack cannot
succeed. White does not even get
time enough to bring his knight
to g3, to say nothing of his other castles in the air.

15.	...	Qd8-a5
16.	Bg2-f1	...

Overprotecting the c-pawn, so
as to be able to meet 16.. Ne5
with 17 f4.

16. ... Nc5-e6

Once again threatening 17..Ne5;
if then 18 f4 N:d4!, followed by
the knight check on f3.

17.	Kg1-g2	h7-h5
18.	f2-f3	h5:g4
19.	h3:g4	...

Dashing one of his hopes: now
he will never get to play h3-h4.

19.	...	Nd7-e5
20.	Nc3-e2	Ne6:d4

Here Gligoric, who has been
playing wonderfully, begins a
direct attack. I would prefer
not to have traded off this
knight yet, moving it instead
to c5 or to f8, and threatening
21.. d5 under still more favorable circumstances.

21. Ne2:d4 d6-d5

Consistently pursuing his plan of opening up the center: his attack will have an easier time finding the king with the e-pawn out of the way.

22.   e4:d5   c6:d5

White had prepared a pretty refutation for 22.. N:g4: 23 fg B:d4 24 B:d4 R:e1 25 Bc3.

23.   Nd4-b5   d5:c4
24.   Nb5-d6   ...

Allowing a remarkable two-piece sacrifice, which would have been a most fitting conclusion for this game.

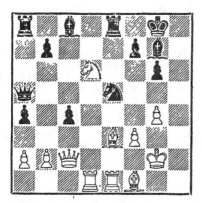

24.   ...   Bc8-e6

The combination begins with 24.. N:f3, and continues 25 K:f3 B:g4+ 26 K:g4 Qh5+ 27 Kg3 Be5+ 28 Kf2 B:d6, threatening 29..Re5; or 25 N:e8 N:e1+ 26 R:e1 Q:e1; or 25 B:c4 N:e1+ 26 R:e1 Be6.

25.   Nd6:e8   Ra8:e8
26.   Qc2-c3   ...

A brave decision, trading queens. It's hard to say whether Euwe saw all of the possible variations after 26.. Qb5 27 Bd4 Bd5, but most likely his intuition told him that he could save himself, and perhaps do even better than that, with the problem move 28 Kg3. Then, if the knight takes on f3, White trades rooks with check and captures the king's bishop; if the bishop takes on f3 instead, White takes

the knight, coming out a piece to the good; and on 28.. f6, White takes first on e5, and then on d5 with the rook. In the line 26..Qb5 27 Bd4 Bd5 28 Kg3 B:f3 29 B:e5 B:d1 30 B:g7 R:e1 31 Q:e1 K:g7 32 Q:d1 Q:b2, Black might have some hope for a draw.

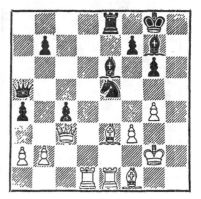

26.   ...   Qa5:c3
27.   b2:c3   Ne5-c6
28.   Be3-b6   ...

The bishop had a much better move: 28 Bc5 would have given White serious winning chances. If 28.. B:c3, 29 Re3 and 30 B:c4; if 28.. Rc8, 29 Re3 Bh6 30 R:e6 fe 31 B:c4 Nd8 32 Bb4 R:c4 33 R:d8+.

28 Bb6 looks strong, since the pawn is blockaded; but as we shall soon see, Euwe has over-looked Black's 29th, which wins the c-pawn for nothing.

28.   ...   Bg7:c3
29.   Re1-e4   Bc3-a5

Euwe had expected to recover the pawn at c4, but now he saw that after the exchange of bishops this pawn will be defended by the knight. White must there-fore reorient himself to a long and arduous defense. The outcome of the game will turn on whether or not Black can succeed in con-necting his passed pawns.

30.   Bb6:a5   Nc6:a5
31.   Re4-e5   b7-b6
32.   Re5-b5   ...

White tries to make the black pawns operate separately, and to keep them from getting too far advanced.

| 32. | ... | c4-c3 |
| 33. | Rd1-c1 | Re8-c8 |

| 34. | Rb5-b4 | ... |

This saves the game. White captures the a-pawn, instead of the relatively harmless b-pawn. After 34 R:b6 B:a2, there would be no defense against the advance of the c-pawn, with Black's bishop and knight clearing its path: for example, 35 Rb5 Nb3 36 Rc2 Bb1.

| 34. | ... | Be6:a2 |
| 35. | Rb4:a4 | Ba2-d5 |

If 35.. Nb3 now, 36 Re1 c2 37 R:a2 c1Q 38 R:c1 R:c1 39 Ra8+ Kg7 40 Rb8, with a draw. The text renews the threat of 36.. Nb3.

36.	Ra4-b4	Na5-b3
37.	Rc1-c2	Nb3-a1
38.	Rc2-c1	Na1-b3
39.	Rc1-c2	Nb3-d2

In time-pressure, Gligoric spurns the repetition of moves, overlooks the loss of a piece, and almost loses, to be saved only by his passed pawn.

40.	Bf1-e2	Bd5-b3
41.	Rc2:d2	c3-c2
42.	Rd2:c2	

DRAW

******

46. Stahlberg—Bronstein
(Queen's Indian Defense)

Stahlberg is a most enjoyable opponent for the King's Indian enthusiast, since he generally prefers sharp, lively continuations over theoretical lines. However, he played the White side of the King's Indian so strongly against Boleslavsky in Round One that I could not muster the courage to repeat that opening against him. So I managed instead to pick another system that he knows very well, from which he secured a sizable advantage.

1.	d2-d4	Ng8-f6
2.	c2-c4	e7-e6
3.	Ng1-f3	b7-b6
4.	e2-e3	Bc8-b7
5.	Bf1-d3	Bf8-e7
6.	Nb1-c3	d7-d5
7.	Qd1-a4+	...

The point to this check is that, of the three possible piece interpositions, none is any good: 7..Nbd7 is met by 8 cd ed 9 Ne5; 7..Qd7 is met by 8 Qc2, and the coming Ne5 will gain a tempo; and finally, if the other knight covers, its colleague is deprived of its natural square. Thus, Black must use his pawn, which closes the bishop's diagonal temporarily. Stahlberg immediately exchanges on d5, forcing the e-pawn recapture, which in turn practically forces an eventual ..c6-c5.

7.	...	c7-c6
8.	c4:d5	e6:d5
9.	0-0	0-0
10.	Qa4-c2	c6-c5

White threatened a favorable opening of the center with 11 e4.

| 11. | b2-b3 | Nb8-c6 |
| 12. | a2-a3 | h7-h6 |

Releasing the king's knight from the defense of the pawn.

| 13. | Bc1-b2 | ... |

I would have preferred 13 Ne2, keeping the option of recapturing on d4 with a knight; and meeting 13.. Rc8 with 14 Qb1.

| 13. | ... | c5:d4 |

Black closes the bishop's diagonal, taking advantage of the

fact that White will be a long
while bringing this piece back
into play at f4. A nearly symmetrical position results, but
White's lightsquare bishop is
still the more actively developed.

14.	e3:d4	a7-a6
15.	Rf1-e1	b6-b5
16.	Qc2-d1	Rf8-e8
17.	Ra1-c1	Be7-d6

DRAW

Of course, with all those
pieces on the board, there's
still lots of play left; but
if White offers the draw in
such a position, Black really
cannot refuse.

******

47. Boleslavsky—Reshevsky
(Ruy Lopez)

1. e4 e5 2. Nf3 Nc6 3. Bb5 a6
4. Ba4 Nf6 5. 0-0 Be7 6. Re1 b5
7. Bb3 d6 8. c3 0-0 9. h3 Na5
10. Bc2 c5 11. d4 cd 12. cd Qc7
13. Nbd2 Nc6 14. Nb3 a5 15. Be3
a4 16. Nbd2 Ba6 17. Rc1 Qb7 18.a3
Bd8 19. b4

Forcing Black to take en passant,
as otherwise the b-pawn would be
blockaded, and with it Black's
entire queenside. But now the game
opens up to White's advantage.

19.. ab 20. N:b3 Bb6 21. Nh4 g6
22. Bb1

DRAW

on Black's offer. Boleslavsky accepted the draw prematurely: he
threatens 23 de de 24 B:b6 Q:b6
25 Qd6 or 24 Nc5, and should at
least have waited to see Black's
move.

******

48. Kotov—Keres
(Grunfeld Defense)

1.	c2-c4	Ng8-f6
2.	d2-d4	g7-g6
3.	Nb1-c3	Bf8-g7
4.	g2-g3	d7-d5

White wanted to hold his e2-e4
for a while yet, but now we see
how Black's King's Indian may
also become a Grunfeld. White's
next move is illogical, allowing

Black to capture the c-pawn under
circumstances which render its
recovery rather problematic.

5.	Bf1-g2	d5:c4
6.	Qd1-a4+	Nf6-d7
7.	e2-e3	...

He ought to have continued in
the same gambit style: 7 Nf3 Nc6
8 0-0 Nb6 9 Qc2 or 8 Q:c4 Nb6
9 Qd3 N:d4 10 N:d4 Q:d4 11 Q:d4
B:d4 12 Nb5 with lively play; if
10.. B:d4, then 11 Bh6, keeping
Black's king in the center as
long as possible, is good.

Kotov wants his pawn back at
all costs, even two tempi; but
that could have cost him the game.

7.	...	0-0
8.	Qa4:c4	c7-c5
9.	Ng1-f3	c5:d4
10.	Nf3:d4	...

Nor was 10 ed any sweeter, considering 10.. Nc6 11 d5 Nde5, or
11 Be3 Nb6 12 Qd3 Bf5.

| 10. | ... | Nd7-e5 |
| 11. | Qc4-e2 | Nb8-c6 |

Black intends a positional pawn
sacrifice, but he might also have
continued his successful policy
of rapid piece development with
10.. Bg4 11 Qd2 Nbc6 12 N:c6 bc.

| 12. | Nd4:c6 | ... |

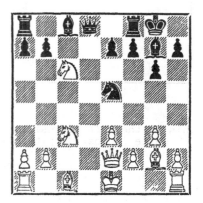

| 12. | ... | Ne5-d3+ |

Keres could not resist giving
this pretty knight check, crown-

ing the knight's far-ranging expedition with the capture of bishop and queen. This mustang's biography was an extensive one: eight of the first fifteen moves, checks to both queen and king, eating queen, bishop and knight, and saddling White with a weak pawn at c3 — certainly enough activity for all of the pieces in any other game!

Even here, 12.. bc 13 0-0 Qb6 14 Rd1 Ba6! 15 Qc2 Rad8 wouldn't have been a bad idea: Black's positional advantage is clear enough.

13. Ke1-d2   ...

Coldly accurate defense! On any other retreat, as we shall see immediately, the c-pawn would not have been defended after move 16, and the king would have stood much worse besides.

13.	...	Nd3:c1+
14.	Nc6:d8	Nc1:e2
15.	Nd8:b7	Ne2:c3
16.	b2:c3	Bc8-e6

This is the sort of position in which White is lost despite his being a pawn ahead. His minor pieces are scattered, his c-pawn is weak, and his rooks are subject to the harassment of the beautifully coordinated black bishops. The proper move for Black here would appear to have been 16..Bf5!, keeping White's rooks from the b-file, and preventing them from doubling on the c-file; he would also be threatening a check

from d8 at his earliest convenience, driving White's king away from its pawn. White would have had to play 17 e4, shutting off his own bishop and making it that much easier for his opponent.

After the text, Kotov manages to keep afloat with amazing skill: for many moves, he maintains his terminally ill pawn _inter vivos_, and eventually pulls himself nearly even.

17.	Rh1-c1	Ra8-c8
18.	Rc1-c2	Rc8-c7
19.	Ra1-c1	Be6-f5
20.	Rc2-b2	Rc7-d7+
21.	Kd2-e2	Rf8-c8

The c-pawn is doomed; the only question is whether White will be able to get any sort of compensation for it. He would be happy, for example, to be able to arrange a trade of knight for bishop, or to clear away all of the minor pieces. (One complicating factor is that, as a result of the unusual opening, both sides were already in time trouble.)

22.	Rb2-b3	Bf5-g4+
23.	Bg2-f3	Bg4:f3+
24.	Ke2:f3	Rd7-c7
25.	c3-c4	...

A beautiful move, the idea being that giving up the pawn in this way allows White to exchange only one rook, while the other gains a tempo to attack the a-pawn.

25.	...	Rc7:c4
26.	Rc1:c4	Rc8:c4
27.	Rb3-a3	h7-h5
28.	Ra3:a7	...

In time-pressure, everybody takes pawns. 28 h4, preventing 28.. g5, could have led to the following pretty line: 28..Rc7 29 R:a7 Kh7 30 a4 Bc3, and the only way White can untangle himself is by giving back the pawn, which leads to a draw.

28.	...	g6-g5
29.	Nb7-a5	Rc4-c2
30.	Na5-b3	g5-g4+
31.	Kf3-g2	e7-e6
32.	a2-a4	Bg7-h6
33.	Kg2-f1	Rc2-b2
34.	Ra7-b7	Rb2-b1+

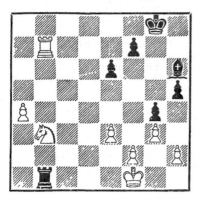

35.	Kf1-g2	Rb1-b2
36.	Kg2-f1	Rb2-b1+
37.	Kf1-g2	Rb1-b2
38.	Nb3-c5	...

Fighting spirit triumphs over common sense: Kotov declines a draw that was his for the taking, in order to obtain by dint of great effort a problem draw some twenty moves later — and the art of chess is the winner. More than likely, though, he simply overlooked, in his fierce time trouble, that Black could take the e-pawn.

38.	...	Rb2-c2
39.	Nc5-e4	Bh6:e3
40.	Kg2-f1	Be3-d4
41.	Rb7-d7	e6-e5

42.	Rd7-d8+	Kg8-g7
43.	Rd8-d6!	...

The beauty of this move becomes evident in the main variation: 43.. f5 44 Rd7+ Kf8 45 Nf6 R:f2+ 46 Ke1. White's 43rd move deserves its exclamation mark, but so does his previous move, which drove Black's king to the seventh rank. Had White played 42 Rd6 immediately (with the black king on g8), Black would have played 42.. f5 and won after 43 Rd8+ Kf7; but if the king tries to go to f7 now, to avoid the perpetual, the f-pawn is lost: 43..f5 44 Rd7+ Kg6 45 Rd6+ Kf7 46 Rf6+ and 47 R:f5. The practical execution of White's plan, then, required a black pawn at f7.

Having safely weathered the worst of the storm, White finds little to fear in the rest of it: by giving up his a-pawn, he secures Black's h-pawn in return, and gets his draw.

43.. Ra2 44. a5 R:a5 45. Nf6 Kf8 46. N:h5 Ke7 47. Rc6 f5 48. Ng7 e4 49. Rc7+ Kf6 50. Nh5+ Ke5 51. Rc2 Ra1+ 52. Kg2 Ra3 53. Nf4 Rf3 54. h3 gh+ 55. N:h3 Ra3 56. Nf4 Kf6 57. Rc6+ Ke7 58. Rc4 Ba7

DRAW

******

49. ᵾeller—Smyslov
(Nimzoindian Defense)

1.	d2-d4	Ng8-f6
2.	c2-c4	e7-e6
3.	Nb1-c3	Bf8-b4
4.	e2-e3	c7-c5
5.	Bf1-d3	0-0
6.	a2-a3	Bb4:c3+
7.	b2:c3	Nb8-c6
8.	Ng1-e2	b7-b6
9.	0-0	...

In Samisch's Attack against the Nimzo-Indian, the plans for both sides are generally determined at an early stage. White accepts doubled pawns, with the c4-pawn especially weak (one might almost say doomed) in order to facilitate a rapid usurpation of the center by means of e3-e4, leading to a kingside attack with f2-f4 (-f5, if Black allows). Master practice has shown that Black gets good counterplay if he gets time for .. f5, blocking the king's wing; while White can only carry his attack through if he can neutralize Black's queen-

side activity and prevent .. f5.
White must play very energetically
to achieve his ends, and from this
standpoint, castling is a waste
of time here.

9.	...	Bc8-a6
10.	e3-e4	Nf6-e8
11.	Qd1-a4	...

I don't see this as being any
place for a queen, which should
be reinforcing White's kingside
threats. More in the spirit of
the system White has selected
would be 11 f4 f5 12 Ng3, with
threats of 13 d5 or 13 e5; or
11 Ng3 first. In any event,
White should be developing his
game in this direction, and not
queenside, where the queen is
so passive. If Black answers
11 f4 with 11.. Na5, attacking
the c-pawn, then 12 dc bc 13 Be3,
when White seizes the b- and d-
files and plays e5 with a very
strong game.

11.	...	Qd8-c8

Smyslov spent about an hour
on this move, and found an excellent plan: he defends c6 and
a6, indirectly attacks the c-
pawn (after an eventual ..c5:d4),
and answers 12 dc with 12.. Ne5.

12.	Bc1-e3	d7-d6
13.	Ra1-d1	Nc6-a5
14.	d4:c5	...

In the new situation, this exchange is not justified, since
Black has had time to play 12..d6
and can now recapture with the d-
pawn. From Geller, one might sooner have expected 14 d5!; although
he might lose the c-pawn later,
this is not all that important —
one pawn is not necessarily the
game. White would also have obtained fair kingside chances then.

14.	...	d6:c5
15.	e4-e5	Qc8-c6
16.	Qa4-c2	...

Of course, White will not exchange queens, since then he would
lose the c-pawn with no compensation.

16.	...	f7-f5
17.	Qc2-a2	...

White retreats into passive defense, which renders his game stra-

tegically lost. Instead, he might
have played 17 ef N:f6 18 Bg5
B:c4 19 B:f6 B:d3 20 R:d3 R:f6
21 c4, keeping the knight out of
c4 and setting up strong pressure
along the d-file. Black's win in
that case would have been far from
simple: for instance, 21.. Raf8
22 f3 Nb7 23 Rfd1, intending Ne2-
g3-e4.

17.	...	Qc6-a4
18.	Ne2-f4	Ne8-c7
19.	Bd3-c2	Qa4-e8

The point to this fine queen
maneuver is that by threatening
to win the c-pawn Black gains
time to deny White's knight the
square h5, and forces White's
bishop to the inferior square b3,
where it will be completely out
of play. Now White cannot return
his bishop to d3.

20.	Bc2-b3	g7-g5

21.	Nf4-h3	h7-h6
22.	f2-f3	Qe8-e7
23.	Nh3-f2	Ra8-d8
24.	Nf2-d3	Qe7-g7
25.	f3-f4	Rd8-d7
26.	Nd3-c1	Rf8-d8
27.	Rd1:d7	Rd8:d7

White's next move exploits an
accidental tactical chance — the
somewhat exposed state of Black's
king — to bring the queen over
to the kingside. However, this
has no material effect on the outcome, since the best White can
achieve out of an attack on the
king with his lone queen is an
exchange of queens and an obvi-

ously lost endgame.

28.	Qa2-e2	Nc7-d5
29.	Be3-d2	Nd5:f4
30.	Bd2:f4	g5:f4
31.	Rf1:f4	Qg7-g5
32.	g2-g3	Kg8-h7
33.	Kg1-f2	Qg5-d8
34.	Qe2-h5	Rd7-g7
35.	Qh5-e2	Rg7-d7

The reason for this repetition is that both sides were in severe time-pressure. White's skilled defense has thus far managed to ward off Black's direct threats, but his resources are gradually running out.

36.	Qe2-h5	Qd8-g5
37.	Qh5-e8	Qg5-e7
38.	Qe8:e7+	Rd7:e7
39.	Bb3-a2	Re7-d7
40.	Kf2-e2	Ba6-b7
41.	Ba2-b1	Kh7-g8

42.	g3-g4	f5:g4
43.	Rf4:g4+	Re7-g7
44.	Rg4-h4	Rg7-g1
45.	Ke2-d2	Kg8-g7
46.	Bb1-d3	Bb7-f3
47.	Rh4-f4	Bf3-h5
48.	Nc1-e2	...

48 Rf6 was possible here, in order to place his pieces a little more effectively.

48.	...	Rg1-g2
49.	Kd2-e3	Rg2-g5
50.	h2-h4	Rg5:e5+
51.	Ke3-d2	Na5-b3+
52.	Kd2-d1	Re5-e3
53.	Kd1-c2	e6-e5
54.	Rf4-f2	e5-e4

WHITE FORFEITED

******

******

ROUND EIGHT

50. Keres—Geller
(King's Indian)

1. d4 Nf6 2. c4 g6 3. Nc3 Bg7
4. Bg5 d6 5. e3 0-0 6. Nf3 c5
7. Be2 h6 8. Bh4 cd 9. N:d4 Nc6
10. 0-0 Bd7 11. Qd2 a6 12. Rfd1
Kh7

Black fairly flaunts his impregnability, daring White to attack him, if he dares. The opportunity is certainly there, but the desire appears to be lacking.

13. Nb3 Be6

Meeting the threat of 14 c5.

14. Nd5 B:d5 15. cd Ne5 16. f4
Ned7 17. Bf3 Rc8 18. Rac1 R:c1
19. R:c1 Qb8 20. e4 Rc8 21. Bf2
Rc7 22. R:c7 Q:c7 23. Qc1

There was no objective reason why Keres should have hurried with this exchange. Could he have been suffering from the previous day's draw with Kotov?

23.. Ne8 24. Q:c7 N:c7 25. Na5
B:b2 26. N:b7 f5

DRAW

******

51. Reshevsky—Kotov
(King's Indian)

1.	d2-d4	Ng8-f6
2.	c2-c4	d7-d6
3.	Nb1-c3	Nb8-d7
4.	Ng1-f3	g7-g6
5.	e2-e4	e7-e5
6.	Bf1-e2	Bf8-g7
7.	0-0	0-0
8.	Rf1-e1	c7-c6
9.	Be2-f1	Nf6-e8
10.	Ra1-b1	...

White prepares 11 b4 in order to hinder the advance of the c-pawn; the square a3 is left for the bishop.

| 10. | ... | Ne8-c7 |
| 11. | b2-b4 | ... |

Seeing that his intended 11.. Ne6 will be met by 12 d5 Nd4 13 N:d4 ed 14 Ne2 c5 15 bc dc 16 f4, when White's monstrous avalanche of pawns would sweep all before it, Kotov decides to carry out his plan with a different move order, playing 11.. c5 first.

11.	...	c6-c5
12.	d4:c5	d6:c5
13.	Bc1-a3	Nc7-e6
14.	b4:c5	Rf8-e8

Recapturing the pawn with either knight would cost Black the exchange after 15 Qd5.

| 15. | Nc3-b5 | Nd7:c5 |

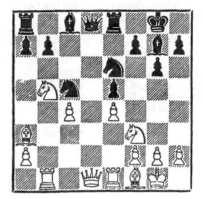

| 16. | Qd1-d5 | ... |

Now Black is forced to transfer his knight to b6, a maneuver as unpleasant as it is futile for him. This maneuver also sets White's c-pawn in motion.

16.	...	Nc5-a4
17.	Rb1-b3	Na4-b6
18.	Qd5-d1	Bc8-d7
19.	c4-c5	Nb6-c8
20.	Rb3-d3	...

Black cannot meet all of the threats: already he must give up a pawn, but that's still not enough to get his pieces coordinated. White breaks into the seventh rank and begins an assault on the king.

20.	...	Ne6-d4
21.	Nb5:d4	e5:d4
22.	Nf3:d4	Qd8-a5
23.	Nd4-b3	...

By trading off his good bishop for Black's bad one, White keeps Black's knight from developing: on c8, this piece is hemmed in by the white pawn at c5, and on e7, by the white pawn at e4. Not only does the knight have

nowhere to go, it interferes with
the rest of the pieces. White's
combination of queen on f3, bishop on c4 and rook on d7 promises
to wind up the game in short order.

23.	...	Qa5:a3
24.	Rd3:d7	Nc8-e7
25.	Rd7:b7	Qa3:a2
26.	Bf1-b5	...

If one may speak of various ways
to win this position, then 26 Qf3
Rab8 27 Bc4 was much quicker:
27.. R:b7 allows mate in a few,
and if 26.. Reb8 instead, then
27 R:e7 Q:b3 28 Re8+.

26.	...	Re8-d8
27.	Qd1-f3	Bg7-f8
28.	Bb5-c4	Qa2-b2
29.	Qf3:f7+	Kg8-h8
30.	e4-e5	...

The rest was played in unbelievable time-pressure: Reshevsky
had literally seconds left, Kotov
a few minutes. Under these circumstances, Kotov found a swindle
which almost brought the house
down.

30.	...	Qb2-c3
31.	Kg1-f1	Ra8-b8
32.	c5-c6	Rb8-c8
33.	Bc4-e6	Qc3-d3+
34.	Kf1-g1	Qd3-e2

The venom this move contains is
displayed in the variation 35 Rf1
Rd1 36 Nd2 Q:d2, when White has
only 37 Bc4, and then 37.. R:f1+
38 B:f1 Qg5 saves Black from the
immediate threats.

Reshevsky seized his head in
his hands, glanced nervously at
his flag (ready to fall at any
moment) and the position, and —
took the bishop with check. Then
Reshevsky asked how many moves
had been made (which is not acceptable grandmaster practice),
and received an answer from one
of the spectators (which is really illegal).

35.	Qf7:f8+	Rd8:f8
36.	Re1:e2	Rc8:c6
37.	Rb7:e7	a7-a5
38.	h2-h4	a5-a4
39.	Nb3-d4	Rc6-c1+
40.	Kg1-h2	Rc1-d1
41.	Nd4-b5	Rd1-b1
42.	Nb5-d6	

As soon as the time-control
moves were finished,

BLACK RESIGNED

******

52. Bronstein—Boleslavsky
(Nimzoindian Defense)

1. d4 Nf6 2. c4 e6 3. Nc3 Bb4
4. Qb3

An antiquated continuation,
which gives White nothing and
has deservedly gone out of favor.

4.. c5 5. dc Na6 6. Nf3 0-0
7. Bg5 B:c5 8. e3 b6 9. Be2 Bb7
10. 0-0 Be7 11. Rfd1 Nc5 12. Qc2
Nfe4 13. B:e7 Q:e7 14. N:e4 N:e4
15. Nd4 d5 16. cd B:d5 17. f3

Rfc8 18. Qa4 Nc5 19. Qa3 Bb7
20. Bf1 h6 21. b4

DRAW

******

53. Gligoric—Stahlberg
(French Defense)

1. e4 e6 2. d4 d5 3. Nc3 Bb4
4. Bd3 de 5. B:e4 c5

An inaccuracy: Black should have
played 5.. Nf6 first. If then
6 Bd3 c5; but if 6 Bf3, he should
prepare ..e6-e5.

6. Ne2 Nf6 7. Bf3 cd 8. Q:d4 Q:d4
9. N:d4 a6 10. 0-0 Nbd7 11. Re1
0-0 12. Bd2 Rd8 13. a3 Bd6 14. Rad1
Bc7

White's positional advantage is
growing. Black is unable to develop his bishop, which in turn
shuts in the rook.

15. Bg5 h6 16. Bh4 g5 17. Bg3
B:g3 18. hg g4

Now Black's pawn weaknesses
become more pronounced.

19. Be2 Nb6 20. Nb3 Bd7 21. Na5
Rab8 22. Rd6 Nc8 23. Rd4 e5
24.Rd2 Re8 25. Ne4 N:e4 26. R:d7
Nc5 27. Rc7 Ne6 28. R:b7 Nd6
29. Rd7 Rb6 30. b4 Nb5 31. Nc4
Rc6 32. N:e5 R:c2 33. B:b5 ab
34. N:f7 Kf8 35. N:h6 Re7 36. Rd5
Nc7 37. Rf5+ Ke8 38. R:e7+ K:e7
39. N:g4 Ra2 40. Rc5 Kd6 41. Rc3

BLACK RESIGNED

******

54. Taimanov—Euwe
(Nimzoindian Defense)

1.	d2-d4	Ng8-f6
2.	c2-c4	e7-e6
3.	Nb1-c3	Bf8-b4
4.	e2-e3	c7-c5
5.	Bf1-d3	d7-d5
6.	Ng1-f3	0-0
7.	0-0	Nb8-c6
8.	a2-a3	Bb4:c3
9.	b2:c3	d5:c4
10.	Bd3:c4	Qd8-c7
11.	Bc4-a2	...

One of many "possible, though
not best" continuations. Its apparent goal — to place the bishop at b1, the queen at c2 and
mate the black king on h7 — is
too lightweight; while its true

aim — advancing the pawns to
c4 and d5, opening the diagonal
for the fianchettoed white
queen's bishop — is somewhat
convoluted, since these same
pawns also close up the diagonal
of his other bishop.

I think White should play here
moves which support the push e3-
e4-e5.

11.	...	e6-e5
12.	Qd1-c2	Bc8-g4
13.	d4-d5	Nc6-e7
14.	c3-c4	Bg4:f3
15.	g2:f3	Qc7-d7

Looking at its structure alone
without regard to the time factor, White's position is good: he
could play Kh1, Rg1, Bb2, Bb1,
etc. The trouble is that Black
has completed his development before White, and can begin his
attack first: already he threatens 16.. Qh3 and .. Ne7-g6-h4. As
a result, White must resort to
desperate measures in order to
avert a swift catastrophe.

16. Ba2-b1   ...

White has not the time to regroup with Kh1 and Rg1, for example: 16 Kh1 Qh3 17 Qe2 e4
18 Rg1 ef 19. Qf1 Ng4 20 Q:h3
N:f2 mate; however, this was the
line he should have chosen, but
with the exchange sacrifice 18 fe!
Ng4 19 f4 N:h2 20 Qg2 Q:g2+
21 K:g2, with strong center pawns.
Now, although White has defended
against the threat of 16.. Qh3
(when there would follow 17 Bb2
Q:f3 18 B:e5), his position is
too passive and his rooks are
disconnected.

16.	...	Ne7-g6
17.	Qc2-f5	Qd7:f5
18.	Bb1:f5	Ng6-h4
19.	Bf5-e4	...

A stock position illustrating
the strength of the two knights
and their advantage over the two
bishops. One bishop is locked in
a cell measuring a3 by c1 by e3;
the other is chained to the pawn
at f3. Both bishops are absolutely impotent, and White has no
useful moves. The knights will
continue to dominate the bishops
as long as the pawn chain remains immobile, so White's best
chance was to retreat the bi-

shop to c2 in an attempt to open the game.

19.   ...   Nf6:e4

Succumbing to the spell of the Two Bishops, Euwe hurriedly exchanges one of them, even though he had the excellent move 19..Rae8.

20. f3:e4   f7-f5
21. e4:f5   ...

Taimanov easily acquired a passed d-pawn in the early opening, and then apparently forgot about it. By itself, certainly, it would cause Black no great discomfort; but if it were to receive a bit of support, its power would grow by leaps and bounds.

21 f4 would have been very much to the point here: however Black might reply, he could not prevent the appearance of the pawn-pair d5-e5 — a chance White would not have had, if Black had not been so hasty with his 20.. f5. 20..Rae8 was still possible, with ..f5 only thereafter. There was no reason to rush matters (since White could hardly have effected any substantial change in the position in one move), and Black's forces would then be completely mobilized.

21.   ...   e5-e4

A slight inaccuracy, affording White an amazing defensive opportunity; his position would have been very difficult after 21..Nf3+ and only then 22.. e4. The threats of 23.. R:f5 followed by .. Rg5+

and .. Rh5, as well as .. Ra8-d8-d6, look so strong and dangerous that it is hard to imagine how White might have wriggled out.

22. f3-f4   ...

A memorable move indeed. Taimanov is the great optimist of the chessboard, always happy with his position, and sometimes a trifle slow to sense approaching difficulties. However, when the wolf is at the door, his resourcefulness, combined with his far-seeing powers of calculation, draws from the deepest reserves of his position such possibilities as to astound not only his opponent, but chess fans everywhere.

The plan he comes up with here dooms all five of his central pawns, in order to reach a position in which rook and two rook pawns successfully hold off rook and four pawns.

22.   ...   e4:f3
23. e3-e4   Ra8-e8
24. Bc1-g5   Re8:e4
25. Bg5:h4   Re4:h4
26. Rf1:f3   Rh4:c4
27. Ra1-e1   Rc4-g4+

A nice in-between check. Its point appears by comparing what might have occurred, had Black merely played his rook to d4 at once: 27.. Rd4 28 Re7 R:d5 29R:b7 Rd:f5 30 R:f5 R:f5 31 R:a7, with a draw. Now, however, White's king must go to the f-file, so that in this line the f-pawn

[83]

falls with check. Thus, White must find a move other than 30 R:b7.

28.	Kg1-f2	Rg4-d4
29.	Re1-e7	Rd4:d5
30.	f5-f6	...

Very good! Many players know how to convert their advantage into a win; it is a far more difficult thing to convert the opponent's advantage into nothing. With 30 f6, White intends to split Black's g- and h-pawns, and I am still not convinced that Euwe's 30.. R:f6 was best. Here's an interesting alternative: 30.. g6 31 Rg7+ Kh8 32 R:b7 c4 33 Rc7 Rd6, etc.

30.	...	Rf8:f6
31.	Rf3:f6	g7:f6
32.	Re7:b7	a7-a5
33.	Rb7-b5	a5-a4

33.. Rf5+ 34 Ke3 Re5+ 35 Kf4 c4 was somewhat better.

34.	Rb5-a5	Rd5-d4
35.	Ra5:c5	...

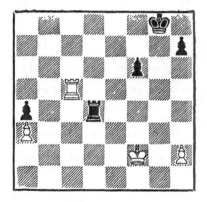

Advising is always easier than playing the game oneself. A more stubborn defense was 37 Ra7, winning control of the seventh rank, but to refuse the c-pawn, with a two-pawn deficit? One can only advise such moves... Nevertheless, the outcome would not have been all that clear, even with Black's two extra pawns: in order to free his king, Black would have had to give back his a-pawn. After that, White's task would be to trade off

his a-pawn for Black's c-pawn, throwing in his h-pawn as well, if necessary: sometimes one can draw the ending against the f- and h-pawns.

After 35 R:c5, White also gets his rook to a7, but Black keeps his a-pawn. The main objection to 35 R:c5, however, is that White doesn't even win his pawn back, since Black's .. Rd4-d3:a3 maneuver reestablishes the two-pawn margin.

35.	...	Rd4-d3
36.	Rc5-a5	Rd3:a3
37.	Ra5-a7	Ra3-a1
38.	Kf2-g3	a4-a3
39.	Kg3-g4	a3-a2

Now Black has only to push his f-pawn to the third rank, and even the best possible position for White — Ra7, Kf2; Black — Ra1, Kh8 — is lost, because of the standard maneuver .. Ra1-h1.

40.	Kg4-h5	f6-f5
41.	Kh5-h6	f5-f4

WHITE RESIGNED

The win is achieved by 42 Ra4 f3 43 Ra3 f2 44 Rg3+ Kh8 45 Ra3 Rg1 46 Ra8+ Rg8, when Black queens one of his pawns.

******

55. Najdorf—Szabo
(Grunfeld Defense)

1.	d2-d4	Ng8-f6
2.	c2-c4	g7-g6
3.	Nb1-c3	d7-d5
4.	c4:d5	Nf6:d5
5.	g2-g3	Bf8-g7
6.	Bf1-g2	Nd5:c3

We all know the basic idea of the Grunfeld is to attack the pawn center, and especially the d-pawn; so why does Black strengthen d4 and open the b-file for White, without being forced to do so?

There are many reasons for it, chief among them the fact that the knight had no good retreat square. Additionally, Black does not lose a tempo, and he removes a strong enemy knight. If the b-file is opened, the c-file is also closed; he may be strengthening the d-pawn, but he is also isolating the a-pawn, and weak-

ening the b-pawn by bringing it
to c3 and detaching it from its
pawn chain. So 6.. N:c3 does
have its logic.

7.	b2:c3	c7-c5
8.	e2-e3	0-0

Of course, Black will have a
difficult time collapsing d4,
but that is not to say it will
be impossible. One of the peculiarities of central pawn tension
is that Black may trade on d4 at
any suitable moment, while White
can almost never take on c5. On
the other hand, as we shall note
more than once, the move 7.. c5
enhances the power of White's
fianchettoed bishop.

9.	Ng1-e2	Nb8-c6
10.	0-0	Qd8-a5

10.. Na5 would have been in the
style of Capablanca, who loved
clear, effective plans: it attacks the weakened square c4,
with a natural followup something
like 11.. Bd7, 12.. cd 13.. Rc8,
14.. Bc6, etc. The text move could
have been met powerfully by 11 a4,
threatening 12 Ba3, when White's
position would glow with all the
colors of the rainbow. (Ba3 must
not be played too hastily, however: 11 a4 Rd8 12 Ba3 Bg4, and
the bishop's diagonal has to be
closed by 13 f3, since 13 B:c5
allows 13.. Q:c5. So the right
move would be 11 a4 Rd8 12 Qb3,
and then 13 Ba3.)

11.	Qd1-b3	...

In Morphy's time, such a move
was played with the intention of
attacking f7; here, the queen's
eye is on b7.

White has apparently attained
his goal first, and retarded the
queen's bishop's development.

11.	...	Bc8-g4!

Following Morphy's example,
Black is ready to sacrifice a
pawn for development: for example, 12 f3 Be6, followed by :

a) 13 d5 c4 14 Q:b7 B:d5;

b) 13 Q:b7 Bc4;

c) 13 Qa3 Bc4 14 Q:a5 N:a5
15 Rd1 Rac8 16 Ba3 b6 17 f4 Rfd8

— in all lines, Black obtains
a fully equal game.

12.	Ne2-f4	e7-e5

If White's knight were not at
f4, his pawn could, passing safely between Scylla and Charybdis,
as it were, cause Black no little anguish; but now White's
stronghold on d4 is attacked from
four sides at once, and his center collapses into formless rub-
ble.

13.	d4:e5	Nc6:e5
14.	h2-h3	...

White has much the worse of it.
He cannot take on b7 with his
queen (14 Q:b7? Rab8 15 Qe7 Q:c3,
and White loses a whole piece),
nor with his bishop (for the
same reason: 14 B:b7 Rab8 15 Qd5
Bf3 or 15.. R:b7, etc., with an
irresistible attack). White's
only chance to equalize is to set
up the formation Nd5 and e3-e4,
but right now he cannot play either 14 Nd5 Be2 15 Re1 Nf3+
16 B:f3 B:f3, when his game is
lost; or 14 e4 Nf3+ 15 Kh1 B:c3
16 Rb1 Nd4 17 Q:b7 Q:a2. So Najdorf's 14 h3 is played to determine the intentions of this bishop.

14.	...	Bg4-f3
15.	Bg2:f3	Ne5:f3+
16.	Kg1-g2	Nf3-e5
17.	e3-e4	b7-b5

Szabo's hot-blooded nature rejects the strong positional line 17.. Qa6, although it is wholly logical and embodies a number of healthy ideas: controlling the light squares, severely weakened by the exchange of the fianchettoed bishop; defending the b-pawn; increasing the queen's radius of activity; and impeding the development of the knight, since 18 Nd5 would be met by 18.. Qe2!

The strength of 17.. Qa6 lies not merely in abstract ideas, but also in concrete variations: for example, 18 Qa3 Qc4, or 18 Ba3 b6, or 18 Be3 c4 19 Qc2 Nd3. If 18 f3, the weakening of the second rank must tell sooner or later (see Game 85, Stahlberg - Szabo).

Szabo's bumptious 17.. b5 leads almost by force to an equal endgame.

| 18. | Bc1-e3 | c5-c4 |
| 19. | Qb3-c2 | Ne5-d3 |

Otherwise 20 Bd4!, and the scales begin to tip in White's favor.

20.	Nf4:d3	c4:d3
21.	Qc2:d3	Bg7:c3
22.	Ra1-d1	Ra8-c8
23.	Qd3-d5	Rf8-e8
24.	Qd5-b3	Rc8-c4
25.	Rd1-d5	a7-a6
26.	Qb3:c4	...

Szabo may have overlooked this move — it happens to grandmasters too, sometimes. Still, there was nothing significantly better.

26.	...	b5:c4
27.	Rd5:a5	Bc3:a5
28.	Kg2-f3	...

DRAW

If the bishop were still on g7, Black would have had some slight winning chances, but now after 28.. Rb8 29 Rc1 c3 30 Bd4 Rb2 31 B:c3 B:c3 32 R:c3 R:a2, the draw is clear.

******

56. Petrosian—Averbakh
(Queen's Gambit)

1.	c2-c4	Ng8-f6
2.	Nb1-c3	e7-e6
3.	Ng1-f3	d7-d5
4.	e2-e3	Bf8-e7
5.	d2-d4	0-0
6.	Bf1-d3	...

White prepares a calm transposition into the Rubinstein Variation, fianchettoing the second bishop; Averbakh finds a good counter, exchanging pawns to transpose into the Queen's Gambit Accepted with an extra tempo for Black, thanks to White's two bishop moves (Bf1-d3 and Bd3:c4).

6.	...	d5:c4
7.	Bd3:c4	c7-c5
8.	0-0	a7-a6
9.	d4:c5	Qd8:d1
10.	Rf1:d1	Be7:c5
11.	a2-a3	b7-b5
12.	Bc4-e2	Bc8-b7
13.	b2-b4	Bc5-e7

DRAW

If one desires an explanation of such quick draws, which occur in every tournament, one must keep in mind that such an event lasts more than one day. Many things happen over the course of thirty rounds that have a bearing on the fighting abilities of the people who play chess. In the present case, Petrosian's peaceable disposition and Averbakh's too, in part, may have been due to the previous round, which went badly for both. After the extra rest day they gave themselves with this eighth-round game, Petrosian went on to win three straight games in good style (an exceptional achievement by any standard in such a strong tourney);

while Averbakh, though perhaps not quite so fortunate, still fought with great verve in the rounds that followed.

In major tournaments, one must ration one's strength, not for the individual game, but for the entire event, taken as a whole. The history of chess events — and that of many other sports as well — contains many cases in which one of the participants forged ahead at the outset, only to lose game after game towards the end (and not against his most powerful opponents, either), finishing far behind the winners.

******

******

ROUND NINE

57. Szabo—Petrosian
(Queen's Gambit)

1.	d2-d4	Ng8-f6
2.	c2-c4	e7-e6
3.	Nb1-c3	d7-d5
4.	Bc1-g5	Bf8-e7
5.	e2-e3	0-0
6.	Ng1-f3	h7-h6
7.	Bg5-h4	b7-b6

The direct and most natural attempt to solve the problem of the queen's bishop. For a long time, White used to get the better of it with 8 cd ed 9 Ne5; Pillsbury won a number of games that way. The system was revived recently when Bondarevsky and Makogonov decided that after 7.. b6 it made little sense to block the diagonal a8-h1 with a pawn; so they began recapturing, after 8 cd, with the knight instead. Now, should White reply to 8.. N:d5 with 9 B:e7 Q:e7 10 N:d5, so that Black must suffer a pawn on d5 anyway, then the bishop shows its flexibility by developing to e6, rather than to b7. Thus, the Bondarevsky-Makogonov Defense proves completely viable, and now on occasion it is White who, as here, deviates from the main line.

8.	Bf1-d3	Bc8-b7
9.	0-0	Nb8-d7
10.	Ra1-c1	...

A little change from the usual 10 Qe2 Ne4 11 Bg3 N:g3 12 fg. After the text move, Black refrains from 10.. Ne4, since White does not retreat to g3, but takes on e7 instead, without fearing 11.. N:c3 12 B:d8 N:d1 (no check) 13 Rf:d1 Rf:d8 14 cd ed 15 R:c7. And if 11..Q:e7 instead, then 12 cd ed 13 N:e4 de 14 R:c7 is possible: after 14.. Bc8 15 Bb5 ef 16 Q:f3 Rb8 17 R:a7, White would have three pawns for the piece plus a powerful position.

10.	...	c7-c5
11.	Qd1-e2	a7-a6

Black has brought out all his minor pieces, but his development is far from complete. He will have a hard time finding good positions for his heavy pieces, while White's rooks and queen are developing very nicely. The text move prepares the maneuver 12.. dc 13 B:c4 b5; then 14.. Qb6, followed by the development of the rooks to c8 and d8. Black still loses an important tempo, however, when 11.. dc 12 B:c4 Ne4 would have eased his defense.

12.	c4:d5	e6:d5

Recapturing with the knight would have suited the spirit of this opening better: if then 13 B:e7 Q:e7 14 N:d5 B:d5, with a comfortable game for Black. On 15 e4, the bishop simply retreats to b7, while if 15 B:a6, Black could recapture at a2, although I would prefer 15.. B:f3 16 gf cd 17 ed Nf6, with good prospects, now that the knight has the d5 and f4 squares.

Petrosian probably disliked 12.. N:d5 because of the simple reply 13 Bg3.

13.	d4:c5	b6:c5
14.	Rf1-d1	Rf8-e8
15.	Bd3-c2	Qd8-b6
16.	Bc2-b3	...

Black's hanging pawns are weak. Szabo carries out a typical maneuver, Bd3-c2-b3, in order to induce the advance of one pawn, which weakens the other, and gives White an important central support point.

16.	...	c5-c4

17.   Bb3-a4   . . .

Now, with the knight pinned a-
gainst the rook, White threatens
18 B:f6 as well as 18 B:d7 and
19 N:d5, forcing Petrosian to
trade off one of the d-pawn's
defenders. However, Szabo should
not have contented himself with
this, when he had an opportunity
to combine his attack on the d-
pawn with threats to Black's
king. Having induced Black to
play his bishop to c6, he ought
to have brought his bishop back
to c2, thus: 17.. Bc6 18 Bc2!
Rab8 19 Nd4 Ba8 20 Rb1, and
Black's game creaks at every
joint: White is threatening both
21 Bg3 and 21 Nf5.

17.   . . .   Bb7-c6
18.   Ba4:c6   Qb6:c6
19.   b2-b3   . . .

Szabo has been bitten by a
fatal idea: to attack the d5-
pawn on the c4 square. With
this one thoughtless move 1)
he weakens an entire cluster
of dark squares in his position; 2) he knocks the supports
out from under his queen's
knight; and 3) he makes Black's
bishop better by giving it the
chance to move out either to b4
or to a3.

Either 19 Nd4 and 20 Nf5,
or 19 Rc2 and 20 Rcd2 would have
been correct here. The pawn
stood quite well at b2, and it
should not have been disturbed.

19.   . . .   Ra8-c8
20.   Nc3-a4   . . .

This must have been the result
of a miscalculation, since the
knight returns at once; but the
queen's position improves meanwhile, and now White must consider how to defend his knight
on c3.

20.   . . .   Qc6-b5
21.   Na4-c3   Qb5-a5
22.   Bh4:f6   Nd7:f6
23.   b3:c4   d5:c4
24.   Nf3-d2   . . .

By now, White's position holds
so many weaknesses that he had
better start thinking about how
he is going to draw; to that end,
his rook should have been sent
in by 24 Rd4, and if then 24..Bb4,

25 R:c4 B:c3 26 R1:c3 Q:c3
27 R:c3 R:c3 28 h3.

24.   . . .   Rc8-c6
25.   Nd2:c4   . . .

Extremely dangerous, for now
White's knights both go straight
under the gun. One gets away with
it, but the other...

25.   . . .   Qa5-c7
26.   Nc3-a4   . . .

The active 26 Nd5 was not good,
since after 26.. N:d5 27 R:d5 Bf6
etc.,there does not seem to be
any way to relieve the pin. What
was required was 26 Nb1, when at
least one knight would be safe;
if then 26.. Rc8 27 N1d2 Bb4
28 Rb1 Nd5 29 R:b4, with some
chances to draw. But now the two
hanging knights give rise to a
combination which wins a piece.

26.   . . .   Re8-c8
27.   Rd1-d4   . . .

Szabo goes overboard in his
desperate attempt to hold the
extra pawn, leaving the queen's
rook thus undefended: 27 Nab6
would have left him some small
drawing chances.

This position illustrates the
power of the pin, based on the
unprotected rook at c1.

27.   . . .   Nf6-e8

The point of this pretty move
is easily seen: Black brings
this knight to d6, freeing the

square f6 for the bishop. From
there, the bishop will attack,
not only the rook at d4, but
also the knight, if it should
move from a4 to b2. 27.. Nd7
would have been an error, in
view of 28 Rc2! Ne5 (the knight
blocks the diagonal of the bishop, giving White time to defend) 29 Nab2, and the rook on
c2 sidesteps to the d-file; on
28.. Bf6 29 R:d7? would be a
mistake, owing to 29.. Q:d7
30 Nab6 Qb7 (29 Re4 would be
the correct move in that case).

28.	e3-e4	Be7-f6
29.	e4-e5	Bf6:e5
30.	Rd4-e4	Ne8-f6

Driving the rook from the
fourth rank wins Black a piece,
since after 31 R:e5 R:c4 32 R:c4
Q:c4 attacks the queen and the
knight and threatens mate, too;
on 33 Qd1 Black calmly "sacrifices" his queen with 33.. Q:a4;
or if 33 Q:c4 R:c4.

31.	Na4-b6	Rc6:b6
32.	Re4:e5	Rb6-c6
33.	Re5-e7	Rc6:c4
34.	Rc1-e1	Qc7-c6
35.	h2-h3	Rc4-c1
36.	Re1:c1	Qc6:e1+
37.	Kg1-h2	Qc1-c4
38.	Qe2-f3	Qc4:a2
39.	Re7-a7	...

WHITE RESIGNED

******

58. Euwe—Najdorf
(King's Indian)

1.	d2-d4	Ng8-f6
2.	c2-c4	g7-g6
3.	g2-g3	Bf8-g7
4.	Bf1-g2	0-0
5.	Nb1-c3	c7-c5
6.	d4-d5	e7-e5
7.	Bc1-g5	h7-h6

Aggressive treatment of the
opening. If Black wants to break
the pin, he must do it at once,
as otherwise White will put his
queen on d2, rendering .. h7-h6
impracticable. And if the pin is
not broken, then White will move
his bishop to h6 and without further ado push his h-pawn — a
serious, though hardly a fatal,
threat. From a purely chessic
viewpoint, then, the logical move
was certainly 7.. d6.

8.	Bg5:f6	Qd8:f6
9.	d5-d6	...

This pawn sortie combines two
strategic ideas: restraint of
Black's queenside development,
and cutting the communications
between the two wings of Black's
position. Additionally, White
gains the valuable square d5 for
both bishop and knight.

Black's retarded development
is due chiefly to the fact that
the pawn which is now nailed to
d7 closes the diagonal c8-h3,
which means that the bishop now
can only get into play on b7 or
a6. But 9.. b6 is not yet playable; first the knight must be
played to c6. Thus, we can deduce
that Black's next three moves
will be: 9.. Nc6, 10.. b6, and
11.. Bb7.

Black's queenside pieces can
only reach the kingside by way
of the square d8, which puts
quite a crimp on their maneuver-
ability.

These are the positive aspects
of 9 d6. There is only one negative aspect: cut off from support, this pawn may die. White's
task is therefore to assail the
kingside with might and main for
as long as the pawn at d6 stands,
depriving Black's kingside of the
necessary support of his queenside pieces. This task Euwe carries out in brilliant style.

9.	...	Nb8-c6

10.	e2-e3	b7-b6
11.	Bg2-d5	Kg8-h8

In order to prepare .. f7-f5.
In his later commentary, Najdorf
suggested a different plan:
11.. Ba6, 12.. Rb8, and 13.. b5.
It seems to me, however, that in
that event the kingside attack
would have developed more quickly and more dangerously.

12.	Nc3-e4	Qf6-d8
13.	h2-h4!	f7-f5
14.	Ne4-g5	...

We would like to draw the reader's attention to this elegant
knight leap; we did not give it
an exclamation mark, simply because we had already given one to
White's previous move.

14.	...	Bc8-b7

Naturally, Black doesn't even
think of saving the exchange, nor
would White dream of taking it:
after 15 Nf7+ R:f7 16 B:f7 Nb4
the initiative would pass to
Black.

15.	g3-g4	...

White continues methodically
clearing the approaches to the
black king. On 15.. Na5, White
could trade bishops and play his
queen to d5, with two threats:
18 Q:b7 and 18 Nf7+; and on
15.. Qf6, White has the choice
between 16 Nf7+, attacking the
queen and winning the exchange
after 16.. R:f7 17 g5, or 16 gf
Q:f5 17 Rh2.

15.	...	e5-e4

Black is not opening the h8-
a1 diagonal in order to capture
the b-pawn, but in order to allow
his king to hie himself to g7,
after which perhaps Black could
risk capturing the knight. But
now a white knight gets to f4.

16.	Ng1-e2	Bg7:b2
17.	Ne2-f4	...

White, in turn, also sacrifices
the exchange. Couldn't Black take
it? That question cannot be answered with variations. White has
a myriad of appealing attacking
continuations. To examine one:
17.. B:a1 18 gf Bc3+ 19 Kf1 is
similar to what actually occurred;

and it would seem to me that
White's threats — 20 N:g6+,
20 Qg4, etc. — would be impossible to withstand, especially
under tournament conditions. Najdorf was apparently of the same
opinion: before anything else,
he aims to shore up the key point
g6. (A note here: White's attack
would congeal very quickly if he
limited his sacrifice to the exchange: 18 Q:a1+? Qf6 19 N:g6+
Kg7.)

17.	...	Qd8-f6
18.	g4:f5!	Bb2:a1

Since White must attain one of
the important squares (g6, h6 or
h5) in any event, Najdorf decides
to take the rook after all, since
this might later allow him to give
up his queen for two pieces or a
piece and a pawn. On 18.. gf,
White would have continued 19 Rb1
Be5 20 Qh5, with a tremendous attack. The next phase of the game
puts one in mind of those ancient
clashes of the masters of the Italian School.

19.	Nf4:g6+	Kh8-g7
20.	Ng5:e4	...

White is practically advertis-
ing that his attack is intuitive,
rather than calculated — otherwise, why would he need the e-
pawn? The simple 20 Nf4, setting
up such fearsome threats as 21 Nh5+,
21 Qh5 and 21 Rg1, seems more appealing, yet Euwe didn't play it.
Why? To put it simply, Euwe did
not want to give his opponent a
choice. White's 20 N:e4 forces

matters: by depriving Black's queen of the square c3, it eliminates the variation 20 Nf4 Qc3+ 21 Kf1 — although, in my opinion, this would only improve White's position. For example: 21.. R:f5 22 Qg4; or 21.. hg 22 hg R:f5 23 Rh7+. But — well, Euwe received a brilliancy prize for this game; the judges were not too strict, and we shall not go nitpicking either. Each grandmaster has his own style, with its strengths and weaknesses.

20.   ...   Ba1-c3+

White has a very strong position, but he is still a whole rook down. 20.. Q:f5 was bad: White would have won right off with 21 Q:a1+ K:g6 22 Rg1+. So first Black pulls his bishop out with check, and then he takes the f-pawn, putting pressure on f2 and removing the protection of the knight at g6.

21. Ke1-f1   Qf6:f5
22. Ng6-f4   ...

Black needs only another move or two to stabilize his position and escape with his extra rook, but these must be good moves. Thus, 22.. Be5 would be answered by 23 Ng3 Qh7 24 Qg4+ Kh8 25 Ng6+; if the queen goes to e5 instead, White's queen checks at g4; and if the bishop retreats to f6, then either 23 Ng3 or 23 Rg1+ wins. I believe that Black must lose here even with the best defense. (Had he wished, White could have forced a draw with 22 Rg1, after which Black must play 22.. Qh3+ 23 Rg2 Qh1+ 24 Rg1 Qh3+, etc.)

22.   ...   Kg7-h8!

(See diagram, next column)

This is a good move. White must take the bishop now, giving his opponent a breath of air, since the consequences of 23 Rg1 are unclear.

23. Ne4:c3   Ra8-e8

But instead of this move, 23.. Nd8 was necessary: the bishop on d5 was long past enduring. Variations like 24 B:b7 N:b7 25 Nce2 Qe4 26 Rg1 Rg8, or 26 Ng3 Q:c4+ 27 Kg2 R:f4 would

(Position after 22.. Kh8!)

have made it very difficult for White, but I believe he might still have turned the trick with 25 Ncd5! in the first variation, instead of the somewhat flaccid 25 Nce2. The pawn on d6 can be let go now, since it has already done its work. Beyond a doubt, however, Euwe's 20 N:e4 put a damper on his attack, whereas Najdorf in turn failed to capitalize on his good fortune.

24. Nc3-e2   Rf8-g8
25. h4-h5   Rg8-g5
26. Ne2-g3   Rg5:g3

Unpleasant, but forced: on 26.. Qg4 there would follow 27 Bf3, and any other retreat gives White far too many pleasant possibilities. At least 26.. R:g3 does not hand over the initiative.

27. f2:g3   Re8:e3

(See diagram, next page)

28. Kf1-f2   ...

There has been no mate as yet, and the material is still even, but the bishop on b7 and the knight on c6 are still mere bystanders; it is this last circumstance that allows White the opportunity to re-form his troops into a new attacking wave and send them in once again to assault the black king's broken position.

28.   ...   Re3-e8

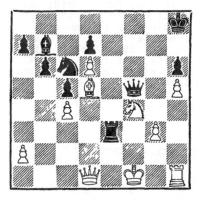

(Position after 27.. R:e3)

29.	Rh1-e1	Re8:e1
30.	Qd1:e1	Kh8-g7
31.	Qe1-e8	...

The poorly sheltered king is a good target, both in the middlegame and in the endgame.

31.	...	Qf5-c2+
32.	Kf2-g1	Qc2-d1+
33.	Kg1-h2	Qd1-c2+
34.	Nf4-g2	Qc2-f5
35.	Qe8-g8+	Kg7-f6
36.	Qg8-h8+	Kf6-g5
37.	Qh8-g7+	...

BLACK RESIGNED,

as mate is inevitable.

******

59. Stahlberg—Taimanov
(Queen's Indian Defense)

1.	d2-d4	Ng8-f6
2.	c2-c4	e7-e6
3.	Ng1-f3	b7-b6
4.	g2-g3	Bc8-a6

Modern thinking in the opening. The move .. b7-b6 does not necessarily mean that Black intends to continue with .. Bb7. He may also attack the pawn at c4; and although there are no less than eleven different defenses to this, each method has its drawbacks. White selects what seems to be the best line.

| 5. | Qd1-a4 | ... |

To this I would eagerly have replied 5.. c5, exploiting the fact that with the queen off-sides, 6 d5 is no longer possible; if 6 Bg2, then 6.. Bb7. As the course of the game will show, Taimanov has other ideas for this pawn.

5.	...	Bf8-e7
6.	Bf1-g2	0-0
7.	Nb1-c3	c7-c6
8.	Nf3-e5	...

8 Bf4! probably looked too primitive to White, but in that case Taimanov would have had nothing better than 8.. Qc8 or 8.. Bb7, since the complications after 8.. b5 would inevitably resolve in White's favor.

8.	...	Qd8-e8
9.	0-0	d7-d5
10.	Rf1-e1	...

White no longer has any advantage. The text move prepares e2-e4, which he never gets the chance to play. Like it or not, he ought to have continued 10 cd cd 11 Q:e8 and 12 Re1, with an approximately equal game.

| 10. | ... | b6-b5 |

Black seizes the initiative.

11.	c4:b5	c6:b5
12.	Qa4-d1	b5-b4
13.	Nc3-b1	...

Obsessed by his desire to play e2-e4 at any cost, White now drops this knight completely out of sight, so as to redevelop it to d2. Doubtless, a4 (with the prospect of getting to c5) would have been a little better square.

13.	...	Nb8-c6
14.	Ne5:c6	Qe8:c6
15.	Nb1-d2	Qc6-b6
16.	e2-e3	...

Stahlberg does not seem to have been in a mood to play chess this evening: 16 Nb3 would have left him with some chances of putting together a defense.

16.	...	Ra8-c8
17.	Bg2-f1	Rc8-c6
18.	Bf1:a6	Qb6:a6
19.	Nd2-f3	Rf8-c8
20.	Qd1-b3	Nf6-e4
21.	Nf3-d2	Rc6-c2

(See diagram on next page)

(Position after 21.. Rc2)

An instructive position which shows us:

1) why, when only one bishop remains, we are told to place our pawns on squares of opposite color. This gives the bishop pawn-trenches to traverse: for example, if White had the light-squared bishop, he would have a fully acceptable game, whereas here his position is hopeless.

2) why it is so clearly advantageous to trade off the enemy's fianchettoed bishop: the square g2 is very weak, and the usual technique of queen to f3, followed by pawn to h5-h4-h3 promises a swift end for White.

3) the importance of seizing the seventh (or second) rank, or even a single square of it. Black could have won two pieces for a rook here with 21.. R:c1 22 R:c1 N:d2, but instead, he simply placed his rook on c2. On the second rank, the rook restricts the enemy pieces, and also sets up sundry combinations, as we shall observe later on.

| 22. | Nd2:e4 | d5:e4 |
| 23. | a2-a3 | ... |

Black could have wound the game up here by 23.. Qd3 24 Q:d3 ed. This threatens to win the bishop, which has yet to make a single move; and if 25 Rd1, then 25..Re2, when the pawn cannot be taken be-

cause of 26.. Re1+, winning the unfortunate bishop. If White, in reply to 23.. Qd3, avoids the exchange of queens by playing 24 Qa4, the simple 24.. b3 underscores his utter helplessness: for example, 25 Q:a7 Bf8 26 a4 Re2 27 Rf1 Rcc2 28 a5 R:f2 29 R:f2 Qd1+ 30 Kg2 Qf3+. However, the text is not a bad idea either.

| 23. | ... | h7-h5 |

| 24. | d4-d5 | Rc8-c4 |

Now White cannot take the e-pawn, since Black's queen would recapture and enter f3 via f6; then, after .. h5-h4, White would have to resign. If, after 25 de Q:e6, White took the b-pawn, then 26.. R:c1 27 Ra:c1 R:c1 28 Q:e6 R:e1+.

25.	Re1-d1	e6:d5
26.	Bc1-d2	Qa6-f6
27.	Ra1-b1	h5-h4
28.	Qb3-a4	Qf6-f5
29.	Qa4:a7	Be7-f8

This chance to exchange queens amounts to a reprieve for White. 29.. Bg5 would have deprived him of this chance, and then nothing could have saved him from ..h4-h3 followed by .. Qf3.

30.	Qa7-b8	g7-g5
31.	g3:h4	g5:h4
32.	Qb8-f4	Qf5:f4
33.	e3:f4	d5-d4
34.	b2-b3	Rc4-c6
35.	a3:b4	f7-f5

Taimanov has managed to drag

[94]

it out a bit, but White's game
is very bad, still: he has five
isolated pawns, and Black's rook
at c2 in conjunction with his
passed pawn assures him the victory.

36.	h2-h3	Rc6-a6
37.	Rb1-c1	Rc2:c1
38.	Rd1:c1	Ra6-a2
39.	Bd2-e1	Ra2-b2
40.	Kg1-g2	Rb2:b3
41.	Rc1-c8	Rb3-b1
42.	Be1-d2	e4-e3

WHITE RESIGNED

******

60. Boleslavsky—Gligoric
(Sicilian Defense)

1.	e2-e4	c7-c5
2.	Ng1-f3	Nb8-c6
3.	d2-d4	c5:d4
4.	Nf3:d4	Ng8-f6
5.	Nb1-c3	d7-d6
6.	Bc1-g5	e7-e6
7.	Qd1-d2	Bf8-e7
8.	0-0-0	Nc6:d4
9.	Qd2:d4	0-0
10.	f2-f4	h7-h6
11.	Bg5-h4	Qd8-a5
12.	e4-e5	d6:e5
13.	Qd4:e5	b7-b6

A strange optical illusion!
Theory holds that the exchange
of queens leads by force to a
favorable endgame for White,
while retreating his queen to
b6 is bad because of 14 Na4 Qc6
15 Bb5 Q:g2 16 Rg1. This is all
true, but only with the black
pawn at h7! Then, indeed, after
13.. Q:e5 14 fe Nd5 15 B:e7 N:e7
16 Bd3, Black could not play
16.. Bd7 because of 17 B:h7+
K:h7 18 R:d7; Black would have
to continue 16.. Nc6 17 Rhe1,
when 17.. Bd7 is once more impossible, and White establishes
a bind. In the present game, however, with the pawn on h6,
16.. Bd7 is quite possible: after 17 Bh7+ K:h7 18 R:d7 Nc6,
the exchange of b-pawn for e-
pawn is not dangerous to Black,
as long as White is no great
endgame enthusiast — which Boleslavsky is not.

Both players overlooked this,
and Gligoric played the novelty
he had prepared for the other
variation.

| 14. | Qe5:a5 | b6:a5 |

Black believes the free game he
gets for his bishops and rooks
compensates for his doubled, isolated pawns; but in my opinion,
White must have the better of it.
He has a 3/2 pawn majority, without the need to create a passed
pawn from it: the passed pawn is
already made for him! The closer
the endgame approaches, the more
the c-pawn's presence will be felt.

| 15. | Bf1-d3 | Bc8-b7 |
| 16. | Rh1-g1 | Rf8-e8 |

16.. Bc5 would give Black nothing, since after 17 Rge1, the
pawn on g2 would still be taboo:
17 Rge1 B:g2? 18 B:f6 gf 19 Rg1,
winning the pair of bishops for
the rook. Nor is 16.. Bc5 17 Rge1
Nd5 attractive, since simplifications are generally unfavorable
to Black here; and besides, White
would stand a great deal better
after 18 N:d5 B:d5 19 Be4 B:e4
20 R:e4.

| 17. | h2-h3 | ... |

White readies 18 g4, which does
not work right away because of
17.. Bc5 and 18.. N:g4.

| 17. | ... | Be7-c5 |
| 18. | Rg1-e1 | Bc5-b4 |

Taking on g2 would still be bad.
Perhaps moving the king to h8
would have been a more useful
16th move: Boleslavsky played it
himself in a later tournament.

19.   f4-f5   ...

Without fearing 19.. B:c3,
which would give White a passed
pawn on the c-file. This observation might come as a surprise
to the reader, since White already has a passed pawn on c2.
Unfortunately for White, this
pawn cannot be considered passed
with so many pieces still on the
board, since it may not stir a
single step without upsetting the
king's disposition. If, however,
Black were to take the knight
here, then the c3-pawn, supported
by the bishop pair, could run for
daylight, while the c2-pawn remained behind to shelter the king.

19.   ...   e6-e5

If Black was not happy with the
19.. ef variation, then 19.. Nd5
was the obvious continuation in
order to play on the pin. This
move costs Black his last point
of support in the center, and
the passed e-pawn is no compensation.

20.   Bd3-b5   Re8-e7
21.   Re1-e3   a7-a6
22.   Bb5-a4   Bb4-c5

The pawn at g2 has been indirectly defended all this time by
the black king's location on the
g-file (.. B:g2; B:f6! gf; Rg1,
pinning the bishop); had the king
gone to f8 here, there might have
followed 23 a3 B:c3 24 R:c3 B:g2
25 Rg3 and 26 Rdg1, and now it is
Black who finds his g-pawn hard
to protect. However, the text
move also says that Gligoric is
unable to find a plan to improve
his position. Meanwhile, Boleslavsky proceeds, in the straightforward style characteristic of
him, to engineer a minor-piece
trade, seize control of d5, and
force the further advance (and
further weakening) of the e-pawn.

23.   Re3-e2   e5-e4
24.   Ba4-b3   Ra8-e8
25.   Bh4:f6   g7:f6
26.   Bb3-d5   e4-e3
27.   Bd5:b7   Re7:b7
28.   Rd1-d5   Bc5-b4
29.   Rd5-d3   Bb4:c3
30.   Rd3:c3   Rb7-e7
31.   Rc3-d3   ...

The four-rook endgame makes
White's advantage very clear.

Black's rooks ride quietly at
anchor, defending their passed
pawn; but White's king stands so
near that it may easily get next
to the pawn, let's say to f3.
Should the e-pawn fall, then
White's win will become a matter
of time. Black's king can neither
come to the aid of its pawn, nor
counterattack the f-pawn. A further demonstration of White's
possibilities is that, were it
his move here, then 32 c4, followed by 33 Rc3, would leave
Black in a completely hopeless
predicament, with the rook on c3
simultaneously attacking the pawn
on e3 and supporting its own
passed pawn. Black's next move is
directed against this threat.

31.   ...   Re7-e4
32.   c2-c3   Kg8-g7
33.   Kc1-c2   Re4-e5

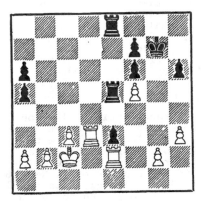

34.   g2-g4   h6-h5
35.   Rd3-d6   ...

Tying the king down to the
f6-pawn —

35.   ...   h5:g4
36.   h3:g4   Kg7-h6

— but the black king refuses
to be tied down! Black is giving
up both his f-pawns in order to
reach the square f3, which will
secure him the draw. Might this
possibility have been prevented?
Yes; the mistake was 34 g4, by
which White transferred the base
of his pawn chain from g2 to g4 —
i.e., closer to Black's king. He
ought to have played 34 g3, with

excellent winning chances: for
instance, 34 g3 R:f5 35 Rd:e3
R:e3 36 R:e3 a4 37 c4 Rf2+
38 Kc3 a3 39 ba R:a2 40 Kb4. In
this line, the winning idea is
not the capture of the e-pawn,
but the exchange of one pair of
rooks in order to secure maximum
activity for his other pieces.

After 34 g4 h5, White no longer has any advantage from either 35 Rd4 or 35 c4: for example, 35 Rd4 Kh6 36 Kd3 Kg5
37 c4 hg 38 hg Kh4.

37.	Rd6:f6+	Kh6-g5
38.	Rf6:f7	Kg5:g4
39.	Rf7-d7	Kg4-f3

Black's king has achieved a
stunning success, becoming the
first to break into the enemy
position.

| 40. | Kc2-d3 | ... |

Luckily, White still has this
move: if not, Black would have
won.

| 40. | ... | Re5:f5 |
| 41. | c3-c4 | a5-a4 |

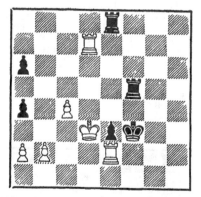

| 42. | Rd7-d6 | ... |

DRAW

— after intensive analysis.

White must move his rook back
and forth along the d-file. After 42 c5, he would lose, and
most instructively. White's king
must defend the rook on e2 and
the pawn on c4 at the same time;
the latter pawn protects the su-
premely important support point
at d5 for the rook, thus defending the king against checks on
the d-file. 42 c5 would allow
Black to double his rooks on the
fifth rank and drive off the
white king, thus: 42.. Ree5
43 c6 Rd5+ 44 Kc4 Rc5+ 45 Kd3
Rfd5+ 46 R:d5 R:d5+ 47 Kc4 Rd2,
and Black wins. There are many
other combinative possibilities
in this ending after 42 c5?,
and all of them favor Black; but
as long as the pawn stands at c4,
the king at d3, and the rook covers the d-file, White can hold
the draw.

******

61. Kotov—Bronstein
(King's Indian)

Everyone loves to attack the
king, but it is often hard to
decide on such an attack, especially when one's opponent can
counterattack on the opposite
wing. The problem is that although the goal of the kingside
attack — mate to the enemy's
king — is more enticing, it is
also far more difficult to achieve than, for example, the creation of a few pawn weaknesses
by means of a queenside attack.
An attack on the king with pieces
alone requires overwhelming numerical superiority and generally
a few sacrifices; and the pawns
cannot always join in the assault.
The present game is an example of
headlong opposite-wing counterattacking. Watch how each side per-
sistently prevents the other's
pawn breaks, c4-c5 and .. f7-f5.
Kotov is the first to achieve his
goal, and his powerful passed pawn
at full career very nearly over-
powers the massed striking force
of the entire black army.

1.	d2-d4	Ng8-f6
2.	c2-c4	g7-g6
3.	g2-g3	Bf8-g7
4.	Bf1-g2	0-0
5.	Nb1-c3	d7-d6
6.	Ng1-f3	Nb8-d7
7.	0-0	e7-e5
8.	e2-e4	Rf8-e8
9.	d4-d5	a7-a6

Usually 9.. Nc5 is played, and
then 10.. a5. For this game,
Black has selected a different
approach, which does not especially require the presence of a
knight on c5; thus there is no
need to move the pawn to a5. The

text move is played mainly to secure the square b5; in conjunction with Black's following move, it may also support a queenside pawn advance.

10.	Nf3-e1	Ra8-b8
11.	Ne1-c2	Qd8-e7
12.	b2-b4	Re8-f8
13.	Nc2-e3	Nf6-e8
14.	Qd1-c2	...

Unhackneyed play. White does not place his knight on d3, where it could have supported the break c4-c5, but on e3, where it helps the queen offer maximum resistance to Black's break .. f7-f5. The ensuing lengthy war of maneuver centers about these two strategically important advances.

14.	...	Nd7-f6
15.	a2-a4	a6-a5
16.	b4:a5	Rb8-a8
17.	Bc1-a3	Nf6-d7
18.	Bg2-h3	h7-h5
19.	Nc3-d1	Ra8:a5
20.	Nd1-b2	Ne8-f6
21.	Ba3-b4	Ra5-a6
22.	a4-a5	Nf6-h7
23.	Bh3-g2	h5-h4
24.	Nb2-d3	...

24.	...	Nd7-f6

Having set up a new defensive line on the c8-a6 diagonal (bishop, pawn and rook), Black throws all his other pieces to the kingside. He might have frozen the c-pawn with 24.. Nc5, but was loath to give up this knight, which is destined to play a lead role in the forth-

coming attack. However, .. Nc5 was the correct move, as it would have left Black with a very solid game.

25.	c4-c5	Nh7-g5
26.	Qc2-c4	Bg7-h6
27.	Bb4-d2	...

Maintaining the option of recapturing with the f-pawn after Black plays .. hg, and freeing b4 for his knight, which will force Black's rook on a6 to beat a quick retreat.

27.	...	Ra6-a8
28.	Rf1-c1	Nf6-h5
29.	c5:d6	c7:d6
30.	Qc4-c7	Qe7-f6
31.	Nd3-e1	h4:g3
32.	h2:g3	Ng5-h3+

Black is forced to rush his attack, as once the white rook gets to b·, Black's position becomes quite uncertain.

33.	Bg2:h3	Bc8:h3
34.	Ne3-g4	...

If White naively picks off the b-pawn, Black penetrates to the king by means of a knight sacrifice on g3: 34 Q:b7 N:g3 35 fg B:e3+ 36 B:e3 Qf1+ 37 Kh2, and now Black has the choice between 37.. Kg7, to clear h8 for the rook, or 37.. Rab8 38 Qc6 Rfc8. 34 Rab1 would not have eliminated the threat of .. N:g3; Kotov's move was best.

34.	...	Bh3:g4
35.	Bd2:h6	Rf8-c8
36.	Qc7:b7	...

| 36. | ... | Rc8-b8 |

Thus, White is the first to reach his goal: he has annexed the weak b-pawn. But now his bishop is trapped.

| 37. | a5-a6 | g6-g5 |

By now it was time for Black to give up thinking about winning the bishop, and concentrate on securing the a-pawn instead, which grows more dangerous with each move. 37.. R:b7 38 ab Rb8 39 Ra8 Qd8 40 Rc8! R:c8 41 R:c8 Q:c8 42 bcQ+ B:c8 would have led to a clear draw; now, however, things get much more complex.

| 38. | Qb7:b8+ | ... |

Black's previous error now allows a beautiful, though far from obvious, combination, reminiscent of a study. A quiet move, 38 Rcb1, is the prelude, with the main variation running: 38.. R:b7 39 ab Rb8 40 Ra8 Qd8 41 B:g5 f6 42 R:b8 Q:b8 43 Be3 Bc8 44 Ba7 Q:b7 45 R:b7 B:b7, and now White wins easily with 46 Bb8, attacking the black pawns from behind. Black would have to continue 38.. Re8 in order to avoid the main variation; on 39 a7, he would have had to retreat his king to h7, as in the game, but this would have left White an important tempo ahead, which he could utilize by playing 40 Qc6, attacking both rooks and threatening to capture either one.

depending upon Black's reply. This would have made matters much more pleasant for White than they turned out in the game.

38.	...	Ra8:b8
39.	a6-a7	Rb8-a8
40.	Rc1-b1	Kg8-h7

The winning move: the king avoids the eighth-rank check, and Black gets queen and minor piece for two rooks (Black could also have transposed with 40.. R:a7 41 Rb8+ Kh7).

41.	Rb1-b8	Ra8:a7
42.	Ra1:a7	Kh7:h6
43.	Rb8-b7	Kh6-g6
44.	f2-f3	Bg4-c8
45.	Rb7-c7	Qf6-d8

The simplest way for Black to win is to break through to the king with his queen. This can be accomplished in either of two ways: by a piece sacrifice, or by a flanking maneuver via d8 and b8; Black chooses the latter. A move earlier, he could also have played 44.. N:g3, but after 45 R:f7 Q:f7 46 R:f7 K:f7 47 fg N:e4 48 Nc2 Nf6 49 Ne3, a knight endgame is reached in which Black has an extra pawn, but White has some drawing chances.

46.	g3-g4	Nh5-f6
47.	Kg1-g2	Bc8-d7
48.	Ne1-c2	Bd7:g4

There's no other way but to sacrifice.

| 49. | f3:g4 | Nf6:g4 |
| 50. | Rc7:f7 | ... |

White can't keep the queen out of b6: if he fails to capture the f-pawn, the queen invades via f6.

50.	...	Qd8-b6
51.	Rf7-g7+	Kg6-h5
52.	Rg7-h7+	Ng4-h6

While the knight covers the king, the queen sets out on a fateful voyage.

| 53. | Ra7-c7 | Qb6-b3 |
| 54. | Kg2-f2 | g5-g4 |

54.. Qd3 55 Ne3 Qd2+ would have won immediately, but the game continuation should also have sufficed to win.

55. Nc2-e3   Qb3-d3

This was the next-to-last move
before the second time control.
Black would have had enough to
win with after 55.. Kg5 56 Rag7+
Kf4 57 Ng2+ K:e4 58 R:h6 g3+, or
58.. Qf3+. Unfortunately, he
gave up his knight too late.

56. Ne3-f5   Qd3-f3+
57. Kf2-g1   Qf3-d1+
58. Kg1-f2   Kh5-g5
59. Nf5:h6   Qd1-d2+

DRAW

******

62. Geller—Reshevsky
(Queen's Gambit)

1.   d2-d4   Ng8-f6
2.   c2-c4   e7-e6
3.   Ng1-f3   d7-d5
4.   Nb1-c3   c7-c5
5.   c4:d5   Nf6:d5
6.   e2-e3   Nb8-c6
7.   Bf1-d3   ...

White had a choice between
7 Bd3 and 7 Bc4. The former,
aiming at quick development and
a piece attack on the kingside,
was in vogue twenty or thirty
years ago, up until a game between Botvinnik and Alekhine, in
which White played 7 Bc4 and won
a beautiful endgame. With 7 Bc4
White emphasizes that although
the black knight on d5 can consider itself safe from pawns after the exchange on d4, it is
not safe from pieces, which
means it's not so well placed

on d5, after all.

However, the game Kotov-Leven-
fish (16th USSR Championship, Moscow 1948) showed an antidote to
7 Bc4 as well: Black immediately
retreated his knight to b6, and
stubbornly refused to play ..c5:d4,
which would have allowed White to
open the diagonal c1-h6 for his
bishop with the recapture e3:d4
(this was the mistake Kotov made
in his game with Boleslavsky).
And, since White's bishop remained on b3, he could not play
b2-b3, so that his queen's bishop
remained a constant source of
worry. At the present time, 7 Bd3
and 7 Bc4 enjoy approximately
equal reputations.

7.   ...   c5:d4
8.   e3:d4   g7-g6

Reshevsky possesses a unique
style, concrete and unprejudiced.
Undeterred by the gaping holes
he creates at f6 and h6, he closes
off the dangerous diagonal b1-h7,
and prepares pressure on the pawn
at d4. Still, not every player
could allow himself such a style,
and not every player would enjoy
it so. I shall note right here
that, despite the draw Reshevsky
obtained in this game, he appears
to have been dissatisfied with
the opening, since in the second
half, against Szabo, he exchanged
knights on c3 in this position,
and then developed his bishop to
e7. A few moves later, however,
he played ..g7-g6 again. Since
Reshevsky did not employ this
variation a third time, it would
seem that the opening of the second game was still less to his
liking.

9.   Bc1-g5   Qd8-a5

Geller would undoubtedly have
answered 9.. Be7 with 10 h4.

10. 0-0   ...

The sacrifice of a pawn after
a knight exchange on c3 is known
from many openings, especially
the Greco Attack of the Giuoco
Piano, which so delights the beginner. In the present instance,
taking the c-pawn with his queen
would soon have left Black hopelessly placed after 12 Bf6.

10. ...   Bf8-g7

| 11. | Nc3-e4 | ... |

Geller skillfully masks his true intentions: he would seem to be threatening 12 Nd6+, when in reality the knight is heading for f6. Naturally, before this point can be secured, he will have to deal with the knight on d5 and the bishop on g7.

| 11. | ... | 0-0 |
| 12. | Bd3-c4 | Qa5-b6 |

Reshevsky plows unswervingly on with his plan of attacking the isolated d-pawn (this was the other idea behind 8.. g6: to allow the bishop to develop to g7); however, no other player I know of would have allowed White his next two moves. Courage alone is insufficient for such a decision.

| 13. | Bc4:d5 | e6:d5 |
| 14. | Ne4-f6+ | Bg7:f6 |

Why didn't the king walk out of the check? Possibly because of 15 Qd2, or the more forcing 15 N:d5 Q:b2 16 Bf6; more probably because Black had already planned his 14.. B:f6 and 15.. Na5.

| 15. | Bg5:f6 | Nc6-a5 |

It is necessary to ascertain the bishop's intentions: Black cannot afford to leave it on f6. There is no time to trade off White's knight, since if 15..Bg4 16 Qd2 B:f3? 17 Qh6 wins.

| 16. | Bf6-e7 | ... |

Many would have played 16 Qd2 here, forcing Black to accept a slightly inferior ending after 16.. Q:f6 17 Q:a5; but as long as Geller can attack, he will do so. After 16 Qd2 Re8 is one of the insufficient replies, in view of 17 Be5, and if 17.. Nc4, then 18 Qh6, and now both 18.. N:e5 and 18.. f6 would be met by 19Ng5. I would have preferred 16 Bg5, intending to re-position the bishop at h6: a bishop on that square not infrequently gives rise to some surprising combinations.

| 16. | ... | Rf8-e8 |
| 17. | Be7-c5 | ... |

17 Re1, with the same idea of playing Qd1-d2-h6, would have been much more interesting: had Reshevsky then taken the pawn at b2, White would have the pretty reply 18 Bb4, and after 18..R:e1+ 19 Q:e1, Black loses the knight on a5 in view of the threatened 20 Qe8+.

17.	...	Qb6:b2
18.	Ra1-b1	Qb2-c3
19.	Rb1-c1	Qc3-b2
20.	Rc1-b1	Qb2-c3
21.	Rb1-c1	Qc3-b2

DRAW

— most unexpectedly.

White, of course, would have risked nothing by continuing his fight for the initiative. His pawn minus would have been virtually meaningless, in view of Black's insecure king.

White had several tempting continuations at his disposal: for instance, I like playing the knight to e5 when the black queen is on c3. Also good is the simple 19 Bb4 Qc7 20 B:a5! Q:a5 21 Qc1, with fierce pressure. If he wanted to force a draw, White could always have done so later. At any rate, Black should had to work a little for it.

******
63. Smyslov—Keres
(Queen's Gambit)

1.	d2-d4	d7-d5
2.	c2-c4	d5:c4
3.	Ng1-f3	Ng8-f6

4.	e2-e3	e7-e6
5.	Bf1:c4	c7-c5
6.	0-0	a7-a6
7.	Qd1-e2	b7-b5
8.	Bc4-b3	Bc8-b7
9.	Rf1-d1	Nb8-d7
10.	Nb1-c3	...

A theoretical position which occurs often in tournament play; for example, Smyslov-Keres, Budapest 1950. Having put off castling for so long, Black ought to exercise his patience a little longer in order to remove his queen from its dangerous opposition to the white rook, to c7 or b6. With 10.. Be7 and 11.. b4, Black enters a line which theory rightly considers inferior for Black. On more than one occasion, Keres has overthrown accepted opinion, infusing new ideas into old variations: as examples, take his games with Boleslavsky and Stahlberg from this tournament. Here, however, he plays a variation of low repute without having any improvement prepared, and his heedlessness lands him in immediate difficulties.*

10.	...	Bf8-e7
11.	e3-e4	b5-b4
12.	e4-e5	...

Of course! The knight has nowhere to go, so Black must enter a line which leads by force to the creation of a powerful white passed pawn.

12.	...	b4:c3
13.	e5:f6	Be7:f6
14.	d4-d5	...

(See diagram, next column)

14.	...	e6-e5
15.	b2:c3	0-0
16.	Nf3-d2	...

Beginning with this move, Smyslov carries out one idea with iron determination and logic: the minor pieces must clear a path for the passed pawn. The knight and the pair of bishops do not defend the pawn; instead, they attack the squares directly in front of it. Seen in this light,

---

*In 1959, Smyslov tried out a new idea — 10..Bd6! — against Petrosian, winning brilliantly.

(Position after 14 d5)

the idea behind the move 16 Nd2 becomes clear: White intends to post this knight on e4 or c4, attacking the square d6.

As the further course of the game shows, it was here that Keres realized the enormity of his error; for the remainder of the game, he displayed amazing resourcefulness, doing literally everything possible to prevent White from capitalizing on his passed pawn.

16.	...	Bf6-e7
17.	Nd2-c4	a6-a5
18.	Nc4:e5	Nd7:e5
19.	Qe2:e5	Be7-f6
20.	Qe5-g3	c5-c4
21.	Bb3-a4	Qd8-e7

Black's pawn sacrifice would appear to have achieved something: White now finds it difficult to complete the development of his queenside, since any move of the queen's bishop (except to b2 or g5, naturally) allows 22..Qa3, winning back the c-pawn.

22. Bc1-f4   ...

Anyway! This is a typical Smyslov move, combining the logical completion of his idea with accurate calculation of its tactical consequences. White disregards his c-pawn in order to secure the forced march of his d-pawn. We should like to draw the reader's attention to the placement of White's bishops, laying down a crossfire in front of the pawn.

On 22..Qa3, White achieves a decisive advantage in the following manner: 23 Bc6 B:c6 24 dc Q:c3 25 Q:c3 B:c3 26 Rac1 and 27 R:c4.

22.   ...   Rf8-d8
23.   d5-d6   Qe7-e4

24.   Rd1-e1   Qe4-f5
25.   d6-d7   h7-h5
26.   Re1-e8+   ...

Now the rook also attacks a square in front of the pawn.

26.   ...   Kg8-h7
27.   h2-h4   Ra8-a6
28.   Bf4-g5   Rd8:d7

The battle is lost. Black can no longer withstand the pressure of White's pieces pushing the pawn forward to queen, and gives up the exchange. The rest is a matter of simple technique.

29. B:d7 Q:d7 30. Rae1 Rd6
31. B:f6 R:f6 32. Qb8 Rf5
33. Rh8+ Kg6 34. Rd8 Qb5 35. Rd6+
Kh7 36. Rd8 Qc5 37. Re3 Bd5
38. Rh8+ Kg6 39. Qd8 Bf3 40. R:f3
R:f3 41. gf

BLACK RESIGNED

******

******

[103]

ROUND TEN

64. Reshevsky—Smyslov
(Nimzoindian Defense)

1. d4 Nf6 2. c4 e6 3. Nc3 Bb4
4. e3 c5 5. Bd3 0-0 6. Nf3 b6
7. 0-0 Bb7 8. Bd2 cd 9. ed d5
10. cd B:c3

An original decision. Smyslov
brings his queen into play, creating long-diagonal pressure
which curtails his opponent's
activity somewhat. After 10..N:d5
there would be no sense for White
in winning a pawn with 11 N:d5
B:d2 12 N:b6, since Black's position would be not one bit inferior after 12.. Q:b6 13 Q:d2
B:f3 14 gf Nc6 15 Be4 Rfd8
16 B:c6 Q:c6. However, White
could continue 11 Qe2, followed
by 12 Qe4, when Black would have
nothing better than to return
his knight to f6.

11. bc Q:d5 12. Re1 Nbd7 13. Qe2
Qh5 14. a4 a6 15. Reb1 Rfd8
16. Be3

Allowing Black to exchange bishops, which vaporizes White's
initiative. However, 16 c4 also
leads nowhere, in view of
16.. B:f3 17 Q:f3 Q:f3 18 gf
Ne5. White might have played
15 c4, though; at least, he
would have kept his two bishops.

16... Be4 17. Bf4 Qf5 18. B:e4
N:e4 19. Bd2

DRAW

More was expected from this
game, but the tournament leaders contented themselves with
extended reconnaissance, postponing their major clash until
the second half.

*****

65. Bronstein—Geller
(Sicilian Defense)

1.	e2-e4	c7-c5
2.	Ng1-f3	Nb8-c6
3.	d2-d4	c5:d4
4.	Nf3:d4	Ng8-f6
5.	Nb1-c3	d7-d6
6.	Bc1-g5	e7-e6
7.	g2-g3	...

A new idea, and not a very
good one, either. Keres often
uses the deployment Qd3, Be2,
Rd1, 0-0, and later even a vol-

untary Bg5-c1. This game works
out rather like that, but with
White having spent an extra tempo (g2-g3) on his king's bishop's
development. Note how smoothly
Black's development proceeds
now. One cannot afford to ignore
the time element even in the qui-
etest opening — how much more
so in the Sicilian!

7.	...	Bf8-e7
8.	Bf1-g2	0-0
9.	0-0	Nc6:d4
10.	Qd1:d4	h7-h6
11.	Bg5-d2	Bc8-d7
12.	Ra1-d1	Qd8-c7
13.	Qd4-d3	Ra8-c8
14.	g3-g4	...

What is wrong with White's
position? His c-pawn is dead;
his queen's knight is just
waiting passively for the stroke
of a pawn from b4; having a 3/2
queenside pawn majority, White
cannot make use of it, and is
reduced to playing with his kingside pawns (which explains why
systems involving long castling
are so popular against the Sicilian: the pawns go precisely
where they are needed). Passive
play would soon involve White in
difficulties, so he sacrifices a
pawn for the sake of the initiative: for example, 14.. N:g4
15 Qg3 h5 16 Kh1, when the center of gravity has shifted to
the kingside. This variation
was easy to accept; however, I
also had to be ready for the
sharp counterattack Black actually undertook on the queenside.

14.	...	b7-b5

Compare this with a similar
move of Geller's, made in his
game with Boleslavsky; then, as
now, Black had no time for the
preliminary 14.. a6.

15.	a2-a3	a7-a5
16.	g4-g5	h6:g5
17.	Bd2:g5	b5-b4
18.	a3:b4	a5:b4
19.	e4-e5	d6:e5
20.	Bg5:f6	Be7:f6

Had Black taken with the pawn,
White would have given perpetual
check immediately. Here and later,
White plays doggedly to open up
Black's king.

21.	Nc3-e4	Rf8-d8

22.   Ne4:f6+   g7:f6

White has achieved his goal, in part: now he induces 23.. f5, to give himself queen checks along the diagonal h4-d8 (otherwise, the black king could hide on e7).

23.   Qd3-f3   f6-f5

On 23.. Kg7, White would have the choice between 24 Re1 and 24 Rd3, not to mention the simple 24 Qg4+ and 25 Q:b4.

24.   Qf3-g3+   Kg8-f8
25.   Qg3-g5   ...

Here Black accepted the

DRAW

White had offered with his 23Qf3. The continuation might have been 25.. Be8 26 Qh6+ Ke7 27 Qh4+ f6 28 Q:b4+ Qc5 29 Q:c5+ R:c5 30 R:d8 K:d8, and now 31 Rc1 gives rise to the following curious position:

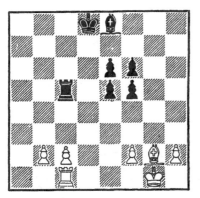

— which each side evaluated in favor of the other. It would be difficult to say with certainty which was right. But Geller thought that 25.. Bb5, and not 25.. Be8, was necessary; then a perpetual check would indeed have ensued.

******

66. Gligoric—Kotov
(Sicilian Defense)

1.   e2-e4   c7-c5
2.   Ng1-f3   d7-d6

3.   d2-d4   c5:d4
4.   Nf3:d4   Ng8-f6
5.   Nb1-c3   a7-a6
6.   g2-g3   e7-e5
7.   Nd4-e2   Bc8-e6
8.   Bf1-g2   b7-b5

With the white king's bishop fianchettoed and the black e-pawn advanced to e5 in this variation, the moves 5.. a6 and 8.. b5 are not intended as part of a queenside attack (since there's nothing there to attack), but rather to gain space for the black pieces: .. Bb7 and ..Nb8-d7-b6. From this point of view, the bishop's deployment at e6 makes little sense. The bishop later takes off for g4, and then h5, as if reproaching Kotov for making it idle aimlessly about the board, instead of taking up its station immediately on the long diagonal.

The ..b7-b5-b4 push makes sense only when Black has a pawn at e6 and White's knight is left without a good retreat. But here, .. b5-b4 will send the knight to the excellent square d5, where Black will be practically forced to trade it off, extending the diagonal of the fianchettoed white king's bishop. These are all the drawbacks of developing the bishop at e6.

9.   0-0   Nb8-d7
10.   a2-a4   b5-b4
11.   Nc3-d5   Nf6:d5
12.   e4:d5   Be6-g4
13.   Bc1-d2   ...

One general rule of chess strategy holds that a target point should be surrounded or isolated before it is attacked. 13 a5 would have been good here, but Gligoric is strongly opposed to pushing pawns; he will decide to play a4-a5 only several rounds later, in Game 120 against Najdorf.

13.   ...   a6-a5
14.   c2-c3   b4:c3
15.   Bd2:c3   Qd8-b6

White has an extra queenside pawn, but making a passed pawn with it would appear to be the last thing on his mind; he wants to do only what is necessary on the queenside in order to free himself to proceed with his at-

tack on the kingside. This was
the aim of the operation: 13 Bd2,
14 c3, and 15 B:c3. Black must
play very alertly in this situation — which he does, in
fact, postponing castling until
move 20 in order to blunt his
opponent's initiative.

16.   h2-h3   Bg4-h5

The further course of the game
will give rise to the natural
question: shouldn't he have taken the knight immediately? Probably not. After 16.. B:e2 17 Q:e2
Be7, White, with the two bishops
already in hand, would have had
no reason to undertake any sort
of kingside operation. It would
be a good idea then to remember
his a-pawn and prepare b2-b4 to
make it a passed one.

17.   Kg1-h2   Bf8-e7

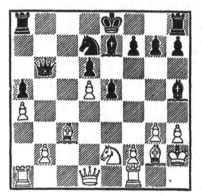

White has secured a definite
advantage, and has made all of
his preparatory moves; now the
time has come to solve the main
problem of which road to choose
in order to get to the win.

Sometimes it's enough merely
to play the so-called "reasonable" and "natural" moves: occupy the open files with your
rooks, move them to the seventh
rank, pile up on a backward pawn,
create a protected passed pawn
and queen it... Many a game has
been won just that automatically:
"By means of simple/logical/ob-
vious moves, White converts his
advantage into a win"; "White's

attack plays itself" — we have
all read such formulas more than
once. However, today's high level
of defensive technique makes it
difficult to believe that a game
will, like a good horse, bring
its player to the desired end by
itself. When one plays an experienced master, who knows all of
the defensive tricks, sometimes
the road to victory is a narrow
path of precise moves.

Gligoric should have converted
his accumulated advantages into
a direct attack, beginning with
18 g4, kicking back the unfortunate bishop before anything else;
after 18.. Bg6 19 f4 would have
been considerably stronger. The
threat of 20 f5 would have forced
19.. f6; then there would follow
20 f5 Bf7 21 Ng3, intending 22 Qf3
and 23 h4, etc. This would lead
to a sharp game, admittedly with
some risk to White, whose king
would not be left all that well
protected; but certainly he would
also have been left with most of
the chances. The halfhearted plan
White actually selects sends his
game down a blind alley.

18.   f2-f4   Bh5:e2

At last, this bishop goes from
words to action, removing the last
of White's knights.

19.   Qd1:e2   Be7-f6
20.   Qe2-c4   ...

After 18 f4, the plan of creating a passed a-pawn lost much
of its punch, since the ever-
present threat of ..ef prevents
White from devoting sufficient
attention to the queen's wing.
Here a combinative player would
certainly have permitted himself
20 g4, threatening 21 g5, 22 Qg4,
and 23 f5; if then 20.. h6 21 h4
is quite possible, and the threat
to advance the g-pawn once again
forces Black's king to remain in
the center. Taking the h-pawn
would not be without risk for
Black either, in view of 22 fe,
opening up the center; in that
event, even Black's best move,
22.. 0-0, would leave him with a
difficult position. White wants
to improve the placement of his
pieces a bit before embarking
upon the pawn storm; but Kotov,
as usual, defends superbly.

| 20. | ... | 0-0 |
| 21. | Qc4-c6 | Rf8-d8 |

White wanted to make a second use of the same technique for extending his bishop's scope. For the present, this bishop is shut in behind the pawn; the exchange of queens would give both bishop and pawn a brilliant future. Kotov, naturally, does not take the queen.

| 22. | Ra1-e1 | ... |

A trap: if 22.. ef 23 B:f6, ignoring the in-between check 23.. fg+ 24 Kh1 gf 25 Re7, when the threats of 26 R:d7 and 26 Q:d6 are hard to meet.

| 22. | ... | Qb6-b8 |

Reculer pour mieux avancer. A few "natural" moves, and already what was Gligoric's initiative is passing to Black. White has carved some holes in his own pawn formation, and as soon as Black gets the chance to play .. ef, forcing the trade of the dark-square bishops, all White's weaknesses will be laid bare.

23.	Re1-b1	Ra8-a7
24.	Qc6-c4	Rd8-c8
25.	Qc4-e4	Qb8-b3

The rebound. Black threatens to win a pawn by 26.. Rc4, as well as by capturing first on f4 and then on c3. If White meets 26.. ef by taking the bishop on f6, then Black would be perfectly justified in giving check on g3 before recapturing on f6 with the knight.

26.	f4:e5	Bf6:e5
27.	Qe4-f5	Rc8-f8
28.	Qf5-f2	...

White's entire advantage has evaporated with these one-movers.

| 28. | ... | Ra7-a8 |
| 29. | Qf2-f5 | Qb3:a4 |

Had the pawn been at a5, it would not have fallen so easily.

| 30. | Rf1-f4 | ... |

Black's position is as solid as a cliffwall. In desperation, White sacrifices the exchange, in hopes that his opponent will grow careless, or commit some oversight in the complications to follow — although these pose much more of a threat to White than to Black.

| 30. | ... | Be5:f4 |
| 31. | g3:f4 | g7-g6 |

Courage based on careful calculation.

32.	Qf5-g5	Ra8-e8
33.	Rb1-g1	Re8-e2
34.	Kh2-h1	Qa4-c2
35.	Qg5-g4	Nd7-c5

The knight enters the fray decisively.

36.	Qg4-h4	Nc5-e4
37.	Bc3-d4	Ne4-f2+
38.	Kh1-h2	Nf2-e4

Time pressure.

39.	f4-f5	Qc2-d3
40.	f5:g6	f7:g6
41.	Bd4-b6	...

After adjourning the game,

WHITE RESIGNED

without continuing. Among other things, Black threatened 41..Nd2 and 42.. Nf3+ .

*****

67. Taimanov—Boleslavsky
(King's Indian)

| 1. | d2-d4 | Ng8-f6 |
| 2. | c2-c4 | d7-d6 |

3.	Ng1-f3	g7-g6
4.	Nb1-c3	Bf8-g7
5.	e2-e4	e7-e5
6.	Bf1-e2	0-0
7.	0-0	Nb8-c6
8.	Bc1-e3	Nf6-g4

Boleslavsky repeats the line
Najdorf so successfully employed
against Taimanov (cf. Game 28,
Round Four), but on this occasion
Taimanov eschews 8 d5, attempting instead to gain the upper
hand by means of 8 Be3. However,
this move is so inoffensive as
to place White in the defender's
position. Further investigation
of this system has shown that
by playing 8.. Re8, Black can
practically force a whole series
of exchanges, thereby solving
his defensive problem (cf. Game
107, Reshevsky - Najdorf). When
this game was played, that improvement had not yet been discovered. After 8.. Ng4 9 Bg5,
Black could play 9.. Bf6, offering to trade off the darksquare bishops; after the move
he actually plays, White carries out a plan which secures
him control of d5 and a definite advantage. So Black's
8.. Ng4 maneuver must be considered not wholly satisfactory,
inasmuch as he intends to continue with 9.. f6; the same
8.. Ng4 would be much better if
Black played it in conjunction
with 9.. Bf6.

9.	Be3-g5	f7-f6
10.	Bg5-c1	e5:d4

Sometimes, in positions like
this, 10.. f5 is not too bad.
Boleslavsky selected the text,
however, and it is hard to say
whether he thought 10.. ed a
better move or simply wished to
obtain some variety

11.	Nf3:d4	Nc6:d4
12.	Qd1:d4	f6-f5
13.	Qd4-d5+	...

(See diagram, next column)

13.	...	Kg8-h8
14.	Be2:g4	f5:g4

Now White has removed one of
Black's pawns from the center,
at the cost of ceding Black the
bishop-pair. White plans to
strengthen his position in approximately the following fash-

ion: Bc1-e3-d4, trading bishops,
Nd5, and the rooks to d1 and c1
or else to d1 and e1. If he is
allowed to carry out all this,
sooner or later Black will be
forced to advance the c-pawn,
after which White can successfully assail the d-pawn.

Black's counterplay is based,
first and foremost, on his bishop-pair, which enable one sometimes to hold a draw even in a
pawn-down endgame; and secondly,
on the shaky status of the e-
pawn, since its defender will
have to reckon with the pawn on
g4.

Let us watch now as the two
plans collide, and what comes
of it.

15.	Bc1-e3	Qd8-f6
16.	Ra1-c1	...

White's plan requires 16 Rfd1,
in order to threaten 17 Bd4, and
so as to be able to meet 16..Be6
17 Q:b7 B:c4 with 18 Q:c7. Black
would probably have replied
16.. Qf7, when 17 Bd4 Q:d5 18 N:d5
would have led to something re-
sembling the desired position for
White which we were discussing.

18 cd was also possible, with
strong pressure on the c-file.

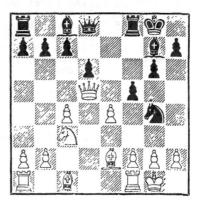

(Position after 13 Qd5+)

16.	...	Qf6-f7
17.	b2-b3	Qf7:d5
18.	Nc3:d5	Rf8-f7
19.	f2-f3	...

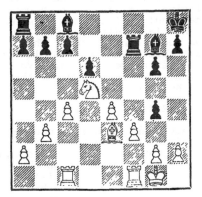

A pretty tactical stroke: on
19.. gf 20 R:f3 R:f3 21 gf c6
22 Nc7 Rb8 23 B:a7 snares the
rook; the same idea also works
in the variation 19.. a6 20 fg
R:f1+ 21 R:f1 c6 22 Nc7, etc.
And if 21.. B:g4 22 N:c7 Rc8,
Black is already a pawn down,
and still saddled with the
weakness at d6.

Black therefore hastens to
drive the knight out of d5 while
his rook is still protecting the
c7 square, White's dream of net-
ting the black queen's rook vanishes like smoke, and the move
19 f3 turns out to be useless.

It's almost sinful to criticize
a move that leads practically by
force to the win of a good pawn,
but it would appear that here,
too, White might well have held
to the positional course with
19 Rfd1, trading bishops on d4
and maintaining a powerful bind.

19.	...	c7-c6
20.	Nd5-f4	g4:f3
21.	g2:f3	Bc8-d7
22.	Rc1-d1	Bg7-e5
23.	Nf4-g2	Ra8-e8

Boleslavsky decides to give up
the a-pawn in order to secure the
trade of his weak d-pawn for
White's center pawn. With Black's
bishop-pair, this accomplishment
practically guarantees him the
draw.

24. f4 Bc3 25. R:d6 R:e4 26. B:a7
Bg4 27. Rd3 Bf6 28. Re3 R:e3
29. N:e3 Bh3 30. Rd1 Be7 31. Ng2

Kg8 32. Be3 Rf8 33. Ne1 Bg4

White's game is not one bit
superior, despite his pawn plus.
After the attack on his rook,
White ought to have accepted the
repetition with Rd1-d3-d1; leaving the d-file puts him into a
cramped position.

34. Rc1 Rd8 35. c5 Bf6 36. Kg2
Re8 37. Bf2 Bf5 38. Kf3 h5 39. h4
Bg4+ 40. Kg3 Bf5 41. Nf3 Re2

DRAW

******

68. Najdorf—Stahlberg
(Queen's Gambit)

1.	d2-d4	Ng8-f6
2.	c2-c4	e7-e6
3.	Nb1-c3	d7-d5
4.	Bc1-g5	Bf8-e7
5.	e2-e3	Nb8-d7
6.	Ng1-f3	0-0
7.	Ra1-c1	c7-c6
8.	Bf1-d3	d5:c4
9.	Bd3:c4	Nf6-d5
10.	Bg5:e7	Qd8:e7

The opening is chiefly of interest for its history. It saw a
lot of use in the Alekhine - Capablanca World Championship match,
where most of the games were drawn
after some positional sparring;
in any event, Black was unable to
win even one. Such biteless defenses are out of fashion nowadays. White's next move was an
Alekhine invention, to which Capablanca's usual reply was
11.. N5f6. Stahlberg plays an
immediate 11.. e5, which fails
to ease Black's defense, but does
allow White to avoid the exchange
of queens he would have to permit
with 11.. N5f6 12 Ng3 Qb4+.

11.	Nc3-e4	e6-e5
12.	0-0	...

Naturally White is not tempted
by the win of a pawn: 12 de N:e5
13 B:d5 N:f3+ 14 gf cd 15 Q:d5,
since Black would then be able
to develop almost all of his remaining pieces with tempo on the
white queen. Nor would 12 B:d5 cd
13 Nc3 amount to anything, in
view of 13.. e4, with a good game
for Black (14 N:d5? Qd6).

12.	...	e5:d4
13.	Qd1:d4	Nd7-b6
14.	Bc4-b3	Bc8-g4

15. Ne4-g3   Bg4:f3

Here and later, Stahlberg holds
to his usual tactic (especially
when playing Black) of wholesale
exchanges, figuring that this will
secure him a draw sooner or later;
if any sort of concrete threat a-
rises, he trusts his experience
and tactical abilities to show
him a way out. However, if Stahlberg intended to trade queens, he
ought to have left himself the
bishop, since the white bishop
will be superior to the black
knight in any minor-piece ending—
though not sufficiently better to
forge a win from that factor alone, of course. Since the black
bishop will disappear in another
half-move, however, this was not
the time to trade queens. 16..Rad8
17 Rfd1 Rfe8 was natural: nothing
really threatens Black, and it is
quite likely that White would then
have tried for the trade of queens
himself by, for example, 18 Nf5
Qg5+ 19 Qg4, when Black could play
19.. Q:g4+, thereby returning the
g-pawn to its original file.

16.   g2:f3   Qe7-f6
17.   Qd4:f6   Nd5:f6
18.   Ng3-f5   Ra8-d8
19.   Rf1-d1   Nb6-c8

He should have returned the
knight to d5; after 20 e4 he
could occupy f4.

20.   Kg1-f1   Rf8-e8
21.   Kf1-e2   Kg8-f8
22.   Rd1:d8   Re8:d8
23.   Rc1-g1   Nf6-e8

A curious picture. Black has
absolutely no intention of ever
playing .. g7-g6, even though
that would relieve him of many
of his later difficulties. In
the succeeding phase of the
game, Black saddles himself with
a number of weaknesses, advancing nearly every pawn but the
one he should have.

24.   Rg1-g4   ...

White has gradually accumulated an uncommon store of positional capital: his king is centralized, his rook is on the
fourth rank, where it will attack Black's pawns, the bishop
controls important squares, and
the knight is actively placed
too. As before, Stahlberg re-
lies on the inner defensive
strength of his position, and
on his ability to repel any danger by tactical means, while
Najdorf breaks down the black
position with a steady alterna-
tion of lefts and rights.

24.   ...   Nc8-e7

Nor should this exchange of
knights be counted an achievement for Black: his one remaining knight cannot hope to pose
White any serious threats, while
two knights working together
might at least have driven the
white bishop from b3, thereby
easing the pressure on d5, which
grows more and more acute with
every exchange. So here too,
24.. g6 ought to have been
played.

25.   Nf5:e7   Kf8:e7
26.   Rg4-e4+   Ke7-f8
27.   Re4-a4   a7-a6
28.   Ra4-f4   f7-f6

It's amazing, how nearly right
Stahlberg's rather careless method of play is. This is apparent from the fact that, despite
a string of inaccurate, and some
just plain bad, moves, Black's
game, positionally speaking, was
still not completely lost. True,
his choices were already limited: neither 28.. Rd7 nor
28.. Nd6 was any good, but after 28.. Nf6 he could still have
held things together. White
would have continued in the same
fashion, improving his position
with e4, f4-f5, then f4 a sec-

ond time, then a4, and then b4 after the bishop retreats, gradually securing more and more space. (An important peculiarity of this position is that after f4-f5 the square e5 is not weakened, thanks to the presence of a second f-pawn, which prevents Black from establishing his knight on e5.) But this plan would still have met a lot of resistance from his opponent; now, however, 28.. f6?, this terrible and completely unnecessary weakening of the e6 square, soon followed by a second, 29.. h6 (which weakens g6), considerably eases White's task.

| 29. | Rf4-h4 | h7-h6 |
| 30. | Rh4-h5 | ... |

An excellent move! Having done its work on the fourth rank, the rook now goes to the fifth, where it restricts Black's pawns to complete passivity. White begins to occupy more space by advancing pawns and bringing up his king.

30.	...	Ne8-c7
31.	f3-f4	Kf8-e7
32.	Rh5-c5	Rd8-d6
33.	Rc5-c1	...

33 f5 suggests itself.

| 33. | ... | b7-b6 |

After White's last inaccuracy, he had to play 33.. f5! 34 h4 h5 35 Rg1 Kf6.

| 34. | f4-f5 | c6-c5 |
| 35. | f2-f4 | Rd6-c6 |

Seeing now that he stands on the very brink of disaster, Black wants to drive off the bishop to give his knight a bit of air, but his decision comes too late.

| 36. | a2-a4 | b6-b5 |
| 37. | Bb3-c2 | ... |

Why wait until you're chased? Now he threatens 38 Be4, and the variations 37.. c4 38 Be4 Rb6 39 b3!, and 38.. Rc5 39 b4 favor White.

37.	...	Nc7-e8
38.	Bc2-e4	Rc6-c7
39.	Be4-d5	...

Now the e-pawn's road is clear.

39.	...	c5-c4
40.	e3-e4	Ne8-d6
41.	a4:b5	a6:b5
42.	Ke2-e3	Rc7-a7
43.	Rc1-g1	Ke7-f8
44.	Ke3-d4	Ra7-c7
45.	Rg1-c1	...

Najdorf is cautious: 45.. b4 and 46.. c3 was the threat. For example, 45 Ra1 b4 46 Ra8+ Ke7 47 Rg8 c3 48 R:g7+ Kd8 49 R:c7 cb 50 Ba2 K:c7.

45.	...	Nd6-b7
46.	Rc1-a1	Nb7-c5
47.	Ra1-a8+	Kf8-e7
48.	e4-e5!	...

A nicely calculated, conclusive combination.

| 48. | ... | Nc5-b3+ |
| 49. | Kd4-c3 | Nb3-c1 |

If 49.. Rc5, then 50 Ra7+ Kf8 51 Rf7+ Ke8 52 Be6 fe 53 R:g7 Nd4 54 Kb4 N:e6 55 fe, with an easily won rook ending.

Black enters the other branch of the combination.

50.	Ra8-g8	Nc1-e2+
51.	Kc3-d2	Ne2:f4
52.	Rg8:g7+	Ke7-d8
53.	e5:f6!	Rc7-d7
54.	Rg7:d7+	Kd8:d7

55. Bd5-c6+!

BLACK RESIGNED — a beautiful game from Najdorf.

69. Petrosian—Euwe
(Reti Opening)

1.	Ng1-f3	Ng8-f6
2.	g2-g3	d7-d5
3.	Bf1-g2	Bc8-f5
4.	d2-d3	e7-e6
5.	Nb1-d2	h7-h6

A loss of time. In such positions, it is better to focus one's attention on piece development, leaving the bishop to fend for itself. If White presses to exchange it off on g6, I believe this can only improve Black's position.

6.	0-0	Bf8-c5
7.	Qd1-e1!	...

A fine move, which trains the queen's fire on both black bishops: now e2-e4 and b2-b4 are both threats. White's system of development is certainly not as harmless as it might seem to be (cf. the second-half game Smyslov - Euwe).

7.	...	0-0
8.	e2-e4	d5:e4
9.	Nd2:e4	Nf6:e4

Black's last two moves seem inconsistent to me. By his 10th move, Black ought to have come up with some sort of plan. The first question to be decided is whether he is going to retain his queen's bishop or trade it off. If it is to be traded, then the bishop, not the knight, ought to have taken on e4: it will now be a long time before this bishop can capture anything more substantial than a pawn. And if it is not to be traded (which, to judge from Black's fifth move, is indeed his intention), then he ought to have retreated it to h7 on the previous move, keeping the pawn tension in the center and restricting the mobility of White's d- and e-pawns — and even of his c-pawn — somewhat. But if, after 9 N:e4, the dark-square bishop were to retreat to e7, then after 10 Nh4! Black would still be forced to part with one of his bishops, since 10.. Bh7 would be impossible in view of 11 N:f6+ and 12 B:b7.

10.	d3:e4	Bf5-h7
11.	b2-b4	Bc5-e7
12.	Bc1-b2	Nb8-a6

Black's heedlessness has brought him into difficulties, although they are not yet insuperable. He needs to develop his queen's knight and to find a good spot for the queen; a task best performed by .. c6, .. Qc7 and ..Nd7. Bringing the knight to c7 looks artificial, and it is difficult even to guess what benefit Dr. Euwe thought he would derive therefrom.

13.	a2-a3	c7-c6
14.	Ra1-d1	Qd8-c8
15.	c2-c4	Na6-c7
16.	Qe1-c3	...

Now White has a clear advantage. All six of Black's pieces stand passively, and routine exchanges on the d-file will not ease his situation, since the fewer pieces remain on the board, the more forcefully will the entombed h7-bishop's absence from the fray be felt. The choice of the plan for the capitalization of White's advantage is a matter for individual taste; already, more than one way is possible. One good idea is 16 c5, followed by bringing the knight via c4 to d6.

16.	...	Be7-f6
17.	Nf3-e5	Rf8-d8
18.	Bg2-f3	...

White waits. 18 Qc1, followed by c4-c5, was more active. Why take over an open file, if one is not going to use it to penetrate the enemy position? While the d-file is under White's control, it ought to be used to get the white knight to d6.

18.	...	Nc7-e8
19.	Rd1:d8	Qc8:d8
20.	Rf1-d1	Qd8-c7
21.	c4-c5	a7-a5

Black opens the a-file, and abandons it forthwith: 23.. Rd8. If that was what he intended, then the a-pawn would have been better left on a7, keeping the possibility of playing .. b7-b6.

22.	Bf3-g2	a5:b4
23.	a3:b4	Ra8-d8
24.	Rd1:d8	Qc7:d8
25.	Qc3-c2	Ne8-c7
26.	Bg2-f1	Nc7-b5
27.	f2-f4	...

White has not maneuvered very
energetically, and Black has succeeded in improving the placement of his pieces — without,
however, solving his biggest
headache: the bishop is as much
out of the picture as ever. This
makes White careless; he has
completely forgotten to look after his e-pawn, and here was
Black's chance to punish him.
Euwe could practically have
equalized by 27.. Qa8, threatening to invade via a2. So the
restrained 26 f3!, instead of
26 Bf1 and 27 f4, was the move
to keep the h7-bishop's horizons
limited.

One way to free the bishop
from its kingside incarcera-
tion would be .. f7-f6 and
.. e6-e5, allowing the bishop
to exit via g8. It is this plan
which Black intends to carry
out now, in fact, and White
must play actively in order to
keep the upper hand. The immediate threat was 27.. Nd4, hitting the queen at c2 and cutting off the queen's bishop from
the knight on e5 — this explains White's last move. Now
Black could have brought about
a trade of queens with 27..Nd4
28 Qd1 Nb5, as the white queen
cannot simultaneously guard the
e-pawn and escape from the
knight. White would therefore
have continued 29 Q:d8+ B:d8,
keeping somewhat the better
ending: 30 Bd3 Kf8 31 Kf2 f6
32 Nc4 Ke7 33 Ke3, and not
only does Black get no chance
to push his e-pawn, he must
now worry about whether White
will push his. So Black chooses
to fight with queens.

27.	...	Kg8-f8
28.	Kg1-f2	Bf6:e5
29.	Bb2:e5	f7-f6
30.	Be5-b2	Kf8-e7
31.	Bf1-c4	Bh7-g6
32.	Kf2-e3	Bg6-f7
33.	g3-g4	Qd8-c7
34.	e4-e5	Qc7-d8
35.	e5:f6+	...

Petrosian continues his assault on f7. The hasty 35 f5
(35.. ef? 36 ef+ gf 37 Q:f5)
would have been a distraction:
35.. fe 36 fe Nd4, and 37 Qh7
N:e6 38 B:e6 seems to be winning, but Black has the surprise reply 38.. Qd1 (very

unpleasant in time pressure),
threatening a perpetual check
(39 B:f7 Qe1+, and 40 Kd3 is
out in view of 40.. Qb1+!).

35.	...	g7:f6
36.	h2-h4	Nb5-c7
37.	Qc2-c3	Nc7-d5+

37.. Qh8 holds out no hope at
all: White could penetrate either
via d6 or through the queenside;
or else he could win the f-pawn
by 38 g5.

38.	Bc4:d5	Qd8:d5
39.	Qc3:f6+	Ke7-e8
40.	Qf6-h8+	Ke8-d7
41.	Qh8-g7	...

The adjourned position. The
winning idea is based on some
beautiful echo-variations where
one bishop defends against the
perpetual check.

41.	...	Kd7-e8
42.	Bb2-f6	Qd5-b3+
43.	Bf6-c3	Qb3-d1
44.	Qg7-h8+	Ke8-d7
45.	Qh8-b8	Qd1-c1+
46.	Bc3-d2	Qc1-g1+
47.	Ke3-d3	Qg1-f1+
48.	Kd3-c2	Qf1-a6

On 48.. Qc4+, the king escapes the checks by 49 Kb2 Qd4+
50 Bc3 Qf2+ 51 Ka3. But now
White has won a tempo for the important 49 h5, fixing the h-
pawn on a dark square. The queen
begins a new series of checks
from the other side, but here
too, the bishop shelters the
king.

49.	h4-h5	Qa6-a2+
50.	Kc2-d3	Qa2-b1+
51.	Kd3-e2	Qb1-e4+
52.	Ke2-f2	Qe4-d4+
53.	Bd2-e3	Qd4:b4
54.	Qb8-f8	...

By forking bishop and pawn, White forces Black's queen to return to f6, after which he carries out the decisive maneuver: exchanging queens and winning the h-pawn.

54.	...	Qb4-b2+
55.	Kf2-g3	Qb2-f6
56.	Qf8-d6+	Kd7-c8
57.	Be3-d4	Qf6-d8
58.	Qd6:d8+	Kc8:d8
59.	Bd4-g7	Kd8-c7
60.	Bg7:h6	b7-b6
61.	c5:b6+	Kc7:b6
62.	Kg3-h4	...

BLACK RESIGNED

******

70. Averbakh—Szabo
(Ruy Lopez)

From the fifth move until its conclusion, this game is a theoretical duel between two excellently prepared and expert advocates of the Open Defense to the Ruy Lopez.

1.	e2-e4	e7-e5
2.	Ng1-f3	Nb8-c6
3.	Bf1-b5	a7-a6
4.	Bb5-a4	Ng8-f6
5.	0-0	Nf6:e4
6.	d2-d4	b7-b5
7.	Ba4-b3	d7-d5
8.	d4:e5	Bc8-e6
9.	c2-c3	Bf8-c5

This is stronger, in my opinion, than 9.. Be7, as Szabo played against Gligoric. Indeed, there can't be very many opening variations in which Black succeeds in developing all of his minor pieces so quickly, to such active positions!

From here on, the knight on e4 draws battle like a magnet. It appears firmly entrenched at present; if it should chance to be driven away, however, Black's entire game will totter.

10.	Nb1-d2	...

After 10 Qd3 Ne7 11 Be3 Bf5!, or simply 10.. 0-0 11 Be3 f5, Black also stands well.

10.	...	0-0
11.	Bb3-c2	f7-f5

An interesting variation, in which the knight is sacrificed at f2, flared, meteor-like, for a moment, and then disappeared. Botvinnik used it against Smyslov in the 1943 Moscow Championship, and a very lively game resulted. Since then, however, no one has come forward who has been willing to repeat the experiment in a game of any importance.

12.	Nd2-b3	...

12 ef was also possible; in that event, the recapture on f6 would have forced Black's knight to leave its outpost at e4, when White could have continued with 13 Nb3 Bb6 14 Nbd4, or 14 Ng5, leading to a game of lively piece play. Averbakh, however, hopes to get more out of the position by retaining the pawn on e5 and driving out the knight with f2-f3. Then, too, 12.. N:f6 is not the only move: 12.. N:f2 is still possible.

12.	...	Bc5-a7

The bishop retreats a bit further, so as not to give White an additional tempo for his a2-a4-a5.

13.	Nf3-d4	Nc6:d4
14.	Nb3:d4	Ba7:d4
15.	Qd1:d4	...

Why not the natural 15 cd? Thereby hangs a tale which we

shall now proceed to elucidate.

For many years — since Fleissig - Mackenzie, Vienna 1882, to be exact — 15 cd f4 16 f3 Ng3 was considered to be unequivocally in Black's favor, since after 17 fg hg, none could see a way to prevent the black queen from getting to h2. Certainly, passive defense allows Black's attack to grow very fierce in a very short time: for example, 18 Be3 Qh4 19 Re1 Qh2+ 20 Kf1 Bh3.

Then Boleslavsky's painstaking investigations forced a re-evaluation of the position. In his well-known games with Botvinnik and Ragozin, he showed that the continuation 18 Qd3 Bf5 19 Q:f5 R:f5 20 B:f5 renders the queen's sortie harmless, since after 20.. Qh4 21 Bh3 Q:d4+ 22 Kh1 Q:e5 23 Bd2, White's pieces set up a combined pressure against the black king which occupies the queen sufficiently to prevent it from supporting the advance of Black's pawns.

After that it was Black who began to avoid this variation, until the Moscow master Yakov Estrin came forward to suggest that Black play, instead of 23.. Q:b2 (Botvinnik) or 23..c5 (Ragozin), an immediate ..d5-d4-d3. With his analyses, some of them worked out to the thirtieth move, Estrin won a number of pretty games by correspondence, achieving what, in all probability, even he had not expected: this chameleon-variation began to be avoided by both White and Black!

(A final note: it would be naive to try to keep White's queen from h7 with 18.. g6, since the queen could still reach h2 for defensive purposes from h6.)

That's a sketch of the reasons why Averbakh recaptured on d4 with the queen instead of the pawn. That's how matters stand today — how will they appear tomorrow? For the present, the search (White's, now) continues. Some Czech players have been analyzing 17 Rf2, instead of capturing the knight. Knowing

Boleslavsky, I am sure he will cross swords with Estrin's line as well, sooner or later.

Let's get back to the game.

15.	...	c7-c5
16.	Qd4-d1	f5-f4
17.	f2-f3	Ne4-g5

The piece sacrifice 17.. Ng3 would clearly have no point here (18 hg fg 19 Qd3 Bf5 20 Q:f5 R:f5 21 B:f5 Qh4 22 Bh3, and Black doesn't even have the queen check at d4), which is why the whole variation, up to and including 17.. Ng5, has been considered unfavorable for Black. Szabo plays the move theory has condemned anyway, and since he shows that the knight does not really stand so badly on g5, he opens, if not a new page, then at least a new paragraph in the opening handbooks.

18.   a2-a4   ...

Black would like very much to get the knight to e6, but White does not allow him the opportunity: 18.. Bf5 19 B:f5 R:f5 20 ab ab 21 R:a8 Q:a8 22 Qd3 forks b5 and f5.

18.   ...   b5-b4

Black is now all set to equalize completely with .. Bf5, for instance: 19 a5 Bf5 20 B:f4 B:c2 21 B:g5 Q:g5 22 Q:c2 Q:e5.

19.   h2-h4   ...

The a- and b-pawns have greeted,

and passed, one another, and the game's culminating moment has almost passed by unnoticed as well. A natural thought was 19 cb cb 20 Qd4; but on 19 cb there comes 19..c4 20 Qd4 Bf5, and the defenseless f-pawn cannot be taken safely by either queen or bishop, while the attempt to pick off the d-pawn also ends badly·for White. Here are the variations:

a) 21 B:f5 R:f5 22 B:f4 Ne6,

b) 21 Q:f4 Nh3+ 22 gh B:c2, and the white king's position is unsafe,

c) 21 B:f5 R:f5 22 Rd1 Ne6 23 Q:d5 Qb6+ 24 Kh1 Rd8, and Black wins, thanks to his pawn on c4, which prevents White from getting his queen back to b3.

Averbakh saw through Szabo's elegant combination; not wanting the knight on e6, however, he invited Black to sacrifice it, although this exposed him to some degree of risk.

19.	...	Ng5-h3+
20.	g2:h3	Qd8:h4
21.	Rf1-f2	Be6:h3
22.	Rf2-h2	Ra8-e8
23.	Qd1:d5+	Kg8-h8
24.	Bc1-d2	...

This is attack and defense at their finest. By defending the pawn at e5, White threatens to throw back the black pieces by 25 Be1. Szabo, by means of a last-ditch rook sacrifice, succeeds in forcing a perpetual check. The attempt to keep his attack going with 24..Re6 would have cost him the game in view of the retort 25 B:f4.

24.	...	Re8:e5
25.	Qd5:e5	Qh4-g3+
26.	Kg1-h1	Qg3:f3+
27.	Kh1-g1	...

DRAW

Averbakh was excellently prepared, but failed to catch his Hungarian opponent napping: both players proved worthy of each other.

*****

*****

ROUND ELEVEN

71. Euwe—Averbakh
(Nimzoindian Defense)

Even with the middlegame at full boil, a master must always be thinking about the endgame. The outcome of many games, even some in which the king barely escaped direct threats and a seemingly inevitable catastrophe, has only been decided deep in the endgame. This game was typical from that standpoint, but a rarity nonetheless. Averbakh chose a plan leading to the creation of a queenside passed pawn. Knowing that a passed pawn generally increases in value as the number of pieces decreases, Averbakh resigned himself to the temporary discomforts of Euwe's frontal assault, concluding the game with an elegant knight sacrifice in precisely the sector where the passed b-pawn had been awaiting its hour.

1.	d2-d4	Ng8-f6
2.	c2-c4	e7-e6
3.	Nb1-c3	Bf8-b4
4.	e2-e3	0-0
5.	Bf1-d3	d7-d5
6.	Ng1-f3	c7-c5
7.	0-0	Nb8-c6
8.	a2-a3	Bb4:c3
9.	b2:c3	b7-b6
10.	c4:d5	e6:d5
11.	Nf3-d2	Bc8-e6
12.	Bc1-b2	c5-c4

By developing his bishop to the long diagonal, White provoked 12.. c4. This makes his intended push of the e-pawn much stronger, since that pawn would no longer need to guard d4. Averbakh is willing to meet him halfway, since he intends a rapid advance of his queenside pawn majority.

13.	Bd3-c2	b6-b5
14.	f2-f3	a7-a5
15.	Rf1-e1	...

I would rather have pushed the e-pawn at once.

15.	...	Qd8-b6
16.	Nd2-f1	b5-b4
17.	Qd1-d2	b4-b3

This practically guarantees Averbakh an advantage in any

sort of endgame. Euwe's plan is certainly unusual, to say the least. The problem is not so much the bishop's retreat to b1, since it remains on the attacking diagonal, but that on the previous move he could have played his rook to c1. However, Euwe thought that Black would be unable to keep the rook imprisoned at a1, so he was unwilling to waste the tempo required to move it.

18.	Bc2-b1	a5-a4
19.	e3-e4	Nc6-e7
20.	Nf1-g3	Kg8-h8
21.	Re1-e2	Nf6-g8

Averbakh prepares to counterattack with ..f5, in order to open some lines, trade a few pieces, and get closer to an endgame.

22.	Ng3-h5	f7-f5
23.	Qd2-g5	Rf8-f7
24.	e4:f5	...

24 e5 looks too risky: getting the queen's rook out would be much more difficult then.

24.	...	Be6:f5
25.	Bb1:f5	Ne7:f5
26.	Ra1-e1	...

The reserve rook now speeds to the battlefront, but it might better have waited until after 26 Re5, tying Black to the defense of the d-pawn and considerably retarding his progress towards the endgame.

[117]

26.	...	Qb6-d8!

Beautiful sacrifices are not the only moves which deserve exclamation marks; such marks should also be placed after moves which are major links in a consistent strategic plan. The tactical justification of 26.. Qd8 is that it would be dangerous for White to avoid the trade, as this would allow Black's queen a very profitable excursion to h4.

27.	Qg5:d8	Ra8:d8
28.	Re2-e8	...

Euwe was roundly criticized for this move, and later he himself recommended 28 Re6; but it is quite evident that he had already formulated his plan of going into a minor-piece endgame and maneuvering the knight via f4 and e6 to c5, followed by the capture of the a-pawn. After 28 Re6, however, the rooks would also have been traded off eventually, with pretty much the same endgame resulting.

28.	...	Rd8:e8
29.	Re1:e8	Rf7-e7

And now the second rook must be exchanged as well, else the bishop is lost.

30.	Re8:e7	Ng8:e7
31.	Kg1-f2	...

On any other move, including 31 Bc1, Black would have replied 31.. Ne3, winning at once.

31.	...	Kh8-g8

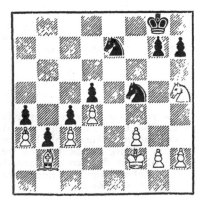

32.	g2-g4?	...

Disappointed at the failure of his original intention, to bring his knight to e6, Euwe insists on having it his way, and starts to push pawns, in hopes of regaining control of e6 and bringing the knight there after all.

No two ways about it: White does have a bad endgame. However, for the moment the position is of a closed nature, and Black must search for a spot to break through. White should play his knight to d2 or b1, and leave his g-pawn at g3. By starting now, White could get this plan carried out just as Black gets set up for the queenside breakthrough: 32 Nf4 Kf7 (otherwise 33 Ne6) 33 g3 Nd6 34 Ng2 Nb5 35 Ne3 Ke6 36 Nf1 Nc8 37 Nd2.

32.	...	Nf5-d6
33.	Kf2-e3	Nd6-b5
34.	f3-f4	Ne7-c8
35.	f4-f5	Nc8-d6
36.	Nh5-f4	...

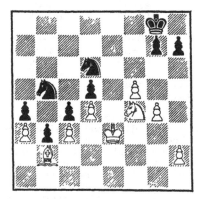

Each side has completed its preparations: White's knight is ready to go to e6, and Black —

36.	...	Nb5:a3!

Averbakh sacrifices his knight to clear the road for his pawns. A most elegant combination.

37.	Bb2:a3	Nd6-b5
38.	Ba3-c1	Nb5-c3
39.	Nf4-e2	Nc3-b1!

WHITE RESIGNED

72. Stahlberg—Petrosian
(King's Indian)

1.	d2-d4	Ng8-f6
2.	c2-c4	g7-g6
3.	g2-g3	Bf8-g7
4.	Bf1-g2	0-0
5.	Nb1-c3	d7-d6
6.	Ng1-f3	Nb8-d7
7.	0-0	e7-e5
8.	e2-e4	Rf8-e8
9.	d4-d5	a7-a5
10.	Nf3-e1	Nd7-c5
11.	Bc1-g5	h7-h6
12.	Bg5:f6	Qd8:f6
13.	a2-a3	...

The first step towards disaster. Having exchanged off his darksquare bishop, White should have redoubled his concern for the vital d4 square; instead, he weakens it — strange as that may sound — with 13 a3, which gives the black knight a bridge to transfer itself from c5 via b3 to d4. But that's still only half a problem.

13.	...	a5-a4
14.	Ra1-b1	Bc8-d7
15.	h2-h4	h6-h5
16.	Kg1-h2	Re8-f8
17.	Bg2-h3	...

The second step, and the fatal one. Although the commentators called this an unbelievable oversight, it may be understood as the conclusion to the plan begun with his 11th move. In fact, were it not for the pawn White will lose after the exchange of bishops, he wouldn't have all that bad a position — but that "were it not" spoils

everything.

17.	...	Bd7:h3
18.	Kh2:h3	Nc5:e4
19.	Nc3:e4	Qf6-f5+
20.	Kh3-h2	Qf5:e4

With only the heavy pieces left, sometimes one pawn is not enough to win with. From here on, Stahlberg offers his young opponent a stubborn but bootless resistance.

21.	Rb1-c1	b7-b6
22.	Ne1-g2	Qe4-f5
23.	Rc1-c2	Qf5-d7
24.	Qd1-d3	Rf8-e8
25.	Rf1-e1	Ra8-b8
26.	Rc2-e2	f7-f5
27.	f2-f3	Kg8-h7
28.	Qd3-c2	Rb8-a8
29.	Qc2-d3	Bg7-h6
30.	Qd3-c2	Qd7-f7
31.	Kh2-h3	f5-f4

Black had the choice of several ways to exploit his advantage; one would be using the a-file, by means of .. Ra8-a5-c5, to prepare .. b5. Petrosian has a different scheme: to open up the kingside and saddle his opponent with isolated f- and h-pawns, and then to localize White's attempt at counterplay on the queenside, leaving him with two more isolated pawns.

32.	g3:f4	Bh6:f4
33.	Ng2:f4	Qf7:f4
34.	Re1-g1	Re8-g8

Taking the f-pawn would have allowed White counterchances: for example, 34.. Q:f3+ 35 Rg3 Qf5+ 36 Q:f5 gf 37 Rg5 Kh6 38 Reg2, or 35.. Qf7 36 Rf2 Qd7+ 37 Kh2 Rg8 38 Rf6.

35.	Qc2-c3	Ra8-f8
36.	Rg1-g3	Rf8-f6
37.	Re2-e4	Qf4-h6
38.	c4-c5	b6:c5
39.	Re4:a4	Qh6-g7

39.. g5 meets a curious rebuttal: 40 Qc2+ Kh8 41 hg R:g5 42 R:g5 Q:g5 43 Ra8+ Kg7 44 Qg2.

40.	Ra4-c4	Qg7-f7
41.	Qc3-d3	Rg8-b8
42.	b2-b4	c5:b4
43.	a3:b4	Rb8-g8
44.	Rc4-c3	Rf6-f4
45.	Rg3-g5	...

This costs White one more pawn, but his game was getting very difficult to defend anyway, against the threat of 45.. Qe7.

45... R:h4+ 46. K:h4 Qf4+
47. Kh3 Q:g5 48. R:c7+ Kh6
49. Rc2 Rf8 50. Rg2 Qf6 51. Qe3+
Qf4 52. Re2 g5 53. Q:f4 R:f4
54. Rc2 R:f3+ 55. Kg2 Rb3 56. Rc6
g4 57. R:d6+ Kg5 58. Re6 R:b4
59. R:e5+ Kh4 60. Kf2 g3+ 61. Kf3
Rb3+ 62. Ke2 Rb2+ 63. Kf1 Rf2+
64. Kg1 Rd2

WHITE RESIGNED

******

73. Boleslavsky—Najdorf
(King's Indian)

1.	d2-d4	Ng8-f6
2.	c2-c4	g7-g6
3.	Nb1-c3	Bf8-g7
4.	e2-e4	d7-d6
5.	f2-f3	0-0
6.	Bc1-e3	e7-e5
7.	d4:e5	d6:e5
8.	Qd1:d8	...

With his ship all fitted out for a long voyage, White unexpectedly heads for a quiet backwater. A contemporary opening does permit this sort of treatment, however: White seeks a small but secure advantage from his control of the d5 square. Now we shall see a curious procession: knight, pawn, bishop, and finally the second knight, all pass through this same square, to be coolly removed by Najdorf. An endgame results in which White still has hopes for an advantage, based on his more active bishop, but these hopes go unrealized.

How is it that Boleslavsky, who relishes a complex game, could have chosen such a biteless line? Presumably, since he plays the Black side of the King's Indian so frequently himself, he was unwilling to divulge his own views on the White side of one of the major variations.

Soon after the position had simplified, Najdorf, who was not at all averse to a draw, asked his opponent:

"Did you play that move for a draw?"

"No."

"Does that mean you played it to win?"

"Mmm ... Partly."

"Maybe you played it to lose?!"

"I played the move which met the needs of the position."

While I will not swear to the literal accuracy of the entire dialogue, I would like to draw the reader's attention to this last retort, which so typifies Boleslavsky's thinking.

8.	...	Rf8:d8
9.	Nc3-d5	Nf6:d5
10.	c4:d5	c7-c6
11.	Bf1-c4	c6:d5
12.	Bc4:d5	Nb8-c6
13.	Ra1-d1	Nc6-d4
14.	Ke1-f2	Bc8-e6
15.	Bd5:e6	Nd4:e6
16.	Ng1-e2	f7-f5
17.	Ne2-c3	f5-f4
18.	Be3-c1	Bg7-f8
19.	Rd1:d8	Ra8:d8
20.	Rh1-d1	Bf8-c5+
21.	Kf2-f1	Bc5-d4
22.	Nc3-d5	...

Two of Black's pawns stand on the same color squares as his bishop: can White turn this microscopic advantage to account?

22.	...	Kg8-f7
23.	Bc1-d2	Rd8-c8
24.	Rd1-c1	Rc8:c1+
25.	Bd2:c1	g6-g5
26.	Kf1-e2	h7-h5
27.	h2-h3	Ne6-f8
28.	b2-b3	Nf8-g6
29.	Bc1-d2	Kf7-e6
30.	Bd2-e1	Ng6-e7
31.	Nd5:e7	Ke6:e7
32.	Ke2-d3	b7-b5

DRAW

******

74. Kotov—Taimanov
(Reti Opening)

1.	c2-c4	Ng8-f6
2.	g2-g3	e7-e6
3.	Bf1-g2	d7-d5
4.	Ng1-f3	d5-d4

This sort of aggression so early in the game cannot hurt

White. ..d5-d4 is not bad in
the Reti, for example, after
1 Nf3 d5 2 c4, but there the
e-pawn is still on e7, and may
later go to e5 in one step. In
this game, a lively skirmish
immediately erupts around the
far-advanced black pawn.

5.   b2-b4!   ...

The idea of using b2-b4 as
a means of fighting for the
d4 square is perhaps reminiscent of the Evans Gambit. In
this position, however, the
b-pawn cannot be taken: 5..B:b4?
6 Qa4+ Nc6 7 Ne5 Be7 8 N:c6,
and if 8..Bd7 9 N:d8 B:a4
10 N:b7, and White has an extra
piece.

5.   ...   c7-c5
6.   Bc1-b2   Qd8-b6
7.   Qd1-b3   Nb8-c6

Black's concern over the fate
of the d-pawn impels him to
spend a tempo in order to induce 8 b5, thus taking the
pressure off the c-pawn and
strengthening his central d-
pawn.

8.   b4-b5   Nc6-a5
9.   Qb3-c2   Bf8-d6
10.   e2-e3   e6-e5
11.   e3:d4   e5:d4

That wasn't the right pawn.
Make the move 11.. c5:d4 on
your board, instead of 11..e5:d4
as played, and you can see how
Black obtains a mobile center
and a lengthy diagonal for his
darksquare bishop. After the
text move, Black's center pawns
are dead, and his bishop's powers much reduced.

12.   0-0   0-0
13.   d2-d3   Bc8-d7

It was time to start thinking
about bringing his knight back
home: 13.. Qc7, followed by ..b6
and ..Nb7.

More than one game has been
lost due to the over-optimistic
assessment of one's own position:
such is the mistake Taimanov
makes here. For the moment, the
chances are about even. It would
be hard to single out any spec-
ific White advantage, but, in
any event, Black has none. Black

will spend the rest of the game
trying to drum up counterplay on
the queenside — against what?
Soon, White will move out his entire herd of pieces from the area
to the left and below the diagonal
pawn-chains; then, after the exchange of rooks (which Black initiates), the question of who controls these squares will cease to
be of any importance whatever. If
Black does not exchange rooks,
however, White will seize the e-
file.

14.   Nb1-d2   h7-h6
15.   Ra1-e1   Ra8-e8
16.   Bb2-c1   Re8:e1
17.   Rf1:e1   Rf8-e8
18.   Re1:e8+   Bd7:e8
19.   Nf3-h4!   ...

The exclamation mark is not
for any one move, but for the
whole of White's original plan,
which is: to remove every single
one of his pieces from the queenside, and set up an attack on
the king, making use of the numerical superiority he enjoys there,
due to the absence from that sector of one black knight.

19.   ...   a7-a6
20.   a2-a4   Qb6-a7
21.   Nh4-f5   Bd6-f8

A strategic technique of which
Taimanov makes frequent use: leaving his king in its keep, under
the protection of his two bishops,
he undertakes the decisive action
on the queenside. The only reason
this technique fails him in this
instance is that there he will
find absolutely nothing and no
one to attack.

22.   Nd2-e4   Nf6:e4
23.   Bg2:e4   ...

(See diagram, following page)

23.   ...   b7-b6
24.   Qc2-d1   ...

Preparing to move out the last
of the troops.

24.   ...   a6:b5
25.   a4:b5   Be8-d7
26.   Qd1-h5   Bd7-e6
27.   Bc1-f4   Na5-b3

27.. Nb7 would have been highly dangerous: for instance,
28 N:h6+ gh 29 B:h6 B:h6 30 Q:h6,

(Position after 23 B:e4)

and now if 30.. Nd6, then
31 Bh7+ Kh8 32 Bf5+ Kg8 33 Qh7+
Kf8 34 B:e6 Qa1+ 35 Kg2 fe
36 Qc7, winning the pawn on b6.
30.. Nd8 obviously fails to
31 Qg5+, and 30.. Qa1+ 31 Kg2
Na5 32 Bh7+ Kh8 33 Bf5+ Kg8
34 B:e6 fe 35 Q:e6+ and 36 Q:b6
is also bad for Black. With the
knight on b3 now, the sacrifice
at h6 would lead only to a perpetual check, since the black
queen could rejoin the defense
via d7.

| 28. | Qh5-d1 | Qa7-a2 |

The continuation of his mistaken plan. Black wants to attack the base of White's pawn
chain at d3 from the rear, but
he also has a weak pawn at b6,
which is easier to assail, being further removed from its
own pieces. In fact, this factor has already forced Black
to avoid the exchange of queens:
28.. Qa1 29 Q:a1 N:a1 30 Bc7,
and the black pawn chain crumbles.

29.	h2-h4	Nb3-a1
30.	h4-h5	Na1-c2
31.	Bf4-e5	Qa2-b2
32.	Be5-c7	Nc2-a3
33.	Qd1-g4	Qb2-c1+

(See diagram, next column)

| 34. | Kg1-g2 | Na3-b1 |

The concluding phase of this
game testifies to the collapse
of Black's plan and the triumph
of White's strategy. The knight
wanders forlornly about the corner of the board, as if trying
to perform the well-known Knight's
Tour, while White methodically
increases the pressure on the
black king's position.

| 35. | Bc7-f4 | Nb1-d2? |

A blunder, of course, but
Black was lost in any event.

| 36. | Qg4-e2 | ... |

BLACK RESIGNED

******

75. Geller—Gligoric
(King's Indian)

1.	d2-d4	Ng8-f6
2.	c2-c4	g7-g6
3.	Nb1-c3	Bf8-g7
4.	e2-e4	d7-d6
5.	f2-f3	...

Samisch's Variation is the
King's Indian's fierce foe. Surrounded by his g2-f3-e4-d5-c4
palisade, White calmly develops
his pieces on the squares left
open, while Black is unable even
to dream of breaking in the center, and must place all his hopes
in a wing attack. Here too, however, life is no bowl of cherries,
since White's king, which is the
chief target of his assault, will

be spirited away to the queenside, robbing Black's pawn press
..f7-f5-f4 of much of its effect by rendering it largely
pointless.

Meanwhile, White has a wider
choice of strategic plans. With
the center closed, he may attack on the kingside with g4,
h4 and h4-h5 etc., or try for
a queenside break by leading
away from his own king with a
pawn attack. Before deciding on
an active plan, both White and
Black engage in a lengthy war
of maneuver, of the sort that
occurs in many contemporary
grandmaster games. Generally
speaking, the ideas behind such
play are: to find the best possible positions for one's pieces,
to restrict the opponent's initiative, to trade off one's own
"bad" bishop for the enemy's
"good" one, and finally, to prepare a break. In the present
game, for example, up until the
42nd move only one piece and
one pawn had been exchanged. At
that moment, however, the game
entered its combinative phase,
and the reader who has followed
the phase preceding that with
diligent attention will be richly rewarded for his pains. He
will see sacrifices, counter-
sacrifices, feints and kingside
attacks — in a word, all the
trappings of a lively game.

5.	...	0-0
6.	Bc1-e3	e7-e5
7.	d4-d5	Nf6-h5

This is not the only plan for
Black. He might also play 7..c6,
attempting to undermine the center, or 7.. a5, to bring a knight
to c5; but as Makogonov showed
in his day, White's attack on
the kingside moves very swiftly.
If Black prepares ..f5 by dropping his knight back to e8, then
8 g4 sometimes follows, giving
White the opportunity to open
the g-file for his rooks with
a later g4:f5.

Black's choice in this game is
the end product of a battle of
ideas of many years' duration.
From h5, the knight mechanically prevents h4-h5, which consequently renders the push h2-h4
at least temporarily useless;
and on 8 g4, then knight goes

to f4, halting White's attack.
7.. Nh5 also prepares 8.. f5:
all logical enough, but no more
than that.

| 8. | Qd1-d2 | f7-f5 |
| 9. | 0-0-0 | f5-f4 |

Black closes the game in the
only sector where he had any
chance to stir up some activity
for his pieces — why? The answer
comes from Gligoric's next two
moves, but it's hardly a satisfactory one. Black wants to trade
off the darksquare bishops with
..Bg7-f6-h4, but he is unable to
achieve this. It is possible that
on 9.. Nbd7 or 9.. Qe8, as Geller
himself usually plays for Black,
Gligoric was afraid of 10 ef gf
11 g4; in that event, he should
continue 11.. fg 12 fg Nf4. White
may get open diagonals, but they
will not be easily occupied, and
Black will get his chances too.
He who plays the King's Indian
must be prepared for dangerous
variations. With his 9.. f4, Black
resigns himself to having less
say in the game.

10.	Be3-f2	Bg7-f6
11.	Ng1-e2	Bf6-h4
12.	Bf2-g1	...

With a pawn chain entirely on
light squares, Geller naturally
does not intend to be deprived
of his darksquare bishop. True,
the rook is shut in, but it takes
two black pieces (the knight on
h5 and the bishop on h4) to keep
it in. (Note that 11.. Bh4 is
made possible by the combination
12 g3 fg 13 hg R:f3).

12.	...	Nb8-d7
13.	Kc1-b1	Bh4-e7
14.	Ne2-c1	Nd7-c5
15.	Nc1-d3	Nc5:d3
16.	Bf1:d3	Bc8-d7

Gligoric considers his position strong enough to withstand
a siege, but against passive play
by Black, sooner or later White
will find a way to break through.
16.. c5 was worth a thought here,
in order to hem in the bishop on
g1 and perhaps give his own bishop an exit via d8. White would
most likely have taken en passant,
leading to a livelier game.

| 17. | Bd3-c2 | Qd8-e8 |

White wanted to carry out the exchanging maneuver 18 Ba4, much like Black's attempt with 11..Bh4, but Gligoric does not allow it.

18.	Bg1-f2	a7-a6
19.	Rd1-c1	Kg8-h8
20.	Bc2-d1	Rf8-f7
21.	Bd1-b3	Rf7-f8

The threat of 22 c5 forces Black to retreat his rook to f8, and on the following move to play 22.. b6. Having already passed up the chance to enliven his game, Black must now wait and watch as White improves his position and prepares his break. Now Black's chances lie in whatever accidental tactical shots may happen to present themselves.

22.	Nc3-e2	b7-b6
23.	Ne2-c3	Nh5-f6
24.	Qd2-d1	Kh8-g7
25.	Qd1-d3	Nf6-h5
26.	Rc1-g1	...

The onslaught White now sets in motion is not so much aggressive as prophylactic in nature. Before breaking on the queenside, White wants to secure the king's wing, fearing that once all of his pieces have left that sector, Gligoric will find a favorable opportunity to play ..g6-g5-g4. But now the base of White's pawn chain is weakened, giving Black the opportunity for a break by means of a piece sacrifice.

26.	...	Kg7-h8
27.	g2-g4	Nh5-f6
28.	h2-h4	Kh8-g7
29.	Rg1-c1	h7-h6
30.	Nc3-e2	Qe8-d8
31.	Rc1-g1	Nf6-h7
32.	Bb3-c2	Bd7-e8
33.	h4-h5	g6-g5

Poor darksquare bishop: off it goes into full retirement, not to make one more move until game's end.

34.	Qd3-d1	Nh7-f6
35.	Bc2-a4	b6-b5

Black cannot allow this bishop to get to c6, and so he is forced to play this active move, resulting in the first exchange of pawns and the opening of the c-file for White. White can no longer play his break at c5, but that's not necessary any longer, since its purpose — to open an attacking line — has already been attained by other means; so he turns to an attack on the c- and b-pawns. The former will be hard to get, since it is easily defended by minor pieces; the latter must be isolated from the bishop at d7, for which purpose the maneuver Ne2-c1-d3-b4-c6 will be useful — but that will mean pulling White's last piece away from the king's wing ...

36.	c4:b5	a6:b5
37.	Ba4-b3	Qd8-b8
38.	Qd1-d2	Qb8-b7
39.	Rg1-c1	Be8-d7
40.	Rc1-c2	Rf8-c8
41.	Rh1-d1	Ra8-a6
42.	Ne2-c1	Nf6:g4!

Unexpectedly wrecking White's maneuvering game. Sacrifices such as this one are always in the air around immobile pawn chains. Not just the pawns, but the pieces behind them also become much more active, and White must go on the defensive for a time.

43.	f3:g4	Bd7:g4
44.	Rd1-h1	...

Geller prefers to give up the exchange, rather than allow his opponent to get three connected passed pawns.

44.	...	Bg4-f3
45.	Qd2-e1	c7-c5
46.	d5:c6	Ra6:c6

How pitiful Black's pieces appeared, cooped up in the narrow space behind their pawn chain; and how his whole position begins to sparkle, once his pawns are set in motion! If Black succeeds in picking up that last center pawn, then of course White would no longer be able to hold the game; otherwise, alas, it is still Gligoric who must strive for the draw.

47.	Bb3-d5	Bf3:h1
48.	Qe1:h1	Qb7-d7
49.	Rc2:c6	Rc8:c6
50.	Bd5:c6	Qd7:c6
51.	Nc1-d3	...

With all of Black's resourcefulness, the position is still uncertain. Geller has held on to his extra piece and his center pawn too; if he can get his knight to d5, then Black must perish. If Black can get in .. d5, obtaining three connected passed pawns, then the battle will flare anew. White's last move aims at seizing control of d5, but it gives Black a second chance. On the other hand, 51 Qf3 would allow Black the possibility 51.. Qd7 and 52..g4.

| 51. | ... | Qc6-c4 |
| 52. | Qh1-f3 | d6-d5 |

53.	Nd3:e5	Qc4-f1+!
54.	Kb1-c2	d5:e4
55.	Qf3:e4	Qf1-f2+

Black has perpetual check, but no more than that, since his own king is too exposed.

56.	Kc2-d3	Qf2-f1+
57.	Kd3-c2	Qf1-f2+
58.	Kc2-d3	Qf2-f1+
59.	Kd3-c2	Qf1-f2+

DRAW

******

76. Smyslov—Bronstein
(Reti Opening)

1.	c2-c4	Ng8-f6
2.	g2-g3	c7-c6
3.	Ng1-f3	d7-d5
4.	b2-b3	Bc8-f5

If Black wants indisputable equality against the Reti, then the setup with ..c7-c6 and developing the bishop to f5 seems best to me, following the classic example Reti - Lasker. There have, of course, been cases in which the bishop ended up out of action on the diagonal b1-h7, but only because Black played in stereotyped fashion, without considering circumstances.

5.	Bf1-g2	e7-e6
6.	0-0	Nb8-d7
7.	Bc1-b2	Bf8-e7
8.	Nb1-c3	0-0

After long thought, Black decided to castle and do without .. h6 for the time being. Someone once said — and many now believe — that loss of time is meaningless in closed positions. If this is true, then it is true only for thoroughly closed positions, not for the kind that now exists upon this board. It seems to me that 8.. h6 would have been an unnecessary waste of time here.

| 9. | Nf3-h4 | ... |

Smyslov reacts immediately to Black's "inaccuracy", intending first to trade off the bishop at g6, then to play c4:d5, and then to prepare e2-e4, in order to clear the center of pawns and secure great activity for his pieces.

| 9. | ... | Bf5-g4 |

A small subterfuge: Black conceals his aggressive intentions behind the mask of forced play.

| 10. | h2-h3 | Bg4-h5 |
| 11. | g3-g4 | ... |

Either White has underrated his

opponent's ideas, or he is simply being careless: Black's long think after 8 Nc3 ought to have forewarned him.

Smyslov probably thought that Black was just putting on a show of intending to sacrifice a piece; and in fact, after 11.. B:g4 12 hg N:g4 13 Nf3, Black would have no threats whatever. A little _zwischenzug_, however, alters the position substantially.

It should be mentioned that Black had just such a turn of events in mind when he pondered his eighth move, keeping in mind that 11.. Bg6 12 N:g6 hg 13 d4 would have left White with a definite advantage.

| 11. | ... | d5-d4 |
| 12. | Nc3-b1 | ... |

Taking the bishop would not be good, in view of 12.. dc 13 B:c3 N:h5 14 Nf3 Bf6 15 d4 Nf4; and after 12 Na4, .. b7-b5 is an immediate threat.

| 12. | ... | Bh5:g4 |
| 13. | h3:g4 | Nf6:g4 |

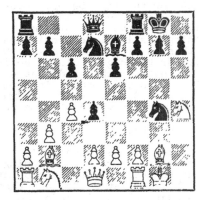

Naturally, I could not calculate all the consequences of the sacrifice, but considering a few of the variations, I felt that Black would have good chances for an attack, or — and sometimes this can be more important — for the steady improvement of his position. For example: 14 Nf3 Bd6, followed by ..f7-f5, ..Qf6, and ..Re8, with the standing threat

of ..e6-e5-e4.

| 14. | e2-e4 | Ng4:f2 |

White mistakenly allowed a tactical shot which could have decided the game at once: 14..Ba3, and if 15 Q:g4, Black recovers his piece, coming out two pawns to the good. On 15 B:a3, Black would get a third pawn with a strengthened attack: 15.. Q:h4 16 Re1 Q:f2+ 17 Kh1 Qh4+ 18 Kg1, and now the quiet 18..c5 is possible, as are the more energetic 18..f5 or 18..Nde5.

In this variation, Black must play for some little time a rook down, which to me seemed excessive. Afraid perhaps of nothing more than having to end this game with a perpetual check, I decided to comfort myself by taking a third pawn for the piece. Evidently, this was an inaccurate assessment of the position.

15.	Rf1:f2	Be7:h4
16.	Rf2-f3	Nd7-e5
17.	Rf3-h3	Bh4-g5

First of all, this retreat to g5 prevents the d-pawn's advance, when there would follow 18..Be3+, 19.. f5 and 20..Ng4; secondly, it prepares 18..d3; and thirdly, it neutralizes the threatened 18 Qh5, in view of the reply 18..h6.

18.	Nb1-a3	Ne5-g6
19.	Na3-c2	Ng6-f4
20.	Rh3-h2	...

White might have given rook

for knight and pawn here: 20 B:d4
N:h3+ 21 B:h3 Bf6, but now 22 e5
fails against 22..B:e5 and
23..Qg5+.

20.   ...   d4-d3!

A decisive maneuver: in conjunction with the trade of bishops that ensues, this puts
White in a difficult position.

21.   Nc2-e3   Nf4-e2+
22.   Kg1-h1   f7-f5

Black here declined White's
offer of a draw, certainly with
some justification: the three
connected passed pawns he now
obtains will be a great danger
to White's pieces.

23.   e4:f5   e6:f5
24.   Bg2-f3   Ne2-g3+
25.   Kh1-g1   Bg5-f6

A positional move, aiming to
exchange off one of the few active white pieces.

26.   Bb2:f6   Qd8:f6
27.   Qd1-e1   ...

27.   ...   f5-f4

A serious error. Having written
the winning move, 27..Rae8, down
on my scoresheet, and with my
hand already reaching for the
rook, I changed my mind at the
last moment, and spent the rest
of the game regretting this lost
opportunity.

28.   Ne3-g4   Qf6-d4+
29.   Kg1-g2   Ra8-e8

30.   Qe1-g1!   Qd4-b2
31.   Qg1-c1   Qb2-d4
32.   Qc1-c3   ...

Smyslov's fighting qualities
must be acknowledged: even in a
slightly inferior position, he
declines a repetition and risks
an immediate loss. Trading queens
here would have given Black four
passed pawns and all sorts of
winning chances. On the other
hand, maybe Smyslov did not like
the idea of retreating his queen
back to g1, after which Black
could play his queen to d6, instead of b2 again.

32.   ...   Qd4-d6
33.   c4-c5   Qd6-g6
34.   Qc3-c4+   Kg8-h8
35.   Rh2-h3   h7-h5

Courage! Black runs up under
the rook's fire to "attack" the
knight with a pinned pawn.

36.   Kg2-h2   Qg6-h7
37.   Ng4-f2   g7-g5
38.   Qc4-d4+   Kh8-g8
39.   Qd4-c4+   Kg8-h8
40.   Qc4-d4+   Kh8-g8

Here the game was adjourned,
and White offered a

DRAW

the next day. I saw no way of
improving the position of my
pieces substantially; for that
matter, I had practically agreed
to the draw with my 30th move.
White needed only the check on
c4 for a three-time repetition,
and so I took Smyslov's offer.

[127]

Imagine my surprise upon discovering that the sealed move had been 41 Ra1-g1: once again Smyslov had declined the draw! It seems to me, however, that this move would have given Black good winning chances once again after 41..Qg6: then Black could answer the check by moving his king to h7, followed by either ..g5-g4 or ..h5-h4. Now White's pieces would remain tied up by Black's pawns; and if White were to carry out the threat implicit in his 41 Rg1, which is: to sacrifice the exchange back with 42 R:g3 fg+ 43 R:g3, Black could keep the initiative by means of the continuation 43.. h4 44 Rh3 Rf4, with strong pressure on the e- and f-files. Smyslov and his second Simagin, however, thought that the immediate 41..h4 42 Ng4, etc. was forced for Black, and it's hard to say which of the two of us was right. When a game is adjourned in a complex position, usually each side unconsciously evaluates the position in his own favor.

What conclusions can be drawn from this tense and interesting struggle? First: even in the most important games, one may, if conditions are right, employ a sacrifice which cannot be analyzed in detail; second: if a mistake or an inaccuracy occurs, there is no need to assume "all is lost" and mope — one must reorient oneself quickly, and find a new plan to fit the new situation.

******

77. Keres—Reshevsky
(Nimzoindian Defense)

If the reader should ask which game I liked the best of all in this tournament, I would have to pass over my own two encounters with onetime American wunderkind Samuel Reshevsky in favor of one of the tournament's most noteworthy games from the viewpoint of its depth of conception, beauty and complexity. This game has been reproduced in chess journals in every language, and has been subjected to dissection by dozens of masters, almost all of the grandmasters, and even Botvinnik himself — and yet we still cannot say with absolute certainty that these analyses represent the final answer. The reader will have the opportunity to examine for himself, and perhaps to add his own contribution to the collective effort of all the world's chessplayers.

1.	d2-d4	Ng8-f6
2.	c2-c4	e7-e6
3.	Nb1-c3	Bf8-b4
4.	e2-e3	c7-c5
5.	Bf1-d3	0-0
6.	a2-a3	Bb4:c3+
7.	b2:c3	b7-b6

Here 7..Nc6 is usually played; after 8 Ne2 b6 9 e4 Ne8, a type of position is reached which is well-known from the games Botvinnik - Reshevsky (Moscow 1948), Bronstein - Najdorf (Budapest 1950), and Geller - Smyslov, from this tournament. Reshevsky repeats the opening he played against Euwe, but where White was unable to summon the courage to play 8 e4 in that game, Keres does so here.

8.	e3-e4	Bc8-b7
9.	Bc1-g5	...

R.G. Ashurov, a Class-A player from Baku, has pointed out a different possibility for White here: 9 e5, and if 9..B:g2, then 10 Bg5 B:h1 11 ef g6 12 B:g6! hg 13 Qg4 with a very strong attack, which Ashurov carries out to mate in several lines. True, some of these variations could be improved for Black, but without a doubt he gets into serious trouble if he takes the pawn and the rook. His best reply to 9 e5 would be to retreat the knight, when White could maintain the pressure with 10 Qh5.

9.	...	h7-h6

Fierce! 9..d6 was also possible: if 10 e5 de 11 de, then Black would not play 11..B:g2, which would lead to a complete collapse of his game in very short order, but 11..Be4! On 9..d6, White would probably have continued 10 f4 Nbd7 11 Nf3 cd 12 cd, with a much more active position; so Black prefers to force matters.

10.	h2-h4	...

Continuing his development. It's easy to see that if Black

were to take the bishop here, he
would have to return it at once,
since 10..hg 11 hg N:e4? 12 Qh5
f5 13 g6 would win quickly.

10.	...	d7-d6
11.	e4-e5	d6:e5
12.	d4:e5	Bb7-e4!

The only move: 12..hg leads to
13 ef Q:f6 14 Bh7+ Kh8 15 hg
Q:c3+ 16 Kf1, and White wins;
if 12..B:g2, then 13 B:f6 gf
14 Qg4+ Kh8 15 Q:g2 Q:d3 16 Rh3,
and Black loses his queen's
rook; and finally, if 12..Qc7,
then 13 ef B:g2 14 fg Qe5+
15 Kd2 Re8 16 Nf3!, and White
saves his rook, coming out a
piece ahead.

| 13. | Rh1-h3! | ... |

The only move: as the reader
can easily determine, taking the
knight with either the bishop
or the pawn would give Black a
favorable ending.

| 13. | ... | Be4:d3 |
| 14. | Rh3:d3 | Qd8-c7 |

The best chance to defend his
difficult position. In such situations, many players are ready
to throw up their hands and play
the first move that comes to
mind; but Reshevsky does not despair.

White has several means of
destroying the black king's pawn
cover. Here Keres concocted an
astounding combination, whose
main variation runs roughly as
follows: 15 B:f6 gf 16 Qg4+ Kh8

17 Qf3 Nd7 18 0-0-0 N:e5 19 Q:f6+
Kh7 20 Rd6 N:c4 21 Nh3 N:d6
22 Ng5+! Kg8 23 Q:h6 f5 24 N:e6
Qh7 25 Q:h7+ K:h7 26 N:f8+ R:f8
27 R:d6 — and the rook ending
will pose few problems for White.

There are certainly many other
possibilities for both sides a-
long the way, which no one could
possibly have calculated; but the
extended conception of unusual
beauty is a hallmark of Keres'
talent.

And now the reader who would
like to poke about with us through
the byways of these combinations
should follow the analysis, as
Nimzovich once recommended, on
two chessboards: one to make the
moves of the game, and the other
to examine the variations.

| 15. | Bg5:f6 | ... |

15 ef hg 16 hg is also quite
good enough here — Najdorf, in
fact, considered it "interesting,
and probably the winning line"—
16..Qe5+ 17 Kf1 Q:g5 18 fg Rc8
19 Rg3 Qf4 20 Rh3 Q:c4+ 21 Ne2
Nc6 22 Qd2.

Nedeljkovic and Vukovic put
forward 19 Qf3 Nc6 20 Qh3 in
this line, as well as the alter-
natives:

a) 16..gf 17 gf Qe5+ 18 Kf1 Q:f6
19 Rg3+ Kh7 20 Qh5+ Qh6 21 Qf3;

b) 16..Qh2 17 Kf1 Qh4 18 Rh3!
Q:c4+ 19 Ne2 e5 20 Qd6 Qe6
21 Qd3 e4 22 Qg3 gf 23 Qh4.

V. Turchuk has rightly up-
braided me for uncritically accepting this analysis, pointing
out that, instead of 21 Qd3,
White could give mate in three
by 21 Rh8+, 22 Q:f8+, and 23 Q:g7.
After that, I critically re-exam-
ined the variation, and came up
with 21 Q:f8+! K:f8 22 Rh8 —
mate again, and in one move less!

Euwe also thinks that the
knight ought to have been taken
with the pawn, but that after
15..hg the proper continuation
is not 16 hg (as Najdorf would
have it), but 16 fg: for example,

a) 16..K:g7 17 Qh5 gh 18 Q:h4,
with the threat of 19 Rg3+;

b) 16..Qe5+ 17 Re3 Q:g7 18 Rg3
f6 19 Nf3, threatening 20 N:g5.

As we can see, all of the commentators agree that this continuation (15 ef) was clearer,
and would have led to a quicker
win. There were indeed two ways
to win, but the line White actually chose was no less forcing
and no less beautiful than those
that were suggested post mortem.
Obviously, once Keres had come
up with a plan that was good enough to win, he carried it out
without distracting himself by
calculating new complexities.

15.   ...   g7:f6
16.   Qd1-g4+   ...

White had an exceptionally
beautiful attacking continuation here: 16 f4!, keeping the
black queen from e5. The main
line runs as follows:

16..Kh7 17 Nh3 Rg8 18 Qh5 Nc6
19 ef Rg6 20 0-0-0 Rd8 21 R:d8
N:d8 22 Ng5+ Kg8 23 R:d8+! Q:d8

(Diagram of hypothetical position)

24 Q:g6+!! fg 25 f7+ Kh8 26 N:e6,
when knight and pawn overcome a
queen.

Such a combination, however, is
not easily calculated over the
board, especially when one takes
into account such diversions as:

a) 16 f4 Kh7 17 Nh3 Qb7, and it
would not be easy for White to
find the proper move, which is
18 Ra2;

b) 16..fe 17 Rg3+ Kh7 18 Qg4 f5
19 Qg6+ Kh8 20 Q:h6+ Qh7 21Q:f8+;

c) 16..Nc6 17 Rd7 Qb8 18 Qg4+
Kh8 19 Qh5.

Grandmaster Botvinnik recommended 16 ef!, and that may be
the most meaningful thing the
reader will learn from these
five pages.

16.   ...   Kg8-h8
17.   Qg4-f3   ...

Keres continues his idea.
17 Rg3 would have been insufficient in view of 17..Q:e5+ 18 Re3
Qc7 19 Rg3 Qe5+; if 18 Kf1 or
18 Ne2, then 18..f5, and Black
can defend. Nothing comes of
17 Nf3 Nd7! 18 R:d7 Q:d7 19 ef
Rg8 20 Qh5 Qd3! 21 Q:h6+ Qh7
22 Qf4 R:g2 either; but 17 0-0-0
Q:e5 18 Nf3 Qc7 19 Rd6 Nc6 20 Qf4
Kg7 21 g4 and 22 g5 looks very
strong: if 17..Nc6, then 18 f4
fe 19 Rd7 Qc8 20 Qh5 Kg7 21 f5!

17.   ...   Nb8-d7
18.   0-0-0   ...

Trifunovic, and Reshevsky himself in later analysis, pointed
out the winning move (in their
opinion), 18 Rd6. Indeed, White
wins after both 18..fe 19 0-0-0
and 18..f5 19 Qf4 Kh7 20 0-0-0;
but the defense 18..Kg7, threatening 19..N:e5 (this was suggested by the German analyst
Rellstab) is sufficient to draw.
For example, 19 ef+ N:f6 20 0-0-0
Qe7, or 19 Qg3+ Kh8 20 Qf4 Kg7,
etc.

18.   ...   Nd7:e5
19.   Qf3:f6+   Kh8-h7
20.   Rd3-d6   Ne5:c4

For the first time in this
game, no doubt, Reshevsky
breathed a sigh of relief. Indeed, he has no worries over
21 Rd7 Qe5 22 R:f7+ R:f7 23 Q:f7+
Qg7, when Black may even threaten
mate in some lines himself: 24 Qf3,
for instance, allows 24.. b5!

21.   Ng1-f3   ...

Reshevsky could have given up
his queen for two rooks and a
better defense here. 21 Nh3 was
more exact; then after the trade
of the queen for two rooks White
could continue 23 f3, followed

by 24 g4 and 25 Nf4, with an undiminished attack, in spite of the attenuated material. Once Reshevsky took the rook with his knight, Keres could finally enter the concluding phase of his outstanding combination.

| 21. | ... | Ne4:d6 |
| 22. | Nf3-g5+ | ... |

If Black takes the knight, nothing can save him from mate.

| 22. | ... | Kh7-g8 |
| 23. | Qf6:h6 | ... |

A glance at the position will reveal a noticeable similarity between it and the position mentioned in the note to Black's 14th. Here, however, Reshevsky sidesteps the main line: instead of 23..f5, he plays

| 23. | ... | f7-f6 |

which, in conjunction with Black's next, is far stronger.

| 24. | Ng5:e6 | Qc7-e7 |
| 25. | Rd1:d6 | ... |

Under severe time pressure, with his emotions in a turmoil from the whole preceding phase of the struggle, Keres fails to find the correct maneuver: 25 Qg6+ Kh8 26 Qh5+ Kg8 27 Rd3! Ne4 (27..Qh7 runs into 28 Q:h7+, 29 N:f8+,and 30 R:d6 — i.e., Keres' main line) 28 N:f8 R:f8 29 Qg4+ Ng5 30 Re3 Qg7 31 Rg3 Kh8 32 hg. However, Keres can-

not be faulted for missing this, since many of the commentators, in quieter circumstances and after lengthy analysis, also failed to discover this winning plan, suggesting instead 28 Qg6+ Kh8 29 N:f8 R:f8 30 Re3, which doesn't work, because Black does not play 30..f5 31 f3!, but 30..Rg8 31 Qh6+ Qh7, or 31 R:e4 R:g6 32 R:e7 R:g2, with a drawn ending.

| 25. | ... | Rf8-f7 |
| 26. | Qh6-d2 | ... |

A time-pressure move, but his selection was already limited. Nothing was to be gained by 26 Qg6+ Kh8 27 Rd5 Rh7, while 26 Rc6 c4! 27 Kb2 Re8 28 f4 Qd7 29 f5 Q:c6 30 Qg6+ Kh8 31 Q:f7 Q:g2+ probably leads to a draw. 26 f4 is also unclear, in view of 26..Rh7 27 Qg6+ Kh8, when 28 f5 is no good in view of 28..Rg8.

Nedeljkovic and Vukovic's recommendation, 26 g4, is not bad.

| 26. | ... | Ra8-e8 |
| 27. | f2-f4 | ... |

27 g4 was better here, answering 27..f5 with 28 g5, and 27..Qb7 with 28 Qd3. White would have retained some winning chances.

| 27. | ... | f6-f5 |

Now Black has fully equal play.

| 28. | Qd2-d5 | Kg8-h8 |

For one thing, Reshevsky could have taken the pawn here: 28..Q:h4 leaves White nothing better than the queen ending after 29 Rd8 R:d8 30 N:d8 Q:f4+ 31 Kb2 Qc7 32 N:f7 Q:f7, where Black obtains winning chances.

29.	Qd5-e5+	Qe7-f6
30.	Kc1-c2	c5-c4
31.	Kc2-d2	Kh8-g8
32.	Qe5-d5	Qf6:h4
33.	Qd5:c4	Qh4-f2+
34.	Kd2-c1	Qf2-g1+
35.	Kc1-c2	Qg1:g2+
36.	Kc2-b3	b6-b5

A trap which also secures the c4 square, where the exchange of queens will shortly take place.

| 37. | Qc4-d4 | ... |

The black queen ought to have

been kept out of f1, which could
have been accomplished by 37 Qd3.

| 37. | ... | Qg2-f1 |
| 38. | Kb3-b4 | Qf1-c4+ |

Reshevsky had only a few seconds left for three moves, so
it is not clear whether he rejected or did not see the tempting move 38..Rf6. The queen could
not take the rook, in view of
39..Qc4+, with mate next; and on
39 Qd5 , of course, Black would
trade queens; but 39 Rd8 R:e6
40 R:e8+ R:e8 41 Qd5+ would appear to save White.

| 39. | Qd4:c4 | b5:c4 |
| 40. | Kb4:c4 | Re8-c8+ |

41. Kc4-b5! ...

Here the game was adjourned.
Both players analyzed all night
and the next day as well — not
the adjourned position, of course,
but the game which led up to it.
Both Keres and Reshevsky knew
there was no need to play off
the adjourned position beyond
the opening of the sealed move;
if they had known better, then
at least one would not have
agreed to the

DRAW

without playing on.

******
******

ROUND TWELVE

78. Bronstein—Keres
(Sicilian Defense)

1.	e2-e4	c7-c5
2.	Nb1-c3	g7-g6
3.	g2-g3	Bf8-g7
4.	d2-d3	Nb8-c6
5.	Bf1-g2	Ra8-b8

Maybe a little bit too straight-forward — an opinion Black soon comes to share himself. On b8 the rook supports the onrush of the b-pawn, which is the sort of forceful assault that makes sense only when conducted in the neighborhood of the white king. In the present game, however, White secures his king in the right-hand corner.

6.	f2-f4	d7-d6
7.	Ng1-f3	e7-e6
8.	0-0	Ng8-e7

General considerations impelled White to push his e-pawn to e5, without worrying about its loss, since this opens at least three lines: White's half of the e-file, the c1-h6 diagonal, and the g2-c6 diagonal. In addition, the excellent post at e4 is cleared for White's queen's knight.

9.	e4-e5	d6:e5

Naturally, Black could also have continued with 9..d5, maintaining a closed position where his lag in development would not have been so important — that's probably how he should have played it.

10.	f4:e5	Nc6:e5

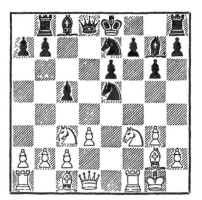

11.	Bc1-f4	Ne5:f3+

The knight seizes its chance to escape with check. Attempting to maintain it on e5 would only mean more trouble for the king, for example:

I. 11..f6 12 B:e5 fe 13 Ng5;

II. 11..N7c6 12 N:e5 N:e5 13 Qe2;

III. 11..0-0 12 N:e5 Qd4+ 13 Kh1 B:e5 14 Nb5 Q:b2 15 Rb1.

12.	Qd1:f3	Rb8-a8

Hitting the bishop with 12..e5 would have been useless, since that piece is aching for a chance to leave the f-file anyway, and taking a pawn en route makes it even better. The bishop also would not be averse to leaving f4 for e5 now, after the rook's return to a8; but in that event Black could castle, thereby exercising his right to "make three moves in one".(We have grown so used to castling that we think of it as just another move, when in fact it is not: the rook moves from h8 to f8, defending f7, while the king leaps from e8 to g8, defending the bishop at g7.)

13.	Bf4-e3	...

White is not above taking the c-pawn. 13 Bc7 would be a mistake, in view of 13..B or Qd4+.

13.	...	0-0
14.	Be3:c5	Bg7-d4+

Symptomatic: in this type of position, White usually spends considerable effort in order to enforce an exchange of dark-square bishops, so that the important squares f6 and h6, so close to Black's king, may be the more easily occupied by White's pieces. The fact that it is Black who initiates the trade of bishops here shows that he is by now unable to think in terms of principles, but only of how to reduce the number of attacking pieces, which nearly always benefits the defender.

15.	Bc5:d4	Qd8:d4+
16.	Kg1-h1	Ra8-b8

As long as White has not yet come up with any concrete threats to mate or to win material, Black should strive to develop his queen's bishop as quickly as possible — that's the idea behind this rook move (..b6 and ..Bb7). Time, however, is an expensive commodity in chess. On b8 the rook is unprotected once again, and soon comes under fire from the queen.

Good or bad, he ought to have played either 16..Nc6 or an immediate 16..e5.

17. Nc3-e4   ...

The knight cannot be kept away from f6. At e4, it simultaneously masks the f4 square, through which the white queen intends to slip into h6; with the queen at h6, Ne4-f6+ would be fatal for Black, so he hits at the knight immediately. Once again, Keres is playing concretely, with hardly a thought for the weak pawn, subject to frontal assault, that he gets on e6.

17. ...   f7-f5
18. Qf3-f4   Bc8-d7

Black's move may be understood in terms of the proverb, "Better late than never". In this case, however, never would have been better.

The only chance to continue fighting lay in 18..Ra8, strange as that might sound. Black would have had serious difficulties, of course, but there seems to be no forced win for White. One could hardly imagine such a game,

where the black rook swings like a pendulum from a8 to b8 and back, and yet even then Black is still able to maintain the balance somehow.

All Black needs now is one small thing — his turn to move.

19. c2-c3   ...

Giving the queen its choice of moving forward, left or right. By going forward to d3, Black risks losing a piece after 20 Nc5 Qb5 21 Qd6; by retreating leftward, to the kingside, Black would allow the knight to get to c5; so therefore, the queen retreats rightward, to the queenside, retaining control of c5 and d6. But now the wolf comes in through a different door — and once again, the queen's rook is the culprit.

19. ...   Qd4-b6
20. Ne4-f6+   Rf8:f6

The importunate knight must be removed regardless of the cost, since otherwise it not only captures the bishop on d7, but also forks all three of Black's heavy pieces (20..Kg7? 21 N:d7!).

21. Qf4:b8+   Bd7-c8

The unfortunate rook has perished at last, leaving behind a shattered army on the battlefield.

22. d3-d4   Rf6-f8
23. Rf1-f2   Ne7-c6
24. Qb8-f4   Bc8-d7
25. Ra1-e1   ...

Black has no compensation at all for his lost exchange, so the rest really requires no comment, except to say that White certainly did not play the second half of the game in the best possible way.

25 .. Nd8 26. d5 Nf7 27. de B:e6 28. b3 Bd7 29. Qd4 Bc6 30. Q:b6 ab 31. B:c6 bc 32. Re6 Rc8 33. Rfe2 Kf8 34. h4 b5 35. a4 ba 36. ba Ra8 37. R:c6 R:a4 38. Rc7 Ra6 39. Rb2 h6 40. c4 f4

The game was adjourned here, to be continued on the day set aside for the completion of all unfinished games.

41. c5 f3 42. Kg1 Ra8 43. Rcb7 Ra1+ 44. Rb1 Ra6 45. Rd7 Ra8 46. Re1 Ra2 47. Re3 Ra1+ 48. Kf2 Ra2+ 49. K:f3 Rc2 50. Rc7 h5 51. Ke4 Nh6 52. Ra3 Re2+ 53. Kf4 Re8 54. Rh7 Kg8 55. R:h6 Kg7 56. c6 K:h6 57. Rc3 g5+ 58. hg+

BLACK RESIGNED

******

79. Gligoric—Smyslov
(Queen's Indian Defense)

1.	c2-c4	Ng8-f6
2.	Nb1-c3	e7-e6
3.	Ng1-f3	c7-c5
4.	g2-g3	b7-b6
5.	Bf1-g2	Bc8-b7
6.	0-0	Bf8-e7
7.	d2-d4	...

The game has transposed into the Queen's Indian, but the transposition has been a favorable one for Black: having gotten his ..c7-c5 in before White's d2-d4, he can now trade off this center pawn without permitting the cramping d4-d5.

7.	...	c5:d4
8.	Qd1:d4	0-0
9.	Rf1-d1	Nb8-c6
10.	Qd4-f4	Qd8-b8

Completely neutralizing White's attempts at any sort of opening advantage.

11.	Qf4:b8	Ra8:b8
12.	Bc1-f4	Rb8-c8
13.	Bf4-d6	...

Is it possible that this harmless attempt to establish himself on d6 was the reason White essayed this whole variation? By this time, 13 Ne5 was the better course.

13.	...	Be7:d6
14.	Rd1:d6	Nc6-e7
15.	Nf3-e5	...

This looks aggressive, but it turns out to be a blunder that costs a pawn. Even blunders, however, have their reasons sometimes. For this encounter, Gligoric chose a cautious opening, in which it is usually difficult to secure an advantage; he also went in for early simplifications, resulting in a completely drawish position. At that moment, suddenly, White began playing for a win! The logic of chess does not permit such things: once a position of clear equilibrium has been established, it takes more than simple will-power to tip the scales.

And it was not yet too late to defend the c-pawn: 15 b3 Nf5 16 Rd3 d5 17 cd N:d5 18 N:d5 B:d5.

15.	...	Bb7:g2
16.	Kg1:g2	Ne7-f5

Naturally! Black drives the rook off first, then the knight, and then takes the c-pawn. Luckily for White, he still has 18 e4, allowing him to double Black's pawns.

17.	Rd6-d2	d7-d6
18.	e2-e4	Nf5:g3
19.	h2:g3	d6:e5
20.	b2-b3	...

There exists a widespread, and therefore dangerous, misconception that the win is automatic once you are a pawn ahead. As a matter of fact, Black's chief advantage in this position lies not so much in his plus pawn, which he is still far from exploiting, as in his control of most of the center squares: d4, d5, c5, f4 and f5.

White has his counterchances: a queenside pawn majority and the d-file. How many similar games have been drawn because of inexact play! Smyslov, however, manages such endings with an iron hand. His plan may be divided into the following phases:

1. The immediate exchange of one
rook, leaving the other to restrain White's queenside pawns
and attack the c- and e-pawns.

2. Deflecting White's rook to
the h-file by the threat to create an outside passed pawn, and
then occupying the ,d-file with
his own rook.

3. Advancing the g-pawn to g4,
undermining the e-pawn's support, which is the f3-pawn.

4. Tying up White's pieces by
attacking the e-pawn.

5. Sending his king in to pick
off the weak pawns.

As we shall see, a simple winning plan — for a Smyslov, naturally!

20.	...	Rf8-d8
21.	Ra1-d1	Rd8:d2
22.	Rd1:d2	Kg8-f8
23.	f2-f3	Kf8-e7

| 24. | Kg2-f2 | h7-h5! |
| 25. | Kf2-e3 | g7-g5 |

The first part of the plan is
complete: White must pull his
rook away.

26.	Rd2-h2	Rc8-d8
27.	Rh2-h1	g5-g4
28.	f3:g4	Nf6:g4+
29.	Ke3-e2	Ng4-f6
30.	Ke2-e3	Rd8-d4

Now the e-pawn is twice attacked; Black intends to continue ..Ke7-f8-g7-g6-g5-g4.

31.	Rh1-f1	Nf6-g4+
32.	Ke3-e2	Ke7-f8
33.	Rf1-f3	Kf8-g7
34.	Rf3-d3	...

White sees the writing on the
wall, and resolves to try his
luck in a knight ending. But
this can only be achieved at
the cost of giving Black a passed
d-pawn.

| 34. | ... | Kg7-f6 |

Now that a rook exchange is in
the offing, Black alters his
king's itinerary. After the automatic 34..Kg6 35 R:d4 ed 36 Nb5
e5 37 N:a7 White has some hope.

35.	Rd3:d4	e5:d4
36.	Nc3-b5	Kf6-e5
37.	Nb5:a7	Ke5:e4
38.	Na7-c8	...

One last swindle: 38..e5?
39 Nd6 is mate! If he wanted to
play on a while longer, however,
38 Nb5 was better. Now the king
is left completely alone against
king, knight and a powerful passed
pawn.

38.	...	d4-d3+
39.	Ke2-d2	Ke4-d4
40.	c4-c5	b6:c5
41.	Nc8-d6	Ng4-e5

WHITE RESIGNED

******

80. Taimanov—Geller
(King's Indian)

Perusal of this meaty game
will acquaint the reader with
two strategic ideas. As a result
of the opening Black obtains the
pawn configuration c5-d6-e5 versus c4-d5-e4; this ensures White
greater freedom to maneuver within his own lines, since he has
three ranks, while Black has only
two. This is an abstract advantage, of course, but it is the
master's task to render it concrete — that is, to find a plan
wherein this will prove useful.
It is instructive to watch as
Taimanov practically clears his
first three ranks of pawns entirely, enabling him to transfer his forces easily from one
wing to the other, while most of
Black's pieces find themselves
jostling one another on the seventh rank, and especially on the

eighth.

And the second idea: White doubles his rooks on the b-file, but cannot turn this to account, since all the good invasion squares are covered by Black's minor pieces. White therefore stirs up some play on the other wing; harmless in itself, this play leads to the exchange of a few pieces and draws the minor pieces away from the b-file, thus allowing White's rooks to invade at b7 and conclude the game within a few moves.

1.	d2-d4	Ng8-f6
2.	c2-c4	g7-g6
3.	Nb1-c3	Bf8-g7
4.	e2-e4	0-0
5.	Ng1-f3	d7-d6
6.	Bf1-e2	e7-e5
7.	0-0	Nb8-d7
8.	Rf1-e1	c7-c6
9.	Be2-f1	Rf8-e8

Geller's ninth move completed his array; now he intends 10..ed, with activization, so Taimanov crosses him up by pushing his center pawn.

| 10. | d4-d5 | ... |

Offering Black the choice of trading on d5 or closing the center — or doing neither. The trade would make sense only if White's bishop were on g2 and Black's rook on f8. Maintaining tension with 10..Qe7 and 11..a5, followed eventually by ..Nc5 and ..f7-f5, looks good here. As to Geller's choice, 10..c5, that's a matter of chessic taste: it seems to me that Black has a harder time obtaining counterplay in the King's Indian with a locked pawn configuration.

| 10. | ... | c6-c5 |
| 11. | g2-g3 | ... |

A far-sighted move whose point will become clear later on.

11.	...	Nd7-f8
12.	a2-a3	Nf6-g4
13.	Nf3-h4	a7-a6

Black refrained from his intended 13..f5, seeing 14 ef gf 15 Bh3, threatening 16 N:f5 and 17 B:g4, and if 15..Qf6, then 16 Ne4 fe 17 B:g4. Thus, 11 g3 was directed against 13..f5:

White gave his knight support at h4, and opened a path for the bishop to h3. Najdorf's suggestion 13..Bf6 14 Ng2 Bg7 is not entirely convincing, inasmuch as 14..B:h4 is not a threat: White can reply to 13..Bf6 with 14 f3 B:h4 15 gh Nf6 16 Bg5 Kg7 17 Qd2.

14.	Bc1-d2	h7-h5
15.	h2-h3	Ng4-f6
16.	b2-b4	b7-b6
17.	b4:c5	b6:c5
18.	Ra1-b1	Nf6-d7
19.	Qd1-a4	Bg7-f6
20.	Nh4-f3	...

White sees that it is not yet time to invade: 20 Qc6 Ra7 21 Q:d6? Rc7!! traps the queen.

| 20. | ... | h5-h4 |

An attack on the king with such limited means can hardly accomplish much. As long as White still has no concrete threats on the queenside, Black might as well have continued his preparations for ..f7-f5.

| 21. | Nc3-d1 | h4:g3 |
| 22. | f2:g3 | Nd7-b8 |

To complete this picture, Black need only "follow through" with ..Bh8. The position illustrates the meaning of the phrase, "freedom of maneuver". A white rook on b3 will control the b-file and simultaneously defend f3 and g3. In some variations, the rook on b1 goes to h1, and the knight on d1 may go to c3, e3 or f2; meanwhile, Black's rooks and knights have only one

move apiece, Black's pieces cannot use the b-file, nor can he
transfer pieces to the kingside.
However, Black's position is solid enough: as we said, White
still has to prove his advantage.

23.	Re1-e3	Nf8-h7
24.	Re3-b3	Bc8-d7
25.	Qa4-a5	Qd8-c8
26.	Nd1-f2	Bf6-d8
27.	Qa5-c3	Bd7-a4

Geller's exceptionally tough,
staunch defense deserves special
mention. He has successfully
driven back the queen, and largely neutralized White's control
of the b-file: on Rb7 he plays
simply ..Re7, and the rook must
either retreat or trade. Now
White directs his knight, bishops and queen toward the king's
wing, forcing Black to divert his
pieces from the b-file.

28.	Rb3-b2	Nb8-d7
29.	h3-h4	Ra8-a7
30.	Bf1-h3	Qc8-c7
31.	Nf3-g5	Nh7:g5
32.	Bd2:g5	Bd8:g5
33.	h4:g5	Kg8-g7
34.	Qc3-f3!	...

This move deserves its exclamation mark, and not just for
itself, but also as the finishing
touch to the game as a strategic
entity. All the moves which follow are based on the quick transfer of pieces from one wing to
the other; the same idea figures
in the present threat of 35 Kg2!
followed by the exchange on d7,
the check on f6, and Rb1-h1, with
unavoidable mate somewhere in the
vicinity of h8.

34.	...	Qc7-d8
35.	Rb2-b7	Ra7:b7
36.	Rb1:b7	...

Now there is a new threat:
37 B:d7 B:d7 38 Qf6+, winning
the key d6-pawn, and with it
the game.

36.	...	Kg7-g8
37.	Bh3:d7	Ba4:d7
38.	Nf2-g4	Qd8:g5

38..Re7 runs into 39 Nf6+,
and on any king move, 40 Qh1.

| 39. | Rb7:d7 | f7-f5 |
| 40. | e4:f5 | Re8-b8 |

Once the time scramble had
ended, and it was established
that White had indeed completed
the required forty moves before
flagfall, then, naturally,

BLACK RESIGNED

******

81. Najdorf—Kotov
(Caro-Kann Defense)

| 1. | e2-e4 | ... |

Initiating a war of nerves.
This was the only game in the
entire tournament that Najdorf
opened with his king's pawn, expecting (as he explained later)
that Kotov would play the Najdorf
Variation of the Sicilian, for
which White had prepared a little surprise.

| 1. | ... | c7-c6 |

After long thought, Kotov replied 1..c7-c6 — also the only
time in the entire tournament
that he deserted his Sicilian.
Kotov proceeded to equalize completely by means of painstakingly accurate play, and then began
considering how to gain the advantage...

2.	d2-d4	d7-d5
3.	Nb1-c3	d5:e4
4.	Nc3:e4	Bc8-f5
5.	Ne4-g3	Bf5-g6
6.	Ng1-f3	Nb8-d7
7.	Bf1-d3	Ng8-f6
8.	0-0	e7-e6
9.	Rf1-e1	Bf8-e7
10.	c2-c4	0-0

11.	Bd3:g6	h7:g6
12.	Bc1-f4	Rf8-e8

Black did not play ..Qc7 before castling; now he prepares ..c7-c5, but clears a spot for his bishop at f8 in anticipation of a possible d4-d5 in reply.

13.	Qd1-c2	c6-c5
14.	Ra1-d1	c5:d4
15.	Nf3:d4	Be7-b4!

Black's threat of ..e6-e5 forces a trade of darksquare bishops, which eases his defense.

16.	Bf4-d2	Bb4:d2
17.	Qc2:d2	a7-a6
18.	b2-b4	Qd8-c7
19.	Rd1-c1	Ra8-d8
20.	Qd2-c3	Nd7-b6

White has one small advantage, his queenside pawn majority; Black has an extra center pawn. This means that in an endgame the chances lie with White, whereas a complex fight with queens promises fully equal play for Black. With this in mind, Kotov should not have been so eager to exchange queens; also, 20..Nb8 and 21..Nc6 was a better idea than his 20..Nb6.

21.	Nd4-f3	Qc7-f4
22.	Qc3-e3	Qf4:e3
23.	Re1:e3	Rd8-c8
24.	Re3-c3	Re8-d8
25.	Kg1-f1	Kg8-f8
26.	Kf1-e2	...

26.	...	Kf8-e7
27.	a2-a3	Rc8-c7
28.	Rc3-c2	Rd8-c8
29.	Ke2-d3	...

It is not clear whether Najdorf was willing to take a draw here, or simply wished to test his opponent's intentions, but in any event after 29..Rd8+ his king would have had to retreat. Of course, the draw would hardly be forced, even after 30 Ke2 Rdc8; White could redeploy his knights to e3 and b3, and try to exploit his queenside preponderance. However, Black would retain powerful support points in the center for his knights — all in all, a stubborn fight would lie ahead.

After 29 Kd3, however, the game took an unexpected turn. Kotov, full of optimism and fighting spirit as usual, decided to push his center pawns, drive off the white king and secure d3. It is our opinion that this plan, even if it could be fully carried out, would not have been especially favorable to Black. However, pushing the e-pawn does deprive the knight on b6 of any chance to go to d5 after White's c4-c5. On e6, the pawn performed an important function by protecting d5.

29.	...	Nf6-d7
30.	Ng3-f1	f7-f5
31.	Nf1-e3	e6-e5
32.	Nf3-d2	e5-e4+
33.	Kd3-e2	Nd7-e5

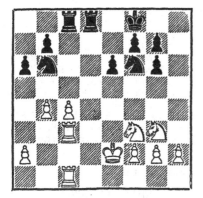

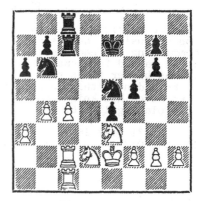

Despite his flurry of activity,

Black has an inferior position. The e-pawn has left behind all the points it ought to have defended, and the knights have no center support. After White's next move, the unpleasant 35 Nd5+ is already threatened.

34.   c4-c5   Ne5-d3
35.   Rc1-d1   Nd3-f4+

An oversight which loses by force. However, 35..Ke6 would also have left Black with the inferior position, in view of 36 g3, with f2-f3 to follow.

36.   Ke2-f1   Ke7-e6
37.   Nd2:e4   ...

After this rather obvious pseudo-sacrifice, Black's game immediately collapses.

37.   ...   Nb6-d7

If the knight is taken, the rook checks at d6.

38.   Ne4-d6   Rc8-h8
39.   g2-g3   Nf4-h3
40.   Ne3-d5   Rc7-c6
41.   Rc2-e2+   ...

BLACK RESIGNED

******

82. Petrosian—Boleslavsky
(English Opening)

1. c4 e5 2. Nc3 d6 3. g3 Nc6
4. Bg2 g6 5. d3 Bg7 6. Bd2 Nge7
7. Nf3 0-0 8. 0-0 Bd7 9. Rb1
Qc8 10. b4 Bh3 11. b5 Nd4 12. a4
B:g2 13. K:g2 Qd7 14. Nd5 c6

White consistently attacks the queenside, whereas Black is committing an inaccuracy here. If he wanted to exchange knights, it was better to do this at d5; if he did not, then he should have moved his knight to f5 before playing 15..c6.

15. N:e7+ Q:e7 16. N:d4 ed
17. Re1 Qd7 18. bc bc 19. Qb3
Rfc8 20. Qb7 Qf5 21. Qa6 h5

DRAW

at White's suggestion, although he had the better of it. A possible continuation might have been 22 Rb7 h4 23 Reb1, etc.

******

83. Averbakh—Stahlberg
(French Defense)

1. e4 e6 2. d4 d5 3. Nd2 c5
4. ed Q:d5 5.Ngf3 cd 6. Bc4 Qd6
7. 0-0 Nf6 8. Nb3 Nc6 9. Re1 a6
10. a4 Be7 11. Nb:d4 N:d4 12. Q:d4
Bd7 13. Bf4 Q:d4 14. N:d4 Rc8
15. Bb3 Nh5 16. Be3 0-0 17. Nf3
Bc5 18. Ne5 Nf6 19. Rad1 Be8
20. B:c5 R:c5 21. c3 Bc6 22. f3
Rb8 23. Rd4 Be8 24. h4 Kf8 25. f4
a5 26. Nd3 Rcc8 27. f5

White departs from the "book" approach to the ending, making a rather adventurous attempt to gain the upper hand. Failing this, he is left with the inferior position.

27 .. ef 28. Re5 Rd8   29. R:f5
R:d4 30. cd b6 31. Rf4 Rd8

Black seizes the initiative.

32. Ne5 Nh5 33. Rf3 R:d4 34. B:f7
Nf6 35. B:e8 K:e8 36. Rb3 Re4
37. Nf3 Nd7 38. Ng5 R:h4 39.Re3+
Kf8

This eases White's defense: the king should have headed for b8: for example, 39..Kd8 40 Ne6+ Kc8 41 Rc3+ Kb8 42 Rc7 Rd4!

40. Ne6+ Kg8 41. Ng5 Kf8 42.Ne6+
Kf7 43. Nd8+ Kg8! 44. Re7 Nf8
45. Rb7 Rh6 46. Nf7 Re6 47. Ng5
Rd6 48. Rb8 h6 49. Ne4 Rd1+ 50. Kh2
Rd4 51. Nc3 Rh4+ 52. Kg1 Rb4
53. Nd5 R:b2 54. R:b6

A mistake, just before the second time control: the knight should have taken the pawn.

54 .. Ra2 55. Nc3 Rc2 56. Nd5
Rc4 57. Ra6 R:a4 58. Ne7+ Kh7
59. Nc6 Ra1+ 60. Kh2 a4 61. Nd4
Nd7 62. Ra7 Nc5 63. Nf5 Kg6
64. g4 Ne6 65. Ra6 Kf7 66. Nd6+
Kf6 67. Nc4 Ke7 68. Ra7+ Kd8
69. Ne5 Nc7 70. Nf7+ Kd7 71. Ne5+
Kc8 72. Nc6 a3 73. Ne7+ Kd8
74. Nc6+ Kd7 75. Nd4 Kc8 76.Kg3
Rd1 77. Nc2 Nb5 78. Ra5 Rc1
79. N:a3 Rc3+ 80. Kh4 g5+! 81.Kh5
Rh3+ 82. Kg6 N:a3 83. Kg7 Nb1!
84. Ra6 Nd2 85. R:h6 R:h6 86.K:h6
Nf3

Just in time.

WHITE RESIGNED

******

[140]

84. Szabo—Euwe
(Queen's Indian Defense)

1.	d2-d4	Ng8-f6
2.	c2-c4	e7-e6
3.	Ng1-f3	b7-b6
4.	Nb1-c3	Bc8-b7
5.	e2-e3	Bf8-e7
6.	Bf1-d3	c7-c5
7.	0-0	...

Before the play gets too live-ly in the center, White decides to secure his king. Black has other ideas: he wants to carry out the typical maneuver in this opening — ..c5:d4 and ..d7-d5 — at once.

Szabo probably figured that Black could not play this be-fore castling because of checks on the a4-e8 diagonal; but Euwe risked it anyway, and equalized.

7.	...	c5:d4
8.	e3:d4	d7-d5
9.	c4:d5	Nf6:d5

Only a player with exception-ally strong nerves could allow himself such opening play.

10.	Bd3-b5+	...

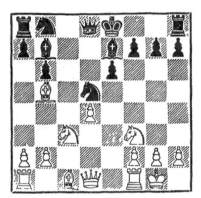

10.	...	Bb7-c6
11.	Bb5:c6+	...

Szabo exchanges bishops too quickly; pressure on the diag-onal with 11 Qa4 was necessary, with the following main varia-tion: 11..B:b5 12 Q:b5+ Qd7 13 N:d5! ed 14 Qb3 or 14 Qe2, when White maintains his lead in development.

11.	...	Nb8:c6
12.	Qd1-a4	Qd8-d7

But now Black's calculations are justified: White is unable to increase the pressure. True, he does make one last attempt, but after

13.	Nc3:d5	

Black naturally does not take back on d5 with the pawn, but instead...

13.	...	Qd7:d5
14.	Bc1-e3	0-0
15.	Rf1-c1	b6-b5

A clear draw takes shape, and is in fact established by repetition of moves.

16.	Qa4-a6	Nc6-b4
17.	Qa6-a5	Nb4-d3
18.	Rc1-c2	Nd3-b4
19.	Rc2-c1	Nb4-d3

DRAW

******

******

ROUND THIRTEEN

85. Stahlberg—Szabo
(Grunfeld Defense)

1.	d2-d4	Ng8-f6
2.	c2-c4	g7-g6
3.	Nb1-c3	d7-d5
4.	Ng1-f3	Bf8-g7
5.	Qd1-b3	...

Black needs ..c7-c5, which White seeks to prevent by applying pressure against the d-pawn, thereby forcing either ..c7-c6 or ..d5:c4. Numerous defensive tries failed to work for Black until Smyslov worked out the plan Black employs in this game.

5.	...	d5:c4
6.	Qb3:c4	0-0
7.	e2-e4	Bc8-g4

This, with the following moves, is the Smyslov System of the Grunfeld.

8.	Bc1-e3	Nf6-d7

This apparently illogical move has its own logic and its own history. When the system first began to be played, 8..Nc6 was usual here; 9 d5 would be answered by the bishop capture at f3, for example: 10 dc b5!, or 10 gf Ne5 11 Qe2 c6! Eventually, White started to get the upper hand in this; then Smyslov (and others) began introducing refinements. This process of "laboratory testing" resulted in the move 8..Nfd7, which combines two ideas: retaining the option of ..c7-c5, and putting pressure on the d-pawn. Now, for example, 9..Nb6 is threatened, and if the queen leaves the d-pawn's protection, then 10..B:f3 followed by 11..B:d4.

There have been several tries here: 9 Nd2, or 9 Be2 Nb6 10 Qd3 followed by long castling, which leads to a double-edged game; or 9 e5, or 9 d5, or 9 Rd1 Nb6 10 Qb3. The conclusion was finally reached that it is better to retreat the queen to b3 before the knight chases it away.

Szabo replies with an extremely complicated variation involving an immediate ..c7-c5.

9.	Qc4-b3	c7-c5

10.	d4-d5	...

If the queen takes the b-pawn, Black first trades his queen's bishop for White's king's knight, and then plays 11..cd, abandoning his queen's rook; one line is 12 Q:a8 dc 13 Q:a7 cb 14 Rb1 Nc6, and Black has a very strong attack on the king for the exchange. The text makes it very uncomfortable for the queen's bishop, which now has the choice of taking on f3 (which would strengthen White's center) or of remaining at its post, to face great peril after 11 Nd2.

10.	...	Nb8-a6
11.	Nf3-d2	e7-e6

Black appears to be locking his own bishop in an escape-proof cell; this is not mere whimsy, however, but the product of analysis which Szabo had already tested in a game from a previous tournament. For example: 12 h3 ed threatening 13..d4, and if 13 ed, then 13..Bf5 14 g4 c4, clearing c5 for the knight, which lets the bishop retreat; if then 15 Q:c4 Ne5 is possible, and the bishop is freed once again.

12.	d5-d6	...

White's pawn has broken free of its support, and will soon be surrounded by the hostile army. A fierce battle erupts around it, but one may already predict that the advantage must swing to Black, whose pieces are all developed, and who has already castled.

12.	...	Bg7-d4

This move is justified by the variation 13 h3 (winning the bishop?!) 13..B:e3 14 fe Qh4 mate! On the other hand, if White exchanges bishops himself and then plays 14 Nb5, Black has the unpleasant reply 14..Ndc5, followed by 15..e5. Black's passed pawn on the d-file would be defended, and therefore a great deal stronger than White s; the black pieces would also be better placed.

13. Bf1:a6 ...

This secures c4 for his knight and wins a tempo for castling, but it also opens the b-file.

13.	...	b7:a6
14.	Nd2-c4	Ra8-b8
15.	Qb3-c2	e6-e5
16.	Nc3-d5	Qd8-h4
17.	0-0	Bg4-e6
18.	g2-g3	...

Stahlberg's characteristically negligent attitude towards the safety of his king. An outstanding tactician who knows how to put up a staunch defense, he has saved so many difficult positions that he sometimes simply ignores such weakenings as this. But his g2-g3 will soon be followed by f2-f3, and a cold wind will begin to blow along the second rank, now open from c- to h-file, which will prove most unhealthy for White's king.

Had White played 18 Rae1 here, or 18 Ne7+ followed by 19 Rae1, his game would still have been far from lost; now it gets very difficult.

18.	...	Qh4-h5
19.	f2-f3	Be6:d5
20.	e4:d5	Nd7-b6
21.	Be3:d4	e5:d4

Although it leaves Black with a protected passed pawn, White could not avoid this exchange, since there was no way to defend the bishop: 21 Rae1 allows 21..N:c4 22 Q:c4 R:b2, with a mate threat at h2 — that second-rank weakness already!

22. Nc4:b6 Rb8:b6!

22..ab was possible too, but Black wanted to keep the b-file open for attacking purposes.

Once again, 23 Q:c5 is impossible on account of 23..R:b2 with a mate threat.

23.	Ra1-c1	Rb6:d6
24.	Qc2:c5	Rd6:d5
25.	Qc5:a7	d4-d3
26.	Qa7-e3	...

The second-rank threat dogs White's every step: he cannot even think of taking the a6-pawn, in view of 26..Re8 with a swift end.

26.	...	d3-d2
27.	Rc1-d1	Rf8-d8
28.	g3-g4	Qh5-h4
29.	Rf1-f2	Rd5-d3
30.	Qe3-f4	Qh4-e7
31.	Qf4-a4	Qe7-f6
32.	Qa4-b4	Qf6-g5
33.	Kg1-g2	Rd3-d4
34.	Qb4-b3	h7-h5

The point of this maneuver is to gain control of g3 — this will become clear after White's forced reply.

35.	h2-h3	h5-h4
36.	f3-f4	Qg5-e7

Naturally White could not allow 36..Qf4, but now comes the decisive maneuver: 36..Qe7 threatens 37..Rd3 followed by 38..Qe3 or 38..Qe1, depending on White's reply.

37.	Rf2-f3	Rd4-d3
38.	Rf3:d3	Qe7-e2+
39.	Kg2-g1	Rd8:d3
40.	Qb3-b8+	Kg8-h7

WHITE RESIGNED

86. Boleslavsky—Averbakh
(Queen's Gambit)

1.	c2-c4	Ng8-f6
2.	Nb1-c3	e7-e6
3.	Ng1-f3	d7-d5
4.	d2-d4	Bf8-b4
5.	c4:d5	e6:d5
6.	Bc1-g5	h7-h6
7.	Bg5:f6	Qd8:f6
8.	Qd1-a4+	Nb8-c6
9.	e2-e3	0-0
10.	Bf1-e2	a7-a6

Black wants to retreat his bishop to d6: this secures it against possible pursuit by Nb5. However, if White had wanted to force this bishop to exchange itself for his queen's knight, he could have played 11 a3; this would have given him much the better game, considering that he could then enforce c3-c4, with powerful pressure on the b- and c-files. So this variation cannot be recommended for Black.

11.	0-0	Bc8-e6
12.	Ra1-c1	Bb4-d6
13.	Qa4-c2	Rf8-d8
14.	Nc3-a4	Nc6-e7

Black's last few moves have aimed at creating a chain of pawns and freeing his pieces from the defense of the pawns at d5 and c7.

15.	Na4-c5	Be6-c8

Black is ready to play the final move to consolidate his position; but now comes an unexpected blow, bringing the combinative element into the game and completely altering the situation. The e-pawn travels from the third rank to the fifth, and brings about a series of favorable simplifications.

16.	e3-e4	...

When one's opponent is well developed, such moves generally are not even considered, since the d4-pawn is "irretrievably" weakened, while Black — well, what does he have to worry about, since he has no weaknesses? In our day, the concept of "weakness" has altered to such an extent that not just pawn structure, but the poor placement of just one piece can be a weakness.

16.	...	Qf6-g6

16..Bf4 would be met by 17 e5 Qc6 18 Nd2!, when 18..b6 would prove unprofitable for Black: 19 Nd3 Q:c2 20 R:c2 B:d2 21 R:d2, reaching an ending similar to the one that occurs in the game, but with a much weaker c-pawn. And on 16..de, the black queen turns out to be badly placed. A sample variation will indicate White's advantage in the fast-paced piece play that ensues: 17 N:e4 Qg6 18 Bd3 Bf5 19 Nh4 Qh5 20 N:f5 N:f5 21 N:d6 N:d6 22 Q:c7.

17.	e4-e5	...

It would seem more logical to continue harrying the queen by 17 Bd3: for example, 17..B:c5 18 Q:c5, or 17..de 18 B:e4 Bf5 19 B:f5, and after the trading on f5 White wins the b-pawn. That's probably what Boleslavsky intended to play, too, until he discovered that Black has the excellent defense 17..Bf4; so he changed his plan.

17.	...	Qg6:c2
18.	Rc1:c2	Bd6:c5
19.	Rc2:c5	c7-c6

A very interesting position has developed. White's natural plan — the minority attack with a4, b4 and b5 — allows Black active counterplay if he exploits White's weakness (the d-pawn), and perhaps carries out the maneuver ..b7-b6 and ..c6-c5.

Black, in turn, will find it profitable to maneuver his rook to support the pawn advance ..f7-f6. If he sticks to passive tactics on both wings, then his game is bound to become difficult.

At the moment, Black threatens 20..Bg4, trading off the knight, and thereby making it harder for his opponent to defend the d-pawn; this explains White's next move.

20. Nf3-d2   a6-a5

Here Black ought to have struck at the d-pawn first by 20..Nf5: his ..a6-a5 would have had more point after 21 Nb3. White could answer with 22 a4, but then comes 22..Bd7, inducing a new White weakness; if 22 Rd1 instead, then 22..a4 23 Nc1 g5!, with such possibilities as ..f7-f6 or ..Nf5-g7-e6.

Averbakh's move prevents 21 b4, followed by Nd2-b3-c5; but we have seen how he could have achieved the same end using far more active means.

21. Rc5-c3   ...

This rook was only passing through c5; now it gives place to the knight.

21. ...   Rd8-f8
22. Rf1-e1   g7-g6

Black's previous move didn't pan out: he wanted to prepare 22..f6, and recapture on f6 with

his rook, but now 22..f6 would be met by 23 e6!, when the white pawn is very strong. So Black reluctantly goes on the defensive.

23. Be2-d3   Bc8-f5
24. Bd3-f1   a5-a4
25. h2-h3   Bf5-d7
26. f2-f4   h6-h5

It takes great skill indeed to induce Averbakh, a well-known endgame expert, to put all of his pawns on the same color squares as his bishop.

27. Nd2-f3   Kg8-g7
28. Kg1-f2   Rf8-h8
29. g2-g3   Kg7-f8
30. Kf2-g2   Ne7-f5
31. Bf1-d3   Nf5-g7
32. Nf3-g5   Bd7-e6

Preventing the possible pawn break 33 e6, and if 33..B:e6 34 B:g6.

33. Bd3-c2   Kf8-e7
34. Rc3-a3   Ng7-f5

Black is very much opposed to advancing his pawn to b5; so he sends up a trial balloon, offering to let White take on f5 and thereby leave himself with knight versus a bad bishop. White, however, calmly retreats his knight to f3, obtaining maximum results. Thus, the a4-pawn draws the pawn to b5 after it, like string from a ball, and the c6-pawn must suffer in turn.

35. Ng5-f3   b7-b5
36. Ra3-c3   Ra8-c8
37. Bc2:f5   Be6:f5

38.   Re1-c1   Bf5-d7

39 e6! would now have been the
logical conclusion of a well-
played endgame: whichever way
Black takes, the white knight
goes to e5, with powerful pressure on both wings. Apparently,
the variation 39..K:e6 40 Ne5
Be8 41 N:c6 Kd6 42 Ne5 R:c3
43 R:c3 f6 44 Nd3 Bd7 appeared
insufficient to Boleslavsky,
so he takes his time.

39.   Nf3-e1   Rc8-b8
40.   Ne1-d3   ...

White has finally gotten what
he was after: as soon as the
knight reaches c5, Black's game
will be nearly hopeless, since
White will have an extra kingside pawn, practically speaking,
and must eventually convert it
into a win. Nevertheless, the
move played gives Averbakh a
problem-like save!

40.   ...   b5-b4
41.   Rc3-c5   ...

Once again the rook is forced
to occupy the square c5 where
White had wanted to place his
knight.

41.   ...   Bd7-f5
42.   Nd3-f2   ...

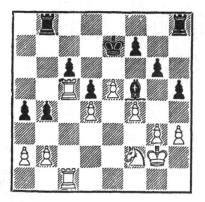

Hoping to force the bishop's
retreat, after which the knight
can support the advance g3-g4,
but —

42.   ...   b4-b3

In his difficult position,
Averbakh finds a brilliant maneuver to set up a drawn position.
If 43 ab, then 43..R:b3 44 R:c6
R:b2 45 Rc7+ Kf8, and White cannot win. Of 43 R:c6, of course,
there follows 43..ba or 43..a3!,
and suddenly it is Black who
wins.

43.   a2-a3   Bf5-c2

The picture has suddenly altered: the weak b-pawn has become strong, and the "bad" bishop now occupies a strong position. There would be no point for
White in taking the c-pawn: 44 R:c6
Rhc8 45 R:c8 R:c8 threatens
46..Rc4, and if White brings his
king up to defend with 46 Kf3,
then 46..Be4+ wins for Black. If
the king were at f1, let's say,
then White could get to e3 via e2
and win. Thus, the ability to
note and exploit the tiniest of
nuances sometimes decides the outcome of a game.

The following maneuvers can
no longer alter the result. The
question arises: was the win ever
possible? And if so, when did
White let it slip?

On move 40, instead of Nd3,
40 Rc5! should have been played,
not allowing Black two tempi for
..b4 and ..Bf5; then, on 40..b4,
he could have replied 41 Ra5; or
if 40..Rhc8 41 Nd3, and now if
41..Bf5 42 Nb2, or if 41..b4,
then 42 Ra5, threatening 43 Nc5.
It seems to me that Black, in
spite of all his resourcefulness,
would have been unable to save
the game then.

44.   Kg2-f3   Ke7-d7
45.   Kf3-e3   Rb8-a8
46.   h3-h4   Ra8-a6
47.   Nf2-h3   Rh8-b8
48.   Nh3-g5   Kd7-e7

DRAW

*****

87. Kotov—Petrosian
(Old Indian Defense)

We should like to draw the
reader's attention to the d4-
pawn in this game: doubled, isolated, and surrounded by enemy
pieces, still it showed an exceptional vitality. Such pawns
were nonexistent in the games of
Morphy, Steinitz, Lasker, Capa-

blanca or Alekhine: they made their debut in contemporary grandmaster games, further enriching the treasury of ideas.

Such pawns appear not only in the King's Indian, but also in the Sicilian Defense after 1 e4 c5 2 Nf3 Nc6 3 d4 cd 4 N:d4 g6 5 c4 Bg7 6 Be3 Nf6 7 Nc3 Ng4 8 Q:g4 N:d4 9 Qd1 e5! 10 Bd3 0-0 11 0-0 d6 12 Ne2 Be6 12 N:d4 ed, and in some other openings as well.

The d-pawn's survivability depends, first and foremost, upon the fianchettoed king's bishop, without which it would be a mere passing fancy; and secondly, upon how effectively Black exploits the open lines adjoining the pawn. And, in fact, such were the themes of the Kotov - Petrosian game.

1.	d2-d4	Ng8-f6
2.	c2-c4	d7-d6
3.	Nb1-c3	Nb8-d7
4.	e2-e4	e7-e5
5.	Ng1-f3	Bf8-e7
6..	g2-g3	...

This is the proper strategy. White begins with the idea that a similar position — except for White's c-pawn at c2 — could arise in the Philidor; there, the bishop would stand on c4, where it plays a leading role in the attack on the king. Here, however, at e2 or d3 it would only interfere with the rooks' actions on the central files. On g2, however, it has an excellent future, since Black will have to cede the d4 square to White eventually, and then the e-pawn will become mobile.

6.	...	0-0
7.	Bf1-g2	c7-c6
8.	0-0	a7-a6
9.	b2-b3	...

A rather patchwork idea. White is apparently anticipating ..b7-b5 by overprotecting c4, but then he brings his knight to d2 so that it may recapture on c4; nor is fianchettoing the queen's bishop particularly favorable with a knight on c3. 9 h3 ought to have been played at once, securing e3 for the bishop and thereby strengthening d4.

| 9. | ... | Rf8-e8 |

| 10. | Bc1-b2 | Be7-f8 |
| 11. | Qd1-d3 | ... |

11 Qc2 and 12 Rad1 was more natural. Why expose the queen to knight harassment from c5 or e5 ?

| 11. | ... | b7-b5 |
| 12. | Nf3-d2 | ... |

Kotov never leaves a plan half-carried out, even when he begins to suspect the plan he has chosen may not have been very good. Here he feels that after 12..ed 13 Q:d4 c5 would be bad for Black, since it would leave White's knight the d5 square in perpetuity; meanwhile, White is preparing an eventual f2-f4. However, Black comes up with a deeply thought out forcing maneuver, leading to the seizure of the d4 square and the appearance of the "hardy" pawn.

| 12. | ... | Bc8-b7 |

12..Qb6 was also possible here, when White would appear to have nothing better than 13 Ne2; but then the question arises: wouldn't the knights have been better developed to d2 and e2 in the first place?

| 13. | Kg1-h1 | ... |

White wants to play f2-f4, but he can't do it right away in view of 13 f4? ed 14 Q:d4 d5!, with the threat of 15..Bc5. The king's retreat does not prevent Black from carrying out his intended maneuver, so some sort of developing move, for instance 13 Re1, was preferable here.

| 13. | ... | e5:d4 |
| 14. | Qd3:d4 | c6-c5 |

(See diagram, next page)

Occupying d5 will be favorable for White if he can secure his knight there or if a trade of minor pieces on that square leaves him with a tangible advantage. In the present instance, neither condition holds, so Petrosian is therefore not afraid to weaken d5. White's queen is forced to beat a slow retreat back into its own camp, with the black knight in hot pursuit.

| 15. | Qd4-d3 | ... |

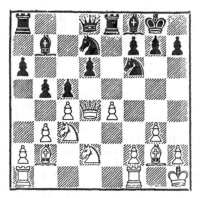

(Position after 14..c5)

After the queen retreats to e3, 15..d5 is possible.

15.	...	Nd7-e5
16.	Qd3-c2	Ne5-c6
17.	Nc3-d5	Nc6-d4

Black uses combinative means to secure a positional advantage: his next move, 18..g6, is an important link. Petrosian had to see all this before playing 13..ed, or else his position would have been quite dubious by this time.

18.	Qc2-d3	g7-g6
19.	Bb2:d4	...

Kotov doesn't quite believe his opponent, so he takes the knight, hoping to be able to

capture the d-pawn later. The more restrained 19 Nf3 would lead to a small advantage for Black: 19..bc 20 bc B:d5! 21 cd N:f3 22 B:f3 Bg7, or 21 ed N:f3 22 Q:f3 Bg7 23 B:f6 B:f6.

19.	...	c5:d4
20.	Nd5:f6+	Qd8:f6
21.	Kh1-g1	Qf6-e5
22.	Rf1-e1	Bf8-g7
23.	Ra1-c1	...

White needs only to bring one of his rooks to d1 in order to win the d4-pawn, but Black has set up such fierce pressure on the c4- and e4-pawns that both rooks are occupied defending them. The plan to win the hardy pawn is not working out, and White's game is hanging by a thread, but Kotov's coolheaded defense stems the tide.

23.	...	Re8-e7
24.	Nd2-f3	Qe5-c5
25.	Bg2-f1	h7-h6
26.	c4:b5	Qc5:b5
27.	Qd3-d1	Qb5-b6
28.	Nf3-d2	Ra8-e8
29.	Bf1-d3	...

The hardy pawn defies all its foes! Not a single piece can attack it, since it takes all of them put together to keep it blockaded. Now it is White's game that looks suspect (29..d5 is a threat), but Kotov finds a courageous pawn sacrifice..

29.	...	d6-d5
30.	e4-e5	Re7:e5
31.	Re1:e5	Re8:e5
32.	Nd2-f3	...

Now the bishop on b7 is firmly entombed, and the two d-pawns turn out to be weaker than one. Black would be more than willing to remove either of them from the board.

| 32. | ... | Re5-e4 |

Petrosian makes one last attempt: an exchange sacrifice, which Kotov of course declines.

| 33. | Qd1-d2 | a6-a5 |

DRAW

Black has difficulty activating his bishops, and White has counterchances, too: a potential passed pawn, and control of the c-file.

Black had so good a position before his 29th move that one feels impelled to speculate as to whether or not he might have had a win.

***** *

88. Geller—Najdorf
(Sicilian Defense)

1.	e2-e4	c7-c5
2.	Ng1-f3	d7-d6
3.	d2-d4	c5:d4
4.	Nf3:d4	Ng8-f6
5.	Nb1-c3	a7-a6
6.	Bf1-e2	e7-e5
7.	Nd4-b3	Bc8-e6
8.	0-0	Nb8-d7
9.	f2-f4	Qd8-c7
10.	f4-f5	Be6-c4
11.	a2-a4!	...

Against this system, a frequently used one by Najdorf, Geller has prepared a plan to occupy the light squares in the center and on the king's wing. By pushing his pawn to f5, he has driven the bishop to c4, where it will shortly be traded off. Now he plays 11 a4 in order to restrict Black's queenside play.

| 11. | ... | Ra8-c8 |
| 12. | Bc1-e3 | Bf8-e7 |

12..d5 13 ed Bb4 or 13 N:d5 N:d5 14 ed B:b3 15 cb Bc5 was more in the spirit of this variation.

| 13. | a4-a5 | h7-h5 |

Najdorf is temperamentally unsuited to a passive game without counterchances. Seeing that his queenside pieces have been hemmed in, he undertakes a kingside diversion, aimed chiefly against the possibility of g2-g4. In a later game, he castled here and held the balance — not because his game was good, but rather thanks to his tactical skill.

14.	Be2:c4	Qc7:c4
15.	Ra1-a4	Qc4-c7
16.	h2-h3	h5-h4
17.	Rf1-f2	...

| 17. | ... | b7-b5 |

Najdorf confidently sacrifices a pawn for a little initiative. His position after the 18th move would indeed have been promising, had Geller taken the a-pawn; but Geller finds a steadier solution to the problem, as we shall see. Denying himself the material, he acquires a great positional advantage instead by a series of fine moves. And although Najdorf gave his 17..b5 an exclamation mark, it is possible that 17..Qc6 was better.

| 18. | a5:b6 | Nd7:b6 |
| 19. | Be3:b6 | ... |

This exchange is aimed at subjugating the light squares, especially d5, since White removes one of the pieces which could defend that square. The next links of his plan will be to bring the rook from f2 to a1, assail the a-pawn with his heavy pieces, tie down Black's rooks and queen to its defense, and finally to bring his knight on b3 to e3, and then to d5.

The first part of this plan takes until move 24, the second part from move 25 to move 27, and the third part is concluded with White's 31st move.

19.	...	Qc7:b6
20.	Qd1-e2	Rc8-a8
21.	Kg1-h2	0-0
22.	Rf2-f1	Ra8-a7
23.	Rf1-a1	Rf8-a8
24.	Ra1-a2	...

Geller is playing an orthodox game to a fault. Here, he protects the b-pawn, in order to free his knight on b3, although he could also have played 24 Qd3, followed by 25 Nd2, when the b-pawn could not have been taken, in view of 26 Rb1. Now White enters the second part of his plan.

24.	...	Be7-d8
25.	Nb3-a5	Ra8-c8
26.	Na5-c4	Qb6-c6
27.	Nc4-e3	a6-a5
28.	Ra4-c4	Qc6-a6
29.	b2-b3	Bd8-b6
30.	Rc4:c8+	Qa6:c8
31.	Ne3-d5	Nf6:d5
32.	Nc3:d5	...

The apotheosis of White's strategy: Geller now holds the keys to Black's castle.

| 32. | ... | Qc8-c5 |
| 33. | Ra2-a1 | ... |

One must always be alert: Qg1

mate was threatened.

| 33. | ... | Qc5-f2 |

There was the chance of 33..a4 34 ba R:a4; however, White would have played 34 Qg4 instead, winning as follows:

I. 34..ab 35 f6 g6 36 Q:h4;

II. 34..Qf2 35 f6 Qg3+ 36 Q:g3 hg+ 37 K:g3 ab 38 R:a7 B:a7 39 cb.

| 34. | Qe2:f2 | ... |

A quicker method was 34 Qg4 Bd8 35 b4 a4, leading to lines covered in the previous note; or even 35 Ra4 and 36 Rc4 or 36 b4. However, Geller wants no complications, not even favorable ones, intending to win this game in positional style.

| 34. | ... | Bb6:f2 |
| 35. | Ra1-f1 | Bf2-d4 |

If the bishop checks, it will never be able to escape from g3.

36.	c2-c3	Bd4-c5
37.	g2-g4	h4:g3+
38.	Kh2:g3	Ra7-b7
39.	Rf1-b1	f7-f6

A classic endgame, with instructional value. The pawns are on squares of their own bishop's color, the knight occupies a powerful position in the center of the board, and the light squares are accessible to the king. There remains only to create an outside passed pawn.

40.	Kg3-f3	Kg8-f7
41.	Kf3-e2	Rb7-b8
42.	b3-b4	g7-g6
43.	Ke2-d3	...

Geller carries his avoidance of combinative play to extremes. 43 fg+ would have won in a few moves: 43..K:g6 44 bc R:b1 45 c6 Rb8 46 c7 Ra8 47 c8Q R:c8 48 Ne7+.

43.	...	g6:f5
44.	e4:f5	a5:b4
45.	c3:b4	Bc5-d4
46.	Rb1-c1	Kf7-g7
47.	Rc1-c7+	Kg7-h6
48.	Kd3-e4	Kh6-g5
49.	Rc7-h7	Bd4-f2
50.	Rh7-g7+	Kg5-h4
51.	Ke4-f3	Bf2-e1

52.	Kf3-g2	Rb8-f8
53.	b4-b5	Be1-a5
54.	b5-b6	Ba5:b6
55.	Nd5:b6	Rf8-b8
56.	Rg7-g4+	Kh4-h5
57.	Nb6-d5	...

BLACK RESIGNED

******

89. Smyslov—Talmanov
(Sicilian Defense)

1. e4 c5 2. Nc3 Nc6 3. g3 g6
4. Bg2 Bg7 5. d3 Nf6 6. Nge2 0-0
7. 0-0 d6 8. Rb1 Rb8 9. a3 b5
10. b4 cb 11. ab

Smyslov "pirated" points for
years with this Closed Variation.

11..Bd7 12. Nf4 e6 13. Bd2 Qc7
14. Nce2 Rfe8 15. Nc1 a5 16. ba
N:a5 17. Nb3 Nb7 18. c3 e5
19. Ne2

DRAW

The pieces on both sides are
so peaceably disposed that not
one of them has yet reached its
fourth or fifth rank. After his
string of victories in the preceding rounds, Smyslov has taken
a "time-out".

******

90. Keres—Gligoric
(Sicilian Defense)

1. e4 c5 2. Ne2 Nf6 3. Nbc3
d6 4. g3 Nc6 5. Bg2 g6 6. d4 cd
7. N:d4 N:d4 8. Q:d4 Bg7 9. 0-0
0-0 10. Qd3 Be6 11. Bd2 Qc7
12. b3 a6 13. Rac1 Rfd8

Intending to meet Nc3-d1-e3
with an immediate 14..d5!

14. Nd5 N:d5 15. ed Bf5 16. Be4
B:e4 17. Q:e4 Bb2 18. Rce1 Bf6
19. c4 Rac8 20. Rc1 Qd7 21. Ba5
R e8 22. Bb6 e5 23. de R:e6
24. Qd3 Rce8 25. Be3 Qe7 26. Rcd1
Bb2 27. Bd2 Qc7 28. Rfe1 Ba3

Playing with fire: the bishop
had no right to leave its post
on the long diagonal.

29. R:e6 R:e6 30. Re1

30 Bc3! would have been stronger.

30..Bc5 31. R:e6 fe 32. b4
Bb6 33. Bf4 e5 34. Bd2 Bd4

35. Be3 B:e3 36. fe Qc6 37. Kf2
b5 38. cb ab 39. e4 Kf7

DRAW

******

91. Reshevsky—Bronstein
(King's Indian)

This game had some influence on
the placement of the leaders,
since I stood 1½ points behind
Reshevsky, and a win for me would
decrease that gap to half a point.
If Reshevsky, who was undefeated
so far, were to win, he would
catch up to Smyslov. So it would
appear that a draw suited none
of us three. (All of these rum-
inations may be considered as
part of the pregame warmup.)

The opening was a well-known
King's Indian, with both sides
striving for the initiative. The
second phase (up to move 23) was
mostly maneuvering; by its close,
a black pawn had appeared on a3,
and a white one on e5. In the
following phase, White tried to
cash in his initiative in the
center and kingside for a mating
attack, inventing a remarkable
combination which sacrificed a
pawn, a rook, and the exchange —
which Black neutralized by exchanging off the enemy knight.
A series of exchanges followed,
which laid bare the deficiencies
of Reshevsky's pawn-pushing.

Queens plus opposite-colored
bishops usually means a very
sharp fight. In the game's concluding phase Black kept up his
mating attack until the very last
move, unwilling to trade queens
anywhere except at b2, which would
have been hopeless for White.

Even after all this, it still
seemed as though Black might not
get his win. He found it, however, by means of a joint maneuver
by queen, bishop and pawn that
left the white pieces in a state
of absolute zugzwang.

1.	d2-d4	Ng8-f6
2.	c2-c4	g7-g6
3.	g2-g3	Bf8-g7
4.	Bf1-g2	0-0
5.	Nb1-c3	d7-d6
6.	Ng1-f3	Nb8-d7
7.	0-0	e7-e5
8.	e2-e4	Rf8-e8
9.	h2-h3	e5:d4

10.	Nf3:d4	Nd7-c5
11.	Rf1-e1	a7-a5
12.	Qd1-c2	c7-c6
13.	Bc1-e3	Nf6-d7
14.	Ra1-d1	a5-a4
15.	Nd4-e2	Qd8-a5

White attacked the d-pawn, but after Black's reply, he sees that the pawn could be recovered favorably by 16..Ne5, when 17 b3 would only make matters worse in view of the surprising stroke 17..B:h3, since taking the bishop would allow the check on f3.

16.	Bg2-f1	Nd7-e5
17.	Ne2-d4	a4-a3
18.	f2-f4	...

Making this active move, Reshevsky offered a draw, although it would appear he was in a fighting mood, and would probably have been quite upset if I had accepted the offer. His inquiry, "Are you playing for a win?" appears to be more in the nature of a probe designed to needle his opponents into some precipitate step.

18.	...	Ne5-d7
19.	b2-b3	Nc5-a6
20.	Be3-f2	Nd7-c5
21.	Re1-e3	Na6-b4
22.	Qc2-e2	Bc8-d7
23.	e4-e5	d6:e5
24.	f4:e5	Ra8-d8
25.	g3-g4	Nc5-e6
26.	Bf2-h4	Ne6-d4
27.	Rd1:d4	Qa5-c5

A key move, justifying Black's entire strategy in this phase. It is very important that the white knight be kept out of f6. The e5-pawn could not have been taken by the bishop, since White would have replied 28 R:e5 and then taken the rook on d8; but now White must give serious consideration to the defense of the e-pawn.

28.	Rd4-e4	Bg7-h6
29.	Kg1-h1	Bd7-e6
30.	g4-g5	...

Initiating the combination. Reshevsky clears f4 for his rook, which clears a spot in turn for his knight.

30.	...	Bh6-g7
31.	Re4-f4	Be6-f5

32.	Nc3-e4	...

White offers the e5-pawn. I was quite tempted to take it, meeting the obvious knight check by sacrificing my queen for rook, knight and pawn. Black's pieces would have acquired tremendous scope, with good prospects for the further strengthening of my position.

However, Reshevsky had prepared a diabolical combination in answer to the pawn capture:

32..Q:e5? 33 R:f5, and now:

a) 33..Q:f5 34 Nf6+ B:f6 35 R:e8+ R:e8 36 Q:e8+ Kg7 37 gf+

b) 33..gf 34 Nf6+ B:f6 35 gf!! Q:e3 36 Qg2 — check and mate.

The beauty of this combination lies in the second line, in which White, already a rook down by move 35, captures, not the queen, but the bishop with a pawn, creating an irresistible threat of mate.

32.	...	Bf5:e4

White's volley has missed its mark.

33.	Rf4:e4	Nb4-a6
34.	e5-e6	f7:e6

Here Reshevsky offered another draw — and this time, I believe he meant it.

Black's position deserves the nod: his a3-pawn is strong, the white king is exposed, and the

black knight is better than the
bad white bishop.

35.	Re4:e6	Re8-f8!
36.	Re6-e7	Bg7-d4
37.	Re3-e6	Qc5-f5

38.	Re7-e8	Na6-c5
39.	Re8:d8	Nc5:e6
40.	Rd8:f8+	Kg8:f8
41.	Bh4-g3	...

Reshevsky thought a long time
before sealing, deciding finally
to give up the doomed pawn, in
hopes that the capture with the
queen would give him an opposite-colored bishops endgame,
while the knight capture would
lead to perpetual check: 41..N:g5
42 Bd6+ Kg7 43 Qe7+.

41.	...	Qf5:g5
42.	Qe2:e6	Qg5:g3
43.	Qe6-c8+	Kf8-e7
44.	Qc8-g4	...

White would very much like to
capture the b-pawn, but this
would lead to an immediate loss,
surprisingly enough, thanks to
a rare circumstance: the king
drives the queen back here! —
44 Q:b7+? Kd8 45 Qa8+ Kc7 46 Qa5+
Bb6, when the queen is en prise
and mate is threatened at g1.

Nonetheless, the check on
move 43 was useful for White:
it brought Black's king out to
e7, so that now Black's queen
may not move to f2 in view of
45 Qe2+, trading queens for a
clear draw.

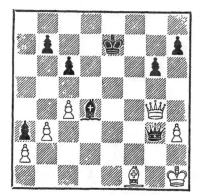

44.	...	Qg3-c3
45.	Kh1-g2	Qc3-b2+
46.	Qg4-e2+	Ke7-d6
47.	Kg2-f3	Bd4-c5
48.	Kf3-e4	Qb2-d4+
49.	Ke4-f3	Qd4-f6+
50.	Kf3-g2	Kd6-c7
51.	Qe2-f3	Qf6-b2+
52.	Qf3-e2	Qb2-d4
53.	Kg2-f3	...

Neither player can afford to
initiate the trade of queens. If
White takes on b2, then Black
needs only to create one more
passed pawn on the kingside to
win; while if Black takes on e2,
the most he will ever be able to
achieve will be the capture of
White's a-pawn. But this would
still not be enough to win for
him, since at that moment the
white king would turn up at c2,
incarcerating its colleague.

| 53. | ... | h7-h5 |

The last reserves enter the
fray.

54.	Kf3-g2	g6-g5
55.	Kg2-g3	Qd4-f4+
56.	Kg3-g2	g5-g4
57.	h3:g4	h5:g4
58.	Kg2-h1	...

(See diagram, next page)

If Black advances his pawn to
g3 now, 59 Bh3 leaves Black no
way that I can see of strengthening his position. The winning
idea is based on zugzwang.

58.	...	Kc7-b6
59.	Kh1-g2	Kb6-c7
60.	Kg2-h1	Bc5-d6
61.	Kh1-g1	Kc7-b6
62.	Qe2-g2	Bd6-c5+
63.	Kg1-h1	Qf4-h6+
64.	Qg2-h2	Qh6-e3
65.	b3-b4	Bc5-d4

There's our zugzwang. Seeing
no way out, Reshevsky allowed
his flag to fall, upon which
he was scored a loss.

******
*****

ROUND FOURTEEN

92. Gligoric—Reshevsky
(Ruy Lopez)

The first twenty moves in this game were right out of theory, and the players added very little of their own to the handbook. It might seem rather dull to the reader, but it does liven up a little when Gligoric offers his queen for rook and bishop on the 29th move. Despite the fact that the resulting balance of forces would favor Black arithmetically, Reshevsky declined this sacrifice.

1. e4 e5 2. Nf3 Nc6 3. Bb5 a6 4. Ba4 Nf6 5. 0-0 Be7 6. Re1 b5 7. Bb3 d6 8. c3 0-0 9. h3 Na5 10. Bc2 c5 11. d4 Qc7 12. Nbd2 Bd7 13. Nf1 Rfe8 14. de de 15. Nh2 g6 16. Ne3 Be6 17. Nhg4 N:g4 18. hg Rad8 19. Qf3 Nc4 20. Nd5 B:d5 21. ed Nb6 22. Be4 c4 23. Bd2 Rd6 24. Rad1 Red8

Both sides continue their leisurely woodshifting: neither wants to rock the boat.

25. Be3 Na4 26. Rd2 a5 27. a3 Nc5 28. g5 f5 29. gf R:f6

30. Be3:c5 Qc7:c5

Had Black taken the queen, 31 B:e7 Q:e7 32 B:f3 would have ensued; now the passed d-pawn would have to be blockaded, but with no more minor pieces at hand, Black would be forced to assign his only rook to the task, leaving White's rooks to pile up on the isolated e-pawn. In this line Black could hope for

no more than a draw.

31. Qe3 Qc7 32. Bf3 Bd6 33. Qh6 Qg7 34. Q:g7+ K:g7

DRAW

******

93. Taimanov—Keres
(Queen's Gambit)

1.	d2-d4	Ng8-f6
2.	c2-c4	e7-e6
3.	Nb1-c3	d7-d5
4.	Bc1-g5	c7-c5

Keres, who stands apart from King's Indianophiles and Nimzolovers alike, has secretly prepared a system for this tournament involving ..c7-c5 at a very early stage of the Queen's Gambit Declined, and employed it successfully against Stahlberg and Geller, and in the last round against Najdorf as well, in reply to 4 Nf3.

5. e2-e3 ...

A practical game is no theoreticians' polemic. Taimanov was undoubtedly aware that after 5 cd theory finds an advantage for White in every variation from "a" to the end of the alphabet — and as a matter of fact, he had won a game himself using precisely that line against Prins at Stockholm 1952. But as Taimanov, who has studied the 5 cd variation extensively, also knows, the last word has not been said here either. So he chooses another line.

Really, is it possible to "prove" that 4..c5 is contrary to the logic of chess with such lines as these:

a) 5 cd cd 6 Q:d4 Be7 7 e4 Nc6 8 Qe3 N:d5 9 ed B:g5 10 f4 Nb4 11 0-0-0 Be7 12 de Qc7 13 ef+ K:f7 14 Nf3 N:a2+; or

b) 5 cd cd 6 Q:d4 Be7 7 e4 Nc6 8 Qd2 ed 9 B:f6 B:f6 10 ed Ne5 11 Bb5 etc.; or

c) 5 cd cd 6 Q:d4 Be7 7 e4 Nc6 8 Qd2 N:e4 9 N:e4 ed 10 B:e7 Q:e7 11 Q:d5 0-0 12 f3 Nb4 13 Qg5 etc.

Note too that after 5 cd Black may try the so-called Peruvian

Variation: 5..Qb6 6 B:f6 Q:b2 etc.

The most precise knowledge of opening theory cannot guarantee one against over-the-board surprises. Therefore, a grandmaster will frequently avoid the "best" continuation in favor of his own, whether accepted by theory or not.

5.	...	c5:d4
6.	e3:d4	Bf8-e7
7.	Ng1-f3	0-0
8.	Ra1-c1	...

A waste of time. White is dallying with the development of his kingside pieces, although the game is now semi-open, which means that White must take care to get his king secured. The more natural move here was 8 Bd3.

8.	...	b7-b6!
9.	Bf1-d3	Nb8-c6
10.	0-0	Nc6-b4
11.	c4:d5!	...

A positional snare. If Black succumbs and takes the bishop — 11.. N:d3 12 Q:d3 ed — then 13 Ne5 gives White a clear advantage: on e5 the knight is better than either bishop. White could have laid a tactical snare as well: 11 Ne5, and if Black takes the bishop, 12 Nc6 Qe7 13 N:e7+ Q:e7 14 Q:d3 Ba6 15 b3 would lead to a lively game with about even chances. The swindle appears if, instead of 12..Qd7, Black tries to snatch a pawn in passing with 12..N:b2 13 Qe2 Qd7 14 N:e7+ Q:e7 15 Q:b2 Ba6. White would not take the knight on move 15, but a doubly defended pawn instead: 15 N:d5, and Black's position would collapse. Black would have to settle for the first variation: 11 Ne5 N:d3 12 Q:d3 Bb7, since an immediate 11..Bb7 12 Bb1 would leave White good attacking prospects against g7 and h7.

11.	...	Nf6:d5
12.	Bg5:e7	Qd8:e7
13.	Bd3-e4	Bc8-b7
14.	Rf1-e1	Ra8-c8
15.	Qd1-d2	h7-h6

Both a prophylactic and a waiting move. Minor piece trades impend: White wishes to induce ..N:c3, so that he can recapture with a pawn and thereby strengthen his d-pawn; Black goes along with this, since the whole pawn constellation will not be any stronger for it. There's no need to hurry with this exchange, however, since it can just as well be played after 16 a3.

16.	a2-a3	Nd5:c3
17.	Be4:b7	Qe7:b7
18.	b2:c3	Nb4-c6
19.	Qd2-d3	Rf8-d8

The classic starting position for an attack against the hanging c- and d-pawns. White must weigh concretely his opponent's threats against his own means for coping with them. In the event White continues passively, Black has several attacking options:

a) Nc6-a5-c4, blockading the c-pawn and pressing on the a-pawn;

b) rook maneuvers on the c- and d-files;

c) undermining the d-pawn by means of ..b6-b5, ..a7-a5, and ..b5-b4.

Black's final plan will depend quite a bit on White's counterplay: whether he settles into a bunker defense, or carries the play to the center with c3-c4 and d4-d5, or attacks the black king.

Taimanov puts off the decision for a move while he opens a vent for his king.

| 20. | h2-h3 | Rc8-c7 |
| 21. | Re1-e4 | ... |

A bold idea. Objectively, it may be that 21 c4 was stronger, but Taimanov does not feel he could defend the hanging c- and d-pawns against a Keres; so he decides to base his defense on the pawn at c3, simultaneously preparing an attack on the king's wing.

| 21. | ... | Nc6-a5 |
| 22. | Nf3-d2 | ... |

Of course it was more appealing to move the knight up: 22 Ne5, but this would have cost the exchange.

| 22. | ... | Qb7-d5 |

Keres insists on inviting c3-c4, since he now threatens to invade at a2. Taimanov, however, is not to be put off his plan, even though by now c3-c4 has become necessary.

| 23. | Re4-g4 | ... |

White has found a vulnerable spot in Black's fortress — g7. Now he wants to attack it twice, following the precepts of chess pedagogy: rook first, queen after. He also threatens the primitive 24 R:g7+, 25 Qg3+ and 26 Q:c7, as well as 24 Ne4.

Some idea of how dangerous the situation could become for Black, should he try to avoid weakening his pawn structure, might be gleaned from the var-

iation 23..Nc4 24 Ne4 Ne5 25 Qg3 N:g4 26 Q:c7 (the rook sacrifice on g7 could boomerang on White here: 25 R:g7+ K:g7 26 Qg3+ Ng6! 27 Q:c7 Q:e4! 28 Q:d8 Nf4, forcing mate).

| 23. | ... | f7-f5 |
| 24. | Rg4-g3 | Rd8-c8 |

Black is not going to be able to break in c3 without the use of his pawns, so the rook move is useless. 24..e5 would have been the proper conclusion to Black's strategy, torpedoing the central d4-pawn. A careful examination of the variations proceeding from 25 Q:f5 ed will convince us that all of them wind up favoring Black. But now the rook on g3 returns to the e-file, fixing Black's newly-created weakness on e6, and the rook's sojourn from e1 to e4 to g4 to g3 to e3 is justified at last.

| 25. | Rg3-e3 | Na5-c4 |

Black goes overboard in his efforts to simplify and win by means of pure technique. If Keres wanted to continue playing for the win, he had to test White with either 25..Qd6 or 25..Qa2.

| 26. | Nd2:c4 | Rc7:c4 |
| 27. | Qd3-d2 | ... |

| 27. | ... | Qd5-c6 |

It's hard for Black to hold his e-pawn, since White has, besides a direct attack on the

pawn, the continual threat to
break with Re5 and d4-d5. Keres
decides to trade the e-pawn for
White's c-pawn, but he chooses
a bad moment to do it: better
to have played 27..R8c6 first,
and then to have retreated his
queen to d7, or even to d6.

For a more general evaluation
of such positions, the reader
should bear in mind that, were
Black's pawn at f7 instead of
f5, White would be in dire
straits after the maneuver ..b6-
b5, ..a7-a5 and ..b5-b4.

28.	Rc1-e1	Rc4:c3
29.	Re3:e6	Qc6-c4
30.	Qd2-f4	Rc3-c1

White's pieces are now very
active, and Black has a hard
time spotting all White's possible plans in time to neutralize them. Here, for example,
31 Re8+ was threatened. So
Black first reduces the number
of pieces on the board.

31.	Qf4:f5	Qc4:d4
32.	Re1:c1	Rc8:c1+
33.	Kg1-h2	...

In a queen-and-heavy-pieces
game, the first thing that must
be seen to is the protection of
the king, since the side which
can combine the advance of its
pawns with threats to the opposing king will hold the initiative in such endings. In this
position, White's advantage boils
down to his having more pawns on
the f- and h-files, with the f-
pawn being especially important,
as it shields the king from
checks on the diagonal h2-b8.
The difference in the positions
of the respective kings is clearly visible from the diagram.

33.	...	Qd4-d7
34.	Qf5-e4	...

(See diagram, next column)

34.	...	Rc1-c8

Keres must now play a dogged
defense, and he does it with skill.

35.	f2-f4	Rc8-f8
36.	Qe4-e5	...

Inviting his opponent to try
the pawn-down rook ending with

36..R:f4 37 Re7 Qd4 38 R:g7+
Kh8 39 Q:d4 R:d4 40 R:a7. Black
could probably have gotten a draw
by trading off all of the queenside pawns, but Keres didn't
want to risk it, since he thought
he could stop White's attack by
simpler means — which, as unfortunately happens so often,
turned out to be more complex.

36.	...	Qd7-d2

Keres assumed that the f-
pawn could not be defended,
for example: 37 Kg3 Qd3+; but
he overlooked the fact that
advancing the pawn would secure the g6 square for White, and
create a new possibility of attacking the g7-pawn. He would
have been better off attacking
the pawn from the other side:
36..Qf7, which also attacks the
f5 square; if then 37 g3 Qf5.

37.	f4-f5	Qd2-a5

In fierce time-pressure, Keres
could not risk 37..Rf7 38 Re8+
Kh7 39 Qb8 R:f5, and decided to
double his queenside pawns. That
could have cost him the game.

38.	Qe5:a5	b6:a5
39.	g2-g4	...

By defending his f-pawn again,
Taimanov slackens his initiative
for a moment and exposes his
king; the latter circumstance
allows Keres to create a threat
to the white a-pawn and force
the draw. With the more active
continuation 39 Re5, Taimanov

would have retained his plus pawn in all lines, with real winning chances.

39. ... Rf8-b8

The rook makes for the open sea; since the pawns are dead even, White's advantage has completely evaporated.

DRAW

******

94. Najdorf—Smyslov
(Nimzoindian Defense)

1. d4 Nf6 2. c4 e6 3. Nc3 Bb4
4. e3 c5 5. Bd3 0-0 6. Nf3 b6
7. 0-0 Bb7 8. a3

8 Bd2 is better here.

8 .. B:c3 9. bc Be4 10. Be2 Nc6 11. Nd2 Bg6 12. Nb3

12 f3 was more in keeping with the position.

12 .. Ne4 13 Qe1 Nd6 14. Qd1

DRAW

******

95. Petrosian—Geller
(Queen's Indian Defense)

1. c4 Nf6 2. Nc3 e6 3. Nf3 c5
4. g3 b6 5. Bg2 Bb7 6. 0-0 Be7
7. d4 cd 8. Q:d4

8 N:d4 offers more chances to sustain an initiative; but then, the Queen's Indian does have a reputation for being a drawish opening...

8 .. 0-0 9. Rd1 Nc6 10. Qf4 Qb8 11. b3 Rd8 12. Q:b8 Ra:b8 13. Bb2 a6 14. Nd2

DRAW

******

96. Averbakh—Kotov
(Old Indian Defense)

The most beautiful game of the Zurich tournament, this game has drawn rave reviews from the entire chess world. "Once in a hundred years..", "Unique in chess literature..", "Exquisite queen sacrifice.." — such were the feelings of commentators of many lands, although none of them could match the reaction in the tournament hall. To this we may add that the Averbakh - Kotov game now has a spot in the golden treasury of chess art.

1.	d2-d4	Ng8-f6
2.	c2-c4	d7-d6
3.	Ng1-f3	Nb8-d7
4.	Nb1-c3	e7-e5
5.	e2-e4	Bf8-e7
6.	Bf1-e2	...

In the previous round, Petrosian had used a similar defense against Kotov and obtained good play. In this tournament, Kotov generally answered 1 d4 with 1..d5, or else played the King's Indian; for this game, however, he adopted Petrosian's idea, employing it impromptu against Averbakh.

In the previous game, White had continued 6 g3, fianchettoing his bishop; here Averbakh uses the other method of developing it, 6 Be2. This would make sense if he followed it up with an advance of his queenside pawns, but he does not carry his plan through to its logical conclusion.

6.	...	0-0
7.	0-0	c7-c6
8.	Qd1-c2	Rf8-e8
9.	Rf1-d1	Be7-f8
10.	Ra1-b1	a7-a5
11.	d4-d5!	...

The immediate 11 a3 would have been a poor idea, since Black would have exchanged in the center, exposing the e-pawn, and then advanced his a-pawn, preventing b2-b4.

11.	...	Nd7-c5
12.	Bc1-e3	Qd8-c7
13.	h2-h3	Bc8-d7
14.	Rb1-c1	g7-g6
15.	Nf3-d2	Ra8-b8

This position is one of dynamic equality, requiring great skill from both sides. Black can undertake a diversion on either the queenside (for example, ..Rec8, ..cd and ..b5) or the kingside (..Kh8, ..Ng8 and..f5). Neither would present any deadly danger to White, provided he takes preventive measures. The only danger would be that he might allow himself to become so wrapped up in meeting the threats on one wing as to miss the critical moment on the other.

16.	Nd2-b3	Nc5:b3
17.	Qc2:b3	c6-c5

This move is the equivalent of an announcement, with fanfares, that Black has chosen the kingside as his main theater of operations. White should now have lost no time preparing a2-a3 and b2-b4: for example, 18 Qc2 Kh8 19 a3 Ng8 20 Bg4, and if 20..Nf6, he can trade bishops and open the b-file.

18.	Kg1-h2	Kg8-h8
19.	Qb3-c2	Nf6-g8
20.	Be2-g4	Ng8-h6
21.	Bg4:d7	...

Since White here declines a possible repetition of the position (21 Be2 Ng8), evidently he feels his chances are not inferior. He is correct, inasmuch as he has the possibility of playing a2-a3, Rb1 and b2-b4; but he is also incorrect, inasmuch as he has something totally different in mind.

21.	...	Qc7:d7
22.	Qc2-d2	Nh6-g8
23.	g2-g4	...

Averbakh is trying to put out the fire with gasoline. Now ..f7-f5 comes with double force, since Black can capture either of two pawns, while neither white pawn may capture on f5.

23.	...	f7-f5
24.	f2-f3	Bf8-e7
25.	Rd1-g1	Re8-f8
26.	Rc1-f1	Rf8-f7
27.	g4:f5	...

Although many commentators gave this move a question mark, it cannot be considered a mistake; actually, it is the continuation of a plan begun much earlier. Averbakh intends an attack along the g-file, and so he opens it. This is all very logical — except that the h-pawn has to be on h2.

27.	...	g6:f5
28.	Rg1-g2	f5-f4
29.	Be3-f2	Rf7-f6
30.	Nc3-e2	...

The creative element of chess is generally thought to consist of three things: logic, accurate calculation, and technique (this last includes a knowledge of theory). There is a fourth ingredient also, however, perhaps the most intriguing of all, although it is often overlooked. I refer to intuition — chess fantasy, if you prefer.

Occasionally a position arises in the course of a game which cannot be evaluated on general principles, such as pawn weaknesses, open lines, better development, etc., since the state of equilibrium has been upset on several counts, rendering an exact weighing of the elements impossible. Attempting to calculate the variations doesn't always work, either. Imagine that White has six or seven different continuations, and Black five or six replies to each move; it's easy to see that no genius on earth could reach even the fourth move in his calculations. It is then that intuition or fantasy comes to the rescue: that's what has given the art of chess its most beautiful combinations, and allowed chessplayers the chance to experience the joy of creating.

It is not true to say that intuitive games were only played in the days of Morphy, Anderssen and Chigorin (as if now, in our era, everything were to be based totally on positional principles and rigorous calculation!): I remain convinced that, even in the games which received the brilliancy prizes at this tournament, not all of the variations were calculated to the end. Intuition has been and remains one of the cornerstones of chess creativity — of which we shall now see proof positive.

| 30. | ... | Qd7:h3+ |

Now the weakness of the pawn at h3 tells. The point of Kotov's remarkable combination, which all his previous play went to prepare, is to drag the white king out to f5, where it will be defenseless against Black's two rooks, knight and bishop; while White's five pieces, deep in his rear echelon, can only look on from afar.

The position has occurred twice, so Black takes a pawn, and begins the count again.

38.	Kg4-f5	Nf6:d5+
39.	Kf5-g4	Nd5-f6+
40.	Kg4-f5	Nf6-g8+
41.	Kf5-g4	Ng8-f6+
42.	Kg4-f5	Nf6-g8+
43.	Kf5-g4	Be7:g5

Black threatens 44..Be7, followed by 45..Nf6+ 46 Kf5 Nd7+ 47 Kg4 Rg8+ and mate next move. White has two tempi in which to organize his defense, but cannot do anything with them, since all communications between the upper and lower halves of the board are either severed by pawn barricades or under the crossfire of Black's pieces. Relatively "best" was 44 Be3 Be7 45 B:f4 ef 46 N:f4 Rh4+ 47 Kg3 R:f4, but even this best would also have been quite hopeless for White.

44.	Kg4:g5	...

44.	...,	Rf8-f7

The threat is mate in two moves by ..Rg7+ and ..Rf6; 45 N:f4 Rg7+ 46 Ng6+ Rg:g6+ 47 Kf5 Ne7 is mate too. White must give up still another piece.

45.	Bf2-h4	Rh6-g6+
46.	Kg5-h5	Rf7-g7
47.	Bh4-g5	Rg6:g5+
48.	Kh5-h4	Ng8-f6
49.	Ne2-g3	...

All of White's battalions fall

31.	Kh2:h3	Rf6-h6+
32.	Kh3-g4	Ng8-f6+
33.	Kg4-f5	...

Like a rabbit hypnotized by a python, the king advances unwillingly to the place of its doom. For an understanding of the next phase of the game, bear in mind that Kotov had very little time left until the time control, and naturally did not wish to spoil such a beautiful and unusual game with some hasty move. Therefore, he decides to give a few checks, in order to get the game past the 40th move and adjourn it. No doubt, there has to be mate in this position; most probably, Kotov saw its basic outlines as far back as his 30th move.

33.	...	Nf6-d7

Here's the proof: had the queen sacrifice been "accurately calculated", Kotov would instead have chosen Stahlberg's postmortem suggestion, 33..Ng4, depriving White of the reply 34 Rg5. After 33..Ng4, White would have had to suffer colossal material losses in order to avert the mate threats.

34.	Rg2-g5	...

The only defense against the threatened mate in three: ..Rf8, ..Rg8 and ..Rf6.

34.	...	Rb8-f8+
35.	Kf5-g4	Nd7-f6+
36.	Kg4-f5	Nf6-g8+
37.	Kf5-g4	Ng8-f6+

one by one, sallying forth
to the aid of their belea-
guered king.

49.	...	Rg5:g3
50.	Qd2:d6	Rg3-g6
51.	Qd6-b8+	...

In reply to thirteen checks,
White gives his first check,
and after

| 51. | ... | Rg7-g8 |

WHITE RESIGNS

A grand game, richly deser-
ving its First Brilliancy Prize.

******

97. Szabo—Boleslavsky
(French Defense)

1. e4 e6 2. d4 d5 3. Nd2 c5
4. ed ed 5. Bb5+ Bd7 6. Qe2+ Be7
7. dc Nf6 8. B:d7+

The logical continuation of
White's opening plan was to
play to retain the pawn with
8 Nb3 0-0 9 Be3. Now Black is
better developed, and will
shortly recover the c-pawn.

8 .. Nb:d7 9. Nb3 0-0 10. Nh3

An unfortunate thought: the
knight never gets to f4.

10 .. Re8 11. 0-0 B:c5 12. Qd1
Bb6 13. c3 h6 14. Bf4 Ne5
15. B:e5 R:e5 16. Re1 R:e1+
17. Q:e1 Qd6 18. Rd1

DRAW

Black has the better of it.
Here is a curious combination
which might occur: 18..Re8
19 Qd2 Ne4 20 Q:d5? N:f2!
21 Q:d6 N:d1+ 22 Q:b6 Re1 mate.

******

98. Euwe—Stahlberg
(Grunfeld Defense)

1.	d2-d4	Ng8-f6
2.	c2-c4	g7-g6
3.	g2-g3	c7-c6

Black meets the flank development of the bishop by advancing
his c-pawn to support ..d7-d5,
setting up a symmetrical position with a fixed pawn structure. Stahlberg is challenging
Euwe the openings theoretician,

by making it very difficult for
White to get an advantage.

Euwe does not try to refute
the opening, which is impossible,
but to upset the statistical balance and create livelier play,
trusting that the advantage of
the first move will make itself
felt somewhere. Stahlberg is
willing to meet Euwe halfway,
and the game which results is
very much like an absorbing nov-
elette.

| 4. | d4-d5 | c6:d5 |
| 5. | c4:d5 | d7-d6 |

The sortie 5..Qa5+ 6 Nc3 Ne4
is insufficient, and meets a
pretty refutation in 7 Qd4 N:c3
8 Bd2 Q:d5 9 Q:c3!

6.	Bf1-g2	Bf8-g7
7.	Nb1-c3	0-0
8.	Ng1-f3	Nb8-d7

It is not entirely clear where
the knight is headed: there
does not seem to be any clear
path leading out of d7. First
he should have let the bishop
out: 8..Bg4 9 Nd4 Qc8!

| 9. | 0-0 | Nd7-b6 |
| 10. | a2-a4 | ... |

Like Tarrasch in his day, Euwe
cannot abide the sight of an enemy knight on b6. But the knight
stands so poorly on that square
that there was no need to disturb it. The quiet 10 Nd4 and
11 b3 would have underscored the
knight's limited mobility, while
the flank deployment of the second bishop would harmoniously
complement the ensemble of white
pieces.

Euwe intends to develop the
bishop at e3: it must have been
in order to rid himself of the
temptation to advance the e-
pawn...

| 10. | ... | Bc8-g4 |
| 11. | Nf3-d4 | a7-a6 |

Here Stahlberg probably wanted
to play 11..Qc8, but didn't like
12 a5 Nc4 13 a6, when White gets
the important square c6 for his
knight.

| 12. | h2-h3 | Bg4-c8 |
| 13. | b2-b3 | Bc8-d7 |

[162]

Stahlberg did not retreat to
d7 immediately, fearing 13 Qb3,
when the attempt to take the
d5-pawn would end very badly
for Black: 12..Bd7 13 Qb3 Nf:d5
14 N:d5 B:d4 15 Bh6, and Black
must cede the exchange, as otherwise White could threaten the
knight at b6 and mate at g7 simultaneously, with serious difficulties for Black. And if, after
13 Qb3, Black does not take the
d-pawn, but continues instead
with 13..Qc7, 14 Be3 Nc4 15 Rfc1
sets up an unpleasant pin on
the c-file.

Thus, the black bishop can
find no fulcrum from which to
exert its leverage, and wanders
mournfully along the diagonal
c8-h3: it has taken three moves
to get from c8 to d7! That's
quite enough to induce White to
start an attack: with 14 a5, the
black knight would have been
driven back to c8, where it interferes with the coordination
of Black's rooks, and would have
had a lot more skulking about to
do, too.

| 14. | Bc1-e3 | Ra8-c8 |
| 15. | Qd1-d2 | Rc8-c5 |

Black is spoiling for a fight!
Stahlberg was probably attracted
less by the prospect of winning
the pawn than by the piquant position of the rook on c5, a square
where it would appear to be vulnerable, yet cannot be attacked.
Evidently, he was not yet willing to sacrifice the rook for
knight and pawn by 15..R:c3
16 Q:c3 Nb:d5, but in his cramped
position he could hardly hope
to obtain anything better. Stahlberg still keeps the possibility
of trading off the rook in this
fashion for the next two moves,
but he stubbornly maintains its
position on c5.

| 16. | Nd4-c6 | ... |

A valiant charge! The knight
may be taken by rook, bishop or
pawn: which is best? Stahlberg
follows the line of greatest resistance: instead of one minor
piece for the rook, he gets two,
but his opponent gets an extremely dangerous passed pawn.
Other possible lines: 16..B:c6
17 dc R:c3 18 Q:c3 Nd5 19 c7;
or 16..Nf:d5 17 N:d8 B:c3, etc.

In either case, White would retain the advantage.

16.	...	b7:c6
17.	Be3:c5	d6:c5
18.	d5:c6	Bd7-e6
19.	Qd2:d8	Rf8:d8
20.	Ra1-d1	Rd8-c8

Black must not exchange rooks
under any circumstances, but he
should have left c8 free for the
knight by retreating the rook to
e8.

| 21. | a4-a5 | Nb6-a8 |
| 22. | Nc3-a4 | ... |

Another pretty combination.
Euwe invites the capture of his
b-pawn, when there would follow
23 Nb6, and White either wins a
piece or queens his pawn. Of
course, Black declines that continuation, but the c-pawn will
fall.

| 22. | ... | Na8-c7 |
| 23. | Na4:c5 | Nf6-d5 |

Black sees that he must bring
up his sleeping kingside pieces
as quickly as possible, and to
that end he sacrifices yet another pawn; however, such dras-
tic measures were as yet unnecessary. 23..Nfe8 was better, intending ..Nd6 and ..Bc3.

| 24. | Nc5:a6 | Nc7:a6 |
| 25. | Bg2:d5 | Be6:h3 |

It would have been tempting
to trade off the bishops as well,
picking up the c-pawn, but this

would have led to a quick finish: one white rook would go
to the eighth rank, while the
other supported the advance of
the b-pawn.

| 26. | Bd5-g2 | Bh3-e6 |

Here too, he cannot exchange
bishops, and for the same reason.

| 27. | Rd1-b1 | Bg7-c3 |

He ought to have found out
where the rook intended to go
after 27..Bf5: the choice was
not great. Stahlberg apparently
feared White would take a draw
by repetition of moves, and he
was loath to abandon a game that
had proven so interesting...

28.	Rf1-d1	Bc3-b4
29.	Rd1-d4	Be6-f5
30.	Rb1-d1	Bb4-d6
31.	Rd4-c4	Bf5-e6
32.	Bg2-d5	Be6:d5
33.	Rd1:d5	...

Black's pointless maneuverings
have allowed White to improve the
positions of his pieces. One of
Black's drawing chances lay in
avoiding an exchange of lightsquare bishops, which keeps the
possibility of giving back the
two pieces for the rook and pawn,
leaving opposite-colored bishops.
For this reason, he should have
brought his lightsquare bishop
to e6 only after the preparatory
31..Nc7.

| 33. | ... | Rc8-b8 |
| 34. | b3-b4 | ... |

Three connected passed pawns
can be a terrible weapon when
they start rolling and smash-
ing all before them. Cases are
known in which such pawns have
defeated two rooks, or even a
queen and rook; so Stahlberg
must take the b-pawn. He cannot
take it with the rook, since after the last black rook is exchanged off, White plays Rd5-
b5-b6 and then queens his a-
pawn. Taking on b4 with the bishop would be bad too, in view
of 35 c7. Luckily for Stahlberg, he can still wriggle out
of his difficult situation by
giving back the two pieces for
rook and pawn to get into a
slightly inferior rook endgame.

34.	...	Na6:b4
35.	Rd5:d6	e7:d6
36.	c6-c7	Rb8-c8
37.	Rc4:b4	Rc8:c7
38.	Rb4-a4	...

The game enters its third, and
most interesting, phase.

The tale of chess tournaments
has furnished us a wealth of material on the theory and practice of rook endgames; this endgame, played by both sides with
a high degree of skill, certainly belongs among the best.
Black's task is a most difficult
one: he has to cope with an outside passed pawn. He does have
counterchances, however: the
possibility of quickly creating
a matching passed pawn on the h-
file, and the fact that there is
so little material left on the
board. This latter circumstance
sometimes allows one to trade
off all his pawns, give up the
rook for the last of the enemy
pawns, and then force one's opponent to repay his debt in the
same coin.

We are largely indebted to
Dr. Euwe's analysis for the following commentaries.

| 38. | ... | Kg8-f8 |

The king would be better
brought via g7 and f6 to e5, but
that doesn't come off: 38..Kg7
39 Kg2 Kf6 40 Kf3 Ke5 41 a6 Ra7
42 Ra5+ d5 43 e4, and White wins
a pawn. The reason this turns
out in White's favor is that
the white rook stands behind its

far-advanced pawn, and thus has
freedom to maneuver; the same
cannot be said of Black's rook,
which stands in front of the
passed pawn and will have fewer
and fewer squares as the pawn
advances further. This is quite
a basic element in the evaluation of rook endings, and will
figure prominently in the struggle at hand.

| 39. | Kg1-g2 | Kf8-e7 |
| 40. | Kg2-f3 | Ke7-d7 |

| 41. | Kf3-e4 | Rc7-a7 |
| 42. | Ke4-d5 | ... |

If Black should succeed in
creating a passed pawn on the
h-file, things will not be so
bad for him.

| 42. | ... | h7-h5 |
| 43. | f2-f4 | ... |

Euwe already sees Black's
plan of ..f7-f6, ..g6-g5 and
..h5-h4, and wishes to keep
in hand the possibility of
creating an outpost at f5,
thereby maintaining winning
chances after a mutual liquid-
ation of passed pawns.

| 43. | ... | Ra7-a6 |

Here Euwe's analysis indicates it would have been better
to begin at once with the creation of a passed pawn by 43..f6,
followed by:

I. 44 a6 g5 45 f5 h4 46 gh gh

a) 47 R:h4 R:a6 48 Rh7+ Ke8

49 Ke6 d5+ 50 K:d5 Ra5+, drawing;

b) 47 Ke4 Kc6 48 Kf4 Kb5 49 Ra3
R:a6 50 R:a6 K:a6 51 Kg4 Kb5
52 K:h4 Kc5, and the pawn ending is drawn, since the king
gets back just in time to defend the pawn on f6;

II. 44 Ra3 g5 45 f5 h4 46 gh gh
47 Ke4 h3 48 Kf3 d5 49 Kg3 Kd6
50 K:h3 Ke5, drawing;

III. 44 e4 Ra6, with the same
ideas as in the game, but with
an extra tempo for Black.

| 44. | e2-e4 | ... |

He shouldn't have taken the
e4 square away from his king.
This is important in the following variation: 44 Ra2 f6 45 Ra3
g5 46 f5 h4 47 gh gh 48 Ke4 h3
49 Kf3 h2 50 Kg2 Kc6 51 K:h2 Kb5
52 Kg3 R:a5 53 R:a5+ K:a5 54 Kh4,
and White picks up the f-pawn
and queens one move before Black.
The same thing occurs after
48..Kc6 49 Kf4 Kb5 50 Kg4 R:a5
51 R:a5+, etc. But now that a
pawn bars the white king's path,
Black can go in for this variation — which, indeed, he does.

44.	...	f7-f6
45.	Ra4-a2	g6-g5
46.	f4-f5	h5-h4
47.	g3:h4	g5:h4
48.	Kd5-c4	Ra6-a8

The crux of this remarkable
endgame, and in fact of the entire game. Stahlberg quite evidently thought that he could sup-

port his passed h-pawn in some lines; how could he have seen that it was precisely the paradoxical 48..Ra7 which would have held the draw? As Euwe shows in his analyses: 49 a6 Kc6, and now:

a) 50 Ra3 h3 51 R:h3 R:a6 52 Rh6 Kd7 53 Rh7+ Ke8 54 Kd5 Ra5+ 55 K:d6 Re5 and draws;

b) 50 Kd4 h3 51 Ra3 h2 52 Ra1 Kd7 53 Kd5 h1Q 54 R:h1 R:a6 55 Rh7+ Ke8 56 Ke6 d5+ 57 K:d5 Ra5+ 58 Kd4 Re5 and draws.

With the rook at a8, White's pawn goes to a7; then, in variation b), after the trade of pawns, White checks at h7 and wins the rook.

| 49. | a5-a6 | Kd7-c6 |
| 50. | a6-a7 | h4-h3 |

The attempt to trade passed pawns by 50..Kb7 51 Rh2 R:a7 52 R:h4 would lose for Black, since his king would not have the time to get back in order to defend his pawns: 52..Kc6 53 Rh6 Rf7 54 Rh8 Re7 55 Kd4 Rf7 56 Rg8, and Black is in zugzwang.

| 51. | Kc4-d4 | Kc6-c7 |

If Black had advanced his passed pawn to the second rank, White would not have taken it off at once, but given check from c2 first; with the black king confined to the b-file, White would have an easy win.

| 52. | Kd4-d5 | Kc7-d7 |

| 53. | Ra2-a3 | h3-h2 |
| 54. | Ra3-a1 | ... |

Underscoring all the shortcomings of Black's position: now he has no useful move. For example, after 54..h1Q 55 R:h1 R:a7 56 Rh7+, White wins the rook at a7. If Black prepares this by retreating his king to the eighth rank, White places his king in opposition, setting up a mate threat after the exchange of pawns. If 54..Ke7, then obviously 55 Kc6 and 56 Kb7. Black tries to play on for a while a pawn down, but that's clearly hopeless.

54.	...	Ra8-e8
55.	Ra1-h1	Re8-e5+
56.	Kd5-d4	Re5-a5
57.	Rh1:h2	Kd7-c6
58.	Rh2-h7	Ra5-a4+

Here Stahlberg might have given his opponent the opportunity to end the game with the following elegant combination, involving back-to-back queen sacrifices: 58..d5 59 e5 Ra4+ 60 Kc3 fe 61 f6 Kd6 62 f7 Ke7 63 f8Q+ K:f8 64 a8Q+ R:a8 65 Rh8+ — but he prefers to lose more prosaically.

59.	Kd4-e3	Ra4-a3+
60.	Ke3-f4	Ra3-a1
61.	Rh7-f7	Kc6-c5
62.	Rf7:f6	Ra1:a7
63.	Rf6-e6	Ra7-a1
64.	f5-f6	Kc5-c6
65.	Kf4-f5	Kc6-d7
66.	Re6-e7+	Kd7-d8
67.	Kf5-e6	...

BLACK RESIGNED

******

*****

ROUND FIFTEEN

99. Boleslavsky—Euwe
(Sicilian Defense)

1.	e2-e4	c7-c5
2.	Ng1-f3	Nb8-c6
3.	d2-d4	c5:d4
4.	Nf3:d4	Ng8-f6
5.	Nb1-c3	d7-d6
6.	Bf1-e2	e7-e5

Euwe plays the Boleslavsky Variation against its inventor: a bit of psychology that often brings good results. To his psychological preparations, the former World Champion has also added a theoretical improvement at the 14th move.

Boleslavsky plays the game peaceably, even somewhat weakly, and Euwe succeeds in equalizing completely.

7.	Nd4-b3	Bf8-e7
8.	0-0	0-0
9.	Bc1-e3	Bc8-e6
10.	Be2-f3	Nc6-a5
11.	Nb3:a5	Qd8:a5
12.	Qd1-d2	Rf8-c8
13.	Rf1-d1	Qa5-b4
14.	Ra1-b1	h7-h6

The players are traveling a well-rutted road: the whole line was played repeatedly at the Stockholm tournament in 1952. There, Black played 14..a6; but after 15 a3 Qc4, White was able to pin Black's knight with 16 Bg5. This move of Black's forestalls that bishop sortie and preserves the knight's freedom of movement. For example, he can play ..Nh7, intending ..Bg5, or ..Nd7 followed by ..Nc5. In the Stockholm games, Black had to spend a tempo defending the bishop by ..Qc7 in order to relieve the pin, and then the knight had to go to e8.

15.	a2-a3	Qb4-c4
16.	Rb1-c1	a7-a6
17.	Bf3-e2	Qc4-c7
18.	f2-f3	Nf6-d7

Here's a surprise: one would think that Black would have to keep two pieces watching the d5 square, so that if White ever occupies it, he would have to recapture with his pawn in the event of an exchange, shutting off his pressure on the d6-pawn. But now Black seems willing to

give up his "good" bishop for White's knight, and it appears that White can now occupy d5 with a piece. Euwe, however, by advancing his queenside pawns and posting his own knight on c5, thwarts White's efforts to install his bishop at d5.

19.	Be2-f1	b7-b5
20.	a3-a4	...

Boleslavsky opens the fight for d5. By attacking Black's pawns, he forces Black either to capture at a4 or to push to b4; in either event, he can bring his bishop to c4.

20.	...	b5-b4
21.	Nc3-d5	Be6:d5
22.	Qd2:d5	Nd7-c5
23.	b2-b3	Be7-g5

Black now executes the idea he planned on the previous move of trading off White's good bishop, ignoring the fact that his d6-pawn appears to be undefended.

24.	Be3:g5	h6:g5

Indirect defense is an often-used technique: it can figure as one of the elements of a combination, or as one of the links in a war of maneuver. In the diagrammed position, the d6-pawn is defended indirectly, since if 25 Q:d6 Q:d6 26 R:d6, Black can snap off the b3-pawn, formerly defended by both the queen and the c-pawn, with his knight. After 26..N:b3 27 Rb1 Nd4

28 R:b4 N:c2 29 Rb7 Ne3 or
28 B:a6 R:c2 29 R:b4 Ne2+,
White could hardly expect to
win the ending. Still, this was
his best shot, as Black would
not have had an easy defense.

25.	Kg1-h1	a6-a5
26.	h2-h3	Ra8-b8
27.	Bf1-b5	Rc8-d8
28.	c2-c3	...

Creating a passed pawn is a
logical plan, but it will be a
difficult pawn to advance:
White's bishop, which would normally support it, has no support points itself.

28.	...	b4:c3
29.	Rc1:c3	Qc7-e7
30.	Qd5-c4	g7-g6
31.	b3-b4	a5:b4
32.	Qc4:b4	Kg8-g7
33.	Qb4-c4	Qe7-a7
34.	Rc3-c2	Nc5-e6
35.	Qc4-c3	Ne6-d4

Euwe has carried out one of
the fundamental ideas of the
Boleslavsky Variation by occupying d4 with his knight. The
pawns at a4 and d6 are approximately equivalent, but Black's
pieces are now better placed,
and soon it will be White who
will have to fight for the draw.

36.	Rc2-b2	Rd8-c8
37.	Qc3-d2	Kg7-f6!
38.	Rd1-c1	Rc8:c1+
39.	Qd2:c1	Qa7-c5
40.	Qc1-d2	Rb8-c8
41.	Kh1-h2	Qc5-a3

The sealed move; after analy-

sis, a

DRAW

was agreed to without further
play. Black stands more actively, but in Euwe's opinion, the
a-pawn gives White sufficient
counterchances.

*****

100. Kotov—Szabo
(King's Indian)

Castling on opposite wings
generally presages pawn assaults
against the opposing kings. An
exception to this rule consists
of the unusual positions arising out of the Samisch King's
Indian. Here both sides, after
castling on opposite wings,
sometimes push the pawns in
front of their own kings. The
present game is an example of
such play. With the center
closed and pawn chains fixed,
Black castles short and sets
up a break on g4 by playing
..f7-f5-f4, ..g6-g5, ..h7-h5,
and ..g5-g4; in the meantime,
White opened the b-file leading
to his own king for his opponent.
This sort of original play on
both sides led to offensive
breakthroughs on opposite wings,
flanking piece maneuvers, and
sharp cut-and-thrust play.

The unusual strategic idea,
the resourceful and daring play
on both sides, and the beautiful concluding combinations
make this game altogether an
exceptionally interesting one.

1.	d2-d4	Ng8-f6
2.	c2-c4	g7-g6
3.	Nb1-c3	Bf8-g7
4.	e2-e4	d7-d6
5.	f2-f3	0-0
6.	Bc1-e3	e7-e5
7.	d4-d5	Nf6-h5
8.	Qd1-d2	f7-f5
9.	0-0-0	Nb8-d7

A substantial improvement on
the Geller - Gligoric game, in
which Black closed the position
with 9..f4. Szabo maintains the
central tension and the possibility of posting his knight at
f4.

| 10. | Bf1-d3 | Nd7-c5 |

And right now was the proper
moment to put this plan into

execution: 10..Nf4!, and if the
bishop goes to c2, then 11..Nb6
(instead of ..Nc5) assails the
weakened c-pawn and induces
12 b3.

| 11. | Bd3-c2 | f5-f4 |

Szabo turns down that same
rocky road as did Gligoric in
the game just mentioned with
Geller, thus consigning himself
to a protracted and difficult
defense, too. In the meantime,
Kotov has a clear plan, which
Makogonov used successfully
again and again in such positions: the king goes to b1, and
the knight on g1 goes to d3,
either squeezing Black's knight
out of c5 or else inducing the
weakening ..b7-b6; meanwhile,
his rooks occupy the c- and d-
files. Gradually, White prepares the break c4-c5, during
which his king will have two
pawns' protection; while Black,
in order to set his kingside
counterbreak in motion, must
strip his king absolutely bare
of pawn cover.

In this game, matters do not
move along quite as smoothly as
we have just described it, but
that's the general scheme; soon
the scales begin to tip in
White's favor. Thus, Black
should not have closed the game
here, either: 11..Nf6 was better, maintaining pressure on
e4 and preventing 12 Nge2 tac-
tically, because of the continuation 12..fe 13 fe Ng4 or
13 B:c5 ef.

| 12. | Be3-f2 | a7-a6 |
| 13. | Ng1-e2 | a6-a5 |

Szabo is on the horns of a
dilemma. Seeing that his intended 13..b5 will not work, in
view of 14 b4 and 15 c5, he
decides to secure the knight's
position, at least. He conducts
the next phase of the game somewhat hesitantly, as though trying to decide what plan he ought
to adopt in the face of White's
growing initiative. After the
20th move, however, he decides
on a pawn assault leading away
from his own king, and plays
va banque.

14.	Kc1-b1	Bc8-d7
15.	Ne2-c1	Rf8-f7
16.	Nc1-d3	b7-b6
17.	Rd1-c1	Bg7-f6
18.	Rh1-f1	Bf6-h4

Obsessed by his desire to exchange off the darksquare bishops, Szabo overlooks White's
simple reply. 18..a4 was necessary, in order to prevent the
trade of lightsquare bishops,
at least, and to deprive White's
pieces of the square b3.

| 19. | Bf2:c5 | ... |

In removing his bishop from
f6, Black left the e5-pawn unprotected, so that now he must
recapture the bishop with his
b-pawn. Strange as it may seem,
the line thus opened will turn
into an artery of communications
for White's pieces, and not for
Black's. The strategy and tactics of chess still hold many a
paradox.

| 19. | ... | b6:c5 |
| 20. | Bc2-a4 | ... |

A maneuver with the same idea
as Black's ..Bg7-f6-h4, but this
one is more successful. Black
cannot sidestep the exchange of
his "good" bishop, since retreating it to c8 would put him
in a squeeze. After 21 Bc6 Ra6
22 Nb5, it would be Black's turn
to seek this exchange.

20.	...	Bd7:a4
21.	Nc3:a4	Qd8-d7
22.	Na4-c3	g6-g5

Black is now in real danger

of losing: the threat is 23 Nb5, 24 Rc3, and 25 Ra3, and there seems to be no way to defend the a-pawn, especially since White can also bring up a second knight to b3. In this position, with its fixed pawn chain, White's knights have great power. Szabo decides to utilize his mobile units where they stand, i.e. on the king's wing; as a result, the game immediately changes character. The preceding unhurried maneuvering gives way to bitter hand-to-hand fighting, requiring a cool head, resourcefulness and accuracy.

| 23. | h2-h3 | Nh5-f6 |

Necessary, in order to play ..g5-g4. 23..Ng3 would not have served the purpose, in view of 24 Rfd1 h5 25 Nf2!, when both black pieces would be nailed down.

| 24. | Nc3-b5 | h7-h5 |
| 25. | Rf1-h1 | ... |

Finding the right plan is nowhere near as difficult as carrying it out by means of accurate — and sometimes "only" — moves, while simultaneously counteracting the enemy plan too. Here and later, Kotov's play is beyond praise. He leaves one rook to withstand the assault, and continuously combines attack with defense.

25.	...	Rf7-h7
26.	Rc1-c3	g5-g4
27.	h3:g4	h5:g4
28.	Rc3-a3	Bh4-g3
29.	Rh1:h7	Qd7:h7

Black defends the a-pawn indirectly, intending to undermine g2, the keystone of the sturdy bridge of white pawns.

| 30. | Nd3-c1 | Qh7-h1! |

By completing the long flanking maneuver ..Qd7-h7-h1, the black queen becomes the first to invade the enemy camp, leaving to its fate not only the c-pawn and the rook, but its king as well. However, Black had no other recourse, since otherwise his a-pawn would have fallen without compensation. Still, White's last move underscored his obvious advantage, which consists of: 1) the better-protected king, 2) his knight, which is a much more dangerous weapon in an attack on the opposing king than Black's bishop; and 3) the pawn White wins in the course of his attack, as well as the tempo he wins by his attack on the rook. All this gives sufficient basis for many combinations; it is the master's skill to select from among those combinations the best and decisive ones.

31.	Nb5:c7	g4:f3
32.	g2:f3	Ra8-a7
33.	Nc7-e6	...

The knight's position is so threatening here that the black king risks death at the first hostile queen check.

33.	...	Bg3-e1
34.	Qd2-d1	Ra7-h7
35.	Ra3-d3	...

Warding off Black's threat of 35..Rh2 and 36..Bd2.

| 35. | ... | Rh7-h2 |
| 36. | a2-a3 | ... |

36 Qb3 would not have been so clear, in view of 36..Qg2, when the check at b8 leads to nothing, since g7 is covered by the queen.

36.	...	Nf6-d7
37.	Qd1-a4	Qh1-g2
38.	Rd3-b3	...

Kotov defends against the threat of mate at b2, and now threatens simply to take off the knight.

38.   ...   Be1-c3

Szabo is setting a trap. Obviously, the bishop cannot be
taken, either by rook or pawn.
If White takes the knight, we
get the well-known "windmill":
39 Q:d7? Q:b2+! 40 R:b2 R:b2+
41 Ka1, and now Black can give
discovered check by moving his
rook to any of a dozen squares.
Generally that would be enough
to give him at least a draw;
here, after 41..Rb7+ 42 Ka2
R:d7, it would even win.

39. Nc1-e2   ...

A beautiful concluding move to
an outstandingly played game.
White attacks the bishop and
closes the second rank. If the
queen takes this knight, then
g7 is left unprotected, and
White has a mating finish by
sacrificing his rook as well:
39..Q:e2 40 Rb8+! N:b8 41 Qe8+,
with mate in three.

BLACK RESIGNED

******

101. Geller—Averbakh
(Sicilian Defense)

1.	e2-e4	c7-c5
2.	Ng1-f3	Nb8-c6
3.	d2-d4	c5:d4
4.	Nf3:d4	Ng8-f6
5.	Nb1-c3	d7-d6
6.	Bf1-c4	Bc8-d7
7.	Bc1-g5	Qd8-a5

The last two moves for both
sides contain a fair number of
opening subtleties. Playing the

Rauzer line against the Sicilian, with its 6 Bg5, 7 Qd2 and
8 0-0-0, White generally does
not get to bring out his lightsquare bishop in the early
stages; in the Scheveningen,
White develops both bishops,
but to humbler posts: e2 and
e3. In this game, Geller decides to develop both his bishops actively, and apparently
he wishes to castle queenside
too. If he could manage all this,
he would stand beautifully. He
began his plan with 6 Bc4, preventing, among other things, the
Dragon Variation, in view of
6..g6 7 N:c6 bc 8 e5!, when capturing is obviously impossible
because of 9 B:f7+, winning the
queen. 8..Ng4 would be necessary instead, when the pawn advances further still: 9 e6 f5
10 0-0, with an active game for
White, following the ancient
game Schlechter - Lasker (Match
1910).

Averbakh's 6..Bd7 prepares to
enter the Dragon Variation.
White could simply have castled
here, the likely continuation
being 7..g6 8 h3 Bg7 9 Be3 0-0
10 Bb3, with a good game. But
he persists with his idea and
plays 7 Bg5.

Averbakh meets this with a
daring and original counterplan:
forcing White to take his king's
knight (there being no other way
to defend both the bishop on g5
and the pawn on e4), and leaving
his king where it stands, he initiates a fierce kingside attack
right out of the opening. Generally, such strategy runs counter to chess principles; but in
this case the open g-file gives
Black two developed major pieces,
and a powerful pawn center as
well. It was just this curious
concatenation of circumstances
that gave rise to such an unusual plan.

Geller regards Black's attack
as of no consequence, and deliberately castles kingside, pushing his kingside pawns as if to
invite his opponent's attack. Of
course, that attack poses no mor-
tal threat to White's king, but
some preventive measures were
still in order. Among other
things, 9 Bd5 would have been
a great deal better than his

9 Nb3: first the queen must be cut off from the kingside, and then 10 Nb3 will be a threat.

8.	Bg5:f6	g7:f6
9.	Nd4-b3	Qa5-g5!
10.	0-0	Rh8-g8!

Along with the witty and subtle finesses aimed at provoking weakenings of the king's pawn cover, one should not forget such things as one-move mate threats.

11.	g2-g3	h7-h5
12.	Nc3-d5	Ra8-c8

Black gives up all thought of castling, but such fortitude was not dictated by necessity. Of course the black king is perfectly safe behind its barbed-wire fence of d6-e7-f7-f6, with all its pieces close by; but under these circumstances, the center pawns are not being exploited to the fullest possible extent. The black king's bishop also will not be able to participate in the game for a long time, and the struggle cannot be won without it.

After 12..0-0-0, intending to continue with ..e7-e6 and ..d6-d5, Black could have opened the center very favorably and obtained definite winning chances.

13.	f2-f4	Qg5-g7
14.	Qd1-d2	h5-h4
15.	Rf1-f3	Qg7-h6
16.	Bc4-f1	h4:g3
17.	Rf3:g3	Rg8-g6
18.	Ra1-e1	f6-f5

Black begins to clear away the underbrush for his bishops. The last white pawn now vanishes from the center.

19.	e4:f5	Bd7:f5
20.	c2-c3	Bf5-e6
21.	Bf1-g2	...

A serious inaccuracy. White's knight is stronger than Black's bishop here, so he ought not to have allowed its exchange, retreating it instead to e3. Averbakh could hardly have put together any decisive threats with all those white pieces coming after his own king.

21.	...	Be6:d5
22.	Bg2:d5	e7-e6
23.	Nb3-d4	...

White's little tactical threat — 24 B:c6+, followed by Nf5 and N:d6+ — is easily repelled: 23 Qg2 was better.

23.	...	Bf8-e7

The bishop takes its first step, and White's position immediately looks suspect (23..Kd7 wasn't bad either).

24.	Bd5-g2	Rg6:g3

Attempting to win the exchange would have been a grievous error: 24..Bh4? 25 Nf5!

25.	h2:g3	Nc6:d4
26.	Qd2:d4	...

If White had taken with the pawn, he would have had a hard time defending both weaknesses, d4 and g3, especially without his darksquare bishop.

26.	...	d6-d5
27.	b2-b4	...

White's position was difficult, but this move makes it hopeless. He might have put up some resistance with 27 Kf1 Bc5 28 Qd3 Qh2 29 Qf3, maintaining drawing chances, especially if the rooks are exchanged.

(See diagram, next page)

27.	...	Rc8-c4
28.	Qd4-e5	Qh6-f6

What for? Why not continue the attack on the king with queen, rook and bishop? 28..Bd8 29 B:d5 Bc7 30 Qg5 Q:g5 31 fg R:c3 or 30 Qe2 R:c3 31 Qg2 Qg6 32 Kh2 Rc2 33 Re2 Qh5+ would have led to a clear win. Now Black's advantage is purely academic.

29.	Qe5:f6	Be7:f6
30.	Bg2:d5	Rc4:c3
31.	Bd5:b7	Rc3:g3+
32.	Kg1-h2	Rg3-g4
33.	Re1-e4	Ke8-e7
34.	f4-f5	...

DRAW

******

102. Smyslov—Petrosian
(Nimzoindian Defense)

1.	d2-d4	Ng8-f6
2.	c2-c4	e7-e6
3.	Nb1-c3	Bf8-b4
4.	e2-e3	0-0
5.	Bf1-d3	d7-d5
6.	Ng1-f3	c7-c5
7.	0-0	Nb8-c6
8.	a2-a3	Bb4:c3
9.	b2:c3	...

Once again, the basic position of the Nimzo-Indian Defense, which occurred so often in this tournament that it was suggested play be started here.

9.	...	b7-b6
10.	c4:d5	e6:d5
11.	Bc1-b2	c5-c4
12.	Bd3-c2	Bc8-g4

13.	Qd1-e1	Nf6-e4
14.	Nf3-d2	Ne4:d2
15.	Qe1:d2	Bg4-h5
16.	f2-f3	Bh5-g6
17.	e3-e4	Qd8-d7
18.	Ra1-e1	f7-f5

We have been following the Round 2 game Reshevsky - Petrosian up through move 18. In that game, White kept a significant positional advantage, although Petrosian put together a fine defense that achieved a draw. Here, in place of his earlier 18..Rae8, Petrosian plays a more active move. The price of that activity, however, is a strong white center pawn with the bishop-pair — and in my opinion, that's too high.

19.	e4:d5	Qd7:d5
20.	a3-a4	Rf8-e8

Black undertakes a series of exchanges, expecting to be left with more pieces available to fight for d5 than his opponent. The battle, however, rages not only for that square, but for the entire board; and the force left to White — a queen and two bishops — is a tremendous one indeed.

21.	Qd2-g5	Qd5-f7
22.	Bb2-a3	h7-h6
23.	Qg5-g3	Re8-e1
24.	Rf1:e1	Ra8-e8
25.	Re1:e8+	Qf7:e8
26.	Kg1-f2	...

Black's strategy has suffered a fiasco. White has the better game, beyond the shadow of a

doubt: his a4-, d4- and c3-
pawns are better than Black's
a7-, b6- and c4-pawns. White
has his passed pawn already,
whereas Black's pawn on a7 can
only become passed over the dead
body of the bishop at a3. The
transfer of the knight to b3 is
played in the faint hope of distracting White's attention from
the events in the center, and
inducing the exchange of at least
one white bishop, but on b3 the
knight is too far from the center of events. Not surprisingly,
it cannot quite get back in time
to prevent the d-pawn from queening.

| 26. | ... | Nc6-a5 |
| 27. | Qg3-f4 | Na5-b3 |

Black is apparently willing to
risk 28 d5 Q:a4 29 d6 Q:a3 30 d7
Qf8 31 Qc7, since he has the save
29..Qc6; in this line, however,
the simple capture 30 B:f5 would
have been quite as strong as it
is in the game continuation.

| 28. | Bc2:f5 | Bg6:f5 |
| 29. | Qf4:f5 | Qe8:a4 |

White's d-pawn becomes more
powerful with every exchange,
and while it advances, the white
queen and bishop will also be
carrying out an attack on Black's
king. The following moves, up
to and including the 40th, were
played by Smyslov with the intention of adjourning the game
without altering the position,
and then finding the surest road
to victory. Play really resumes
on the 41st move, and it will
take a chess miracle to save
Black's game then.

30.	Qf5-f8+	Kg8-h7
31.	Qf8-f5+	Kh7-g8
32.	Qf5-e6+	Kg8-h7
33.	Qe6-e4+	Kh7-g8
34.	Qe4-a8+	Kg8-h7

Smyslov checks from a different
square each time, so as not to
repeat the position three times
by accident.

35.	Qa8-e4+	Kh7-g8
36.	Qe4-d5+	Kg8-h7
37.	Ba3-e7	Nb3-c1
38.	Qd5-f5+	Kh7-g8
39.	Qf5-f8+	Kg8-h7
40.	Qf8-f5+	Kh7-g8
41.	d4-d5	...

Smyslov plays a move that he
will have to make anyway before
adjournment, so as to make his
opponent do the thinking before
sealing, and also to make it
harder for him to analyze the
adjourned position.

| 41. | ... | Qa4-a2+ |

Chess miracles, as opposed to
the other sort, still happen on
occasion, thanks to chessplayers'
fantasy and the game's endless
possibilities. In this — to
all appearances, absolutely
lost — position, Petrosian com-
poses a study: Black to move
and draw, and demonstrates the
solution to Smyslov after adjournment.

| 42. | Kf2-g3 | Qa2-d2 |
| 43. | d5-d6 | ... |

If 43 Qe6+, to prevent the
check on e1, then 43..Kh8 44 d6
Ne2+ 45 Kg4 Qf4+ 46 Kh5 Q:h2+
is perpetual check — and on
46 Kh3, it is mate to White's
king.

43.	...	Qd2-e1+
44.	Kg3-g4	Nc1-d3
45.	Qf5-d5+	...

If White pushes his pawn to
d7 at once, then the draw is
attained with the problem-like
45..h5+! 46 K:h5 Q:e7 47 Qd5+
Kh7 48 d8Q Nf4+; if instead
48 Qe4+, then 48..Q:e4 49 fe
Nf4+, and Black even wins.

| 45. | ... | Kg8-h7 |
| 46. | d6-d7 | Qe1-e5! |

[174]

A move of rare beauty. If
White queens, he is mated in
two moves; if he trades queens,
he loses the d-pawn; and if he
retreats by 47 Qd4, Q:h2 forces
perpetual check.

Convinced that a genuine miracle had come to pass, Smyslov
resigned himself to the loss of
a half-point, and forced the
draw with a sham queen sacrifice.

47. Qd5:d3+   c4:d3
48. d7-d8Q   ...

DRAW

In turn, Black's attempt to
play for the win would be easily
rebuffed: 48..Qe2 49 Kh3 d2
50 Qd7 d1Q 51 Qf5+.

However, as it turns out, miracles are sometimes no more than
optical illusions in chess as
well: 47 Qd6 would have allowed
White to defend the h-pawn, skew-
er-fashion, through Black's
queen. On 47..Nf2+ there follows
48 Kh4 g5+ 49 Kh5; and on any
other Black reply to 47 Qd6
White simply makes another queen,
and his king easily escapes the
checks.

Curiously, neither of the players, nor the tournament participants, nor the spectators, noticed this possibility for White.
47 Qd6 was discovered by a Swedish amateur some months after
the end of the tournament.

******

103. Keres—Najdorf
(Sicilian Defense)

1.	e2-e4	c7-c5
2.	Ng1-e2	Ng8-f6
3.	Nb1-c3	d7-d6
4.	g2-g3	Nb8-c6
5.	Bf1-g2	g7-g6
6.	d2-d3	Bf8-g7

A quiet line of the Sicilian.
The play, as you can see, leads
to a nearly symmetrical position, the only difference being
that the black pawns face the
queen's wing, while White's
face the center. This factor
predetermines further planning
on both sides. Keres does not
employ this unhurried maneuvering system very often, and he
later commits a number of inaccuracies, allowing Black, first
to equalize, and then to get the
better of it.

7.	Bc1-e3	0-0
8.	h2-h3	...

Smyslov, who best knows the
Closed System and plays it like
a virtuoso, prefers 8 Qc1 here,
intending to trade off the darksquare bishops; if Black forestalls this by 8..Re8 9 Bh6 Bh8,
only then 10 h3. The queen's
move to c1, instead of d2, is
made with the idea of answering
8..Ng4 by 9 Bd2.

8.	...	Nf6-e8

Black clearly intends to put
a knight on d4. Now was White's
last opportunity for 9 d4; failing to play it, he cedes his
opponent a spatial advantage.

9.	Qd1-d2	Nc6-d4
10.	Nc3-d1	Ra8-b8

Black is already prepared to
advance the b-pawn, while White
hasn't even castled yet. His
next maneuver has as its aim
the removal of the knight from
d4 and the advance of his pawn
to that square, but this plan
is doomed to fail. The best plan
now was simply to take the
knight and play 12 Bh6, so that
Black's pawn advance would at
least be deprived of the support of his king's bishop.

11.	Ne2-f4	Ne8-c7
12.	c2-c3	e7-e5!

A fine example of the use of a tactical stroke to overturn an opposing strategic plan. If Black's knight were to retreat, then after 13 d4 White would stand well. Now, however, it is White's knight which must retreat, and d3-d4 will never occur. More: Black immediately plays ..d6-d5 and ..f7-f5, taking over the center completely.

13. Nf4-e2 ...

13 cd would not have suited White any better, since Black would then occupy important central points.

| 13. | ... | Nd4:e2 |
| 14. | Qd2:e2 | b7-b6 |

White has lost the first skirmish: his pieces are poorly posted, with the knight in particular having not a single move.

15.	0-0	d6-d5
16.	c3-c4	d5:e4
17.	d3:e4	...

17. ... f7-f5

Najdorf gives his opponent no rest! The pawn must be taken, as 18..f4 is threatened, and if its path is blocked by 18 f4, then 18..Ne6, and the knight enters the fray with tremendous effect. After the exchange of pawns at f5, Black is suddenly threatening 19..Bd3; and so the white knight, for the sake of whose freedom White played 16 c4, never gets to c3 at all.

18.	e4:f5	Bc8:f5
19.	Rf1-e1	Bf5-d3
20.	Be3-g5	Qd8-d4

The triumph of centralization.

| 21. | Qe2-e3 | Bd3:c4 |
| 22. | Ra1-c1 | ... |

White's game is lost: he has no advantages whatsoever to compensate him for the pawn. The continuation 22 Nc3 Ne6 23 Rad1 Q:e3 24 B:e3 Nd4 would hold out no prospects for him, so he seeks somehow to change the normal course of events. He offers Black the option of winning another pawn, with 22..B:a2, or sacrificing the exchange himself. Both the one and the other would favor Black:

1) 22..B:a2 23 b3 Ne6 24 Q:d4 N:d4 25 Bd5+ Kh8 26 Re3 e4!, with an easy win;

2) 22..Bf7 23 Q:d4 ed! 24 Bf4 Rbc8 25 Bb7 Nd5! 26 B:c8 N:f4 27 gf R:c8, with a winning position; or if White plays 26 Bd6 (instead of 26 B:c8), then 26..Nb4, or 27 Ba6 (instead of 27 gf) 27..d3 is not bad.

Najdorf disdains both acquiring and sacrificing material, expecting the win to be a matter of simple technique after the trade of queens. However, this exchange substantially improves White's position, chiefly by bringing his knight back into the game; later, Black also allows White's rook to reach the seventh.

22.	...	Qd4:e3
23.	Nd1:e3	Bc4:a2
24.	Rc1-a1	Ba2-b3
25.	Ra1-a3	Bb3-e6
26.	Ra3:a7	Nc7-b5
27.	Ra7-e7	Nb5-d4
28.	Ne3-g4	Be6:g4
29.	h3:g4	Nd4-f3+
30.	Bg2:f3	Rf8:f3
31.	Re1-d1	...

Black has simplified the game and held onto his pawn, but the quality of his position has been so debased that the win is already in doubt.

31. ... Rf3-f7

There was something to be said

for 31..Bf8, too — mainly that
after 32 Ra7 Rf7 33 R:f7 K:f7
34 Rd7+, he could bring his
king to the center. Of course,
Black could expect to lose a
pawn in the line 32 R:e5 Bg7
33 Re2 Rb3, but he would still
be left with all of the chances.

32.	Re7:f7	Kg8:f7
33.	Rd1-d7+	Kf7-g8
34.	b2-b3	b6-b5

Black induced 34 b3 by his
threat of 34..c4 and 35..e4;
now he is able to set about
creating his passed pawn by
making use of the following
standard technique: 35..c4
36 bc, and now he does not recapture White's pawn, but instead pushes his own pawn on
to queen with 36..b4. Why must
Black continue this way? Because, by recapturing at c4,
he allows White's rook, by
going to c7, to force him to
defend his pawn from the side,
after which the pawn could no
longer take even one step further; White could then move
his king up and take it.

After the inevitable ..c5-c4
and ..b5-b4, White will be in a
real spot. Within three moves,
Black's pawn will reach the
first rank, so its march must
be halted, and not later than
b2. In these circumstances, the
proper plan would be: 35 Kf1 c4
36 bc b4 37 Bc1 b3 38 Rd2 (perhaps also 38 c5 b2 39 B:b2 and
40 c6) and 39 Bb2, when the
pawn is stopped; or 37..Rc8
38 Rb7 R:c4 39 Bd2 Bf8 40 g5,
when Black could hardly hope
to win.

With 35 Rc7, White places his
rook in front of his pawn, and
also deprives himself of the opportunity of playing Rd2. Now
the above variations are no longer operative, and White must
give up a piece for the pawn.

35.	Rd7-c7	c5-c4
36.	b3:c4	b5-b4
37.	Bg5-c1	e5-e4
38.	c4-c5	b4-b3
39.	c5-c6	b3-b2

(See diagram, next column)

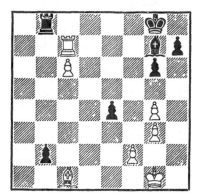

| 40. | Bc1:b2 | Rb8:b2 |

The fortieth move! By recapturing with his bishop, Black
would have entered a difficult,
but still most probably won,
endgame: 40..B:b2 41 Rd7 Rc8
42 c7 Bf6 43 Kf1 Kf8, followed
by ..Be7 and ..Ke8; if 44 R:h7,
then 44..Bg7.

| 41. | Rc7-d7 | ... |

DRAW

Despite his extra piece,
Black cannot win. After 41..Rc2
42 c7, Black's only reasonable
move is 42..Bf8. Now the bishop
cannot move anywhere, because
of the check on d8, the king
cannot cross the seventh rank,
and the rook can only move up
and down the c-file. Remember
this position!

✶✶✶✶✶

104. Reshevsky—Taimanov
(Nimzoindian Defense)

1.	d2-d4	Ng8-f6
2.	c2-c4	e7-e6
3.	Nb1-c3	Bf8-b4
4.	e2-e3	0-0
5.	Ng1-e2	d7-d5
6.	a2-a3	...

White seeks to extract the
maximum from this opening by
obtaining the advantage of the
two bishops without the doubled
c-pawns that usually accompany
them.

6.	...	Bb4-e7
7.	c4:d5	e6:d5
8.	Ne2-g3	...

Reshevsky likes this opening position, even though theory does not, considering that Black equalizes with 8..c5. Reshevsky obviously has his own opinions on that score, since he has always been willing to enter the Ng1-e2-g3 line, and plays it outstandingly well.

His opponents in this tournament — Taimanov, and Averbakh in Round 18 — declined to play 8..c5 in favor of their own more intricate, which is not to say better, systems. I still think that 8..c5 is the simplest solution.

8.	...	Rf8-e8
9.	b2-b4	c7-c6
10.	Bf1-d3	b7-b5

No very high level of chess erudition is required to brand this move anti-positional, and to give it a fat question mark, as almost every commentator has done. Its bad points are quite obvious. But the move was played by an international grandmaster, and he undoubtedly saw some good in the move, this being that Black fixes the pawn at b4, and prepares to break with ..a7-a5, aiming to isolate one of the queenside pawns. As for the weakness of the pawn at c6, Black expects to close the c-file with the maneuver ..Nb8-d7-b6-c4, simultaneously bringing this knight to a strong position also.

Perhaps Taimanov would not have been quite so roundly condemned, had it been recalled that the thoughtless 10..b5 was played by Reshevsky himself against Gligoric in a game from their match in New York 1951.

11.	Bc1-d2	...

Gligoric also played in this fashion against Reshevsky. The modest bishop move is exceptionally strong, and destroys both of Black's hopes. The push 11..a5 would now be risky, on account of 12 ba R:a5 13 a4! b4 14 Na2 Na6 15 B:a6; so Taimanov tries bringing his knight to c4 first.

11.	...	Nb8-d7
12.	a3-a4	

White would also have met 11..a6 with 12 a4, and even though 12..Bb7 would allow Black to maintain b5, 13 Qb3 Nbd7 14 a5 would have prevented him from getting his knight to c4.

12.	...	Be7:b4
13.	a4:b5	c6-c5
14.	0-0	c5-c4

White has the freer game. In the present instance, this means that the b5-pawn is a strong damper on the opposing position, the black d-pawn needs piece protection, and Black must also be on his guard against a possible knight incursion on f5. Exchanging on d4 would not change the basics of the position, but merely open another line for the bishop at d2. Taimanov takes an optimistic approach to the position by creating a protected passed pawn, but this gives White some other trumps. Above all, by removing the central tension, he frees his opponent from worrying about his pawn chain, and allows him to concentrate on active minor piece play. As for the passed pawn, its protector is itself in need of protection, and will cause Black no end of worry.

I would have preferred the waiting move 14..Nb6.

15.	Bd3-c2	a7-a5
16.	b5:a6	Ra8:a6
17.	Ra1:a6	Bc8:a6
18.	Qd1-a1	...

Beginning a powerful strategic maneuver aiming at the occupation of the a- and b-files by his heavy pieces; especially pretty is the concluding 21 Rb2, which refutes Black's defensive play.

18.	...	Nd7-b8
19.	Qa1-a4	Bb4-f8
20.	Rf1-b1	Re8-e6

(See diagram, next page)

21. Rb1-b2 ...

Black intended to wrest the
b-file away with 21..Rb6, but
now this move would achieve
nothing, since 22 Qa5 would
follow, when the rook must return to d6 (22..Nbd7 23 Na4
Rb8 24 Q:a6), and White then
definitely takes over the b-
file with 23 Na4. Such moves,
easily passed over, can frequently be more important than
a combination, and decide the
outcome of a game.

Black's position has clearly
deteriorated. White's further
plan is to step up the pressure
on the d5-pawn; Black does not
feel he can tolerate the knight
on f4, and so he exchanges it.

21.	...	g7-g6
22.	Ng3-e2	Bf8-d6
23.	Ne2-f4	Bd6:f4
24.	e3:f4	...

Despite this apparent weakening of his d-pawn, White submits
to the exchange, since it leaves
him master of the dark squares.
Utilizing the weakening ..g7-g6
he had earlier forced upon Black,
his kingside pawn majority and
the growing power of his pair of
bishops, Reshevsky storms the
enemy king position with exceptional energy.

Nothing remains for Black but
to try to cut down the number
of active pieces on the board,
and to ward off the direct tactical threats.

24.	...	Nb8-d7
25.	h2-h3	Re6-b6
26.	Qa4-a5	Qd8-b8

Black did not have this possibility earlier, when b8 was
occupied by a knight. Apropos
of this, it should be noted that
Black had no need to return the
knight to b8 on move 18: the
bishop on a6 was better defended
with 18..Qa8.

| 27. | Rb2:b6 | Qb8:b6 |

Here White could have won a
pawn by 28 N:d5 Q:a5 29 N:f6+
N:f6 30 B:a5; his position is
so strong, however, that he has
no need to distract himself by
consideration of the endgame after 30..Nd5.

28. Qa5-a3 ...

| 28. | ... | Nd7-f8 |
| 29. | Bd2-e3 | Ba6-c8 |

Black defends himself against
30 f5, but after 30 g4 he will
have to start looking after his
d-pawn, in view of the threatened 31 g5. Losing time doesn't
really mean very much here, since
Black can't make any effective
improvement in the positioning
of his pieces. Taimanov defends
very resourcefully, as usual: his
play shows no sign of despondan-
cy. He tries constantly to set
his opponent some new problem —
not all that complex, perhaps,
but at least it takes up time,
and there's very little of that
left!

30.	g2-g4	Bc8-b7
31.	f4-f5	g6-g5
32.	Qa3-e7	h7-h6
33.	Nc3-a4	Qb6-c6
34.	Na4-c5	Bb7-c8
35.	Qe7-d8	Kg8-g7

Here the time-pressure scramble reached its zenith: Reshevsky had literally seconds for the last five moves, whereas Taimanov had a full minute!

36.	Be3-d2	...

By leaving both his bishops on the second rank for a moment Reshevsky allows Taimanov to pull his queen away from the defense of the bishop at c8, and thereby destroys the fruits of all his skillful play. Instead, 36 Ba4 Qa8 37 Kg2 would have placed Black in complete zugzwang.

36.	...	Qc6-b5

37.	Qd8:c8	...

In time-pressure, Reshevsky sees a mate, so he gives up the bishop at c2 and retains the darksquare one. But Taimanov incontestably refutes this idea, forcing Reshevsky, at adjournment time, to give serious consideration to how he can keep from losing this game.

Objectively, 37 Bc3 was best, keeping the queen from b2. If then 37..Qe8, White could even trade queens, keeping a sizable advantage in spite of Black's protected passed pawn.

37.	...	Qb5-b2
38.	Kg1-g2	Qb2:c2
39.	Bd2-b4	Nf6-e4!

In such positions, counter-attack is the best means of defense.

40.	Nc5:e4	Qc2:e4+
41.	Kg2-g3	...

Reshevsky sealed this strong move. The game was not resumed, the

DRAW

being agreed to without further play, in view of the following main variation: 41..Nh7 42 Bd6 Q:d4 43 Qc7 Nf6 44 Be5 Qd3+ 45 Kg2 Qe4+ — perpetual check.

*****

105. Bronstein—Gligoric
(King's Indian)

If, having castled, you see that your opponent has closed the center and is preparing a direct pawn storm, then it's a good idea to open a line beforehand in the region where his king is or intends to be. On that principle, Gligoric sets up some interesting queenside play as early as the ninth move, and obtains a strong counter-initiative.

1.	d2-d4	Ng8-f6
2.	c2-c4	g7-g6
3.	Nb1-c3	Bf8-g7
4.	e2-e4	d7-d6
5.	h2-h3	0-0
6.	Bc1-e3	...

Another form of the Samisch Attack, with 5 h3 instead of 5 f3. The advantages of this system are: two dark diagonals are not weakened, the diagonal d1-h5 remains open, and the square f3 as well — Black will find it difficult to establish his knight on h5, when it can always be driven away by Be2. There are disadvantages, too, chief among them the fact that e4 has no pawn protection, which Gligoric skillfully exploits later on.

6.	...	e7-e5
7.	d4-d5	Nb8-d7
8.	g2-g4	Nd7-c5

| 9. | Qd1-c2 | c7-c6 |

White is all set to castle long and follow this up by storming Black's king position. Gligoric chooses this moment to remind him that with the c-file opened, the white king won't be entirely safe, either.

| 10. | Ng1-e2 | c6:d5 |
| 11. | c4:d5 | Qd8-a5 |

Black attacks the e-pawn indirectly, using the c-file, as may be seen from the variation 12 Rb1 Nc:e4 13 b4 Qc7.

| 12. | Ne2-g3 | Bc8-d7 |
| 13. | Be3-d2 | ... |

Now Black has to reckon with b2-b4, since the pawn will have to be taken, and the queen could find itself lost among the white pieces.

| 13. | ... | Rf8-c8 |

An exchange of courtesies. Black invites his opponent to carry out his threat of 14 b4, but White declines the invitation, since after 14 b4 Q:b4 15 Nb5, Black is not obliged to continue 15..Qa4 16 Q:a4 N:a4 17 N:d6, with a somewhat inferior endgame; instead, he can sacrifice his queen with 15..Q:b5 16 B:b5 B:b5, and White's king would be in a pitiable state.

| 14. | Ra1-b1 | Qa5-d8 |
| 15. | Qc2-d1 | ... |

Both queens go home, in order to resume their duel, after a short while, on the king's wing.

15.	...	a7-a5
16.	Qd1-f3	Ra8-b8
17.	g4-g5	Nf6-e8
18.	h3-h4	...

Black's queenside initiative threatens to spill over into a major offensive. White hurries to distract his opponent's attention, and partly succeeds.

18.	...	f7-f6
19.	Bf1-e2	Ne8-c7
20.	Ke1-f1	Qd8-e7
21.	g5:f6	Qe7:f6
22.	Qf3:f6	Bg7:f6
23.	h4-h5	...

Thanks to Black's foresight, this move, which might have been aggressive, is finally played after the exchange of queens, and now serves only to rid White of a weakness which might otherwise become palpable after ..h7-h5.

23.	...	Rc8-f8
24.	h5:g6	h7:g6
25.	Kf1-g2	Bf6-g7
26.	Bd2-e3	b7-b5
27.	Rb1-c1	Nc7-a6
28.	Nc3-d1	Rf8-c8
29.	Nd1-c3	a5-a4
30.	Rc1-d1	b5-b4

Both sides are now playing to win an approximately level position. White shuffles his pieces while Black pushes his pawns, trying to get through to the b-pawn. He clears the b5 square in order to trade off White's king's bishop there and open an entry for the knight to d3. However, Black's accomplishments are temporary, while their drawbacks will be permanent. The knight, which now retreats to the first rank, will later be aiming for c4.

31.	Nc3-b1	Bd7-b5
32.	Be2:b5	Rb8:b5
33.	Kg2-f3	Rb5-b7
34.	Kf3-e2	...

The king, which fled the center the moment danger loomed, is back. Now the drawbacks of the King's Indian Defense begin to assert themselves: the dark-square bishop, if it does not have its say in the middlegame, usually finds little to do in the endgame.

34.	...	Rb7-c7
35.	Rd1-c1	Nc5-d7
36.	Rc1:c7	Rc8:c7
37.	Rh1-c1	...

Clearing the king's road to the queenside.

37.	...	Rc7:c1
38.	Be3:c1	Na6-c5
39.	Bc1-e3	Kg8-f7
40.	Nb1-d2	Nd7-b6

(See diagram, next page)

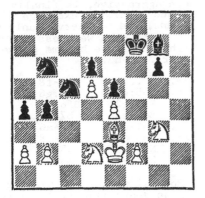

White had his move to seal
here, and he could not find
enough strength to resist
playing 41 B:c5: first, because
it gave him a protected passed
pawn; and second, because it
gave his opponent a weak, blockaded pawn at c5, and made it
easier for his own king to get
to b5. Nevertheless, this. was
not the best move; although it
did not let the win slip, it
complicated it considerably.
The bishop was a good one, and
this was not yet the time to
trade it. 41 Nf1 was correct,
bringing back this knight which
has stood for thirty moves doing nothing, while maintaining
all his threats. The difference
is that while it is on e3 the
bishop keeps Black's king out
of g5, so that White can spend
some time quietly improving his
position by transferring the
knight, let us say, via h2 to
g4; after that, B:c5 dc; Kd3
would lead to an easy win.

41.	Be3:c5	d6:c5
42.	Ke2-d3	Kf7-f6
43.	Nd2-c4	Nb6-d7
44.	Ng3-f1	Kf6-g5
45.	Kd3-e3	Bg7-h6
46.	Nf1-h2	Kg5-f6+

46..Kh4+ would be met, not by
47 Kf3 Bf4, with good drawing

chances, but by 47 Ke2!, leaving
f3 free for the knight's decisive transfer to d3.

47.	Ke3-e2	Bh6-f4
48.	Nh2-g4+	Kf6-e7

The black king's attempt at
counterattack has failed: 48..Kg5
would be met by 49 f3.

49.	Ke2-d3	Ke7-d8
50.	Nc4-d6	Kd8-c7
51.	Nd6-f7	a4-a3

Gligoric wearies of passive
defense, and makes an attempt
to break things up, which unfortunately leads to a quick
loss. If Black had simply stood
in place, White would have continued with f2-f3, brought his
knight to d3, and then broken
up Black's pawn bastions with
a2-a3, etc., according to all
the rules of endgame theory.
Black's impatient move appre-
ciably hastens the end.

52.	b2:a3	b4:a3
53.	Kd3-c4	Kc7-b6
54.	Kc4-b3	Kb6-a5
55.	Nf7-d6	Bf4-c1
56.	Nd6-c4+	Ka5-b5
57.	Ng4:e5	...

BLACK RESIGNED

******

******
******

This round opened the second half of the tournament. After three

days' rest, the grandmasters resumed battle...

ROUND SIXTEEN

106. Bronstein—Taimanov
(Queen's Indian Defense)

1. d4 Nf6 2. c4 e6 3. Nf3 b6
4. g3 Ba6 5. Nbd2 c5 6. Bg2 Nc6
7. dc B:c5 8. 0-0 0-0 9. a3 Bb7

The bishop's foray to a6 forced
White to slow his usual tempo of
development in the Queen's Indian. But Black's accomplishments
are fleeting: one bishop has already returned to its accustomed
place, and now the b-pawn's advance forces the other's retreat
as well!

10. b4 Be7 11. Bb2 Rc8 12. Qb3
Rc7 13. Rac1 Qa8 14. Qd3 h6
15. Rfd1 Rd8 16. e4 d6

White has kept the pawn from
going to d5; and if his knight
were on c3, he could strengthen
his position still further. With
the knight on d2, however, I
could find no plan that had any
future in it, either at the board
or at home. Black's pieces may
indeed be cramped, but they are
well coordinated; together with
Black's pawns, they form a very
solid structure. On the whole,
it seems to me that the best way
to meet the Queen's Indian is
not to allow it. White won two,
and Black six, of the fifteen
Queen's Indians played in this
tournament: an unenviable result. It was also an atypical
one: a more typical result would
have been for all fifteen to
have ended as draws.

17. Qe2 a5 18. Ra1 ab 19. ab
Qc8 20. Bc3 Nd7 21. Nd4 N:d4
22. B:d4 Bf6 23. B:f6 N:f6
24. Qe3 d5

DRAW

(Diagram of final position)

*****

107. Reshevsky—Najdorf
(King's Indian)

1.	d2-d4	Ng8-f6
2.	c2-c4	g7-g6
3.	Nb1-c3	Bf8-g7
4.	e2-e4	d7-d6
5.	Bf1-e2	0-0
6.	Ng1-f3	e7-e5
7.	0-0	Nb8-c6
8.	Bc1-e3	...

Najdorf's next two moves, introduced in this game, must be rated
an important theoretical achievement, since Black obtains a draw
practically by force.

8. ... Rf8-e8

Najdorf apparently came upon
this move while analyzing the
King's Indians played not very
long before this tournament in
his long match against the same
opponent. In two of those games,

Najdorf defended with 8..Ng4, though unsuccessfully. Whether 8..Re8 or 8..Ng4 is the better move, however, is a question that will have to be left open for the time being.

| 9. | d4-d5 | ... |

This appears to win a tempo, but the knight unexpectedly goes forward, instead of backward.

9.	...	Nc6-d4
10.	Nf3:d4	e5:d4
11.	Be3:d4	Nf6:e4
12.	Bd4:g7	Kg8:g7
13.	Nc3:e4	Re8:e4

| 14. | Qd1-c2 | Re4-e8 |

DRAW

Black may have slightly the better of it: in the endgame, his king can reach a good position via the dark squares. Evidently, in reply to 7..Nc6, should the attempts of a few theoreticians to demonstrate an advantage for White after 8 de prove unsuccessful, we shall have to return to 8 d5.

******

108. Keres—Petrosian
(King's Indian)

1.	d2-d4	Ng8-f6
2.	c2-c4	g7-g6
3.	Nb1-c3	Bf8-g7
4.	Ng1-f3	d7-d6
5.	Bc1-f4	...

A peaceful system, especially unpleasant to those players who essay the King's Indian in search of double-edged combinative play. It differs from Smyslov's system (see Games 139 and 184) in that here the pawn is on c4 instead of c3.

Theoreticians tell us that ..e7-e5 is difficult to get in against this line, so Black generally plays for ..c7-c5 instead, following up with a gradual advance of his queenside pawns. Petrosian carries out only the first part of this plan, and then both sides spend a lot of time in slow maneuvering, trying to induce weaknesses.

It still seems to me that Black has no reason not to try for ..e7-e5. But even with the plan he uses in this game, his 5..Nbd7 is a poor choice: 5..0-0 would be better, in order to continue, after 6 e3, with 6..c5, followed by ..Nc6!

5.	...	Nb8-d7
6.	h2-h3	c7-c5
7.	e2-e3	0-0
8.	Bf1-e2	b7-b6
9.	0-0	Bc8-b7
10.	d4-d5!	a7-a6

After some small opening inaccuracies, Black has drifted into a positional squeeze.

11.	a2-a4	Nf6-e8
12.	Qd1-d2	Nd7-e5
13.	Nf3-h2	e7-e6
14.	Ra1-d1	Qd8-e7
15.	Qd2-c2	Ra8-d8
16.	Qc2-b3	...

An interesting psychological motif is becoming apparent here. By making only "natural" and "necessary" moves, Keres is trying to deceive his opponent into thinking that he plans nothing more than the steady improvement of his position. In fact, he has something completely different in mind: Keres wants (it's hard to believe this) to whip up an attack on the h-file! To that end, he keeps the knight at h2 for a long time, waiting for the moment when its appearance at g4 will force Black to take it off. Meanwhile, for form's sake, he "presses" on b6, d6, etc.

| 16. | ... | Qe7-c7 |

17.	Rd1-d2	e6:d5
18.	Nc3:d5	Bb7:d5
19.	Rd2:d5	Ne8-f6
20.	Rd5-d1	Ne5-c6
21.	Be2-f3	Rf8-e8

And here is that small inaccuracy (21..Nb4 was necessary); now comes —

22.	Nh2-g4	...

Now 22..h5 23 N:f6+ B:f6 24 B:c6 Q:c6 25 Rd5 would be bad for Black; that leaves him small choice between 22..Nb4 23 Bg5 and 22..N:g4. Petrosian chooses the latter line, as it leaves him with a relatively sounder position.

22.	...	Nf6:g4
23.	h3:g4	Nc6-b4
24.	Rd1-d2	Qc7-e7
25.	Rf1-d1	Bg7-e5
26.	g4-g5	a6-a5
27.	g2-g3	Qe7-e6
28.	Kg1-g2	Qe6-e7
29.	Rd1-h1	Qe7-e6

Petrosian has no great choice: he must shuffle back and forth, waiting for the next wave of Keres' attack.

30.	Rh1-h4	Re8-f8
31.	Qb3-d1	Be5:f4
32.	e3:f4	f7-f6
33.	Rd2-e2	Qe6-f7
34.	g5:f6	Qf7:f6

In order to defend the h-pawn, Black has had to loosen his king position somewhat.

35.	Qd1-e1	Rd8-d7
36.	Re2-e6	Qf6:b2
37.	Re6-e7	Rd7:e7
38.	Qe1:e7	Qb2-g7
39.	Qe7:d6	Qg7-f6
40.	Qd6-d7	Qf6-f7
41.	Qd7-d6	Qf7-f6
42.	Qd6-c7	Rf8-f7
43.	Qc7-c8+	Rf7-f8
44.	Qc8-d7	Qf6-f7

This position already occurred after Black's 40th move.

45.	Qd7-d2	Qf7-e6
46.	Rh4-h1	Qe6:c4
47.	Qd2-d6	...

47.	...	Qc4-d4
48.	Qd6-e6+	Kg8-h8

Boleslavsky pointed out an amusing move here: 48..Rf7 49 R:h7 Qf6: Black forces the exchange of queens and draws, against all logic! A rare case indeed!

However, after the problem move ..Rf7 White has the no less original reply 49 Be2. This chance should still have been explored, however, since the "more solid" 48..Kh8 leads to the immediate loss of his extra pawn, and he never does manage to trade queens.

49.	Qe6:g6	Qd4-g7
50.	Qg6-e4	Nb4-a2
51.	Qe4-c4	Na2-b4
52.	Bf3-e4	Rf8:f4
53.	Qc4-e6	Rf4:e4
54.	Qe6:e4	Qg7-d7
55.	Qe4-e5+	Kh8-g8
56.	Rh1-h5	...

BLACK RESIGNED

******

109. Smyslov—Averbakh
(Queen's Gambit)

1.	c2-c4	Ng8-f6
2.	Ng1-f3	e7-e6
3.	Nb1-c3	d7-d5
4.	d2-d4	Bf8-b4
5.	c4:d5	e6:d5

6.	Bc1-g5	h7-h6
7.	Bg5:f6	Qd8:f6
8.	Qd1-b3	Qf6-d6
9.	a2-a3	Bb4:c3+
10.	Qb3:c3	0-0

The minority attack is not just an opening idea most frequently employed in the Exchange Variation (actually the Carlsbad Variation) of the Queen's Gambit Declined, but a general strategic idea, which under the right circumstances may be employed at any stage of the game, and not just on the queenside. The point of this attack is to give the opponent weaknesses in the sector where he holds a quantitative pawn majority, and then to attack the weak pawns with pieces.

Here the circumstances are exceptionally favorable for a White minority attack on the queen's wing. Generally Black, in order to equalize, must undertake a piece attack on the king.

11.	Ra1-c1	c7-c6
12.	e2-e3	Bc8-f5
13.	Bf1-e2	Nb8-d7
14.	0-0	...

Why is White delaying his b2-b4? Black would reply 14..Be4, when 15 Nd2 would be impossible, with the g-pawn loose. White does not want to give up his knight for Black's bishop either, since that bishop is hampered by its own pawns. However, Black's next move puts a long-time crimp on the white b-pawn's

advance.

14.	...	a7-a5

In order to prevent the minority attack, the pawn separates from its base and becomes a target itself. Sometimes it happens that such a pawn draws a string of black pawns after it, like a needle pulling thread; in the present situation, however, Averbakh isn't concerned with its defense yet. What he has accomplished is that White must now set about regrouping his pieces toward a new goal (assailing the a-pawn); Black uses this time to be the first to create threats on the kingside.

15.	Nf3-e1	Nd7-f6
16.	Ne1-d3	Bf5:d3

The knight has come under the bishop's guns after all. The attempt to get the knight to c5 by way of b3, avoiding the b1-f5 diagonal, would have failed, since Black would have answered 15 Nd2 with 15..a4.

17.	Qc3:d3	Rf8-e8
18.	Be2-f3	Nf6-e4
19.	Bf3:e4	Re8:e4
20.	Qd3-b3	Qd6-d7
21.	Rc1-c5	Re4-g4

This transfer of the rook to g4 illustrates Black's counter-chances in this type of position. Usually during the minority attack White's king is left either completely devoid of piece protection or else covered by just one minor piece. It's not easy, though, to break through to the king by means of a pawn storm, so the most popular method is the direct frontal assault, especially when g2 and h2 provide such excellent targets for the pieces. Should White have to advance his g- or h-pawn, only then should Black bring in his pawns. The success of such an operation depends upon the concrete peculiarities of the position. In the present instance, Smyslov was not in a risk-taking mood: calling off his attempt to win the a-pawn, he decides to force the draw. A moral victory for Black.

22.	h2-h3	Rg4-g6
23.	Kg1-h1	a5-a4
24.	Qb3-b4	Rg6-f6
25.	Kh1-g1	...

DRAW

******

110. Geller—Szabo
(Nimzoindian Defense)

1.	d2-d4	Ng8-f6
2.	c2-c4	e7-e6
3.	Nb1-c3	Bf8-b4
4.	e2-e3	0-0
5.	Bf1-d3	d7-d5
6.	Ng1-f3	b7-b6
7.	0-0	c7-c5

Although the c-pawn does attack the white center, its presence on c5 also has the drawback of cutting off the king's bishop's retreat. The more restrained 7..Bb7 seems more appropriate to me.

8.	Qd1-e2	Nb8-d7
9.	c4:d5	e6:d5
10.	a2-a3	Bb4-a5
11.	b2-b4	...

Black did not want to give up his bishop, but will soon discover that the white knight is worth more. The assault White now begins against c7 and d6 has the self-evident justification of excluding the darksquare bishop from play. In such cases, the opening of lines generally favors the better developed side. The pawn sacrificed in order to achieve this functions as bait.

| 11. | ... | c5:b4 |
| 12. | Nc3-b5 | a7-a6 |

13.	Nb5-d6	Nd7-b8
14.	Nd6:c8	Qd8:c8
15.	Bc1-d2	b4-b3

The quality of a position does not always depend on the quantity of pawns. In this case, Black has enough weaknesses to give White a clear advantage. The thematic line here would be 15..ba 16 B:a5 ba 17 Rfc1, when White could look forward to a good harvest, not only of the three a-pawns, but of the d-pawn as well. Naturally, Szabo does not like this variation, so he decides on a counter-sacrifice, to "clutter" the b-file a bit.

16.	Ra1-b1	Nb8-c6
17.	Rb1:b3	Ba5:d2
18.	Qe2:d2	b6-b5
19.	Rf1-c1	Qc8-d7
20.	Rb3-c3	Rf8-c8
21.	Nf3-e5	...

Geller gives his opponent no rest. After the forced exchange on e5, Szabo has new problems, one of them being where to put the knight now on f6. The leap to e4 appears compromising, but in fact it is his best practical chance. Should the knight retreat, the pack of e- and f-pawns would charge unstoppably into the black king's fortress.

21.	...	Nc6:e5
22.	d4:e5	Rc8:c3
23.	Qd2:c3	Nf6-e4
24.	Qc3-d4	...

White decides he can catch the knight, but that was hardly necessary. 24 Qc7 was simple and good, occupying all the key positions. On the other hand, White's position is so good that it is hard to spoil with just one move.

24.	...	Qd7-b7
25.	h2-h4	h7-h6
26.	Rc1-c2	Ra8-c8
27.	Rc2:c8+	Qb7:c8
28.	Qd4:d5	Ne4-c3
29.	Qd5-d6	...

The knight on e4 has gone on, but the pawn on d5 is no more. Naturally, Black cannot afford to wait until the e- and f-pawns start to roll, so he attempts to get in first with a desperate try at creating a

passed pawn on the queenside.
The game unexpectedly turns com-
binative; still more unexpectedly,
Szabo obtains real saving chances.

29.	...	a6-a5
30.	f2-f4	h6-h5
31.	f4-f5	Nc3-d1
32.	e5-e6	Nd1:e3

Anyway.

| 33. | Kg1-f2 | ... |

The intended 33 e7 is refuted
by a queen invasion of White's
rear echelons (33..Qc1+, etc.):
an excellent idea from Szabo in
severe mutual time-pressure.

33.	...	Ne3-g4+
34.	Kf2-f3	Qc8-c1
35.	e6:f7+	...

The queen check on the eighth
rank would not have had the desired effect. Feeling that his
win is gone, Geller ensures
against loss by guaranteeing
himself a perpetual check.

35... K:f7 36. Qd7+ Kf8 37. Qd8+
Kf7 38. Qd7+ Kf8 39. Qd6+ Kf7
40. Qe6+ Kf8 41. Qd6+ Kf7 42. Qe6+
Kf8

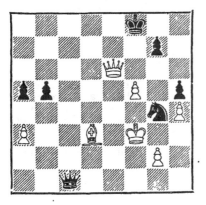

43. Bd3:b5   ...

This was a mistake. The game
was adjourned here, with White
having not the slightest advantage: Black's queen and knight
stand too near his king. Apparently unwilling to analyze the
position, Szabo called the arbiter and told him that the po-

sition had been repeated three
times, and was therefore drawn.
No one had kept score during
time-pressure, so it was only
with great difficulty that Geller was able to demonstrate to
Szabo the error of his ways, and
obtain the right to continue the
game. However, the move he sealed
was so poor as to require him,
once the game was resumed, to
expend quite as much energy to
demonstrate to Szabo that the
position was still a draw. In
the hurly-burly of tournament
play, it's not difficult to over-
estimate one's own chances — or
the other fellow's, for that matter.

43.   ...   Qc1:a3+

Black would have had more
winning chances by not taking
the a-pawn here, and playing
43..Qc3+ instead. The enticing
endgame Szabo is aiming for
turns out, contrary to his expectations, to be a draw.

44. Ke4 Qe3+ 45. Kd5 Nf6+ 46. Kc6
Q:e6+ 47. fe Ke7 48. Bc4 Ne4
49. Kb6 a4 50. Ka5 Nd6

The position is a splendid
illustration of a bishop's power over a knight: despite having an outside passed pawn,
Black cannot win.

51. Bd5 Nf5 52. K:a4 N:h4 53. Kb3
Nf5 54. Kc3 Kd6 55. Bf3 h4 56. Kd3
K:e6 57. Ke4 Kf6 58. Bg4 Nh6
59. Bd7 Kg5 60. Kf3 Nf7 61. Bc8
Ne5+ 62. Ke4 Nc4

Szabo will not believe that
the position cannot be won, and
tries advancing his g-pawn later — which White does not even
deign to notice.

63. Kf3 Ne5+ 64. Ke4 Kf6 65. Kf4
g6 66. Ke4 g5 67. Ke3 Kg6 68. Ke4
Nc4 69. Kf3 Nd2+ 70. Ke3 Nf1+

Even checks don't help!

71. Kf2 Ng3 72. Kf3 Kf6 73. Kg4
Nf1 74. Ba6 Ne3+ 75. Kh3 Nf5
76. Bd3 Ng3 77. Kg4 Nh1 78.Bc2

DRAW

******

111. Kotov—Euwe
(Reti Opening)

1.	c2-c4	Ng8-f6
2.	g2-g3	e7-e6
3.	Bf1-g2	d7-d5
4.	Ng1-f3	d5:c4
5.	0-0	a7-a6

In his theoretical works, Euwe advises against playing to retain the pawn, recommending 5..Nbd7 6 Na3 Nb6 7 N:c4 N:c4 8 Qa4+ Bd7 9 Q:c4 Bc6 10 b3 Bd6 instead, with approximately equal play. With 5..a6, apparently, he is trying for more.

6.	Qd1-c2	b7-b5
7.	Nf3-e5	Nf6-d5
8.	d2-d3	...

An experienced fighter's decision. Rather than spend a lot of effort trying to regain the pawn, Kotov would rather try for active piece play.

8.	...	c4:d3
9.	Ne5:d3	Bc8-b7
10.	Rf1-d1	Qd8-c8
11.	a2-a4	Nb8-d7
12.	a4:b5	a6:b5
13.	Ra1:a8	Bb7:a8
14..	Nb1-a3	Bf8:a3

Black doesn't want to trouble himself over the defense of his b-pawn, so he rather cavalierly parts with his king's bishop. However, by trading off this bishop, Euwe presents Kotov with too many of the dark squares. 14..Qb8 was more conservative, although even then White would stand very well after 15 Qb3 c6 16 e4 N5b6 17 Bf4.

15.	b2:a3	0-0
16.	Nd3-c5	...

Of course, it will not be easy to drive the knight out of here, and it is not in Black's best interests to trade it off. White is still a pawn down, but the powerful position of his pieces outweighs that.

16.	...	Nd7-b6
17.	e2-e4	Nd5-e7
18.	Bg2-f1	Ba8-c6
19.	f2-f3	...

By allowing Black to exchange the second pair of rooks, White immediately dissipates his advantage. 19 Bb2 was correct, and

then 19..Rd8 would be poor, in view of 20 Qc3 f6 21 R:d8+ Q:d8 22 N:e6. The line 19..Na4 20 N:a4 ba 21 Qc5 Re8 22 Bh3, with the threat of 23 Qe5, would also be in White's favor.

19.	...	Rf8-d8
20.	Bc1-g5	Rd8:d1
21.	Qc2:d1	Ne7-g6
22.	Qd1-d8+	Bc6-e8
23.	Qd8:c8	Nb6:c8
24.	Bg5-d8	c7-c6

White's positional advantage still fully counterbalances Black's extra pawn, but not a bit more than that.

25.	f3-f4	e6-e5
26.	f4-f5	Ng6-f8
27.	Kg1-f2	Nf8-d7
28.	Nc5-b7	f7-f6
29.	Kf2-e3	Kg8-f8
30.	h2-h3	Be8-f7

Black cannot show any great activity: White does have two bishops, after all, and they have to be reckoned with.

31.	Bd8-a5	Kf8-e8
32.	g3-g4	Nd7-b6
33.	Ba5-b4	Bf7-c4
34.	Bf1-g2	Bc4-a2
35.	Bg2-f1	Ba2-c4
36.	Bf1-g2	Bc4-a2

DRAW

A game without much excitement.

*****

112. Boleslavsky—Stahlberg
(French Defense)

1.	e2-e4	e7-e6
2.	d2-d4	d7-d5
3.	Nb1-c3	Bf8-b4

Stahlberg is unwilling to play his usual 3..Nf6, apparently fearing to walk into some sort of preparation. But playing 3..Bb4 is like jumping out of the frying pan into the fire, since Boleslavsky plays the Nimzovich Variation quite a lot himself, and is thoroughly conversant with every Black weakness.

Of course, Stahlberg does make a few changes in Black's normal defensive layout, but he gets into difficulties just the same.

4.	e4-e5	c7-c5
5.	a2-a3	Bb4:c3+
6.	b2:c3	Ng8-e7
7.	a3-a4	...

A flexible move: depending upon Black's reply, White may continue with 8 Ba3, 8 Qd2, 8 Qg4, or the game line, 8 Nf3.

7.	...	Nb8-c6
8.	Ng1-f3	Bc8-d7
9.	Bf1-e2	Ra8-c8
10.	0-0	0-0
11.	Bc1-a3	b7-b6
12.	Be2-a6	Rc8-c7

13.	Ba6-d3	h7-h6
14.	Rf1-e1	Nc6-a5
15.	Ba3-c1	c5-c4

Black has skillfully masked his actual intentions, which has, in turn, prevented White from putting together a concrete plan of attack; but here he mistakenly lets himself be seduced by the opportunity to open the f-file. It brings him no benefit whatever, and after a few defensive moves, White renews his onslaught. Black would have been better advised to keep to his waiting tactics, fitting his actions to those of his opponent.

16.	Bd3-f1	Ne7-g6
17.	g2-g3	f7-f6
18.	e5:f6	Qd8:f6
19.	Bf1-g2	Rc7-c8
20.	Qd1-e2	Rf8-f7
21.	h2-h4	...

The tocsin sounds. The dark

squares are hopelessly weak, and Boleslavsky begins methodically to increase his pressure. The bishop on c1 will return to its appointed attacking diagonal a3-f8, the rooks will gather on the f-file, the knight will enter e5, and the pawns, supported by the bishop at h3, will advance for the decisive break. What can Black find to oppose this? Very little, other than passive defense.

21.	...	Na5-c6
22.	h4-h5	Ng6-f8
23.	Nf3-h2	Nf8-h7
24.	f2-f4	Rc8-e8
25.	Nh2-f3	Qf6-d8
26.	Nf3-h4	Nh7-f8
27.	Re1-f1	Nc6-e7
28.	Nh4-f3	Ne7-c6
29.	Bc1-a3	Bd7-c8
30.	Rf1-f2	Nf8-d7
31.	Ra1-f1	Nc6-e7
32.	Bg2-h3	Ne7-f5
33.	Kg1-h2	Nd7-f6
34.	g3-g4	Nf5-d6
35.	Nf3-e5	Rf7-c7

36.	Bh3-g2	...

Having achieved a won position, White hesitates. 36 g5 immediately, or after the preparatory 36 B:d6, suggests itself: in either case, the g-file is opened, and thanks to his great advantage in maneuvering space, White would be able to set up a winning attack. Now Black gets time to pull his knight off the f6 square, so that g4-g5, although it is still playable, no longer wins a tempo.

36.	...	Nd6-e4
37.	Rf2-f3	Nf6-d7
38.	Ne5-g6	...

The knight could have been harried a bit with 38 Re3, but White appears to be making a habit of forgetting to open files — the f-file, in this case.

38.	...	Nd7-f6
39.	Ng6-e5	Nf6-d7
40.	Kh2-g1	Nd7:e5
41.	f4:e5	Ne4-g5

Black has managed to fortify himself on the exact spot where a breakthrough seemed inevitable. The position has now closed up, which deprives White's bishops of the greater part of their effectiveness. White's best course here would have been to content himself with an immediate draw, but he could not resist the temptation of winning the queen.

| 42. | Rf3-f8+ | Re8:f8 |

Naturally, 42..Kh7 43 R:e8 Q:e8 44 Rf8 would leave White with a powerful attack; now, however, only Black can have any winning chances.

But Stahlberg does not like exhausting adjournments, so after analyzing the position, he offered a

DRAW

which Boleslavsky accepted.

******

******

113. Stahlberg—Kotov
(Old Indian Defense)

1.	d2-d4	Ng8-f6
2.	c2-c4	d7-d6
3.	Ng1-f3	Nb8-d7
4.	Nb1-c3	e7-e5
5.	e2-e4	c7-c6
6.	Bf1-e2	Bf8-e7

The King's Indian bishop belongs at g7 — which is where it ends up later.

7.	0-0	0-0
8.	Qd1-c2	Rf8-e8
9.	b2-b3	...

White is also not developing his bishop to its best square. A more active plan would be to bring his rook to d1 first, and then to play 10 h3, preparing to develop the bishop to e3.

9.	...	Be7-f8
10.	Bc1-b2	Nf6-h5
11.	g2-g3	g7-g6
12.	Ra1-d1	Nh5-f6
13.	d4-d5	...

The position begins to take on the aspect of a "normal" King's Indian. Not wishing to allow the opening of the center after 13..ed, White pushes his pawn, and the war of maneuver continues.

13.	...	c6-c5
14.	Nf3-h4	Bf8-g7
15.	a2-a3	Nd7-b6
16.	Be2-f3	Re8-f8
17.	Nc3-e2	Bc8-d7
18.	Bb2-c3	Nf6-e8
19.	Bc3-a5	Qd8-e7
20.	Rd1-e1	Ra8-c8
21.	Ba5-d2	Qe7-d8
22.	Qc2-c1	Bg7-f6
23.	Nh4-g2	Bf6-e7
24.	Bd2-h6	Ne8-g7

There's no denying the fact that Kotov has made better use of the last ten moves: his forces have been most harmoniously regrouped. Now the pawns enter the fray.

25.	h2-h4	f7-f5
26.	e4:f5	g6:f5
27.	Ne2-c3	Bd7-e8
28.	Bf3-d1	Nb6-d7
29.	Bh6:g7	Kg8:g7
30.	Qc1-e3	Be7-f6
31.	Bd1-c2	Be8-g6

32.	Qe3-e2	e5-e4

Soon both sides will begin trading threats — a boon to the reader who, after this rather tedious overture, will now see a delightful combination and a delicate endgame.

The pawn advances in order to secure f3 for the knight which is now on d7. Since the fianchettoed bishop also threatens White's queen's knight, it might seem that the maneuver ..Nd7-e5-f3+ could not be prevented. Stahlberg dissipates that illusion by means of a forcing variation.

33.	Ng2-f4	Rf8-e8
34.	Nf4-e6+	Re8:e6
35.	d5:e6	Bf6:c3
36.	e6:d7	Qd8:d7

So now White has won the exchange; but that was not the reason his knight invaded e6 with check. If Black had time to get in 37..h5, White's initiative would wither, so:

37.	h4-h5	Bc3:e1
38.	h5:g6	Be1-c3
39.	g6:h7	Rc8-h8

An innocent-looking move that conceals a dastardly trap. The game is about even here, and after 40 Kg2 and 41 Rh1, the draw would have been quite obvious. But with his last move in time-pressure, Stahlberg trustingly attacks the bishop, no doubt expecting that Black would find nothing better than 40..Bf6.

40.   Qe2:e3   Kg7-g6!

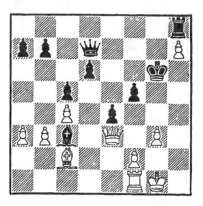

role in the fight.

The king fulfills three tasks with one move: defending g5, clearing the queen's path to h7, and avoiding the check — that's important too! — in the event of 41 Q:c3. What is memorable is not just the idea of the combination, but the cleverness with which it is carried out. Suddenly, unexpectedly, the white king is in trouble.

3) Nor are the pawns on f2 and g4 equivalent: where the pawn on f2 is weak and needs protection, the pawn on g4 stands ready to assist its pieces in their assault on the pawn at f2.

All of these advantages would lose their importance if White could just manage to get the rooks traded off, but he can't. The game's concluding phase is most instructive.

41.	Rf1-d1	Bc3-d4
42.	Qe3-f4	Qd7:h7
43.	Kg1-f1	Qh7-h1+
44.	Kf1-e2	Qh1-h5+!

Kotov plays this second part of the game with uncommon energy and resourcefulness. White, it would seem, was just waiting for the chance to play g3-g4; yet here is Black, giving him the opportunity to play it with tempo!

45.	g3-g4	Qh5:g4+
46.	Qf4:g4+	f5:g4
47.	Bc2:e4+	Kg6-g5

Here's the rub: despite the bishops of opposite color, White has a lost game. Let's see why:

1)Black's bishop is supported, and stands very well at d4, while the same cannot be said of the bishop at e4.

2) Black's king is far more active than its white counterpart, and in fact assumes a leading

48.	Rd1-h1	Rh8-e8
49.	f2-f3	b7-b5
50.	Ke2-f1	b5:c4
51.	b3:c4	g4-g3
52.	Rh1-h7	Re8-b8
53.	Be4-b7	...

Stahlberg is doing everything he can. Before all else, he denies the black rook entry into his camp. Were it not for the passed g-pawn, that might have been enough to save the game.

53.	...	Bd4-e5
54.	Kf1-g2	Kg5-f4
55.	Rh7-f7+	Kf4-e3

The decisive inroad by the black king.

56.	f3-f4	Be5:f4
57.	Rf7-e7+	Bf4-e5
58.	Re7-f7	a7-a5
59.	a3-a4	Ke3-d4
60.	Bb7-d5	Rb8-b2+
61.	Kg2-f1	Rb2-a2

Here,

WHITE RESIGNED

******

114. Euwe—Geller
(King's Indian)

1. d4 Nf6 2. c4 g6 3. g3 Bg7
4. Bg2 0-0 5. Nf3 d6 6. 0-0 Nbd7
7. Qc2 e5 8. Rd1 Re8 9. Nc3 c6
10. de de 11. Ng5 Qe7 12. Nge4
Nc5 13. Nd6 Rd8 14. N:c8 R:d1+
15. N:d1 R:c8 16. Bd2 Nfd7
17. Bc3 f5 18. Ne3 Ne6 19. b4 Nd4

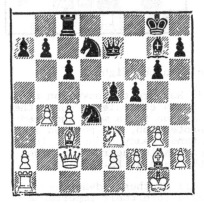

20 Qb2 Qf7 21 a4 Rf8

Euwe's passive play has allowed
Geller to set up a good attacking
position. Sooner or later, the
knight on d4 will have to be tak-
en by the bishop, which will give
Black still more positional advantages.

22. a5 f4 23. gf Q:f4 24. Rf1
Nf6 25. c5 Ne4

Black's knights are insuffer-
able, but —

26. B:e4 Q:e4 27. B:d4 cd

— the advantage of the two
bishops in this case came down
to their being able to get rid
of two good knights in two moves.

28. Ng2 a6 29. Qb3+ Kh8 30. Qd3
Qe5 31. f4

Euwe intends to set up an impregnable fortress.

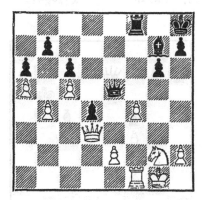

31..Qe6 32. Rf3 Re8 33. Kf2
Rf8 34. Kf1 Kg8 35. Kf2 Rf7
36. Kf1 Rf5 37. Kf2 Bf6 38. Kg1
Rd5 39. Kf2 Kg7 40. Kf1 Rh5
41. Kg1 Rd5 42. h3 Kf7 43. Kf2
Ke7 44. Kf1 Kd8 45. Ne1 Kc7
46. Nc2 Kb8

An important element of
Black's plan. Concluding that
simple means will not suffice
against White's position, Black
first removes his king to the
opposite wing, where it will
not be exposed by his upcoming
pawn storm. White's knight follows, and takes up station, so
Black's king will not forget the
possibility of a deadly check on
the eighth rank.

47. Na3 Bd8 48. Nc4 Bc7 49. Nb6
Rd8 50. f5 gf

Euwe loses his patience, and
eases Black's task.

51. Q:f5 Qh6 52. Qf7 Qc1+
53. Kf2 Bh2!

Black has found the white
king's Achilles heel: the g1
square.

54. Qg7 Bf4 55. Kg2 Be3 56. Rf1

White loses without a fight.
56 Rf7 had to be tried, and then
Black would have had to find the
complex line 56..Qg1+ 57 Kf3
Qf1+ 58 Kg3 Bf4+! 59 Kh4 Qf2+

60 Kg4 h5+. Now, everything is
much simpler.

56..Qd2 57. Rf7 Q:e2+ 58. Kg3
Qe1+ 59. Kf3 Qh1+ 60. Kg3 Qg1+
61. Kf3 Qf2+ 62. Ke4 Re8+
63. Re7 Qh4+

WHITE RESIGNED

******

115. Szabo—Smyslov
(Queen's Gambit)

1.	d2-d4	d7-d5
2.	c2-c4	c7-c6
3.	Ng1-f3	Ng8-f6
4.	Nb1-c3	d5:c4
5.	a2-a4	Bc8-f5
6.	e2-e3	e7-e6
7.	Bf1:c4	Bf8-b4
8.	0-0	Nb8-d7
9.	Qd1-e2	0-0
10.	e3-e4	Bf5-g6
11.	Bc4-d3	...

Repeating the opening of Game
34, Boleslavsky - Smyslov, but
Szabo finds an improvement, 11 Bd3,
over Boleslavsky's 11 e5, which
gave White nothing.

| 11. | ... | Qd8-a5 |

Not a very good move. In Game
128 against Stahlberg, two
rounds later, Smyslov played
11..h6, and quickly achieved
full equality, while in his match
with Geller Smyslov successfully employed 11..Bh5. Since White
cannot achieve anything with this
variation, the thought comes to
mind that perhaps 10 e4, or even
5 a4, may not be best.

12.	Nc3-a2	Bb4-e7
13.	Bc1-d2	Qa5-h5
14.	Na2-c3	Rf8-d8
15.	Bd2-f4	c6-c5
16.	d4-d5	...

The standard break in such positions. First White closes d5
to Black's knight; then he drives
it away with 17 e5, after which
he can recapture the d-pawn, obtaining a strong central position
for his own knight.

16.	...	e6:d5
17.	e4-e5	Bg6:d3
18.	Qe2:d3	Nf6-e8
19.	Nc3:d5	Be7-f8
20.	Qd3-b3	Qh5-g6
21.	a4-a5	...

White nails down the b-pawn,
but he cannot take it yet, owing to the ensuing "perpetual
check" to his queen: ..Ra8-b8-
a8. His next move strengthens
the threat to the b-pawn.

21.	...	h7-h6
22.	Nd5-e3	b7-b6
23.	Rf1-d1	Ne8-c7
24.	Bf4-g3	...

Black must now find a defense
to the threatened 25 Bh4. Szabo
is playing with great verve, and
Black's position grows critical.

24.	...	b6-b5
25.	Bg3-h4	c5-c4
26.	Qb3-c3	f7-f6
27.	Ne3:c4	...

White wins a pawn, but renders his win more difficult.
Black would have had a rough-
er go of it after 27 b3 N:e5
28 N:e5 R:d1+ 29 R:d1 fe 30 bc
bc 31 Q:c4+ Ne6 32 Ng4 — his
best chance would have been
30..b4.

27.	...	b5:c4
28.	Qc3:c4+	Qg6-f7
29.	Qc4:c7	Nd7:e5

30.	Qc7:f7+	Ne5:f7
31.	Bh4-g3	a7-a6
32.	Kg1-f1	Ra8-c8
33.	Rd1-c1	Bf8-b4

DRAW

— at White's instigation.

Szabo would have retained significant winning chances in the endgame after, let's say, 34 R:c8 R:c8 35 Ra4, when Black would be unable to recover the b-pawn: 35..Rc1+ 36 Ke2 Rc2+ 37 Kd1 R:b2 38 Kc1 Rb3 39 Kc2 Rc3+ 40 Kb2 Rc4 41 Kb3. He would have had to retreat his bishop: 35..Bf8; then White replies 36 Ne1, slowly improves the position of his pieces, and still retains excellent chances to make something out of his extra pawn.

******

116. Averbakh—Keres
(Ruy Lopez)
1. e4 e5 2. Nf3 Nc6 3. Bb5 a6
4. Ba4 Nf6 5. 0-0 Be7 6. Re1 b5
7. Bb3 0-0 8. c3 d6 9. h3 Na5
10. Bc2 c5 11. d4 Qc7 12. Nbd2
Bb7 13. d5

White closes the center, in order to begin storming the kingside.

13.. Bc8 14. Nf1 Bd7 15. b3 g6
16. Bh6 Rfb8 17. g4

White made one attacking move,

and stopped there. Averbakh is giving notice that he will continue his aggression only in the event Keres starts pushing his queenside pawns.

17.. Bf8 18. Qd2 Kh8 19. Ng5
Kg8 20. Nf3 Kh8 21. Ng5 Kg8
22. Nf3

DRAW

Black is unable to break the repetition, since after Nf3 White threatens B:f8 and Qh6, followed by Ng5 once again. Therefore, Black moves his king to h8, so as to answer Qh6 by ..Ng8. But of course White is by no means obligated to repeat moves...

******

117. Petrosian—Reshevsky
(Reti Opening)

1.	Ng1-f3	Ng8-f6
2.	g2-g3	g7-g6
3.	Bf1-g2	Bf8-g7
4.	0-0	0-0
5.	d2-d3	d7-d5
6.	Nb1-d2	c7-c5
7.	e2-e4	...

This is a King's Indian with reversed colors; consequently, White has an extra tempo. This is a structure which has been heavily used of late by Soviet masters, and which demands a great deal of alertness from Black. Schemes which White can well employ against the King's Indian can prove lethal when Black employs them a move behind. Reshevsky chooses an exchange of center pawns, which is approximately equivalent to the line in which White plays d4:e5. This generally leads to complete leveling, but here White manages to carry out the advance of his e- and f-pawns to the fifth rank.

7.	...	d5:e4
8.	d3:e4	Nb8-c6
9.	c2-c3	h7-h6
10.	Qd1-e2	Bc8-e6
11.	Nf3-e1	Qd8-b6
12.	h2-h3	Ra8-d8
13.	Kg1-h2	Nf6-h7
14.	f2-f4	...

White already stands somewhat

superior, thanks to his advantage in terrain. His next task is to regroup his pieces, presently posted on the first two ranks, in order to support the further advance of his e- and f-pawns. One very important factor in this is that his opponent has no active plan; indeed, Black's pieces spend the next seven moves nearly inactive, unless you consider the transfer of the bishop to the other long diagonal — which of course could have been done earlier, without wasting time on the maneuver ..Bc8-e6-d7-c6.

14.	...	Nc6-a5
15.	Ne1-f3	Be6-d7
16.	Rf1-e1	Qb6-c7
17.	Nd2-f1	b7-b6
18.	Nf1-e3	Bd7-c6
19.	Ne3-g4	Nh7-f6
20.	Ng4-f2	Bc6-b7
21.	e4-e5	Nf6-h7
22.	h3-h4	...

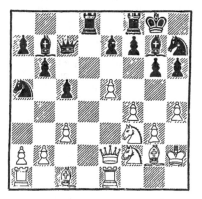

White has already won the strategic battle: his opponent's pieces have been driven back to the last two ranks. The natural plan now for White would be to advance his f- and g-pawns for a breakthrough on the kingside. Petrosian takes a somewhat different course: by threatening h4-h5:g6 etc., he induces the blockading ..h6-h5; then he sacrifices a pawn with f4-f5! If Black accepts, White's knight on f2 goes, with great profit, to f4 — an excellent stratagem.

| 22. | ... | h6-h5 |
| 23. | f4-f5 | Qc7-d7 |

Reshevsky declines the sacrifice, of course, but now the e-pawn enters the fray. Black manages to ward off White's onslaught, but his e- and h-pawns become isolated.

24.	e5-e6	Qd7-d5
25.	e6:f7+	Qd5:f7
26.	f5:g6	Qf7:g6
27.	Nf3-g5	Bb7:g2
28.	Kh2:g2	e7-e5
29.	Qe2-e4	Rf8-f5
30.	Ng5:h7	Kg8:h7

DRAW

White's position is far superior, of course. If queens are exchanged, Black's weak pawns will be excellent targets; and if they are not exchanged, Black's exposed king and the continual need to watch over its safety would tie Black hand and foot.

*****

118. Najdorf—Bronstein
(Nimzoindian Defense)

1.	d2-d4	Ng8-f6
2.	c2-c4	e7-e6
3.	Nb1-c3	Bf8-b4
4.	e2-e3	c7-c5
5.	Bf1-d3	b7-b6
6.	Ng1-f3	Bc8-b7
7.	0-0	0-0
8.	Bc1-d2	d7-d6
9.	Qd1-c2	Nb8-d7

Here Black refrained from the tempting 9..B:f3, as he felt he would not be able to exploit the weakening of White's king protection: e.g., 9..B:f3 10 gf cd 11 ed Nc6 12 Be3, when the king is quite secure. Nevertheless, Black should still have played this, but with the idea of attacking, not the king, but the opposing center. After 12..B:c3 13 Q:c3 d5 or 13..e5, we would have had some interesting play, whereas now White develops a clear advantage, and Black must employ all of his alertness.

10.	a2-a3	Bb4:c3
11.	Bd2:c3	Ra8-c8
12.	Nf3-d2	h7-h6
13.	Ra1-c1	d6-d5
14.	b2-b3	d5:c4
15.	b3:c4	Qd8-c7

Black's chief worry is how to

prevent d4-d5. He must also keep an eye out to prevent White from entrenching his knight at e5, or setting up the battery Bb1 and Qc2; if that does happen, he must have ..Nf8 ready. Black has plenty of worries, as may be seen. But it is a bore to think only about defense: Black's 14..dc carries with it the hope of exploiting the active position of his fianchettoed bishop, and perhaps the relative weakness of the pawns at c4 and d4. Black would very much like one of those two pawns to advance. White also has the threat of ..Nf6-g4 to deal with here.

| 16. | Rf1-d1 | ... |

White is not placing his rooks right: he ought to occupy the e- and d-files.

16.	...	Rf8-e8
17.	Nd2-f1	c5:d4
18.	e3:d4	Qc7-f4
19.	Nf1-g3	h6-h5

Black must hurry before White plays 20 Re1 and tries to bring one of his rooks to g3, after his knight goes to e4. A rook on g3, in conjunction with the bishop on c3, could demolish g7.

| 20. | h2-h3 | h5-h4 |
| 21. | Ng3-f1 | Nf6-e4 |

DRAW

The knight at e4 must be taken, and after 22 B:e4 B:e4, White's advantage disappears.

******

119. Taimanov—Gligoric
(Sicilian Defense)

The sacrifice of a pawn for the initiative is one of the most complex problems of chess strategy — and perhaps of its psychology as well. The positions that occur as the result of a sacrifice are so varied that no generalizations can possibly be made. Some grandmasters, possessing the faculty of quick calculation, not infrequently give up a pawn or two simply to alter the nature and balance of a position, even if this is perhaps not in their favor. I don't think this manner of playing has much of a future. I myself have sacrificed, all told, several dozen pawns, but still I think that the master who sacrifices a pawn ought to have at least a general idea of the nature of the initiative he will thereby obtain, and what sort of game will ensue.

Once in a while, a pawn must be given up, or even an exchange or a piece, against one's will — the point being that any other course leads to a difficult position. Playing White, Taimanov sacrificed a pawn in the opening, but obtained no more of an initiative thereby than he might have obtained by keeping the same number of pawns as his opponent. Throughout the game, White put himself through agonies trying to regain his pawn, but never quite succeeded; eventually, Black's extra pawn went on to queen.

1.	e2-e4	c7-c5
2.	Ng1-f3	d7-d6
3.	Bf1-b5+	...

The exchange of lightsquare bishops on the fourth move is part of a far-seeing strategic idea. Gligoric has placed his pawns on dark squares, so Taimanov thinks that with the lightsquare bishop gone Black will find it hard to maintain the positional balance. Of course, Black can advance his center pawns to e6 and d5, but that will take time.

3.	...	Bc8-d7
4.	Bb5:d7+	Qd8:d7
5.	0-0	Nb8-c6
6.	Rf1-e1	...

After the exchange of bishops, I think it makes more sense to put the pawn on the light square d3 and the knight on c3 (where it controls the light square d5), and after Black plays ..e7-e6 or ..g7-g6, to prepare the advance f2-f4-f5. Taimanov acts illogically in selecting a plan which helps Black to clear the c5-f8 diagonal, presently cluttered with black pawns.

6.	...	Ng8-f6
7.	d2-d4	c5:d4
8.	Bc1-g5	...

White decides not to recapture the d-pawn, choosing instead a sharp move he had prepared previously; he expects 8..e5 9 B:f6 gf 10 c3!, or 8..g6 9 B:f6 ef 10 N:d4, or 8..Ng4 9 N:d4 h6 10 Bc1. However, Gligoric finds an excellent plan which knocks the last white pawn out of the center and secures active positions for Black's pieces.

| 8. | ... | d6-d5 |
| 9. | Bg5:f6 | ... |

There's not much choice: Black would answer 9 e5 with 9..Ne4.

9.	...	g7:f6
10.	e4:d5	Qd7:d5
11.	Nb1-c3	Qd5-d7
12.	Nc3-e4	0-0-0

| 13. | c2-c3 | ... |

Of course, Taimanov sees that his strategic plans have come a cropper: Black has a pawn more, with the possibility of setting up a powerful center, while the white knights have no points of support. The ability to make exceptionally objective assessments of events as they are occurring is one of Taimanov's outstanding traits — a trait to be envied, and certainly imitated as well. Here, White's only hope lies in creating complications, and Taimanov is ready to answer 13..dc with 14 Qb3, giving up his b-pawn into the bargain. However, Gligoric not only declines further acquisitions, he even gives back his extra pawn temporarily, securing his advantage by advancing his pawns to f5 and e5.

| 13. | ... | f6-f5 |
| 14. | Ne4-c5 | Qd7-d5 |

The interesting complications that arise after 14..Qc7 would work out in Black's favor, but these would be complications nonetheless, which is precisely what Taimanov is aiming for; so Gligoric sticks with the strong move 14..Qd5, centralizing his queen. On 14..Qc7, White would have replied 15 cd e5 16 Rc1 e4 17 Ne5 R:d4 18 Qb3, but Black had a better alternative in 17..N:e5! 18 Ne6 fe 19 R:c7+ K:c7 20 Qb3 Nc6 21 Q:e6 N:d4 22 Qe5+ Bd6.

| 15. | c3:d4 | e7-e5 |
| 16. | Ra1-c1 | e5:d4 |

Taimanov's relentless play for complications has borne fruit: Black plays inexactly here. 16..e4 was correct, when 17 Ne5 would be out because a piece would be lost, and 17 Nh4 would run into 17..Be7 18 Qh5 B:h4 19 Q:h4 Q:d4 20 Qh5 Qf6. Now Black's extra pawn has no great role to play, since it is blockaded, and his isolated pawns on the kingside are weak.

| 17. | Nc5-d3 | Bf8-d6 |

(See diagram, next page)

(Position after 17..Bd6)

18. Nf3-e5   ...

White seeks his chances precisely where they will be the
hardest to find: he can extract
nothing from the pinned knight
at c6, so he ought to have attacked the f5-pawn with 18 Nh4
and 19 Qh5.

18.	...	Rh8-e8
19.	Ne5:c6	Re8:e1+
20.	Nd3:e1	b7:c6
21.	Qd1-d3	...

What has White achieved? The
d-pawn is no longer isolated,
and the knight which blockaded
it has had to be replaced with
the queen.

| 21. | ... | Kc8-b7 |
| 22. | b2-b4 | ... |

Too bold. Taimanov should have
recalled his third move, Bb5+,
which deprived his opponent of
his lightsquare bishop, and
tried to keep the black pawns on
dark squares. For this purpose,
22 b3 was best, followed by the
transfer of his knight to c4.

22.	...	Bd6-f4
23.	Rc1-d1	Bf4-c7
24.	a2-a3	Bc7-b6
25.	Ne1-f3	Qd5-e4
26.	Nf3-g5	Qe4:d3
27.	Rd1:d3	a7-a5!

This excellent move decides the
game. Black returns his extra
pawn at the best possible moment.

In a few moves, he picks up the
b-pawn, after which his two connected passed pawns will bring
him victory.

28.	Ng5:f7	Rd8-d5
29.	Kg1-f1	a5:b4
30.	a3:b4	Kb7-a6
31.	f2-f4	Ka6-b5
32.	Nf7-e5	Bb6-c7
33.	Rd3-d1	Bc7-d6

33..B:e5 34 fe K:b4 would have
been a gross blunder, in view of
35 e6!, when the threat to support the advance of this passed
pawn with a rook would have
forced Black to seek the draw.

34.	Kf1-e2	Bd6:e5
35.	f4:e5	Rd5:e5+
36.	Ke2-d3	Kb5:b4
37.	Rd1-c1	Kb4-b5
38.	Kd3:d4	Re5-d5+
39.	Kd4-e3	c6-c5
40.	Rc1-b1+	Kb5-a4
41.	Rb1-b7	h7-h5
42.	Ke3-f4	c5-c4
43.	Kf4-g5	c4-c3
44.	Kg5:h5	Rd5-d2
45.	g2-g3	Rd2:h2+
46.	Kh5-g5	Rh2-f2

WHITE RESIGNED

******

******

120. Gligoric—Najdorf
(Sicilian Defense)

1.	e2-e4	c7-c5
2.	Ng1-f3	d7-d6
3.	d2-d4	c5:d4
4.	Nf3:d4	Ng8-f6
5.	Nb1-c3	a7-a6
6.	g2-g3	e7-e5
7.	Nd4-e2	Bc8-e6
8.	Bf1-g2	b7-b5

Najdorf repeats the move Kotov played against Gligoric in Game 66. This time, Gligoric begins immediate operations on the queenside. As one of the spectators pointed out, however, he could have played still more sharply: 9 Nf4, and if Black accepts the sacrifice, 10 e5 simultaneously attacks a8 and f6; while if he does not accept, the knight makes a triumphal entrance at d5.

9.	a2-a4	b5-b4
10.	Nc3-d5	Nf6:d5
11.	e4:d5	Be6-f5
12.	0-0	Nb8-d7
13.	Bc1-d2	Ra8-b8
14.	f2-f4	Bf5-g6
15.	h2-h3	f7-f6
16.	Kg1-h2	Bf8-e7
17.	a4-a5	Qd8-c7
18.	c2-c3	b4-b3
19.	f4-f5	Bg6-f7

A curious moment: in the middlegame, the rook occupies an open line, though not a file, as is usual; this time it's the fourth rank, completely cleared of both white and black pieces. Najdorf could have prevented this by 16..a5, but of course it never entered his head that his opponent might intend, in the middle game with a board full of pieces, to open the fourth rank and occupy it with a rook.

20.	Ra1-a4	...

As he played this original move, Gligoric offered a draw, which Najdorf declined, although his position gave him no grounds for so optimistic an appraisal, as he himself later concluded. For example, after 20..0-0 21 Nc1 Nc5 22 Rb4! Q:a5 23 N:b3, White has good play.

20.	...	Nd7-c5
21.	Ra4-g4	g7-g6
22.	Rg4-b4	...

Unexpected, and foolhardy: White abandons the f-pawn, hoping to regain the b-pawn. In this game, Gligoric's normally strict style is unrecognizable.

22.	...	g6:f5
23.	Bd2-e3	0-0
24.	Ne2-c1	Bf7-g6
25.	Nc1:b3	Rb8:b4
26.	c3:b4	Nc5-e4
27.	Qd1-e2	Qc7-b7
28.	Nb3-d2	...

And now it was Najdorf who offered the

DRAW

which was accepted, although White still has the superior position. Black would be ill-advised to take the b-pawn, in view of 28..Q:b4 29 N:e4 fe 30 Bh6 Rb8 31 Rf2, with the threat of h3-h4-h5; also possible is 30 Q:a6 Q:b2 31 Qb6, when the exchange of queens would lose for Black.

Black might have been able to wriggle out of his difficulties by means of the piece sacrifice 28..N:g3 29 K:g3 f4+ 30 B:f4 ef+ 31 R:f4 f5; Najdorf carries his analysis to move 51. The variations are interesting, no doubt, but it would have been more interesting still had the game continued.

121. Bronstein—Petrosian
(Old Indian Defense)

1.	d2-d4	Ng8-f6
2.	c2-c4	d7-d6
3.	Nb1-c3	Nb8-d7
4.	Bc1-g5	h7-h6
5.	Bg5-h4	g7-g5

This is the sort of move that radically alters the course of a game, forcing the opponent to rethink all the details of the position. Mechanically, the move ..g7-g5 is simple to explain: Black exchanges off the bishop on g3 for his knight, thereby enhancing the prospects of his own king's bishop. However, "pawns do not move backward", and moving the pawn from g7 to g5 defines the pawn structure in this sector too early, making it easier for White to formulate a concrete plan.

6.	Bh4-g3	Nf6-h5
7.	e2-e3	Nh5:g3
8.	h2:g3	Bf8-g7
9.	Bf1-d3	Nd7-f6
10.	Qd1-d2	c7-c6
11.	0-0-0	Qd8-a5

White's last three "attacking" moves offered his opponent no problems whatever: he is making his preparations to attack in the wrong sector. The drawbacks of Petrosian's defense might have stood out if White had played 9 f4, assailing the g-pawn.

12.	Kc1-b1	Bc8-d7
13.	Ng1-e2	e7-e6
14.	Ne2-c1	0-0-0
15.	Nc1-b3	Qa5-c7
16.	Qd2-e2	Rh8-e8
17.	e3-e4	...

White has wasted a lot of time in preparing for this advance, which now encounters Black's excellent defensive formations.

17.	...	c6-c5
18.	e4-e5	d6:e5
19.	d4:e5	Nf6-g8
20.	f2-f4	...

Now, ten moves too late, this misses the point completely, and allows Black to open the game in his favor.

20.	...	g5:f4
21.	g3:f4	f7-f6
22.	Nc3-b5	Bd7:b5
23.	c4:b5	Kc8-b8
24.	Rd1-c1	b7-b6
25.	Bd3-g6	Re8-f8
26.	Rh1-e1	...

White sacrifices a pawn in the mistaken hope of being able to entice the black rook to e5; however, White will be unable to exploit either the h1-a8 diagonal or the open d-file, in view of the unfortunate position of his knight on b3. One cannot help but recall Tarrasch's famous dictum (see Preface)!

26.	...	f6:e5
27.	f4:e5	Rd8-d5
28.	Bg6-e4	Rd5:e5
29.	Qe2-c2	Rf8-d8
30.	Re1-d1	Rd8:d1
31.	Rc1:d1	Ng8-e7
32.	Nb3-d2	...

DRAW

White's position would be not a bit inferior, if his knight could only manage to maintain itself on c4. However, with 32..c4!, Black would prevent this: 33 N:c4 R:b5 or 33 Q:c4 Q:c4 34 N:c4 R:e4. On the other hand, White need not take the pawn: his best course would be to continue 33 a4, retreat his bishop to f3, and keep trying to work up counterthreats against the black king. In time-pressure, Petrosian failed to notice 32..c4, and therefore agreed to the draw.

******

122. Reshevsky—Averbakh
(Nimzoindian Defense)

1.	d2-d4	Ng8-f6
2.	c2-c4	e7-e6

3.	Nb1-c3	Bf8-b4
4.	e2-e3	0-0
5.	Ng1-e2	d7-d5
6.	a2-a3	Bb4-e7
7.	c4:d5	e6:d5
8.	Ne2-g3	Bc8-e6

Since White has not prevented ..c7-c5, Black ought to have exploited this in the interests of freer development: among other things, his knight could have gone to c6 instead of d7. Averbakh opts for a solid but passive deployment, which allows Black too few counterchances for him to have hopes for anything more than a draw. With 8..c5, Black would have knocked the d-pawn out of the center, opened the c-file, and cleared the e5 square for his pieces.

9.	Bf1-d3	Nb8-d7
10.	0-0	c7-c6
11.	Bc1-d2	Rf8-e8

Black feels he has fulfilled his primary goal in the Nimzo-Indian by putting a long-term crimp on e3-e4. White begins unhurried preparations for the e-pawn's advance, while Black holds to his siege tactics: the value of his sortie ..a7-a5-a4 is more symbolic than real. Against this backdrop, Black's position declines noticeably over the next ten or twelve moves: the bishop's dithering from c8 to e6 to d7 to c8 to e6 again does not involve any sort of strategy, serving only to demonstrate the impregnability of Black's position. Meanwhile, White marshals his forces for the decisive stroke.

12.	Qd1-c2	a7-a5
13.	Nc3-e2	Nd7-b6
14.	Ne2-f4	Be6-d7
15.	Rf1-e1	Be7-f8
16.	f2-f3	Bd7-c8

Black has so far managed to prevent e3-e4, but Reshevsky will push his plan through.

17.	Ra1-c1	g7-g6
18.	Nf4-e2	Bf8-g7
19.	h2-h3	a5-a4
20.	e3-e4	d5:e4
21.	f3:e4	Bc8-e6
22.	Bd2-e3	Be6-b3
23.	Qc2-d2	...

White has created a powerful center. The next part of his plan will be an attack on the king, but it is not yet the time for the pieces to enter the fray: first the h-pawn must advance, to breach the fortress walls.

This game is vintage Reshevsky: instead of flinging himself head over heels into the attack, he methodically accumulates advantages, while trying not to give his opponent any counterchances. Averbakh misconstrues the gradual development of White's attack, taking his caution for indecision. The position already requires Black to take energetic action on the queenside.

23.	...	Nf6-d7
24.	Be3-g5!	f7-f6

An unpleasant weakening of the king's wing. With the pawn at f7, the routine attack h2-h4-h5 would lose much of its effectiveness, inasmuch as the capture h5:g6 could always be met by recapturing with the f-pawn. 24..Bf6 was bad, of course, since White would take the bishop, bring his rook to the f-file, and then push his pawn to e5. And retreating the queen to c7 would place that piece in a most uncomfortable position.

Averbakh's only hope is to counterattack the white center (30..c5).

25.	Bg5-e3	Nd7-f8
26.	h3-h4	Bb3-f7

The h-pawn could have been stopped here with 26..h5, so 26 Bh6!, followed by 27 h4, was more accurate.

27.	h4-h5	Nf8-e6

The defenders of the fortress place themselves in readiness for battle with the maneuvers ..Ne6, ..Bf8 and ..Nd7, preparing to sell their lives dearly (Black is also preparing ..c5).

28.	Re1-f1	Bg7-f8
29.	Rf1-f2	Nb6-d7
30.	Rc1-f1	c6-c5

At last, at last! (Wouldn't this have been better played at

move eight?)

31.	d4-d5	Ne6-c7
32.	h5:g6	h7:g6

The e5 square Black has obtained for his pieces doesn't come anywhere near compensating for White's control of the h-file. It's only a question of how soon White can manage to double or triple his heavy pieces there.

33.	Rf2-f4	b7-b5
34.	Rf4-h4	Nd7-e5
35.	Kg1-h1	Qd8-d7?

Black is in an unenviable position, of course, but a grandmaster should not fall apart like this, simultaneously giving up both a pawn and a key point in his position. White might have begun the conquest of h6 and g7 on his 35th move with 35 Bh6! Instead, he played a waiting move, 35 Kh1, for which there was no particular need, since nothing threatened the white king where it stood. Quite evidently Reshevsky had still not completely made up his mind to force through the attack. Since matters were proceeding through one of his accustomed time-shortages, he wanted to play a few nondescript moves to reach the time control. It was precisely these circumstances that made it imperative for Averbakh to play 35..b4, stirring up some complications, at least. One time-pressure possibility might have been 36 Bh6 N:d3 37 B:f8 K:f8 38 Q:d3, when Black

holds things together somehow. And if White should delay his Bh6 long enough to play, shall we say, 36 ab, then 36..a3 would give Black some serious counterchances. After Averbakh's blunder, White's problem finds an easier solution.

36.	Rf1:f6	Ne5-g4
37.	Be3-g5!	Bf8-g7

Accepting the exchange sacrifice would lead to a quick checkmate: for example, 37..N:f6? 38 B:f6 Bg7 39 B:g7 K:g7, and the queen checks from c3, with decisive threats. Play would have proceeded similarly had Black chosen 36..Be7 instead of his 36..Ng4.

38.	Rf6-f4	Ng4-e5
39.	Bg5-f6	Bg7:f6
40.	Rf4:f6	Kg8-g7
41.	Qd2-g5	Re8-h8
42.	Ng3-f5+	Qd7:f5
43.	Rf6:f5	Rh8:h4+
44.	Kh1-g1	...

BLACK RESIGNED

This game is a classic example of how one should undermine the foundation of a solid position. Reshevsky considered it his best game of the tournament.

******

123. Keres—Szabo
(Sicilian Defense)

1.	e2-e4	c7-c5
2.	Ng1-f3	d7-d6
3.	d2-d4	c5:d4
4.	Nf3:d4	Ng8-f6
5.	Nb1-c3	a7-a6
6.	Bf1-e2	e7-e5
7.	Nd4-b3	Bf8-e7
8.	Bc1-e3	Bc8-e6
9.	0-0	Nb8-d7
10.	f2-f4	...

The various lines of this system of development are distinguished chiefly by the placement of the f- and a-pawns, In Game 88, Geller played f2-f4 and a2-a4 against Najdorf, with an active position for White, but somewhat insecure in the center. In Game 36, Smyslov pushed both pawns one square against Kotov. In this game, Keres plays f2-f4, but leaves the a-pawn in place for the time being. I myself prefer a2-a4 and f2-f3.

Thus are the masters' tastes revealed even in the opening. So let the reader be properly skeptical of such notes as:"Better a2-a4", or "f2-f3 was more circumspect." In the beginning of the game, there are many roads, and most of them lead straight to Rome.

| 10. | ... | Ra8-c8 |
| 11. | Kg1-h1 | Be6-c4 |

Contrary to the rules of positional play, here Szabo offers the exchange of his good bishop — and rightly so. In the first place, this bishop is living in constant fear of White's threat to advance the f-pawn, which means it's not so good after all. And in the second place, Szabo wishes to use the rather shaky condition of White's e-pawn to fight for the square d5, which would make his other bishop "good".

12.	Nb3-d2	Bc4:e2
13.	Nc3:e2	0-0
14.	Ne2-g3	d6-d5
15.	f4:e5	Nd7:e5

15..N:e4 would not be good in view of 16 Nd:e4 de 17 Bd4.

| 16. | Be3-d4 | ... |

Keres stirs up some interesting complications, but Black still has sufficient counterchances. White's best lines arise after 16..Nc6 or 16..Ng6; for example:

1) 16..Nc6 17 B:f6 B:f6 18 ed Q:d5 19 Nde4;

2) 16..Ng6 17 e5 Nd7 18 Nf3, or 17 B:f6 as in the first variation.

As usual, Szabo finds the most active continuation.

| 16. | ... | Nf6-g4 |
| 17. | Rf1-f4 | ... |

(See diagram, next column)

This gets White two knights for his rook and two pawns. As for 17 h3, that's no threat: Black replies 17..Bc5 here, too, and can always meet hg with the queen check at h4.

17.	...	Be7-c5
18.	Bd4:c5	Rc8:c5
19.	Rf4:g4	Ne5:g4
20.	Qd1:g4	Rc5:c2
21.	Nd2-f3	d5:e4
22.	Qg4:e4	Rc2:b2
23.	h2-h3	Rf8-e8
24.	Qe4-a4	...

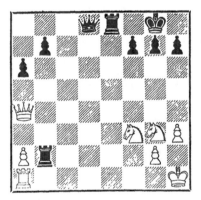

We shall have occasion to compare the relative strengths of queen, rook and knight again

in Game 186, Kotov - Najdorf.
Knights and queens complement
each other, knights being strong
in the center and around enemy
pawns; while rooks come into
their own in the endgame, where
they find plenty of space for
their straightforward maneuvers.
Proceeding from these ideas,
White ought to utilize his
knights on the kingside, without trading queens, trying for
something such as the following:
24 Qg4 Qf6 25 Rf1 Qg6 26 Ng5
Qc2 27 Qf3, or 24 Qg4 Qc8 25 Nf5
Qc3 26 N3d4.

24.	...	Qd8-c8
25.	Ng3-f5	Qc8-c6
26.	Qa4-d4	...

Here too, 26 Qg4 Qf6 (26..Qg6?
27 Ne7+!) 27 Rd1 was good. However, the queen exchange was most
tempting: White's knights gain
permanent sway over f5, and it
was hard to foresee that fate
would send them somewhere else
altogether.

26.	...	Qc6-f6
27.	Qd4:f6	g7:f6
28.	a2-a4	Rb2-b4
29.	a4-a5	...

The knight's active position
on f5 might have been exploited
for an attack on f7. For this
purpose, the rook at a1 would
have to be brought to d7; the
loss of the a-pawn would be inconsequential, since the b-pawn
would be recovered immediately:
29 Rd1 R:a4 30 Rd7, with the
double threat 31 Nh6+ and 31 R:b7.
White's actual move, powerful
though it might appear, leads,
amazingly enough, to a difficult endgame for him.

29.	...	Rb4-f4
30.	Nf5-d6	Re8-b8
31.	Ra1-b1	Rf4-a4
32.	Rb1:b7	Rb8:b7
33.	Nd6:b7	...

In the middle of the board,
supported by a pawn, one knight
may sometimes be as strong as a
rook. Here, however, on the edge
of the board, the knights cannot
work at full strength, and one
rook can deal successfully with
two knights. Black's plan — to
bring up his king, drive off the
knight, or else force the trade
of both knights for his rook —

looks very dangerous indeed.
Keres' following maneuvers,
creating unbreachable defensive
positions with two knights and
a pawn, without the aid of the
king, are beautiful beyond comparison.

33.	...	Kg8-f8
34.	Nf3-d2	Kf8-e7
35.	Nd2-b3	Ra4-b4
36.	Nb3-c5	...

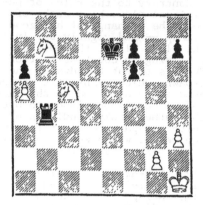

A wonderful position!

The knights fend off their foes.
Now Black pushes his pawn to f5,
and opens a route for his king
to go via f6 and e5 to d4.

| 36. | ... | f6-f5 |
| 37. | Kh1-g1 | Rb4-b5 |

Otherwise, the knight forks
when his king gets to e5.

38.	Kg1-f2	Ke7-f6
39.	Nc5-d7+	Kf6-e6
40.	Nd7-b6	...

The knights have regrouped,
and are once again unapproachable. Now the black rook attempts to penetrate from the
flank.

| 40. | ... | Ke6-e5 |
| 41. | Kf2-g3 | Rb5-b3+ |

Here Black had an interesting
try: 41..f4+, intending after
42 Kh4 to play for the win of a
pawn by ..Rb5-b3-g3. During this
time White could probably pick
up the a-pawn, and the outcome
of the game would probably not
have been altered.

| 42. | Kg3-h4 | Rb3-c3 |
| 43. | Nb7-c5! | Rc3:c5 |

The knight must be taken now, like it or not, but although Black will be a pawn up in the endgame, there is no win.

44.	Nb6-d7+	Ke5-d6
45.	Nd7:c5	Kd6:c5
46.	Kh4-g5!	...

Typical of pawn endings. The king, of course, is headed for the h-pawn, but if Black advances his king to d4 instead of b5, then White also keeps the option of taking the f5-pawn first.

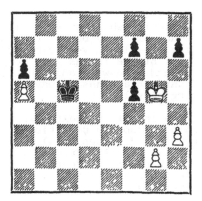

46.	...	Kc5-b5
47.	Kg5-h6	Kb5:a5
48.	Kh6:h7	Ka5-b4
49.	h3-h4	a6-a5
50.	h4-h5	a5-a4
51.	h5-h6	a4-a3
52.	Kh7-g8	a3-a2
53.	h6-h7	a2-a1Q
54.	h7-h8Q	...

Black was just one tempo shy of a win.

| 54. | ... | Qa1-a8+ |
| 55. | Kg8-h7 | Qa8:g2 |

55..Q:h8+ 56 K:h8 Kc3 57 Kg7 is a draw too.

| 56. | Qh8-d4+ | Kb4-b3 |
| 57. | Qd4-d3+ | ... |

DRAW

*****

124. Smyslov—Euwe
(Reti Opening)

Sacrificing a pawn in order to seize an open line in the center is one of the oldest strategic ideas known: it may be found in the classical games of Greco, Morphy, Anderssen, Chigorin, Spielmann and Alekhine. Occasionally, a pawn is given up to obtain a line for a bishop, the most obvious example being the Danish Gambit: 1 e4 e5 2 d4 ed 3 c3 dc 4 Bc4 cb 5 B:b2. The most promising sacrifices, however, are those which open lines for the rooks, especially when this involves a direct attack on the king. Our forebears knew of another Muzio Gambit besides the usual one, called the "Double (or "Wild") Muzio": 1 e4 e5 2 f4 ef 3 Nf3 g5 4 Bc4 g4 5 0-0 gf 6 B:f7+ K:f7 7 Q:f3, which is occasionally encountered even today. Of course, masters and grandmasters take a rather skeptical attitude toward such play, but it has a sizable following among players of middling strength. For example, this gambit was a most fearsome weapon in the hands of a Moscow first-category player, Volodya Smirnov (whose untimely passing we all mourn), in school and college tournaments, where he employed his own analyses and variations.

But where pieces and pawns were formerly sacrificed on the second or third move, nowadays such early skirmishings in the center are avoided. It's certainly not because players fear risk — in plain terms, the King's Indian is a greater risk for Black than the King's Gambit for White. Nevertheless, not one of us is afraid to play the King's Indian, while the advocates of the King's Gambit grow fewer and fewer, as do those of the Scotch, Italian and Vienna Games. The problem with all these openings is that after a short fight in the center, the pawn structure simplifies, and the fight which follows becomes flat and featureless. Players of our day know how to sacrifice a pawn or a piece as well as Morphy or Anderssen did; but it is a characteristic of the present state of the art that sacrifices must be postponed while shielding one's combinative yearnings behind a mask of positional play.

The Smyslov - Euwe game, filled with combinative ideas that flow organically from the position, deserves to be counted among the finest examples of the art of chess.

1.	Ng1-f3	Ng8-f6
2.	g2-g3	d7-d5
3.	Bf1-g2	Bc8-f5
4.	0-0	Nb8-d7
5.	d2-d3	c7-c6
6.	Nb1-d2	h7-h6

With his queen's pawn supported by 5..c6, it makes more sense to occupy the center with 6..e5. The problem with this move is that his king's bishop remains shut in behind its own pawns, making it impossible for Black to castle kingside for some time. Smyslov exploits this with his 7 e4! — somewhat later than Morphy was accustomed to play this move, it is true, but with no less effect.

7.	e2-e4	d5:e4
8.	d3:e4	Nf6:e4
9.	Nf3-d4	Ne4:d2

Was it the fear of giving up his two bishops that prevented the former World Champion from playing 9..Nd6, and prompted him instead to develop still another enemy piece? After 9..Nd6 10 N:f5 N:f5 11 Re1 g6 12 Ne4, or 11..e6 12 Bh3 Nd6 13 Qh5, White would still have had to prove the correctness of his pawn sacrifice.

| 10. | Bc1:d2 | Bf5-h7 |

11.   Bd2-c3   ...

In the bygone days of chess, when today's finely-tuned techniques of positional play had not yet been worked out to such a degree, and having a piece or a pawn more was considered the mark of a cad — in those days, I do not doubt that White would, without much hesitation, have sacrificed a knight on c6, and knocked apart the black king's insecure shelter. The strategic basis for this sacrifice would be the complete isolation of Black's bishop and rook. Some concrete variations:

I. 11 N:c6 bc 12 B:c6 Rc8 13 Ba5!

II. 12..Bf5 13 Qf3 Rc8 14 Ba4, following which White would place his rook on d1, obtaining a position very similar to that of the famous game Morphy — Duke of Brunswick and Count Isouard; Black has no way of freeing himself.

The indecisive text turns the game in another direction for a while, and forces Smyslov to put forth a lot of ingenuity later on, in order to create once again the opportunity for a combinative attack.

11.	...	Qd8-c7
12.	Qd1-f3	e7-e5
13.	Rf1-e1	0-0-0
14.	Nd4-b3	f7-f6

Euwe sets up a pawn chain on the dark squares, without giving a thought to what will protect the light ones — a circumstance Smyslov later exploits beautifully. 14..f5 should have been played at once.

15.   Bc3-a5   Nd7-b6

Black overestimates his position and plays too dogmatically, without giving an inch. 15..b6 16 Bc3 Nc5 should have been played. After 17 N:c5 B:c5 18 a4 Bd4 19 a5, etc., White would have had some chances, but the risks in that case would have been mutual. Now, White is home free.

16.   c2-c4   Rd8-d3

One more Black retreat: the bishop now no longer controls c5.

26. Nb3-c5   Kb8-a8

On 26..Nb6 there would follow 27 Rd7!, but now the end comes at once.

27. Nc5:b7   Ka8:b7
28. Rd1-d7+   Kb7-a8
29. Qe3-c5   ...

This was enough to win, but every chessplayer from beginner to grandmaster would have gotten more enjoyment out of the variation 29 Bg2 Re8 30 B:e5 R:e5 31 Q:e5! Q:e5 32 B:c6+ Kb8 33 Rb7+ Ka8 34 Rb-any mate. For the same reason, the prosaic 30 R:g7 Q:g7 31 B:c6+ and 32 B:e8 was not as strong.

29. ...   Nc8-b6
30. Rd7:g7   Qf6:g7
31. Bc3-e5   Qg7-d7
32. Be5:h8   ...

An extra pawn plus the two bishops means the outcome of the game is assured. The phase which follows is not especially interesting: here or there Smyslov might have played more accurately, for instance by not exchanging queens.

32. ...   Ka8-b7
33. Bh8-d4   Qd7-e6
34. Bh3-f1   Bh7-g8
35. b2-b3   f5-f4
36. a2-a4   f4:g3
37. h2:g3   Bg8-f7

17. Qf3-h5   Qc7-e7
18. Bg2-f1   g7-g6

It is unpleasant to have to shut in one's own bishop, but after the rook's only possible retreat — to d7 — the threat was Bh3, so ..f6-f5 had to be prepared.

19. Qh5-e2   Rd3-d7
20. Qe2-e3   Kc8-b8
21. Ra1-d1   Nb6-c8

Clouds are beginning to gather over the black king's position. Euwe and Stahlberg's recommendation of 21..Bg8 would not have made any substantial change in the position: for example, 22 B:b6 ab 23 Q:b6 threatens 24 Na5.

22. Bf1-h3   ...

A consequence of 11..f6?: the diagonal h3-c8 is very weak, and so Black, who did not want to play ..f7-f5, must play it now; but now it only half helps.

22. ...   Rd7:d1
23. Re1:d1   f6-f5
24. Ba5-b4!   ...

Initiating a series of combinative blows. With this move, White exposes: 1) the insufficiently protected e-pawn, and 2) the weakness of the h-pawn (in the variation 24..Qc7 25 B:f8 R:f8 26 Q:h6).

24. ...   Qe7-f6
25. Bb4-c3   Bf8-g7

| 38. | a4-a5 | Nb6-c8 |
| 39. | Bf1-g2 | ... |

39 a6+ K:a6 40 Qb4 would have decided immediately; now the game will drag on for quite some time.

39.	...	Qe6-d6
40.	a5-a6+	Kb7:a6
41.	Bg2:c6	Qd6:c5
42.	Bd4:c5	Nc8-b6
43.	Kg1-f1	Bf7-e6
44.	Kf1-e2	Nb6-d7
45.	Bc5-d4	Ka6-a5
46.	Bd4-c3+	Ka5-b6
47.	Bc6-e4	g6-g5
48.	Bc3-d4+	Kb6-a5
49.	Bd4:a7	Ka5-b4
50.	Be4-c2	Kb4-c3

Black has not stood so well in quite a long time, but that's cold comfort since, as before, he's two pawns down.

51.	Bc2-d1	Nd7-e5
52.	Ke2-e3	Ne5-c6
53.	Ba7-b6	g5-g4
54.	Ke3-f4	h6-h5
55.	Bb6-e3	Nc6-a5
56.	Kf4-e5	Be6-c8
57.	c4-c5	Na5:b3
58.	Bd1-e2	Nb3-a5
59.	Be2-b5	Na5-c4+
60.	Ke5-f4	Nc4:e3
61.	f2:e3	Kc3-b4
62.	Bb5-e8	h5-h4
63.	g3:h4	Kb4:c5
64.	h4-h5	g4-g3
65.	Kf4:g3	Kc5-d5
66.	h5-h6	Bc8-f5
67.	Kg3-f4	Bf5-h7
68.	Kf4-g5	...

BLACK RESIGNED

******

125. Geller—Stahlberg
(French Defense)

1.	e2-e4	e7-e6
2.	d2-d4	d7-d5
3.	Nb1-d2	c7-c5
4.	e4:d5	e6:d5
5.	Ng1-f3	Ng8-f6
6.	Bf1-b5+	Bc8-d7
7.	Bb5:d7+	Nb8:d7
8.	0-0	Bf8-e7
9.	d4:c5	Nd7:c5
10.	Nf3-d4	...

White has given his opponent a weak pawn on d5, but his plans for the next few moves do not involve an attack on it. White's play will revolve around the fact that the square in front of the d-pawn has passed completely into his hands, and makes a good base for his pieces: from this square, pieces could exercise strong influence over both wings. A somewhat vague idea, of course; one cannot win a game, even by controlling the best square on the board, without attacking anything from it. In the present game, concrete targets became quite highly visible after Black's ..g7-g6 and ..f7-f5, but Stahlberg found sufficient defensive resources, one of them being his centralized knight at e4.

10.	...	0-0
11.	Nd4-f5	Rf8-e8
12.	Nd2-b3	Nc5-e6
13.	Bc1-e3	Qd8-c7
14.	c2-c3	Ra8-d8
15.	Qd1-f3	...

The a-pawn obviously cannot be taken.

15.	...	Nf6-e4
16.	Nf5:e7+	Re8:e7
17.	Rf1-d1	a7-a6
18.	Nb3-d4	g7-g6

Such moves are not to everyone's taste, but Stahlberg always plays without preconceptions. Generalizations about weak dark squares do not frighten him.

19.	h2-h4	Ne6-g7
20.	g2-g3	f7-f5
21.	Kg1-g2	Qc7-e5
22.	Rd1-d3	Qe5-f6
23.	Ra1-d1	Re7-d7
24.	Nd4-e2	Qf6-c6
25.	Be3-d4	...

White has succeeded in setting up a strong position. He may invade the king's wing with his queen, setting up threats on the dark squares, or he may precede this by cutting up the kingside pawns with h4-h5. True, the outcome of either course of action is not entirely clear, but in any event White ought not to have submitted to the queen exchange he allows in a few moves. Apparently Geller expected he would win the ending by pure technique, but Stahlberg puts up his usual stubborn defense, attaining an unbreachable position.

25.	...	Ng7-e6
26.	Ne2-f4	Ne6:f4+
27.	Qf3:f4	Rd8-e8
28.	Rd3-e3	...

If 28 h5 instead, then 28..Qd6
29 Q:d6 R:d6 30 hg hg 31 f3 Ng5,
and White has achieved nothing —
but perhaps it would have been
worthwhile to drive out the
knight first, and only then to
play h4-h5.

28.. Qd6 29. Q:d6 N:d6 30. R:e8+
N:e8 31. Be5 Kf7 32. f3 Nf6
33. Kf2 Ke6 34. Bd4 Ng8 35. Ke3
Ne7 36. Kd3 Nc6 37. Re1+ Kf7
38. a4 Re7 39. R:e7+ K:e7 40. Ke3
Ke6 41. Bh8 h5

DRAW

White's pieces can find no
way into the enemy camp.

******

126. Kotov—Boleslavsky
(King's Indian)

1.	c2-c4	Ng8-f6
2.	Nb1-c3	g7-g6
3.	g2-g3	Bf8-g7
4.	Bf1-g2	d7-d6
5.	Ng1-f3	0-0
6.	0-0	c7-c5
7.	d2-d4	Nb8-c6
8.	d4-d5	...

Against someone who likes to
play the Black side of the King's
Indian because it leads to a
complicated struggle, the most
unpleasant choice would be 8 dc,
but for this game both players
were aggressively inclined.

8.	...	Nc6-a5
9.	Qd1-d3	a7-a6
10.	Nf3-d2	Ra8-b8
11.	b2-b3	b7-b5

Black is developing harmoniously: already he threatens
12..b4, followed by 13..N:d5.
Evidently, White's was not the
strongest system of development.

12.	Ra1-b1	b5:c4
13.	Nd2:c4	Na5:c4
14.	Qd3:c4	...

Kotov refuses to give an inch,
but it was already high time for
him to consider maintaining the
balance, which he could have done
with 14 bc R:b1 15 Q:b1 Bd7

16 Bd2 Qc7 17 Qc2 Rb8 18 Rb1.
After the text move, Black's
initiative grows. Already he
has a target in the white d-
pawn, deprived of pawn protection.

14.	...	Nf6-e8
15.	Bc1-b2	Ne8-c7
16.	Nc3-d1	Rb8-b4
17.	Qc4-c2	Bg7:b2
18.	Nd1:b2	Bc8-f5

Black induces e2-e4 to short-
en the diagonal of the fianchettoed bishop; then he resets himself for an attack on the e-
pawn.

19.	e2-e4	Bf5-d7
20.	Nb2-d3	Rb4-d4
21.	Rf1-e1	e7-e5

22.	d5:e6	...

If White does not capture en
passant, he will never get the
rook out of d4.

22.	...	Nc7:e6
23.	Rb1-d1	Bd7-b5
24.	Nd3-c1	Qd8-a5
25.	Bg2-f1	Rf8-e8
26.	Bf1:b5	a6:b5

The most cursory inspection
of the position will show that
Black's pieces hang like clouds
over White's position. But how
to turn this to account? Boleslavsky wants the key to the
white fortress: the e-pawn.

27.	Nc1-e2	Rd4:d1
28.	Re1:d1	Ne6-g5
29.	Kg1-g2	Ng5:e4

30.	f2-f3	Ne4-g5
31.	Rd1:d6	Qa5-a8

Kotov has won his pawn back, but Boleslavsky relentlessly turns to attack the next pawn on the diagonal, at f3. What happens if this pawn falls, or moves on? Behind the pawn on f3 stands the king, which Black has marked down as the next and final target of his attack.

32.	Rd6-d3	Ng5-e6
33.	Qc2-d2	b5-b4
34.	Kg2-f2	Qa8-b8
35.	Rd3-e3	Qb8-a7
36.	f3-f4	Re8-d8
37.	Qd2-c2	Qa7-d7
38.	Kf2-e1	Qd7-d5
39.	Ne2-g1	Qd5-d4

Black's pretty maneuvers have set up irresistible threats: the rook cannot move, so it must be defended. If 40 Ke2, then 40..Re8!, threatening 41..N:f4+; if then 41 Qd3 Ra8 42 Qb1 c4!

40. Qc2-e2 ...

40 Kf2 Re8 41 Nf3 Q:e3+ 42 K:e3 Nd4+ 43 Qe4, or 40..Ra8 41 Nf3 Qa1 42 Re2 Nd4 43 N:d4 cd 44 Qc6! would have been better.

40.	...	Qd4-a1+
41.	Ke1-f2	Rd8-a8
42.	Qe2-d3	...

42. ... Ra8:a2+

Taking pawns with check is not always the best. Here, as the saying goes, 42..Nd4 43 Ne2 R:a2 "deserved attention"; considering Black's threat of 44..Qh1, it is doubtful that he would have had to play on for another twenty-five moves.

43. Ng1-e2 Qa1-d4

Now 43..Qh1 does not work in view of 44 R:e6, but 43..Nd4 would still have decided immediately.

44. Kf3 Q:d3 45. R:d3 Kf8 46. Re3 Ke7 47. g4 f5 48. gf gf 49. Ng3 Kf6 50. Re5 Nd4+ 51. Ke3 Rc2 52. Nh5+ Kg6 53. Ng3 h5 54. h4 Rc3+ 55. Kf2 Rf3+ 56. Kg2 R:f4 57. R:c5 R:h4 58. Rc4 Rg4 59. Kh3 N:b3 60. Rc8 Nd4 61. Rg8+ Kh6 62. Rh8+ Kg5 63. Rg8+ Kf4 64. N:h5+ Kf3 65. Rb8 Ne6 66. Rb5 Ng5+ 67. Kh2 Rh4+ 68. Kg1 Nh3+

WHITE RESIGNED

******

******

ROUND NINETEEN

127. Boleslavsky—Geller
(Sicilian Defense)

Mutual forcing attacking play against opposite-wing castled positions is one of the sharpest forms of the chess struggle. In this it is equally important not to throw oneself too hastily into the attack and not to be excessively concerned with the defense of one's own king. The harmonious blending of attack and defense, based upon experience, knowledge and intuition, is what we find in this game between two masters of the aggressive style.

1.	e2-e4	c7-c5
2.	Ng1-f3	Nb8-c6
3.	d2-d4	c5:d4
4.	Nf3:d4	Ng8-f6
5.	Nb1-c3	d7-d6
6.	g2-g3	Bc8-g4
7.	f2-f3	Bg4-d7
8.	Bc1-e3	g7-g6
9.	Qd1-d2	Bf8-g7
10.	0-0-0	0-0
11.	g3-g4	...

With his 6..Bg4, Geller forced White to advance his f-pawn to f3; making a virtue of necessity, Boleslavsky then played the Rauzer Attack against his opponent's Dragon Variation, in which White plays f2-f3 of his own volition.

11.	...	Ra8-c8
12.	Kc1-b1	Nc6-e5
13.	h2-h4	...

The position is of exceptional interest, both for theory and for the practice of the middlegame.

White has a powerfully centralized knight, making a good counterweight to the bishop on d7 and ready to meet a queen sortie to a5 by retreating to b3. White started his pawn storm first, and has already gotten in g3-g4 and h2-h4; his own king position has no weaknesses, while Black's pawn at g6 forms a hook for White's advancing army to seize upon.

While Black may be starting his pawn advance later than White's, he already has a line open against the enemy king. His centralized knight is very powerful too: it attacks the weak link in White's pawn chain—the pawn which is, in fact, the only support of White's whole chain (and very shaky, too!).

Black controls, and may soon occupy, the important square c4, which carries about the same value as the f5 square does for Black; meanwhile, White still does not control one square in the immediate area of Black's king. Finally, the powerful bishop at g7 may give rise to dangerous combinations on the long diagonal.

As may be seen, a complex position; at the moment, it lies in a state of dynamic equality. Great skill is necessary in order to maneuver the entire mass of pawns and pieces, while simultaneously countering the enemy's operations. In this game, we shall follow the struggle move by move.

13. ... b7-b5

Black answers blow for blow. This prepares ..b5-b4, as well as .. Nc4, after which he could now answer B:c4 with ..b5:c4, opening the b-file, which is more dangerous to White than the c-file.

14. Be3-h6 ...

Taking the b-pawn would be madness, of course. And h4-h5 is ineffective, so long as Black's pieces solidly defend the squares h7 and h8; so first

White wants to trade off one of
the most important defensive
pieces.

14.   ...   Bg7:h6

..Bh8 is sometimes possible in
such positions: at the moment,
the rook is less valuable than
the bishop. The long diagonal,
at present loaded with pieces,
may be cleared quickly with,
for instance, 14..Bh8 15 B:f8
R:c3 16 bc N:f3 17 N:f3 N:e4 —
not a forced line by any means,
and a clear loss for Black here
as well, but presented merely
as an illustration of the ideas
that may come up in the course
of battle.

15.   Qd2:h6   Rc8:c3

h4-h5 was a real threat now,
so this exchange of rook for
knight, which also breaks up
the king's cover, was practically forced.

16.   b2:c3   ...

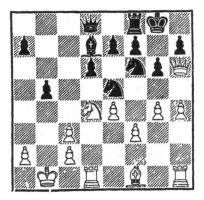

16.   ...   Qd8-a5

The natural attacking continuation.

17.   Qh6-e3   ...

White's king position is loos-
ening, and his queen must now
return to the defense. On the
other hand, the position is still
in balance, since White has the
exchange as compensation.

17.   ...   Qa5-a3

Nothing comes of 17..Nc4
18 B:c4 bc 19 Ka1 Rb8 20 Rb1.
Now 18..b4 is a threat.

18.   h4-h5   b5-b4
19.   Qe3-c1   Qa3:c3
20.   Qc1-b2   Rf8-c8

Black refrains from 20..Qe3,
which could result in a repetition of moves after 21 Qc1
Qc3. Black has no advantage,
and after the exchange of queens
his game becomes perhaps even
a bit inferior.

21.   h5:g6   ...

This forces Black to initiate
the trade, as 21..hg allows
22 Qc1, with the threat of 23 Qh6.

21.   ...   Qc3:b2+
22.   Kb1:b2   h7:g6
23.   a2-a3   ...

An inaccuracy, which leads up
to Boleslavsky's following one-
move oversight, the only such
occurrence in his tournament
practice in the last fifteen
years. Correct was 23 Bd3 or
23 Be2, and only then 24 a3. In
that event, White would have had
winning chances.

23.   ...   b4:a3+
24.   Kb2:a3   ...

Even here, nothing fearsome
would have occurred after 24 Ká2,
but Boleslavsky bravely follows
the variation he calculated:
24..N:f3 25 N:f3 Rc3+ 26 Rd3?!?!
As Boleslavsky explained it later, he of course saw that the
black knight could take the f-
pawn, followed by the rook check
at c3, forking king and knight;
but he thought his 26 Rd3 would
protect both attacked pieces —
including the king!

24.   ...   Ne5:f3
25.   Nd4:f3   Rc8-c3+
26.   Ka3-b2   Rc3:f3
27.   e4-e5   Nf6:g4

The foundation cracks, and
the entire edifice comes tum-
bling down.

28.   Bf1-e2   Rf3-f2
29.   Be2:g4   Bd7:g4
30.   Rd1-f1   Rf2:f1
31.   Rh1:f1   d6:e5

No rook can fight a bishop and four pawns. If it were not for the a-pawn, perhaps White might scare up some sort of chances, but it will take him a couple of moves to win that pawn, and in that time, the black pawns can go a long way...

32.	c2-c4	Kg8-f8
33.	Rf1-a1	Bg4-f3
34.	c4-c5	g6-g5
35.	Ra1:a7	g5-g4
36.	Ra7-a3	Kf8-e8
37.	Kb2-c1	f7-f5
38.	Kc1-d2	f5-f4
39.	Ra3-a6	g4-g3
40.	Kd2-e1	Bf3-e4

WHITE RESIGNED

******

128. Stahlberg—Smyslov
(Queen's Gambit)

1.	d2-d4	d7-d5
2.	c2-c4	c7-c6
3.	Ng1-f3	Ng8-f6
4.	Nb1-c3	d5:c4
5.	a2-a4	Bc8-f5
6.	e2-e3	e7-e6
7.	Bf1:c4	Bf8-b4
8.	0-0	Nb8-d7
9.	Qd1-e2	Bf5-g6
10.	e3-e4	0-0
11.	Bc4-d3	h7-h6

Making a draw with Black sometimes becomes a necessity due to one's tournament standing or the approach of more important games. When he needed to draw a game, Smyslov used the Slav Defense, and neither Boleslavsky, nor Szabo, nor Stahlberg in this game

could make any headway against it.

True, Szabo found the interesting move 11 Bd3, and obtained a significant advantage after 11..Qa5?, but two rounds later Smyslov already had an improvement for Black, 11..h6; and his subsequent maneuver ..Nd7-b8-c6 gave him full equality.

12.	Rf1-d1	Qd8-e7
13.	h2-h3	Ra8-d8
14.	e4-e5	Nf6-d5
15.	Nc3:d5	c6:d5
16.	Bd3:g6	...

This exchange could have been delayed, with the developing 16 Bd2 played first.

16.	...	f7:g6
17.	Bc1-d2	Nd7-b8!
18.	Bd2:b4	Qe7:b4
19.	a4-a5	Rd8-c8
20.	Qe2-d3	g6-g5
21.	Qd3-g6	...

21.	...	Qb4-e7
22.	Rd1-c1	a7-a6
23.	Rc1-c3	Nb8-c6
24.	Ra1-c1	Qe7-d7
25.	Qg6-c2	Qd7-f7
26.	Qc2-d2	Qf7-f5
27.	b2-b4	...

DRAW

But perhaps not quite so simply as the reader might think. In view of the threatened 28 b5 ab 29 a6, Black must play 27..Rce8! here, in order to meet 28 b5 ab 29 a6 with 29..Na5! The exchange sacrifice 28 R:c6

bc 29 R:c6 would fail to 29..Rc8!
30 R:a6 Rc2 or 30 Qc3 R:c6 31 Q:c6
h5!

Thus, White's relatively best
line would be 28 Re3 followed by
29 b5 ab 30 a6. Sometimes the
draw two grandmasters agree to
conceals many pretty possibilities.

******

129. Euwe—Keres
(Grunfeld Opening)

1.	d2-d4	Ng8-f6
2.	c2-c4	g7-g6
3.	g2-g3	Bf8-g7
4.	Bf1-g2	d7-d5
5.	c4:d5	Nf6:d5
6.	e2-e4	Nd5-b6
7.	Ng1-e2	c7-c5
8.	d4-d5	e7-e6

Why does Black voluntarily
create this breach in his position, as if to invite the further advance of the d-pawn? The
answer to this must be sought in
Keres' first few moves. Black's
entire system is aimed at enticing the white pawn to d6,
there to be attacked and eliminated. For the time being,
White restrains himself long
enough to castle; but eventually
he decides to exploit this
breach in the pawn wall by pushing his pawn to d6. It appears
to me that the pleasure of attacking the encircled pawn is
won at too great a price: a
conclusion which the further
course of this game supports.

9.	0-0	0-0
10.	Ne2-c3	...

We have seen a similar maneuver in Game 19, Euwe - Smyslov:
the knight on b1 stays at home
temporarily, so as to come out
later at either a3 or d2, or to
replace the other knight when
it leaves c3, depending upon
circumstances.

10.	...	e6:d5
11.	e4:d5	Nb8-d7
12.	Nc3-e4	...

Now White has an obvious advantage, consisting of the great
mobility of his d-pawn by comparison with the clear weakness of
the black pawn at c5. In addition, White has more space avail-

able for maneuvering.

12.	...	Nd7-f6
13.	Nb1-c3	Nb6-d7
14.	d5-d6	...

The battle waxes very hot after this pawn's advance. Trading the c-pawn for the d-pawn
would be unfavorable for Black:
for example, 13..N:e4 14 N:e4!
N:d5 15 N:c5, and I cannot see
how Black is to maintain his
position at b7 and d5 without
sacrificing either position or
material.

14.	...	Ra8-b8
15.	Bc1-g5	h7-h6
16.	Bg5:f6	Bg7:f6

A necessity, and a sad one
too, since it will be difficult
to fight that passed pawn without his darksquare bishop.

Black's opening idea has been
a fiasco.

17.	Ne4:f6+	Nd7:f6
18.	Rf1-e1	Bc8-e6
19.	Qd1-f3	b7-b5
20.	Qf3-f4	Kg8-h7
21.	Ra1-d1	Rb8-b6

(See diagram, next page)

[216]

22. a2-a3 ...

Every positional achievement —
in this case, the pawn at d6,
which commands the attention of
the black pieces — is important,
but not so much of itself as in
conjunction with other combinative or positional motifs. In
the diagrammed position, the motifs for White are:

1) the undefended c5-pawn,

2) the Black king's weakened
cover,

3) the ever-present possibility of the advance d6-d7,

4) control of the c7 and e7
squares; coupled with this,
the idea of trying for control
of either the c-file or the e-
file.

And for Black:

1) the possibility of surrounding the d-pawn from three sides,

2) a queenside majority attack,

3) the possibility of ..Nh5,
which would force White's queen
away from its strong position
on f4.

It is by means of this matching up and balancing of the
chances for both sides that the
master generally arrives at more
or less objective conclusions,
which are called an "evaluation
of the position".

If coefficients could be found
for that sort of evaluation, then
machines could also play chess.

By now it is clear that White,
whose pieces are more actively
placed, should try to exploit
his opponent's weaknesses, while
not forgetting his main threats.
There were two ways for Euwe to
accomplish this. One was 22 b3,
in order to slow Black's pawn
roller: ..b5-b4, ..c5-c4 and
..c4-c3; but Black's position
would still have been difficult
to crack, chiefly due to the
bishop at e6. So 22 R:e6 suggests itself, in order to eliminate the only black piece that
has any freedom of action, and
thus fling open the door to the
black king's shelter along the
seventh rank, while turning
Black's three good pawns at f7,
g6 and h6 into two weak ones at
e6 and g6. White's attack could
then develop as follows: 22..fe
23 Qe5 Qd7 24 Bh3, or 23..Re8
24 Q:c5.

At all events, the text move
had little to recommend it. It
does nothing to further White's
plans, and needlessly weakens
b3. Keres exploits this skillfully.

22. ... Rf8-e8

An excellent defensive maneuver. The bishop threatens to
exit to b3, when the rook at d1
will be overburdened, having to
defend the d-pawn as well as
the king's rook.

23. Nc3-e4 Nf6:e4
24. Re1:e4 Qd8-d7

Completing the encirclement,
and more importantly the blockade, of the d-pawn: without mobility, it holds no further terrors. Meanwhile, the c5-pawn is
awakening from its slumber, so
Euwe hurries to trade it for the
d-pawn before it starts to advance.

25. Qf4-e5 Re8-d8
26. Qe5:c5 Rb6:d6

Now the fire has died, and
there is no cause for further
argument. The DRAW comes as
the natural conclusion to a
battle flamed — and faded.

(Queen's Gambit)

1.	d2-d4	Ng8-f6
2.	c2-c4	e7-e6
3.	Ng1-f3	d7-d5
4.	Nb1-c3	c7-c5
5.	c4:d5	Nf6:d5
6.	e2-e3	Nb8-c6
7.	Bf1-d3	Nd5:c3

If Black wanted to trade on c3, he should have played 7..cd first.

8.	b2:c3	Bf8-e7
9.	Qd1-c2	g7-g6

Black prepares to castle. Considering White's threat of B:h7, this or some other weakening was practically unavoidable, and it is hard to say whether Reshevsky would have had less of a problem after 9..h6. Szabo would then have tried to have his king's bishop and his queen trade places as quickly as possible, and what would Black do then? Further weakening of his pawn barricade with ..g7-g6 or ..f7-f5 would be fatal, and Black obviously would not have enough time to bring his knight to f8. On the other hand, that same ..Nf8 would be not only his one chance, but his one hope as well. So we must conclude that the combination of 6..Nc6 with 7..N:c3 was unfortunate. The text move weakens a whole cluster of squares, and gives White the basis for a successful attack.

10.	h2-h4	h7-h5
11.	Ra1-b1	Ra8-b8
12.	Bd3-e4	...

The first consequence of Black's carelessness: on 12..Bd7, White sacrifices a piece with 13 B:g6 fg 14 Q:g6+ Kf8 15 e4, with the threat of 16 Bh6+.

12.	...	Qd8-c7
13.	0-0	Bc8-d7
14.	d4-d5	e6:d5
15.	Be4:d5	Be7-f6
16.	Nf3-g5	Nc6-d8
17.	c3-c4	Bd7-c6
18.	Ng5-e4	...

Szabo has obtained an excellent attacking position, while Black's pieces stand passively, and his king still has not castled.

18.	...	Bf6-g7
19.	Bc1-b2	0-0
20.	Ne4-f6+	Bg7:f6?

21.	Bb2:f6	...

This has not happened in tournament play in a long time: both grandmasters have overlooked a mate in two by 21 Q:g6+ Bg7 22 Q:g7 mate. Black's only move was 20..Kh8, when White would have continued his attack by 21 f4, followed by f4-f5 or e3-e4-e5, with a relatively easy win. Those with a penchant for beauty might try 21 Qc3, threatening 22 Ne8; 21..B:d5 would be well met by 22 N:d5.

21.	...	Bc6:d5
22.	c4:d5	Qc7-d6
23.	Qc2-c3	Qd6:d5
24.	Rf1-d1	Qd5-f5
25.	e3-e4	Qf5-e6
26.	Bf6-g7	b7-b6

White's position was so powerful that despite his unbelievable oversight on the 21st move, he still has more than enough to win here. Once again, it comes down to a mate threat at g7, for which purpose he need only have retreated his bishop by 27 Bh6. The only reply would be 27..f6, when 28 Qg3 would have won at least a rook.

Szabo played otherwise:

27. Bg7:f8?   Kg8:f8

immediately saw his error, and became so distraught that, after using up nearly all his remaining time, and still without making a move, he accepted the

DRAW

Reshevsky had offered nearly half an hour before — right after White took the rook at f8 with his bishop. After such a traumatic experience, Szabo was a long time regaining his confidence, which naturally affected his play for the remainder of the tournament.

******

131. Averbakh—Bronstein
(King's Indian)

1. d4 Nf6 2. c4 g6 3. g3 Bg7 4. Bg2 0-0 5. Nc3 d6 6. Nf3 Nbd7 7. 0-0 e5 8. e4 Re8 9. h3 ed 10. N:d4 Nc5 11. Re1 a5 12. Qc2 Ng4 13. Red1 Ne5 14. Nce2 c6 15. Be3 Qe7

The threat was 16 N:c6 and 17 B:c5.

16. b3 h5 17. Nc3 Ned7 18. Re1 Qd8 19. Rab1 Nf8 20. Red1 Qe7

Neither player is putting much life into this well-known and thoroughly analyzed variation: White plays his cards close to the vest, and Black follows his example. Sometimes excessive peaceableness can be justified, but not here.

21. a3 Nfe6 22. h4 Nd7 23. N:e6 Q:e6 24. Na4 Bf8 25. c5 dc 26. N:c5 N:c5 27. B:c5

DRAW

******

132. Petrosian—Gligoric
(King's Indian)

1.	d2-d4	Ng8-f6
2.	c2-c4	g7-g6
3.	Nb1-c3	Bf8-g7
4.	e2-e4	d7-d6
5.	f2-f3	0-0
6.	Bc1-e3	e7-e5
7.	d4-d5	...

White is not obliged to close the center: he could also have continued with 7 Nge2 ed 8 N:d4 c6 9 Nc2 Re8 10 Qd2 d5 11 0-0-0, which wins the d-pawn eventually, but gives Black the initiative.

7.   ...   Nf6-h5

This move is not obligatory either, but a lot of people seem to think that in the King's Indian the f-pawn must go to f5 as quickly as possible. I don't believe that's always true. The ..f7-f5 or ..f7-f5-f4 attack is good, provided it achieves some substantive end; if not, then it's better to postpone ..f7-f5 until it is most effective. For this reason, 7..Nbd7 and 7..a5 were not at all inferior to the text move.

8.	Qd1-d2	f7-f5
9.	0-0-0	f5-f4
10.	Be3-f2	Bg7-f6
11.	Ng1-e2	Bf6-h4
12.	Bf2-g1	g6-g5!

A new move: compare this with Game 75, Geller - Gligoric, in which Black played 12..Nd7, and then pulled his bishop back to e7. Since Black had to endure a long and difficult defense in that game, Gligoric decides to waste no time opening the g-file for kingside counterplay. In reply, Petrosian exploits the knight's absence from d7 to break on the left flank.

13.	c4-c5!	g5-g4
14.	Kc1-b1	g4:f3
15.	g2:f3	Nb8-a6

With part of the board blockaded, Black appears to be all set for the long haul after his ..f5-f4. So there was no reason for haste here, either: the coolheaded 15..Kh8 would have forestalled White's next threat, and made possible the plan ..Rg8, ..Be7, ..a5 etc.

16.   c5-c6   ...

This energetic move secures
White's advantage. If 16..b6,
then 17 a3 followed by 18 b4
takes away all the black knight's
squares, and the queen's bishop's
as well; if 16..bc 17 dc, when
the a2-g8 diagonal is opened,
and White's pieces gain the d5
square, for example: 17..Qe8
18 Nc1 Q:c6? 19 Bb5 Qb7 20 B:a6
Q:a6 21 Qd5+.

16.   ...   Nh5-f6
17.   c6:b7   Bc8:b7
18.   Ne2-g3   ...

A transparent sacrifice which
only slows down the attack. White
thinks that his threat of 19 Nf5
will force Black to enter the
unfavorable line 18..fg 19 hg
B:g3 20 Qg5+ Kh8 21 Q:g3. Gligoric's quiet reply, however,
forces the knight to retreat and
try a different route.

18.   ...   Bb7-c8
19.   Ng3-e2   Na6-c5

This allows White to dismember Black's pawn formation totally by trading his bishop for
the knight, which leaves Black
in a more or less lost position.
Black might have exploited his
opponent's loss of time with
19..Nd7, and only then ..Nac5
and ..a5.

20.   Bg1:c5!   ...

White instantly exploits his
opponent's inaccuracy.

20.   ...   d6:c5
21.   Ne2-c1   Qd8-e7
22.   Nc1-b3   Bc8-d7

Directed against the threatened 23 Na4 and 24 Qc2. However,
Petrosian now finds an original
queen maneuver to win the c5-
pawn.

23.   Qd2-g2+!   Kg8-h8
24.   Qg2-g1   Nf6-e8
25.   Qg1:c5   Ne8-d6
26.   Rd1-c1   ...

Petrosian correctly declines
the second pawn: after 26 Q:c7
Rfc8 27 Qa5 Bf2! Black would
have some serious counterchances.

26.   ...   Bd7-e8
27.   Bf1-h3   a7-a5

Black's only hope is an attack on White's king. So he
gives up another pawn to open
a line and remove one of the
pieces covering the king.

28.   Nb3:a5   Bh4-f2
29.   Qc5:f2   Ra8:a5
30.   Rh1-g1   Be8-g6
31.   Bh3-f1   Rf8-b8
32.   Rc1-c2   Nd6-f7
33.   h2-h4   Nf7-d6
34.   Bf1-d3   Rb8-b4

White plays rather hesi-
tantly in time-pressure (Rh1-
g1-c1, Bh3-f1-d3-f1), which,
while it does not let the win
slip away, still allows his
opponent to improve the position of his pieces. The idea
of transferring his rook to
the fourth rank is very good,
but it does not get carried
through to its logical conclusion.

35.   Rg1-c1   Rb4-d4
36.   Bd3-f1   Qe7-d8
37.   Nc3-e2   ...

37.   ...   Rd4-a4

During the past fifteen
moves Black has tried by every
means available to complicate
the game, but Petrosian's solid preventive measures have
taken their toll: Gligoric loses
faith, and just at the very moment when blind luck offers him
an unexpected — I might even
say unbelievable — opportunity
to complicate, and mix things
up. The idea of giving a rook
for "only" two pawns with

37..R:e4 seemed just too risky.
But when one sacrifices, one
does not count pawns, but rather
accrued advantages and concrete
variations.

Had Gligoric not lost heart,
and found within himself the
strength to sacrifice the rook,
the continuation might have
been very interesting; I am
sure that Petrosian would have
had reason to regret his carelessness.

First, some considerations
of a general nature. After 38 fe
N:e4, the only White reply that
makes any sense is 39 Qe1, defending against the newly created threat of 39..Nd2+ 40 Ka1
R:a2+ 41 K:a2 Qa8 mate. Nor is
this all: Black's queen now takes
on d5, and White's king is quite
suddenly and quite obviously in
a mating net.

For just one rook (of questionable usefulness), Black clears
away all pawn obstructions in
the center; along with the three
pawns he gets as material compensation, he also obtains two
diagonals, one file and a powerful knight in the very middle of
the board. White's material advantage would probably have allowed him to save his king from
direct threats, but finding the
solution to this task would have
presented him no small difficulties.

For those who enjoy complicated, pretty variations, we
present a summary analysis,
giving a good illustration of
the possibilities for both
sides in this head-breaking
position. (In addition to the
author's variations, we have
made use here of those arising
from the correspondence polemic between Soviet grandmaster
Tigran Petrosian and the Yugoslav master Vukovic, commentator for "Sahovski Glasnik".

I. 40 b3 Nd2+ 41 Kb2 R:a2+
42 K:a2 Q:b3+ 43 Ka1 Qa3+,
and mate next; or 41 Ka1 N:b3+
42 Kb2 N:c1.

II. 40 b4 Nd2+ 41 Ka1 Nb3+
42 Kb1 R:a2 43 K:a2 (43 N:f4
Nd2+ 44 Q:d2 Qb3 mate!) 43..N:c1+
44 Ka1 Qa8+ 45 Kb1 Qa2+!

III. 40 a3 Nd2+ 41 Ka1 Nb3+
42 Kb1 N:c1 43 N:c1 Rc5 44 Bd3
B:d3 45 N:d3 Q:d3 46 Qe2 Q:e2
47 R:e2 Kg7 48 b4 Rd5, or:

a) 43 K:c1 B:c2 44 K:c2 Qe4+

b) 43 Q:c1 Qb3 44 Qd2 Rd5
45 Qc1 Q:c2+ 46 Q:c2 Rd1+

IV. 40 Q:a5 Q:a5 41 Ka1 f3
42 Nc3 Ng3 43 Rf2 e4.

Of course Gligoric could not
calculate all of these variations through in time-pressure,
and therefore was unable to bring
himself to give up a rook on
"spec". On the other hand, considering that Black ended up re-
signing the game four moves later, the rook doesn't appear to
have been worth keeping.

```
38.  Ne2-c3    Ra4-d4
39.  b2-b3     ...
```

Whether by intuition or by
conscious choice, Petrosian is
not about to allow Black to play
something as tempting as ..R:e4
twice. In the game of chess as
in life, opportunity knocks but
once.

```
39.  ...        Qd8-b8
40.  h4-h5      Bg6:h5
41.  Qf2-h4     ...
```

and Gligoric

RESIGNED

After 41..Bg6 42 Qf6+ and
43 Q:e5, Black's entire pawn
chain is destroyed, while after 41..Qe8 there would follow
Bf1-h3-e6 , followed by rook
to g2.

******

133. Najdorf—Taimanov
(Nimzoindian Defense)

```
1.   d2-d4     Ng8-f6
2.   c2-c4     e7-e6
3.   Nb1-c3    Bf8-b4
4.   e2-e3     0-0
5.   Bf1-d3    d7-d5
6.   Ng1-f3    b7-b6
7.   0-0       Bc8-b7
8.   Bc1-d2    d5:c4
9.   Bd3:c4    Nb8-d7
10.  Qd1-e2    c7-c5
11.  Rf1-d1    c5:d4
12.  Nf3:d4    Qd8-e7
```

White's slow opening play has allowed Black time to complete his development.

13.	Ra1-c1	a7-a6
14.	a2-a3	Bb4-c5
15.	Bd2-e1	b6-b5
16.	Bc4-a2	Ra8-c8
17.	f2-f3	Nd7-e5
18.	Be1-f2	Nf6-d7
19.	Ba2-b1	Bc5-a7
20.	f3-f4	...

Weakening the h1-a8 diagonal is not a good idea for White: driving out the knight did not require such strong measures. Within two moves, Najdorf gives up a pawn in order to enforce an exchange of queens; then, his two bishops restore approximate equality.

20.	...	Ne5-g6
21.	g2-g3	Ba7:d4!

That's the point! If the rook takes, Black gets his main reserve, the e-pawn, very successfully into the fray with a sudden onslaught against White's king: 22 R:d4 e5 23 R4d1 R:c3! 24 R:c3 ef — you need only set up this position to understand why White hurriedly recaptured with the pawn, and then closed the bishop's diagonal with d4-d5.

22.	e3:d4	Nd7-f6

23.	d4-d5	Nf6:d5

Black might also have been tempted to set up a death-dealing battery against White's king with 23..Ba8, threatening 24..Qb7.

24. N:d5 ed 25. Q:e7 N:e7 26. Bc5 Rfe8 27. Ba2 h6 28. Kf2 Rc6 29. Bb4 R:c1 30. R:c1 Nc6 31. Bd2 Nd4

Black's extra pawn is of no significance, so the draw is foreordained. By continuing his stubborn pursuit of the win, Taimanov gets into an inferior position. But after some small agitation, everything comes out all right in the end.

32.Be3 Nf5 33. Ba7 Rc8 34. Bc5 Rc7 35. Rc3 h5 36. Bb1 Nh6 37. h4 Bc8 38. Bd4 Rc4 39. Bd3 R:c3 40. B:c3 Bf5 41. Be2 g6 42. a4 ba 43. B:a6 Bc2 44. Bc8 Kf8 45. Bb4+

DRAW

******

******

ROUND TWENTY

134. Taimanov—Petrosian
(Nimzoindian Defense)

One of the tournament's most beautiful games, in which White, without resorting to a pawn storm, managed to break down a solid defensive position by combinative means.

The reader will note that this is not the first time we have referred to a game as being "one of the most beautiful of the tournament". Indeed, a great number of beautiful games were produced here. True beauty in chess can only be a creation by both players: should one player's mastery of the game considerably exceed that of his opponent, the resulting creation cannot afford us complete esthetic satisfaction.

There were only three brilliancy prizes given at the Zurich tournament; but even if there had been ten times that many, the jury could still have found worthy recipients for them.

1.	d2-d4	Ng8-f6
2.	c2-c4	e7-e6
3.	Nb1-c3	Bf8-b4
4.	e2-e3	c7-c5
5.	Bf1-d3	0-0
6.	Ng1-f3	d7-d5
7.	0-0	Nb8-c6
8.	a2-a3	Bb4:c3
9.	b2:c3	b7-b6
10.	c4:d5	e6:d5

A defensive system that saw a lot of use in this event — in Games 12, 71, 102 and 160, for example. In each case, Black found sufficient counterchances, thanks to his extra queenside pawn.

In this game, Taimanov spends two moves in order to trade off the black queen's knight, which enables him to carry out his intended f2-f3 and e3-e4 quickly, by eliminating the pressure on the d4-pawn.

11.	Nf3-e5	Qd8-c7
12.	Ne5:c6	Qc7:c6
13.	f2-f3	Bc8-e6
14.	Qd1-e1	Nf6-d7
15.	e3-e4	...

In no other Nimzo-Indian was

White able to get in e3-e4 so quickly and effectively, opening diagonals for both his bishops at once. The slightest misstep from Black could result in his king's falling under a powerful attack — Qh4 is already threatened.

15.	...	c5-c4

Petrosian decides to turn to defense exclusively, based upon the strong point at e6. This decision was not at all forced: using his temporary lead in development and the central pawn tension, he might have stirred up sharp play by means of 15..f5.

For example:

I. 16 ed Q:d5 17 Be3 Ne5 — 17..f4 and 17..cd are good too.

II. On 16 e5, Black has kept the c4 square open for his knight, and would reply 16..b5, with the threat of ..Nd7-b6-c4.

III. Perhaps Petrosian disliked the continuation 16 c4 fe 17 fe dc 18 d5, but this is not dangerous for Black either, after 18..Qd6:

a) 19 B:c4 Ne5 20 Be2 Bg4 21 Bb2 B:e2 22 Q:e2 Rae8, and the white pawns are blockaded;

b) 19 de Q:d3 20 ed R:f1+ 21 Q:f1 Qd4+;

c) Black would get a tremendous attack after 19 R:f8+ R:f8 20 de Ne5, when the bi-

shop cannot retreat to b1 or
e2 because of 21..Qd4+, while
if it retreats to f1 or c2,
then 21..Ng4, and I see no
way of stopping both 22..Q:h2
mate and 22..Qd4+.

16.	Bd3-c2	f7-f5
17.	e4-e5	Rf8-f7
18.	a3-a4	a7-a5
19.	f3-f4	b6-b5

White has a clear plan of attack: h3, Kh2, Rg1, g4, Qg3 or
Qh4, and Black cannot meet this
on the kingside in any way. Petrosian's attempt to divert his
opponent with his extra queenside pawn is understandable, but
now a breach appears in his fortress, through which the enemy
bishops will assail Black's position from the flank, while the
queen and the other rook continue their frontal assault.

20.	a4:b5	Qc6:b5
21.	Bc1-a3	Nd7-b6
22.	Qe1-h4	Qb5-e8
23.	Rf1-f3	Nb6-c8
24.	Bc2-a4	...

White's pieces are coordinating beautifully. The bishop
obviously cannot be taken, while
on 24..Bd7 there follows 25 e6
Q:e6 26 Qd8+.

24.	...	Rf7-d7
25.	Ra1-b1	...

White disdains the exchange,
rather than allow Black to untangle himself.

25.	...	Qe8-d8

26.	Ba4:d7	...

If Black takes the queen, then
after 26..Q:h4 27 B:e6+ Kh8
28 B:d5 Ra7 he will be unable to
stop White's pawn phalanx, to
say nothing of the fact that
White could also win the knight
with 29 Rb8 Qd8 30 e6 or 30 Be6.

26.	...	Qd8:d7
27.	Rf3-g3	...

Taimanov attacks in classic
style, quickly creating irresistible threats of mate. On
the other hand, he could also
have won with 27 Rh3 h6 28 Rg3
Kh7 29 Bf8; or if 27..g6, then
28 Rb7!, forcing mate.

27.	...	Nc8-a7
28.	Ba3-e7	Be6-f7
29.	Qh4-g5	Bf7-g6
30.	h2-h4	Na7-c6
31.	Be7-a3	Nc6-d8
32.	h4-h5	Nd8-e6
33.	Qg5-h4	Bg6-f7
34.	h5-h6	g7-g6
35.	Qh4-f6	Qd7-d8
36.	Ba3-e7	Qd8-c7

37.	Rg3:g6+	...

The conclusive combinative
blow: if 36..B:g6, then 37 Q:e6+
Bf7 38 Qf6.

37.	...	h7:g6
38.	h6-h7+	...

The finish is a trifle crude:
38 Kf2 was more delicate, with
mate in no more than four moves
after any Black reply, even
38..Q:e7 or 38..Kh7.

38.	...	Kg8:h7
39.	Qf6:f7+	Ne6-g7
40.	Kg1-f2	...

BLACK RESIGNED

******

135. Gligoric—Averbakh
(Sicilian Defense)

1.	e2-e4	c7-c5
2.	Ng1-f3	Nb8-c6
3.	d2-d4	c5:d4
4.	Nf3:d4	Ng8-f6
5.	Nb1-c3	d7-d6
6.	Bc1-g5	e7-e6
7.	Qd1-d2	a7-a6
8.	0-0-0	Bc8-d7

The starting point for much theoretical research. Latest analyses give White the nod, perhaps without sufficient grounds for doing so. The point of Black's defense 7..a6 and 8..Bd7 is that with the white queen on d2 and bishop on g5, Black always has the stroke ..N:e4 available.

| 9. | f2-f4 | ... |

It is difficult to get any sort of attack against the Sicilian without this move, but now comes the main variation of Black's defense.

9.	...	h7-h6
10.	Bg5-h4	Nf6:e4
11.	Qd2-e1	...

This move was discovered not too long ago — perhaps fifteen years back. 11 B:d8 N:d2, etc., was formerly considered obliga-

tory, but that gives Black an excellent endgame. Retreating the queen to e1 opened up new possibilities for further creativity on both sides.

| 11. | ... | Ne4-f6 |
| 12. | Nd4-f5 | Qd8-a5 |

In days of yore, people were not as preoccupied with pawns as they are today, counting them up after every half-move — no, pawns used to be sacrificed at the drop of a hat for various, occasionally questionable and even dubious ends. Even then, however, they were not given away. Steinitz, for example, used to suffer an awful lot for the chance to hang on to, and then bring home, one extra pawn. He probably would not have parted quite so lightly with his d-pawn; on the other hand, one may sympathize with Averbakh's distaste for 12..Qc7, since after 13 B:f6 gf 14 Nd5, the queen has to lose a tempo and retreat to d8: a prospect unlikely to appeal to anyone. However, positions do occur whose solution lies precisely in such a modus operandi — could this be one such? At any rate, after 14..Qd8 I see no immediate dangers for Black, and perhaps he will be able to rid himself of the e-file pin with the curious move ..Nc6-e5!

13.	Nf5:d6+	Bf8:d6
14.	Rd1:d6	0-0-0
15.	Qe1-d2	...

The game immediately loses all interest for theory and goes into the trenches for a war of maneuver, where neither side wants to undertake any active plan.

15 B:f6 gf 16 Qh4 is very interesting here, but I believe the strongest course would be the simple retreat of the rook from d6 to d2. Only after seeing Black's reply should White decide whether he will play on the black pawn weaknesses after B:f6 or keep this bishop for an attack on the squares round about the black king. Lately this variation has become the rage.

15..Ne7 16. Bd3 Bc6 17. R:d8+ R:d8 18. Rd1 Qh5 19. g3 Nf5 20. B:f6 gf 21. Qf2 Nd4 22. Be4

Qc5 23. Kb1 f5 24. B:c6 Q:c6
25. a3 Qf3 26. Qg1

Can one possibly hope to win
a game by such moves? Gligoric
remains true to himself: not
one unnecessary pawn move; but
this occasionally gives his
play an excessively cautious
turn. It is no surprise that
this game is shortly drawn.

26..Nc6 27. R:d8+ K:d8 28. Kc1
Kc7 29. Kd2 h5 30. Qe3 Q:e3+
31. K:e3 Kd6 32. Nd1 f6 33. Kd3
Ne7 34. c4 h4 35. b4 hg 36. hg
b6 37. Ne3 Nc6 38. Nc2 a5 39. Kc3
ab+ 40. ab Nb8 41. Nd4 Na6
42. Kb3 Nc7

DRAW

******

136. Bronstein—Szabo
(Nimzoindian Defense)

1.	d2-d4	Ng8-f6
2.	c2-c4	e7-e6
3.	Nb1-c3	Bf8-b4
4.	Ng1-f3	c7-c5
5.	e2-e3	0-0
6.	Bf1-e2	...

Since the main variation with
6 Bd3 gives White neither the
push e3-e4 nor a mating attack
on the b1-h7 diagonal, he leaves
the d-file open.

6.	...	d7-d5
7.	0-0	Nb8-c6
8.	c4:d5	...

This trade reveals White's
intentions:

I. 8..N:d5 9 N:d5 ed 10 a3 Ba5
11 dc

II. 8..N:d5 9 N:d5 Q:d5 10 a3
Ba5 11 dc Q:c5 12 b4.

Black must therefore submit to
an isolated pawn, which gives
White a small but secure advantage after 8..ed 9 dc B:c5 10 a3
or 10 b3. The author's idea was
adopted successfully by Gligoric
in a later game against Euwe.

8.	...	c5:d4
9.	d5:c6	d4:c3
10.	Qd1-b3	...

Every chess primer teaches the
importance of controlling the
long diagonal, which is why nei-

ther side wishes to capture the
other's b-pawn. However, White
is a move ahead, and Szabo, like
it or not, must finally give way.

10.	...	Qd8-e7

It would have been better to
maintain the symmetry by the
sacrifice of a pawn with 10..Qb6.
Now White secures a sizable advantage with a curious knight
maneuver.

11.	Nf3-e5	Bb4-d6
12.	Ne5-c4	c3:b2
13.	Bc1:b2	Bd6-c5

Now that the position has
opened up, it would make no
sense at all for Black to give
up his better bishop for the
knight.

14.	Be2-f3	Nf6-d5
15.	Nc4-e5	b7:c6

16.	e3-e4	...

Taking on c6 with the knight
was better, leaving Black's
queen with no good square: 16 N:c6
Qd6 17 e4 or 16..Qc7 17 B:d5 ed
18 Qc3. I failed to see that, on
16..Qg5, 17 h4 wins.

16.	...	Nd5-f6
17.	Rf1-c1	Bc8-d7
18.	Qb3-c3	Bc5-b4
19.	Ne5:c6	Bd7:c6
20.	Qc3:c6	...

A series of exchanges has left
White with the pure form of the
two-bishop advantage.

20.	...	Ra8-d8
21.	Rc1-c4	Rd8-d2
22.	Bb2-c1	Rd2-d7
23.	Bc1-e3	Bb4-d6
24.	Qc6-a6	Rf8-d8
25.	Ra1-b1	Nf6-e8
26.	g2-g3	Bd6-e5
27.	Kg1-g2	h7-h6

One cannot maneuver forever. While there is still time, both sides improve the positions of their kings.

28.	Rc4-b4	Kg8-h7
29.	Rb4-b7	Ne8-d6

The only way to save the a-pawn, but the knight is doubly pinned on the d-file.

30.	Rb7:d7	Rd8:d7
31.	Be3-c5	Rd7-c7
32.	Bc5-a3	...

Once more White fails to rise to the occasion. The pin on the knight could have been strengthened by 32 Qa3.

32.	...	Qe7-d7
33.	Rb1-c1	Rc7:c1
34.	Ba3:c1	Be5-d4
35.	e4-e5	...

A pawn sacrifice to keep the initiative. Black's sole weakness is the a-pawn, so Black's bishop must be pulled off the g1-a7 diagonal at any cost.

35.	...	Bd4:e5
36.	Bc1-e3	Nd6-c8
37.	a2-a4	...

It is very important for White that he get this pawn to a5, depriving Black's pieces of the square b6. Black puts his bishop on b8 in order to free his knight on c8 — but that's six of one, half a dozen of the other...

37.	...	Be5-b8
38.	a4-a5	Nc8-d6

After 37..Ne7 38 Bb7, the a-pawn would fall; now the knight gets pinned again.

39.	Be3-f4	f7-f6
40.	Qa6-d3+	Kh7-g8
41.	a5-a6	...

Nailing the a7-pawn in place. Now the outcome of the game

hinges on whether White has the means to prevent ..e6-e5.

41.	...	Kg8-h8
42.	Qd3-b3	...

Beginning an uninterrupted assault by the queen and the lightsquare bishop. White is determined to force ..f6-f5, while Szabo is playing for ..e6-e5.

42.	...	Qd7-e8
43.	Bf3-h5	...

A combination based on the theme of overloading the queen: one black pawn must fall.

43.	...	Qe8-g8
44.	Bh5-f7	...

44.	-...	Qg8:f7
45.	Qb3:b8+	Nd6-e8
46.	Qb8-b7	...

This shows the usefulness of that white pawn at a6. Curiously, both white bishops end up behind black pawns.

46.	...	Qf7-h5
47.	h2-h3	Kh8-h7
48.	Qb7:a7	e6-e5
49.	Bf4-e3	e5-e4
50.	Qa7-e7	...

BLACK RESIGNED

******

137. Reshevsky—Euwe
(Nimzoindian Defense)

In Game 17 against Averbakh, Reshevsky was unable to solve

his defensive problems in the
opening; so he decided to employ
a similar system here as White.
He had to wait quite a while —
from the third to the twen-
tieth round — since no one
wanted to play the main-line
Nimzo-Indian against him.

1.	d2-d4	Ng8-f6
2.	c2-c4	e7-e6
3.	Nb1-c3	Bf8-b4
4.	e2-e3	c7-c5
5.	Bf1-d3	d7-d5
6.	Ng1-f3	0-0
7.	0-0	Nb8-c6
8.	a2-a3	Bb4:c3
9.	b2:c3	d5:c4
10.	Bd3:c4	Qd8-c7
11.	Rf1-e1	e6-e5

Reshevsky played 11..Rd8 against
Averbakh, in order to prevent 12d5,
but Euwe does not consider this
push to be dangerous, and he may
be right.

12.	d4-d5	e5-e4

Euwe had an energetic counterblow ready, but there was no
need for it. Simply moving the
knight to a5 would have left the
d5-pawn in a precarious position,
cut off from its own camp. For
example, 12..Na5 13 d6 Qc6 14 N:e5
Qe4 recovers the pawn with good
play. Also possible is Euwe's
postmortem suggestion of 13..Qb6
14 N:e5 N:c4 15 N:c4 Qa6.

13.	d5:c6	e4:f3
14.	Qd1:f3	Bc8-g4
15.	Qf3-g3	Qc7:c6

White holds his usual small
positional advantage in this
variation: a kingside pawn majority, which can drive the black
knight from f6, after which the
bishop-pair will have attacking
prospects against the king. As
for Black's extra pawn on the
queenside, that must wait for
an endgame.

16.	e3-e4	Bg4-h5
17.	e4-e5	Nf6-d5
18.	a3-a4	a7-a6

Euwe resolutely undertook the
maneuver ..Bg4-h5-g6 in order to
cover his king, anticipating the
coming attack; but then he failed
to carry it through, beginning
another plan instead: ..a7-a6
and ..b7-b5. The bishop, left

untended, allows White the
opportunity for an interesting
maneuver of his own. Better to
complete one plan (by playing
..Bg6 now or after ..Nc7) before beginning another.

19.	a4-a5	b7-b5
20.	a5:b6	Nd5:b6
21.	Ra1:a6	Ra8:a6
22.	Bc4:a6	...

Not everyone would decide to
take such a pawn: after 22..c4,
23..Nd5 is threatened, or
23..Ra8, and the bishop might
disappear in a wink. But Reshevsky is prepared, if he sees
a chance to win, to think it
over for two hours and twenty-
five minutes, if it means he
will then be able to exploit
that chance and fashion a win
out of it.

22.	...	c5-c4
23.	Qg3-h4	...

Thus, Reshevsky exploits the
undefended black bishop. If
now 23..Bg6 24 Be3, and Black
will be in trouble; so Euwe
forces matters.

23.	...	Rf8-a8
24.	Bc1-e3	h7-h6
25.	Qh4:h5	Ra8:a6
26.	Be3-d4	Nb6-d5

Now the game enters a new
phase, wherein Black, despite
his pawn minus, has fair drawing chances, especially if the
queens are exchanged. The problem for White is that he only
has one bishop now, and that one

not the better of the two, since his pawns stand on dark squares; additionally, White has a weak pawn at c3, and Black has the more active rook.

White, in turn, can prepare and carry out a maneuver to extend his bishop's diagonal: pushing his e-pawn to e6 when the time is right. This advance will be even stronger if the f-pawn gets to f5 first.

These are the underlying motifs of the struggle that follows.

27.	Qh5-g4	Qc6-e6
28.	Qg4-f3	Nd5-e7
29.	h2-h3	...

Rather slow: invading b7 immediately with the queen promised more.

29.	...	Qe6-d5

Now White must trade, since 30..Rg6 is threatened. After the exchange of queens, Black's task is much simplified.

30.	Qf3:d5	Ne7:d5
31.	g2-g3	Nd5-c7

This destroys the fruits of his dogged defense. The obvious 31..Ra3 would have yielded sizable drawing chances. Euwe gives the following variation: 31..Ra3 32 e6 fe 33 R:e6 N:c3 34 Re7 Kf8! 35 Bc5! Ra5! 36 Rc7+ Kg8 37 Bb4 Ra1+ 38 Kg2 Nd5, which secures Black the draw.

32.	Re1-b1	...

This flanking maneuver and subsequent infiltration of the rook to the seventh rank decides the game in short order.

32.	...	Nc7-e6
33.	Rb1-b8+	Kg8-h7
34.	Rb8-c8	Ra6-a4
35.	Bd4-e3	Ne6-g5
36.	Kg1-g2	Ng5-e4
37.	Be3-d4	Ne4-d2
38.	e5-e6	...

This breakthrough, properly timed, sets up an irresistible threat of mate.

38.	...	f7:e6
39.	Rc8-c7	Kh7-g6

40.	g3-g4	...

BLACK RESIGNED

******

138. Keres—Stahlberg
(Queen's Gambit)

1.	d2-d4	Ng8-f6
2.	c2-c4	e7-e6
3.	Nb1-c3	d7-d5
4.	Bc1-g5	Bf8-e7
5.	e2-e3	Nb8-d7
6.	Ng1-f3	0-0
7.	Qd1-c2	c7-c6
8.	Ra1-d1	Rf8-e8
9.	a2-a3	d5:c4
10.	Bf1:c4	Nf6-d5
11.	Bg5:e7	Qd8:e7
12.	0-0	Nd5:c3
13.	Qc2:c3	b7-b6
14.	Nf3-e5	...

The exchange of bishops and knights has simplified Black's position; now, by preparing ..c6-c5, he wishes to solve Black's basic problem in the Orthodox Defense: the development of his queen's bishop. White has several different ways to proceed here. One good line involves placing his rook on e1, and pushing his e-pawn to e4, meeting ..c5 with d4-d5. He may also retreat the bishop to a2, and bring his rooks to the c-file. Keres likes to set his knights in central positions, and occasionally succeeds with an attack based on such favorable placement.

Exchanging knights at e5 might tempt Black — in fact, if all the pieces could be cleared from the board then, the pawn ending would be much superior for him, perhaps even a win, thanks to his three-to-two on the queen-side. However, no one has yet found the way to remove all the pieces. After 14..N:e5 15 de Bb7 16 Rd6, White occupies d6 and the rest of the file as well. The exchange of rooks could only take place on d6 after that, and White would recapture with his pawn, obtaining a powerful passed pawn.

So Black develops his bishop first, which creates a threat to trade knights, since after 14..Bb7 15 Ba2 N:e5 16 de Rad8!, for instance, the d-file would become a trading-ground.

14.	...	Bc8-b7
15.	f2-f4	Nd7:e5
16.	f4:e5	c6-c5

Certainly the opening has been a success for Black: having secured full equality, he now enters an engrossing full-scale battle, despite the rather slim material available. He has two open files at his disposal (c- and d-), while White has only one (the f-).

Open files are important when they contain targets, or when they serve as avenues of communication for the transfer of pieces, usually rooks, to the main theater of action. In this case, the f-file satisfies both conditions; more importantly, however, it lies close to the king, which makes Stahlberg nervous.

The Swedish grandmaster decides to swing his bishop over to the defense of the king's wing via e4, and thereafter to concentrate on his attack against the d-pawn and on using the c-file for flanking maneuvers against the white king. Such a plan is certainly feasible, but I do think Black would have obtained more from the position if he had exchanged on d4 immediately, and then tried to invade the second rank with his rooks. His threats against g2 might have curtailed the activities of the white rooks.

17.	Qc3-e1	Bb7-e4
18.	Rf1-f4	Be4-g6
19.	h2-h4	c5:d4
20.	e3:d4	Ra8-c8
21.	Qe1-e2	Rc8-c7

Naturally, it would have made no sense for Black to trade off his bishop with 21..Bh5 22 Q:h5 R:c4, since that piece traveled here for the express purpose of protecting his king. After 23 Rd3, White's attack gets there first.

| 22. | Rd1-f1 | ... |

(See diagram, next column)

| 22. | ... | h7-h5 |

Such moves can and should only be played when there is no longer any other way to defend the king. Here Black had wholly sufficient — and not quite so violent — means: 22..Rec8 23 Ba6 Rc2 24 Qf3 Rf8, and if 25 h5 Bf5 26 g4 Qh4.

23.	Rf1-f3	Re8-c8
24.	Bc4-d3	Bg6:d3
25.	Rf3:d3	g7-g6

Black's pawn at h5 has drawn the g-pawn after it, and already White's pieces are preparing to invade on the weakened squares h6, g5 and f6.

| 26. | Rd3-g3 | Kg8-h7 |

Now the forcing play begins: 27 Q:h5 was threatened, and White's next move sets up the threat of 28 R:h5+.

27.	Rg3-g5	Qe7-f8
28.	Qe2-e4	Qf8-h6
29.	d4-d5	...

Keres rushes to crown his heavy-piece attack with this pawn breakthrough, but in so doing, he gives his opponent a counterchance. 29 Rf6 was correct, nailing the kingside down, after which there would no longer be a defense to the threat of 30 Qf4 and 31 d5!

[230]

29.	...	e6:d5
30.	Qe4:d5	Qh6-f8
31.	e5-e6	...

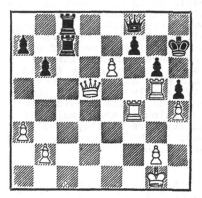

| 31. | ... | Qf8-c5+ |

Psychologically speaking, one can understand why Black should seize the first opportunity to exchange queens and rid himself of White's mating threats, but the resulting endgame is hopeless for him. 31..f5 instead would have given him good drawing chances.

In order to keep his attack from flickering out, Keres would probably have sacrificed a rook at f5, but after 32 Rf:f5 gf 33 R:h5+ Kg6 34 Rg5+ Kh6, White appears to have no better move than 35 Qf3, when Black could reply 35..Rc1+ 36 Kh2 Qd6+ 37 g3 Qd2+, forcing an approximately even ending after 38 Kh3 Q:g5 39 hg+ K:g5 40 e7 Rh8+ 41 Kg2 Rc2+ 42 Kg1 Rc1+, etc.

32.	Qd5:c5	b6:c5
33.	e6:f7	Kh7-g7
34.	f7-f8Q+	Rc8:f8
35.	Rf4:f8	Kg7:f8
36.	Rg5:g6	c5-c4
37.	Rg6-g5	Rc7-b7
38.	Rg5:h5	Rb7:b2
39.	Rh5-c5	Rb2-c2
40.	Kg1-h2	Kf8-e7
41.	h4-h5	c4-c3
42.	Rc5-c6	...

BLACK RESIGNED

******

139. Smyslov—Boleslavksy
(King's Indian)

1. d4 Nf6 2. Nf3 g6 3. Bf4 Bg7 4. Nbd2 d6 5. h3 0-0 6. e3

An unusual system against the King's Indian, which Smyslov employs whenever he does not want to give Black the slightest chance of obtaining an initiative. White firmly anchors his d4-pawn, and controls e5 three times, preventing Black from carrying out the traditional King's Indian advance, ..e7-e5. 5 h3 is thrown in to safeguard the queen's bishop against possible exchange via ..Nh5.

In this game, Boleslavsky demonstrates the best method of combating this solid, although rather indolent, system: he plays ..c7-c5, occupies the c-file, and builds a barricade of pawns before the darksquare bishop. Any other course would have left Black in the throes of a positional squeeze.

6..c5 7. Be2 Nc6 8. Bh2

No one was chasing it! 8 c3 was more in the spirit of the system, intending to recapture at d4 with the c-pawn.

8..cd 9. ed Bd7 10. 0-0 Rc8 11. Re1 a6 12. Bf1 b5 13. c3 Na5 14. Ng5 Re8 15. Nde4 N:e4 16. N:e4 Nc4 17. Rb1

DRAW

******

140. Geller—Kotov
(Nimzoindian Defense)

1.	d2-d4	Ng8-f6
2.	c2-c4	e7-e6
3.	Nb1-c3	Bf8-b4
4.	e2-e3	c7-c5
5.	Bf1-d3	0-0
6.	Ng1-f3	d7-d5
7.	0-0	Nb8-c6
8.	a2-a3	Bb4:c3
9.	b2:c3	d5:c4
10.	Bd3:c4	Qd8-c7
11.	Qd1-c2	e6-e5
12.	Bc4-a2	Bc8-g4
13.	Nf3:e5	...

Geller has repeated the opening of Game 54, Taimanov - Euwe;

but, having learned from White's
unfortunate experience with
13 d5, he uses a different continuation here, intending e3-e4.

13.	...	Nc6:e5
14.	d4:e5	Qc7:e5
15.	e3-e4	...

A sharp and original idea: exploiting the bishop's temporary
position at g4 to push his pawn
to e4 without the support of his
minor pieces. White could right-
fully lay claim to a strategic
victory — if he could also secure the advance of his f-pawn
two squares. However, since he
has to keep f2-f3 in reserve in
order to prevent Black from picking off the e-pawn, White's only
pawn in the center will be pretty
shaky. This shows, for instance,
in the fact that White cannot reply to Black's next move, 15..Rfe8,
with the natural 16 Re1 in view
of 16..N:e4! 17 f3 Q:c3 18 Q:c3
N:c3 19 R:e8+ R:e8 20 fg Re1+
21 Kf2 Re2+ 22 Kf3 R:a2. In this
line, 20..N:a2, recommended by
some commentators, does not work,
since White, instead of taking
the knight, plays 21 Bd2!, when
the knight remains trapped.

| 15. | ... | Rf8-e8 |
| 16. | Ba2-b1 | ... |

This would have some point, if
there were any way at all of en-
forcing f2-f4.

16.	...	Ra8-d8
17.	f2-f3	Bg4-d7
18.	Bc1-b2	Bd7-c6

19.	Bb1-a2	Nf6-h5
20.	Ra1-d1	Nh5-f4
21.	Rd1-d2	...

While White has spent his time
maneuvering bishops, Black has
brought his knight to a strong
position. The laws of chess allow
that it may be driven off with
a pawn move, but the laws of
strategy categorically forbid
such a move as 21 g3, since this
would fatally weaken the second
rank. Thus, White should have
begun thinking about maintaining
equality here by playing 21 Bc1
since, to White's great good fortune, 21..Bb5 still does not
work.

Geller is unwilling to believe
that he does not have the better
game, and so he seeks to gain
the upper hand on the d-file,
which allows Kotov to carry out
a beautiful combination on the
themes of deflection of the
queen and cooperation of queen
and knight. We have already mentioned that queen and knight can
sometimes be stronger than queen
and bishop, and occasionally they
are no weaker than queen and rook.
This will be easier to comprehend
if one bears in mind that the bishop's capabilities parallel
the queen's, while the knight's
complement them.

| 21. | ... | Bc6-a4 |

Prelude. This drives the queen
into a dark cell, where it may be
attacked by a knight from either
d3 or e2.

| 22. | Qc2-c1 | Qe5-g5 |

(See diagram, next page)

[232]

Now the threat is 23..R:d2 and 24..Nh3+. If 23 Kh1, then 23..Nd3, and White has to give up the exchange.

| 23. | Ba2-d5 | Nf4:d5 |

Black has the better position, and now wins a pawn. He might have tried to exploit the active position of his pieces another way, by 23..R:d5 24 ed Re2, etc.

| 24. | e4:d5 | Rd8:d5 |
| 25. | Rd2:d5 | Qg5:d5 |

26.	c3-c4	Qd5-d3
27.	Rf1-e1	f7-f6
28.	Re1:e8+	Ba4:e8
29.	Qc1-c3	Qd3-e2
30.	Bb2-c1	Be8-f7
31.	Qc3-d2	Qe2-e7

Black declines the trade of queens, in view of 31..Q:d2 32 B:d2 B:c4 33 Be3; and after White induces ..b7-b6, his bishop can attack the black pawns from behind. However, he could still have traded queens, but without capturing the c-pawn immediately, continuing instead with 32..Kf8 33 Be3 b6 34 Bf4 Ke7 35 Bb8 Kd7, and if the bishop takes the pawn now, 36..Kc7 catches it!

32.	Qd2-e3	Kg8-f8
33.	h2-h4	Qe7:e3+
34.	Bc1:e3	b7-b6
35.	a3-a4	...

On 35 Bf4, Black returns to the bishop-catching theme with 35..Ke7.

35.	...	Kf8-e7
36.	a4-a5	Bf7:c4
37.	a5:b6	a7:b6
38.	Kg1-f2	Ke7-d6
39.	Be3-f4+	Kd6-c6
40.	Kf2-e3	Bc4-f7
41.	g2-g4	b6-b5

Against two connected passed pawns, White is helpless.

| 42.. | h4-h5 | b5-b4 |

WHITE RESIGNED

******

******

ROUND TWENTY-ONE

141. Kotov—Smyslov
(English Opening)

1. c4 e6 2. Nf3 d5 3. e3 Nf6
4. b3 g6 5. Bb2 Bg7 6. d4 0-0
7. Bd3 c5 8. 0-0 cd 9. N:d4

9 ed was better, to maintain the important center pawn.

9..e5 10. Nb5 a6 11. N5c3 dc
12. B:c4 b5 13. Be2 Bb7 14. Nd2 e4

Black has resolved all of his opening problems well; the only thing left to do now is develop his queen's knight so that he can get into the fight for the c- and d-files. Desiring complications, White plays the double-edged 15 b4, with the idea of getting his knight to c5; however, this allows Black the opportunity to invade at c4. Play now revolves around the following themes: the control and occupation of c4 and c5, the opposition of the bishops on the long diagonal, and the control of the open files.

15. b4 Qe7 16. a3 Rfd8 17. Qc2 Nbd7 18. Nb3 Rac8 19. Rfd1 Nd5

Is it possible that Smyslov actually thought he was winning the pinned white knight? Kotov, unable to believe his eyes, spent forty minutes in thought before taking off the knight with his rook.

20. R:d5 B:c3

Smyslov does not see that he is losing two pieces for a rook. The knight had to be removed by other means: 20..R:c3 21 B:c3 B:d5. White would not relish 21 R:d7 R:c2 22 R:e7 R:b2 23 R:b7 R:b3, as this would come nearer to favoring Black. White's best line would be 20..R:c3 21 B:c3 B:d5 22 B:g7 K:g7 23 Rc1, maintaining some advantage.

21. R:d7! R:d7

Smyslov had seen 21 R:d7, of course; what he probably had not seen was that 21..B:b2 is met by 22 R:d8+.

22. B:c3 Bd5 23. Nc5 Rd6 24. Bb2 f6 25. Bd4 Qf7 26. h3 Re8 27. Rc1 h5 28. a4 f5 29. Bb2 Kh7 30. Qc3 Bc4 31. B:c4 bc 32. Q:c4 Rd1+ 33. Kh2 Q:c4 34. R:c4 Rd2 35. Bf6 R:f2 36. Rd4 f4 37. Rd7+ Kh6 38. h4 g5 39. B:g5+ Kg6 40. B:f4

BLACK RESIGNED

******

142. Boleslavsky—Keres
(Ruy Lopez)

1.	e2-e4	e7-e5
2.	Ng1-f3	Nb8-c6
3.	Bf1-b5	a7-a6
4.	Bb5-a4	Ng8-f6
5.	0-0	Bf8-e7
6.	Rf1-e1	b7-b5
7.	Ba4-b3	0-0
8.	c2-c3	d7-d6
9.	h2-h3	Nc6-a5
10.	Bb3-c2	c7-c5
11.	d2-d4	Qd8-c7
12.	Nb1-d2	Rf8-d8

Introducing a variation Keres prepared especially for this game. The point behind this move is that on 12..Bb7 White usually closes up the center with 13 d5, leaving the bishop nothing better to do than return to c8. After 12..Re8 13 de is possible, when the black rook eventually goes to the d-file. But after this move it would make no sense at all for White to play either 13 d5 (while the bishop still stands on c8) or 13 de (since the rook is already on the d-file). So instead White continues the traditional knight's tour, from b1 via d2 and f1 to g3 or e3.

13. Nd2-f1   d6-d5!

And here is the novelty Keres prepared. The position this creates cannot be exhaustively analyzed, since every move gives rise to three or four different possibilities, none worse than any other. So a calculation five moves deep would entail checking out around twenty thousand variations, stopping periodically along the way to decide whether this or that intermediate position would favor one side or the other. Such a calculation could probably be performed only by a computer — but a computer does not possess intuition.

If we try to evaluate the position on the basis of general principles, we conclude that White has good attacking chances: both his bishops, both his knights, and his queen can be mobilized quickly to the battlefield, while the rook hinders the black king's flight. There are only two tactical counterchances for Black that we can see: his queen attacks the bishop on c2, and his rook may eventually threaten the white queen.

Therefore, there has to be a line White can play that will give these possibilities concrete expression. In that case, why does 12..Rd8, and the whole variation, deserve an exclamation mark? It's for Keres' astute psychological preparations. Knowing beforehand what line

was to be played, he set Boleslavsky the sort of problem that would be very difficult to solve over the board. Under these circumstances, Keres ran no great risk of losing, while his winning chances were very good indeed.

14.   e4:d5   ...

Master Vasiukov later suggested a clever solution: 14 de de 15 N1d2! ef 16 ef B:f6 17 Q:f3 Be6 18 Ne4 Be7 19 Qh5, or 14..N:e4 15 Ne3! Be6 16 Qe2.

14.   ...   e5:d4
15.   c3:d4   Nf6:d5
16.   Qd1-e2   Bc8-b7
17.   Nf1-g3   c5:d4
18.   Nf3:d4   ...

Many commentators thought this move a waste of time, and recommended 18 Nf5 instead; but after 18..Bb4 it is not clear just how White is to continue the attack, not just for the sake of attacking, but in order to win. There was a loss of time, true, but not here; 16 Qe2, as played, instead of the correct 16 Ng5.

18.   ...   g7-g6

Simple and good. White threatened to bring in his knights at f5 or h5, and then to reinforce them with the queen. By this one modest move, Keres immediately solves several defensive problems by depriving White's pieces of the f5 and h5 squares. Bear in mind that White's advantage is of a temporary sort, and that if it is not put into some concrete form within the next two or three moves, Black will bring up his reserve (the knight on a5) to solidify his king's position. After Black's powerful move, I don't believe Boleslavsky had any way to continue his attack other than 19 Ndf5! If Black takes the knight, he:

1) opens the g-file,

2) opens the b1-h7 diagonal,

3) lets the queen get to h5, and most importantly,

4) must tolerate a white knight at f5 anyway!

If Black could defend himself
successfully in this line, then
already there was nothing to be
done for White! But in that case
Keres would also have had no
easy time of it, whereas here
White's game worsens move by
move.

19.	Bc1-h6	Be7-f6
20.	Nd4-b3	Na5-c4
21.	Ng3-e4	Bf6:b2
22.	Nb3-c5	...

White decides to give up the
exchange, since after 22 Rab1 or
22 Rad1 Black's piece pressure
against the queenside would
have been unbearable.

22.	...	Bb2:a1
23.	Re1:a1	f7-f5
24.	Nc5:b7	Qc7:b7
25.	Ne4-c5	Qb7-c6
26.	Nc5-d3	Nd5-c3
27.	Qe2-e1	Qc6-f6
28.	f2-f4	Nc3-e4
29.	Kg1-h2	Qf6-c3
30.	Qe1-b1	Nc4-d2
31.	Qb1-c1	Rd8:d3
32.	Bc2:d3	Qc3:d3
33.	Qc1-c7	Nd2-f3+!

WHITE RESIGNED

******

143. Stahlberg—Reshevsky
(King's Indian)

Even among the strongest of
the contemporary masters, we still
find the sort of player who is
far stronger with the white
pieces than with the black. With
Black, such a player thinks
about getting a draw from the
opening moves. When he has
White, certain positions inspire
in him flights of fancy, and a
desire to win at any cost; when
he has Black, the same positions
seem to inspire nothing but bore-
dom, and calculations aimed at
"equalizing". This quality is
a strong characteristic in
Reshevsky, which the reader will
note for himself from a study of
his games. I will mention only
this statistic: in this tournament, Reshevsky won seven games
with White, lost only one and
drew six; while with Black, he
could only win one, losing three
and drawing ten!

In the present game Reshevsky

played dull chess, not even attempting to make use of the
counterchances inherent in the
King's Indian Defense.

1. d4 Nf6 2. c4 g6 3. g3 Bg7
4. Bg2 0-0 5. Nc3 d6 6. Nf3
Nbd7 7. 0-0 e5 8. e4 ed 9. N:d4
Re8 10. h3 Nc5 11. Re1 a5 12. Qc2
Ng4

Up to here, everything has
gone according to theory. In
Game 131, Averbakh - Bronstein,
White continued 13 Rd1. After
the text move, 13 Nb3, Reshevsky could have stirred up a
sharp fight with 13..Ne5.

13. Nb3 N:b3 14. ab Ne5 15. Be3
Nc6 16. Rad1 Nb4 17. Qc1

17 Qd2 was much more active
here, intending f2-f4 and Qf2.

17..Bd7 18. Kh2 Qe7 19. f4
Bc6 20. Qd2 Qf8 21. Qf2 f5
22. Bd4 B:d4 23. R:d4 Qf6 24. Rd2
Re7 25. ef R:e1 26. Q:e1 Re8
27. Re2 R:e2 28. Q:e2 Q:f5
29. B:c6 bc 30. Qe7 Qf7 31. Qe3
Qf5 32. Qe7 Qf7 33. Qe3 Qf5
34. Qe7

DRAW

******

144. Euwe—Bronstein
(Dutch Defense)

| 1. | d2-d4 | e7-e6 |
| 2. | c2-c4 | f7-f5 |

What else but 2..f5 against
the Dutch champion? However,
this failed to surprise him;
after a few introductory moves
the game took on the aspect of
a theoretical discussion.

3.	g2-g3	Ng8-f6
4.	Bf1-g2	Bf8-e7
5.	Ng1-f3	0-0
6.	0-0	d7-d6
7.	Nb1-c3	Qd8-e8
8.	Rf1-e1	...

An old continuation which has
been resurrected, thanks to the
discovery of the rook sacrifice
at e4.

| 8. | ... | Qe8-g6 |
| 9. | e2-e4 | ... |

Some theoreticians believe this

move opens the e-file; chess practitioners, however, know that two files are opened: the e-file for White and the f-file for Black as well. The player who is the first to reap some tangible benefit from "his" file gains the initiative.

```
 9.   ...        Nf6:e4
10.   Nc3:e4     f5:e4
11.   Re1:e4     ...
```

```
11.   ...        e6-e5
```

Of course Black will not take the rook (11..Q:e4? 12 Nh4!), sacrificing a pawn instead, for the sake of quick development. The correctness of the sacrifice would be fully tested, not by its acceptance, but by the quiet retreat 12 Re1; however, White has other ideas.

```
12.   Qd1-e2     Bc8-f5
13.   Nf3-h4     ...
```

Euwe probably underestimated Black's position. White's desire to trade off one of the bishops is wholly understandable, but the rook will not be well placed at h4.

```
13.   ...        Be7:h4
14.   Re4:h4     Nb8-c6
```

White's position is now a trifle difficult. If he gives up his fianchettoed bishop for the black knight, his light squares will become weak, but how else can he defend the d4 square? 15 Be3 seems the simplest solution, but after 15..Bd3 16 Bd5+

Kh8, Black would have the initiative. White decides to exchange pawns.

```
15.   d4:e5     d6:e5
```

After playing the opening sharply, Black is unable to make the switch to positional chess quickly enough; the knight recapture, followed by ..Rae8, was better.

```
16.   Bc1-e3    Ra8-d8
17.   Be3-c5    Rf8-e8
18.   Bg2-d5+   ...
```

White's bishops have found the opportunity to display their powers.

```
18.   ...       Kg8-h8
19.   Qe2-h5    ...
```

A prelude to interesting complications.

```
19.   ...       Qg6:h5
20.   Rh4:h5    g7-g6
21.   Rh5:f5!   g6:f5
22.   Bd5-f7    ...
```

Now Black faces a difficult decision: which of the white bishops is more valuable? After lengthy consideration, he decided to take the darksquare bishop, chiefly because of the possibility of invading at d2 with his rook.

(See diagram, next page)

22.	....	Re8-e7
23.	Bc5:e7	Nc6:e7
24.	Bf7-h5	...

The only possibility. Now
24..Rd2 would be met by 25 Rd1,
and if 25..R:b2 26 Rd7. The
question is whether Black will
have time to play ..e4 and bring
his king directly to the center
via g7-f6-e5. He begins this
plan with great expectations,
but meets with a clever riposte.

24.	...	Ne7-c6
25.	Ra1-d1	Nc6-d4
26.	Rd1-e1	e5-e4

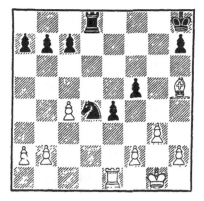

The thought of accepting the
repetition by 26..Nc6 27 Rd1 Nd4
28 Re1 was repellent, but Euwe
elegantly demonstrates that this
courageous pawn push also cannot
alter the outcome.

27.	f2-f3	Nd4-c2
28.	Re1-c1	...

DRAW

The invasion at c2 with the
knight was thoughtless, of course.
Time-pressure was not a factor
yet, and there was no reason for
me to suppose that Euwe had decided to hand me the game with
his 27 f3. Indeed, after 27..Nc2
28 Re2 is bad because of 28..Rd1+;
consequently, I should have giv-
en more thought to 28 Rc1. Instead, I glanced over two variations: 28 Rc1 Rd2 29 fe fe, and
28 Rc1 e3 29 R:c2 Rd1+ 30 Kg2
Rd2+. Both seemed to have their
good points, and so I decided to
postpone the final decision until after White's reply.

The choice, however, turned
out to be a difficult one. In
the first line, after 30 Rd1!,
White gets the better endgame;
in the second line, after 31 R:d2
ed, the d-pawn never queens at
all, as Black hoped, in view of
the simple 32 f4, when White
still has his bishop, while
Black no longer has his knight.
So 28..Nb4 would probably have
been correct, but after that it
would have been White's turn to
assume the offensive. Quite evidently, Euwe was feeling peaceable that day. All's well that
ends well.

******

145. Szabo—Gligoric
(English Opening)

Saying something like " the
contemporary way of handling the
opening" still does not explain
how the opening was played. Sometimes, the opening is sharp, and
the first mistake decides the
outcome. In this case, both sides
reveal their plans at the outset:
one attacks, let's say, on the
kingside, while the other does
the same on the queenside. This
has always been one of the most
popular scenarios, in our day
as much as it was in the past.

In the present game, we meet
a new approach, one which has
begun appearing relatively recently in tournaments, and which
Konstantinopolsky aptly termed
"the clash of openings". Both
sides bring their troops out

according to a chosen scheme, making no contact with the opposition for the moment, and in most cases not crossing the demarcation line between the fourth and fifth ranks.

Such an unhurried attitude, however, frequently foreshadows an interesting game — as it does here.

1.	c2-c4	Ng8-f6
2.	g2-g3	g7-g6
3.	Bf1-g2	Bf8-g7
4.	e2-e4	d7-d6
5.	Ng1-e2	0-0
6.	0-0	c7-c5
7.	Nb1-c3	Nb8-c6
8.	d2-d3	Bc8-d7
9.	h2-h3	Nf6-e8
10.	g3-g4	Ne8-c7
11.	f2-f4	Ra8-b8

A position has been reached which is reminiscent of a Closed Sicilian, with the only difference being that the pawn on c2 has jumped to c4. White's pawns occupy good starting positions for a strong attack on the king. As soon as Szabo plays his 12 f5, Black plays his 12..b5, and — they're off!

12.	f4-f5	b7-b5
13.	Nc3:b5	Nc7:b5
14.	c4:b5	Rb8:b5
15.	Ne2-c3	Rb5-b8
16.	g4-g5	Nc6-e5

On d4 this knight would have blockaded the base of the white pawn chain and controlled more important squares than it does here. Among other things, it would have made White's next move impossible, and forced Szabo to decide what he wants to do with his f-pawn.

17.	Nc3-d5	e7-e6
18.	f5-f6	e6:d5
19.	f6:g7	...

The reader who is thoroughly acquainted with opening theory will recall this "little combination" of White's without difficulty as being similar to one that occurred in a game Milner-Barry - Capablanca. In a similar position, Black recaptured on g7, but some Moscow players later showed that ..Re8 would have been better. Perhaps that would have been the better

move here as well; if then 20 d4 cd 21 Q:d4 de (instead of 21..Qb6) with good counterplay.

| 19. | ... | Kg8:g7 |

| 20. | d3-d4 | ... |

An energetic move in Szabo's characteristic style, leading to a favorable ending for White.

| 20. | ... | c5:d4 |
| 21. | Qd1:d4 | Qd8-b6 |

The exchange of queens is Black's best defense — but not on b6. Why not the maneuver 21..Qc8 (threatening 22..B:h3) 22 Kh2 Qc4, winning a tempo for Black?

22.	Qd4:b6	Rb8:b6
23.	e4:d5	Bd7-f5
24.	b2-b3	f7-f6
25.	Bc1-e3	Rb6-b7
26.	g5:f6+	Kg7:f6
27.	Ra1-c1	...

White can now strike a positional balance: he has the open c-file, the two bishops, and an extra pawn on the queenside; Black has a strongly centralized knight and an extra pawn on the kingside. White will have the easier time trying to turn his advantages to account, if only because, in such positions:

1) the two bishops can do more than bishop and knight, even when the knight is centralized;

2) White's passed pawn on the a- or b-file will be more dan-

gerous than Black's, since the
latter can easily be stopped
by the white king;

3) the relative weakness of
Black's a- and d-pawns will
be of no small significance.

27.	...	Rf8-e8
28.	Rc1-c3	Rb7-e7
29.	Be3-d4	Kf6-g5
30.	Rc3-g3+	Kg5-f6
31.	Bg2-e4	Re7-f7

A picturesque position. Black's
pieces are all tied up, but White
cannot reap anything tangible
from that, since he is bereft of
pawns precisely where he needs
them, on the f- and g-files.

| 32. | Rg3-c3 | Kf6-g7 |
| 33. | Be4-g2 | ... |

The two bishops should be
treasured, but never hoarded.
After 33 B:f5! gf 34 Rc6, I
don't see how Black will find
a decent defense for the weak
pawns at a7, d6 and f5; for
example: 34..Rd8 35 R:d6 R:d6
36 B:e5+, or 34..Rd7 35 R:f5;
and on 34..Rf6 35 Ra6 or
35 Rc7+ is sufficient. Trading
off a pair of rooks with 33..R:f5
34 R:f5 gf is also bad for Black,
if for no other reason than
35 B:a7.

33.	...	Kg7-f8
34.	b3-b4	Re8-b8
35.	a2-a3	Rb8-b5
36.	Rf1-d1	Rf7-e7
37.	Rc3-e3	Kf8-f7
38.	Rd1-e1	Re7-d7
39.	Re1-c1	...

Szabo again disdains the win
of a pawn, by 39 B:e5 de 40R:e5,
and if 40..a5 41 Bf1 would be
the simplest means of nipping
all possible complications in
the bud. But he does come back
to this idea, all the same, a
few moves later.

39.	...	Ne5-d3
40.	Rc1-f1	Nd3-e5
41.	Rf1-c1	Ne5-d3
42.	Rc1-c8	Nd3-e5
43.	Bd4:e5	...

Here I would no longer want
the pawn: 43 Bf1 Rb7 44 Rec3
looks more convincing.

43.	...	d6:e5
44.	Re3:e5	Kf7-f6
45.	Re5-e3	Kf6-g5
46.	Rc8-c5	Rb5-b8
47.	Kg1-f2	h7-h5
48.	Re3-g3+	Kg5-h6
49.	h3-h4	Rb8-f8
50.	Rg3-f3	Rf8-f7
51.	Rc5-a5	Rd7-c7
52.	Kf2-g3	Rc7-c4
53.	Bg2-h3	...

Carelessness. Szabo allowed
Black's rook onto the c-file,
and now he allows it behind his
passed pawn, which makes his
task a bit more complicated.

53.	...	Rf7-g7
54.	d5-d6	Rc4-d4
55.	Bh3:f5	g6:f5+
56.	Kg3-f2	f5-f4!

White apparently forgot such
a possibility existed. Now the
white king must retreat to the
first rank, which practically
nullifies his material advantage.

57.	Ra5-a6	Kh6-g6!
58.	d6-d7+	Kg6-f5
59.	Ra6:a7	Rd4-d2+
60.	Kf2-e1	...

(See diagram, next page)

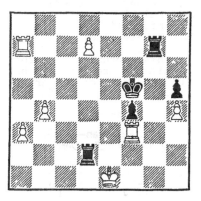

60.   ...   Rg7-g2

..Rg:d7 was probably all right too, but the text move is more convincing. White must now give up his pride and joy, the d-pawn, since Black is threatening ..Ra2, or ..Rge2+ and ..Rh2.

61.   d7-d8Q   Rd2:d8
62.   Ra7-f7+   Kf5-e5
63.   Rf3:f4   Rg2-a2
64.   Rf4-f3   Rd8-d2

The last difficult move of this endgame, which practically seals the draw.

65.   Rf3-f2   Rd2:f2
66.   Rf7:f2   Ra2:a3
67.   Rf2-g2   Ra3-a1+
68.   Ke1-f2   Ra1-a2+
69.   Kf2-g1   Ra2-a1+
70.   Kg1-f2   Ra1-a2+
71.   Kf2-g1   Ra2-a1+
72.   Kg1-h2   Ra1-b1
73.   Rg2-g5+   Ke5-f4
74.   b4-b5   Kf4-f3

DRAW

*****

146. Averbakh—Taimanov
(Sicilian Defense)

1.   e2-e4   c7-c5
2.   Ng1-f3   Nb8-c6
3.   d2-d4   c5:d4
4.   Nf3:d4   Ng8-f6
5.   Nb1-c3   d7-d6
6.   Bf1-c4   ...

White gives notice of his intent to break down the impregnable "Sicilian" center by means

of a direct attack, which is one of the strategic ideas behind the move 6 Bc4. One must also keep the human factor in mind: Averbakh is hot for revenge on Taimanov for their game from the first half.

6.   ...   e7-e6
7.   0-0   a7-a6
8.   Bc1-e3   Qd8-c7
9.   Bc4-b3   ...

White is spending two moves developing a bishop that Black can easily exchange with ..Nb8-c6-a5:b3, but there is a point to this. The exchanging operation also consumes a great deal of time, leaving White a strong knight at d4, while Black's bishops will not exert much influence for the moment.

9.   ...   Bf8-e7
10.   f2-f4   Nc6-a5
11.   Qd1-f3   b7-b5

This is not Taimanov's first experience with this opening: he played all of this against Lipnitsky in the XX USSR Championship in 1952. There White continued 12 e5 and achieved nothing.

12.   e4-e5!   ...

The exclamation mark is not for the quality of the move, but for Averbakh's courage. In his comments to the Lipnitsky game, Taimanov pointed out the best defensive method for Black, and wrote that White could safely consign the entire variation to the dustbin. Averbakh wants to find a better use for it.

12.   ...   Bc8-b7
13.   Qf3-g3   d6:e5
14.   f4:e5   Nf6-h5
15.   Qg3-h3   ...

On 15 Qf2 Black sacrifices a piece: 15..0-0! 16 g4 N:b3 17 ab Q:e5 18 gh Q:h5, with a very powerful attack.

15.   ...   Qc7:e5

Just what Averbakh was waiting for! It was later established that the correct line is 15..N:b3 16 N:b3 Q:e5 17 Na5, and here neither 17..Bd5 nor 17..Nf6 is any good, but 17..b4! leads to

a highly interesting fight after
18 Nc4 Qc7! 19 Q:h5 0-0 20 Nb6
bc 21 N:a8 B:a8.

| 16. | Bb3:e6! | f7:e6 |

Sometimes this type of pretty
sacrifice can be refuted simply
by castling. Here, however,
16..0-0 runs into 17 Rf5 Nf4
18 R:e5 N:h3+ and the bishop
recaptures at h3.

| 17. | Nd4:e6 | Bb7-c8 |

Black meets the threat of
18 Bd4, but the second threat
remains in force:

| 18. | Qh3:h5+ | Qe5:h5 |
| 19. | Ne6:g7+ | ... |

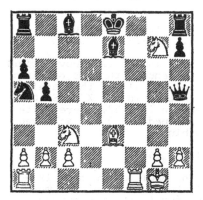

| 19. | ... | Ke8-d7 |
| 20. | Ng7:h5 | ... |

Naturally, two extra pawns
would be enough for White to
win with, but add to that his
attack on the king...

20.	...	Na5-c4
21.	Be3-d4	Rh8-g8
22.	Nc3-d5	Rg8-g5
23.	Nh5-f6+	Be7:f6
24.	Nd5:f6+	Kd7-c6
25.	Nf6:h7	Rg5-g6
26.	Ra1-e1	b5-b4
27.	b2-b3	Nc4-a3
28.	Re1-e5	Na3-b5
29.	Bd4-e3	Nb5-c3
30.	Nh7-f8	...

White's pieces are creeping
closer and closer to the king.

| 30. | ... | Rg6-g7 |

31.	Rf1-f6+	Kc6-c7
32.	Be3-h6	Rg7-g4
33.	Re5-e7+	Kc7-d8
34.	Re7-h7	Ra8-b8
35.	Nf8-e6+!	Bc8:e6
36.	Rf6-f8 mate	

In this tournament, Averbakh
and Taimanov produced two beautiful specimens of the art of
chess.

******

147. Petrosian—Najdorf
(Queen's Indian Defense)

1.	d2-d4	Ng8-f6
2.	c2-c4	e7-e6
3.	Ng1-f3	b7-b6
4.	Nb1-c3	Bc8-b7
5.	e2-e3	Bf8-e7
6.	Bf1-d3	d7-d5

In Game 84, Szabo - Euwe,
which also ended in a quick
draw, Black played 6..c5; 6..d5
makes the game a Queen's Gambit
Declined, with no particular advantages for White.

7.	0-0	0-0
8.	Qd1-e2	Nb8-d7
9.	b2-b3	a7-a6

Black wants his bishop on a
more active square, so he secures it against Nb5.

10.	Bc1-b2	Be7-d6
11.	Ra1-d1	Nf6-e4
12.	c4:d5	e6:d5
13.	Nf3-e5	Qd8-e7
14.	Ne5:d7	Qe7:d7
15.	Nc3-b1!	...

DRAW

The sort of position in which
almost any pawn advance leaves
a weakness, and the pieces
alone are not enough to wrest
an advantage.

******

******

ROUND TWENTY-TWO

148. Najdorf—Averbakh
(Queen's Indian Defense)

Middlegame and endgame cannot be separated, one from the other; in the middlegame — and sometimes even in the opening — the master discerns the outlines of the forthcoming endgame. Many of Averbakh's creations are very logical and consistent because he is such a great authority on, and enthusiast of, the endgame. Here, by moves 12-15 he had already visualized the coming knight vs. bishop endgame, and did everything possible thereafter to assure his knight the best possible working conditions for its struggle against the bishop. We know the knight is strong: a) when the pawns are fixed, b) when it has points of support, and c) when the enemy pawns are on squares of the same color as his bishop.

Averbakh achieves all of this by means of some fine maneuvers, leaving Najdorf in complete zugzwang.

1.	c2-c4	Ng8-f6
2.	Ng1-f3	e7-e6
3.	g2-g3	b7-b6
4.	Bf1-g2	Bc8-b7
5.	0-0	Bf8-e7
6.	d2-d4	0-0
7.	Nb1-c3	Nf6-e4
8.	Qd1-c2	Ne4:c3
9.	b2:c3	...

It has been said that this move weakened the c4-pawn, and that therefore the usual 9 Q:c3 was better. I do not think that such a weakening would have had very much of an effect on the overall pawn mass, had White only taken the status of this pawn (at c4) into account when making his further plans, and not allowed Black to attack it unimpeded. Black's knight will now try to get to a5 via c6, which White should endeavor to meet by the timely posting of his knight to b3. Play could proceed approximately as follows: 9..Nc6 10 Nd2 Na5 11 B:b7 N:b7 12 Nb3. White now plans an immediate advance of his a-pawn to a4 and a5, thus forcing Black to play ..a7-a5 himself, which deprives his knight of that square. Should the knight then try for d6, it would be met by the very pawn it was trying to attack, advancing from c4 to c5.

9.	...	Nb8-c6
10.	Nf3-e5	Nc6-a5
11.	Bg2:b7	Na5:b7
12.	Qc2-a4	...

Of course, this position is far less appealing for White than the one obtained in the preceding variation. The role of pawn-keeper is hardly a becoming one for the queen, and queens may also be exchanged..

12.	...	d7-d6
13.	Ne5-d3	Nb7-a5
14.	c4-c5	Qd8-e8
15.	Qa4:e8	Rf8-e8
16.	Ra1-b1	Re8-c8
17.	h2-h4	d6-d5
18.	Bc1-f4	f7-f6
19.	Nd3-b4	a7-a6
20.	c5:b6	c7:b6
21.	Bf4-d2	...

White has an unenviable position — but why?

1) Above all, because his a2- and c3-pawns are clearly weaker than their opposite numbers at a6 and b6; the c-pawn especially needs constant defense;

2) White's position contains a gaping hole at c4, which Black will find perfectly fitted to his knight, and perhaps to his rook as well;

3) the darksquare bishop is passively placed — compare it with Black's!

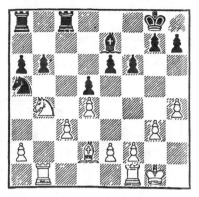

White's only chance is an attack on the weak pawn at b6, but this is illusory, since it can always advance to b5, and the knight on c4 protects it anyway.

Of course, Black cannot hold on to all the advantages his position contains, but he doesn't need them all in order to win. Shortly White eliminates his weakness at c3, but only by entering precisely the sort of endgame Averbakh has been striving for. A more solid position would be obtained by 21 Nd3 Nc4 22 Rfc1 Rc6 23 Kf1.

21.	...	Na5-c4
22.	Bd2-e1	Be7:b4
23.	c3:b4	...

This position must be considered lost for White. Black's pieces now have access into White's camp: soon the rook turns up at c2, where in conjunction with the knight at c4 it completely dominates the surrounding squares.

23.	...	Nc4-a3
24.	Rb1-b3	Na3-b5
25.	e2-e3	Rc8-c2
26.	a2-a4	Nb5-d6
27.	a4-a5	b6-b5

White has nothing better than to make the first offer to exchange rooks, as otherwise there follows 28..Rac8.

28.	Rb3-c3	Ra8-c8
29.	Rc3:c8+	Nd6:c8
30.	f2-f3	Nc8-e7

31.	Be1-f2	...

Hoping that Black will go after the pawn with 31..Rb2 32 Rc1, but Averbakh simply brings up his king.

31.	...	Kg8-f7
32.	Rf1-b1	Ne7-f5
33.	Kg1-f1	Nf5-d6
34.	Rb1-b3	Nd6-c4
35.	Kf1-g2	f6-f5

White is in absolute zugzwang. If 36 f4 Nd2 and 37..Ne4; if 36 e4 fe followed by 37..Nd2 and 38..N:e4; the king cannot move, because of 36..Nd2 and 37..N:f3; and if the rook goes to d3, then 36..Rb2 and 37..R:b4. The move White actually plays allows Black to pick off an important center pawn for nothing, which ends the game for all practical purposes.

36.	Rb3-b1	Nc4:e3+
37.	Kg2-g1	f5-f4
38.	g3:f4	Ne3-f5
39.	Kg1-f1	g7-g6
40.	Rb1-b3	Kf7-e7
41.	Rb3-b1	Ke7-d7

WHITE RESIGNED

After the obvious 42..Rc4, one of the pawns on the fourth rank falls, with more to follow.

******

149. Taimanov—Szabo
(Dutch Defense)

1.	d2-d4	e7-e6
2.	c2-c4	f7-f5
3.	Nb1-c3	Ng8-f6

4.	e2-e3	d7-d5
5.	Bf1-d3	c7-c6
6.	f2-f4	Bf8-e7
7.	Ng1-f3	0-0
8.	0-0	...

An unusual and rarely-seen system, the so-called "Double Stonewall", which once enjoyed great popularity. The blocked state of the center pawns enforces a complex maneuvering game, which gains a measure of sharpness from the positions of the knights at e4 and e5 and the possibility (never actually carried out in this game) of a sudden g2-g4 or ..g7-g5. The position is not wholly symmetrical: White's pawn at c4 gives him some queenside initiative, so Black usually builds on the kingside. Both sides have "bad" queen's bishops, and would be happy to trade them off, even if "only" for knights, or gradually bring them into play on the kingside. These basic motifs underlie the play for the next 8-10 moves.

8.	...	b7-b6
9.	Bc1-d2	Bc8-a6

This move would have had some point, if Black could have traded off the lightsquare bishops, but it quickly becomes clear that he cannot exchange on c4 without giving up the center.

10.	Qd1-e2	...

Since 10..B:c4 11 B:c4 dc 12 Q:c4 would leave serious weaknesses at e6 and c6, the bishop goes right back to b7.

10.	...	Ba6-b7
11.	c4:d5	...

In many such positions it suits White to trade on d5 when Black cannot recapture with the e-pawn. Such a moment occurs now, and Taimanov seizes the c-file.

11.	...	c6:d5
12.	Rf1-c1	...

12 Rac1 was more accurate.

12.	...	a7-a6
13.	Nc3-a4	Nf6-e4
14.	Nf3-e5	Be7-d6
15.	b2-b4	Bd6:e5

This trade is more or less forced, as otherwise it would be difficult for Black to complete the development of his queenside. On 15..Nd7 there could follow 16 Nc6 B:c6 17 R:c6, hitting the bishop at d6 and threatening the a-pawn, as well as 18 Rac1, sealing his control of the open file.

16.	f4:e5	Bb7-c6
17.	Na4-b2	...

Not a proper place for the knight. It should have returned to c3, and traded off the knight on e4 at the earliest convenient moment.

17.	...	Bc6-e8
18.	Rc1-c2	Nb8-d7

Szabo wishes to free himself from the coils of the positional squeeze that now menaces him. If 19 B:a6, then 19..Qg5 threatens 20..Bh5 or 20..N:d2; also, when the bishop leaves a6, Black's rook will be able to invade at a3. So Taimanov declines the pawn.

19.	a2-a4	Qd8-g5
20.	Ra1-f1	...

So the rook ought not to have left here at move 12. In any event, Taimanov is now even with his opponent in time lost (9..Ba6 and 10..Bb7).

20.	...	b6-b5

Szabo cleverly continues his

search for the initiative, once
more offering a pawn: 21 ab ab
22 B:b5 Ra3!, with good chances;
for example: 23 Bd3 Bh5 24 Qe1
Rfa8.

Thus, a not overly prolonged
maneuvering stage is followed
by a period during which combinative motifs appear more and more
frequently.

21.	a4-a5	Be8-h5
22.	Qe2-e1	Rf8-d8
23.	Rc2-c6	Nd7-f8
24.	Bd3-b1	Rd8-c8
25.	Rc6:c8	Ra8:c8
26.	Nb2-d3	Nf8-d7

Black's active play has reaped
some not inconsiderable positional fruits: his "inferior" lightsquare bishop is better developed than the enemy's passive
darksquare bishop, he has wrested
control of the c-file away, and
the threatened Nc5 is not dangerous due to 27 Nc5 Ne:c5 28 bc
Qe7, followed by ..Nd7-b8-c6.

27.	Nd3-f4	Bh5-f7
28.	Bb1:e4	f5:e4
29.	Qe1-b1	Rc8-c4
30.	Rf1-c1	Qg5-f5
31.	Nf4-e2	Bf7-g6
32.	Rc1-f1	Qf5-g5
33.	Ne2-f4	Bg6-f5
34.	Bd2-e1	Nd7-b8
35.	Qb1-b2	Nb8-c6

Black has completed his regrouping and now stands better:
he attacks the b-pawn, and controls the c-file, and his queen
is active too. All that saves
White is the fact that the bishop
is somewhat insecure at f5, since
White's next move sets up a
threat of 37 N:d5 followed by
38 Q:f5.

36.	Qb2-f2	...

Now White wins a pawn by the
threat of 37 N:e6, but remains
with the inferior position. When
the gunfire dies down a bit, we
shall explain why this is so.

36.	...	h7-h6
37.	Nf4:d5	e6:d5
38.	Qf2:f5	Qg5:e3+
39.	Be1-f2	Qe3-g5
40.	Qf5-e6+	Kg8-h7
41.	Qe6:d5	...

41.	...	Qg5-g6

Black refrains from advancing
his e-pawn for the moment, so
as not to give White's queen
access to the kingside.

Now he threatens ..N:b4, ..Rc2,
and ..e4-e3, in this or some
other order. The strength of
Black's position is that his
pieces stand ready to attack
the king, and his pawn at e4
is worth a piece. White's pawn,
by contrast, can only advance:
it supports nothing, and needs
protection itself as well.

These are all general ideas,
however; the actual play here-
abouts requires great accuracy
and farseeing calculation. The
next few moves by both sides
are the best possible — from
the viewpoint of the respective
opponents — since the game was
adjourned at this point, and
resumed after painstaking analysis.

42.	e5-e6	Nc6:b4
43.	Qd5-d6	...

This is stronger than 43 Qd7,
when there would follow 43..e3,
and if 44 B:e3 Qe4, or if 44 Bg3
e2 45 Re1 Qg4. In both these
lines Black wins, as has been
demonstrated by detailed analysis, whose variations run to
the 53rd move; we shall present
only one of them: 44 Bg3 e2
45 Re1 Qg4 46 Qf7 Q:d4+ 47 Kh1

Qd5 48 R:e2 Rc2 49 Qf1 Qd3 50 Re1
Q:f1+ 51 R:f1 Re2 52 Re1 R:e1+
53 B:e1 Nd5, and wins.

43.	...	Nb4-d3
44.	h2-h3	Rc4-c2
45.	Bf2-g3	e4-e3
46.	e6-e7	Qg6-e4
47.	Rf1-f3	e3-e2
48.	Qd6-d7	...

After analyzing the adjourned
position, Taimanov ought to have
realized the seriousness of
Black's counterchances and made
some attempt at reaching a peaceable conclusion. Now was precisely the right time: 48 e8Q!
Q:e8 49 R:d3 e1Q+ 50 B:e1 Q:e1+
51 Kh2 is a forced draw. The
text move not only fails to improve White's winning chances,
but might actually have lost.

| 48. | .... | e2-e1Q+ |

At the last moment, Szabo's
nerves failed him — he may have
been short of time — and he too
failed to see the pretty and
thematic 48..Nf4, when even two
queens would not be enough to
save White from mate. For example:
49 e8Q e1Q+ 50 B:e1 R:g2+ 51 Kh1 Q:f3
or 49 Be1 Rc1 50 e8Q R:e1+ 51 Kh2
Rh1+ 52 K:h1 e1Q+ 53 Kh2 Q:e8, or
49 Qf5+ Q:f5 50 e8Q e1Q+ 51 B:e1
R:g2+ 52 Kf1 Rh2 53 Qe5 Qc2.

49.	Bg3:e1	Rc2:g2+
50.	Kg1:g2	Nd3:e1+
51.	Kg2-f2	...

DRAW

— it's perpetual check. A pret-

ty game, and a complex one.

*****

150. Gligoric—Euwe
(Nimzolndian Defense)

"The basic position of the Nimzo-Indian" (after 1 d4 Nf6 2 c4
e6 3 Nc3 Bb4 4 e3 c5 5 Bd3 d5
6 Nf3 Nc6 7 0-0 0-0) occurred
eleven times in this tournament
prior to this twenty-second
round; of those games, six were
drawn, with the results of the
remaining five favoring Black
slightly.

You will not find Gligoric's
name listed among those who are
considered "main-line enthusi-
asts"; those would be Reshevsky,
Euwe and Averbakh.' For this game
Gligoric came as close to the
main line as he ever did
in the course of the tournament,
but he gave it a different treatment, more like a Queen's Gambit: developing the bishop at e2,
he traded off the center pawns
so as to leave Black an isolated
d5-pawn. The game's chief interest lies in the ebb and flow
of the positional struggle that
revolves around this pawn.

Heavy-piece fighting for an
isolated pawn is one of the central elements of positional play.
Much more is involved than the
simple formula:"White attacks
twice, Black defends twice — and
a draw is the outcome". Woven
into the struggle are such motifs as: pinning the isolated
pawn (should the heavy pieces
defend it from behind), a sudden switch to an attack on the
king, or an attempt to occupy
the seventh rank at some point
when the heavy pieces are tied
to the defense of the isolated
pawn. Isolated pawn endings were
played with great skill by the
classicists Lasker, Capablanca
and Rubinstein. In the present
game, Gligoric and Euwe come
forearmed with their knowledge
of the old masters' legacy.
The reader who immerses himself
in this battle's fine points, who
examines the techniques used here,
and who familiarizes himself with
the basic ideas behind this type
of ending, will have made a great
stride forward in positional play.

The game's concluding phase, a

"four-vs-three" rook endgame, is also of great theoretical interest.

1.	d2-d4	Ng8-f6
2.	c2-c4	e7-e6
3.	Nb1-c3	Bf8-b4
4.	e2-e3	c7-c5
5.	Ng1-f3	d7-d5
6.	Bf1-e2	0-0
7.	0-0	Nb8-c6
8.	c4:d5	e6:d5
9.	d4:c5	Bb4:c5
`10.	a2-a3	...

It is Black's task to rid himself of the isolated pawn — that is, to push it to d4 and trade it off. This, however, is impossible for the moment, due to 11 Na4. The natural thing for Black to do would therefore be to prepare this advance with ..a7-a6 and ..Ba7. It is White's task to use these two tempi to bring out another piece to control the d4 square, intending to occupy it later on with a knight. Following this plan, one must consider 10 b3! a6 11 Na4 Ba7 12 Bb2 more logical; if then 12..b5 13 Rc1!, followed by 14 Nc5. The square d4 would have remained under White's control, a strategic accomplishment of no small importance.

10.	...	a7-a6
11.	b2-b4	Bc5-d6

In his detailed comments to this game for a Yugoslav magazine, Gligoric's second, Trifunovic, indicates that 11..Ba7 should have been played here: on 12 Bb2, Black could have continued 12..d4; and on 12 b5 (after 11..Ba7), Trifunovic gives a pretty variation: 12..d4 13 bc dc 14 Qb3 Qc7 15 Q:c3 Bd7 16 Ne5 Nd5. Here too, however, White could continue 17 Qb2 B:c6 18 N:c6 Q:c6 19 Bf3, and hold a definite plus, thanks to his bishop pair, open files and extra center pawn.

12.	Bc1-b2	Bc8-g4
13.	Ra1-c1	Bd6-c7
14.	Nc3-a4	...

Gligoric has completed the first part of his plan: the d-pawn is now fixed firmly in place. Euwe hopes to stir up some play on the kingside, but White easily repels Black's threats, and by steadily trading off minor pieces, draws

closer and closer to his goal: a battle of heavy pieces for the isolated pawn.

14.	...	Qd8-d6

15.	g2-g3	Nf6-e4
16.	Na4-c5	...

The centralized knight must go first. 16 Nd4 would have been inferior, owing to 16..Bh3 17 Re1 Qf6.

16.	...	Ne4:c5
17.	Rc1:c5	Ra8-d8
18.	Nf3-d4	...

Now White has a solid grip on the d4 square, and Black's attack can no longer come to anything, in view of the small amount of material left on the board.

18.	...	Bg4:e2
19.	Qd1:e2	Nc6:d4
20.	Bb2:d4	Bc7-b6
21.	Rf1-d1!	...

This move is the tactical justification for White's whole plan. If the rook were forced to retreat from c5 here, the exchange of bishops would leave White with an isolated pawn as well, and there would be no further reason why he should think about winning.

21.	...	Bb6:c5
22.	Bd4:c5	Qd6-e5
23.	Bc5:f8	Kg8:f8
24.	Rd1-d4	g7-g6
25.	b4-b5	...

In order to understand what follows, one must keep in mind that rook endings with four pawns to three, all on one side, generally cannot be won. So if all of the queenside pawns disappear, Black would be risking very little even if he does lose the isolated d-pawn. With this in mind, 25 b5, which leads to exchanges, is not a very good move: 25 Qd2 would be more consistent, threatening 26 e4 and forcing 25..f5.

Attacking the isolated pawn on the file with the threat of e3-e4 is a technique common to such endings.

25.	...	a6:b5
26.	Qe2:b5	Qe5-c7
27.	Qb5-b2	Kf8-g8
28.	Qb2-d2	Qc7-c5

Euwe defends excellently. Here, 29 e4 was threatened, and if 28..Ra8 29 R:d5 R:a3, White would have continued 30 Rd8+ Kg7 31 Qd4+ Kh6 32 Rg8. By inducing the further advance of the a-pawn, Black increases the likelihood of its exchange, and hopes thereby to turn the game into a drawn ending.

29.	a3-a4	Qc5-a3
30.	a4-a5	Rd8-c8

The pawn can no longer be defended; by giving it up now, Black hopes to get the queens traded off, at least.

31.	Rd4:d5	...

Here, Gligoric, who has managed the game very consistently and powerfully up to now, commits a small inaccuracy, but a very common one. Having forced Black to abandon the d-pawn's defense, he ought not to have taken it just yet, as this gives Euwe the chance to bring his rook to a good position. 31 Kg2 was correct; if then 31..Qc1, he should avoid trading queens for the moment by playing his queen to b4. Here it is important that the variation 31..Qc1 32 Qb4 Rc2 33 R:d5 Q:e3 does not work for Black, in view of 34 Rd8+, 35 Qf8+ and 36 Rd6+.

31.	...	Qa3-c1+
32.	Qd2:c1	Rc8:c1+
33.	Kg1-g2	Rc1-b1

With this rook maneuver, Black ensures the exchange of his last queenside pawn. It is elementary, but important, that White can accomplish nothing by attacking the pawn from behind: 34 Rd8+ Kg7 35 Rb8 Rb5, and White cannot play 36 a6.

And so, in a few moves we shall see the theoretically drawn four vs. three-pawn rook endgame. Gligoric wants to test theory's conclusion, to see how much truth there is in it; so he plays on for a while, risking nothing. For the moment, he simply places his pawns more actively.

34.	g3-g4	Kg8-g7
35.	h2-h4	b7-b6
36.	h4-h5	b6:a5
37.	Rd5:a5	Rb1-b7
38.	g4-g5	...

Opinions vary on this move. Euwe gave it an exclamation mark, calling it "a pawn sacrifice rich with possibilities", while Trifunovic considered it a serious mistake, allowing Black to trade off two pawns. He recommended postponing g4-g5 in favor of the preparatory moves Kg3, f3, e4, Kf4 and Ra6. I submit that neither of them is completely correct: Black need not lose here, regardless of whether or not White plays g4-g5.

The move g4-g5 is interesting from a psychological standpoint. It was played just before the time-control, leaving Euwe to decide whether to reply 38..gh, which weakens his pawn formation — "but who would have imagined that this would play such an important role in the resulting — three vs. three! — endgame?" (Euwe). Instead, he could have played 38..h6, which would have led to a much clearer draw after the exchange of two pawns.

| 38. | ... | g6:h5 |

| 39. | Ra5-a6 | ... |

Beautifully played! Now ..h7-h6 will be impossible, of course, but White is also threatening to bring up his pawn to e4, his king to f5, and his rook to h6. White wins this ending, if he can capture the h5-pawn while keeping the pawns at f7 and h7 in place.

| 39. | ... | Rb7-b3 |

Either Euwe had no time left to think, or else he considered he could draw as he pleased; in any case, he was not paying sufficient attention to his opponent's plan. The rook had to be brought to e6, when it turns out that exchanging rooks results in a king and pawn endgame that Black can just barely draw: 39..Re7 40 Kg3 Re6 41 R:e6 fe 42 Kh4 Kg6 43 f4 h6. If White does not take on e6, then Black plays ..h7-h6; and if White answers 39..Re7 with 40 Rh6, then 40..Re5 41 R:h5 Kg6. Curiously, the rook can only be transferred

to e6 via e7: Euwe's recommendation 39..Rb4 40 f4 Re4 41 Kf3 Re6, etc., is refuted by 40 f3, by which White covers both g4 and e4, keeping Black's rook off the sixth rank and threatening 41 Rh6.

| 40. | Ra6-h6 | Rb3-a3 |
| 41. | Kg2-g3 | Ra3-a1 |

Black meets the threatened 42 R:h5 by threatening to reply with 42..Kg6.

42.	e3-e4	Ra1-g1+
43.	Kg3-f4	Rg1-h1
44.	e4-e5	h5-h4

Euwe might have adjourned the game on move 40, but continued playing until the 44th move, during which time he succeeded in committing his final mistake. Advancing this pawn gave White's king the square g4 and shortened the range of his own rook enough to give White sufficient basis for a real winning attempt. With the black pawn at h5, I do not believe a win would have been possible. If, for instance, White sets up this position: Kf5, Rb7, and pawns at f4, e5 and g5, with the threat of e5-e6, then Black puts his rook on the e-file, which renders the pawn advance unplayable, and White's king has no move either.

| 45. | Kf4-g4 | Rh1-g1+ |
| 46. | Kg4-f5 | ... |

White does not fall into the trap 46 K:h4 Rh1+, when Black draws the pawn endgame after 47 Kg4 R:h6 48 gh+ K:h6 49 Kf5 Kg7 50 f3 h6 51 f4 h5 52 Kg5 f6+ 53 ef+ Kf7, etc.

46.	...	Rg1-h1
47.	Kf5-g4	Rh1-g1+
48.	Kg4-f5	Rg1-h1

From now on, this position will be included in every endgame textbook. The winning method, discovered by Gligoric in actual play, is not only pretty and logically consistent, but a valuable addition to theory as well.

Reaching the final position will require White to advance his pawn from e5 to e6 with his rook on the seventh rank, but

this is not immediately playable. Gligoric's plan to make
it so may be divided into the
following stages:

1) induce the black h-pawn to
advance, and then capture it;

2) bring his own rook to d1
and drive the enemy rook from
the e-file;

3) carry out the final maneuver by pushing the f-pawn to
f5 and the e-pawn to e6 with
the support of the king and
rook.

49.   f2-f4   h4-h3

It was noted in the first edition of this book that Black
advanced this pawn to h3 in view
of the threat of 50 Kg4, since
the white king could now capture the h-pawn while his f-pawn
is on f4: 50 Kg4 Rg1+ 51 K:h4 Rh1+
52 Kg4 R:h6 53 gh+ K:h6 54 f5,
when the pawn ending is won for
White.

But as Orlov, an amateur from
Leningrad, has pointed out, this
is not so: the ending is a draw!
Black continues 54..Kg7 55 Kg5
f6+ 56 ef+ Kf7. He also notes
that the text move (49..h3) is
necessary, but for a different
reason: 50 Kg4 Rg1+ 51 Kh3! Rh1+
52 Kg2, which wins the pawn.

50. Kf5-g4   Rh1-g1+
51. Kg4-f3   Rg1-f1+
52. Kf3-g3   Rf1-g1+
53. Kg3-f2   Rg1-h1
54. Rh6-f6   ...

A pretty move, which aims by
the use of zugzwang either to
force the king to retreat or to
force the rook to move, after
which the white king can attack
and capture the h-pawn. White's
rook had to go to f6 in order
to defend the f-pawn.

An interesting line is 54..Kg8
55 Kg3 Kg7 56 Kg4 Kg8 57 Rh6,
and the pawn falls, since if the
rooks are exchanged by 57..Rg1+
58 K:h3 Rh1+ 59 Kg4 R:h6 60 gh,
the black king can no longer
reach the pawn at h6.

54.   ...   Rh1-a1
55. Kf2-g3   Ra1-h1
56. Kg3-g4   Kg7-g8

57. Rf6-h6   ...

Now White is threatening to
take the pawn with his rook;
if 57..Rg1+, then 58 K:h3 is
also possible, with the same
ideas mentioned in the preceding note.

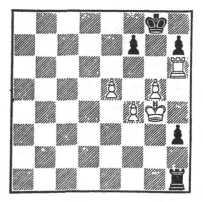

57.   ...   h3-h2

In Orlov's opinion, this was
the decisive mistake by Black,
who let the draw slip here. This
could have been obtained, he
says, by 57..Rg1+ 58 K:h3 Rh1+
59 Kg4 R:h6 60 gh f6 61 ef Kf7
62 Kf5 Kf8 63 Ke6 Ke8 64 f7+
Kf8.

I was just preparing myself
to argue with this capable Leningrad analyst, when my thunder
was stolen by the well-known expert on pawn endgames, Igor Maizelis, who pointed out that in
exactly the position where Orlov
ends his analysis in the belief
that it is an obvious draw White
can win with a maneuver reminiscent of a composed study: 65 Kd6!!
K:f7 66 Kd7 Kf8 67 Ke6, etc.
And if Black plays 62..Ke8 in
Orlov's line (instead of 62..Kf8),
then 63 Ke6 Kf8 64 Kd7 Kf7
65 Kd8 Kf8 66 f7 K:f7 67 Kd7
Kf6 68 Ke8, and the white king
attacks and captures the last
black pawn, and then shepherds
its own pawn through to h8.

Additionally, Master Fridstein
has pointed out that, in Orlov's
line with 57..Rg1+ instead of
57..h2, White is not obliged to
take on the pawn ending, but can

capture the pawn by a different route: 58 Kf3 Rf1+ 59 Kg3 Rg1+ 60 Kf2 Rh1 61 Rh4. All that remains is for me to thank Messrs. Orlov, Maizelis and Fridstein for their interesting and valuable comments.

58.	Kg4-g3	Rh1-g1+
59.	Kg3:h2	Rg1-g4

White has now completed the first part of his plan, but the win is not easy even yet: his king is cut off, and the f-pawn needs protection.

As a matter of fact, couldn't Black cut off the white king on the h-file permanently? No, because after 60 Rf6 Kg7 61 Kh3 Rg1 62 Ra6 the threat to advance the e-pawn (with the king at h5 and the rook at a7) would force Black's rook off the g-file.

60.	Rh6-f6	Kg8-g7
61.	Kh2-h3	Rg4-g1
62.	Kh3-h4	Rg1-h1+
63.	Kh4-g4	Rh1-g1+
64.	Kg4-f5	Rg1-f1

Black has selected the defensive plan of tying White's king to the f-pawn. By attacking the f-pawn from behind, Black leaves his king relatively free to maneuver (..Kg7-f8-g7), while also preventing the white king from occupying f6; with White's rook on the seventh rank, this would decide the game at once. When White's king comes out, Black's rook will check on the files, but Gligoric finds a skillful maneuver to drive Black's rook from the f-file and secure the win.

As Euwe points out, 64..Ra1, Black's other possible plan here, would not have saved him either: 65 Rc6 Ra4 66 Rc7 Kf8 67 Kg4 Ra1 68 f5, and now comes a series of checks, which the king escapes on c8: 68..Rg1+ 69 Kf4 Rf1+ 70 Ke4 Re1+ 71 Kd5 Rd1+ 72 Kc6 Rc1+ 73 Kd7 Rd1+ 74 Kc8 Rd5 75 f6 R:e5 76 Kd7, and by forcing the trade of rooks White reaches a won pawn ending: 76..Rd5+ 77 Kc6 Rd8 78 Rd7. And if 74..Rg1, then 75 f6 R:g5 76 Kd7, etc.

65.	Rf6-c6	Kg7-f8

Had Black not played 64..Rf1, then the simple 66 Kf6 would have decided here. If 66 Rc4 to prepare this, then naturally the black king returns to g7.

66.	Rc6-c8+	Kf8-g7
67.	Rc8-d8	...

Zugzwang again. What can Black do?

I. 67..h6 68 gh+ K:h6 69 Rg8. With Black's king cut off, White wins easily.

II. 67..Ra1 68 Rd7, threatening 69 e6, and Black is lost, considering:

a) 68..Ra5 69 Kg4 Kf8 70 Rd8+ Kg7 71 f5 R:e5 72 f6+, with mate next;

b) 68..Kf8 69 Kf6 Ra6+ 70 Rd6!, etc.;

c) 68..Ra6 69 Kg4 h6 70 f5 Kg8 71 Rd8+ Kh7 72 g6+ fg 73 f6.

All that's left is the text.

67.	...	Rf1-f2

But after White's reply,

68.	Rd8-d1	...

Black has no more checks, nor can his rook return to f1.

Thus, White has now completed the second part of his plan, and is all ready to push his pawns to f5 and e6, once the black rook has been forced off the f-file. If the rook does not leave the file, then the king must go either to g8 or to f8, which would leave it perilously placed indeed after White's f4-f5-f6; for example: 68..Kf8 69 Kg4 Re2 70 Kf3 Ra2 71 f5.

68.	...	Rf2-f3
69.	Kf5-e4	Rf3-f2
70.	Ke4-e3	Rf2-a2
71.	f4-f5!	...

The concluding phase: White's pawns are set in motion.

71.	...	Ra2-g2

71..Ra7 would be met by 72 Ke4,

[252]

73 Rd8, and e5-e6 or f5-f6+.

72. Rd1-d7 ...

By now White had another way to win: 72 g6 hg 73 f6+.

72. ... Rg2:g5

White would have won beautifully after 72..Kf8: 73 f6 Ke8 74 Re7+ Kf8 75 Rb7 Ke8 76 Rb8+ Kd7 77 Rf8 Ke6 78 Re8+ Kf5 79 e6!

73.	Ke3-f4	Rg5-g1
74.	e5-e6	Rg1-f1+
75.	Kf4-e5	Rf1-e1+
76.	Ke5-d6	h7-h5
77.	Rd7:f7+	Kg7-g8
78.	Kd6-e7	...

BLACK RESIGNED

78..h4 is met by 79 Kf6 h3 80 Rg7+ Kh8 81 Rg3.

An endgame that will repay close study.

*****

151. Bronstein—Stahlberg
(Queen's Gambit)

1.	d2-d4	d7-d5
2.	c2-c4	e7-e6
3.	Ng1-f3	Ng8-f6
4.	Nb1-c3	Nb8-d7
5.	c4:d5	e6:d5
6.	Bc1-g5	Bf8-e7
7.	e2-e3	c7-c6
8.	Qd1-c2	Nd7-f8
9.	Bf1-d3	Nf8-e6
10.	h2-h4	...

In my preparations for the Stahlberg game, I set great store by this flank attack, which seemed to refute Black's plan of bringing a knight to e6. On 10..g6, 11 B:f6 B:f6 12 h5 is very strong, and on 10..h6 I intended to continue 11 B:f6 B:f6 12 g4, followed by queenside castling and g4-g5; I felt such an attack would have to succeed. But Stahlberg played

10. ... h7-h6

anyway, and immediately I saw my mistake.

11. Bg5:f6 Be7:f6
12. 0-0-0 ...

Unfortunately, after 12 g4 Nc7! White is short the one tempo he needs in order to continue with his pawn storm. He should still have played 12 g4, however, but with the idea, after 12..Nc7, of laying aside temporarily his ideas of a crushing attack, in favor of a plan to accumulate positional advantages, beginning with 13 Bf5. White's irrepressible urge to complicate soon forces him back on the defensive.

12. ... Ne6-c7
13. h4-h5 Bc8-g4
14. Kc1-b1 0-0

The decision of a great master. Not everyone would dare to castle when his opponent had already pushed his pawn to h5, but Stahlberg has accurately calculated that the c-file will be

opened before a white pawn can
get even as far as g5.

15.	Nc3-e2	Nc7-b5
16.	Nf3-e5	Bf6:e5
17.	d4:e5	Qd8-b6

17..a6 was more logical: then
18 B:b5 ab would open the a-
file, which would cause White a
lot of worry in connection with
a possible pawn storm.

18.	Bd3:b5	Qb6:b5
19.	f2-f3	Bg4-f5
20.	Qc2:f5	Qb5:e2
21.	Rh1-e1	...

Offering Black's queen a
choice: either leave the area,
and thereby allow White's g-
pawn to proceed with a boarding
expedition, or remain in the
area of the upcoming skirmishes.

| 21. | ... | Qe2-f2 |

Black's decision turned on his
assessment of the line 22 Qg4 f5
23 ef R:f6 24 f4, when the queen
appears about to be trapped, but
Black escapes damage by exploiting a pin: 24..Re8 25 Re2 R:f4.

| 22. | Qf5-g4 | ... |

The same initial move as in
the variation presented above,
but with the more modest goal
of creating a passed e-pawn.
His trust in the almighty powers
of this pawn nearly ends up cost-
ing White the game, but finally
it saves him as well. Another
possible plan, 22 g4, would have
resulted in a sharp game; how-

ever, White's attacking fires had
been damped by move twenty.

22.	...	f7-f5
23.	Qg4-h3	Ra8-d8
24.	f3-f4	d5-d4

Returning the queen to active
duty.

25.	e3:d4	Qf2:f4
26.	Qh3-b3+	Rf8-f7
27.	d4-d5	c6:d5
28.	e5-e6	...

The remainder of the game may
almost be said to follow from
this advance. If the rook simply recaptures at d5, 28..R:d5
29 Q:d5 Qh4 would force White's
rook to abandon the e-file; thus,
28 e6, which clears e5 for the
white queen. All very properly
thought out, except that White
completely forgot about his h-
pawn, which could have been saved
by 31 Qd1.

28.	...	Rf7-e7
29.	Rd1:d5	Rd8:d5
30.	Qb3:d5	Qd4-h4
31.	Qd5-e5	Qh4:h5
32.	Qe5-b8+	Kg8-h7
33.	Qb8-d6	...

Not 33 Qf8 R:e6!

33.	...	Qh5-g5
34.	g2-g3	Qg5-f6
35.	a2-a3	h6-h5
36.	Kb1-a2	g7-g5
37.	Qd6-d5	Kh7-g6
38.	Qd5-d8	...

White has no sense of the danger — such is the power of his
faith in the amulet on e6. While
the white queen dances back and
forth, Black is making a passed
pawn of his own; thereafter,
White's affairs take a sharp
turn for the worse. Of course,
the pawn at e6 does constrict
Black's forces powerfully, but
White's pieces are tied to it
as well. The only real advantage
it confers on White is the greater mobility of his rook. Therefore, before Black finds time to
regroup, the king should be sent
out to save the pawn, especially
now that the road that leads to
it (a2-b3-c4-d5), although completely open, is also completely
safe. But a king-march to the
middle of the board with queens
and rooks still on the board is

nothing to be lightly undertaken;
White — mistakenly — hesitates to
make the decision.

38.	...	Kg6-g7
39.	Qd8-d6	Kg7-g6
40.	Qd6-d8	Kg6-h6

Unlike its white counterpart,
the black king may even be a bit
too active. In the heat of the
time-scramble, Black cannot decide on the proper way to open
up his fortress.

| 41. | Qd8-d5 | f5-f4 |

Now Black's two pawns far out-
weigh White's singleton.

42.	g3:f4	Qf6:f4
43.	Re1-e5	Qf4-f6
44.	Qd5-e4	b7-b5!

Preventing 45 a4, which would
have bolstered White's position
a little, and setting up a threat
to exchange queens at c4. So now
White must push his pawn anyway,
but that gives Black two pawns
plus.

45.	Qe4-e2	a7-a6
46.	a3-a4	b5:a4
47.	Qe2-e3	h5-h4

On 47..Qf4, White would have
attacked the rook with 48 Qc5.
Had White not taken the b-pawn
away from its protection of the
c4 square, then 47..Qf4 48 Qc5
Qc4+ would have won easily here.

48.	Re5-e4	Kh6-g6
49.	Qe3-e2	h4-h3
50.	Re4-e3	...

Retreat all along the line. Now
White has troubles with Black's
g- and h-pawns to add to his worries over the e-pawn.

50.	...	Kg6-g7
51.	Qe2-h2	Re7-b7
52.	Qh2-e2	Rb7-e7
53.	Qe2-h2	a4-a3

White's defensive resources are
running out, and Black, with two
pawns plus, decides to return one,
since 54 ba would completely denude the white king, and capturing with the king is also not
without its dangers, in view of
possible checks along the diagonal a3-f8 or from the squares
a5 or a4. However, the white king

has no choice now, so this time
he throws himself into the river without a second thought. A
move earlier, Black could have
placed White in zugzwang with
52..Kf8! (53 Rf3 R:b2+!), but
such moves frequently escape
notice in the course of a game.

54.	Ka2:a3	Re7:e6
55.	Qh2-c7+	Qf6-f7
56.	Qc7-c3+	...

This maneuver, which Black may
have underestimated, saves
White's game. With the black
king exposed, the advantage of
the g-pawn cannot be turned to
account.

56.	...	Re6-f6
57.	Re3:h3	Qf7-e7+
58.	Ka3-a2	Qe7-e6+
59.	Ka2-a1	Kg7-g8
60.	Rh3-h1	Qe6-c6
61.	Qc3-h3	...

White's queen and rook are
free to roam once more, so
Black decides that it's time to
settle the issue peaceably by
perpetual check.

61.	...	Qc6-a4+
62.	Ka1-b1	Qa4-e4+
63.	Kb1-a1	...

DRAW

******

152. Reshevsky—Boleslavsky
(King's Indian)

Chess is a limitless game; to
avoid losing his way in it, the

chessplayer will use certain guideposts to orient himself in the evaluation of a position and the selection of a plan, such as weak pawns, open files, a lead in development, good and bad bishops, a poorly placed king, and so on. It is worth noting that one will not find in every game such guideposts as will allow one to compare a position's good and bad points and to choose a proper plan on that basis. Either chess theory has not yet found a quantity of guideposts sufficient to exhaust the game's diversity, or else there are positions in which the balance has been upset more than once, and guideposts are hard to discern. In any event, one frequently finds the sort of game which must be played for quite some time on nothing more than gut feeling and calculation, and this is the hardest sort of game to play, even for a grandmaster.

1.	d2-d4	Ng8-f6
2.	c2-c4	g7-g6
3.	g2-g3	Bf8-g7
4.	Bf1-g2	0-0
5.	Nb1-c3	d7-d6
6.	Ng1-f3	c7-c5
7.	d4-d5	Nb8-a6

This move is, of course, not classical. A piece is developed somewhere out on the rim, immediately makes another move, and winds up at c7, which has never been considered a very good square for a knight. However, ideas such as this occur frequently in the modern type of game, where they are dangerous precisely because of their seeming illogic and, at the same time, their preeminent practicality.

The whole point to the maneuver ..Nb8-a6-c7 and ..Ra8-b8 is that Black wants to play ..b7-b5 without recourse to ..a7-a6. Why play ..b7-b5, when White can reply simply b2-b3? Not so fast: in order to play b2-b3, White must first remove two of his pieces from the long diagonal; after that, however, Black can trade pawns on c4, followed by bishop to a6 and rook to b4, when White will have a very difficult time defending his c-pawn. It is for that reason — to keep a6 clear for the bishop — that

Black does not wish to play ..a7-a6.

8.	0-0	Na6-c7
9.	Nf3-d2	Ra8-b8
10.	a2-a4	e7-e6

Now Black attacks the c4-pawn from the other side. Playing e2-e4 would block the diagonal of White's own bishop, so he takes on e6; after

| 11. | d5:e6 | Bc8:e6 |

he has the choice of either leaving his knight tied to the defense of his c-pawn, or

| 12. | Nd2-e4! | ... |

From here until approximately the 23rd move, the game follows a long and complicated course of tactical calculation, for which no all-inclusive general rules have yet been formulated. In the art of complex combinative calculation, these two are worthy foes — in fact, at the time this tournament was played they were, along with Geller and Taimanov, the best calculating players in the world. Naturally, this does not by any means lessen their stature as positional players.

Let's examine a few of the combinative motifs that will occur during the creative process. Black's rook, having left a8, now defends the b7-pawn, but the knight and the rook are now subject to diagonal attack. After the white queen's bishop

leaves c1, the b2-pawn will be
left undefended, and the black
king's bishop will be able to
capture it with tempo. After
White's knight captures the d6-
pawn, the squares e8 and c8
will be closed to Black's rooks,
and moving the bishop to e7 will
win White the exchange; and so
forth, and so on. This is far
from being a complete listing,
of course: merely fragmented
glimpses of the sort of general
ideas that take shape in the
chessplayer's mind as he makes
his choice of possible continuations.

12.	...	Nf6:e4
13.	Nc3:e4	Be6:c4
14.	Bc1-g5	Qd8-d7

Boleslavsky is trying to entice his opponent inside the
walls of the fortress, but Reshevsky stoutly resists the temptation: 15 Nf6+ B:f6 16 B:f6
Qe6 brings White no special re-
wards, while further losses will
not be long in coming his way.
If Black had played 14..f6,
White could have replied 15 Bf4
g5 16 N:d6.

15.	Qd1:d6	Qd7:d6
16.	Ne4:d6	Bc4:e2
17.	Rf1-e1	Be2-d3
18.	Bg5-e7	...

The prospect of giving up a
rook for the darksquare bishop
and picking up a pair of pawns
as interest, naturally, doesn't
disturb Black at all. But Reshevsky has spotted an important
peculiarity of the forthcoming
endgame: his rooks will be able
to act in concert against Black's
bishop and two pawns. The only
thing that gives him some slight
pause is Black's possession of
two powerful bishops.

| 18. | ... | Bg7:b2 |
| 19. | Ra1-a2 | Bb2-g7 |

(See diagram, next column)

| 20. | Bg2-f1 | ... |

A pretty move to conclude this
game's combinative phase: Black's
assets will no longer include
the pair of bishops. His rook
can no more leave f8 than his
queen's bishop can avoid exchange. Now White can exploit
his lead in development and the
strong position of his rooks. On
the other hand, Black's position
is by no means lost: it is his
overassessment of his own chances
that costs him the game later.

| 20. | ... | Bd3:f1 |
| 21. | Kg1:f1 | Nc7-d5 |

A knight's strength is doubled when it has pawn support.
Had Boleslavsky played 21..Ne6,
he would have obtained a solid
position, with the knight cutting short all of White's attempts to win the queenside pawns,
moving to d4 also if necessary.

| 22. | Be7:f8 | Bg7:f8 |
| 23. | Ra2-e2! | ... |

Beautiful play! White threatens to trade off Black's rook
and attack the pawns from behind. This combination would
obviously have been impossible
if the knight stood at e6, which
is why it was so important to
close the e-file with the knight.
Now Black has to take the knight,
since 23..Kg7 allows 24 Ne8+ and
25 Re5.

| 23. | ... | Bf8:d6 |
| 24. | Re2-d2 | Bd6-f8 |

Had Black gone after the g-pawn, he would have lost to 24..B:g3 25 hg Nc7 26 Re7 Ne6 27 Rdd7. However, it's difficult to believe that with two pawns for the exchange, Black could think of no more active move than 24..Bf8. He might have tried picking off a third pawn with 24..Nb6, for instance. On the other hand, if the author had been playing Black here, and had moved his knight to b6, and then lost, Boleslavsky might then have written in his notes that 24..Bf8 should have been tried — and he, in his turn, would have been right also.

| 25. | Rd2:d5 | c5-c4 |

Black wants to push this pawn to c3 so it can be defended by the bishop. If 25..a6, Euwe recommends 26 Rde5 b5 27 a5, with the idea of winning the a-pawn. To my way of thinking, 26 a5 is a sounder line for White.

| 26. | Re1-e4 | ... |

Refuting Black's idea. 26 Rc1 Rc8, followed by ..c3 and ..Bg7, would leave Black with no worries; but now 26..Rc8 would be met by 27 Rdd4 c3 28 Rc4, and after the rooks are exchanged, the pawn must fall: 28..R:c4 29 R:c4 Bg7? 30 Rc8+.

The same result follows 26..c3 27 Rc4 Bg7 28 Rdc5!, and after the unavoidable exchange of rooks, White wins easily by bringing his king to d3, after which his unchained rook begins to reap the defenseless black a- and b-pawns.

| 26. | ... | a7-a6 |

Boleslavsky has one last chance: to trade off White's a-pawn and advance his one remaining compensating pawn as far as possible.

27.	Re4:c4	b7-b5
28.	a4:b5	a6:b5
29.	Rc4-c7	b5-b4
30.	Rd5-d7	Rb8-a8

The pawn cannot be pushed further just yet, in view of 30..b3? 31 Rb7.

31.	Kf1-g2	Ra8-a2
32.	Rd7:f7	b4-b3
33.	Rc7-b7	Bf8-c5

To understand the following curious events, one must know, first of all, that they occurred while Reshevsky was in tremendous time-trouble; and secondly, that all of this occurred very late at night. The twenty-second round fell on a Saturday. For religious reasons, Reshevsky started his Saturday games some hours after the usual time — after the rise of the evening star; on Fridays, he played his games during the day, so as to finish before the rise of that same star.

Fearing to leave something hanging in time-pressure, Reshevsky decides to play Rf7-f3-d3-d7-f7, which was playable with Black's pawn at b3, but allowed Black a saving clause when the pawn went to b2.

| 34. | Rf7-f3 | b3-b2 |
| 35. | Rf3-d3 | Bc5-f8 |

Now the win could have been attained with 36 Rd8, but Reshevsky follows his "plan".

| 36. | Rd3-d7 | ... |

And here, Black might have saved his game with the clever rook retreat from a2 to a7. Boleslavsky still had a few minutes, and in the light of day he would no doubt have seen and played that move; but at 2:00 a.m., and after a tense and exhausting struggle, he played automatically:

| 36. | ... | Bf8-c5? |

and after

| 37. | Rd7-d8+ | Bc5-f8 |
| 38. | Rd8-b8 | |

BLACK RESIGNED

******

153. Keres—Kotov
(Catalan Opening)

1.	d2-d4	Ng8-f6
2.	c2-c4	e7-e6
3.	g2-g3	d7-d5
4.	Bf1-g2	Bf8-e7
5.	Ng1-f3	0-0
6.	0-0	c7-c6

After this, Keres transposes into a classical Reti configuration in which Black has no particular need of the move ..c7-c6. Kotov could also have used another, perhaps more accurate, move order: 6..Nbd7, and if 7 b3 c5.

7.	b2-b3	Nb8-d7
8.	Bc1-b2	b7-b6
9.	Nb1-d2	Bc8-b7
10.	Ra1-c1	Ra8-c8
11.	e2-e3	c6-c5

There exists a barely perceptible difference between White's position and Black's. How much is "barely"? White's bishop is on g2, while Black's is on e7. Keres asks himself, "How may this affect the further course of play?", and answers, "The white queen has the square e2, while the symmetrical square e7 is occupied by Black's bishop, and his queen will be uncomfortable on an open file." Thus, White's plan begins with the moves e3, Qe2 and Rfd1 — but this is only a beginning.

12.	Qd1-e2	c5:d4
13.	Nf3:d4	Nd7-c5
14.	Rf1-d1	Qd8-d7

Black must clear d8 for his rook, and then quit the d-file. This costs him two moves, and his queen on e8 is still not so well posted as White's on e2.

| 15. | Nd2-f3 | Rf8-d8 |

| 16. | Nf3-e5 | Qd7-e8 |
| 17. | c4:d5 | ... |

Keres initiates a multi-branched combination of unusual complexity, based on pinning possibilities along the c-file, the activity of his fianchettoed king's bishop, and in one variation even a threat of mate at g7!

| 17. | ... | Bb7:d5 |

| 18. | Nd4-c6 | ... |

A brilliant move, completely unexpected. The knight is now triply attacked, and only the knight at e5 defends it! As it turns out, however, the c6 square is also controlled by the bishop at g2 "through" the bishop at d5, and by the rook at c1 "through" the knight at c5!

If 18..B:c6 19 R:d8 B:d8 20 N:c6 R:c6 21 B:c6 Q:c6 22 b4, the knight is pinned and White wins the exchange for a pawn. And if 18..B:g2 19 N:d8 Ba8 20 N8:f7.

| 18. | ... | Rc8:c6 |
| 19. | Ne5:c6 | Qe8:c6 |

On 19..B:c6 we get the variation mentioned in the preceding note.

| 20. | Bg2:d5 | ... |

White also wins the exchange for a pawn this way — a pedestrian return for a combination on such a grand scale. He would

have gotten a good deal more
out of 20 B:f6 B:f6 21 e4 B:e4
22 R:d8+ B:d8 23 B:e4 Q:e4
24 Q:e4 N:e4 25 Rc8, or 20..B:g2
21 B:e7 Re8 22 B:c5 Bf3 23 B:b6,
and White comes out two pawns
ahead.

20.	...	e6:d5
21.	b3-b4	Nf6-e4
22.	b4:c5	b6:c5
23.	Qe2-g4	...

23.	...	g7-g6
24.	h2-h4	Qc6-e6
25.	Qg4:e6	f7:e6

White has the better position,
but Black has excellent counterchances. Now White must overcome
Kotov's unflagging resourcefulness all over again in order to
win the game — no small order,
considering the energy and imagination Keres expended on the
preceding stage.

26.	Bb2-e5	c5-c4
27.	Rc1-c2	...

27 Bd4 would have been better
here, in order to keep the knight
out of c5 and d3.

27.	...	Ne4-c5
28.	Rd1-b1	Kg8-f7
29.	Be5-d4	Rd8-d7
30.	Rc2-b2	...

30..e5 had to be prevented, so
30 Kf1 was the move. However, one
cannot see everything.

30.	...	e6-e5

Having succeeded in advancing

this pawn by combinative means
and bringing up his king, Kotov
need no longer have any fears
as to the outcome of this game.

31.	Bd4:c5	Be7:c5
32.	Rb2-c2	Rd7-c7
33.	e3-e4	...

Keres still tries for the win,
but he may have missed the boat
already. With this move, he prevents 33..d4, so he can return
his rook to c1 and pick up the
pawn at c4.

33.	...	Kf7-e6
34.	Kg1-f1	Bc5-d4
35.	f2-f3	c4-c3
36.	Kf1-e2	Rc7-f7

A little reminder that Black
still has a rook.

37.	Rb1-f1	Ke6-d6
38.	Ke2-d3	Kd6-c5
39.	Rc2-e2	Rf7-b7
40.	f3-f4	d5:e4+
41.	Re2:e4	...

If 41 K:e4 Kc4 42 fe B:e5.

41.	...	Rb7-d7
42.	Kd3-c2	Kc5-d5
43.	Rf1-e1	Rd7-b7

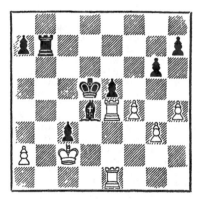

44.	Kc2-c1	...

After 44 fe Black would be unable to stop the passed pawn;
however, he would have good
chances to win, not to draw,
with 44..Rb2+ 45 Kc1 R:a2 46 e6
Kc4 47 Kb1 Rb2+ 48 Ka1 Kb3.
White would have better in 47 R1e2,
but then Black could also im-

prove on 45..R:a2, by playing
45..Bf2 46 R1e2 Bc5 instead.

44.   ...   Rb7-b2

With the same threats. Now
the fires of battle slowly begin to subside, and after one
more harmless try the game
winds up a draw.

45. R4e2 e4 46. R:e4 R:a2
47. g4 Rg2 48. f5 gf 49. gf
Rf2 50. Re7 Kc4 51. R1e4 Kd3
52. R:d4+ K:d4 53. R:h7 a5
54. Rd7+ Ke4 55. h5 R:f5 56. h6
Rh5

DRAW

******

154. Smyslov—Geller
(King's Indian)
One of the postulates of opening theory reads as follows: In
the opening, White should always
play to gain the advantage, while
Black should always play to equalize. I do not know the precise
formulation of Geller's views, but
to judge from his games, he apparently believes that whichever side
he happens to be playing is the
side that ought to get the better
of the opening.

The chief characteristics of
Geller's creativity are an amazing ability to extract the very
maximum from the opening and a
readiness to abandon positional
schemes for an open game rife
with combinations, or vice ver-
sa, at any moment.

1.	d2-d4	Ng8-f6
2.	c2-c4	g7-g6
3.	Nb1-c3	Bf8-g7
4.	e2-e4	d7-d6
5.	Ng1-f3	0-0
6.	Bf1-e2	e7-e5
7.	0-0	c7-c6
8.	Rf1-e1	e5:d4
9.	Nf3:d4	Rf8-e8
10.	Be2-f1	Nf6-g4

Having developed his pieces
harmoniously, Smyslov now wishes
to set about a straightforward
siege of Black's position, without incurring any weaknesses himself. He would like to make the
first breach in the fortress
wall at d6 — but now this sudden knight sortie, with its un-
mistakable threat of 11..Qh4,

forces Smyslov to recast his
plans.

11.   h2-h3   Qd8-f6

11..Qb6 comes to the same thing
after 12 hg Q:d4 (but not 12..B:d4
because of 13 Qd2, when the threat
of 14 Na4 forces Black into full
retreat).

12.   h3:g4   Qf6:d4
13.   g4-g5   ...

An outstanding idea! Smyslov
establishes an outpost in the
immediate vicinity of the enemy army's general headquarters.
And although this cheeky pawn
is cut off from its own chain,
directly or indirectly it holds
back three of the enemy. Most
importantly, it holds down the
thematic King's Indian thrust
..f7-f5.

13.   ...   Nb8-d7
14.   Bc1-f4   Qd4:d1
15.   Ra1:d1   Bg7-e5
16.   Bf4-e3   Nd7-c5

With the queens exchanged,
Black is ready to trade bishop
for knight as well, if he can
get a pawn into the bargain: for
example, 17 f4 B:c3 18 bc N:e4.
So White contents himself with
the more modest 17 f3, waiting
for the right moment to drive
the bishop from e5 and take the
d-pawn. A position of dynamic
equilibrium results. Black now
advances his queenside pawns,
but all the while he must keep
an eye on the central grouping

of his own and the enemy forces.

17.	f2-f3	Bc8-e6
18.	Rd1-c1	a7-a5
19.	Rc1-c2	a5-a4
20.	a2-a3	Re8-b8

White's last move was to defend the b-pawn, so he could transfer the knight via e2 to d4. Geller intended to meet this maneuver with the following aggressive line: 21 Ne2 Nd3 22 Rb1 b5 23 cb Ba2 24 Ra1 Bb3, with interesting complications. If Geller had been in a peaceable mood, he would probably have played 20..f6, and after 21 gf B:f6 the game would most likely have been drawn.

21.	Re1-b1	h7-h6

Geller decides to liquidate the unpleasant g5-pawn at the precise moment when both White's rooks are located on the same diagonal, as though to invite an attack from the bishop at f5. However, Smyslov refutes Black's idea by means of an accurately calculated counterblow.

22.	g5:h6	f7-f5
23.	f3-f4	...

Geller evidently missed the fact that 23..B:c3 could now be met by 24 B:c5 dc 25 R:c3 fe 26 Re3 Bf5 27 Be2 Re8 28 Rd1, with a won position.

23.	...	Be5-f6
24.	e4-e5	Bf6-e7
25.	e5:d6	Be7:d6
26.	Rb1-d1	Bd6-f8
27.	Nc3-d5	...

A pretty stroke, in Smyslov's characteristic style, which leads to complications favoring White. If Black takes the knight with his pawn, he gets into a hopeless position: 27..cd 28 cd Ne4 29 de B:h6 30 Rc7, or 28..B:d5 29 R:d5 Ne4 30 Rc7, intending 31 Bc4, etc.

27.	...	Rb8-d8
28.	Nd5-f6+	Kg8-f7

28..Kh8 was much better: on the natural continuation 29 Bd4 he could have sacrificed the exchange with 29..R:d4 30 R:d4 Be7 and trap the knight. White would have to give some thought to the extrication of that knight, but it could probably be accomplished by 29 Re1 Be7 30 Bf2: White's position remains somewhat superior, but Black has defensive possibilities.

29.	Rd1:d8	Ra8:d8
30.	Nf6-h7	Nc5-e4
31.	Nh7-g5+	Kf7-f6
32.	g2-g4	Rd8-d1
33.	Ng5:e4+	f5:e4
34.	g4-g5+	...

Now White's passed pawn is solidly defended, which assures him the victory.

34.	...	Kf6-f7
35.	Kg1-f2	Rd1-d7
36.	Rc2-d2	Rd7:d2+
37.	Be3:d2	Bf8-c5+
38.	Bd2-e3	Bc5-d6
39.	Be3-d4	Kf7-g8
40.	Kf2-e3	Be6-f5
41.	c4-c5	Bd6-c7
42.	Bf1-e2	Bc7-a5

| 43. | Be2-d1 | Ba5-e1 |
| 44. | Bd1:a4 | ... |

BLACK RESIGNED

******

******

ROUND TWENTY-THREE

155. Geller—Keres
(Queen's Gambit)

1.	d2-d4	Ng8-f6
2.	c2-c4	e7-e6
3.	Nb1-c3	d7-d5
4.	Ng1-f3	c7-c5
5.	c4:d5	c5:d4
6.	Qd1:d4	e6:d5
7.	e2-e4	...

Once again Keres employs the new defense, specially prepared for this tournament, which he used successfully against Stahlberg (see Game 33). Geller's plan of attack with 7 e4 takes us out of the realm of the positional schemes of the Queen's Gambit and into the sphere of the open games of the Italian School. On 7..de, White trades queens and continues 9 Ng5, attacking the pawns at f7 and e4.

7.	...	Nb8-c6
8.	Bf1-b5	Nf6:e4
9.	0-0	...

Geller plays in classical style. Having sacrificed a pawn, he is in no hurry to recover it, bringing out his pieces instead for an attack on the king.

9.	...	Ne4-f6

Black's task must be to remove his king from the center at all costs, otherwise an extra pawn or even an extra piece will not save him from a fierce attack. The task is not solved by exchanging knights at c3, since 9..N:c3 10 Q:c3 would leave the g7-pawn under fire from the white queen, as before, and the dark-square bishop would remain unable to move and clear the way for castling kingside.

10.	Rf1-e1+	Bf8-e7
11.	Qd4-e5	...

One who plays an open game must not only search for and invent various attacks and combinations, but also keep a sharp eye on his opponent, and never forget that he may also come up with a clever idea himself. Thus, at first Geller's move looks quite strong: it pins the bishop and delays Black's castling, and on 11..Be6 12 Nd4 is very uncomfortable.

However, Keres finds a pretty combinative solution: even though he "cannot" castle, he does so anyway! Immediately, White's position is practically hopeless, since he no longer has either his attack or his pawn. So Geller's correct strategical idea must have fallen victim to an incorrect tactical execution.

Geller could have kept the king in the center for quite some time by means of the maneuver 11 B:c6+ bc 12 Qe5, when his threats of 13 Nd4 and 13 b3 followed by 14 Ba3 would have forced an immediate 12..Kf8.

11.	...	0-0

Suddenly, Black's knight is mobile again: 12 B:c6 Bd6!, and then 13..bc.

12.	Qe5-e2	Rf8-e8
13.	Bc1-g5	Bc8-g4
14.	Ra1-d1	h7-h6
15.	Bg5-h4	...

White might have won back his pawn instead: 15 B:f6 B:f6 16 Q:e8+ Q:e8 17 R:e8+ R:e8 18 R:d5 — but he could hardly have had any hopes of saving the endgame then. White's knights would have had no points of support, and would have had to stay tied to their posts, while Black's bishops would hold absolute sway over the board. Sooner or later, White's a- and b-pawns would have fallen.

15.   ...   Nf6-e4

Another little combination: if
16 B:e7, Black simplifies with
16..N:c3 17 B:d8 N:e2+ 18 R:e2
R:e2 19 B:e2 R:d8, and eventually
wins, being a pawn ahead. If
16 B:c6 first, then 16..bc defends the d-pawn. 16 R:d5 is
also met by 16..N:c3, with simplifications favorable to Black,
or even the win of the exchange.

16.	Bh4-g3	Ne4:c3
17.	b2:c3	Be7-f6
18.	Qe2:e8+	Qd8:e8
19.	Re1:e8+	Ra8:e8
20.	Rd1:d5	Re8-c8
21.	Rd5-d3	...

This allows a third and final
"little combination" — adding
up to the equivalent of one
"grand combination". Although
21 Rd3 was condemned by the
annotators, it does not alter
the outcome, but merely hastens
it. After 21 Rc5 Be7 22 Rc4 Be6
23 Ra4 a6 also, Black has an
easy win.

21.	...	Nc6-b4
22.	Rd3-e3	Nb4:a2
23.	h2-h3	Bg4:f3
24.	g2:f3	Na2:c3
25.	Bb5-d7	Rc8-d8
26.	Bd7-f5	g7-g6
27.	Bf5-d3	Nc3-d1

WHITE RESIGNED

******

156. Kotov—Reshevsky
(Queen's Indian Defense)

1.	d2-d4	Ng8-f6
2.	c2-c4	e7-e6
3.	Ng1-f3	b7-b6
4.	e2-e3	Bc8-b7
5.	Bf1-d3	Bf8-e7
6.	0-0	0-0
7.	Nb1-c3	d7-d5
8.	Qd1-e2	Nb8-d7
9.	b2-b3	a7-a6
10.	Bc1-b2	Be7-d6

This is too pacific. White is
preparing to open the center with
11 e4, and from a Reshevsky one
might sooner have expected
10..Bb4 11 a3 B:c3 12 B:c3 dc
13 bc c5 or 13..Be4.

11.	e3-e4	d5:e4
12.	Nc3:e4	Nf6:e4
13.	Bd3:e4	Bb7:e4
14.	Qe2:e4	...

White has the freer position,
with significantly more lines
available for various regroup-
ings. Since his darksquare bishop is on the a1-h8 diagonal,
it looks very tempting to bring
a rook to g3, but he must also
counter Black's efforts to increase the scope of his own
pieces by ..c7-c5 or ..e6-e5.

14.	...	Qd8-e7
15.	Ra1-e1	Rf8-e8
16.	Re1-e2	a6-a5
17.	Rf1-e1	Bd6-b4
18.	Re1-d1	Ra8-d8
19.	Rd1-d3	f7-f6
20.	Rd3-e3	Qe7-f7
21.	g2-g3	Bb4-d6
22.	Qe4-c6	Nd7-b8
23.	Qc6-b5	Nb8-d7
24.	Kg1-g2	Bd6-f8
25.	a2-a3	Rd8-c8
26.	Qb5-c6	Nd7-b8
27.	Qc6-b7	Qf7-d7
28.	Qb7-e4	Qd7-f7

Lengthy maneuvers on interior
lines have not brought about any
substantial change in the position. White's next move is a
careless one that allows Reshevsky to assume the initiative.

29.	Qe4-g4	h7-h5!
30.	Qg4-e4	c7-c5!

Well played. Now Black knocks
White's d-pawn out of the cen-

ter and obtains full play.

| 31. | Re3-d3 | Nb8-c6 |
| 32. | Re2-d2? | ... |

White absent-mindedly puts the rook on a bad square. He should have taken the c-pawn first.

32.	...	c5:d4
33.	Nf3:d4	Nc6-e5
34.	Rd3-c3	Rc8-d8

35.   f2-f4   ...

A very risky decision. The plan to take over the d-file should have been implemented with something like 35 Rc1 and 36 Rcd1. This foolhardy push of the f-pawn could have cost White the game. It decisively weakens two diagonals, both of them vital to White's health and safety: c5-g1 and a8-h1.

35.   ...   Ne5-g4

Of course. Black immediately has a number of combinative threats; among other things, the threat of 36..e5 forces White's knight to abandon d4 at once.

| 36. | Nd4-f3 | Rd8:d2+ |
| 37. | Nf3:d2 | Re8-d8 |

This returns the favor. Reshevsky feels that White will have a harder time defending the pawns at a3 and b3 once the rooks are exchanged, but Kotov manages to hold on. I would have selected the more obvious 37..f5, especially since the rook already occupies the e-file. After '38 Qf3

e5 39 h3 e4, or 39 fe N:e5 40 Qd5 Bc5, Black's pieces would be quite excellently placed, while White's would have no useful moves. His best would have been 38 Qc6.

38.	Rc3-d3	Rd8:d3
39.	Qe4:d3	Qf7-b7+
40.	Qd3-e4	Qb7-d7
41.	Nd2-f3	Bf8-c5
42.	Bb2-d4	Bc5:d4
43.	Nf3:d4	Kg8-f7
44.	h2-h3	f6-f5
45.	Qe4-d3	Ng4-f6
46.	Nd4-f3	Qd7:d3

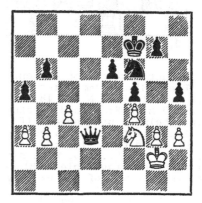

46..Qe7, aiming at the a-pawn, offered somewhat better chances. As the game's further course will make clear, Reshevsky overestimated his chances in his home analysis. Well, there's no need for us to regret that, since the knight ending that results is most interesting.

47.	Nf3-e5+	Kf7-e7
48.	Ne5:d3	Nf6-e4
49.	b3-b4	Ke7-d6
50.	Nd3-e5	a5-a4

50..ab would have secured the draw, but Black wants to retain his own a-pawn while removing that of his opponent. One cannot fault Reshevsky's logic, except that Kotov finds an astonishing defense.

51.   Kg2-f3   g7-g5

Black is giving it all he's got. Kotov's position now looks critical, in view of the threatened 52..Nd2+ 53 Ke3 Nb1 54 Kd3 h4, or 52..g4+ 53 hg hg+ 54 N:g4

Nd2+ 55 Ke2 N:c4, etc.; but by means of a sharp left-hand turn, his king escapes the danger zone.

52. Kf3-e3   ...

A very pretty move — and here are the variations (with the first one very much like a novel):

I. 52..Nc3 — a hunt for the a-pawn — 53 Kd3 Nb1 54 Kc2 N:a3+ 55 Kb2 — the knight perishes, but the breakthrough comes on the other side — 55..h4 56 K:a3 hg; and if the knight hurries to assist with 57 Nf3?, then 57..gf, and the wave of pawns from e6 to f5 to f4 to g3 rolls unopposed to the first rank. But the knight can ride "round-about": 57 Nf7+!, and after Nf7:g5-f3, the g-pawn is stopped at the very threshold.

II. 52..N:g3 53 Nf7+ Ke7 54 N:g5, and once again, the black knight is mired.

Reshevsky nevertheless finds a way to get to the a-pawn.

52.	...	g5-g4
53.	h3:g4	h5:g4
54.	Ne5:g4	Ne4-c3
55.	Ng4-e5	Nc3-b1
56.	Ke3-d3	Nb1:a3
57.	b4-b5	...

This allows Black to give up his knight for two pawns and obtain some real drawing chances. Wouldn't the simple 57 Kc3 have been better? No, since it turns out that 57..b5 would give Black

an immediate draw: 58 c5+ Kd5 59 c6 Kd6 60 Kb2 Nc4+.

57.	...	Na3:b5
58.	c4:b5	Kd6-c5
59.	Ne5-f3	Kc5:b5
60.	Nf3-d4+	Kb5-b4
61.	Kd3-c2	e6-e5
62.	f4:e5	Kb4-c5
63.	e5-e6	Kc5-d6
64.	Kc2-c3	b6-b5
65.	Kc3-b4	Kd6-e7
66.	Kb4-c5	a4-a3
67.	Kc5-d5	...

BLACK RESIGNED

******

157. Boleslavsky—Bronstein
(English Opening)

1.	c2-c4	e7-e5
2.	Nb1-c3	d7-d6
3.	Ng1-f3	f7-f5
4.	d2-d4	e5-e4
5.	Nf3-d2	c7-c6

Black's method of play, using only his pawns, is hardly likely to attract imitators. Not surprisingly, Black soon finds himself in difficulties.

6.	e2-e3	Ng8-f6
7.	Bf1-e2	g7-g6
8.	0-0	Bf8-h6
9.	b2-b4	0-0
10.	b4-b5	Rf8-e8
11.	Nd2-b3	Nb8-d7
12.	Qd1-c2	Qd8-c7
13.	Bc1-d2	c6-c5

So as to avoid the opening of the b-file, at least.

14.	d4:c5	d6:c5
15.	Nc3-d5	Qc7-d6
16.	Ra1-d1	b7-b6
17.	f2-f4	Nf6:d5
18.	c4:d5	Nd7-f6

(See diagram, next page)

19.	Bd2-c3	Bc8-b7
20.	Qc2-b2	...

White has an obvious position-al advantage. Here the transfer of the knight from b3 via d2 to c4 suggests itself; Black would of course be ill-advised to take the d-pawn, since the opening of the d-file and the a2-g8 diago-nal would kill him. By missing this opportunity, White cedes the initiative.

20.	...	Nf6-g4
21.	Qb2-c1	Bh6-g7
22.	h2-h3	Bg7:c3
23.	Qc1:c3	Ng4-f6
24.	Be2-c4	Ra8-d8
25.	Rd1-d2	h7-h6
26.	Nb3-c1	Kg8-h7
27.	Nc1-e2	Qd6-f8
28.	Rf1-d1	Rd8-d6
29.	Qc3-b3	Re8-d8
30.	Ne2-c3	Qf8-e7
31.	Rd2-f2	Bb7-c8
32.	Nc3-e2	Bc8-e6
33.	Ne2-c3	Be6-f7
34.	a2-a4	...

White's position has become dubious; he is opening this im-portant operating file for his pieces just in the nick of time.

34.	...	Nf6-e8
35.	a4-a5	Qe7-f6
36.	Rf2-a2	g6-g5
37.	Rd1-f1	Qf6-g6
38.	a5:b6	a7:b6
39.	Ra2-a7	Rd8-d7
40.	Ra7-a8	Ne8-f6
41.	Qb3-b2	g5-g4

42.	h3:g4	Qg6:g4
43.	Rf1-d1	Qg4-h5

And here it is Black who misses his chance: 43..Qg3 ought to have been attempted. In view of the threat of 44..Ng4, White would have had to defend himself with 44 Qf2, but after 44..Q:f2+ 45 K:f2 N:d5 46 N:d5 B:d5 47 B:d5 R:d5 48 R:d5 Black goes into the rook ending a pawn up. On the other hand, I don't think this ending could have been won.

44.	Qb2-f2	Qh5-g6
45.	Ra8-c8	Nf6-g4
46.	Qf2-e1	Rd7-a7
47.	Rc8-c6	Ra7-a3
48.	Rd1-c1	Qg6-f6
49.	Bc4-e2	...

DRAW

******

158. Stahlberg—Gligoric
(King's Indian)

1.	Ng1-f3	Ng8-f6
2.	c2-c4	g7-g6
3.	g2-g3	Bf8-g7
4.	Bf1-g2	0-0
5.	0-0	d7-d6
6.	d2-d4	c7-c5
7.	h2-h3	...

Sometimes White can permit him-self this kind of tempo-loss in the opening, especially when, as here, the move is not altogether useless. Stahlberg intends to de-velop his bishop to e3 without fear of ..Ng4.

7.	...	Nb8-c6
8.	Nb1-c3	Bc8-d7

Here and later Gligoric avoids exchanges, in order to keep the game complicated. 8..cd 9 N:d4 N:d4 10 Q:d4 Be6 was also good; if then 11 B:b7 B:h3.

9.	d4:c5	d6:c5

Possibly White should have initiated this exchange with his seventh move.

10.	Bc1-e3	Qd8-c8
11.	Kg1-h2	Rf8-d8
12.	Qd1-c1	...

The endgame after 12 B:c5 B:h3 13 B:h3 R:d1 14 B:c8 R:a1 15 R:a1 R:c8 seems to favor Black.

12.	...	Nc6-d4
13.	Rf1-d1	Bd7-c6
14.	Nf3-e1	...

After playing a rather slow opening, White now removes an important piece from the center unnecessarily and falls into a difficult position. A few exchanges would have been more to the point here: 14 N:d4 cd 15 R:d4 R:d4 16 B:d4 B:g2 17 K:g2 Q:c4 18 e3, or 15 B:d4 Ng4+ 16 hg R:d4 17 R:d4 B:d4 18 e3.

14.	...	b7-b6
15.	Be3-g5	Bc6:g2
16.	Ne1:g2	Qc8-e6!

Coupled with his next move, this is an outstanding maneuver which leads to the win of a pawn. Its precision appears in the following variations: 17 Qe3 Q:c4 18 Q:e7 Rd7 19 Qe3 Re8, and White is in a hopeless predicament; or 17 Ne3 Ne4, when Black threatens to trap the bishop.

17.	Ng2-e3	Nf6-e4
18.	Nc3:e4	Qe6:e4
19.	Ne3-d5	...

The courage of despair. The white pieces are very poorly placed: the rooks lack scope, the queen is buried, and every pawn stands quite as passively as the next. Even the bishop stands alone, in the middle of Black's pieces. It is therefore understandable that the Swedish grandmaster should wish to see his knight set free, at least.

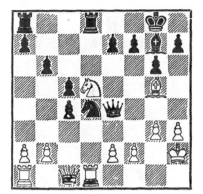

19.	...	Qe4:e2
20.	Qc1-e3	...

The check at e7 would lead to still greater difficulties: 20 N:e7+ Kf8 21 Qe3 Q:e3 22 fe Nf3+; or 21 N:g6+ hg 22 B:d8 Q:f2+.

20.	...	Qe2:e3
21.	Bg5:e3	e7-e6
22.	Be3:d4	Bg7:d4
23.	Nd5-e7+	Kg8-f8
24.	Ne7-c6	Rd8-d6
25.	Nc6:d4	Rd6:d4
26.	Rd1:d4	c5:d4
27.	Ra1-d1	e6-e5

An extra protected passed pawn in the center, with chances of making it two connected passed pawns — that's more than enough to win with. The rest is a matter of uncomplicated technique. Black brings his king to the center, creates a second passed pawn, and by advancing his pawns with the support of the rook, he forces his opponent to lay down his arms.

28.	Kh2-g2	Kf8-e7
29.	f2-f4	f7-f6
30.	Kg2-f3	Ke7-e6
31.	Rd1-c1	Ra8-d8
32.	f4:e5	f6:e5
33.	Kf3-e4	...

Stahlberg is giving his opponent all the hindrance he can. For the moment, the pawns are blockaded, and the only way to win is to get the rook around in back; in that event, however, White threatens to advance his

c-pawn. White is finally betrayed by the undefended status
of his rook and Black's threat
to mate on e3 when his rook
reaches the second or third
rank.

33.	...	Rd8-c8
34.	a2-a3	a7-a5
35.	b2-b3	Rc8-f8
36.	c4-c5	Rf8-c8

Destroying his last hope: 37 cb
R:c1!

37.	b3-b4	b6:c5
38.	Rc1-c4	Ke6-d6
39.	b4-b5	Rc8-b8
40.	a3-a4	Rb8-f8
41.	Rc4-c1	Rf8-f2
42.	Rc1-b1	c5-c4

WHITE RESIGNED

******

159. Euwe—Taimanov
(Nimzoindian Defense)

1.	d2-d4	Ng8-f6
2.	c2-c4	e7-e6
3.	Nb1-c3	Bf8-b4
4.	Qd1-c2	c7-c5
5.	d4:c5	0-0
6.	Bc1-f4	...

One of Euwe's numerous opening novelties, this one does not
try for any sort of big advantage, but it does introduce some
diversity into this well-known
line.

6.	...	Bb4:c5
7.	e2-e3	Nb8-c6
8.	Ng1-f3	d7-d5

9.	a2-a3	Qd8-e7
10.	Bf4-g5	Rf8-d8
11.	Ra1-d1	d5:c4
12.	Rd1:d8+	Qe7:d8
13.	Bf1:c4	Bc5-e7
14.	0-0	Bc8-d7
15.	Rf1-d1	Qd8-e8

By forcing Black to waste time
on the maneuver ..Qd8-e7:d8-e8,
White has obtained a small edge
in development.

| 16. | Bg5:f6 | Be7:f6 |

White has now removed one of
the main defenders of the h7
square. After Black's bishop
recapture (instead of the pawn
recapture), Euwe believes 17 Nb5
was worth a look: the knight aims
for c7, and if 17..Rd8 18 Nd6.
However, after 17..Qe7! 18 Nd6
Be8, White's advantage evaporates.

| 17. | Nc3-e4 | Bf6-e7 |
| 18. | Nf3-g5 | ... |

As we leave the opening for
the middlegame stage, the chances
lie with White. His advantage
consists of the more active placement of his pieces and his control of the d-file. White now
essays a curious combination,
which unfortunately falls short
of its mark; so playing the other knight straightforwardly out
to g5 was therefore better. After
18 Neg5, Black would have had
nothing better than to play
18..g6, and after 19 h4 and 20 h5,
the black king's position might
become very unsafe, in view of
White's standing threat to sacrifice a piece at e6 and enter

at g6 with his queen. Besides, after 18 Neg5 g6 the square f6 would be seriously weakened, and Black would not have enough time to bring his bishop to g7: 19 h4 Bf6 20 Ne4 Bg7 21 Nd6 Qb8 22 N:f7.

18. ... h7-h6

Taimanov courageously meets his opponent's idea head-on, having more accurately judged the endgame which now arises by force.

19. Ne4-d6   Be7:d6
20. Qc2-h7+   Kg8-f8
21. Rd1:d6   h6:g5

By removing this dangerous knight, Black is obviously avoiding all manner of possible surprises.

22. Rd6:d7   Qe8:d7
23. Qh7-h8+   Kf8-e7
24. Qh8:a8   Qd7-d1+

White's queen is temporarily blocked out of play, and Black quickly goes after the defenseless white pawns.

25. Bc4-f1   Qd1-b3
26. h2-h3   ...

White is too complacent: 26 Qh8 was necessary, followed by an immediate 27 h4. Euwe apparently hoped to close the b-file with Bb5, in which case his queen should certainly be at a8.

26. ...   Qb3:b2
27. a3-a4   Qb2-b6
28. Qa8-h8   ...

A pawn down, White nevertheless has some compensation in his queen, which is very active on the eighth rank.

28. ...   Ke7-f6

Would you believe that the humble h-pawn would become a queen in just a few moves? 28..g6 29 h4 gh 30 Q:h4+ Kd7 31 Qf6 Nd8 32 Bb5+ Kc8 was necessary, maintaining his extra pawn with a safe king.

29. h3-h4   Qb6-c5

Suspecting nothing.

30. h4-h5   ...

But now what is he to do? How to defend against the threat of h5-h6-h7-h8Q?

30. ...   g5-g4
31. h5-h6   Qc5-g5
32. h6-h7   ...

Suddenly the black king is feeling a good deal less than comfortable. A catastrophe appears to be imminent, but "first aid" (..g5-g4-g3) arrives just in time to save "his majesty's" health.

32. ...   g4-g3

Now, in view of the threatened 33..gf+ 34 K:f2 Qh4+, White's queen cannot leave the h-pawn.

33. Qh8-g8   g3:f2+
34. Kg1:f2   Nc6-e7
35. h7-h8Q   ...

The h-pawn has truly had a brilliant career. Now White even wins a piece.

| 35. | ... | Ne7:g8 |
| 36. | Qh8:g8 | Qg5-h4+ |

DRAW

agreed, since White's minimal material advantage is not enough to exploit. By means of his resourceful play, Taimanov neutralized his mistake on the 28th move.

******

160. Szabo—Najdorf
(Nimzoindian Defense)

1.	d2-d4	Ng8-f6
2.	c2-c4	e7-e6
3.	Nb1-c3	Bf8-b4
4.	e2-e3	0-0
5.	Ng1-f3	d7-d5
6.	a2-a3	Bb4:c3+
7.	b2:c3	b7-b6
8.	c4:d5	e6:d5
9.	Bf1-d3	c7-c5
10.	0-0	Nb8-c6
11.	a3-a4	...

By maintaining the pawn tension in the center, Black prevents White's e3-e4, so Szabo seeks an exit for his bishop on the a3-f8 diagonal. As soon as he plays 11 a4, however, Najdorf immediately closes the center and stations his knight at e4, giving White the choice of trading off his bishop or worrying over his c3-pawn. This game is significant for opening theory, since Najdorf's 12th

move is an improvement on the game Taimanov - Botvinnik from the XX USSR Championship.

| 11. | ... | c5-c4 |
| 12. | Bd3-c2 | Nf6-e4 |

Botvinnik played 12..Bg4, but his opponent ignored the threat to double his pawns and played 13 Qe1!

| 13. | Qd1-e1 | ... |

This allows Black to entrench himself firmly at e4. 13 B:e4 de 14 Nd2 was more in the spirit of the position, since a later f2-f3 would open the f-file for his rook and give his queen an exit to g3.

13.	...	Rf8-e8
14.	Bc1-b2	Bc8-f5
15.	Nf3-d2	Qd8-g5

Black's pieces are much more actively posted. If Black can hold firm in the struggle for the strategically vital e4 square, then clearly he will have the whip hand.

| 16. | Nd2:e4 | Bf5:e4 |

Black's major task would have been solved by the pawn recapture, which makes use of the fact that the e3-pawn is twice attacked and f2-f3 is therefore impossible. After 16..de, both White's bishops would remain blockaded for some time. Black could exploit this to create threats against the white king: for example, 17 Qd2 Bg4 (threatening ..Bf3) 18 Kh1 Re6 19 Bd1 Rh6 20 B:g4 Q:g4 21 f3 Qg3 22 h3 ef 23 R:f3 R:h3+.

| 17. | Bc2:e4 | Re8:e4 |
| 18. | Bb2-a3 | Re4-g4 |

(See diagram, next page)

19.	g2-g3	Rg4-e4
20.	Ra1-b1	Ra8-e8
21.	Rb1-b5	Qg5-d8
22.	Qe1-e2	a7-a6
23.	Rb5-b2	Nc6-a5
24.	Rf1-b1	Re4-e6

24..Nb3 was also possible;
White would then have probably
replied 25 R:b3 cb 26 Q:a6, and
with a couple of pawns for the
exchange, he would not be too
badly off. So Black holds back
on ..Nb3 for a while, waiting
until the queen no longer attacks
the a6-pawn.

25.	Kg1-g2	h7-h6
26.	Qe2-h5	Na5-b3
27.	Rb2-e2	Qd8-d7
28.	Ba3-b2	Kg8-h7
29.	h2-h3	g7-g6
30.	Qh5-f3	Re6-e4
31.	g3-g4	...

31.	...	f7-f5

The f-pawn is the only weak
spot in Black's position. Why
not play simply 31..Kg7, defending f6 at the same time? That
would have assured the fall of
White's a-pawn, for no compensation, and Black's win would
then have been quite easy.

32.	g4:f5	g6:f5
33.	Rb1-g1	Re8-g8+
34.	Kg2-h1	Rg8:g1+
35.	Kh1:g1	Re4-e7
36.	Kg1-h1	Qd7-e6
37.	Qf3-f4	Re7-g7

Najdorf wants to force a decision by occupying the g-file.
Exchanging queens and pushing his
queenside pawns was a sounder
idea.

38.	Kh1-h2	Qe6-g6

White's game appears hopeless.

39.	Qf4-g3	Qg6-h5
40.	Qg3-f4	...

A lucky find: White can leave
his rook hanging, as long as the
black king cannot avoid the perpetual check.

40.	...	Qh5-g6
41.	Qf4-g3	Qg6-e8
42.	Qg3-f4	Qe8-e4
43.	f2-f3	Qe4-d3

DRAW

Indeed, White plays 44 Rg2,
and after the rooks are exchanged Black can win the bishop, but not the game, in view

of the perpetual check. 43..Qb1
leads nowhere for the same reason. Instead of his actual last
move, however, Black could have
tried 43..Q:f4+ 44 ef Kg8, when
45 Re5 fails to 45..Nd2!, threatening mate in two. If Black's
king gets to the queenside, he
will have real winning chances,
since he will have an extra pawn,
for all practical purposes.
Black's position was so strong
that not even two inaccuracies
could spoil it completely.

******

161. Averbakh—Petrosian
(Sicilian Defense)

1.	e2-e4	c7-c5
2.	Ng1-f3	d7-d6
3.	d2-d4	c5:d4
4.	Nf3:d4	Ng8-f6
5.	Nb1-c3	g7-g6
6.	Bf1-e2	Bf8-g7
7.	Bc1-e3	0-0
8.	0-0	Nb8-c6
9.	Qd1-d2	d6-d5

With this standard d-pawn advance, Black wants to bring about
a series of exchanges to ease his
defense; however, some risk is
involved in this, due to the possibility 10 N:c6 bc 11 e5 Nd7
12 f4 e6 13 Na4, when White is
better. 11..Ng4 12 B:g4 B:g4
13 f4 would also leave Black in
a ticklish position, in view of
the threatened 14 Bc5. Averbakh
chooses a different course.

10.	e4:d5	Nf6:d5
11.	Nc3:d5	Nc6:d4
12.	c2-c4	...

This is more interesting than
the obvious 12 B:d4 Q:d5 13 Rad1,
etc.: it leaves Black with the
problem of whether to keep his
knight on d4 or to take the bishop at e2. If he should play
12..N:e2+ 13 Q:e2 e6, then the
quiet 14 Nc3 retains the better
chances for White, despite the
pair of black bishops, thanks
to White's queenside majority of
pawns and his control of most of
the central squares. Black finds
the best move.

12.	...	e7-e5
13.	f2-f4	Bc8-e6
14.	f4:e5	Nd4:e2+
15.	Qd2:e2	Be6:d5

16.	Ra1-d1	Bd5:c4
17.	Qe2:c4	Qd8-c8

I suppose it's time to let
the reader in on our little secret: up to and including Black's
17th move, both sides have been
replaying a game from the Szcza-
wno-Zdroj tournament of 1950, in
which Averbakh was Black. There
Geller continued 18 Qd5, and after 18..Qe6 19 Q:e6 fe 20 Rd7,
secured not the slightest advantage. Now Averbakh is playing
White, and has prepared an improvement — however, it does
not lead to anything substantial either.

18.	Qc4:c8	Ra8:c8
19.	Rd1-d7	Bg7:e5
20.	Rd7:b7	Rc8-b8
21.	Rb7:b8	Rf8:b8
22.	b2-b3	...

DRAW

******

******

ROUND TWENTY-FOUR

162. Petrosian—Szabo
(English Opening)

1.	c2-c4	Ng8-f6
2.	Nb1-c3	c7-c5
3.	Ng1-f3	d7-d5
4.	c4:d5	Nf6:d5
5.	g2-g3	Nd5:c3
6.	b2:c3	g7-g6
7.	Qd1-a4+	Nb8-d7
8.	h2-h4	h7-h6
9.	Ra1-b1	Bf8-g7
10.	Bf1-g2	...

The opening of this game has been quite characteristic of contemporary strategy. The energetic moves Qa4+, h2-h4, and Rb1 were only a means to create a more favorable position from which to enter the middlegame.

10.	...	0-0
11.	c3-c4	e7-e5
12.	d2-d3	Nd7-b6
13.	Qa4-c2	Bc8-d7

For a few moves, both sides maneuver quietly, each in his own camp.

14.	Bc1-e3	Qd8-e7
15.	Nf3-d2	f7-f5
16.	Nd2-b3	Ra8-c8
17.	Bg2:b7	Rc8-c7
18.	Bb7-g2	f5-f4

19.	Be3-c1	Bd7-c6
20.	Bg2:c6	Rc7:c6
21.	Nb3-d2	f4:g3

For the price of a pawn, Black has managed to hold White's king in the center. Far more important in this situation, however, is the opening of the f-file, since even before ..f4:g3, castling would not have been without danger to White, in view of his weakened pawn wall f2-g3-h4. Petrosian plays the next part of the game very resourcefully, and succeeds in warding off his opponent's threats while retaining his material advantage.

22.	f2:g3	Nb6-c8
23.	Rb1-b8	Nc8-d6

Of course it would have been difficult to calculate accurately all the consequences of 23..e4, but it would have brought about a completely muddled position, in which Black is not without chances — and that was precisely what Szabo aimed for in sacrificing the first pawn.

24.	Rb8:f8+	Qe7:f8
25.	e2-e4	...

Black's bishop is now firmly entombed — a consequence of Black's inability to decide on 23..e4.

25.	...	Qf8-c8
26.	Nd2-f1	h6-h5
27.	Nf1-e3	Rc6-a6
28.	Ne3-d5	Qc8-g4
29.	Qc2-g2	Nd6:c4

White has consolidated quite well, and there's nothing left for Black but the battering ram..

30.	d3:c4	Ra6:a2
31.	Qg2:a2	Qg4:e4+
32.	Qa2-e2	Qe4:h1+
33.	Qe2-f1	Qh1-h2
34.	Bc1-e3	Qh2:g3+

Black has managed to liquidate all White's pawn reserves. If only his bishop could help the queen, just a little! Concluding that now, at last, it's time to come out of the shadows, the bishop shoulders its pawn aside, but — alas! — too late. White's pieces begin their counterattack, and thanks to their numerical superiority, they sweep all before them.

(See diagram, next page)

35.	Qf1-f2	Qg3-h3
36.	Ke1-d2	e5-e4
37.	Nd5-f6+	Kg8-h8
38.	Nf6:e4	Qh3-e6
39.	Kd2-d3	Qe6-d7+
40.	Kd3-e2	Qd7-e6
41.	Ne4-d2	...

BLACK RESIGNED

******

163. Najdorf—Euwe
(Nimzoindian Defense)

1.	d2-d4	Ng8-f6
2.	c2-c4	e7-e6
3.	Nb1-c3	Bf8-b4
4.	e2-e3	c7-c5
5.	Bf1-d3	b7-b6
6.	Ng1-f3	Bc8-b7
7.	0-0	0-0
8.	Nc3-a4	...

For some reason, the masters in this tournament seemed to favor defensive systems with a queen's bishop fianchetto against Najdorf (see, for example, Games 94 and 118). In this game, Najdorf employs one of the best continuations, which forces Black to exchange pawns under most unfavorable circumstances.

8.	...	c5:d4
9.	e3:d4	Qd8-c7
10.	a2-a3	Bb4-e7
11.	Na4-c3	...

White leaves the correct road, and theory can no longer extract anything useful from this game. 11 b4! was more logical, using the knight to support a possible

c4-c5. On 11 b4, of course, there might follow 11..Ng4, forcing 12 g3, but there's nothing terrible about that. Now Black gets in ..d7-d5.

11.	...	d7-d5
12.	c4:d5	Nf6:d5
13.	Nc3:d5	Bb7:d5
14.	Nf3-e5	Qc7-b7
15.	Rf1-e1	Nb8-c6
16.	Qd1-h5	f7-f5
17.	Ne5:c6	Qb7:c6

Both sides have a pair of bishops and one approximately equivalent weakness (at d4 and e6, respectively), which equalizes the possibilities for attack and defense.

18.	Bc1-f4	Be7-f6
19.	Ra1-c1	Qc6-a4
20.	Bf4-e5	Bf6:e5
21.	d4:e5	Ra8-c8
22.	Qh5-e2	Qa4-f4

Black's queen now occupies a square that by rights ought to belong to White's, and creates a threat to take over the c-file.

| 23. | Qe2-e3 | ... |

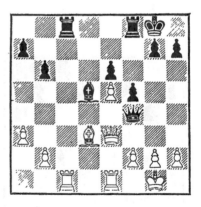

An excellent reply, with the idea of controlling the central light squares with his bishop and the dark squares with his pawns. Despite the fact that this exchange doubles and isolates the white pawns, it is precisely this queen exchange that makes them no longer weak, since the rook will be unable to reach them.

23.	...	Qf4:e3
24.	f2:e3	Rf8-d8
25.	Bd3-a6	Rc8-c1
26.	Re1:c1	Bd5-e4

Black has had to cede the c-file, but has seized the neighboring file as compensation, and will be the first to reach the seventh rank. The game gradually levels out, eventually winding up with a perpetual check.

27.	Ba6-c8	Rd8-d2
28.	Bc8:e6+	Kg8-f8
29.	Rc1-c7	Rd2:g2+
30.	Kg1-f1	Rg2:b2
31.	Rc7-f7+	Kf8-e8
32.	Rf7:a7	Rb2-b1+
33.	Kf1-f2	Rb1-b2+

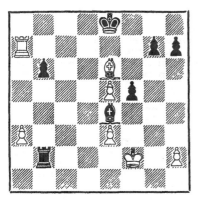

White's whole problem is that his king cannot escape via g3 because of 34..Rg2+ 35 Kh4 Rg4+ 36 Kh5 Bf3 or 35 Kh3 Rg4; in both cases, the mate threat wins for Black.

34.	Kf2-f1	Rb2-b1+
35.	Kf1-e2	Rb1-b2+
36.	Ke2-e1	Rb2-b1+
37.	Ke1-d2	Rb1-b2+
38.	Kd2-c3	Rb2-c2+
39.	Kc3-d4	Rc2-d2+
40.	Kd4-c4	Rd2-c2+
41.	Kc4-d4	...

The king finds no shelter on the other wing either: 41 Kb5 Rc5+, and Black picks up the e5-pawn; or 41 Kb3 Rc5 42 Bd7+ Kd8 43 e6 Ra5, forcing the

DRAW

******

164. Taimanov—Stahlberg
(Reti Opening)

1.	c2-c4	e7-e6
2.	g2-g3	Ng8-f6
3.	Bf1-g2	d7-d5
4.	Ng1-f3	d5:c4
5.	Qd1-a4+	Nb8-d7
6.	Qa4:c4	a7-a6
7.	0-0	Bf8-d6

7..Bd6 and 9..Qe7 must be intended as a preparation for ..e6-e5; if that is so, then 6..a6 was a waste of time.

8.	d2-d4	0-0
9.	Rf1-d1	Qd8-e7
10.	Qc4-c2	Ra8-b8

Inconsistent again: by this advance, the b-pawn will leave the c-pawn far behind, and soon the latter will fall — on the d6 square, it's true, but that's a mere detail. 10..e5 should have been played at once, and if 11 de N:e5 12 N:e5, he should recapture with the bishop, and not with the queen.

11.	Nb1-c3	b7-b5
12.	e2-e4	b5-b4
13.	Nc3-a4	e6-e5
14.	d4:e5	Nd7:e5
15.	Nf3:e5	Qe7:e5
16.	Bc1-f4	Qe5-a5
17.	Rd1:d6	...

When one has two equivalent ways to win a pawn, it's hard to resist a little joke (Black could not retreat to e7, in view of 17 e5).

17.	...	c7:d6
18.	Bf4:d6	Bc8-e6
19.	Bd6:f8	Rb8:f8
20.	b2-b3	Rf8-c8
21.	Qc2-d2	Be6-d7
22.	Na4-b2	Bd7-e6

(See diagram, next page)

23.	Nb2-d3	Be6:b3
24.	Qd2:b4	Qa5:b4
25.	Nd3:b4	Bb3-c4
26.	e4-e5	Nf6-d7
27.	f2-f4	...

Clearing a path for the king to d4. As for the e-pawn, it did not need defending, as the following variation serves to illustrate: 27 Rc1 N:e5? 28 Nc6! N:c6 29 R:c4 Ne7 30 R:c8+ N:c8 31 Bb7 Nb6 32 B:a6.

27.	...	g7-g6
28.	Ra1-d1	Nd7-b6
29.	Rd1-d6	...

White is dead set against taking a second pawn from Black with 29 Bb7. By allowing the a-pawns to be exchanged, Taimanov lengthens the game considerably, and is forced to seek his win in a protracted knight endgame.

29.	....	Nb6-a4
30.	a2-a3	Rc8-b8
31.	Bg2-d5	Bc4:d5
32.	Rd6:d5	...

32 N:d5 was better.

| 32. | ... | Na4-b6 |
| 33. | Rd5-a5 | ... |

33 Rc5 would have restricted the knight.

33.	...	Nb6-c4
34.	Ra5:a6	Nc4:a3
35.	Nb4-d5	Na3-c2
36.	Ra6-a4	Kf8-g7
37.	Ra4-c4	Rb8-d8
38.	Nd5-f6	Nc2-e3

Black is doomed to passive defense. Stahlberg's last move somewhat fortifies the knight's position at f5, and makes its rotation between f5 and h6 easier.

| 41. | Nf6-e4 | Rd8-e8 |
| 42. | Kg1-f2 | Re8-e7 |

White's perpetual threat against the f7-pawn has forced Black to allow the exchange of rooks, thus depriving Stahlberg of the hope still beating in his breast of securing a draw in the "three-vs-four" rook and pawn ending already known to us. As for the knight and pawn "three-vs-four" ending, that, as we shall see, is a win.

43.	Rc7:e7	Nf5:e7
44.	Kf2-f3	Kg7-f8
45.	Ne4-d6	Ne7-c6
46.	Kf3-e4	Kf8-e7
47.	f4-f5	Nc6-b4

(See diagram, next page)

48. f5-f6+   Ke7-f8

The king must fall back to the
eighth rank: on 48..Ke6 49 Nb7
threatens 50 Nd8+ or 50 Nc5 mate.

49. Nd6-b7   Nc5-a6
50. Ke4-d5   Na6-c7+
51. Kd5-d6   Nc7-b5+
52. Kd6-d7   ...

Apparently, even a lone knight
is not so easily avoided.

52. ...   Nb5-d4
53. Nb7-c5   Nd4-f5
54. Kd7-d8   ...

After the eighth rank, there's
nowhere else to go. The author
wishes to take this opportunity
to dispel a mistaken notion cur-
rent among some beginners that
according to the laws of chess,
if a king reaches the eighth
rank, one captured pawn may be
taken back. In this tournament,
several kings made it to the
eighth rank, and the reader may
see for himself that no pawns
appeared on the board as a result. This is a nonexistent
"rule", artificial and contrary to the logic of chess, whose
laws are the product of many
years' experience.

54. ...   Nf5-d4
55. Nc5-d7+   ...

The next phase of the struggle sees White pushing back the
black king and beginning a rightward movement of his own.

55. ...   Kf8-g8
56. Kd8-e8   Nd4-e6
57. Ke8-e7   g6-g5

Zugzwang: the king is tied to
the f7-pawn, and the knight is
trying to blockade the e5-pawn;
Black's defensive resources,
however, have finally run out.

58. Ke7-e8   Ne6-c7+
59. Ke8-d8   Nc7-e6+
60. Kd8-e7   Ne6-d4
61. Nd7-c5   ...

Now all is in readiness for
the decisive e5-e6.

61. ...   Nd4-c6+
62. Ke7-d6   Nc6-a5
63. e5-e6   f7:e6
64. Kd6-e7   ...

This looks like the end, but
Stahlberg, as ever, resourcefully searches out the tiniest
chance.

64. ...   Na5-c6+
65. Ke7-e8   Nc6-e5
66. Nc5:e6   Ne5-f7

Black has taken up his final
defensive line; behind that is
the abyss.

67. Ke8-e7   g5-g4
68. Ne6-g7   Nf7-h6
69. Ng7:h5   Nh6-f5+

If one held a contest among
knights for the most checks giv-
en, Stahlberg's would surely
hold the record.

70. Ke7-e8   Nf5-d6+
71. Ke8-d7   Nd6-f5
72. Nh5-g7!   Nf5-h6

The pawn ending is certainly
nothing Black is interested in.

73. Kd7-e7   Nh6-f7
74. Ng7-f5   ...

BLACK RESIGNED

******

165. Gligoric—Boleslavsky
(Sicilian Defense)

1. e2-e4   c7-c5
2. Ng1-f3   d7-d6
3. d2-d4   c5:d4
4. Nf3:d4   Ng8-f6

5.	Nb1-c3	a7-a6
6.	g2-g3	e7-e6

Boleslavsky declines to enter the 6..e5 line, since Gligoric is known to favor that system for White, and can be expected to have an improvement prepared over his Round 18 game with Najdorf.

7.	Bf1-g2	Bf8-e7
8.	0-0	0-0
9.	b2-b3	Qd8-c7
10.	Bc1-b2	Nb8-c6
11.	Nc3-e2	Bc8-d7
12.	c2-c4	...

White wants to control d5. To meet this, Black first removes all his pieces and pawns from the long diagonal, which greatly decreases the effectiveness of the fianchettoed bishop; then he undermines the c4-pawn, and secures full equality.

12.	...	Ra8-c8
13.	Ra1-c1	Qc7-b8
14.	Bb2-a3	Rf8-d8
15.	Qd1-d2	b7-b5!
16.	c4:b5	a6:b5
17.	Ba3-b2	Nc6:d4
18.	Ne2:d4	Qd8-b6
19.	a2-a3	...

DRAW

******

166. Bronstein—Kotov
(Queen's Indian Defense)

1.	c2-c4	Ng8-f6
2.	Ng1-f3	b7-b6
3.	g2-g3	Bc8-b7
4.	Bf1-g2	c7-c5
5.	0-0	e7-e6
6.	Nb1-c3	Bf8-e7
7.	d2-d4	c5:d4
8.	Nf3:d4	Bb7:g2
9.	Kg1:g2	...

In the Queen's Indian we occasionally see a fianchettoed ... king. What would impel White to develop his bishop at g2 and then trade it off immediately? Certainly it is not that the king is so well placed on g2. No, the explanation lies in the fact that in the Queen's Indian the positional battle hinges on the advance ..d7-d5. If White can restrain it, he has the better game; if Black enforces it, he equalizes. White therefore trades bishops in order to neu-

tralize the queen's bishop's support of this advance, and the king ends up on g2.

In other lines, White plays Nf3-e1, recapturing on g2 with the knight.

9.	...	Qd8-c8

Another typical maneuver in such positions. Black exploits the hanging c-pawn and the king's position to bring his queen to the long diagonal without loss of time.

10.	Qd1-d3	Nb8-c6
11.	b2-b3	0-0
12.	Bc1-b2	Rf8-d8

An unhurried move which underscores the strength of Black's position. White no longer has the means to keep the d-pawn in its place.

13.	Ra1-c1	Nc6:d4
14.	Qd3:d4	Be7-c5
15.	Qd4-f4	Qc8-b7+
16.	Kg2-g1	d7-d5
17.	c4:d5	...

DRAW

White's try for advantage was made with too cautious, and therefore harmless, means.

******

167. Reshevsky—Geller
(Nimzoindian Defense)

1.	d2-d4	Ng8-f6
2.	c2-c4	e7-e6
3.	Nb1-c3	Bf8-b4
4.	Qd1-c2	d7-d5
5.	c4:d5	e6:d5
6.	Bc1-g5	h7-h6
7.	Bg5:f6	Qd8:f6
8.	a2-a3	Bb4:c3+
9.	Qc2:c3	...

What made Reshevsky aim for such a position out of the opening? Isn't it symmetrical, with no advantage of any kind for White? Symmetrical, yes — but not entirely. Geller has pawns on light squares; consequently, the squares in front of them are dark squares, and White will be able to establish his knight on these squares, where the light-square bishop Geller is now left with cannot drive it away. Further, Black cannot avoid having

to play ..c7-c6, and this will
create a notch which White's
attacking pawns can grapple.
Thus, White has prospects of
further strengthening his position, while Black must operate
on the kingside whether he will
or no — here, however, the modus operandi is not so clear.

9.	...	0-0
10.	e2-e3	c7-c6
11.	Ng1-e2	Bc8-f5
12.	Ne2-f4	Nb8-d7
13.	Bf1-e2	Rf8-e8
14.	0-0	Nd7-f8
15.	b2-b4	Nf8-e6
16.	Nf4-h5	...

The obverse of the standard
minority attack appears if White
simply trades knights: 16 N:e6
R:e6 17 b5 Qg5 18 bc R:c6 19 Qb3
Bh3 20 Bf3 B:g2!,and Black's
queenside holds, while White's
kingside is already in ruins.
The ability to temper attack with
defense is one of the chessmaster's most valued, essential
skills. Total immersion in one's
own plan generally leads to un-
derestimating that of one's opponent. Forgetting this axiom cost Reshevsky a half-point
after adjournment.

16.	...	Qf6-g6
17.	Nh5-g3	Ra8-c8
18.	Ra1-c1	Ne6-g5

Black should always play ..a7-
a6 in these cases to induce White
to play a2-a4; then, if the "minority" advances any further, it
will involve a pawn exchange. The
more pawns Black can trade off,
the fewer his queenside weaknesses.

19.	b4-b5	...

This break is based on the
fact that after 19..cb 20 Qb3,
no matter how Black replies,
White not only wins his pawn
back, but gains another as well.

19.	...	Ng5-e4
20.	Qc3-a5	...

The queen attacks the a-pawn.
Had Black moved it up to a6 at
the proper time, he would be in
a great deal less trouble now.

20.	...	c6-c5!

In his difficult position, Geller does not lose his resourcefulness or presence of mind. Seeing that "normal" play will result in a slow death for Black,
he gives up the pawn and allows
White two connected passed pawns,
but creates an interesting counterchance in the form of a far-
advanced c-pawn. If 21 Q:a7, for
example, then 21..c4.

21.	Ng3:f5	Qg6:f5
22.	d4:c5	b7-b6!
23.	Qa5:a7	...

Of course not 23 cb? R:c1
24 R:c1 Q:f2+.

23.	...	b6:c5
24.	Be2-d3	c5-c4
25.	Bd3:e4	Qf5:e4
26.	Rf1-d1	c4-c3
27.	Qa7-d4	...

Now Geller's tactics are justified. Fearing the c-pawn's
swift advance, followed by the
d-pawn, Reshevsky hurriedly exchanges queens, and now real
drawing possibilities begin to
appear. Black would have had a
harder job after 27 b6 or 27 Rd4,
for example: 27 b6 c2 28 Rf1
(but not 28 Re1 d4!).

27.	...	Rc8-c4
28.	Qd4:d5	c3-c2
29.	Rd1-d2	Qe4:d5
30.	Rd2:d5	Re8-a8
31.	b5-b6	Ra8-b8

One of those rare cases in
Geller's career where he overlooks a saving combination, this

one based on the white king's
lack of an "airhole": 31..R:a3
32 b7 Rb4 33 Rd8+ Kh7 34 b8Q
R:b8 35 R:b8 Rd3 36 Rf1 Rc3!
Now White has nothing better than
to enter a "four-vs.-three" rook-
and-pawn ending, which theory
considers drawn (cf. Game 150,
Gligoric - Euwe).

32.	Rd5-d6	Rc4-a4
33.	Rc1:c2	Ra4:a3
34.	h2-h3	Ra3-b3
35.	Rc2-c6	Rb3-b2
36.	e3-e4	h6-h5
37.	e4-e5	h5-h4
38.	Rd6-d4	...

And here it might seem that
nothing could save Black. Nevertheless, I would not have
traded my b-pawn for the insignificant h-pawn. Couldn't
White have relocated his rook
on the seventh rank? After
38 e6 f6 39 Rc7 R:b6 40 R6d7,
it seems White's idea has jelled
(and this, by the way, is the
same sort of sudden assault on
g7 Reshevsky used once before in
this tournament, against Euwe).

38.	...	Rb2:b6
39.	Rc6:b6	Rb8:b6
40.	Rd4:h4	...

In order to understand what
follows, keep in mind that there
are some rook endings in which
two extra pawns are not enough
to win. As an example, sometimes
it is impossible to win the ending with rook and f- and h-pawns
against rook, or rook and two
connected passed pawns against
rook, if the pawns can be blockaded. Geller is hoping to transpose into one of these endgames.

40.	...	Rb6-b1+
41.	Kg1-h2	Rb1-e1
42.	f2-f4	Re1-e3
43.	Rh4-g4	Kg8-h7
44.	Rg4-g3	Re3-e2
45.	h3-h4	Re2-e4
46.	Rg3-f3	f7-f6
47.	e5:f6	g7:f6
48.	Kh2-g3	...

Believing he can win as he
pleases, Reshevsky plays carelessly: 48 g4 was the proper
continuation. Now Black gets in
the important blockading move
49..f5.

48.	...	Kh7-g6

49.	Rf3-a3	f6-f5

Black has achieved a great deal:
his rook and king are active,
while White's pawns are immobil-
ized. Still, had White played
50 Ra8, his two extra pawns
would have won in a walk.

50.	Ra3-a6+	Kg6-h5

51.	Ra6-f6	...

Another inaccuracy, which
throws away the win for certain
in an amazing fashion: 51 Ra8
was still the right move. Now
Black's king is restricted —
too much so, in fact.

51.	...	Re4-e3+
52.	Kg3-f2	Re3-a3
53.	g2-g3	...

After 53 R:f5+ K:h4, we reach
one of the drawn positions with
two extra pawns for White.

53.	...	Ra3-f3+!

54 K:f3 or 54 Kg2 R:g3+ 55 K:g3
is stalemate! The king makes for
the e-file, but it doesn't make
any difference. (If the white
rook were on a8, there would
be no stalemate; White would
win.)

54.	Kf2-e2	Rf3:g3
55.	Rf6:f5+	Kh5:h4
56.	Ke2-f2	Rg3-a3
57.	Rf5-g5	Ra3-b3
58.	Rg5-g1	Kh4-h5
59.	Kf2-e2	Rb3-a3
60.	f4-f5	Ra3-a5

DRAW

168. Keres—Smyslov
(English Opening)

On the eve of the 24th round, Keres was a half-point behind Smyslov, but Keres was due for his bye in the 25th round. In the event of a draw with Smyslov, he would fall either a point or a point and a half behind Smyslov, depending on how the latter scored against Reshevsky in Round 25. Thus, we can see the psychological circumstance which impelled Keres to try his luck with a strange, sharp kingside attack, using only his two rooks without the aid of his pawns.

Keres either could not or would not make methodical and logical preparations for his attack. As early as the 19th move, he offered a rook, as the English expression goes, "for nothing". Our understanding of sacrifices usually involves some resounding check — B:h7+ or R:g7+ — forcing one's opponent to capture the piece. However, the finest sacrifices are a bit different: the rook is attacked, but it does not move...

1.	c2-c4	Ng8-f6
2.	Nb1-c3	e7-e6
3.	Ng1-f3	c7-c5
4.	e2-e3	Bf8-e7
5.	b2-b3	0-0
6.	Bc1-b2	b7-b6
7.	d2-d4	c5:d4
8.	e3:d4	d7-d5
9.	Bf1-d3	Nb8-c6
10.	0-0	Bc8-b7
11.	Ra1-c1	...

On 11 Qe2, Black could play for the win of a pawn without running too much of a risk: 11..Nb4 12 Bb1 dc 13 bc B:f3 followed by 14..Q:d4.

11.	...	Ra8-c8
12.	Rf1-e1	Nc6-b4
13.	Bd3-f1	Nf6-e4
14.	a2-a3	Ne4:c3
15.	Rc1:c3	...

White unveils his original plan to transfer the rook to the kingside. On the other hand, 15 B:c3 was obviously out of the question, in view of 15..Na2.

15.	...	Nb4-c6
16.	Nf3-e5	Nc6:e5
17.	Re1:e5	...

Both rooks are ready for the plunge.

17.	...	Be7-f6
18.	Re5-h5	g7-g6

It would not be out of place to mention here that White was already threatening 19 R:h7 K:h7 20 Qh5+ Kg8 21 Rh3 Bh4 22 R:h4 f5 23 Qh7+, with an irresistible attack.

19. Rc3-h3   ...

"I thought for a long time," said Smyslov afterwards, "over whether or not I should give in, and accept the rook — the more so, in that I was unable to see how White would be able to win here..." Indeed, to take a whole rook for nothing! The worst of it is, what if I don't take it, and then lose? And look: next move, the rook will take off the h-pawn — well, then, grab it! Calculating all the variations over the board is obviously not possible; all one can do is to examine the main lines and trust in oneself.

19. ...   d5:c4

Smyslov's intuition did not deceive him: as later analysis was to show, he made the best move here. But how did he arrive at it? What sort of mechanism, if one may so call it, operates a grandmaster's intuition? Did Smyslov reason it out, or did he simply guess, as one might do in a lottery, and pull out a winning number?

Of course the text move resulted from a deep study of the position. First of all, Black is opening his bishop's diagonal, creating the possibility of transferring that piece via e4 to f5 or g6. Secondly, the d-file is opened, creating the possibility of moving the queen to d5 and attacking the square g2 along the diagonal, or simply taking the d4-pawn with the queen. And thirdly, a passed c-pawn temporarily makes its appearance; it may go on to c3, closing the diagonal of the dangerous white bishop... Meanwhile, the white rook is still <u>en prise</u>, and now the basic threat of ..g6:h5 is a real one; for on 20 bc, for example, 20..gh 21 Q:h5 Be4.

Still, we are all curious to see what might have happened if Black had taken the rook right away — wouldn't 19..gh 20 Q:h5 Re8 have saved him, by opening an escape hatch for the king? No, since White would have cut off his escape with the startling 21 a4!!, threatening 22 Ba3. Some sample lines:

I. 21..dc 22 Q:h7+ Kf8 23 Ba3+ Re7 24 Rg3;

II. 21..Qd6 22 c5, and now:

a) 22..bc 23 Qh6 Bg7 24 Q:h7+ Kf8 25 dc,

b) 22..Qd8 23 c6 R:c6 24 Ba3 Rd6 25 Qh6 B:d4 26 Bd3, or

c) 22..Qf4 23 Q:h7+ Kf8 24 Ba3 bc 25 B:c5+ Re7 26 Rg3 Ke8 27 Bb5+.

20. Rh5:h7 ...

Keres could still have forced a draw by 20 Qg4 c3 21 B:c3 R:c3 22 R:c3 Q:d4 23 Q:d4 B:d4 24 Rc7 gh 25 R:b7, but he was not looking for a draw when he undertook this attack.

20. ... c4-c3

Now the bishop can neither take the pawn — 21 B:c3? R:c3 — nor retreat — 21 Bc1 Q:d4. Keres finds the best chance.

21. Qd1-c1 Qd8:d4

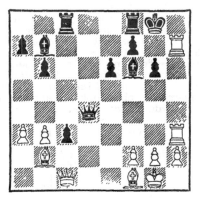

Taking the bishop would be a bad idea in view of 22 Qh6 Q:d4 23 Rh8+ B:h8 24 Qh7 mate.

22. Qc1-h6 Rf8-d8
23. Bb2-c1 Bf6-g7
24. Qh6-g5 Qd4-f6
25. Qg5-g4 c3-c2
26. Bf1-e2 Rd8-d4

Accuracy to the end. Black forces 27 f4, opening the diagonal for a check.

27. f2-f4 Rd4-d1+
28. Be2:d1 Qf6-d4+

WHITE RESIGNED

******

******

ROUND TWENTY-FIVE

169. Smyslov—Reshevsky
(Reti Opening)

In his battle for the right to play a match for the world's championship, Smyslov had just survived a fierce struggle with Keres; his next opponent, Reshevsky, was just as aggressively inclined.

At this moment, Reshevsky had half a point less than Smyslov, with one more game played. So, strictly speaking, even a win would not have allowed Reshevsky to overtake the leader, while a draw would clearly have been unsuitable. So, like Keres, the American also set himself the task of winning at all costs.

1.	c2-c4	Ng8-f6
2.	Nb1-c3	e7-e6
3.	Ng1-f3	Bf8-b4
4.	g2-g3	b7-b6
5.	Bf1-g2	Bc8-b7
6.	0-0	0-0
7.	Qd1-b3	Bb4:c3

The rather unusual 3..Bb4, followed by the exchange on c3, was evidently something Reshevsky had prepared with the intention of obtaining a position bearing the least possible resemblance to anything in theory, and of carrying on the fight with his knights against the enemy's bishops.

8.	Qb3:c3	d7-d6
9.	b2-b3	Qd8-e7
10.	Bc1-b2	c7-c5
11.	d2-d4	Nb8-d7
12.	Ra1-d1	Bb7-e4

A proper move, typical of a Queen's Indian Defense: Black places his bishop in front of its pawn chain, so that now he need no longer fear White's d4-d5. If the bishop had remained on b7, it would have been doomed to passivity, whereas now it is fully the equal of White's bishop on g2.

13.	d4:c5	Nd7:c5
14.	Qc3-e3	...

A powerful move, combining the tactical threat of 15 B:f6 and 16 b4 with the positional idea of either driving the bishop out or inducing the e-pawn's advance.

14.	...	e6-e5

Black has now more or less neutralized the two bishops. The bishop on e4 stands guard over one, while the other is hemmed in by Black's pawns. Of course, the d-pawn will be a source of worry, but this is no great danger, as long as Black's position contains no other weaknesses. White's following maneuvers aim at getting the black bishop for his knight.

15.	Bg2-h3	a7-a5
16.	Nf3-h4	Rf8-e8
17.	f2-f3	...

White could also have achieved his ends without this move, since 17 Nf5 would have forced Black to give up the bishop; but Smyslov leaves himself the option of taking the bishop on g6 at a later time, under more favorable circumstances.

17.	...	Be4-g6
18.	Rd1-d2	Ra8-d8
19.	Rf1-d1	Qe7-c7
20.	Nh4:g6	h7:g6
21.	Bh3-g2	...

Even here, it cannot be said that White's bishop-pair confers on him any kind of substantial advantage. This is a balanced position, which here presages, not a draw, but rather an interesting struggle. In the course of the next ten or twelve moves, both sides maneuver, while hiding their plans from each other, and await the moment when the constellation of pieces will allow them to take decisive action.

21.	...	Nf6-h5
22.	Qe3-c3	...

(See diagram, next page)

(Position after 22 Qc3)

22.   ...   Nh5-f6

White's bishops are still restricted, but his darksquare bishop can go to e3, which is the
intersection point of two important diagonals. Black should have
forestalled this while attempting
to seize the initiative on the
kingside with 22..f5!

One may imagine that perhaps
Reshevsky deliberately refrained
from playing this here, in order
to play it after White had played
e2-e4, and closer to the time-
control, for the sake of further
complicating matters. However,
this tactic proved unsuccessful
against Smyslov's clear, logical
play.

23.	e2-e4	Nf6-h5
24.	Qc3-e3	Nh5-f6
25.	Bg2-h3	Nf6-h7
26.	Rd2-e2	Nh7-f6
27.	Rd1-f1	Nf6-h5
28.	Bh3-g2	Qc7-e7
29.	Bb2-c1	Qe7-c7
30.	Rf1-d1	Kg8-h7
31.	Qe3-f2	Nh5-f6
32.	Bc1-e3	Nf6-h5
33.	Re2-c2!!	...

We must give this move two exclamation marks, as otherwise we
would have to give one to each
of Smyslov's moves. He emerges
as the winner of this game from
both the chessplaying and the
psychological point of view.
Reshevsky was unable to fathom
the plan behind his moves. Here,

Smyslov only feinted at f3-f4,
while he was really preparing a
battery on the diagonal g1-a7.
Now a2-a3 and b3-b4 is the threat,
driving the knight away so as
to attack the b-pawn. 33 Rc2 was
played to eliminate the reply
..N:b3 after his 34 a3, and to
support the break c4-c5 in some
lines. As for Black's pieces,
the only difference between their
positions now and what it was
eleven moves ago is that the king
has gone from g8 to h7 — and
even this slight change is not
to Black's advantage.

33.   ...   f7-f5

Reshevsky now executes his
long-delayed thrust, when he
no longer has any real choice.
The rest follows quite swiftly,
presenting a sharp contrast to
the deliberate maneuvers of the
preceding stage.

| 34. | e4:f5 | g6:f5 |
| 35. | g3-g4 | Nh5-f4 |

Reshevsky sacrifices a pawn,
but achieves his goal: complications at any price.

| 36. | Be3:f4 | e5:f4 |
| 37. | Qf2-h4+ | Kh7-g8 |

| 38. | g4:f5 | d6-d5 |

A second pawn follows the
first, in order to attain the
sort of position where, temporarily, the pawn count will be
meaningless. If White plays this
stage calmly and accurately, his
two extra pawns must tell. And,

once again, Smyslov comes out on top, despite all of his opponent's tactical skill.

| 39. | c4:d5 | ... |

If 39 R:d5 R:d5 40 cd Qe5, threatening 41..Qa1+ or 41..Nd3, or simply 41..Q:f5.

| 39. | ... | Qc7-e5 |
| 40. | Rc2-d2 | ... |

40 Rc4 Qe3+ 41 Kh1 Nd3 would be a mistake for White.

| 40. | ... | Rd8-d6 |
| 41. | Rd2-d4 | Qe5-e3+ |

41..Q:f5 42 Q:f4 Q:f4 43 R:f4 Re2 would have been stronger. We get the same position in another three moves, but White retains his f5-pawn. And if White answers 41..Q:f5 with 42 R:f4, then 42..Qc2 43 Re1 R:e1+ 44 Q:e1 Nd3, with complications.

42.	Kg1-h1	Re8-e5
43.	Qh4:f4	Qe3:f4
44.	Rd4:f4	Re5-e2
45.	Rf4-g4	...

Threatening 46 f6 and 47 d6. White's pawns get underway now, and now they are six against three!

45.	...	Kg8-f8
46.	Rg4-g6	Nc5-b7
47.	Rg6-e6	Re2:a2
48.	f3-f4	Ra2-b2
49.	Rd1-e1	Rd6:e6
50.	d5:e6	Nb7-d6
51.	e6-e7+	Kf8-f7
52.	Bg2-d5+	Kf7-e8

53.	Bd5-c6+	Ke8-f7
54.	e7-e8Q+	Nd6:e8
55.	Bc6:e8+	Kf7-f6
56.	Be8-g6	...

BLACK RESIGNED

This game (and the one that follows) decided first prize, for all practical purposes. Smyslov displayed all his best qualities, while I played this important game with Geller in a manner far beneath any possible criticism.

******

170. Geller—Bronstein
(Queen's Gambit)

| 1. | d2-d4 | e7-e6 |
| 2. | Ng1-f3 | Ng8-f6 |

2..f5 was a more suitable move in order to play for a win, but Black was peaceably inclined.

3.	c2-c4	d7-d5
4.	c4:d5	e6:d5
5.	Nb1-c3	c7-c6
6.	Qd1-c2	Bc8-g4
7.	Bc1-g5	Nb8-d7
8.	e2-e3	Bf8-d6
9.	Bf1-d3	Qd8-c7
10.	0-0-0	h7-h6
11.	Bg5-h4	Bd6-b4
12.	Kc1-b1	Bb4:c3
13.	Qc2:c3	0-0

There was no reason to delay the knight invasion of e4; after 13..Ne4 14 Qc2 Bf5 White would have had to reckon with 15..g5.

14.	h2-h3	Bg4-h5
15.	Qc3-c2	Nf6-e4
16.	Bd3:e4	d5:e4
17.	g2-g4	Bh5-g6
18.	Nf3-d2	...

After 18 Bg3, the queen sacrifice 18..Q:g3 19 fg ef 20 e4 Nf6 comes into consideration: bishop, knight and the pawn at f3 would be adequate compensation.

18.	...	Nd7-b6
19.	Nd2-c4	Nb6-d5
20.	Bh4-g3	Qc7-d7
21.	Nc4-e5	Qd7-e6
22.	Qc2-b3	Bg6-h7
23.	Rd1-c1	...

Black may already have gone too far in his unwillingness to undertake anything active. White has cleverly exploited his partner's weak play to work up some queenside pressure, although there were no real threats as yet. So the following blunder of a pawn was totally uncalled for.

23.   ...   a7-a5

24.   Qb3:b7   ...

Of course! I had completely overlooked that the b8 square was controlled by White's bishop on g3. Now Black's game slides rapidly downhill.

24.	...	Nd5-b4
25.	Ne5-c4	c6-c5
26.	d4:c5	Nb4-d3
27.	c5-c6	f7-f5
28.	g4:f5	Bh7:f5
29.	Rh1-g1	Bf5-g6
30.	Rc1-c2	Ra8-c8
31.	Bg3-d6	Rf8-e8
32.	Qb7-d7	Qe6-f6
33.	c6-c7	Bg6-f5
34.	Qd7-b5	Bf5:h3
35.	Bd6-g3	Bh3-e6
36.	Nc4-d6	Nd3-b4
37.	Nd6:e8	Be6:a2+
38.	Kb1-c1	Qf6-e7
39.	Ne8-d6	Nb4-d3+
40.	Kc1-d2	Rc8:c7
41.	Qb5-e8+	Qe7:e8
42.	Nd6:e8	Rc7-d7
43.	Rc2-c7	...

BLACK RESIGNED

******

171. Kotov—Gligoric
(King's Indian)

In the struggle that is chess, the blockade is not just an important technique, but also one of the elements in the strategic plan. The methods for dealing with any enemy piece may be ranked in descending value as follows: capture (or elimination), exchange, attack, blockade. The attacked piece may be defended in any of several ways: retreat is the simplest, but it may also be shielded, or the attacking piece may be captured. The idea behind the blockade is first to deprive the target piece of its mobility before actually attacking it.

In the most general sense, a blockade may be employed against any piece, including the king, but when we speak of the blockade in practical terms, generally it is in reference to pawns. They are the easiest to blockade, and the most dangerous pieces when set in motion.

Which pieces best fill the role of blockader? First and foremost, of course, the knight, since while it blocks the path of the pawn it also attacks the squares diagonally behind it. The bishop is also useful for this purpose, since it can prevent the advance of several pawns simultaneously. One may also blockade a pawn with a pawn, but that is a double-edged weapon, since the blockading pawn becomes blockaded itself.

These are the blockade's simplest facets; the reality of chess is a great deal more complicated. In the Kotov - Gligoric game, Black succeeded in maintaining a blockade of a considerable length of pawn chain, thereby severely restricting, not only the pawns, but the pieces too. Naturally, Gligoric did not achieve all this for nothing: it cost him a great deal of thought—and two pawns.

1.	d2-d4	Ng8-f6
2.	c2-c4	g7-g6

3.	Nb1-c3	Bf8-g7
4.	e2-e4	d7-d6
5.	f2-f3	0-0
6.	Bc1-e3	e7-e5
7.	d4-d5	c7-c5

After the sufferings he en-
dured in his games with Geller
and Petrosian from White's continual threat of c4-c5, Gligoric decides to close the center.
Although this does deprive his
knight of the square c5, it also
retains solid control of d4, even
if his e5-pawn should go else-
where. Kotov's 8 Bd3 is the natural reaction for White, intending to create threats on the diagonal b1-h7 in the event of
..f7-f5.

8.	Bf1-d3	Nf6-h5
9.	Ng1-e2	f7-f5
10.	e4:f5	g6:f5
11.	Qd1-c2	e5-e4!

The first link in Black's plan
of blockade: he brings a white
pawn to e4, which remains there
until the end of the game, hampering any effort by White to
obtain the initiative on the diagonal where his queen and bishop are so threateningly posted.
Meanwhile, he frees e5 for his
own pieces, and clears an important operating diagonal for
his "Indian" bishop, in the
event White castles long. For
all these advantages, Black has
only given up one pawn: an insignificant price, considering
the circumstances.

12.	f3:e4	f5-f4
13.	Be3-f2	Nb8-d7

The black knight wants to get
to e5, and White has to get it
out of there at any cost, which
explains his knight's retreat to
its original square.

White saw nothing attractive
in the line 14 e5 N:e5 15 B:h7+
Kg8; although White keeps his
extra pawn and the semblance of
an attack on the king, his position is actually quite hopeless,
in view of Black's threats of
..N:c4, ..f4-f3, and ..Qg5.

14.	Ne2-g1	Qd8-g5
15.	Bd3-f1	Nd7-e5

Black has won the first skirmish, and thrown back the enemy
forces, but he has yet to win
the campaign. After regrouping,
White's pieces move out once
again to more active positions.

16.	Ng1-f3	Qg5-e7
17.	Nf3:e5	Qe7:e5
18.	0-0-0	Nh5-f6
19.	h2-h3	Bc8-d7

Gligoric loves a well-prepared
breakthrough. A less patient
player would have been unable to
restrain himself from playing
19..a6 20 Bd3 b5 21 cb ab 22 B:b5
Ba6, with a fearsome attack on
the a- and b-files and the long
diagonal.

20.	Bf1-d3	a7-a6
21.	Nc3-b1	...

Outstanding! Now, after ..b7-
b5, White does not take the pawn,
but replies Nb1-d2, threatening
to drive away the queen, one
way or another, from the main
blockading square.

21.	...	f4-f3!!

Beautiful play. The maneuver
Nb1-d2-f3 could have led to the
collapse of Black's entire blockading position. Gligoric demonstrates that he is a true chess
artist in the creative sense by
giving up a second pawn in order
to deprive the knight of the f3
square and expand the radius of
his blockade.

22.	g2:f3	Nf6-h5
23.	Nb1-d2	Nh5-f4

A classic example of a block-aded position. The blockade's immediate effect embraces four white pawns, but its influence penetrates much deeper: the lightsquare bishop has been turned into a pawn, the knight's own pawns occupy all of its best squares, and even so mobile a piece as White's queen is almost totally blockaded as well! Now Black threatens no more and no less than mate in two; and the best defensive move is answered, at last, by the well-prepared breakthrough.

One can only marvel at the great defensive power of White's position, and at Kotov's masterful ability to stay on his feet come what may, considering the circumstances.

24.	Bd3-f1	b7-b5
25.	h3-h4	Kg8-h8
26.	Rh1-g1	Bg7-f6
27.	Nd2-b3	Ra8-b8

At the critical juncture, Black fails to show the necessary resoluteness. He had to calculate the variations and advance one of his pawns. If 27..a5 fails against 28 cb a4 29 Nd2 a3 30 Nc4 ab+ 31 Kb1 Qe7 32 e5, when the blockade is broken, then 27..b4 28 Na5 Ba4 29 b3 would be very strong for Black, guaranteeing him at least a perpetual check. He could, however, also retreat his bishop to d7, continuing the attack.

28.	Bf2-e1	b5-b4
29.	Kc1-b1	Rb8-a8

Black's rook returns, but White has improved his position considerably: the knight can now go to c1 and thence to d3, lifting the blockade a little.

30.	Be1-g3	Rf8-g8
31.	Qc2-h2	...

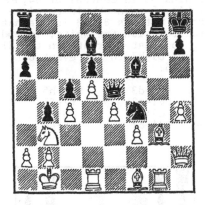

| 31. | ... | Rg8:g3 |

An exchanging combination on the theme of "interference and decoy". Once the white f- and e-pawns started moving, Black's game would crumble.

32.	Rg1:g3	Nf4-e2
33.	Qh2:e2	Qe5:g3
34.	Nb3-c1	a6-a5
35.	Nc1-d3	Bf6-d4

The bishop must get closer to the center, in view of the threatened 36 e5.

36.	h4-h5	Qg3-h4
37.	Bf1-g2	Ra8-g8
38.	Rd1-h1	Qh4-g3
39.	Bg2-f1	a5-a4

The last moves before the time-control were made in a hurry. Black could also have pushed his a-pawn without moving his queen about; nor was White's next move with his king necessary.

| 40. | Kb1-c2 | ... |

40.   ...   a4-a3

Gligoric could have maintained good winning chances with 40..b3+ 41 ab ab+ 42 K:b3 Qg7 43 h6 Ba4+ 44 K:a4 Qb7, or 43 Kc2 Rb8 44 Qg2 Ba4+ 45 Kc1 Qb7.

41.   b2-b3   ...

DRAW

After careful analysis, both sides concluded that Black had no win.

******

172. Boleslavsky—Taimanov
(Queen's Indian Defense)

Does White get the advantage from his right to the first move? Every chessplayer asks himself that question, and the answer is not easily discovered.

One is forcefully reminded in this connection of Vsevolod Rauzer, one of our most noted master-theoreticians, whose motto was, "1 e2-e4!, and White wins". He was probably joking when he said that, but every joke contains its share of truth. This conviction that moving the king's pawn first gave White the better of it, while 1 d2-d4 led only to a draw, inspired Rauzer to work out amazingly deep and forceful attacking systems in a number of openings: the Sicilian, French, Ruy and Caro-Kann, and many others. Later, of course, it developed that many of his

wins owed less to the objective strength of his 1 e2-e4 than to Rauzer's own creative talent, the exceptionally logical pattern of his thinking, and the accuracy of his calculations. Rauzer's Attacks and Variations live on, and are still employed to this day, even though it is possible for Black to defend himself successfully against them. So working up forcing lines for use in the opening battle, a fearsome weapon in the hands of such players as Morphy, Chigorin, Pillsbury, Alekhine, Fine and Botvinnik, is a method that works equally well for White or Black. The player who uses a prepared forcing line may very well run into a forced refutation, as indeed happened in some games from the present tournament. There is no player, past or present, who has never made a mistake — an axiom that holds just as true for home analysis as it does for over-the-board play. Which, in turn, means that one cannot, as a rule, gain the advantage this way in the opening.

So there exists a different concept of opening strategy, which may briefly be summarized as follows: that it is not necessary to make the very best moves — only good ones.

This was the creative attitude of Lasker and Capablanca, for example, and it is Smyslov's too. The advantage of the opening, in this case, is understood to be the right to choose a system of development more suited to the White player's taste, and which gives him the greatest possible liberty to express his creative ability.

Statistics — a sound approach to the study of mass phenomena — show that White's opening advantage is quite real. In the various eras of history, in every strong tournament for which records were kept, White held a persistent edge in the number of wins. This advantage of White's should be considered as a tendency, which manifests itself in the course of dozens or hundreds of games, but which has no bearing on the outcome of any particular game. It would be tremendously interesting to examine this tendency in historical cross-section: has the percentage of games won by White increased or decreased by comparison with what it was, say, 20, 50 or 100 years ago? One peculiar feature should be noted: the stronger the tournament, the weaker the influence of the advantage of the first move. As examples to demonstrate this, one may cite the 1948 World's Championship Match-Tournament, the 1951 World's Championship Match (in which White won four games and Black six), and a few other events. Does this mean that eventually the right of the first move will give no advantage at all? Time will tell...

In this game, the reader will find a sample of Boleslavsky's well-prepared and accurately-calculated opening play, followed by a natural transition into a combinative middle stage, and then an interesting endgame which is a win for White. In conclusion, we have a witty counter-combination by Taimanov.

1.	d2-d4	Ng8-f6
2.	c2-c4	e7-e6
3.	Ng1-f3	...

The first of White's "merely good" moves. 3 Nc3 is universally considered "best".

3.	...	b7-b6
4.	g2-g3	Bc8-b7
5.	Bf1-g2	Bf8-e7
6.	0-0	0-0
7.	Nb1-c3	Nf6-e4

In contrast to the King's Indian, where the placement of the white e-pawn makes no difference to Black, in the Queen's Indian Black has to keep close watch on the e4 square. The difference is easily explained: in the King's Indian, Black places his center pawns on d6 and e5, leaving his queen's bishop the excellent diagonal c8-h3 to work on, whereas here the queen's bishop is developed to b7, with a different working diagonal, a8-h1. Consequently, it follows that the fewer pawns stand in the way from b7 to f3, the better Black's prospects will be. The next phase of the game could be headed,"The Battle For e2-e4", and it is Boleslavsky who comes out the victor. Unlike Taimanov, he does not forget his other option, that of shutting the fianchet-toed bishop out with d4-d5.

| 8. | Qd1-c2 | Ne4:c3 |
| 9. | Qc2:c3 | ... |

White's second and third "merely good" moves. Stubborn attempts to secure an advantage by means of 8 Bd2 or 9 bc are still being tried — although the latter move does encounter the powerful rejoinder 9..Nc6 (cf. Najdorf - Averbakh).

| 9. | ... | f7-f5 |

Opinions are sharply divided over this fashionable move. It is enough to note that some consider it to be a defensive move; others, attacking.

The author possesses a rather limited knowledge of the Queen's Indian, and although 9..f5 did occur in the third and last encounter between the previous and the present World Champions (Amsterdam 1938, Alekhine - Botvinnik), it would seem to me that Keres is more correct in preferring the unhurried transfer of this bishop to a better square with 9..Be4. In this opening formation, the f-pawn probably belongs at f7: the pawns at d7, e6 and f5 overload the diagonal c8-h3.

| 10. | b2-b3 | Be7-f6 |
| 11. | Bc1-b2 | Nb8-c6 |

Of course, Black understands that the knight does not belong at c6; he is merely using that square as a springboard to bring the knight to the king's wing. However, this costs Black another move, which enhances White's initial advantage.

With his advantage in time, White methodically prepares, and then carries out, the important push d4-d5, cutting the black bishop's mobility to nil.

12.	Ra1-d1	Qd8-e8
13.	Qc3-c2	Nc6-d8
14.	d4-d5	...

Black could no longer prevent this aggression: on 13..Ne7 14 d5 would also have been the

reply, since 14..B:b2 15 Q:b2
ed 16 Ng5 Qg6 17 Nh3 favors
White.

| 14. | ... | Bf6:b2 |
| 15. | Qc2:b2 | e6:d5 |

White's pawn must be removed
from d5 at all costs: if Black
plays passively, then 16 Nd4,
and the opening of the center
with e2-e4 is not to be prevented.

16.	c4:d5	c7-c5
17.	d5:c6	d7:c6
18.	Nf3-e5!	Rf8-f6

One can only describe Black's
position as "ailing". As you
can see, one need not make gross
blunders in order to lose a
game; sometimes it is enough
merely to have played the opening superficially. Still, beginning with this move, Taimanov
starts to play at full power,
demonstrating his customary resourcefulness and invention.

| 19. | f2-f4 | ... |

Boleslavsky's combinative style
has one feature peculiar to himself: strict logic intertwined
with his tactical strokes. A
player of Smyslov's or Makogonov's style would probably have
played the more cautious 19 Rd2
followed by 20 Rfd1, and if
19..Re6, then the temporary retreat 20 Nd3.

| 19. | ... | Nd8-f7 |
| 20. | Rd1-d7 | ... |

Forcing a series of exchanges.

20.	...	Nf7:e5
21.	f4:e5	Qe8:d7
22.	e5:f6	...

(See diagram, next column)

A most unusual position for
the white f-pawn, which has now
gotten behind the f5-pawn's
back!

22.	...	Ra8-f8
23.	f6:g7	Qd7:g7
24.	Qb2:g7+	Kg8:g7
25.	e2-e4!	f5:e4
26.	Rf1:f8	Kg7:f8
27.	Bg2:e4	...

And is that all? — the reader
asks. Yes, and that's not so
little, either. It is a well-
known truth that the importance
of a weakness increases as the
number of pieces on the board
decreases.

Here, White has at least three
advantages:

1) his bishop is active, while
Black's is not;

2) he can create a passed pawn
on the g- or h-file before
Black can create one;

3) he can also get his king to
the center more quickly.

These advantages are quite
sufficient to win.

27.	...	h7-h6
28.	Kg1-f2	Kf8-e7
29.	Kf2-f3	a7-a5
30.	Kf3-g4	Bb7-c8+

This is proper: Black sacrifices a pawn to activate his bishop. With the passive 30..Kf6 31 Kh5 Kg7 32 g4, followed by 33 g5, Black would lose without a struggle.

| 31. | Kg4-h5 | c6-c5 |
| 32. | Kh5:h6 | Ke7-f6! |

Black is defending excellently. White's king will be pinned to the h-file, where it blocks the pawn's advance.

| 33. | Be4-f3 | a5-a4 |

A trial balloon: White must now decide whether the black threat of ..a4-a3 followed by ..Bc8-f5-b1:a2 or ..Bc8-e6:b3 is dangerous or not.

| 34. | b3:a4 | ... |

Boleslavsky has concocted an interesting combination, but Taimanov finds a surprising loophole. The immediate 34 g4 was better, since White gets his pawn to g8 before Black can set up his breakthrough on the opposite wing.

34.	...	c5-c4
35.	g3-g4	c4-c3
36.	g4-g5+	Kf6-e5
37.	Bf3-d1	Bd7-g4
38.	Bd1-c2	Bg4-f5
39.	g5-g6!	Bf5:c2
40.	g6-g7	...

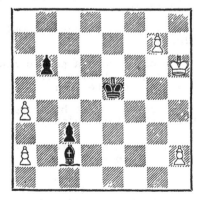

Doubtless expecting 40..Bb3 41 ab c2 42 g8Q c1Q 43 Qg5+, trading queens, after which White's h-pawn queens.

| 40. | ... | Bc2-h7 |

Taimanov's improvement. Black succeeds in avoiding the exchange of queens, since the white king has to abandon the g5 square.

41.	Kh6:h7	c3-c2
42.	g7-g8Q	c2-c1Q
43.	Qg8-b8+	...

The queen ending is none too pleasant for Black either, but still it is a queen ending, with all of its attendant drawing chances. This sudden turn in a game which White had thought was already over knocks him off his stride. For the remainder of the game, Boleslavsky appears to be playing somewhat planlessly; eventually, he overlooks a drawing queen exchange himself.

43.	...	Ke5-d5
44.	Qb8-b7+	Kd5-e5
45.	Qb7-g7+	...

He ought to have chopped off the b-pawn without further ado.

45.	...	Ke5-d5
46.	Qg7-f7+	Kd5-e5
47.	h2-h4	Qc1-c2+
48.	Kh7-g7	Qc2:a4
49.	Qf7-f6+	Ke5-e4
50.	Qf6-e6+	...

And here he ought to have sent his pawn a-queening. White is only driving the black king closer to his h-pawn.

50.	...	Ke4-f4
51.	h4-h5	Kf4-g5
52.	Qe6-e5+	Kg5-g4
53.	h5-h6	Qa4-d7+
54.	Kg7-f6	Qd7-d8+
55.	Kf6-f7	Qd8-d7+
56.	Qe5-e7	Qd7-d3
57.	Qe7-e6+	Kg4-h5
58.	Kf7-e8	b6-b5

This pawn advance looks harmless for White; does it make any difference whether it's on b6 or b4? White carelessly repeats moves.

| 59. | Ke8-e7 | b5-b4 |
| 60. | Ke7-e8 | Qd3-g6+! |

DRAW

agreed: after 61 Q:g6+ K:g6 62 Kd7 K:h6 63 Kc6 Kg6 64 Kb5

Kf7 65 K:b4 Ke8 66 Kb5 Kd8 67 Kb6
Black's king reaches c8 just in
time. With Black's pawn at b6 (or
b5), the exchange of queens would
not have been playable, since the
white king would have time to occupy b7, securing the route a2-
a4...a8Q.

******

173. Stahlberg—Najdorf
(King's Indian)

1.	d2-d4	Ng8-f6
2.	c2-c4	g7-g6
3.	g2-g3	Bf8-g7
4.	Bf1-g2	0-0
5.	Nb1-c3	c7-c5
6.	d4-d5	e7-e5

A defense which Najdorf used
frequently prior to this tournament, up until its demolition
at the hands of Euwe in Game 58.
After a lengthy recess, Najdorf
is employing it again, without
fear of Euwe's 7 Bg5, which he
intends to meet with 7..d6 8 Ne4
Qa5+, or 8 Qd2 a6.

7.	Ng1-f3	d7-d6
8.	0-0	Nb8-d7
9.	Qd1-c2	Qd8-e7
10.	e2-e4	a7-a6
11.	a2-a4	Nf6-h5
12.	Bc1-d2	Kg8-h8

Black is preparing for the
freeing and counterattacking
move ..f7-f5 by playing the maneuver ..Nd7-f6-g8. The immediate 12..f5 would be a poor
move in view of 13 Ng5 Ndf6 14 ef
B:f5 15 Nge4, and the pin is
not dangerous to White, with
his knight so well defended.
In this line, 14 Ne6!? is also
interesting: after 14..B:e6
the king's bishop's diagonal
ould be opened.

13.	a4-a5	...

While Black is busily executing
his complicated maneuvers on the
kingside, White threatens to
block the queenside, and then to
continue with 14 Na4 and 15 b4,
outstripping his opponent's attack. So Najdorf's next sharp
move is practically his only
means of holding the balance.

13.	...	b7-b5
14.	c4:b5	...

Stahlberg decides to give up

the exchange for a strong passed
a-pawn; later, he was to conclude that the simple 14 ab was
better, retaining a positional
advantage. This self-criticism
is commendable, but I do not
consider the move Stahlberg actually made in any way inferior
to 14 ab.

14.	...	a6:b5
15.	Nc3:b5	Bc8-a6
16.	Nb5-a3	...

If White had been afraid to
lose, he could have continued
16 Nc7 B:f1 17 B:f1 Rac8 18 Nb5,
when Black would have nothing
better than to return his rook
to a8. Stahlberg goes for the
win.

16.	...	Ba6:f1
17.	Ra1:f1	...

Having given up the exchange,
White ought to advance his passed
pawn as quickly as possible; for
this purpose the rook is better
placed at a1, and the bishop at
f1. If Black can blockade the a-
pawn, he will probably have the
advantage.

17.	...	Nh5-f6
18.	Na3-c4	Nf6-e8
19.	Bg2-h3	Ra8-a7
20.	Bd2-e3	Ra7-b7

White was threatening 21 b4.

21.	Rf1-a1	...

Most unhappily, Stahlberg returns his rook to a1. Had he recaptured with the bishop at move

17, then here he might have
played (other things being
equal) 21 a6, when everything
would have looked quite a bit
different.

21.   ...   Ne8-c7

Just in time to head off the
threatened a5-a6-a7.

22. Qc2-a4   Nd7-b8
23. Nc4-b6   f7-f5
24.   e4:f5   g6:f5
25. Qa4-h4   Qe7-f7
26. Be3-h6   Nb8-a6
27. Nb6-c4   Nc7-b5
28. Nc4-e3   f5-f4

With the a-pawn blockaded,
Black begins his attack on the
other wing.

29. Bh6:g7+   Qf7:g7
30. Ne3-f5   Qg7-g6
31. Qh4-g4   Qg6:g4
32. Bh3:g4   Rb7-a7
33. Nf3-d2   Na6-b4
34. Nd2-c4   Rf8-f6
35. Ra1-d1   Kh8-g8

The exchange of queens has
led to a difficult endgame, in
which the chances clearly lie
with Black, but the play is
very complicated, with eight
pieces wandering about the
board, any one of them capable
of surprises.

It is instructive to follow
the way both players try to
cut down the mobility of the
opposing pieces by tying them
down to the defense of weak
points. Black's rook and knight
are tied to the d-pawn, while
White's knight, bishop and rook
defend the pawn at a5, the pawn
at d5, and the knight at f5.
Black's king now approaches the
battlefield.

36. Bg4-h3   Kg8-f8
37. Kg1-g2   Ra7-f7
38. Nf5-h4   f4:g3
39.   f2:g3   Nb5-d4
40. Bh3-e6   ...

An interesting, although insufficient, chance, which serves
to complicate yet again what
would appear to be a rather simple position. If 40..N:e6, then
41 de R:e6 42 N:d6 Rd7 43 Rf1+,
etc. Najdorf finds an equally
interesting rebuttal.

40.   ...   Rf6-f2+
41. Kg2-h3   Rf2-f1

The game was adjourned here;
after analysis, Black confidently converted his advantage
into a win.

White has his choice of rooks.
Had Stahlberg played 42 B:f7,
the continuation might have been:
42..R:d1 43 Bh5 Ra1 44 N:d6 N:d5
45 Nb7 e4 46 N:c5 e3 47 Ng2 e2
48 Nd3 Nf6 49 Bg4 h5 50 Bc8 Nf3,
and Black wins a piece. This
variation is Najdorf's, and bears
witness to the way he spent the
time between the first and second sessions.

42. Rd1:f1   Rf7:f1
43. Nc4:d6   Nd4:e6
44.   d5:e6   Kf8-e7
45. Nd6-e4   Ke7:e6
46. Ne4:c5+   Ke6-d5
47. Nc5-a4   e5-e4
48. Kh3-g2   Rf1-a1
49. Na4-c3+   Kd5-e5
50.   g3-g4   Ra1:a5
51. Nh4-f5   Nb4-d5
52. Nc3-d1   Ra5-a1
53. Nd1-f2   Nd5-f4+
54. Kg2-g3   Ra1-g1+
55. Kg3-h4   Rg1-g2
56. Nf2-d1   Rg2:h2+
57. Kh4-g3   Rh2-h3+
58. Kg3-f2   Rh3-f3+
59. Kf2-e1   h7-h5
60. Nd1-e3   h5-h4
61.   g4-g5   h4-h3

WHITE RESIGNED

******

[296]

174. Euwe—Petrosian
(Old Indian Defense)

1. d4 Nf6 2. c4 d6 3. Nc3 e5
4. Nf3 Nbd7 5. Bg5 Be7 6. e3 0-0
7. Qc2 c6 8. Bd3 ed 9. ed Re8
10. 0-0 h6 11. Bd2 Nf8 12. h3
Ne6 13. Rae1 d5 14. cd cd 15. Qb3
Bf8 16. Re2 Qd6 17. Bc1

Neither tired player can muster the strength for any show of aggression.

17..a6 18. Rfe1 b5 19. Bf5 Bd7
20. a3 Rac8 21. Qd1 Nc7 22. B:d7
N:d7 23. Ne5

                    DRAW

                  ******

175. Szabo—Averbakh
(Sicilian Defense)

A curious game. Szabo twice overlooked the same sort of "little combination" on the same square, d4; after Averbakh's inaccuracies, however, he was still able to achieve a draw.

1.	e2-e4	c7-c5
2.	Ng1-f3	Nb8-c6
3.	Bf1-b5	g7-g6
4.	0-0	Bf8-g7
5.	Nb1-c3	d7-d6
6.	d2-d3	...

A comparatively rare and not a very active system of the Sicilian. White is not in a hurry to play d2-d4; and since his pawns all stand on light squares, he makes no secret of his willingness to exchange his light-square bishop.

6.	...	Bc8-d7
7.	Nc3-d5	e7-e6
8.	Nd5-e3	Ng8-e7
9.	c2-c3	0-0
10.	d3-d4	Nc6:d4

An unpinning technique, which consists of an attack on a different enemy piece with the pinned piece, while simultaneously attacking the pinning piece. Another example of this technique occurs with the black queen at d8, the knight at f6, White's bishop at g5 and his queen at c3: Black plays ..Ne4, attacking the queen with his knight and also the bishop with his queen.

This "little combination" does not cost White material, but it

does free Black's game.

11.	Nf3:d4	c5:d4
12.	Bb5:d7	d4:e3
13.	Qd1:d6	...

This rather risky continuation is the only way to avoid losing a pawn.

13.	...	e3:f2+
14.	Rf1:f2	Ne7-c6
15.	Bc1-f4	Qd8-b6
16.	Ra1-d1	...

It was time for White to end this foolishness, capture on c6, and play his other bishop to g5.

16.	...	Ra8-d8
17.	Qd6-c7	Bg7-d4

Once again, in the same spot! Black closes the rook's line of fire, which deprives the bishop on d7 of protection. Then he swiftly doubles rooks, winning the d-pawn: a most elegant combination.

18.	c3:d4	Qb6:c7
19.	Bf4:c7	Rd8:d7
20.	Bc7-g3	f7-f5

Averbakh no doubt thought he could always take the pawn. If he takes it at once, there would be complications: 20..R:d4 21 R:d4 N:d4 22 Be5 Nc6 23 Bf6, or 22..Rd8 23 Bf6 Rd7 24 Kf1 Nc6 25 Rc2. On 20..Rfd8 there could follow 21 Rdf1 N:d4 22 Bh4 Rc8 23 Bf6, and in either case the win for Black is unclear, despite his pawn to the good.

Black wants to ensure the best possible conditions for his knight, while preventing the above-mentioned possibility Bf6.

21.   d4-d5!   ...

Black expected to force either the exchange or advance of White's e-pawn, which would have meant a further strengthening of the knight's position at c6; for example, 21 ef R:f5 22 R:f5 gf 23 Bf2 Rd5! and 24..e5. However, Szabo has found a clever counter: if 21..fe? 22 R:f8+ K:f8 23 Rf1+ and 24 dc. So Black must take on d5, and an equal ending results.

21.	...	e6:d5
22.	Rd1:d5	Rd7-f7
23.	e4:f5	Rf7:f5
24.	Rf2:f5	Rf8:f5
25.	Rd5-d7	Rf5-f7
26.	Rd7-d6	Kg8-f8
27.	a2-a3	...

DRAW

******

******

ROUND TWENTY-SIX

176. Averbakh—Euwe
(Nimzoindian Defense)

1.	d2-d4	Ng8-f6
2.	c2-c4	e7-e6
3.	Nb1-c3	Bf8-b4
4.	e2-e3	c7-c5
5.	Ng1-f3	0-0
6.	Bf1-d3	d7-d5
7.	0-0	Nb8-c6
8.	a2-a3	Bb4:c3
9.	b2:c3	d5:c4
10.	Bd3:c4	Qd8-c7
11.	Be4-d3	e6-e5
12.	Qd1-c2	Qc7-e7

Toward the end of the tournament, the grandmasters began to lose some of their inventiveness in the openings. Here, Averbakh repeats the opening of Game 39, Bronstein - Euwe, which led to a position rife with chances for White. Euwe played 12..Re8 in that game, hoping thereby to prevent White's e3-e4 for some time; however, it turned out to be playable after all, since the opposition of queens allowed White to answer (after 13 e4) 13..ed 14 cd cd with 15 N:d4 (12..Qe7 is no more effective in this regard). After Zurich, everyone plays 12..Re8!, hoping for the continuation 13 e4 c4!

13.	d4:e5	Nc6:e5
14.	Nf3:e5	Qe7:e5
15.	Rf1-e1	Bc8-d7

Now the opening is over. The advance e3-e4 remains the underlying theme for the present, but there will be other themes as well, for example: White's queen's bishop is walled in by its own pawns, and Black later sacrifices a pawn in order to keep it imprisoned; White no longer has his king's knight, that sturdy defender of the king's wing, which inspires Euwe to devise and execute a sharp attack against the white king. In general, Black must be acknowledged to have solved his opening problems successfully; his last move (15..Bd7), however, is really a tactical trap, and does not fit into the greater plan: if now 16 e4, then 16..Ba4! 17 Q:a4? Q:c3. But Black's intended kingside attack would have become much stronger after 15..Re8, intending to meet 16 e4 with 16..Ng4 17 f4 Qh5 18 h3 c4, obtaining good play. 16 Bb2 would

be met as in the game with 16..c4.

16.	Bc1-b2	c5-c4

A brave move, and a beautiful one, too: White's c-pawn is nailed down — he never does play c3-c4 in this game — and eventually the white queen's bishop falls without ever having attacked anything. There is an element of tactics here as well: Averbakh must pay close attention to the diagonal c5-g1, since a check by Black's queen at c5, attacking the bishop on c4, could prove most unpleasant for White.

17.	Bd3:c4	Nf6-g4
18.	f2-f4	...

On 18 g3 Black invades the light squares by means of a technique which should be familiar to every chessplayer: 18..Qh5 19 h4 Ne5 20 Be2 Bg4.

18.	...	Qe5-c5

Put the bishop back on c8, put the rook on e8 instead, and you will see that, after 15..Re8, the move 16 Bb2 would have been simply bad for White.

19.	Qc2-d3	Ra8-d8
20.	Ra1-d1	...

In conjunction with his previous move, this is a bold and original idea, marking Averbakh as a genuine artist (it goes without saying that deep calculation was necessary too). Many would have fallen for the move

Najdorf recommends here, 20 Qd4, but this leads to immediate destruction by 20..Qh5 21 h3 Bc6! 22 hg Q:g4, when Black wins the queen for rook and minor piece.

20 Bd5 was tempting, but then one of the symmetrical bishop retreats (to e6 or c6, f5 or b5), combined with the threat of ..N:e3, would probably have given Black, if not the better of it, then at least the opportunity to enter a quiet endgame. Now, however, in spite of Euwe's outstanding defense, White maintains his extra pawn.

20.   ...   Qc5-b6

Black defends the rook, and once again threatens ..Ba4, while simultaneously hitting the bishop.

21.   Qd3-e2   ...

White gets his queen out of danger, defends his queen's bishop, and attacks the knight, forcing a quick resolution.

21.   ...   Ng4:e3
22.   Qe2:e3   Qb6:b2
23.   Re1-e2   Qb2-b6!

Attack and defense are both at their peak. Black brings about an exchange of queens, as if he did not see White's threat of doubling on the d-file, winning a piece. However, this exchange is Black's only means of holding the game: the bishop does not fall, since Black can attack White's bishop with his rook and unpin (25 Red2 Rc8).

24.   Qe3:b6   a7:b6
25.   Re2-e7   ...

(See diagram, next column)

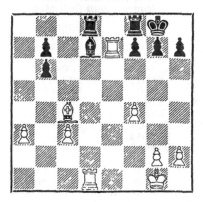

25.   ...   Bd7-e6
26.   Rd1:d8   Rf8:d8
27.   Bc4:e6   f7:e6
28.   Re7:b7   Rd8-c8
29.   Rb7:b6   Rc8:c3
30.   Rb6-a6   Kg8-f7

So now it's an ending, in which White has an extra rook's pawn, but Black can attack it from behind with his rook: such endings are generally drawn. The pawn is unable to advance without the aid of the king; and in the time it takes for the king to get to the a-file, Black's rook or king can pick off a brace of kingside pawns. After that, if worse comes to worst, Black can always give up his rook for the passed pawn.

31.   Kg1-f2   h7-h5
32.   a3-a4   Rc3-a3
33.   h2-h4   Kf7-f6
34.   Ra6-a5   g7-g6
35.   Kf2-e2   Ra3-g3?

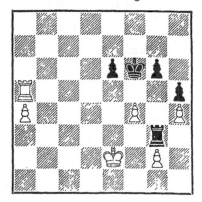

The textbook maneuver 35..Ra2+ would have secured an easy draw.

36. Ra5-g5!   ...

Now the white rook defends both pawns, freeing the king to support the passed a-pawn.

36.	...	Rg3-a3
37.	a4-a5	Kf6-f7
38.	Ke2-d2	Kf7-e7
39.	Kd2-c2	Ke7-d7
40.	Kc2-b2	Ra3-a4
41.	g2-g3	Kd6-c6
42.	Kb2-b3	Ra4-a1
43.	Kb3-b4	Ra1-b1+
44.	Kb4-c4	Rb1-a1
45.	Kc4-b3	...

BLACK RESIGNED

******

177. Petrosian—Stahlberg
(Sicilian Defense)

This entire game is an excellent illustration of Petrosian's style: its highly individual positional pattern and its logical consistency combine to create a harmonious whole and an artistic achievement. Curiously, not one of the annotators of this game, Stahlberg among them, could find a single sizable error on Black's part! The contemporary game operates on such fine nuances that they prove difficult to isolate, even in analysis, to say nothing of over-the-board play.

1.	e2-e4	c7-c5
2.	d2-d3	Nb8-c6
3.	Ng1-f3	g7-g6
4.	g2-g3	Bf8-g7
5.	Bf1-g2	d7-d6
6.	0-0	Ng8-f6
7.	Nb1-d2	0-0
8.	a2-a4	Bc8-d7
9.	Nd2-c4	Qd8-c8
10.	Rf1-e1	...

The reader will doubtless have noted that Petrosian is playing a King's Indian Defense with the White pieces. Defense against what? The King's Indian is usually played in reply to 1 d4, but here Black has not played the corresponding 1..d5; his setup looks more like a Dragon Sicilian. Thus, we are dealing once again with our old friend the clash of openings, in which both sides arrange their pieces in

accordance with predetermined schemes, and bide their time, each occupying only his own half of the board, without as yet encountering the other.

10.	...	Nf6-g4
11.	c2-c3	h7-h6
12.	Qd1-e2	Kg8-h7
13.	Nf3-d2	f7-f5

Lulled by his opponent's apparently pacific deployment, Black initiates the conflict. This is a serious inaccuracy, whereby he weakens not only his kingside, but the central squares too. It would have been most sensible for him to place his queen on c7 (instead of c8), his rooks on e8 and d8, and prepared gradually for ..d6-d5.

14.	f2-f4	f5:e4
15.	d3:e4	Ng4-f6
16.	Nd2-f3	Bd7-g4
17.	Nc4-e3	Bg4-h3
18.	Nf3-h4	Bh3:g2
19.	Qe2:g2	e7-e6
20.	Qg2-c2	...

White's position is uncoiling like a spring: his pieces and pawns turn out to be as harmoniously placed for action in the center as on the right flank. Black has weak pawns at d6 and e6, and a tornado threatens to sweep away all obstacles on the b1-h7 diagonal as well.

20.	...	Nc6-e7
21.	Ne3-c4	Nf6-e8
22.	Bc1-d2	Qc8-c6
23.	Re1-e2	Ra8-d8
24.	Ra1-e1	b7-b5

Pressed by White's central and kingside superiority, Stahlberg seeks chances on the other side, but White's position is solid here too.

25.	a4:b5	Qc6:b5
26.	Nc4-e3	Rd8-b8
27.	Bd2-c1	Bg7-f6
28.	Nh4-f3	c5-c4
29.	Kg1-g2	...

There's no rush: he knows what his position is worth.

29.	...	Bf6-g7
30.	h2-h4	Kh7-g8
31.	Re1-d1	Rb8-c8
32.	e4-e5	...

An elegant breakthrough! Now
35..d5 36 h5 leads to a completely hopeless position for
Black. Taking the pawn looks
relatively harmless, and would
appear to give Black counterchances, for example: 32..de
33 N:e5 B:e5 34 fe Qc6+. Petrosian's idea, however, is much
subtler.

32.	...	d6:e5
33.	Qc2-e4	Rc8-c5
34.	f4:e5	Qb5-c6
35.	Ne3-c2	Qc6:e4
36.	Re2:e4	Ne7-c6
37.	Nc2-e3	Nc6-a5

The e-pawn hangs by a thread,
but Black cannot take it, either
here or on the next move. For
example, if 37..N:e5 38 N:e5 R:e5
39 R:e5 B:e5 40 N:c4 Bg7 41 Be3,
and White wins the a-pawn: 41..a6
42 Ra1 Nc7 43 Bb6.

38.	Nf3-d2	Ne8-c7
39.	Ne3:c4	Rf8-d8
40.	Rd1-e1	Na5:c4
41.	Nd2:c4	Nc7-d5
42.	Nc4-d2	Rd8-b8
43.	Re4-a4	Rc5-c7
44.	Nd2-f3	Nd5-b6
45.	Ra4-g4	Kg8-h7
46.	Nf3-d4	Rb8-e8

Black has lost a pawn, but his
weaknesses still remain. So
White can fully expect to win,
but some accuracy is still required: the queenside pawns must
be secured, and if the e-pawn
really must be given up, then
only in exchange for the a-pawn,
so as to set up connected passed
pawns as quickly as possible.
This is the point of his next
few moves.

47.	Rg4-e4	a7-a6
48.	Re1-e2	Nb6-d7
49.	Nd4-f3	Re8-b8
50.	Bc1-e3	Bg7-f8
51.	Re4-a4	Rc7-c6
52.	Be3-d4	Rb8-b5
53.	b2-b4	Bf8-g7
54.	Re2-a2	Nd7:e5
55.	Nf3:e5	Bg7:e5
56.	Bd4:e5	Rb5:e5
57.	Ra4:a6	...

| 57. | ... | Rc6:a6 |

If Black could take the c-pawn
here, he would be saved, but —
57..R:c3? 58 Ra7+ Kg8 59 Ra8+
Kf7 60 R2a7+ Kf6 61 Rf8 is mate!

58.	Ra2:a6	Kh7-g7
59.	c3-c4	Kg7-f6
60.	b4-b5	Re5-e2+
61.	Kg2-f3	Re2-c2
62.	Ra6-c6	Rc2-c3+
63.	Kf3-f4	Rc3-c1
64.	b5-b6	Rc1-b1
65.	g3-g4	Kf6-e7
66.	Kf4-e5	Rb1-e1+
67.	Ke5-d4	...

BLACK RESIGNED

******

178. Najdorf—Boleslavsky
(King's Indian)

1.	d2-d4	Ng8-f6
2.	c2-c4	g7-g6
3.	g2-g3	Bf8-g7
4.	Bf1-g2	0-0
5.	Ng1-f3	d7-d6
6.	0-0	c7-c5
7.	d4:c5	d6:c5
8.	Nf3-e5	...

An important innovation by
Najdorf. Moving the knight on
f3 to e5 injects new possibilities into an apparently harmless variation. After the tour-

nament, the conclusion was
reached that 8..Nfd7! 9 Nd3
Nc6 is Black's best line here.
The move Boleslavsky selected
is more natural, but it's
exactly what Najdorf was counting on.

8.	...	Qd8-c7
9.	Ne5-d3	Nb8-c6
10.	Nb1-c3	Bc8-f5
11.	Bc1-f4	Qc7-a5
12.	Bf4-d2	...

The harrying of the black
queen continues. Black must now
make the important concession
of his lightsquare bishop, leaving White's fianchettoed bishop
without an opponent. The effects
of this will be felt for the
rest of the game.

12.	...	Bf5:d3
13.	e2:d3	Qa5-c7
14.	Bd2-e3	Rf8-d8

Nowadays a player will select
a move not according to the ex-
ternal characteristics of a position, but by concretely evaluating its possibilities. Here,
Black could occupy d4 with his
knight, but he sees that this
would leave him with insufficient prospects for the further
strengthening of his position.
Meanwhile, White could play
Rab1 and b4, etc.; and with his
bishop working on the diagonal
h1-a8, he could work up some
serious threats to Black's
queen's wing. During all this,
practically the only thing the
knight on d4 would accomplish
would be to cover the weak pawn
on d3 from frontal attacks along
the d-file. This is why, instead
of the "strategic" ..Nd4, Black
selects the combinative ..Rfd8,
aiming directly at the d-pawn.

15.	Be3:c5	Nc6-e5
16.	d3-d4	Ne5:c4
17.	Qd1-e2	Nc4-d6

A series of subtle changes
has occurred. White's queen's
bishop has migrated to c5, where
it cramps Black's activities.
White's d-pawn has moved up a
square, but it remains just as
isolated, and therefore just as
weak, as it was before.

But is it really weak? It is
common practice to talk about
an isolated pawn's shortcomings
and neglect its positive aspects.
One such aspect is the absence
of pawns on the neighboring
files, which is a point for the
"isolated" side, as long as he
can bring his major pieces to
those files. And so it is
here: the absence of pawns on
the c- and e-files is clearly
not favorable to Black. The
queen, for example, stands quite
uncomfortably at c7, and the far-
reaching power of White's bishops is also making itself felt.
Under these circumstances, Black
takes the only proper decision:
to attack and eliminate the d-
pawn supporting White's center
as quickly as he can.

18.	a2-a4	e7-e6
19.	a4-a5	Nd6-f5
20.	a5-a6	Nf6-d5

Black mistakenly stops halfway. 20..b6 would have achieved
both of Black's goals by driving
the bishop from c5 and eliminating the d-pawn. After 20..b6
21 B:a8, Black would also have
had the pleasant choice of which
bishop he wishes to leave White;
I would have left him the darksquare bishop, since after 21..R:a8
22 Ba3 N:d4 the position compli-
cates in a manner unfavorable to
White. However, the intermediary
22 Nb5 strengthens the defense,
so perhaps Black would be better
advised to take the other bishop:
21..bc, and after 22 Bg2 cd he
has a strong passed pawn.

Then Black's pressure on the
b-file, combined with the advance of his d- and e-pawns supported by his fianchettoed king's
bishop, would have assured him
even chances, despite his small
material deficit. Boleslavsky selects another, quieter continuation, but it leaves the bishop
at c5 undisturbed, and creates
two new weaknesses for Black at
a7 and d5.

21.	a6:b7	Qc7:b7
22.	Nc3:d5	e6:d5
23.	Ra1-a4	a7-a5
24.	Qe2-d3	Ra8-b8
25.	Rf1-b1	Qb7-b3

White's pressure is becoming
unbearable, so Black seeks to
exchange queens; however, this
should have cost him a pawn.

26.	Qd3:b3	Rb8:b3	
27.	Ra4:a5	...	

The chief drawback of this exchanging operation is that it costs White his most active piece, that being the bishop at c5. He could have maintained his two bishops with 27 g4, which would have led to the loss of a pawn for Black in a considerably inferior position: 27..Nh4 28 Be7, or 27..Nh6 28 h3, and the pawns on d5 and a5 will not long survive.

27.	...	Bg7:d4	
28.	Bc5:d4	Nf5:d4	
29.	Bg2:d5	Rb3-b4	
30.	Kg1-g2	...	

White has now the very difficult task of queening his b-pawn, a task rendered more complicated by all those enemy pieces on dark squares, where they are very hard to drive out. Now White's king will approach the battlefield. Black decides to enforce the exchange of the last pair of minor pieces, which completely immobilizes the b-pawn.

30.	...	Nd4-b3	
31.	Bd5:b3	Rb4:b3	
32.	Ra5-a3	Rb3-b4	

An interesting rook endgame, and beyond doubt an instructive one as well. White wants to achieve the following, if possible: bring his king over to the b-pawn, trade off one rook, and not allow the black king to reach his pawns.

33.	Ra3-f3	Rd8-b8	
34.	b2-b3	Rb8-b7	
35.	Kg2-f1	Kg8-g7	
36.	Kf1-e2	Rb4-b6	
37.	Ke2-d2	Rb7-b8	
38.	Kd2-c2	Rb6-c6+	

The first part of the plan is now complete, but Boleslavsky's clever rook maneuver once again throws White's king back to the d-file.

39.	Rf3-c3	Rc6-e6	
40.	Rc3-e3	Re6-c6+	
41.	Kc2-d2	g6-g5	

The point of this move is to break up White's pawn structure, and most probably White should have replied with the same pawn advance: 42 g4. Of course, after that Black could have maneuvered ..Rc6-h6-f6-h6, to try to tie one of White's rooks to the h-pawn, but as long as White did not swerve from his basic plan of advancing his b-pawn, Black's defense would still have been very difficult. For example: 42 g4 Rh6 43 h3 Rf6 44 f3 Rh6 45 b4 R:h3 46 b5!, and if 46..Rb6, the king goes after the rook.

42.	Re3-e4	Rb8-d8+	
43.	Kd2-e1	Rc6-h6	
44.	h2-h4	g5:h4	
45.	g3:h4	f7-f5	

Najdorf has, somewhat overconfidently, allowed Black to dismember White's f-, g- and h-pawns, resulting in the exposure of White's king. Black's rooks can now threaten to check on the ranks as well as on the files, and the black king's chances are also greatly enhanced. In such circumstances, it is hard to fix your attention on any one thing in particular, and so the pawn at b3 takes only one more forward step.

46.	Re4-c4	Rh6-e6+	
47.	Ke1-f1	...	

The king returns home — and immediately a black rook comes knocking.

47.	...	Rd8-d2	
48.	b3-b4	Re6-e2	
49.	Rc4-f4	Kg7-f6	

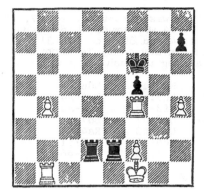

50. Rb1-b3 ...

Black's clever defense has won his pieces a great deal of activity. The fact that he no longer blockades the b-pawn does not mean at all that he is letting it slip away from his attention. Two rooks on the second rank are a powerful force. Here, for example, on 50 b5 there could follow 50..Rb2, when 51 Rfb4 is not playable due to 51..R:f2+. In addition, Black threatened 50..Ke5, driving White's rook from f4, which is the intersection of the lines f4-b4 and f4-f2. White's last move meets that threat, since 50..Ke5 51 Rbf3 would cost Black the f-pawn.

| 50. | ... | Rd2-b2 |
| 51. | Rb3:b2 | Re2:b2 |

51 Rff3 would have been met by 51..R:f2+!

52. Kf1-g2 ...

The b-pawn cannot get far without the king's help — but how can he throw his f- and h-pawns away? If he leaves them to the black king, then even if he succeeds in queening his b-pawn, Black will be able to give up his rook at the queening square and draw by keeping either his f- or his h-pawn.

52.	...	Rb2-c2
53.	Rf4-d4	Kf6-e5
54.	Rd4-d7	Rc2-c4
55.	Rd7:h7	Rc4:b4
56.	h4-h5	Ke5-f6

57. Kg2-g3 ...

DRAW

******

179. Taimanov—Kotov
(Queen's Gambit)

1.	d2-d4	Ng8-f6
2.	c2-c4	e7-e6
3.	Ng1-f3	d7-d5
4.	Nb1-c3	Bf8-b4
5.	c4:d5	e6:d5
6.	Qd1-a4+	Nb8-c6
7.	Bc1-g5	h7-h6
8.	Bg5:f6	Qd8:f6
9.	e2-e3	0-0
10.	Bf1-e2	Bc8-e6
11.	0-0	a7-a6

In Ragozin's Defense, the abstract concept of White's opening advantage assumes a concrete form: the black knight stands in front of the pawn at c7, which must sooner or later become the target of an attack, and the d-pawn remains artificially isolated for some time. In return, Black obtains what is referred to as good piece play. There is no disputing that in the eyes of Schlechter, Teichmann or even Rubinstein, the backward pawn was something more substantial than lively piece play, but in our day the latter is more often preferred.

Taimanov's next move initiates a plan of gradually accumulating small positional advantages. First he secures control of his open file.

12.	Rf1-c1	Bb4-d6
13.	Qa4-d1	Nc6-e7
14.	Nc3-a4	...

14..c5 must be prevented, and he would like to induce 14..b6.

| 14. | ... | b7-b6 |
| 15. | Na4-c3 | ... |

Having carried out both tasks efficiently, the knight returns.

| 15. | ... | Rf8-d8 |
| 16. | Qd1-f1 | ... |

An interesting positional maneuver. By this threat to the a-pawn, White induces still another weakening of Black's pawn skeleton. This maneuver would have been more effective on the

previous move, however, instead
of 15 Nc3.

| 16. | ... | c7-c6 |
| 17. | Nc3-a4 | ... |

If he takes the a-pawn, his
bishop will be trapped.

17.	...	Rd8-b8
18.	Rc1-c3	a6-a5
19.	Ra1-c1	Be6-d7
20.	a2-a3	...

An invitiation to Black to
"free himself" with 20..c5, to
which White would reply 21 dc
B:a4 22 cd Q:d6 23 Nd4, with an
excellent position.

20.	...	Ne7-g6
21.	Be2-d3	Qf6-e6
22.	Qf1-d1	Bd6-c7
23.	Qd1-c2	Ng6-e7
24.	Rc1-e1	...

Having squeezed as much as he
could out of his pressure on the
c-pawn, and seeing that it is,
nevertheless, still standing,
White switches to the e-file.
The immediate 24 e4 would not
have been effective, since the
black knight could go to d5.
White must create conditions such
that a trade of pawns on e4 will
lead to an immediate attack on
the black queen.

| 24. | ... | f7-f5 |

One more positional achievement for White: Black's f-pawn
now hinders the mobility of his
own pieces, and the weakening
of the diagonal a2-g8 will make
itself felt later. On the other
hand, Kotov played this move in-
tentionally: had he feared the
difficulties just mentioned, he
could have played 24..Qf6.

| 25. | b2-b4 | ... |

This was more or less forced.
Attempting to strengthen his
grip on e4 with something like
Nd2, f2-f3 and e3-e4 would have
led to a powerful reactivation
of Black's pieces, which have
been observing the white kingside for some time.

The text move conceals a trap:
25..ab 26 ab c5 27 Nb2 c4
28 N:c4! dc 29 B:c4 Nd5 30 B:d5
Q:d5 31 R:c7.

25.	...	a5:b4
26.	a3:b4	Bc7-d6
27.	Re1-b1	b6-b5

This was almost forced: 27..c5
28 b5 c4 was impossible due to
29 R:c4! dc 30 B:c4 Nd5 31 Qb3,
and, in any case, Taimanov was
planning to push his pawn to b5.

28.	Na4-c5	Bd6:c5
29.	Rc3:c5	Ra8-a4
30.	Nf3-e5	Rb8-a8
31.	Qc2-e2	Bd7-e8
32.	Qe2-f3	Ra4-a1
33.	Rc5-c1	Ra1:b1
34.	Rc1:b1	g7-g6

Thus, White has achieved all
a positional player could ask
for. With lightsquare bishops
on the board, five of Black's
pawns stand on light squares;
White's knight occupies an ideal
position in the center, and cannot be driven away; and Black's
pieces are tied down to defending the weak g- and c-pawns,
which stand on open files. If
only White could also occupy
the a-file with his rook!

What sort of attacking plan
should White select? Since his
opponent's weaknesses are fixed
on light squares, he should attack the light squares, following
this rough scheme (and adjusting,
naturally, for his opponent's re-
actions): h2-h3, Kh2, Rg1 and
g2-g4; or he can retreat his
queen and then play f2-f3 and
e3-e4. Taimanov's following
moves, f2-f4 and h2-h4, destroy
the possibility of a breakthrough on the light squares,

and about three-quarters of
his chances as well.

35.	h2-h4	Kg8-g7
36.	Qf3-g3	Qe6-d6
37.	f2-f4	h6-h5
38.	Bd3-e2	Ra8-a4?!

Convinced that White has no
threats any more, Kotov takes
the game out of the realm of
chess and into that of psychology, inviting his opponent to
take the h-pawn, expecting something like this: 39 B:h5 R:b4
40 R:b4 Q:b4 41 B:g6 B:g6 42 h5
Qd6 43 Kf1, etc. — but even this
is hardly advantageous to Black,
especially as White also has
39 B:h5 R:b4 40 Rc1.

It should be noted here that
this psychological experiment
owed its existence in large measure to the sporting situation:
had he won this game, Kotov
would have improved his tournament standing substantially, ov-
ertaking Keres and settling just
a half-point behind Reshevsky.

39.   Be2-d1!!   ...

A brilliant rejoinder. Without deciding yet whether or not
he will take the h-pawn, Taimanov forces the rook to declare
itself. If it abandons the a-
file, then he will take the pawn.
The position of the white bishop, and its simultaneous action against a4 and h5 are
strongly reminiscent of the powers of the king in Russian
draughts — could that be where
the bishop's move was taken from?

39.	...	Ra4:b4
40.	Rb1-a1	...

White's dreams have come true:
the rook rips through to the
eighth rank, and sows utter
turmoil.

| 40. | ... | Ne7-c8 |

The power of White's rook and
the shortcomings of Black's position become clear in the following line: 40..Bf7 41 Ra7 Rb1
42 Qg5 (now White doesn't even
need his bishop) 42..R:d1+ 43 Kh2
Kf8 44 Qh6+.

41.	Ra1-a8	Qd6-e6
42.	Bd1:h5	Kg7-f8

43.	Bh5:g6	Be8:g6
44.	Ne5:g6+	Kf8-e8
45.	Ng6-e5	Ke8-d8
46.	Qg3-g7	Rb4-a4
47.	Ra8-b8	c6-c5
48.	Rb8-b7	...

BLACK RESIGNED

******

180. Gligoric—Geller
(King's Indian)

The second game between these
two players bore a great deal of
resemblance to their first: the
same opening with colors reversed,
the same sort of difficult, engrossing endgame — the only difference was the result.

1.	d2-d4	Ng8-f6
2.	c2-c4	g7-g6
3.	Nb1-c3	Bf8-g7
4.	e2-e4	d7-d6
5.	Ng1-f3	0-0
6.	Bf1-e2	e7-e5
7.	0-0	c7-c6
8.	d4-d5	...

Driving a wedge between two
wings, White splits the arena
of battle into two independent
sectors. Geller immediately begins his operations in the region nearest the enemy king,
while Gligoric comes up with a
roundabout maneuver: first he
breaks on the queen's wing, and
only then does he go after the
king. The next few moves are
easy to understand, but this is
not a position amenable to precise evaluation. In such cases,
the player who puts more fantasy,
courage and logic into his plan
will be the winner.

8.	...	c6-c5
9.	Nf3-e1	a7-a6
10.	Bc1-e3	Nf6-e8
11.	Ne1-d3	f7-f5
12.	f2-f3	f5-f4
13.	Be3-f2	g6-g5
14.	b2-b4	...

With this, Gligoric intends to
exploit the opening of the b-
file: there is no chance of a
break at c5.

14.	...	b7-b6
15.	b4:c5	b6:c5
16.	Ra1-b1	Rf8-f6

The rook is shunted to g6, to
support the pawns' assault.

17.	Nc3-a4	Nb8-d7
18.	g2-g4	f4:g3
19.	h2:g3	Rf6-g6
20.	Nd3-e1	Nd7-f6
21.	Na4-b6	Ra8-b8
22.	Nb6:c8	Rb8:b1
23.	Qd1:b1	Qd8:c8
24.	Kg1-g2	g5-g4

Both sides have gotten closer to their goals: Black now begins a determined assault on g3, while White mounts an invasion, beginning with Qb6.

25.	Ne1-c2	g4:f3+
26.	Be2:f3	Bg7-h6
27.	Qb1-b6	Qc8-d7
28.	Qb6:a6	Qd7-g7
29.	Rf1-h1	Bh6-f4
30.	Rh1-h3	h7-h5

White has shored up g3 as well as he could. Now Black's last reserve, the h-pawn, comes running to the aid of his pieces.

31.	Kg2-h2	Nf6-g4+
32.	Bf3:g4	h5:g4
33.	Rh3-h5	Bf4-g5
34.	Qa6-c8	...

Who has the better of it? There is good and bad in both positions: for instance, White has a pawn more, but his rook stands poorly at h5. We generally say such positions are in a state of dynamic balance.

34.	...	Qg7-f7
35.	Kh2-g1	Rg6-g7
36.	Rh5-h2	Qg7-d7

A brilliant decision, based on an exceptionally profound under-

standing of the position. Geller takes on an endgame in which, despite his pawn minus, he can make Gligoric fight hard for the draw.

37.	Qc8-a8	Qd7-d8
38.	Qa8:d8	Bg5:d8
39.	Nc2-e3	Rg7-a7
40.	Bf2-e1	Ne8-f6

Underscoring the weakness of White's pawns at c4, d5 and e4. For once it turns out not to be such a good idea to put pawns on squares not controlled by one's own bishop. As long as there are other pieces on the board, the pawns frequently get into difficulties.

41.	Rh2-b2	...

41.	...	Bd8-c7

Despite the limited amount of material remaining, Black has dealt successfully with his main concern: keeping the white rook out of his back rank.

42.	Kg1-f1	Kg8-f7
43.	Kf1-e2	Nf6:e4

Otherwise, the king gets to d3.

44.	Ne3:g4	Kf7-g6
45.	Ke2-d3	Ne4-g5
46.	Ng4-e3	Ra7-a3+
47.	Kd3-e2	Bc7-d8
48.	Be1-d2	e5-e4
49.	Rb2-b8	...

Gligoric has spent too much time pondering and waiting, while Black has, by his consistent

play, strengthened his pieces'
positions to the maximum. Since
White's a- and g-pawns, though
passed, are practically motion-
less, not surprisingly Black
is in firm control of the initiative. White attempts to rec-
tify his error by means of this
rook incursion, and nearly succeeds.

49.	...	Bd8-f6
50.	Ne3-g4	Ng5-f3
51.	Ng4:f6	Kg6:f6
52.	Bd2-f4	Nf3-d4+
53.	Ke2-f1	e4-e3

White should not have allowed
the black pawn to reach e3 so
easily. 53 Kf2 was the proper
move, and after 53..R:a2+ 54 Kf1
Black could no longer play
54..e3; White would then have
enough time to attack the pawn
from the rear with Re8. The reason for keeping the e-pawn under restraint will become clear
shortly.

54.	Rb8-e8	e3-e2+
55.	Kf1-f2	Ra3-f3+
56.	Kf2-g2	Rf3-f1

It seems quite likely that in
his preliminary calculations Gligoric assumed that he need not
fear this position, intending
simply to take the e-pawn off
with his rook. Only later did
he notice that the reply to this
would be, not 57..N:e2, but
57..R:f4.

57.	Bf4-d2	Rf1-d1
58.	Bd2-c3	Rd1-c1
59.	Bc3:d4+	...

The final error: he should not
have traded his bishop. White now
rids himself of the pawn at e2,
but the d-pawn becomes still more
dangerous. If the bishop had
simply moved back and forth along
the diagonal, I do not see how
Black could have won. For example: 59 Bd2 Rd1 60 Ba5, or
59..R:c4 60 Kf2 Rc2 61 Be1 R:a2
62 Bc3.

59.	...	c5:d4
60.	Re8:e2	d4-d3
61.	Re2-f2+	Kf6-e5

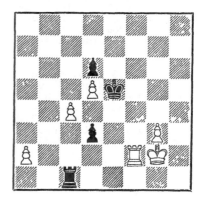

62.	Kg2-f3	Ke5-d4

This pawn, with support of
rook and king, will cost White
his rook in a move or two.

63.	g3-g4	...

White remembers his own passed
pawns too late.

63.	...	Kd4-c3
64.	Kf3-e4	Rc1-e1+
65.	Ke4-f5	d3-d2
66.	Rf2:d2	Kc3:d2
67.	g4-g5	Kd2-d3
68.	c4-c5	d6:c5
69.	d5-d6	Re1-e8
70.	d6-d7	Re8-a8

WHITE RESIGNED

A textbook rook-vs-separated-
passed-pawns position. White is
one move short of a draw: 71 Ke6
c4 72 Ke7 c3 73 d8Q R:d8 74 K:d8
c2 75 g6 c1Q 76 g7 Qg1.

******

181. Bronstein—Smyslov
(Ruy Lopez)

1. e4 e5 2. Nf3 Nc6 3. Bb5 a6
4. B:c6

One of World Champion Dr. Emanuel Lasker's favorite variations; he employed it at the St.
Petersburg tournament of 1914 to
score a famous victory over Capa-

blanca. Since then, Black's defensive strategies have been worked out to the tiniest details; consequently, this variation is seldom employed any more, and is considered drawish.

4 .. dc 5. Nc3 f6 6. d4 ed
7. Q:d4 Q:d4 8. N:d4 Bd7 9. Be3
0-0-0 10. 0-0-0 Ne7 11. h3 Ng6
12. Nb3 Bb4 13. Ne2 Rhe8 14. a3
Bf8 15. Nc3 Be6 16. R:d8+ R:d8
17. Rd1 R:d1+ 18. K:d1 Ne5
19. Bc5 Bd6 20. B:d6 cd 21. Nd4

DRAW

******

182. Reshevsky—Keres
(Nimzoindian Defense)

1. d4 Nf6 2. c4 e6 3. Nc3 Bb4
4. e3 b6 5. Ne2 Ba6 6. Ng3

Now the pawn threatens to run from e3 up to e5, which Black cannot prevent by 6..d5 because of 7 Qa4+. Keres takes an interesting, though not an outstandingly good, decision: he allows the pawn to advance, and then counterattacks on d4.

6 .. 0-0 7. e4 d6 8. Bd2 c5

9. a3 Ba5

Wrong: he should have taken on c3 without further ado, following this up with 10..Nc6.

10. d5 ed 11. cd B:f1 12. K:f1
Nbd7 13. h4 Re8 14. f3

DRAW

If the reader ever has such a position with White, he should never accept a draw; and if he has Black, he should never offer one. White has the better position. He may attack as he chooses, on either flank, with good prospects in either case. So why did Reshevsky offer a draw? Obviously, he was making his own calculations: there remained three rounds, with no chance for him to take first, and second place now seemed assured. Perhaps psychology had something to do with it, too, as well as arithmetic: after all, the three previous rounds had brought him only one half-point...

******

******

ROUND TWENTY-SEVEN

183. Keres—Bronstein
(King's Indian)

1.	d2-d4	Ng8-f6
2.	c2-c4	g7-g6
3.	Nb1-c3	Bf8-g7
4.	e2-e4	d7-d6
5.	f2-f4	...

The Four Pawns' Attack. This variation has an interesting history. When it first appeared, it struck terror into the hearts of King's Indian players. By the aggregate efforts of many masters, this attack's steamroller tendencies were neutralized, and soon it was Black who began to score the points. The variation disappeared for quite some time, giving place to the more conservative setups with g2-g3 and Bg2, etc., or the "riskier" attack with 5 f2-f3, 6 Be3 and 7 Qd2.

Recently, the storming variation has reappeared, with new aspirations and new goals, of course, and decked out with an array of modern positional ideas.

In this game Black employs a thirty-year-old defensive line recommended by Alekhine. Not surprisingly, the line has gone stale since his day, and Black saves himself only by calling a timely halt to, and making some alterations in, his originally intended plan.

5.	...	c7-c5
6.	d4:c5	...

This pawn used to be pushed to d5, but praxis has shown the line 6 d5 0-0 7 Nf3 e6 8 Bd3 ed 9 cd b5 to be acceptable for Black.

6.	...	Qd8-a5
7.	Bf1-d3	Qa5:c5
8.	Ng1-f3	...

This is how the variation is played nowadays. White has good play for his pieces; unless he is prevented, he will not find it too difficult to put together a decisive mating attack.

8.	...	0-0
9.	Qd1-e2	Nb8-c6
10.	Bc1-e3	Qc5-h5

The queen went to the kingside in order to attack the bishop, in the event that White castles, with ..Ng4. The bishop could not retreat to d2 then, in view of 12..Nd4! (using the well-known technique of decoying both the queen and the knight from the defense of h2). However, White does have a better move.

11.	h2-h3	Nf6-g4
12.	Be3-d2!	...

Now Black must beat a sad retreat, so as not to suffer a worse fate. From the course indicated by his 10..Qh5 and his 11..Ng4, one might logically expect 12..Nd4 here, but then the well-considered 13 Qf1! would set Black insoluble problems.

Black's defensive system has failed to justify itself.

12.	...	Ng4-f6
13.	0-0	Nf6-d7

Having suffered a fiasco on the kingside, Black's knight journeys to the queenside. Black must be very careful, continuously calculating all the variations beginning with f4-f5, since his queen at h5 makes a very tempting target for the white minor pieces.

14.	Ra1-d1	Qh5-a5
15.	Bd3-b1	Qa5-b4

White straightforwardly im-

proves his position, and Black, who has lost a great deal of time on the maneuver ..Qa5-h5-a5, is finding it most difficult to come up with a plan of equal value. The queenside diversion he undertakes places his queen in jeopardy once again, but it turns out to be the only means of maintaining the balance. 15..Qb4 is indeed the thread which holds Black's game together.

16. Bd2-e3   ...

Now comes rapid simplification.

16.	...	Nd7-b6
17.	Nc3-d5	Qb4:b2
18.	Qe2:b2	Bg7:b2
19.	Nd5:b6	a7:b6
20.	Rf1-f2	...

DRAW

King's Indian players will have to find a better antidote to the Four Pawns' Attack.

******

184. Smyslov—Gligoric
(King's Indian)
1. d4 Nf6 2. Nf3 g6 3. Bf4

Two points in front of his nearest rivals, Smyslov employs quiet, solid lines for his last games, and does not avoid a draw, whether he has White or Black. For this game, he employs, once again, the variation he used in Game 139 against Boleslavsky.

3 .. Bg7 4. Nbd2 d6 5. h3 0-0 6. e3 c5 7. Be2 Nc6 8. Bh2 b6 9. 0-0 Bb7 10. c3 Qd7 11. Re1 Rfd8 12. Qc2 Rac8 13. Rad1 cd 14. N:d4 d5 15. N:c6 Q:c6 16. Qb3 Qc5 17. Qb5

This is the sort of position where it is very difficult to create any kind of complications.

17 .. Q:b5 18. B:b5 Ne8 19. Bd3 Nd6 20. f3 Bh6 21. Bf4

DRAW

******

185. Geller—Taimanov
(Ruy Lopez)

Why is it that today — as compared to ten years ago, let's say — so few masters will go in for fierce combinative attacks, with piece sacrifices? More than any other reason, it is because the art of combinative defense these days has reached such a high level that in the heat of the battle it occasionally becomes difficult to determine who is attacking whom. Of course it's fun to crumble the defenses of an opponent's king move by move, to create irresistible threats, and to wind up the game with a mating attack. But how sad it can be to end up minus both piece and attack, to sit and wonder:"How did all this happen? Where did I go wrong?"

This is, roughly, the psychological backdrop of the Geller - Taimanov game; but at the very end, fortune favored the brave.

1.	e2-e4	e7-e5
2.	Ng1-f3	Nb8-c6
3.	Bf1-b5	Bf8-b4

In the Evans Gambit, White sacrifices a pawn in order to lure the black bishop to b4, so that he can play c2-c3 and d2-d4 with tempo. Here the bishop is going to b4 of its own accord, and White can carry out the same idea free of charge, so to speak. Geller comes to an unexpected conclusion: since he is not required to sacrifice one of his own pawns, he takes one of his opponent's.

| 4. | 0-0 | Ng8-e7 |

5.	c2-c3	Bb4-a5
6.	Bb5:c6	Ne7:c6
7.	b2-b4	Ba5-b6
8.	b4-b5	Nc6-a5
9.	Nf3:e5	0-0
10.	d2-d4	d7-d5

I would prefer 10..Qe8, intending 11..d6.

11.	Bc1-a3	Rf8-e8
12.	Qd1-h5	...

White has decided to sacrifice a piece for the attack. Naturally, he has plenty of grounds for this: the black king's knight has been driven to a5, and the bishop at b6 is also out of play. And the combined force of the bishop at a3, the rook on the f-file, and the queen bodes nothing good for Black's king. Nevertheless, 12 Nd2 first was better, since complete success will never be attainable without this knight.

12.	...	f7-f6
13.	f2-f4	...

The further course of the game will demonstrate that this move should have lost by force.

13.	...	f6:e5
14.	f4:e5	Bc8-e6

The main line of Geller's combination ran as follows: 14..Nc4 15 Qf7+ Kh8 16 Bf8, forcing mate. It was not his fault that Taimanov's sharp eye spotted and neutralized this combination. On the other hand, White still has quite a few attacking possibilities.

15.	Nb1-d2	d5:e4
16.	Nd2:e4	Bb6:d4+

A powerful positional move that brings Black's bishop into the game. The fact that a pawn is also gained, and with check at that, is mere circumstance.

17.	Kg1-h1	...

After 17 cd Q:d4+ 18 Nf2 Nc4, White's attack would come to a swift and bitter conclusion. Now 17..B:e5 would run into 18 Ng5, while after 17..Be3, the rook occupies the d-file·with tempo, creating boundless possibilities for the attacker's fantasy involving 19 Rf3 or 19 Rd3.

Once again, Taimanov finds the best move.

17.	...	Be6-d5
18.	Ne4-f6+	...

Another sacrifice; this one is forced, since the knight hasn't the time to retreat.

18.	...	g7:f6
19.	c3:d4	Qd8-d7

This is enough for a defense, but bringing up the reserves with 19..Nc4 was better.

20.	e5:f6	Qd7-f7
21.	Rf1-f5	...

White must submit to this exchange of queens and continue the fight with his two pawns against Black's piece.

21.	...	Qf7:h5
22.	Rf5:h5	Bd5-f7
23.	Rh5-g5+	Bf7-g6
24.	Ba3-e7	Kg8-f7
25.	Ra1-c1	Ra8-c8
26.	h2-h4	Re8-g8

Having successfully carried off his complex defensive task and achieved a winning position, Taimanov begins to play carelessly. Here the enemy pawn ought to have been stopped with 26..h5; if then 27 g4 hg 28 h5 Rh8.

27.	Rg5-e5	b7-b6
28.	g2-g4	Bg6-d3
29.	g4-g5	Rg8-e8

Another inaccuracy. 29..Nc4 30 R5e1 Nd6 was necessary.

30.	Rc1-c3	Bd3-c4

The last mistake. He could have held on with 30..Bg6.

31.	Rc3-g3	c7-c6
32.	h4-h5	Re8-g8
33.	Be7-b4	Rc8-e8
34.	Rg3-e3	Re8:e5
35.	Re3:e5	Bc4-e6

(See diagram, next page)

36.	Bb4:a5	b6:a5
37.	b5:c6	Rg8-d8
38.	c6-c7	Rd8-c8
39.	d4-d5	Be6-g4
40.	Re5-e7+	Kf7-f8
41.	g5-g6	h7:g6
42.	h5:g6	...

BLACK RESIGNED

Worth noting is Geller's fierce determination in seeking every chance available to him in the two-pawns-vs-piece endgame. Following his Round 24 draw with Reshevsky, Geller won three in a row, and in the next round he was to add a fourth — the longest winning streak of the tournament. This brilliant finish assured Geller of a good place after his disastrous start.

******

186. Kotov—Najdorf
(King's Indian)

1.	c2-c4	Ng8-f6
2.	Nb1-c3	g7-g6
3.	d2-d4	Bf8-g7
4.	e2-e4	d7-d6
5.	f2-f3	0-0
6.	Bc1-e3	e7-e5
7.	d4-d5	c7-c5
8.	g2-g4	...

After his unhappy experience with the opening as White in Game 171, Kotov - Gligoric, in which he played 8 Bd3, Kotov switches to the more aggressive continuation 8 g2-g4 and 9 h2-h4, intending to break down the black king's fortress at once.

8.	...	Nf6-e8
9.	h2-h4	f7-f5
10.	e4:f5	g6:f5
11.	g4-g5	e5-e4
12.	f3-f4	...

The advantage of advancing this pawn to f4 is that Black's pieces are denied the square e5. On the other hand, this move also has serious drawbacks: Black obtains a protected passed pawn in the center, the darksquare bishop is blocked, and White's knight loses the f4 square.

Ng1-h3-f4, creating the ever-present threat of sinking the knight at e6 and also of a possible excursion to h5, was much better.

12.	...	b7-b5
13.	c4:b5	a7-a6

Encouraged by his preponderance in the center, Najdorf undertakes a powerful wing demonstration.

14.	Qd1-d2	a6:b5
15.	Bf1:b5	Bc8-a6
16.	Bb5:a6	Nb8:a6
17.	Ng1-e2	...

The threat of ..Na6-b4-d3+ forces White to castle hurriedly on the short side, which means that his main strategic idea — an attack on the kingside — has come a cropper. Now his whole game looks dubious. Black's queen can travel the Great White Way, f7-h5-g4, to approach the exposed white king, the d5-pawn looks very lonely indeed, and the white bishop has no prospects. In such a position, an extra pawn is small consolation.

17.	...	Na6-b4
18.	0-0	Ne8-c7
19.	Ne2-c1	Qd8-e8
20.	a2-a3	Qe8-h5

A pretty maneuver. Najdorf's threat of ..Qg4+ and ..Q:h4+ brings the white rook to f2. White is willing to give up the h-pawn without a check, but Najdorf has other ideas.

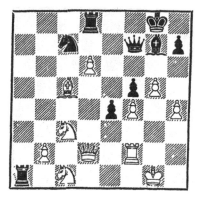

21.	Rf1-f2	Qh5-f7

And here's the idea! Now the
rook can no longer reach d1, so
the d-pawn is defenseless. And
with the d5 outpost gone, Black
advances his pawn from d6 to d4,
and the game will end almost instantly. Naturally, Kotov ob-
jects to such an immediate and
painful end; so with his usual
defensive resourcefulness, he
gives up an exchange for a pawn,
casting the game into a sea of
interesting complications. Najdorf, who probably thought his
win would now be a matter of
technique, must begin the fight
all over again. Psychologically,
this is sometimes very difficult.

22.	a3:b4	Ra8:a1
23.	b4:c5	d6:c5

The first inaccuracy. There
was a fairly simple win after
23..B:c3 24 bc N:d5 25 cd N:e3
26 Q:e3 Qd5, but who likes to
give away his "Indian" bishop?

24.	Be3:c5	Rf8-d8
25.	d5-d6	...

(See diagram, next column)

25.	...	Nc7-e8

A second inaccuracy, and this
one probably costs him the win.
After 25..Ne6 26 Bb6 Rd7 27 Rf1
Ra6, White would lose his passed
pawn without getting any counterchances in return for it. The
text move looks stronger, but it
allows Kotov an amazing resource
later on.

26.	Kg1-g2	Bg7-f8
27.	Nc1-e2	Ne8:d6
28.	Qd2-d5	Nd6-b7
29.	Qd5:f7+	Kg8:f7
30.	Bc5:f8	Rd8:f8
31.	Ne2-g3	Nb7-d6

Had Najdorf foreseen White's
idea, he might have played
31..Ke6, followed by ..Nc5-d3; however, fully confident that this
position was an automatic win,
he continued his incautious play..

32.	Rf2-d2	Kf7-e6
33.	Rd2-d5	Rf8-b8

And now Najdorf is ready to
reap the harvest. First he will
pick up the pawn at b2; then his
rooks will put the squeeze on
White's knights; then the e-pawn
will go on to queen — but as the
Eastern proverb has it:"If it
weren't for the wolves, our goat
could make it to Mecca." But now
two howling wolves appear, in
the form of a pair of white
knights...

We should point out that in the diagrammed position 34 N:f5 N:f5 35 Re5+ Kd7 36 R:f5 fails to 36..R:b2+ 37 Kg3 Rb3. Black could also take the b-pawn at once with 34..R:b2+ 35 Kh3 N:f5 36 Re5+ Kd7 37 R:f5 Ra3 .

34.	Rd5:d6+!	Ke6:d6
35.	Ng3:f5+	Kd6-c6
36.	Nc3-e4	Rb8:b2+
37.	Kg2-f3	Rb2-b4
38.	Nf5-g3	Ra1-a4
39.	h4-h5	Ra4-a3+

Najdorf's chief difficulty is that he is not sure whether he ought to be playing for the win or giving thought to saving the game. At any moment, one of the knights may come up with a fatal fork, so he keeps his rooks at a respectful distance.

40.	Kf3-g4	Kc6-d7

41.	g5-g6	h7:g6
42.	h5:g6	Kd7-e7
43.	Ng3-f5+	Ke7-e6
44.	Nf5-g7+	Ke6-e7
45.	Ng7-f5+	Ke7-e6
46.	g6-g7	Ra3-a8
47.	Ne4-g3	Ra8-g8
48.	Ng3-h5	Rb4:f4+

A fitting conclusion to a most interesting game! Where Kotov took a knight and a pawn for each of his rooks, Najdorf gets only a pair of pawns for his pair of rooks, leaving Kotov the knights as interest, so to speak. However, two knights cannot mate, as we know: they can only stalemate.

49.	Kg4:f4	Rg8:g7
50.	Nh5:g7+	...

DRAW

This game might better belong in an adventure magazine than in a tournament book.

******

187. Boleslavsky—Petrosian
(Caro-Kann Defense)

1.	e2-e4	c7-c6
2.	Nb1-c3	d7-d5
3.	d2-d4	d5:e4
4.	Nc3:e4	Bc8-f5

This is Black's standard continuation in this opening. Although theory considers it completely sound, I have a weakness for the impudent 4..Nf6 5 N:f6+ gf. If the reader who wishes to trap me in my words

should ask why I never played
this, even once, in the thirty
rounds of this tournament, I
would pick one reason out of
many, and reply that nobody
played 1 e2-e4, even once,
against me.

5.	Ne4-g3	Bf5-g6
6.	Ng1-h3	e7-e6
7.	Nh3-f4	Bf8-d6
8.	c2-c3	Ng8-f6
9.	h2-h4	Qd8-c7

Now White has the choice of
10 Qf3, stirring up interesting
double-edged complications such
as 10..Nbd7 11 h5 Bc2 12 h6 g6
13 Bc4 e5 14 Qe2 0-0-0; or 10 h5,
which sacrifices a pawn, but
leaves Black with a permanent
weakness at e6. Boleslavsky
chooses the second, and better,
continuation.

10.	h4-h5	Bd6:f4
11.	Bc1:f4	Qc7:f4
12.	h5:g6	f7:g6
13.	Qd1-d2	...

A curious decision: White offers to exchange queens, even
though he is a pawn down! Petrosian may have entertained the
hope that Boleslavsky would
yield to the temptation to play
13 Qb3, hitting b7 and e6 simultaneously; the text destroys his
illusions (13 Qb3 Ng4 14 Q:e6+
Kd8).

13.	...	Qf4:d2+
14.	Ke1:d2	Nb8-d7
15.	Ra1-e1	Ke8-f7
16.	Bf1-c4	Ra8-e8
17.	Bc4-b3	c6-c5
18.	Ng3-e4	Nf6:e4+
19.	Re1:e4	Nd7-f6
20.	Re4-e5	c5:d4
21.	c3:d4	Re8-e7

Black's pieces are tied down
to e6; however, White is unable
to improve his position either,
and since he is a pawn down, the
game is quickly drawn.

22.	Rh1-e1	Rh8-e8
23.	Kd2-d3	h7-h6
24.	f2-f4	...

DRAW

******

188. Stahlberg—Averbakh
(Queen's Indian Defense)

1.	d2-d4	Ng8-f6
2.	c2-c4	e7-e6
3.	Ng1-f3	b7-b6
4.	g2-g3	Bc8-b7
5.	Bf1-g2	Bf8-e7
6.	Nb1-c3	Nf6-e4
7.	Bc1-d2	...

This is not a bit weaker than
the usual 7 Qc2. The bishop move
awakened pleasant memories in
the chief arbiter of the tournament, the Czech veteran Karel
Opocensky, who introduced this
line long ago.

7.	...	f7-f5
8.	0-0	0-0
9.	Qd1-c2	Ne4:c3
10.	Bd2:c3	Bb7-e4
11.	Qc2-b3	a7-a5
12.	Nf3-e1	...

Beginning the fight for e4.

12.	...	a5-a4
13.	Qb3-d1	Be4:g2
14.	Ne1:g2	Be7-f6
15.	Qd1-d3	Nb8-c6
16.	e2-e4	f5:e4
17.	Qd3:e4	Qd8-e8
18.	Ra1-d1	Qe8-f7
19.	Ng2-e3	Qf7-g6

Black should not have detached
his a-pawn from its fellows. Now
he accepts an exchange of queens
in order to avoid the loss of
his pawn after 19..Rae8 20 Qc2.

20.	Qe4:g6	h7:g6
21.	Rf1-e1	Nc6-a5
22.	Re1-e2	Rf8-e8
23.	Re2-c2	d7-d6
24.	Kg1-g2	Kg8-f7
25.	Rd1-d3	Kf7-e7
26.	h2-h4	Ke7-d7
27.	f2-f4	Na5-b7
28.	Ne3-g4	Nb7-a5
29.	Ng4-e5+	...

(See diagram, next page)

[317]

29.   ...   Kd7-c8

Black cannot take the knight:

I. 29..de 30 de+ Ke7 31 ef+ gf
32 Rcd2 Rd8 33 B:f6+

II. 29..B:e5 30 de N:c4 31 ed
N:d6 32 B:g7, and although the
pawns are still even, Black's
game is lost, since he cannot
stop White from creating a
passed pawn on the h-file.

Averbakh finds the best defense, comparatively speaking.

30.   Bc3:a5   ...

He could have taken the g6-
pawn with his knight, but after
30..N:c4 31 Bb4 Black could sacrifice a piece with 31..a3!
32 R:c4 ab 33 Rb3 R:a2, muddying
the waters considerably. Stahlberg's choice is more conservative.

30.   ...   d6:e5
31.   f4:e5   Ra8:a5
32.   e5:f6   g7:f6
33.   c4-c5   b6:c5
34.   d4:c5   Re8-d8

A waste of time; after 34..e5,
Black would have had every reason to expect a drawn outcome.
But now White's rook reaches e5
by force, completely blocking the
e- and f-pawns.

35.   Rd3-f3   ...

The winning move. Black's rook
must assume a passive position,

which is a most unpleasant thing
to have to do in a rook ending.

35.   ...   f6-f5
36.   Rf3-e3   Rd8-e8

Active defense is too late now:
36..Rd5 37 R:e6 Rd:c5 38 Rf2.

37.   Re3-e5   ...

37.   ...   Kc8-d8
38.   Rc2-e2   Ra5-b5
39.   Kg2-f3   Rb5-b4
40.   c5-c6   ...

40 a3 was a calmer choice.
Black's only counterchance is
in the hope that he can somehow
obtain White's a- and b-pawns
in exchange for his e- and g-
pawns. In that event, White would
be better off losing his a-pawn
on the third rank.

40.   ...   Rb4-e4

This is completely worthless.
The pawn should have been attacked with 40..Rb6; the continuation 41 R:e6 R:e6 42 R:e6 R:b2
leaves Black some hope, at least.

41.   Re2:e4   f5:e4+
42.   Re5:e4   a4-a3
43.   Re4-d4+   Kd8-c8
44.   Rd4-a4   ...

BLACK RESIGNED

******

189. Euwe—Szabo
(King's Indian)

1.	d2-d4	Ng8-f6
2.	c2-c4	g7-g6
3.	g2-g3	Bf8-g7
4.	Bf1-g2	0-0
5.	Nb1-c3	c7-c5
6.	d4-d5	d7-d6
7.	Ng1-f3	Nb8-a6
8.	Nf3-d2	Na6-c7
9.	Qd1-c2	Ra8-b8
10.	b2-b3	e7-e6

White's brief weakening of the long diagonal brings on the natural reaction from Black.

11.	Bc1-b2	e6:d5
12.	c4:d5	b7-b5
13.	0-0	Rf8-e8

Black has gotten in ..b7-b5 without hindrance, and stands quite well. For this reason, it would be premature, even foolhardy, to make an attacking gesture at this time: 13..b4 14 Nce4 Nc:d5 15 Rd1, and Black cannot maintain his extra pawn.

14.	e2-e4	Bc8-a6
15.	Rf1-e1	Nf6-g4
16.	Nc3-e2	Ng4-e5
17.	Ra1-b1	...

While Black plays on the wings, White methodically gathers his forces in the center.

17.	...	b5-b4
18.	Nd2-c4	Nc7-b5
19.	f2-f4	...

Having bolstered his position sufficiently, White can undertake this step as well.

19.	...	Ne5:c4
20.	b3:c4	Nb5-d4

The black pawn at d4 is doomed, but the c-file will be opened, and the pawn at c4 will also be a target for sundry assaults. It would be very tempting to put his knight on a3: after 21 B:a3 ba Black would control the important square b2 — but not for long, since 22 Qa4 would attack the pawn and the bishop at a6. So the knight takes the other path. As regards so-called "doomed" pawns, we know — from Game 87, for instance — that sometimes they can prove to be very hardy indeed. In this game too, despite all the bloodletting that fol-

lows, the d4-pawn manages to outlive many.

21.	Ne2:d4	c5:d4
22.	Bg2-f1	Rb8-c8
23.	Bf1-d3	...

The bishop stands well here: it defends the c- and e-pawns, and prevents the enemy pawn from advancing. Now White may consider besieging that pawn.

23.	...	Qd8-b6
24.	Qc2-b3	...

Black's previous move stepped up the pressure on the c-pawn. 24 Qa4 would have been wrong, therefore, in view of 24..B:c4 25 B:c4 d3+ 26 Kg2 d2 27 Red1 B:b2, when the White position is in ruins.

24.	...	Re8-e7
25.	Kg1-g2	Qb6-c5
26.	Qb3-a4	Ba6-b7
27.	a2-a3	a7-a5
28.	Bb2-c1	...

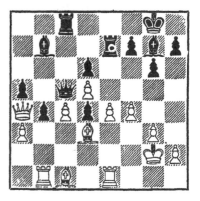

From the diagram, one might find it hard to believe that there might be a chink in White's position, and especially that it might be at d5, which appears to be his strongest point, resting as it does on two firm pillars and immune to pawn attack. In this position, however, a combinative motif appears: by means of a series of exchanges, Black draws both of White's rooks away from the defense of his queen's bishop, and then the c-pawn, which covers this bishop on the file, can no longer play

its role as defender of the
d-pawn.

28.	...	f7-f5
29.	a3:b4	a5:b4
30.	Qa4:b4	Qc5:b4
31.	Rb1:b4	f5:e4
32.	Re1:e4	Bb7:d5

White was unable to prevent
..B:d5; had he captured on e4
with his bishop, he would have
risked a possibly fatal pin:

32 B:e4 Rce8 33 Kf3 Bc8 34 Bd2 h5.

Now everything comes off.

33.	c4:d5	Re7:e4
34.	Bd3:e4	Rc8:c1

DRAW

******

******

190. Szabo—Stahlberg
(Queen's Gambit)

1.	c2-c4	e7-e6
2.	Ng1-f3	Ng8-f6
3.	d2-d4	d7-d5
4.	Nb1-c3	Nb8-d7
5.	c4:d5	e6:d5
6.	Bc1-g5	Bf8-e7
7.	e2-e3	c7-c6
8.	Qd1-c2	Nd7-f8

Stahlberg's favorite defense, with which we are already acquainted from Game 8.

9.	Bf1-d3	Nf8-e6
10.	Bg5-h4	g7-g6
11.	0-0	0-0
12.	Ra1-b1	...

The b-pawn is headed for b5; its mission is to disorganize the enemy pawn formation.

12.	...	a7-a5
13.	a2-a3	Ne6-g7
14.	b2-b4	a5:b4
15.	a3:b4	Bc8-f5
16.	b4-b5	Bf5:d3
17.	Qc2:d3	Nf6-d7
18.	b5:c6	...

The pawns are fighting hand-to-hand now. White's b-pawn perishes, but the bastion at c6 holds firm, since the c-pawn is immediately replaced by its comrade from b7.

White has succeeded in giving his opponent a weak pawn on the open c-file, but the rooks will certainly never take it, provided the cavalry can defend it from

the rear.

18.	...	b7:c6
19.	Bh4:e7	Qd8:e7
20.	Qd3-c2	Ng7-f5
21.	Nc3-a4	Qe7-d6
22.	Na4-b6	Nd7:b6
23.	Rb1:b6	Nf5-e7

The knight takes up its post.

24.	g2-g3	Rf8-b8
25.	Rf1-b1	Rb8:b6
26.	Rb1:b6	f7-f6

Securing e5 against the white knight and clearing f7 for his king.

27.	Kg1-g2	Kg8-f7
28.	Nf3-d2	Ra8-b8
29.	Qc2-b2	Rb8:b6
30.	Qb2:b6	Qd6-a3
31.	h2-h4	Qa3-d3

DRAW

Finding it difficult to shelter his king from Black's insistent checks, Szabo lays aside his aggressive aspirations and settles for a peaceable conclusion.

******

191. Averbakh—Boleslavsky
(Dutch Defense)

1.	d2-d4	e7-e6
2.	Ng1-f3	f7-f5
3.	g2-g3	Ng8-f6
4.	Bf1-g2	Bf8-e7
5.	0-0	0-0
6.	c2-c4	d7-d6
7.	b2-b3	...

The question of the "solidity" of Black's system could only be debated after the strictly theoretical 7 Nc3; the text makes Black's task a great deal easier. Time is an excellent gift in the opening.

7.	...	a7-a5
8.	Bc1-b2	Qd8-e8
9.	Nb1-d2	Nb8-c6
10.	a2-a3	Be7-d8

A quick look at the new grouping of Black's pieces reveals a curious picture: the queen has taken the place of the king, and the bishop, the queen's. It is a typical deployment in these positions where Black prepares for ..e6-e5.

11.	Nf3-e1	e6-e5
12.	e2-e3	Bc8-d7
13.	Ne1-c2	e5:d4

Averbakh's insipid play has allowed Black the chance to mount a successful kingside attack. Black intended a pawn sacrifice here: 14 ed f4!, opening the queen's bishop's diagonal. Deciding that this would be a dangerous line, White recaptures with his knight, despite the temptation to open the e-file for his pieces.

| 14. | Nc2:d4 | Nc6:d4 |
| 15. | Bb2:d4 | Bd7-c6 |

By bringing this bishop out to an active position, and then obtaining his opponent's consent to its exchange, Boleslavsky scores a weighty positional success. In the Dutch Defense, Black's lightsquare bishop is considered bad (especially in the Stonewall Variation), while White's fianchettoed king's bishop is the mainstay of his position. The exchange of these bishops creates an unpleasant situation around the white king.

16.	Nd2-f3	Bc6-e4
17.	Nf3-e1	b7-b6
18.	a3-a4	Nf6-d7
19.	Ne1-d3	...

| 19. | ... | g7-g5! |

In the Dutch Defense, the g-pawn is a necessary ingredient in all attacks on the king: its

advance renders the entire position dynamic. Had Black played 20..Bf6, he would have strengthened his position still further.

20.	Nd3-c1	Nd7-e5
21.	Bg2:e4	f5:e4
22.	Bd4:e5	Qe8:e5
23.	Qd1-d5+	Qe5:d5
24.	c4:d5	...

Boleslavsky absent-mindedly overlooked the obvious queen check, thereby falling out of a promising middlegame into a dubious endgame. Now he must buckle himself down to a laborious defense.

| 24. | ... | Ra8-b8 |

This, coupled with the pawn advance that follows, is Black's best chance.

25.	Rf1-d1	b6-b5
26.	g3-g4	Bd8-f6
27.	Ra1-a2	Bf6-e5
28.	Kg1-g2	Rf8-f7
29.	a4:b5	Rb8:b5
30.	Ra2-a4	Be5-b2
31.	Ra4:e4	...

DRAW

in view of 31..B:c1 32 R:c1 R:d5.

******

192. Petrosian—Kotov
(King's Indian)

1.	d2-d4	Ng8-f6
2.	c2-c4	d7-d6
3.	Ng1-f3	g7-g6
4.	Nb1-c3	Bf8-g7
5.	g2-g3	0-0
6.	Bf1-g2	Nb8-d7
7.	0-0	e7-e5
8.	Qd1-c2	c7-c6
9.	Rf1-d1	Rf8-e8
10.	d4:e5	d6:e5
11.	Nf3-g5	Qd8-e7
12.	Ng5-e4	Nf6:e4

After his fierce two-day battle with Najdorf, Kotov decided to take a little time-out; thus, this series of simplifying exchanges. First, the enemy horse is liquidated; then the rooks disappear, and a drawish wind begins to blow. One might add that Black's activities were the more successful, in that they received Petrosian's wholehearted support and cooperation.

13.	Nc3:e4	Nd7-c5
14.	Ne4-d6	Re8-d8
15.	Nd6:c8	Rd8:d1+
16.	Qc2:d1	Ra8:c8
17.	Bc1-e3	Rc8-d8
18.	Qd1-c2	f7-f5
19.	Ra1-d1	...

DRAW

******

193. Najdorf—Geller
(King's Indian)

This game was identical to the Najdorf - Petrosian game until move 12: again, Najdorf gave up his central pawn for the black b-pawn, and thereby abandoned the struggle to solve one of the basic problems of the opening. But where Petrosian, in the sixth-round game alluded to, immediately committed a serious positional error by playing ..c7-c5 and deprived his knight of its best square, Geller takes a lesson from that game, and carries out a successful queenside attack here.

1.	d4-d4	Ng8-f6
2.	c2-c4	g7-g6
3.	g2-g3	Bf8-g7
4.	Bf1-g2	0-0
5.	Ng1-f3	d7-d6
6.	0-0	Nb8-c6
7.	Nb1-c3	Bc8-g4
8.	h2-h3	Bg4:f3
9.	Bg2:f3	Nf6-d7
10.	Bf3-g2	Nc6:d4
11.	Bg2:b7	Ra8-b8
12.	Bb7-g2	Rb8-b4
13.	e2-e3	Nd4-e6
14.	Qd1-e2	Nd7-e5!

In some openings — Alekhine's Defense, for example, or the Grunfeld — Black moves an un-protected piece into the center to induce the hypertrophied ad-vance of White's pawns, intend-ing to attack them later. Geller here executes a similar idea in the middlegame. He is trying to induce White's pawns to advance to f4 and to b3, which he soon accomplishes. Later, he will work up an attack against the pawn at b3, for which purpose he will set his rooks on the b-file and his knight at c5, supporting the a-pawn's advance to a4. The reader should note that Petrosian was unable to carry out the same idea only because he had no piece that could control the a4 square: the queen, of course, is not a proper piece for this purpose, and the knight needs the square c5 — which, as we saw, had been oc-cupied by his pawn.

15.	f2-f4	Ne5-d7
16.	Nc3-d5	Rb4-b8

Despite the white knight's threatening posture, and the rather humble status of Black's pawns, we consider Black's po-sition preferable. The knight will not keep its place on d5 for very long, while Black's pawns harbor a great deal of potential energy. White will have trouble developing his rooks, and his wing attack on the kingside has fewer prospects than Black's attack on the queen-side.

17.	Qe2-c2	c7-c6
18.	Nd5-c3	Qd8-c7
19.	Ra1-b1	a7-a5
20.	Bc1-d2	Ne6-c5
21.	Nc3-e2	Qc7-b6
22.	Kg1-h2	Rf8-c8
23.	Bd2-c3	...

Najdorf follows roughly the same scheme he used against Pe-trosian: exchanging bishops in order to weaken the king's posi-tion and pave the way for a pawn assault.

23.	...	Bg7:c3
24.	Ne2:c3	Qb6-a6

The strategic idea is proper; its tactical execution is faul-ty. The weakening 25 b3 could also have been induced by 24..Qb4, and the queen would have been much more actively placed.

25.	b2-b3	Rb8-b6
26.	Nc3-e4	Nc5:e4
27.	Qc2:e4	Rc8-e8

Black is going to extremes in his effort to avoid the advance of his center pawns. This was exactly the proper moment to answer White's flank attack, in accordance with classical principles, with a counterstroke in the center: 27..e6! 28 g4 d5; now White's first attacking wave has been beaten off, and the black pawn cannot be prevented from advancing to a4.

| 28. | f4-f5 | Nd7-e5 |
| 29. | f5-f6! | Qa6-a7 |

Now it becomes clear that in his singleminded pursuit of his queenside idea Black has neglected his chances in the center, thereby handing over the initiative to his opponent.

| 30. | Rb1-d1 | Rb6-b4 |

This could have led to serious difficulties. 30..Qc7 was necessary, to defend the d-pawn.

| 31. | Qe4-d4 | c6-c5 |

Trading queens would correct White's pawn structure, and cost Black his c-pawn and the game.

| 32. | Qd4-h4 | ... |

White's goal would have been attained with 32 Qf4, with the same idea of penetrating to h6, but without losing sight of the knight on e5, and maintaining pressure on the pawn at d6. Then Black would have had to turn his entire attention to defense, whereas now he succeeds in carrying out his plan of breaking into the White position through b3.

| 32. | ... | a5-a4 |
| 33. | Rd1:d6 | a4:b3 |

Here is the difference between putting the queen at h4 and at f4: in the latter case, Black's last move would have been met by 34 Q:e5.

34.	a2:b3	Rb4:b3
35.	f6:e7	Qa7:e7
36.	Qh4:e7	Re8:e7
37.	Bg2-d5	Rb3:e3
38.	Rd6-d8+	Kg8-g7
39.	Rd8-c8	Ne5-d3
40.	Rc8-a8	Re3-e2+
41.	Kh2-g1	Re2-d2
42.	Ra8-a1	Nd3-b4

WHITE RESIGNED

******

194. Taimanov—Smyslov
(Catalan Opening)

1.	d2-d4	Ng8-f6
2.	c2-c4	e7-e6
3.	g2-g3	d7-d5
4.	Bf1-g2	d5:c4
5.	Qd1-a4+	Bc8-d7
6.	Qa4:c4	Bd7-c6
7.	Ng1-f3	Bc6-d5
8.	Qc4-a4+	Qd8-d7

9. Qa4:d7+   ...

Any queen retreat would have allowed 9..c7-c5, when Black has solved the two basic problems of the Catalan: the development of his queen's bishop, and counterattacking the pawn at d4. After the exchange of queens, further simplifications quickly follow, and the game winds up drawn. One must conclude, then, that the queen's meanderings from d1 to a4 to c4 and back to a4 again, in search of the sacrificed pawn, were absolutely harmless to Black.

Rapid development of White's kingside (5 Nf3) holds out more promise. The c4-pawn would not run away, and Black could not try to hold on to it without creating weaknesses in his position.

```
 9.    ...        Nb8:d7
10.    0-0        c7-c5
11.    Nb1-c3     Bd5-c6
12.    d4:c5      Bf8:c5
13.    Bc1-f4     0-0
14.    Ra1-d1     Rf8-d8
15.    Bf4-d6     Bc5:d6
16.    Rd1:d6     Kg8-f8
17.    Rf1-d1     Kf8-e7
18.    Rd6-d2     Nd7-c5
19.    Rd2:d8     Ra8:d8
20.    Rd1:d8     Ke7:d8
21.    Nf3-e5     Bc6:g2
22.    Kg1:g2     ...
```

DRAW

******

195. Gligoric—Keres
(Nimzoindian Defense)

```
1.    d2-d4      Ng8-f6
2.    c2-c4      e7-e6
3.    Nb1-c3     Bf8-b4
4.    e2-e3      b7-b6
5.    a2-a3      Bb4:c3+
6.    b2:c3      Bc8-b7
7.    f2-f3      Nb8-c6
8.    e3-e4      ...
```

Five pawn moves in a row! Strictly speaking, one should never play like this, but here the white pawns' inchworm progression is justified by the introverted character of the position. White wants to kill three birds with one stone, putting Black's knights under threat of a pawn press, giving

his bishop an exit to g5, and simultaneously closing off the fianchettoed black queen's bishop's diagonal.

However, all of these White achievements would pale to insignificance if Black would recall his own chances, particularly against the chronically sick pawn at c4.

So we can see that both sides are entering the middlegame with roughly even chances: everything turns on which player handles his pieces better.

```
 8.    ...        d7-d6
 9.    Bf1-d3     Nc6-a5
10.    Ng1-e2     ...
```

White decides not to defend his c-pawn, in the interests of mounting his attack on f6 sooner. One must eventually consider the development of one's pieces also.

```
10.    ...        Qd8-d7
11.    0-0        Bb7-a6
12.    Ne2-g3     Ba6:c4
13.    Bd3:c4     Na5:c4
14.    Qd1-e2     Qd7-c6
15.    Bc1-g5     h7-h5
```

A powerful move. White wished to take at f6 with his bishop, and then to play his knight out to h5. Black does not object to this turn of events, but he wishes to introduce a small but substantial change: 15..h5. Now the knight can only reach h5 by capturing this pawn, and this small detail changes the picture completely: after White plays N:h5, Black will have two attacking lines, instead of one.

```
16.    Bg5-h4     0-0-0
17.    f3-f4      Rd8-g8
18.    Bh4:f6     g7:f6
19.    Ng3:h5     ...
```

(See diagram, next page)

19.   ...   f6-f5

Inviting the knight in to f6; however, after 20 Nf6 Rg6 21 e5, Black's return visit with 21..Ne3 would not suit White at all.

20.   Nh5-g3   ...

The merits of Black's plan may be seen in the thematic variation 20 ef R:h5 21 Q:h5 Q:g2 mate. If Black had left his pawn at h7, the white knight at h5 would have been unassailable. All this was very nicely played by Keres.

20.	...	f5:e4
21.	Ng3:e4	Rh8-h3
22.	Ne4-g3	Rh3-h6
23.	Rf1-f3	Rg8-h8

Having broken out into the open, Black's rooks search for weak points.

24.	h2-h3	f7-f5
25.	Ng3-f1	Rh8-g8
26.	Rf3-g3	Rg8:g3
27.	Nf1:g3	a7-a5
28.	a3-a4	...

White's a-pawn sat for quite some time under attack by the knight at c4, hampering the mobility of White's queen's rook; but now Black's a-pawn threatened to go to a4, fixing White's a-pawn as a permanent target.

28.	...	Rh6-g6
29.	Kg1-h2	Kc8-b7
30.	Ra1-a2	d6-d5

Gligoric's accurate defense

has successfully beaten back the first wave of the attack; his king now stands quite securely. But what is he to do about his tattered queenside?

31.	Qe2-h5	Qc6-e8
32.	Ra2-e2	Nc4-d6
33.	Re2-e5	...

A knight usually stands well at e5. Gligoric's attempt to centralize his rook could have resulted in an immediate loss. However, saying that White committed an oversight is about the same as saying nothing at all; it is a great deal more interesting to speculate on the causes of White's oversight. During a lengthy war of maneuver, it not infrequently happens that one's combinative alertness is dulled. I think that this is precisely what happened here, to both players.

33.   ...   Qe8-f7

This is not like Keres; in such cases, the commentator generally justifies the oversight with "time-pressure". By trapping the rook with 33..Ne4, Black could have either forced 34 R:e4 or captured the knight on g3, since the knight could not leave that square in view of the obvious combination 34..R:g2+! 35 K:g2 Q:h5.

34.	Qh5-f3	Qf7-d7
35.	Qf3-h5	Qd7-f7
36.	Qh5-f3	Rg6-h6
37.	Re5-e2	Qf7-d7
38.	Re2-a2	Qd7-c6
39.	Ra2-a1	Qc6-c4

The queen finds a roundabout route behind White's pawns. White has dug himself in thoroughly, but Black's advantage is of a lasting sort, expressed less in the activity of his pieces than in his better pawn position. Specifically:

a) all of Black's pawns form a single strand, while White's are broken into three "islands", to use Botvinnik's expression;

b) the pawns at d5 and f5 secure e4 for Black's knight; if White should trade knights on that square, Black gets a protected passed pawn;

c) if Black wins the a-pawn,
his passed a-pawn will queen
without opposition; the "ready-
made" passed h-pawn cannot do
this, since the white pieces
are unable to clear its path.

These are the major features
of the position, and they serve
to explain why Black is constantly on the offensive, while
White can only defend himself
passively. Under the circumstances,
White's defense must crack sooner or later.

| 40. | Kh2-g1 | Qc4-b3 |
| 41. | Ng3-e2 | Qb3-c2 |

A powerful position for the
queen: from here, it attacks the
pawns at a4, c3 and g2.

| 42. | g2-g4 | ... |

The courage of despair: White
already had no good defense to
Black's plan of ..Rg6, ..Ne4,
etc. Now Keres finds a series
of pretty moves to force the
win.

42.	...	f5:g4
43.	h3:g4	Rh6-h4
44.	Ra1-c1	Qc2-h7

45.	c3-c4	Rh4-h3
46.	Qf3-g2	Qh7-d3
47.	c4:d5	Nd6-e4
48.	d5:e6	Qd3-e3+
49.	Kg1-f1	Rh3-f3+

WHITE RESIGNED

******

196. Bronstein—Reshevsky
(Ruy Lopez)

1.	e2-e4	e7-e5
2.	Ng1-f3	Nb8-c6
3.	Bf1-b5	a7-a6
4.	Bb5-a4	Ng8-f6
5.	0-0	Bf8-e7
6.	Rf1-e1	b7-b5
7.	Ba4-b3	d7-d6
8.	c2-c3	0-0
9.	h2-h3	Nc6-a5
10.	Bb3-c2	c7-c5
11.	d2-d4	Qd8-c7
12.	Nb1-d2	Na5-c6
13.	d4:c5	d6:c5
14.	Nd2-f1	Rf8-d8
15.	Qd1-e2	Nf6-h5
16.	a2-a4	Ra8-b8
17.	a4:b5	a6:b5
18.	g2-g3	...

Up to and including Black's
17th move, this variation is
well-known to theory. Here 18 g4
Nf4 19 B:f4 ef 20 e5 is recommended, and White wins a pawn
due to his threat of 21 Qe4.
Theory needs only a pawn ahead
to come up with its ±, but that's
not quite enough for the chessplayer sitting at the board. It
is frequently possible to win a
pawn with such moves as g2-g4 or
..g7-g5, but how then does one
convert that pawn into a full
point?

In this instance, is 18 g4
justifiable? I think not. After
18 g4 Nf4 19 B:f4 ef 20 e5, for
example, Black could play 20..Bb7
21 Qe4 g6, and if 22 Q:f4 f6,
when the game opens up in a manner clearly favorable to Black,

who is always assured of at least a draw.

Such were the considerations by which I came gradually to the conclusion that 18 g4 was not the move. However, I could not allow a knight on f4, either. Thus arose the move 18 g3; so far as my memory serves, this has never before appeared in a tournament game.

Black, of course, cannot take the h-pawn, since after 19 Ng5 White wins in all lines: the bishop at h3 and the knight at h5 are both _en prise_.

18.   ...   g7-g6
19. Kg1-h2   ...

19 Ne3 B:h3 20 Nd5 was not enough to retain the advantage, but there is no need for White to be in a hurry: the square d5 is preordained for the knight, and will not run away.

19.   ...   Bc8-e6
20. Nf1-e3   c5-c4
21. Re1-d1   ...

White fears a black knight's invasion at d3, and therefore strives to reduce the number of pieces controlling that square.

21.   ...   Rd8:d1
22. Qe2:d1   Rb8-d8
23. Qd1-e2   Qc7-c8
24. Ne3-d5   ...

A pawn sacrifice typical of such positions; in order to accept it, Black must give up his lightsquare bishop. Now White will be able to disturb his opponent in various areas of the board.

24.   ...   Be6:d5
25. e4:d5   Rd8:d5
26. b2-b3   ...

White tries to open the position as much as possible; this will make the advantage of his two bishops more tangible. Black seeks the reverse: to keep his defense at least semi-closed.

26.   ...   Nh5-f6
27. Nf3-g5   ...

Black was ready to play 27..e4 and bring his rook over to h5.

White has not yet forgotten the golden rule: Always combine attack with defense. Unfortunately, he did forget this rule later.

27.   ...   Nc6-d8
28. b3:c4   Qc8:c4
29. Qe2:c4   b5:c4
30. Ra1-a4   Nf6-d7
31. Ra4:c4   Nd7-c5

Black's pieces are now so well posted that White's rook can find no way to penetrate. Still, White has achieved something: he has created a passed pawn (although it is not far advanced), which in conjunction with his two bishops represents a force to be reckoned with.

32. Ng5-e4   Nd8-e6
33. Ne4:c5   Ne6:c5
34. Rc4-b4   Nc5-d3

Just as White feared, the knight has reached d3. However, now the white rook reaches the eighth rank as well, and gives the game's first check.

35. Rb4-b8+   Kg8-g7
36. Bc1-e3   e5-e4
37. Rb8-e8   Be7-f6
38. Re8-c8   ...

In terrific time-pressure, White declined to play 38 c4 in view of 38..Rf5, failing to see that after 39 R:e4 N:f2 40 Rf4! the knight would be trapped. The proper reply for Black would be 38..Re5, when White could hardly have hoped to exploit his minimal advantage.

| 38. | ... | Nd3:f2 |

Unexpected, and quite pretty. If the knight is taken — which is what White should have done — the rook goes to the second rank and picks up one of White's bishops. Striving for a win at all costs, White rejected this variation in favor of a subtle trap; then, holding his breath, he waited to see if Reshevsky would fall into it.

| 39. | c3-c4 | Rd5-a5 |

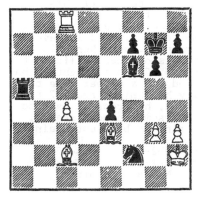

| 40. | Bc2-b3 | Ra5-a3 |

Black is absolutely determined to attack two bishops simultaneously. With this move — while I was still writing it down, in fact — Reshevsky offered a draw (for the third time this game).

| 41. | Be3-c5 | ... |

Threatening mate after 42 Bf8+. The rest is understandable: White wins the exchange, and the game with it.

| 41. | ... | Bf6-e7 |

41..R:b3? 42 Bf8+ Kh8 43 Bh6+ Bd8 44 R:d8 mate.

| 42. | Bc5:a3 | Be7:a3 |
| 43. | c4-c5 | ... |

This pawn will shortly cost Black his bishop.

43.	...	e4-e3
44.	c5-c6	Nf2-e4
45.	Rc8-e8	f7-f5
46.	Bb3-c4	Ba3-d6
47.	c6-c7	Bd6:g3+
48.	Kh2-g2	Bg3:c7
49.	Re8-e7+	Kg7-f6
50.	Re7:c7	f5-f4
51.	Kg2-f3	...

BLACK RESIGNED

******

******

ROUND TWENTY-NINE

197. Reshevsky—Gligoric
(King's Indian)

1.	d2-d4	Ng8-f6
2.	c2-c4	g7-g6
3.	g2-g3	Bf8-g7
4.	Bf1-g2	0-0
5.	Nb1-c3	d7-d6
6.	Ng1-f3	c7-c5

We are indebted to the Yugoslavs for the introduction of this move to serious international practice. White has to decide here whether to push his pawn to d5 or allow the black knight to develop to c6 and then drive it at once to a5. In either event, the game will be very interesting. Of course, White's opening advantage will not be neutralized immediately, but Black has no need to fear: although White does stand a bit more actively, Black still disposes of sufficient possibilities for the most diverse creative efforts.

Among Soviet players, the Leningrad grandmaster Korchnoi is a virtuoso in this variation.

7.	d4-d5	Nb8-a6
8.	Nf3-d2	Na6-c7
9.	Qd1-c2	Ra8-b8
10.	b2-b3	...

Reshevsky copies Euwe's play in the latter's game with Szabo. I do not think it proper to allow Black to get in ..b7-b5 so easily: 9 a4 might have been played, even though this weakens the b4 square — but how important is that, if Black cannot extract anything from it? On the other hand, Reshevsky had played just that move some days earlier against Boleslavsky. And although he obtained an advantage there, he tries for more here — and winds up with nothing!

10.	...	b7-b5
11.	Bc1-b2	b5:c4
12.	Nd2:c4	...

If this knight had a chance of reaching c6 later, then this recapture would be justified. But since the variation 12..Ba6 13 Na5 N7:d5 14 Nc6 Nb4 is in Black's favor, the pawn recapture would have made more sense: d5 and b5 would have been more solidly de-

fended, and the rook on b1 would have turned out to be well placed after all.

12.	...	Bc8-a6
13.	Nc4-e3	Rb8-b4
14.	0-0	Qd8-d7
15.	h2-h3	Rf8-b8
16.	Ra1-b1	Qd7-c8
17.	Kg1-h2	Nc7-e8

Black obtained a very good game out of the opening, but he is totally incapable of deciding which side is the better one from which to begin his assault on the d5-pawn; thus he continues to shuffle his pieces back and forth. This sort of cat-and-mouse play allows Reshevsky time for a singularly favorable regrouping, and then White can give his opponent a little trouble too. Gligoric ought to have picked out a proper time to bring his knight from c7 to d4; instead, he drops it back to e8 for some unknown reason, only to bring it back out again.

18.	Bb2-a3	Rb4-b7
19.	Rf1-c1	Qc8-d8
20.	Nc3-a4	Nf6-d7
21.	Bg2-e4	...

White wants to trade off the hampering black queen's bishop. In such positions, I like the break with a2-a3 and b3-b4.

21.	...	Ne8-c7
22.	Ba3-b2	Nd7-f6
23.	Be4-d3	Bg7-h6

Gligoric unexpectedly loses his patience, and comes up with a very dangerous plan to open the game with ..e7-e6 — dangerous because, while the e-file does fall into Black's hands, the combination of ..Bh6 and ..e7-e6 hands White the important diagonal a1-h8 and the key square f6. Later, Reshevsky takes faultless advantage of this "generosity".

24.	f2-f4	Qd8-d7
25.	Na4-c3	e7-e6
26.	Nc3-e4	...

The refutation of Black's idea. It's a real shame that the d-pawn is now attacked three times, not even defended once — and yet it cannot be taken.

| 26. | ... | Nf6:e4 |

White threatened simultaneous check to the queen and the king, so the knight had to be removed. Other lines would lead to still greater advantage for White, for instance: 26..Nfe8 27 Qc3 Bg7 28 Q:g7+ N:g7 29 Nf6+, or 26..Nf:d5 27 N:d5 B:d3 28 Nf6+, or, finally, 26..Nfe8 27 Qc3 e5 28 fe B:e3 29 e6.

27.	Bd3:e4	f7-f5
28.	d5:e6	Qd7:e6
29.	Be4:b7	Rb8:b7

Recapturing with the bishop would do little to improve Gligoric's position, since after 30 Qc4 Nd5 31 Ng2, followed by 32 Rd1, Black's attack would soon run out.

| 30. | Qc2-c3 | Nc7-e8 |
| 31. | Qc3-d2 | ... |

In time-pressure, Reshevsky could not bring himself to try the forcing line, although Black's resistance would have been speedily crushed after 31 Qh8+ Kf7 32 Q:h7+ Bg7 33 B:g7 N:g7 34 Rc3 d5 35 Ng2. Now, Black gets drawing chances.

31.	...	Rb7-e7
32.	Ne3-d5	Qe6:e2+
33.	Qd2:e2	Re7:e2+
34.	Kh2-g1	Kg8-f8
35.	Rc1-e1	Re2-d2
36.	Re1-d1	Rd2-e2
37.	Nd5-f6	...

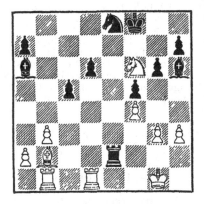

| 37. | ... | Bh6-g7 |

The last error in time-pressure: he should have taken off the knight at f6, retreated his rook to e6, and tried to get his bishop to e4, after which the battle might have begun afresh. White would still have won with 38 R:d6, sacrificing two pieces for a rook, but activating his own pieces to the maximum: 38..Ne4 39 R:a6 Nd2 40 Rc1 Nf3+ 41 Kf1 R:b2 42 R:c5, or 38..Bb7 39 B:f6 Rg2+ 40 Kf1 R:g3 41 Rd8+ Kf7 42 Be5: here there would have been some practical chances, whereas now the game is over.

38.	Nf6:h7+	Kf8-g8
39.	Bb2:g7	Kg8-g7
40.	Nh7-g5	Re2-e3
41.	Rd1-e1	...

BLACK RESIGNED

******

198. Keres—Taimanov
(Sicilian Defense)

1.	e2-e4	c7-c5
2.	Ng1-f3	Nb8-c6
3.	d2-d4	c5:d4
4.	Nf3:d4	Ng8-f6
5.	Nb1-c3	d7-d6
6.	Bf1-c4	...

Sozin's sharp system, which we have already seen. Theoretical opinion concerning this variation has changed more than once.

It was played three times in the Zurich tournament; today it is the favorite weapon of young Robert Fischer.

6.	...	e7-e6
7.	0-0	a7-a6
8.	Bc1-e3	Qd8-c7
9.	Bc4-b3	Nc6-a5

In Game 146 Taimanov played 9..Be7 here against Averbakh, and lost. Now he returns to the older system with 9..Na5, so as to be sooner rid of that pernicious bishop. Later, once he had rehabilitated 9..Be7, Taimanov used it successfully in one of his games at the XXI USSR Championship.

| 10. | f2-f4 | b7-b5 |
| 11. | f4-f5 | ... |

An old idea in a new setting.

In the final round of the 1935 Moscow International Tournament, the 67-year-old Emanuel Lasker destroyed Pirc's position right out of the opening with a similar all-out attack, and received a brilliancy prize for his play. Keres carries out a similar idea, but he is not following Lasker so much as Tolush, who also employed 11 f5, not too long before this tournament, in his game with Taimanov in the Leningrad Championship that year.

| 11. | ... | Na5:b3 |
| 12. | c2:b3 | Bf8-e7 |

One of the positional rules — capture toward the center — is being broken frequently of late. In this position, the idea is clear: to open the c-file for the white rooks. However, in the endgame, the disadvantages of his pawn structure could cause White considerable embarrassment.

Black must exercise some caution in completing his development. Such moves as 12..b4, or 12..e5, followed by 13..b4, may win the e-pawn, it is true; but they contradict Black's strategy.

| 13. | Ra1-c1 | Qc7-d7 |

Here is Taimanov's prepared improvement. The continuation in the Tolush - Taimanov game alluded to was 13..Qb7 14 b4 0-0 15 fe fe 16 Qb3, with some pressure; here Black covers e6 with two pieces, and then quietly castles.

14.	f5:e6	f7:e6
15.	b3-b4	0-0
16.	Qd1-b3	...

A rare place for the queen in the Sicilian. Keres hopes either to induce ..d6-d5, or else to pin Black's bishop down to c8. Taimanov finds still another solution: he prepares ..e6-e5.

| 16. | ... | Kg8-h8 |

Black does not wish to become active too soon, while his king is still exposed. Indeed, after 16..Ng4 White has the pretty stroke 17 Nd5, when Black would be in some difficulty.

| 17. | h2-h3 | e6-e5 |

Combinations can be part of the defense, as well as the attack. Here we see the start of a combination whose final goal is to wrest away the initiative from his opponent.

| 18. | Nd4-f5 | ... |

18 Nc6? would be a mistake in view of 18..Q:c6 19 Nd5 Qe8 20 Nc7 Qg6 21 N:a8 B:h3.

| 18. | ... | Bc8-b7 |
| 19. | Nf5:e7 | ... |

White must begin this series of exchanges, since retreating to g3 would mean going on the defensive.

Keres may have hoped he would have the time to secure d5 by means of 19 Bg5, followed by 20 B:f6; only now did he notice that 19 Bg5 loses a pawn after 19..N:e4 20 N:e7 N:g5 or 20 B:e7 R:f5. So White takes the bishop first, and then plays Bg5. And to avoid finding himself in an inferior position, he shores up his e-pawn with a number of exchanges, attempting simultaneously to press his claim on the d-pawn.

19.	...	Qd7:e7
20.	Be3-g5	h7-h6
21.	Bg5:f6	Rf8:f6
22.	Rf1:f6	Qe7:f6
23.	Rc1-f1	Qf6-g6

White has made no obvious error, but nonetheless the initiative has gradually passed over to Black. It appears evident that attacking the e-pawn with 16 Qb3 took too much time, while not giving White any real chances. A different and more promising plan was adopted by Geller in his game against Taimanov from the XXI USSR Championship. Instead of opening the f-file with 14 fe, he played 14 Qf3, continuing his attack with g2-g4-g5. It would seem that somewhere along these lines the fate of Taimanov's defense to 6 Bc4 will be decided.

In the meantime, however, Keres must find the simplest means of neutralizing Taimanov's pressure in the difficult endgame that lies ahead. He decides to give up his e-pawn for Black's d-pawn, and to retain the heavy pieces for play against the passed (and "almost extra") e-pawn.

| 24. | Qb3-d1 | Ra8-c8 |

Black does not fear the white piece invasion of his eighth rank: after the e-pawn falls, it is White's king which will be the first to come under a mating attack.

25.	Qd1-f3	Rc8-c4
26.	Rf1-d1	Kg8-h7
27.	a2-a3	Bb7:e4

Keres has managed to plug the holes in his position by means of some accurate play, and Taimanov can find nothing better than to go into a queen ending in which White has a useless doubled pawn on the queenside.

28.	Nc3:e4	Rc4:e4
29.	Rd1:d6	Re4-e1+
30.	Kg1-f2	Qg6:d6
31.	Kf2:e1	Qd6-g6
32.	Ke1-d2	e5-e4
33.	Qf3-f2	...

A quick glance at this position might leave one wondering how even Keres, with all his skill in queen endings, could save this game. However, there are two peculiarities in this position which ease White's task a bit: the black king's scanty cover, which means White is always threatening a perpetual check, and the solid position of White's queenside pawns — after all, they <u>are</u> three against

two! The meaning of this latter circumstance will soon become clear.

| 33. | ... | Qg6-g5+ |

33..Qf6 is useless, since White would bravely proceed to exchange queens, continuing — not with 35 g4, certainly (which would be good after 35..Kg6 36 Ke3 f5, but would be refuted by 36..Kg5) — with 35 Ke3!, which forces 35..f5. After 36 g4, there would be very few chances left, it is true, but they'd all be White's.

| 34. | Kd2-e2 | Qg5-d5 |
| 35. | Ke2-e3! | ... |

This saves the game. All of White's pawns turn out to be placed precisely where they are needed. If it were not for the pawn at b4, 35..Qc5+ would win; the b2-pawn defends the a3-pawn, which would otherwise be lost to 35..Qd3+.

| 35. | ... | Qd5-d3+ |

White threatened to attack the e-pawn with 36 Qc2, and 35..Kg6 fails to 36 Qc2 Kf5 37 Qc8+.

| 36. | Ke3-f4 | g7-g5+ |
| 37. | Kf4-e5! | |

DRAW

—since Black has no good defense against the perpetual check.

******

199. Smyslov—Najdorf
(King's Indian)

1.	d2-d4	Ng8-f6
2.	Ng1-f3	g7-g6
3.	g2-g3	Bf8-g7
4.	Bf1-g2	0-0
5.	0-0	d7-d6
6.	b2-b3	e7-e5
7.	d4:e5	Nf6-g4
8.	Bc1-b2	Nb8-c6
9.	c2-c4	Rf8-e8
10.	Nb1-c3	Ng4:e5
11.	Nf3:e5	...

DRAW

This quick draw assured Smyslov of a clear first in the Candidates' Tournament, regardless of the outcome of any of the other games of the last two rounds.

******

200. Geller—Petrosian
(Nimzoindian Defense)

1.	d2-d4	Ng8-f6
2.	c2-c4	e7-e6
3.	Ng1-f3	Bf8-b4+
4.	Nb1-c3	c7-c5
5.	e2-e3	0-0
6.	Bf1-e2	b7-b6
7.	0-0	Bc8-b7
8.	Qd1-b3	c5:d4
9.	Qb3:b4	Nb8-c6
10.	Qb4-a3	d4:c3
11.	Qa3:c3	Nf6-e4
12.	Qc3-c2	f7-f5

While White made five queen moves in pursuit of the bishop-pair, Black has completed his development and established a knight in the center. Petrosian now brings his rook to h6, blockades the white queenside pawns, and obtains an outstanding position.

13.	a2-a3	Rf8-f6
14.	b2-b4	Rf6-h6
15.	Bc1-b2	d7-d6
16.	Ra1-d1	Qd8-e7
17.	Be2-d3	a7-a5!
18.	b4-b5	...

Black's wing-pawn push is a well-known technique used against pawns at a3, b4 and c4 (or the corresponding pawns at a6, b5 and c5). 18 ba would have been met by 18..N:a5, attacking the c-pawn down the file. Geller's reply weakened the c5 square. Black's knight heads for it immediately, forcing White to take it off next move. This helps, but only by half, since Black still has his other knight.

On 18 Qb3, White's queen would remain tied to the defense of the b-pawn, a circumstance which Black could exploit by preparing a kingside attack. Nevertheless, he should not have weakened c5.

18.	...	Nc6-b8
19.	Bd3:e4	Bb7:e4
20.	Qc2-e2	Nb8-d7
21.	Nf3-e1	e6-e5
22.	f2-f3	Be4-b7
23.	Qe2-f2	Ra8-c8
24.	Rd1-c1	˙Qe7-e6

White has taken the necessary

defensive measures on the king-side (among other things, he has covered d3 against a possible knight incursion from c5), but he still does not have a good defense for his c-pawn. So he decides to sacrifice it.

25.	f3-f4	e5-e4
26.	Ne1-c2	Nd7-c5

Complications such as 26..Q:c4 27 Nd4 Qf7 28 Qg3 Rg6 29 R:c8+ B:c8 30 Qh4 evidently appeared double-edged to Black, so Petrosian declined the sacrifice. White has passed the dangerous corner in safety, and now pulls confidently in for a drawn finish.

27.	Nc2-d4	Qe6-f7
28.	Qf2-g3	...

DRAW

******

201. Kotov—Averbakh
(Nimzoindian Defense)

1.	d2-d4	Ng8-f6
2.	c2-c4	e7-e6
3.	Nb1-c3	Bf8-b4
4.	e2-e3	0-0
5.	Ng1-e2	d7-d5
6.	a2-a3	Bb4-e7
7.	c4:d5	e6:d5
8.	Ne2-g3	Rf8-e8
9.	Bf1-d3	Nb8-d7
10.	0-0	a7-a6

After playing an unsuccessful long-term waiting game against Reshevsky, Averbakh plays a more logical system with ..c7-c5 this time, and quickly achieves complete equality. The cautious 10..a6 is directed against any possible incursion of white pieces on b5.

11.	Qd1-c2	Be7-f8
12.	Bc1-d2	c7-c5
13.	d4:c5	Nd7:c5
14.	Ra1-d1	Bc8-g4

The immediate 14..Be6 was more accurate. On e2 White's bishop is better placed than it was on d3.

15.	Bd3-e2	Bg4-e6
16.	Ng3-f5	Ra8-c8
17.	Nf5-d4	Bf8-d6
18.	Be2-f3	Nc5-e4
19.	Nd4:e6	f7:e6
20.	Qc2-b3	Ne4-c5

21.	Qb3-a2	Qd8-c7
22.	g2-g3	Qc7-f7
23.	Bd2-c1	Bd6-e5
24.	Nc3-e2	Rc8-c7
25.	Bf3-g2	...

White cannot work up any initiative anywhere; so he keeps to a waiting game, taking care not to allow Black any important local superiority.

25.	...	g7-g6
26.	Qa2-b1	Nc5-b3
27.	Bc1-d2	Nb3:d2
28.	Rd1:d2	Re8-c8
29.	h2-h3	Rc7-c4
30.	Rf1-c1	Qf7-c7
31.	Rc1:c4	Qc7:c4
32.	f2-f4	Be5-b8
33.	Ne2-d4	Qc4-c1+
34.	Qb1:c1	Rc8:c1+

DRAW

******

202. Boleslavsky—Szabo
(Queen's Indian Defense)

1.	d2-d4	Ng8-f6
2.	c2-c4	e7-e6
3.	Ng1-f3	c7-c5
4.	Nb1-c3	c5:d4
5.	Nf3:d4	Bf8-b4
6.	Qd1-b3	Nb8-a6
7.	e2-e3	...

White wants to sacrifice a pawn for quick development. The present position offers little grounds to recommend such an experiment: Black is well developed, and his king solidly protected. 7 Bg5 would have led to some curious complications, for example: 7..Qa5 8 Bd2 Nc5 9 Qc2 Nce4! 10 N:e4 N:e4 11 Nb3 B:d2+ 12 N:d2 d5, and Black is more actively placed.

7.	...	Nf6-e4
8.	Bf1-e2	Qd8-a5
9.	0-0	Na6-c5

This refutes White's idea. If the bishop had taken on c3 at once, then White's development after 10 bc Q:c3 11 Bb2 would be full compensation for Black's extra pawn. Nor would the trade of queens at b3 have hurt White, since this would reunite the a- and c-pawns. But now the queen must move to c2, and the exchange will take place under circumstances unfavorable to White.

10.	Qb3-c2	Bb4:c3
11.	b2:c3	Qa5:c3
12.	Qc2:c3	Ne4:c3
13.	Be2-f3	Ke8-e7
14.	Nd4-b3	...

White's darksquare bishop is unable to exert its influence due to the excessively powerful position of the knight at c5. Boleslavsky's next few moves are aimed at ousting that knight.

14.	...	Nc3-a4
15.	Bc1-a3	d7-d6
16.	Nb3-a5	e6-e5
17.	Rf1-c1	Ra8-b8
18.	Ra1-b1	Bc8-f5
19.	Rb1:b7+	...

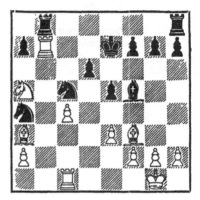

The job turned out to be a tough one, and White had to resort to forceful measures.

19.	...	Nc5:b7
20.	Na5:b7	Rb8:b7
21.	Bf3:b7	Rh8-b8
22.	Bb7-c6	...

White has improved his position somewhat, and he has won back his pawn. However, his pawns are split; so despite his two bishops, he still has a tough ending.

22.	...	Na4-c5
23.	f2-f3	Rb8-b6
24.	Ba3:c5	d6:c5
25.	Bc6-d5	Rb6-b2
26.	Rc1-c3	Rb2:a2
27.	Rc3-b3	Bf5-d7
28.	Rb3-b7	Ke7-d6!

Szabo plays this ending well.

Naturally, 28..f6 would not work in view of 29 Bc6 Rd2 30 R:a7.

29.	Bd5:f7	Bd7-c6
30.	Rb7-b1	a7-a5
31.	Bf7-d5	Bc6:d5
32.	Rb1-d1	a5-a4
33.	Rd1:d5+	Kd6-c6
34.	h2-h4	Ra2-c2
35.	Rd5:e5	a4-a3
36.	Re5-e6+	Kc6-b7
37.	Re6-e7+	Kb7-b6
38.	Re7-e6+	Kb6-a5
39.	Re6-e8	a3-a2
40.	Re8-a8+	Ka5-b4
41.	Kg1-h2	Kb4-b3
42.	Ra8-b8+	Kb3:c4

WHITE RESIGNED

******

203. Stahlberg—Euwe
(Nimzoindian Defense)

1.	d2-d4	Ng8-f6
2.	c2-c4	e7-e6
3.	Ng1-f3	b7-b6
4.	Nb1-c3	Bc8-b7
5.	Bc1-g5	Bf8-b4
6.	Ra1-c1	...

White wants to maintain the connections between his queen-side pawns: against the threatened ..B:c3, he circumspectly defends the knight with his rook (since after 7 bc, the a-pawn would be cut off from the main group).

6.	...	h7-h6
7.	Bg5:f6	Qd8:f6
8.	e2-e3	0-0
9.	Bf1-e2	d7-d6
10.	0-0	Bb4:c3
11.	Rc1:c3	Nb8-d7
12.	Nf3-d2	e6-e5
13.	Be2-f3	Bb7:f3
14.	Nd2:f3	...

DRAW

******

******

ROUND THIRTY

204. Averbakh—Geller
(King's Indian)

1. d4 Nf6 2. c4 g6 3. g3 Bg7
4. Bg2 0-0 5. Nf3 d6 6. 0-0 Nbd7
7. Nc3 e5 8. e4 Re8 9. h3 ed
10. N:d4 Nc5 11. Re1 a5 12. Qc2
Nfd7

The idea underlying this move
is to bring the knight via e5
and d3 to b4, after White's Be3.

13. Rd1 c6 14. Be3 a4 15. Rab1
Qe7 16. Re1 Ne5 17. b3 ab 18. ab
Ned3 19. Re2 Nb4 20. Qd1 Qc7
21. Rd2 Qa5

White has zeroed in on the
pawn at d6; in order to capture
it, however, he must bring his
bishop to f4 — when Black could
develop the threat of ..f7-f5.

22. Nde2 Bf8 23. g4 Ne6 24. Ng3
Qe5 25. Nce2 Ra3 26. Nd4 Qa5

26..Nf4 was impossible, in
view of 27 Nf3 Qf6 28 g5.

27. Nc2 N:c2 28. R:c2 Qb4
29. Bd2 Qb6 30. Be3 Qb4 31. Bd2
Qb6 32. Be3 Qb4

DRAW

******

205. Petrosian—Smyslov
(Queen's Gambit)

1. d4 d5 2. c4 c6 3. cd cd
4. Nc3 Nf6 5. Nf3 Nc6

Another form of Four Knights'
Game, which is not as harmless
as it might seem to be. A symmetrical position does not mean
that neither side wants a fight;
perhaps it is only being postponed to a later stage. In the
present case, it is being postponed to a later tournament.

6. Bf4 Bf5 7. e3 e6 8. Qb3 Bb4

This continuation was discovered by Trifunovic. Even Botvinnik, who had White in 1947
against Trifunovic, had to take
a draw as early as move 13. Petrosian follows his example
against Smyslov.

9. Bb5 Qa5 10. B:c6+ bc 11. a3
B:c3+ 12. Q:c3 Q:c3+ 13. bc

DRAW

206. Taimanov—Reshevsky
(King's Indian)

1.	d2-d4	Ng8-f6
2.	c2-c4	d7-d6
3.	Ng1-f3	g7-g6
4.	Nb1-c3	Bf8-g7
5.	e2-e4	0-0
6.	Bf1-e2	Nb8-d7
7.	0-0	e7-e5
8.	Rf1-e1	e5:d4
9.	Nf3:d4	Nd7-c5
10.	Be2-f1	Rf8-e8
11.	f2-f3	Nf6-d7
12.	Bc1-e3	c7-c6
13.	Qd1-d2	a7-a5
14.	Ra1-d1	a5-a4
15.	Nd4-c2	...

| 15. | ... | Bg7-e5 |

A well-known technique for the
defense of the d-pawn in the
King's Indian.

16.	Be3-d4	Nc5-e6
17.	Bd4:e5	...

A self-assured weakening of
his d4. Fortunately for Taimanov, this is not too dangerous,
in view of White's good development.

17.	...	d6:e5
18.	Qd2-f2	Qd8-e7
19.	g2-g3	Nd7-f6

The weakness at d4 can only
be exploited in an ending; and,
strictly speaking, now was the
time to start thinking about
exchanging queens. The variation 19..Qc5 20 Q:c5Nd:c5 seems
to meet the needs of the position, since the knight on d7
goes to c5, and the threat of

the other knight to go to a4
would force White to keep a
knight posted at c2 to guard
that square. However, Reshevsky declined the queen trade,
since after 20 b4 ab 21 ab
Q:f2+ 22 K:f2 Black's minimal advantage would not have
been sufficient to win.

| 20. | b2-b4 | ... |

This strong move equalizes
the game completely; now f3-f4
is a threat. So Reshevsky was
forced to accept the

DRAW

here. It seems to me that the
American grandmaster committed
his mistake even before the
start of this game: he should
have chosen a different variation, or perhaps even a different opening. The line that
occurred in the game was too
well known to Taimanov.

***

207. Euwe—Boleslavsky
(King's Indian)

1.	d2-d4	Ng8-f6
2.	c2-c4	g7-g6
3.	g2-g3	Bf8-g7
4.	Bf1-g2	0-0
5.	Nb1-c3	d7-d6
6.	Ng1-f3	Nb8-d7
7.	0-0	e7-e5
8.	b2-b3	...

An ancient line which has now
gone out of fashion. The bishop
never does get to b2.

8.	...	Rf8-e8
9.	Qd1-c2	c7-c6
10.	Rf1-d1	e5-e4
11.	Nf3-e1	...

On 11 Nd2, Black could bravely proceed with 11..d5!, when
White's attempt to exploit the
fork motif by 12 cd cd 13 Nb5
would be met by 13..Re6 14 Qc7
Qe8. And on 11 Ng5, Black could
sacrifice a pawn for good prospects with 11..e3, and if 12 B:e3
R:e3 13 fe Ng4, or 12 fe Ng4 at
once, with good piece play.

11.	...	Qd8-e7
12.	h2-h3	a7-a6
13.	a2-a4	d6-d5
14.	c4:d5	c6:d5
15.	a4-a5	b7-b5

16.	a5:b6	Nd7:b6
17.	Qc2-d2	Bc8-e6
18.	Ne1-c2	Qe7-d7
19.	Kg1-h2	h7-h5
20.	Nc3-a4	Nb6:a4
21.	Ra1:a4	Qd7-c7

Black is now threatening ..h5-
h4, so White retreats his king
to g1.

22.	Kh2-g1	Re8-b8
23.	Nc2-a1	Kg8-h7
24.	Qd2-a2	Rb8-b6
25.	Bc▲-f4	Qc7-d7
26.	Kg1-h2	Nf6-e8
27.	Rd1-c1	Ne8-d6
28.	Bf4:d6	...

Another achievement for Black,
this one induced by his threat
of 28..Nf5. The absence of this
bishop makes itself felt later.

28.	...	Qd7:d6
29.	e2-e3	h5-h4
30.	b3-b4	...

Boleslavsky's attack has grown
quite ominous. Euwe decides to
sacrifice a pawn in the hope of
distracting his opponent from
his king long enough so that he
can free himself a bit.

30.	...	Bg7-h6
31.	Rc1-c3	Rb6:b4
32.	Na1-b3	Rb4-a4
33.	Qa2:a4	Be6-d7
34.	Qa4-a5	Bd7-b5

The lightsquare bishop, having
sat for so long in reserve, now
enters the fray.

35.	Nb3-c5	Ra8-b8 (
36.	Qa5-a1	Bh6-g5
37.	Qa1-d1	h4:g3+
38.	f2:g3	f7-f5
39.	Qd1-e1	Bb5-c4
40.	Kh2-g1	Bg5-d8

Now the other bishop also joins
in the attack, heading for c7,
where it supports the queen in
its activities along the diagonal b8-h2. Boleslavsky plays
this phase of the game with
great skill.

| 41. | Rc3-c2 | Bd8-c7 |
| 42. | Bg2-f1 | ... |

Euwe offers Black his g-pawn
in exchange for the a-pawn, hoping to get the queens exchanged
and thereby relieve himself of

worrying over mate threats.
On 42 Kh2, Black had the
elegant rook sacrifice 42..Rb1
43 Q:b1 Q:g3+ 44 Kg1 Qh2+. In
addition to this threat to invade on the b-file with his rook,
Black also had the simpler plan
..g6-g5 and ..f5-f4, so White's
position must be untenable.

| 42. | ... | Bc4:f1 |

Black could have brought his
other bishop decisively into
the game here by 42..Ba5 43 Q:a5
(43 Qf2 Rb1) 43..Q:g3+ 44 Rg2
Q:e3+ 45 Kh1 Rb1 46 Qc7+ Kh6
47 Ne6 Q:h3+!

43.	Kg1:f1	Qd6:g3
44.	Qe1:g3	Bc7:g3
45.	Nc5:a6	Rb8-b3
46.	Kf1-e2	g6-g5
47.	Na6-c5	Rb3-b6
48.	Rc2-a2	f5-f4
49.	Ra2-a7+	Kh7-g6
50.	Ra7-a6	f4-f3+
51.	Ke2-f1	Rb6:a6
52.	Nc5:a6	Bg3-d6

This is why the bishop is
stronger than the knight.

| 53. | Kf1-f2 | Kg6-f7 |

WHITE RESIGNED

******

208. Gligoric—Bronstein
(Nimzoindian Defense)

1.	d2-d4	Ng8-f6
2.	c2-c4	e7-e6
3.	Nb1-c3	Bf8-b4
4.	e2-e3	0-0

5.	Ng1-e2	d7-d5
6.	a2-a3	Bb4-e7
7.	c4:d5	e6:d5
8.	Ne2-g3	c7-c5

Alekhine played this as far
back as his 25th match game
against Euwe in 1937. By this
counterattack against the white
center Black removes White's
pawn from d4, and obtains the
possibility of settling down at
e5.

9.	Bf1-d3	Nb8-c6
10.	0-0	Rf8-e8
11.	d4:c5	Be7:c5
12.	b2-b4	Bc5-d6
13.	Bc1-b2	Bd6-e5
14.	Nc3-a4	Be5:b2

The battle is raging for d4.
However, this is not an end in
itself, since controlling the
square in front of an isolated
pawn is only important in those
cases where White can establish
a piece on that square and has
no weaknesses himself.

Black's further play is directed towards the enticement of
White's pieces as far as possible from d4, and the creation of
weaknesses in White's queenside
pawn position. For example, this
trade of darksquare bishops is
favorable to White, but Black
could not allow White to control
the long diagonal. And besides,
the white knight ends up in an
out-of-the-way location, from
which it would require at least
four moves to reach d4.

| 15. | Na4:b2 | Bc8-g4 |
| 16. | Bd3-e2 | ... |

White's queen had no good
retreat square, but the exchange
of this pair of bishops favors
Black, not White.

16.	...	Bg4:e2
17.	Ng3:e2	Qd8-d6
18.	Nb2-d3	a7-a6
19.	Ra1-c1	a6-a5

Just in time. On the pre-
vious move White could have
played 19 b5 to good effect;
since it was important to
maintain his knight at c6 then,
Black played 18..a6. But now
White's a-pawn is insufficiently protected, and Black can redeploy his knight to e6, where

it will hold a great deal of
influence over the squares g7,
f4, d4 and c5.

20.	b4-b5	Nc6-d8
21.	a3-a4	Nd8-e6
22.	Ne2-g3	...

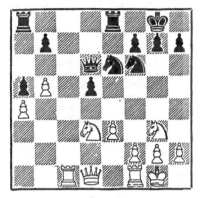

| 22. | ... | Qd6-a3 |

Black's queen gets behind
the a-pawn. White drives it
away, but it goes to c3; the
rook hits it again, and it returns...

23.	Rc1-a1	Qa3-c3
24.	Ra1-c1	Qc3-a3
25.	Rc1-a1	Qa3-c3

DRAW

******

209. Szabo—Kotov
(Nimzoindian Defense)

1.	d2-d4	Ng8-f6
2.	c2-c4	e7-e6
3.	Nb1-c3	Bf8-b4
4.	e2-e3	0-0
5.	Bf1-d3	d7-d5
6.	Ng1-f3	c7-c6
7.	0-0	Nb8-d7
8.	Qd1-e2	a7-a6
9.	a2-a3	c5:d4
10.	e3:d4	d5:c4
11.	Bd3:c4	Bb4-e7
12.	Bc4-a2	...

Black prepares to fianchetto
his queen's bishop. White's bishop retreats a little way, so
as to be able to answer ..b7-b5
with d4-d5.

| 12. | ... | Nd7-b6 |

| 13. | Bc1-g5 | Nf6-d5 |

White's plan of setting up a
powerful attacking position
with Rfe1, Rad1, Bb1, Ne5 and
f2-f4 induces Black to start
this exchanging operation, resulting in a lessening of the
number of pieces on the board.
Thus, the threat of an immediate mating attack is gone, but
White's advantage remains, merely altering its form.

14.	Bg5:e7	Nd5:c3
15.	b2:c3	Qd8:e7
16.	c3-c4	...

16.	...	Nb6-a4
17.	Ba2-b3	Bc8-d7
18.	Qe2-c2	Na4-b6
19.	c4-c5	Ra8-c8
20.	Nf3-e5	Rf8-d8
21.	Qc2-e4	...

White's positional advantage
is indisputable. He may choose
between the advance of his a-
pawn to the fifth rank, permanently nailing down the pawn at
b7, or an immediate attack with
f2-f4-f5, or the development of
his rooks to the d- and e-files.
All of these are good plans, except that they are not forceful
enough, and allow Black the opportunity to put together a stout
defense. Szabo prefers to simplify a little, leaving himself
one concrete advantage: pressure
on the open file against the
pawn at b7.

21.	...	Nb6-d5
22.	Bb3:d5	e6:d5
23.	Qe4-f4	f7-f6

24.	Ne5:d7	Qe7:d7
25.	Ra1-b1	Rd8-e8
26.	f2-f3	Re8-e7
27.	Rf1-f2	Rc8-e8
28.	Rf2-b2	Re7-e1+

By the exchange of one rook, Black removes the piece that controls e1, so that later he can set up some counterplay on that file.

29.	Rb1:e1	Re8:e1+
30.	Kg1-f2	Re1-e8
31.	Rb2-b6	...

White's threats are assuming concrete form: 32 Rd6. Kotov undertakes a raid with his queen, in order to distract his opponent by threatening the safety of his king.

31.	...	Qd7-e7
32.	Qf4-d2	Re8-d8

There was absolutely no reason to give up the e-file for nothing, especially when he must submit to an exchange of queens as well. The only means of resisting White's pressure was 32..f5, for example: 33 g3 f4 34 Rd6 fg+ 35 hg Rd8, or 33 h3 Qh4+ 34 Kf1 f4. White would still have held the advantage, but he would also have had a difficult time coordinating his attack on the b- and d-pawns with the defense of his king.

After the trade of queens that follows next move, Black winds up in a difficult rook ending.

33.	Qd2-e3	Qe7:e3+
34.	Kf2:e3	Rd8-d7
35.	h2-h4	...

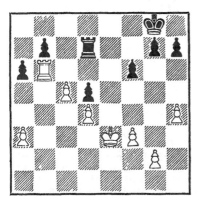

Black's rook is tied to the defense of the b- and d-pawns. White wants to get his king to f5 or e5; Black's next few moves prevent this, but with them he contracts a fresh weakness: the pawn at f6.

35.	...	Kg8-f7
36.	h4-h5	g7-g5
37.	h5:g6+	Kf7:g6
38.	Ke3-f4	h7-h5
39.	g2-g3	Rd7-h7
40.	Kf4-e3	Rh7-e7+
41.	Ke3-f4	Re7-h7

After analyzing the adjourned position, Kotov came to the conclusion that his position was hopeless, and that his only chance lay in activating his rook.

42.	a3-a4	h5-h4
43.	g3:h4	Rh7:h4+
44.	Kf4-e3	Rh4-h7
45.	Rb6-d6	Rh7-e7+
46.	Ke3-d3	Kg6-g5
47.	Rd6:d5+	Kg5-f4
48.	Rd5-d6	f6-f5
49.	Rd6-f6	Re7-e1
50.	Rf6-f7	Re1-b1
51.	a4-a5	Rb1-b3+

Black has done everything possible: his king has broken in, his rook is active, and the f-pawn is now twice attacked. But it's all too late: the d-pawn will cost him the game.

52.	Kd3-c4	Rb3-b1
53.	Rf7-f6	Rb1-h1
54.	Rf6-b6	Rh1-h7
55.	Rb6-b3	Rh7-d7
56.	d4-d5	Kf4-e5
57.	d5-d6	f5-f4

58.	Rb3-b1	Rd7-h7
59.	Rb1-e1+	Ke5-f6
60.	c5-c6	b7:c6
61.	Kc4-c5	Rh7-h2
62.	Re1-d1	...

BLACK RESIGNED

******

210. Najdorf—Keres
(Queen's Gambit)

1.	d2-d4	Ng8-f6
2.	C2-c4	e7-e6
3.	Nb1-c3	d7-d5
4.	Ng1-f3	c7-c5
5.	c4:d5	c5:d4
6.	Qd1:d4	e6:d5
7.	e2-e4	Nb8-c6
8.	Bf1-b5	a7-a6

Keres loves to play <u>va banque</u>, and does so with a great deal of skill, especially at the end of a tournament, when his final standing is in the balance. One can hardly help recalling the last-round wins that secured him first places in such strong tournaments as the XV, XVIII, and XIX USSR Championships, and the 1952 Budapest International.

The word "tournament" probably awakens in Keres visions of armored knights galloping towards each other with lances at the ready (and certainly not offering any draws!). Perhaps he saw himself as just such a knight when, in the final round, he elected to try for clear second place, and for the third time adopted this double-edged weapon, his new defense — or, more accurately, counterattack — to the Queen's Gambit. The risk was very great, since his game against Geller had already looked dubious; and now Najdorf, who is known to specialize in forcing lines, would be well prepared, beyond the shadow of a doubt.

8..a6 is an improvement on the Geller-Keres game (No. 155), in which 8..N:e4 was played.

| 9. | Bb5:c6+ | b7:c6 |
| 10. | Nf3-e5 | ... |

This is better than castling here, when Black could reply 10..de 11 Q:d8+ K:d8 12 Ng5 Ke8. The text forces Black's bishop to a passive position.

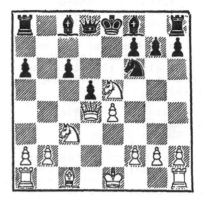

| 10. | ... | Bc8-b7 |
| 11. | e4:d5 | Nf6:d5 |

11..Be7 has been suggested instead of the text. White might have replied 12 d6 Q:d6 13 Q:d6 B:d6 14 Nc4, with the better game, due to the weakness of the black a- and c-pawns. Still, this was better than 11..N:d5, since Black could thereby have avoided subjecting himself to the perils of the direct attack that now encircles his king.

| 12. | 0-0 | Bf8-e7 |
| 13. | Ne5:c6 | ... |

A pretty piece sacrifice, with the idea of keeping Black's king in the center and attacking it there with White's rooks, queen and minor pieces. Keres has caught a Tartar, indeed!

13.	...	Bb7:c6
14.	Qd4:g7	Rh8-f8
15.	Rf1-e1	Qd8-d6

(See diagram, next page)

| 16. | Nc3:e4 | ... |

DRAW

Najdorf did not play 16 N:d5, in view of 16..Q:d5; on almost any White reply, Black castles queenside, and then plays ..Rg8,

with very dangerous threats, for example: 17 Bh6 0-0-0 18 Qg4+ f5, or 18 R:e7 Rg8, and White cannot defend g2.

The next day, after the tournament had already ended, Najdorf, with his usual Argentine fervor, showed all the participants that 17 Bf4 would have won anyway: 17..0-0-0 would be met by 18 R:e7 Rg8 19 Rc7+. And if 16..B:d5 instead, then 17 Bg5 Be6 18 Rad1 Qb4 19 Bh6, with a powerful attack. In reply, Keres just smiled...

******

******

******

CROSSTABLE

	Participants	1	2	3	4	5	6	7	8
1	Smyslov	x	½½	11	½1	½½	11	½½	½0
2	Bronstein	½½	x	1½	11	½½	½0	½½	½½
3	Keres	00	0½	x	½½	½1	½1	½½	½½
4	Reshevsky	½0	00	½½	x	½½	½½	½½	10
5	Petrosian	½½	½½	½0	½½	x	½½	0½	½½
6	Geller	00	½1	½0	½½	½½	x	11	½0
7	Najdorf	½½	½½	½½	½½	1½	00	x	1½
8	Kotov	½1	½½	½½	01	½½	½1	0½	x
9	Taimanov	½½	0½	½½	½½	11	10	0½	01
10	Averbakh	½½	½½	1½	½0	½½	½½	½1	0½
11	Boleslavsky	½½	½½	00	½0	½½	10	½½	11
12	Szabo	½½	10	0½	0½	00	0½	½½	01
13	Gligoric	0½	0½	½0	½0	½0	½0	½½	0½
14	Euwe	00	½½	½½	00	0½	10	1½	1½
15	Stahlberg	0½	½½	00	0½	00	½½	00	10

9	10	11	12	13	14	15	Total	Place
½½	½½	½½	½½	1½	11	1½	18	I
1½	½½	½½	01	1½	½½	½½	16	II-IV
½½	0½	11	1½	½1	½½	11	16	II-IV
½½	½1	½1	1½	½1	11	1½	16	II-IV
00	½½	½½	11	½1	1½	11	15	V
01	½½	01	1½	½1	01	½½	14½	VI-VII
1½	½0	½½	½½	½½	0½	11	14½	VI-VII
10	1½	00	10	1½	0½	01	14	VIII-IX
x	10	½½	½½	½0	0½	11	14	VIII-IX
01	x	½½	½½	0½	11	00	13½	X-XI
½½	½½	x	½0	½½	½1	½½	13½	X-XI
½½	½½	½1	x	1½	½½	1½	13	XII
½1	1½	½½	0½	x	½1	11	12½	XIII
1½	00	½0	½½	½0	x	1½	11½	XIV
00	11	½½	0½	00	0½	x	8	XV

INDEX OF PLAYERS

(The numbers refer to games)

PETROSIAN -
- Averbakh   56
- Boleslavsky   82
- Bronstein   16
- Euwe   69
- Geller   95
- Gligoric   132
- Keres   3
- Kotov   192
- Najdorf   147
- Reshevsky   117
- Smyslov   205
- Stahlberg   177
- Szabo   162
- Taimanov   29

RESHEVSKY -
- Averbakh   122
- Boleslavsky   152
- Bronstein   91
- Euwe   137
- Geller   167
- Gligoric   197
- Keres   182
- Kotov   51
- Najdorf   107
- Petrosian   12
- Smyslov   64
- Stahlberg   38
- Szabo   25
- Taimanov   104

SMYSLOV -
- Averbakh   109
- Boleslavsky   139
- Bronstein   76
- Euwe   124
- Geller   154
- Gligoric   184
- Keres   63
- Kotov   36
- Najdorf   199
- Petrosian   102
- Reshevsky   169
- Stahlberg   23
- Szabo   10
- Taimanov   89

STAHLBERG -
- Averbakh   188
- Boleslavsky   7
- Bronstein   46
- Euwe   203
- Geller   20
- Gligoric   158
- Keres   33
- Kotov   113
- Najdorf   173
- Petrosian   72
- Reshevsky   143
- Smyslov   128
- Szabo   85
- Taimanov   59

SZABO -
- Averbakh   175
- Boleslavsky   97
- Bronstein   31
- Euwe   84
- Geller   1
- Gligoric   145
- Keres   18
- Kotov   209
- Najdorf   160
- Petrosian   57
- Reshevsky   130
- Smyslov   115
- Stahlberg   190
- Taimanov   44

TAIMANOV -
- Averbakh   41
- Boleslavsky   67
- Bronstein   5
- Euwe   54
- Geller   80
- Gligoric   119
- Keres   93
- Kotov   179
- Najdorf   28
- Petrosian   134
- Reshevsky   206
- Smyslov   194
- Stahlberg   164
- Szabo   149

Player	1	2	3	4	5	6	7	8	9	10	11	12	13	14	15
1 Smyslov	½	1	2	3	3½	4	5	<u>5</u>	6	6½	7	8	8½	9	9½
2 Bronstein	1	1½	2	2½	2½	3	3½	4	4½	5	5½	6½	7½	<u>7½</u>	8½
3 Keres	½	½	1½	2	3	4	4½	5	5	<u>5</u>	5½	5½	6	6½	7
4 Reshevsky	½	1	1½	2½	3½	4½	5	6	6½	7	7½	<u>7½</u>	7½	8	8½
5 Petrosian	½	1	1½	2	2	2	<u>2</u>	2½	3½	4½	5½	6	6½	7	7½
6 Geller	1	1	1½	1½	2	<u>2</u>	2	2½	3	3½	4	4	5	5½	6
7 Najdorf	½	1	1½	2½	<u>2½</u>	3½	4	4½	4½	5½	6	7	7	7½	8
8 Kotov	0	0	0	<u>0</u>	½	1	1½	1½	2	3	4	4	4½	5½	6½
9 Taimanov	0	½	<u>½</u>	½	1½	2½	3	3	4	4½	4½	5½	6	6½	7
10 Averbakh	½	1½	2	2½	2½	2½	3	3½	<u>3½</u>	4	5	5	5½	5½	6
11 Boleslavsky	½	½	1½	2½	3	3	3½	4	4½	5	5½	6	6½	7	7½
12 Szabo	0	½	½	½	1½	2½	3	3½	3½	4	<u>4</u>	4½	5½	6	6
13 Gligoric	_	½	1	1½	2½	2½	3	4	4½	4½	5	5	5½	6	6
14 Euwe	1	2	2	2½	2½	3	3½	4½	5½	5½	5½	6	<u>6</u>	7	7½
15 Stahlberg	½	1½	2	2	2	2	2½	2½	2½	2½	2½	3½	3½	3½	<u>3½</u>

Underscoring (__)

PROGRESSIVE SCORES

16	17	18	19	20	21	22	23	24	25	26	27	28	29	30
10	10½	11½	12	12½	12½	13½	<u>13½</u>	14½	15½	16	16½	17	17½	18
9	9½	10	10½	11½	12	12½	13	13½	13½	14	14½	15½	<u>15½</u>	16
8	8½	9	9½	10½	11½	12	13	13	<u>13</u>	13½	14	15	15½	16
9	9½	10½	11	12	12½	13½	13½	14	14	14½	<u>14½</u>	14½	15½	16
7½	8	8½	9½	9½	10	<u>10</u>	10½	11½	12	13	13½	14	14½	15
6½	7½	8	9	9	<u>9</u>	9	9	9½	10½	11½	12½	13½	14	14½
8½	9	9½	10	<u>10</u>	10½	10½	11	11½	12½	13	13½	13½	14	14½
7	8	8	<u>8</u>	9	10	10½	11½	12	12½	12½	13	13½	14	14
7½	7½	<u>7½</u>	8	9	9	9½	10	11	11½	12½	12½	13	13½	14
6½	7	7	7½	8	9	10	10½	<u>10½</u>	11	12	12	12½	13	13½
8	<u>8</u>	9	9	9½	9½	9½	10	.10½	11	11½	12	12½	12½	13½
6½	7	7½	8	8	8½	9	9½	9½	10	<u>10</u>	10½	11	12	13
<u>6</u>	7	7½	7½	8	8½	9½	10½	11	11½	11½	12	12	12	12½
8	8	8	8½	8½	9	9	9½	10	10½	10½	11	<u>11</u>	11½	11½
4	4	4½	5	5	5½	6	6	6	6	6	7	7½	8	<u>8</u>

indicates bye.

[349]

A CATALOG OF SELECTED
DOVER BOOKS
IN ALL FIELDS OF INTEREST

A CATALOG OF SELECTED DOVER BOOKS IN ALL FIELDS OF INTEREST

100 BEST-LOVED POEMS, Edited by Philip Smith. "The Passionate Shepherd to His Love," "Shall I compare thee to a summer's day?" "Death, be not proud," "The Raven," "The Road Not Taken," plus works by Blake, Wordsworth, Byron, Shelley, Keats, many others. 96pp. $5\frac{3}{16}$ x $8\frac{1}{4}$. 0-486-28553-7

100 SMALL HOUSES OF THE THIRTIES, Brown-Blodgett Company. Exterior photographs and floor plans for 100 charming structures. Illustrations of models accompanied by descriptions of interiors, color schemes, closet space, and other amenities. 200 illustrations. 112pp. $8\frac{3}{8}$ x 11. 0-486-44131-8

1000 TURN-OF-THE-CENTURY HOUSES: With Illustrations and Floor Plans, Herbert C. Chivers. Reproduced from a rare edition, this showcase of homes ranges from cottages and bungalows to sprawling mansions. Each house is meticulously illustrated and accompanied by complete floor plans. 256pp. $9\frac{3}{8}$ x $12\frac{1}{4}$. 0-486-45596-3

101 GREAT AMERICAN POEMS, Edited by The American Poetry & Literacy Project. Rich treasury of verse from the 19th and 20th centuries includes works by Edgar Allan Poe, Robert Frost, Walt Whitman, Langston Hughes, Emily Dickinson, T. S. Eliot, other notables. 96pp. $5\frac{3}{16}$ x $8\frac{1}{4}$. 0-486-40158-8

101 GREAT SAMURAI PRINTS, Utagawa Kuniyoshi. Kuniyoshi was a master of the warrior woodblock print — and these 18th-century illustrations represent the pinnacle of his craft. Full-color portraits of renowned Japanese samurais pulse with movement, passion, and remarkably fine detail. 112pp. $8\frac{3}{8}$ x 11. 0-486-46523-3

ABC OF BALLET, Janet Grosser. Clearly worded, abundantly illustrated little guide defines basic ballet-related terms: arabesque, battement, pas de chat, relevé, sissonne, many others. Pronunciation guide included. Excellent primer. 48pp. $4\frac{3}{16}$ x $5\frac{3}{4}$. 0-486-40871-X

ACCESSORIES OF DRESS: An Illustrated Encyclopedia, Katherine Lester and Bess Viola Oerke. Illustrations of hats, veils, wigs, cravats, shawls, shoes, gloves, and other accessories enhance an engaging commentary that reveals the humor and charm of the many-sided story of accessorized apparel. 644 figures and 59 plates. 608pp. $6\frac{1}{8}$ x $9\frac{1}{4}$. 0-486-43378-1

ADVENTURES OF HUCKLEBERRY FINN, Mark Twain. Join Huck and Jim as their boyhood adventures along the Mississippi River lead them into a world of excitement, danger, and self-discovery. Humorous narrative, lyrical descriptions of the Mississippi valley, and memorable characters. 224pp. $5\frac{3}{16}$ x $8\frac{1}{4}$. 0-486-28061-6

ALICE STARMORE'S BOOK OF FAIR ISLE KNITTING, Alice Starmore. A noted designer from the region of Scotland's Fair Isle explores the history and techniques of this distinctive, stranded-color knitting style and provides copious illustrated instructions for 14 original knitwear designs. 208pp. $8\frac{3}{8}$ x $10\frac{7}{8}$. 0-486-47218-3

Browse over 9,000 books at www.doverpublications.com

ALICE'S ADVENTURES IN WONDERLAND, Lewis Carroll. Beloved classic about a little girl lost in a topsy-turvy land and her encounters with the White Rabbit, March Hare, Mad Hatter, Cheshire Cat, and other delightfully improbable characters. 42 illustrations by Sir John Tenniel. 96pp. 5³⁄₁₆ x 8¼. 0-486-27543-4

AMERICA'S LIGHTHOUSES: An Illustrated History, Francis Ross Holland. Profusely illustrated fact-filled survey of American lighthouses since 1716. Over 200 stations — East, Gulf, and West coasts, Great Lakes, Hawaii, Alaska, Puerto Rico, the Virgin Islands, and the Mississippi and St. Lawrence Rivers. 240pp. 8 x 10¾.

0-486-25576-X

AN ENCYCLOPEDIA OF THE VIOLIN, Alberto Bachmann. Translated by Frederick H. Martens. Introduction by Eugene Ysaye. First published in 1925, this renowned reference remains unsurpassed as a source of essential information, from construction and evolution to repertoire and technique. Includes a glossary and 73 illustrations. 496pp. 6⅛ x 9¼. 0-486-46618-3

ANIMALS: 1,419 Copyright-Free Illustrations of Mammals, Birds, Fish, Insects, etc., Selected by Jim Harter. Selected for its visual impact and ease of use, this outstanding collection of wood engravings presents over 1,000 species of animals in extremely lifelike poses. Includes mammals, birds, reptiles, amphibians, fish, insects, and other invertebrates. 284pp. 9 x 12. 0-486-23766-4

THE ANNALS, Tacitus. Translated by Alfred John Church and William Jackson Brodribb. This vital chronicle of Imperial Rome, written by the era's great historian, spans A.D. 14-68 and paints incisive psychological portraits of major figures, from Tiberius to Nero. 416pp. 5³⁄₁₆ x 8¼. 0-486-45236-0

ANTIGONE, Sophocles. Filled with passionate speeches and sensitive probing of moral and philosophical issues, this powerful and often-performed Greek drama reveals the grim fate that befalls the children of Oedipus. Footnotes. 64pp. 5³⁄₁₆ x 8 ¼. 0-486-27804-2

ART DECO DECORATIVE PATTERNS IN FULL COLOR, Christian Stoll. Reprinted from a rare 1910 portfolio, 160 sensuous and exotic images depict a breathtaking array of florals, geometrics, and abstracts — all elegant in their stark simplicity. 64pp. 8⅜ x 11. 0-486-44862-2

THE ARTHUR RACKHAM TREASURY: 86 Full-Color Illustrations, Arthur Rackham. Selected and Edited by Jeff A. Menges. A stunning treasury of 86 full-page plates span the famed English artist's career, from *Rip Van Winkle* (1905) to masterworks such as *Undine, A Midsummer Night's Dream,* and *Wind in the Willows* (1939). 96pp. 8⅜ x 11.

0-486-44685-9

THE AUTHENTIC GILBERT & SULLIVAN SONGBOOK, W. S. Gilbert and A. S. Sullivan. The most comprehensive collection available, this songbook includes selections from every one of Gilbert and Sullivan's light operas. Ninety-two numbers are presented uncut and unedited, and in their original keys. 410pp. 9 x 12.

0-486-23482-7

THE AWAKENING, Kate Chopin. First published in 1899, this controversial novel of a New Orleans wife's search for love outside a stifling marriage shocked readers. Today, it remains a first-rate narrative with superb characterization. New introductory Note. 128pp. 5³⁄₁₆ x 8¼. 0-486-27786-0

BASIC DRAWING, Louis Priscilla. Beginning with perspective, this commonsense manual progresses to the figure in movement, light and shade, anatomy, drapery, composition, trees and landscape, and outdoor sketching. Black-and-white illustrations throughout. 128pp. 8⅜ x 11. 0-486-45815-6

THE BATTLES THAT CHANGED HISTORY, Fletcher Pratt. Historian profiles 16 crucial conflicts, ancient to modern, that changed the course of Western civilization. Gripping accounts of battles led by Alexander the Great, Joan of Arc, Ulysses S. Grant, other commanders. 27 maps. 352pp. 5⅜ x 8½. 0-486-41129-X

BEETHOVEN'S LETTERS, Ludwig van Beethoven. Edited by Dr. A. C. Kalischer. Features 457 letters to fellow musicians, friends, greats, patrons, and literary men. Reveals musical thoughts, quirks of personality, insights, and daily events. Includes 15 plates. 410pp. 5⅜ x 8½. 0-486-22769-3

BERNICE BOBS HER HAIR AND OTHER STORIES, F. Scott Fitzgerald. This brilliant anthology includes 6 of Fitzgerald's most popular stories: "The Diamond as Big as the Ritz," the title tale, "The Offshore Pirate," "The Ice Palace," "The Jelly Bean," and "May Day." 176pp. 5⅜ x 8½. 0-486-47049-0

BESLER'S BOOK OF FLOWERS AND PLANTS: 73 Full-Color Plates from Hortus Eystettensis, 1613, Basilius Besler. Here is a selection of magnificent plates from the *Hortus Eystettensis,* which vividly illustrated and identified the plants, flowers, and trees that thrived in the legendary German garden at Eichstätt. 80pp. 8⅜ x 11. 0-486-46005-3

THE BOOK OF KELLS, Edited by Blanche Cirker. Painstakingly reproduced from a rare facsimile edition, this volume contains full-page decorations, portraits, illustrations, plus a sampling of textual leaves with exquisite calligraphy and ornamentation. 32 full-color illustrations. 32pp. 9⅜ x 12¼. 0-486-24345-1

THE BOOK OF THE CROSSBOW: With an Additional Section on Catapults and Other Siege Engines, Ralph Payne-Gallwey. Fascinating study traces history and use of crossbow as military and sporting weapon, from Middle Ages to modern times. Also covers related weapons: balistas, catapults, Turkish bows, more. Over 240 illustrations. 400pp. 7¼ x 10⅛. 0-486-28720-3

THE BUNGALOW BOOK: Floor Plans and Photos of 112 Houses, 1910, Henry L. Wilson. Here are 112 of the most popular and economic blueprints of the early 20th century — plus an illustration or photograph of each completed house. A wonderful time capsule that still offers a wealth of valuable insights. 160pp. 8⅜ x 11. 0-486-45104-6

THE CALL OF THE WILD, Jack London. A classic novel of adventure, drawn from London's own experiences as a Klondike adventurer, relating the story of a heroic dog caught in the brutal life of the Alaska Gold Rush. Note. 64pp. 5³⁄₁₆ x 8¼. 0-486-26472-6

CANDIDE, Voltaire. Edited by Francois-Marie Arouet. One of the world's great satires since its first publication in 1759. Witty, caustic skewering of romance, science, philosophy, religion, government — nearly all human ideals and institutions. 112pp. 5³⁄₁₆ x 8¼. 0-486-26689-3

CELEBRATED IN THEIR TIME: Photographic Portraits from the George Grantham Bain Collection, Edited by Amy Pastan. With an Introduction by Michael Carlebach. Remarkable portrait gallery features 112 rare images of Albert Einstein, Charlie Chaplin, the Wright Brothers, Henry Ford, and other luminaries from the worlds of politics, art, entertainment, and industry. 128pp. 8⅜ x 11. 0-486-46754-6

CHARIOTS FOR APOLLO: The NASA History of Manned Lunar Spacecraft to 1969, Courtney G. Brooks, James M. Grimwood, and Loyd S. Swenson, Jr. This illustrated history by a trio of experts is the definitive reference on the Apollo spacecraft and lunar modules. It traces the vehicles' design, development, and operation in space. More than 100 photographs and illustrations. 576pp. 6¾ x 9¼. 0-486-46756-2

A CHRISTMAS CAROL, Charles Dickens. This engrossing tale relates Ebenezer Scrooge's ghostly journeys through Christmases past, present, and future and his ultimate transformation from a harsh and grasping old miser to a charitable and compassionate human being. 80pp. 5⅜₆ x 8¼. 0-486-26865-9

COMMON SENSE, Thomas Paine. First published in January of 1776, this highly influential landmark document clearly and persuasively argued for American separation from Great Britain and paved the way for the Declaration of Independence. 64pp. 5⅜₆ x 8¼. 0-486-29602-4

THE COMPLETE SHORT STORIES OF OSCAR WILDE, Oscar Wilde. Complete texts of "The Happy Prince and Other Tales," "A House of Pomegranates," "Lord Arthur Savile's Crime and Other Stories," "Poems in Prose," and "The Portrait of Mr. W. H." 208pp. 5⅜₆ x 8¼. 0-486-45216-6

COMPLETE SONNETS, William Shakespeare. Over 150 exquisite poems deal with love, friendship, the tyranny of time, beauty's evanescence, death, and other themes in language of remarkable power, precision, and beauty. Glossary of archaic terms. 80pp. 5⅜₆ x 8¼. 0-486-26686-9

THE COUNT OF MONTE CRISTO: Abridged Edition, Alexandre Dumas. Falsely accused of treason, Edmond Dantès is imprisoned in the bleak Chateau d'If. After a hair-raising escape, he launches an elaborate plot to extract a bitter revenge against those who betrayed him. 448pp. 5⅜₆ x 8¼. 0-486-45643-9

CRAFTSMAN BUNGALOWS: Designs from the Pacific Northwest, Yoho & Merritt. This reprint of a rare catalog, showcasing the charming simplicity and cozy style of Craftsman bungalows, is filled with photos of completed homes, plus floor plans and estimated costs. An indispensable resource for architects, historians, and illustrators. 112pp. 10 x 7. 0-486-46875-5

CRAFTSMAN BUNGALOWS: 59 Homes from "The Craftsman," Edited by Gustav Stickley. Best and most attractive designs from Arts and Crafts Movement publication — 1903–1916 — includes sketches, photographs of homes, floor plans, descriptive text. 128pp. 8¼ x 11. 0-486-25829-7

CRIME AND PUNISHMENT, Fyodor Dostoyevsky. Translated by Constance Garnett. Supreme masterpiece tells the story of Raskolnikov, a student tormented by his own thoughts after he murders an old woman. Overwhelmed by guilt and terror, he confesses and goes to prison. 480pp. 5⅜₆ x 8¼. 0-486-41587-2

THE DECLARATION OF INDEPENDENCE AND OTHER GREAT DOCUMENTS OF AMERICAN HISTORY: 1775-1865, Edited by John Grafton. Thirteen compelling and influential documents: Henry's "Give Me Liberty or Give Me Death," Declaration of Independence, The Constitution, Washington's First Inaugural Address, The Monroe Doctrine, The Emancipation Proclamation, Gettysburg Address, more. 64pp. 5⅜₆ x 8¼. 0-486-41124-9

THE DESERT AND THE SOWN: Travels in Palestine and Syria, Gertrude Bell. "The female Lawrence of Arabia," Gertrude Bell wrote captivating, perceptive accounts of her travels in the Middle East. This intriguing narrative, accompanied by 160 photos, traces her 1905 sojourn in Lebanon, Syria, and Palestine. 368pp. 5⅜ x 8½. 0-486-46876-3

A DOLL'S HOUSE, Henrik Ibsen. Ibsen's best-known play displays his genius for realistic prose drama. An expression of women's rights, the play climaxes when the central character, Nora, rejects a smothering marriage and life in "a doll's house." 80pp. 5⅜₆ x 8¼. 0-486-27062-9

Browse over 9,000 books at www.doverpublications.com

DOOMED SHIPS: Great Ocean Liner Disasters, William H. Miller, Jr. Nearly 200 photographs, many from private collections, highlight tales of some of the vessels whose pleasure cruises ended in catastrophe: the *Morro Castle, Normandie, Andrea Doria, Europa,* and many others. 128pp. 8⅞ x 11¾. 0-486-45366-9

THE DORÉ BIBLE ILLUSTRATIONS, Gustave Doré. Detailed plates from the Bible: the Creation scenes, Adam and Eve, horrifying visions of the Flood, the battle sequences with their monumental crowds, depictions of the life of Jesus, 241 plates in all. 241pp. 9 x 12. 0-486-23004-X

DRAWING DRAPERY FROM HEAD TO TOE, Cliff Young. Expert guidance on how to draw shirts, pants, skirts, gloves, hats, and coats on the human figure, including folds in relation to the body, pull and crush, action folds, creases, more. Over 200 drawings. 48pp. 8¼ x 11. 0-486-45591-2

DUBLINERS, James Joyce. A fine and accessible introduction to the work of one of the 20th century's most influential writers, this collection features 15 tales, including a masterpiece of the short-story genre, "The Dead." 160pp. 5³⁄₁₆ x 8¼. 0-486-26870-5

EASY-TO-MAKE POP-UPS, Joan Irvine. Illustrated by Barbara Reid. Dozens of wonderful ideas for three-dimensional paper fun — from holiday greeting cards with moving parts to a pop-up menagerie. Easy-to-follow, illustrated instructions for more than 30 projects. 299 black-and-white illustrations. 96pp. 8⅜ x 11. 0-486-44622-0

EASY-TO-MAKE STORYBOOK DOLLS: A "Novel" Approach to Cloth Dollmaking, Sherralyn St. Clair. Favorite fictional characters come alive in this unique beginner's dollmaking guide. Includes patterns for Pollyanna, Dorothy from *The Wonderful Wizard of Oz,* Mary of *The Secret Garden,* plus easy-to-follow instructions, 263 black-and-white illustrations, and an 8-page color insert. 112pp. 8¼ x 11. 0-486-47360-0

EINSTEIN'S ESSAYS IN SCIENCE, Albert Einstein. Speeches and essays in accessible, everyday language profile influential physicists such as Niels Bohr and Isaac Newton. They also explore areas of physics to which the author made major contributions. 128pp. 5 x 8. 0-486-47011-3

EL DORADO: Further Adventures of the Scarlet Pimpernel, Baroness Orczy. A popular sequel to *The Scarlet Pimpernel,* this suspenseful story recounts the Pimpernel's attempts to rescue the Dauphin from imprisonment during the French Revolution. An irresistible blend of intrigue, period detail, and vibrant characterizations. 352pp. 5³⁄₁₆ x 8¼. 0-486-44026-5

ELEGANT SMALL HOMES OF THE TWENTIES: 99 Designs from a Competition, Chicago Tribune. Nearly 100 designs for five- and six-room houses feature New England and Southern colonials, Normandy cottages, stately Italianate dwellings, and other fascinating snapshots of American domestic architecture of the 1920s. 112pp. 9 x 12. 0-486-46910-7

THE ELEMENTS OF STYLE: The Original Edition, William Strunk, Jr. This is the book that generations of writers have relied upon for timeless advice on grammar, diction, syntax, and other essentials. In concise terms, it identifies the principal requirements of proper style and common errors. 64pp. 5⅜ x 8½. 0-486-44798-7

THE ELUSIVE PIMPERNEL, Baroness Orczy. Robespierre's revolutionaries find their wicked schemes thwarted by the heroic Pimpernel — Sir Percival Blakeney. In this thrilling sequel, Chauvelin devises a plot to eliminate the Pimpernel and his wife. 272pp. 5³⁄₁₆ x 8¼. 0-486-45464-9

AN ENCYCLOPEDIA OF BATTLES: Accounts of Over 1,560 Battles from 1479 B.C. to the Present, David Eggenberger. Essential details of every major battle in recorded history from the first battle of Megiddo in 1479 B.C. to Grenada in 1984. List of battle maps. 99 illustrations. 544pp. 6½ x 9¼. 0-486-24913-1

ENCYCLOPEDIA OF EMBROIDERY STITCHES, INCLUDING CREWEL, Marion Nichols. Precise explanations and instructions, clearly illustrated, on how to work chain, back, cross, knotted, woven stitches, and many more — 178 in all, including Cable Outline, Whipped Satin, and Eyelet Buttonhole. Over 1400 illustrations. 219pp. 8⅜ x 11¼. 0-486-22929-7

ENTER JEEVES: 15 Early Stories, P. G. Wodehouse. Splendid collection contains first 8 stories featuring Bertie Wooster, the deliciously dim aristocrat and Jeeves, his brainy, imperturbable manservant. Also, the complete Reggie Pepper (Bertie's prototype) series. 288pp. 5⅜ x 8½. 0-486-29717-9

ERIC SLOANE'S AMERICA: Paintings in Oil, Michael Wigley. With a Foreword by Mimi Sloane. Eric Sloane's evocative oils of America's landscape and material culture shimmer with immense historical and nostalgic appeal. This original hardcover collection gathers nearly a hundred of his finest paintings, with subjects ranging from New England to the American Southwest. 128pp. 10⅝ x 9.
0-486-46525-X

ETHAN FROME, Edith Wharton. Classic story of wasted lives, set against a bleak New England background. Superbly delineated characters in a hauntingly grim tale of thwarted love. Considered by many to be Wharton's masterpiece. 96pp. 5³⁄₁₆ x 8 ¼. 0-486-26690-7

THE EVERLASTING MAN, G. K. Chesterton. Chesterton's view of Christianity — as a blend of philosophy and mythology, satisfying intellect and spirit — applies to his brilliant book, which appeals to readers' heads as well as their hearts. 288pp. 5⅜ x 8½. 0-486-46036-3

THE FIELD AND FOREST HANDY BOOK, Daniel Beard. Written by a co-founder of the Boy Scouts, this appealing guide offers illustrated instructions for building kites, birdhouses, boats, igloos, and other fun projects, plus numerous helpful tips for campers. 448pp. 5³⁄₁₆ x 8¼. 0-486-46191-2

FINDING YOUR WAY WITHOUT MAP OR COMPASS, Harold Gatty. Useful, instructive manual shows would-be explorers, hikers, bikers, scouts, sailors, and survivalists how to find their way outdoors by observing animals, weather patterns, shifting sands, and other elements of nature. 288pp. 5⅜ x 8½. 0-486-40613-X

FIRST FRENCH READER: A Beginner's Dual-Language Book, Edited and Translated by Stanley Appelbaum. This anthology introduces 50 legendary writers — Voltaire, Balzac, Baudelaire, Proust, more — through passages from *The Red and the Black, Les Misérables, Madame Bovary,* and other classics. Original French text plus English translation on facing pages. 240pp. 5⅜ x 8½. 0-486-46178-5

FIRST GERMAN READER: A Beginner's Dual-Language Book, Edited by Harry Steinhauer. Specially chosen for their power to evoke German life and culture, these short, simple readings include poems, stories, essays, and anecdotes by Goethe, Hesse, Heine, Schiller, and others. 224pp. 5⅜ x 8½. 0-486-46179-3

FIRST SPANISH READER: A Beginner's Dual-Language Book, Angel Flores. Delightful stories, other material based on works of Don Juan Manuel, Luis Taboada, Ricardo Palma, other noted writers. Complete faithful English translations on facing pages. Exercises. 176pp. 5⅜ x 8½. 0-486-25810-6

Browse over 9,000 books at www.doverpublications.com

FIVE ACRES AND INDEPENDENCE, Maurice G. Kains. Great back-to-the-land classic explains basics of self-sufficient farming. The one book to get. 95 illustrations. 397pp. 5⅜ x 8½. 0-486-20974-1

FLAGG'S SMALL HOUSES: Their Economic Design and Construction, 1922, Ernest Flagg. Although most famous for his skyscrapers, Flagg was also a proponent of the well-designed single-family dwelling. His classic treatise features innovations that save space, materials, and cost. 526 illustrations. 160pp. 9⅜ x 12¼. 0-486-45197-6

FLATLAND: A Romance of Many Dimensions, Edwin A. Abbott. Classic of science (and mathematical) fiction — charmingly illustrated by the author — describes the adventures of A. Square, a resident of Flatland, in Spaceland (three dimensions), Lineland (one dimension), and Pointland (no dimensions). 96pp. 5³⁄₁₆ x 8¼. 0-486-27263-X

FRANKENSTEIN, Mary Shelley. The story of Victor Frankenstein's monstrous creation and the havoc it caused has enthralled generations of readers and inspired countless writers of horror and suspense. With the author's own 1831 introduction. 176pp. 5³⁄₁₆ x 8¼. 0-486-28211-2

THE GARGOYLE BOOK: 572 Examples from Gothic Architecture, Lester Burbank Bridaham. Dispelling the conventional wisdom that French Gothic architectural flourishes were born of despair or gloom, Bridaham reveals the whimsical nature of these creations and the ingenious artisans who made them. 572 illustrations. 224pp. 8⅜ x 11. 0-486-44754-5

THE GIFT OF THE MAGI AND OTHER SHORT STORIES, O. Henry. Sixteen captivating stories by one of America's most popular storytellers. Included are such classics as "The Gift of the Magi," "The Last Leaf," and "The Ransom of Red Chief." Publisher's Note. 96pp. 5³⁄₁₆ x 8¼. 0-486-27061-0

THE GOETHE TREASURY: Selected Prose and Poetry, Johann Wolfgang von Goethe. Edited, Selected, and with an Introduction by Thomas Mann. In addition to his lyric poetry, Goethe wrote travel sketches, autobiographical studies, essays, letters, and proverbs in rhyme and prose. This collection presents outstanding examples from each genre. 368pp. 5⅜ x 8½. 0-486-44780-4

GREAT EXPECTATIONS, Charles Dickens. Orphaned Pip is apprenticed to the dirty work of the forge but dreams of becoming a gentleman — and one day finds himself in possession of "great expectations." Dickens' finest novel. 400pp. 5³⁄₁₆ x 8¼. 0-486-41586-4

GREAT WRITERS ON THE ART OF FICTION: From Mark Twain to Joyce Carol Oates, Edited by James Daley. An indispensable source of advice and inspiration, this anthology features essays by Henry James, Kate Chopin, Willa Cather, Sinclair Lewis, Jack London, Raymond Chandler, Raymond Carver, Eudora Welty, and Kurt Vonnegut, Jr. 192pp. 5⅜ x 8½. 0-486-45128-3

HAMLET, William Shakespeare. The quintessential Shakespearean tragedy, whose highly charged confrontations and anguished soliloquies probe depths of human feeling rarely sounded in any art. Reprinted from an authoritative British edition complete with illuminating footnotes. 128pp. 5³⁄₁₆ x 8¼. 0-486-27278-8

THE HAUNTED HOUSE, Charles Dickens. A Yuletide gathering in an eerie country retreat provides the backdrop for Dickens and his friends — including Elizabeth Gaskell and Wilkie Collins — who take turns spinning supernatural yarns. 144pp. 5⅜ x 8½. 0-486-46309-5

Browse over 9,000 books at www.doverpublications.com

HEART OF DARKNESS, Joseph Conrad. Dark allegory of a journey up the Congo River and the narrator's encounter with the mysterious Mr. Kurtz. Masterly blend of adventure, character study, psychological penetration. For many, Conrad's finest, most enigmatic story. 80pp. 5³⁄₁₆ x 8¼. 0-486-26464-5

HENSON AT THE NORTH POLE, Matthew A. Henson. This thrilling memoir by the heroic African-American who was Peary's companion through two decades of Arctic exploration recounts a tale of danger, courage, and determination. "Fascinating and exciting." — *Commonweal.* 128pp. 5⅜ x 8½. 0-486-45472-X

HISTORIC COSTUMES AND HOW TO MAKE THEM, Mary Fernald and E. Shenton. Practical, informative guidebook shows how to create everything from short tunics worn by Saxon men in the fifth century to a lady's bustle dress of the late 1800s. 81 illustrations. 176pp. 5⅜ x 8½. 0-486-44906-8

THE HOUND OF THE BASKERVILLES, Arthur Conan Doyle. A deadly curse in the form of a legendary ferocious beast continues to claim its victims from the Baskerville family until Holmes and Watson intervene. Often called the best detective story ever written. 128pp. 5³⁄₁₆ x 8¼. 0-486-28214-7

THE HOUSE BEHIND THE CEDARS, Charles W. Chesnutt. Originally published in 1900, this groundbreaking novel by a distinguished African-American author recounts the drama of a brother and sister who "pass for white" during the dangerous days of Reconstruction. 208pp. 5⅜ x 8½. 0-486-46144-0

THE HUMAN FIGURE IN MOTION, Eadweard Muybridge. The 4,789 photographs in this definitive selection show the human figure — models almost all undraped — engaged in over 160 different types of action: running, climbing stairs, etc. 390pp. 7⅞ x 10⅝. 0-486-20204-6

THE IMPORTANCE OF BEING EARNEST, Oscar Wilde. Wilde's witty and buoyant comedy of manners, filled with some of literature's most famous epigrams, reprinted from an authoritative British edition. Considered Wilde's most perfect work. 64pp. 5³⁄₁₆ x 8¼. 0-486-26478-5

THE INFERNO, Dante Alighieri. Translated and with notes by Henry Wadsworth Longfellow. The first stop on Dante's famous journey from Hell to Purgatory to Paradise, this 14th-century allegorical poem blends vivid and shocking imagery with graceful lyricism. Translated by the beloved 19th-century poet, Henry Wadsworth Longfellow. 256pp. 5³⁄₁₆ x 8¼. 0-486-44288-8

JANE EYRE, Charlotte Brontë. Written in 1847, *Jane Eyre* tells the tale of an orphan girl's progress from the custody of cruel relatives to an oppressive boarding school and its culmination in a troubled career as a governess. 448pp. 5³⁄₁₆ x 8¼.
0-486-42449-9

JAPANESE WOODBLOCK FLOWER PRINTS, Tanigami Kônan. Extraordinary collection of Japanese woodblock prints by a well-known artist features 120 plates in brilliant color. Realistic images from a rare edition include daffodils, tulips, and other familiar and unusual flowers. 128pp. 11 x 8¼. 0-486-46442-3

JEWELRY MAKING AND DESIGN, Augustus F. Rose and Antonio Cirino. Professional secrets of jewelry making are revealed in a thorough, practical guide. Over 200 illustrations. 306pp. 5⅜ x 8½. 0-486-21750-7

JULIUS CAESAR, William Shakespeare. Great tragedy based on Plutarch's account of the lives of Brutus, Julius Caesar and Mark Antony. Evil plotting, ringing oratory, high tragedy with Shakespeare's incomparable insight, dramatic power. Explanatory footnotes. 96pp. 5³⁄₁₆ x 8¼. 0-486-26876-4

Browse over 9,000 books at www.doverpublications.com

THE JUNGLE, Upton Sinclair. 1906 bestseller shockingly reveals intolerable labor practices and working conditions in the Chicago stockyards as it tells the grim story of a Slavic family that emigrates to America full of optimism but soon faces despair. 320pp. 5³⁄₁₆ x 8¼. 0-486-41923-1

THE KINGDOM OF GOD IS WITHIN YOU, Leo Tolstoy. The soul-searching book that inspired Gandhi to embrace the concept of passive resistance, Tolstoy's 1894 polemic clearly outlines a radical, well-reasoned revision of traditional Christian thinking. 352pp. 5³⁄₁₆ x 8¼. 0-486-45138-0

THE LADY OR THE TIGER?: and Other Logic Puzzles, Raymond M. Smullyan. Created by a renowned puzzle master, these whimsically themed challenges involve paradoxes about probability, time, and change; metapuzzles; and self-referentiality. Nineteen chapters advance in difficulty from relatively simple to highly complex. 1982 edition. 240pp. 5⅜ x 8½. 0-486-47027-X

LEAVES OF GRASS: The Original 1855 Edition, Walt Whitman. Whitman's immortal collection includes some of the greatest poems of modern times, including his masterpiece, "Song of Myself." Shattering standard conventions, it stands as an unabashed celebration of body and nature. 128pp. 5³⁄₁₆ x 8¼. 0-486-45676-5

LES MISÉRABLES, Victor Hugo. Translated by Charles E. Wilbour. Abridged by James K. Robinson. A convict's heroic struggle for justice and redemption plays out against a fiery backdrop of the Napoleonic wars. This edition features the excellent original translation and a sensitive abridgment. 304pp. 6⅛ x 9¼.
0-486-45789-3

LILITH: A Romance, George MacDonald. In this novel by the father of fantasy literature, a man travels through time to meet Adam and Eve and to explore humanity's fall from grace and ultimate redemption. 240pp. 5⅜ x 8½.
0-486-46818-6

THE LOST LANGUAGE OF SYMBOLISM, Harold Bayley. This remarkable book reveals the hidden meaning behind familiar images and words, from the origins of Santa Claus to the fleur-de-lys, drawing from mythology, folklore, religious texts, and fairy tales. 1,418 illustrations. 784pp. 5⅜ x 8½. 0-486-44787-1

MACBETH, William Shakespeare. A Scottish nobleman murders the king in order to succeed to the throne. Tortured by his conscience and fearful of discovery, he becomes tangled in a web of treachery and deceit that ultimately spells his doom. 96pp. 5³⁄₁₆ x 8¼. 0-486-27802-6

MAKING AUTHENTIC CRAFTSMAN FURNITURE: Instructions and Plans for 62 Projects, Gustav Stickley. Make authentic reproductions of handsome, functional, durable furniture: tables, chairs, wall cabinets, desks, a hall tree, and more. Construction plans with drawings, schematics, dimensions, and lumber specs reprinted from 1900s *The Craftsman* magazine. 128pp. 8⅛ x 11. 0-486-25000-8

MATHEMATICS FOR THE NONMATHEMATICIAN, Morris Kline. Erudite and entertaining overview follows development of mathematics from ancient Greeks to present. Topics include logic and mathematics, the fundamental concept, differential calculus, probability theory, much more. Exercises and problems. 641pp. 5⅜ x 8½. 0-486-24823-2

MEMOIRS OF AN ARABIAN PRINCESS FROM ZANZIBAR, Emily Ruete. This 19th-century autobiography offers a rare inside look at the society surrounding a sultan's palace. A real-life princess in exile recalls her vanished world of harems, slave trading, and court intrigues. 288pp. 5⅜ x 8½. 0-486-47121-7

Browse over 9,000 books at www.doverpublications.com

THE METAMORPHOSIS AND OTHER STORIES, Franz Kafka. Excellent new English translations of title story (considered by many critics Kafka's most perfect work), plus "The Judgment," "In the Penal Colony," "A Country Doctor," and "A Report to an Academy." Note. 96pp. 5³⁄₁₆ x 8¼. 0-486-29030-1

MICROSCOPIC ART FORMS FROM THE PLANT WORLD, R. Anheisser. From undulating curves to complex geometrics, a world of fascinating images abound in this classic, illustrated survey of microscopic plants. Features 400 detailed illustrations of nature's minute but magnificent handiwork. The accompanying CD-ROM includes all of the images in the book. 128pp. 9 x 9. 0-486-46013-4

A MIDSUMMER NIGHT'S DREAM, William Shakespeare. Among the most popular of Shakespeare's comedies, this enchanting play humorously celebrates the vagaries of love as it focuses upon the intertwined romances of several pairs of lovers. Explanatory footnotes. 80pp. 5³⁄₁₆ x 8¼. 0-486-27067-X

THE MONEY CHANGERS, Upton Sinclair. Originally published in 1908, this cautionary novel from the author of *The Jungle* explores corruption within the American system as a group of power brokers joins forces for personal gain, triggering a crash on Wall Street. 192pp. 5⅜ x 8½. 0-486-46917-4

THE MOST POPULAR HOMES OF THE TWENTIES, William A. Radford. With a New Introduction by Daniel D. Reiff. Based on a rare 1925 catalog, this architectural showcase features floor plans, construction details, and photos of 26 homes, plus articles on entrances, porches, garages, and more. 250 illustrations, 21 color plates. 176pp. 8⅜ x 11. 0-486-47028-8

MY 66 YEARS IN THE BIG LEAGUES, Connie Mack. With a New Introduction by Rich Westcott. A Founding Father of modern baseball, Mack holds the record for most wins — and losses — by a major league manager. Enhanced by 70 photographs, his warmhearted autobiography is populated by many legends of the game. 288pp. 5⅜ x 8½. 0-486-47184-5

NARRATIVE OF THE LIFE OF FREDERICK DOUGLASS, Frederick Douglass. Douglass's graphic depictions of slavery, harrowing escape to freedom, and life as a newspaper editor, eloquent orator, and impassioned abolitionist. 96pp. 5³⁄₁₆ x 8¼. 0-486-28499-9

THE NIGHTLESS CITY: Geisha and Courtesan Life in Old Tokyo, J. E. de Becker. This unsurpassed study from 100 years ago ventured into Tokyo's red-light district to survey geisha and courtesan life and offer meticulous descriptions of training, dress, social hierarchy, and erotic practices. 49 black-and-white illustrations; 2 maps. 496pp. 5⅜ x 8½. 0-486-45563-7

THE ODYSSEY, Homer. Excellent prose translation of ancient epic recounts adventures of the homeward-bound Odysseus. Fantastic cast of gods, giants, cannibals, sirens, other supernatural creatures — true classic of Western literature. 256pp. 5³⁄₁₆ x 8¼. 0-486-40654-7

OEDIPUS REX, Sophocles. Landmark of Western drama concerns the catastrophe that ensues when King Oedipus discovers he has inadvertently killed his father and married his mother. Masterly construction, dramatic irony. Explanatory footnotes. 64pp. 5³⁄₁₆ x 8¼. 0-486-26877-2

ONCE UPON A TIME: The Way America Was, Eric Sloane. Nostalgic text and drawings brim with gentle philosophies and descriptions of how we used to live — self-sufficiently — on the land, in homes, and among the things built by hand. 44 line illustrations. 64pp. 8⅜ x 11. 0-486-44411-2

Browse over 9,000 books at www.doverpublications.com

ONE OF OURS, Willa Cather. The Pulitzer Prize–winning novel about a young Nebraskan looking for something to believe in. Alienated from his parents, rejected by his wife, he finds his destiny on the bloody battlefields of World War I. 352pp. 5³⁄₁₆ x 8¼. 0-486-45599-8

ORIGAMI YOU CAN USE: 27 Practical Projects, Rick Beech. Origami models can be more than decorative, and this unique volume shows how! The 27 practical projects include a CD case, frame, napkin ring, and dish. Easy instructions feature 400 two-color illustrations. 96pp. 8¼ x 11. 0-486-47057-1

OTHELLO, William Shakespeare. Towering tragedy tells the story of a Moorish general who earns the enmity of his ensign Iago when he passes him over for a promotion. Masterly portrait of an archvillain. Explanatory footnotes. 112pp. 5³⁄₁₆ x 8¼. 0-486-29097-2

PARADISE LOST, John Milton. Notes by John A. Himes. First published in 1667, *Paradise Lost* ranks among the greatest of English literature's epic poems. It's a sublime retelling of Adam and Eve's fall from grace and expulsion from Eden. Notes by John A. Himes. 480pp. 5³⁄₁₆ x 8¼. 0-486-44287-X

PASSING, Nella Larsen. Married to a successful physician and prominently ensconced in society, Irene Redfield leads a charmed existence — until a chance encounter with a childhood friend who has been "passing for white." 112pp. 5⅜ x 8½. 0-486-43713-2

PERSPECTIVE DRAWING FOR BEGINNERS, Len A. Doust. Doust carefully explains the roles of lines, boxes, and circles, and shows how visualizing shapes and forms can be used in accurate depictions of perspective. One of the most concise introductions available. 33 illustrations. 64pp. 5⅜ x 8½. 0-486-45149-6

PERSPECTIVE MADE EASY, Ernest R. Norling. Perspective is easy; yet, surprisingly few artists know the simple rules that make it so. Remedy that situation with this simple, step-by-step book, the first devoted entirely to the topic. 256 illustrations. 224pp. 5⅜ x 8½. 0-486-40473-0

THE PICTURE OF DORIAN GRAY, Oscar Wilde. Celebrated novel involves a handsome young Londoner who sinks into a life of depravity. His body retains perfect youth and vigor while his recent portrait reflects the ravages of his crime and sensuality. 176pp. 5³⁄₁₆ x 8¼. 0-486-27807-7

PRIDE AND PREJUDICE, Jane Austen. One of the most universally loved and admired English novels, an effervescent tale of rural romance transformed by Jane Austen's art into a witty, shrewdly observed satire of English country life. 272pp. 5³⁄₁₆ x 8¼. 0-486-28473-5

THE PRINCE, Niccolò Machiavelli. Classic, Renaissance-era guide to acquiring and maintaining political power. Today, nearly 500 years after it was written, this calculating prescription for autocratic rule continues to be much read and studied. 80pp. 5³⁄₁₆ x 8¼. 0-486-27274-5

QUICK SKETCHING, Carl Cheek. A perfect introduction to the technique of "quick sketching." Drawing upon an artist's immediate emotional responses, this is an extremely effective means of capturing the essential form and features of a subject. More than 100 black-and-white illustrations throughout. 48pp. 11 x 8¼. 0-486-46608-6

RANCH LIFE AND THE HUNTING TRAIL, Theodore Roosevelt. Illustrated by Frederic Remington. Beautifully illustrated by Remington, Roosevelt's celebration of the Old West recounts his adventures in the Dakota Badlands of the 1880s, from round-ups to Indian encounters to hunting bighorn sheep. 208pp. 6¼ x 9¼. 0-486-47340-6

Browse over 9,000 books at www.doverpublications.com

THE RED BADGE OF COURAGE, Stephen Crane. Amid the nightmarish chaos of a Civil War battle, a young soldier discovers courage, humility, and, perhaps, wisdom. Uncanny re-creation of actual combat. Enduring landmark of American fiction. 112pp. 5³⁄₁₆ x 8¼. 0-486-26465-3

RELATIVITY SIMPLY EXPLAINED, Martin Gardner. One of the subject's clearest, most entertaining introductions offers lucid explanations of special and general theories of relativity, gravity, and spacetime, models of the universe, and more. 100 illustrations. 224pp. 5⅜ x 8½. 0-486-29315-7

REMBRANDT DRAWINGS: 116 Masterpieces in Original Color, Rembrandt van Rijn. This deluxe hardcover edition features drawings from throughout the Dutch master's prolific career. Informative captions accompany these beautifully reproduced landscapes, biblical vignettes, figure studies, animal sketches, and portraits. 128pp. 8⅜ x 11. 0-486-46149-1

THE ROAD NOT TAKEN AND OTHER POEMS, Robert Frost. A treasury of Frost's most expressive verse. In addition to the title poem: "An Old Man's Winter Night," "In the Home Stretch," "Meeting and Passing," "Putting in the Seed," many more. All complete and unabridged. 64pp. 5³⁄₁₆ x 8¼. 0-486-27550-7

ROMEO AND JULIET, William Shakespeare. Tragic tale of star-crossed lovers, feuding families and timeless passion contains some of Shakespeare's most beautiful and lyrical love poetry. Complete, unabridged text with explanatory footnotes. 96pp. 5³⁄₁₆ x 8¼. 0-486-27557-4

SANDITON AND THE WATSONS: Austen's Unfinished Novels, Jane Austen. Two tantalizing incomplete stories revisit Austen's customary milieu of courtship and venture into new territory, amid guests at a seaside resort. Both are worth reading for pleasure and study. 112pp. 5⅜ x 8½. 0-486-45793-1

THE SCARLET LETTER, Nathaniel Hawthorne. With stark power and emotional depth, Hawthorne's masterpiece explores sin, guilt, and redemption in a story of adultery in the early days of the Massachusetts Colony. 192pp. 5³⁄₁₆ x 8¼.
0-486-28048-9

THE SEASONS OF AMERICA PAST, Eric Sloane. Seventy-five illustrations depict cider mills and presses, sleds, pumps, stump-pulling equipment, plows, and other elements of America's rural heritage. A section of old recipes and household hints adds additional color. 160pp. 8⅜ x 11. 0-486-44220-9

SELECTED CANTERBURY TALES, Geoffrey Chaucer. Delightful collection includes the General Prologue plus three of the most popular tales: "The Knight's Tale," "The Miller's Prologue and Tale," and "The Wife of Bath's Prologue and Tale." In modern English. 144pp. 5³⁄₁₆ x 8¼. 0-486-28241-4

SELECTED POEMS, Emily Dickinson. Over 100 best-known, best-loved poems by one of America's foremost poets, reprinted from authoritative early editions. No comparable edition at this price. Index of first lines. 64pp. 5³⁄₁₆ x 8¼. 0-486-26466-1

SIDDHARTHA, Hermann Hesse. Classic novel that has inspired generations of seekers. Blending Eastern mysticism and psychoanalysis, Hesse presents a strikingly original view of man and culture and the arduous process of self-discovery, reconciliation, harmony, and peace. 112pp. 5³⁄₁₆ x 8¼. 0-486-40653-9

SKETCHING OUTDOORS, Leonard Richmond. This guide offers beginners step-by-step demonstrations of how to depict clouds, trees, buildings, and other outdoor sights. Explanations of a variety of techniques include shading and constructional drawing. 48pp. 11 x 8¼. 0-486-46922-0

SMALL HOUSES OF THE FORTIES: With Illustrations and Floor Plans, Harold E. Group. 56 floor plans and elevations of houses that originally cost less than $15,000 to build. Recommended by financial institutions of the era, they range from Colonials to Cape Cods. 144pp. 8⅜ x 11. 0-486-45598-X

SOME CHINESE GHOSTS, Lafcadio Hearn. Rooted in ancient Chinese legends, these richly atmospheric supernatural tales are recounted by an expert in Oriental lore. Their originality, power, and literary charm will captivate readers of all ages. 96pp. 5⅜ x 8½. 0-486-46306-0

SONGS FOR THE OPEN ROAD: Poems of Travel and Adventure, Edited by The American Poetry & Literacy Project. More than 80 poems by 50 American and British masters celebrate real and metaphorical journeys. Poems by Whitman, Byron, Millay, Sandburg, Langston Hughes, Emily Dickinson, Robert Frost, Shelley, Tennyson, Yeats, many others. Note. 80pp. 5³⁄₁₆ x 8¼. 0-486-40646-6

SPOON RIVER ANTHOLOGY, Edgar Lee Masters. An American poetry classic, in which former citizens of a mythical midwestern town speak touchingly from the grave of the thwarted hopes and dreams of their lives. 144pp. 5³⁄₁₆ x 8¼.
0-486-27275-3

STAR LORE: Myths, Legends, and Facts, William Tyler Olcott. Captivating retellings of the origins and histories of ancient star groups include Pegasus, Ursa Major, Pleiades, signs of the zodiac, and other constellations. "Classic." — *Sky & Telescope.* 58 illustrations. 544pp. 5⅜ x 8½. 0-486-43581-4

THE STRANGE CASE OF DR. JEKYLL AND MR. HYDE, Robert Louis Stevenson. This intriguing novel, both fantasy thriller and moral allegory, depicts the struggle of two opposing personalities — one essentially good, the other evil — for the soul of one man. 64pp. 5³⁄₁₆ x 8¼. 0-486-26688-5

SURVIVAL HANDBOOK: The Official U.S. Army Guide, Department of the Army. This special edition of the Army field manual is geared toward civilians. An essential companion for campers and all lovers of the outdoors, it constitutes the most authoritative wilderness guide. 288pp. 5³⁄₁₆ x 8¼. 0-486-46184-X

A TALE OF TWO CITIES, Charles Dickens. Against the backdrop of the French Revolution, Dickens unfolds his masterpiece of drama, adventure, and romance about a man falsely accused of treason. Excitement and derring-do in the shadow of the guillotine. 304pp. 5³⁄₁₆ x 8¼. 0-486-40651-2

TEN PLAYS, Anton Chekhov. *The Sea Gull, Uncle Vanya, The Three Sisters, The Cherry Orchard,* and *Ivanov,* plus 5 one-act comedies: *The Anniversary, An Unwilling Martyr, The Wedding, The Bear,* and *The Proposal.* 336pp. 5³⁄₁₆ x 8¼. 0-486-46560-8

THE FLYING INN, G. K. Chesterton. Hilarious romp in which pub owner Humphrey Hump and friend take to the road in a donkey cart filled with rum and cheese, inveighing against Prohibition and other "oppressive forms of modernity." 320pp. 5⅜ x 8½. 0-486-41910-X

THIRTY YEARS THAT SHOOK PHYSICS: The Story of Quantum Theory, George Gamow. Lucid, accessible introduction to the influential theory of energy and matter features careful explanations of Dirac's anti-particles, Bohr's model of the atom, and much more. Numerous drawings. 1966 edition. 240pp. 5⅜ x 8½. 0-486-24895-X

TREASURE ISLAND, Robert Louis Stevenson. Classic adventure story of a perilous sea journey, a mutiny led by the infamous Long John Silver, and a lethal scramble for buried treasure — seen through the eyes of cabin boy Jim Hawkins. 160pp. 5³⁄₁₆ x 8¼.
0-486-27559-0

Browse over 9,000 books at www.doverpublications.com